Jon E. Lewis is a writer and historian. His journalism has appeared in the *Independent*, the *Guardian* and *Time Out*. His books include *The Mammoth Book of War Correspondents* and *The Mammoth Book of How It Happened in Britain*.

Also available

THE MAMMOTH BOOK OF
JOURNALISM

Edited by Jon E. Lewis

ROBINSON
London

Constable & Robinson Ltd
3 The Lanchesters
162 Fulham Palace Road
London W6 9ER
www.constablerobinson.com

First published in the UK by Robinson,
an imprint of Constable & Robinson Ltd 2003

A copy of the British Library Cataloguing in
Publication Data is available from the British Library.

ISBN 1–84119–686–X

Printed and bound in the EU

10 9 8 7 6 5 4 3 2 1

CONTENTS

INTRODUCTION

It was the Romans who started it. In 59 BC the authorities in Rome issued the *Acta Diurna*, a daily round-up of important social and political events which was displayed publicly for the information of the citizens.

Some might say it was all downhill thereafter, journalism, let us be frank, is not a highly regarded endeavour. In Victorian England certain professions were barred to those who had sunk so low as to sell their pens to the newspapers. The reason for the low popular esteem of journalism is not hard to fathom. Sometimes it is official propaganda, and too often it is lurid and highly improbable entertainment of the "I Was the Love Child of Martians" – type. Today's "red-top" tabloids and *National Inquirers* are the direct descendants of the London *Universal Spectator* of 1728 (which boasted that it covered "the Progress of Wit and Humour, Free from Politicks and Raillery, Religious Controversy, or Dulness") and the infamous "yellow" newspapers *The World* and *The Journal* of 1890s New York.

There is, of course, an utterly different sort of journalism, and it is that which concerns us here. This is the journalism of *reportage*, the eyewitness capture and compression in words of events.

What makes for good *reportage*? The answer is a paradox. The journalist must render an objective report – but in a highly individual manner. In other words, the best reportage is the truth, and nothing but the truth, as refracted through the language skills of the journalist. There were, for instance, many reporters covering the schools integration crisis at Little Rock in 1957, but only one Relman Morin. Similarly the Vietnam War was overrun by journalists but there was only one Michael Herr, whose reports used the cadences of rock music ("Airmobility, dig it, you weren't going anywhere. It made you feel safe, it made you feel Omni, but it was only a stunt, technology") to capture the world's first rock 'n' roll war. But naturally, *reportage* has an even better edge – the edge of the "scoop" – if you just happen to be the only reporter at an incident of significance, as Humphrey Tyler was at Sharpeville.

Which leads to the importance of *reportage*. As an eyewitness record it is the first draft of history, but more prosaically the information it imparts is essential for the knowledge of the citizen. And only an informed citizenry can make proper political choices. Democracy and reportage go hand in hand, hence the battles by journalists and citizens against the tendency of government to control the press. Perhaps the most dramatic pay-off of press freedom was Carl Bernstein and Bob Woodward's investigation for the *Washington Post* into Watergate which brought the downfall of a president, but there have been many others, including William Howard Russell's exposé in *The Times* of the conditions of British troops in the Crimean War which led to public outcry and then to army reforms.

Russell, incidentally, was a key figure in journalism. While journalism was as old as the Romans, *mass* journalism was a Victorian phenomenon courtesy of improvements in literacy and technology. Not until the mid-19th century and the education acts was there widespread literacy (in 1850 3 million American children were in school). The newspapers now had their public. Changes in papermaking and printing technology enabled newspapers to produce their goods cheaply and in abundance. By 1827 the London *Times* was printed on a single press (as opposed to rows of presses) at the heady rate of 5000 copies an hour. Yet, what was printed could scarcely be called "news", for much of it was written by hand and posted. Sometimes, especially if sent from abroad, the dispatch took weeks to arrive. It was not until the invention of the electric telegraph that there arrived the technological means of instantly communicating a report to the editorial office. Russell was one of the pioneers in the use of the telegraph, using it for his dispatches from the ringside of war from several corners of the globe.

War *reportage* – including articles from William Henry Russell – is well represented in the pages which follow. I make no apologies for this (nor indeed for stretching *reportage* into the occasional piece of humour, opinion and journalist's memoir). War, dealing as it does with Death and the Destiny of nations, is always the big story. Yet, there is also travel, art, sport, politics, disasters, crime and murder. No subject is alien to good reporting.

All human life is here.

CHARLES DICKENS

A MAN IS GUILLOTINED IN ROME

Pictures from Italy, 1845

Charles Dickens (1812–70) began his writing career as a reporter for the *Morning Herald*, and never quite gave up journalism even in the years of his greatest output as a novelist. The travel sketch below was written for the *Daily News*, the paper Dickens founded in 1845. The piece never made it to the newspaper, but went instead "straight to book" in *Pictures from Italy*.

On one Saturday morning (the eighth of March) a man was beheaded here. Nine or ten months before, he had way-laid a Bavarian Countess, travelling as a pilgrim to Rome – alone and on foot, of course – and performing, it is said, that act of piety for the fourth time. He saw her change a piece of gold at Viterbo, where he lived; followed her; bore her company on her journey for some forty miles or more, on the treacherous pretext of protecting her; attacked her, in the fulfilment of his unrelenting purpose, on the Campagna, within a very short distance of Rome, near to what is called (but what is not), the Tomb of Nero; robbed her; and beat her to death with her own pilgrim's staff. He was newly married, and gave some of her apparel to his wife: saying that he had bought it at a fair. She, however, who had seen the pilgrim countess passing through their town, recognized some trifle as having belonged to her. Her husband then told her what he had done. She, in confession, told a priest; and the man was taken, within four days after the commission of the murder.

There are no fixed times for the administration of justice or its execution, in this unaccountable country; and he had been in prison ever since. On the Friday, as he was dining with the other prisoners, they came and told him he was to be beheaded next

morning, and took him away. It is very unusual to execute in
Lent; but his crime being a very bad one, it was deemed advisable
to make an example of him at that time when great numbers of
pilgrims were going towards Rome, from all parts, for the Holy
Week. I heard of this on the Friday evening, and saw the bills up
at the churches, calling on the people to pray for the criminal's
soul. So I determined to go, and see him executed.

The beheading was appointed for fourteen and a half o'clock
Roman time: or a quarter before nine in the forenoon. I had two
friends with me; and as we did not know but that the crowd might
be very great, we were on the spot by half past seven. The place of
execution was near the church of San Giovanni Decollato (a
doubtful compliment to Saint John the Baptist) in one of the
impassable back-streets without any footway, of which a great
part of Rome is composed – a street of rotten houses, which do
not seem to belong to anybody, and do not seem to have ever been
inhabited, and certainly were never built on any plan, or for any
particular purpose, and have no window-sashes, and are a little
like deserted breweries, and might be warehouses but for having
nothing in them. Opposite to one of these, a white house, the
scaffold was built. An untidy, unpainted, uncouth, crazy-looking
thing of course; some seven feet high, perhaps: with a tall,
gallows-shaped frame rising above it in which was the knife,
charged with a ponderous mass of iron, all ready to descend, and
glittering brightly in the morning sun, whenever it looked out,
now and then, from behind a cloud.

There were not many people lingering about; and those were
kept at a considerable distance from the scaffold, by parties of the
Pope's dragoons. Two or three hundred foot soldiers were under
arms, standing at ease in clusters here and there; and the officers
were walking up and down in twos and threes, chatting together
and smoking cigars.

At the end of the street, was an open space, where there would
be a dust heap, and piles of broken crockery, and mounds of
vegetable refuse, but for such things being thrown anywhere and
everywhere in Rome, and favouring no particular sort of locality.
We got into a kind of wash-house, belonging to a dwelling-house
on this spot; and standing there in an old cart, and on a heap of
cart-wheels piled against the wall, looked, through a large grated
window, at the scaffold, and straight down the street beyond it,

until, in consequence of its turning off abruptly to the left, our perspective was brought to a sudden termination, and had a corpulent officer, in a cocked hat, for its crowning feature.

Nine o'clock struck, and ten o'clock struck, and nothing happened. All the bells of all the churches rang as usual. A little parliament of dogs assembled in the open space, and chased each other in and out among the soldiers. Fierce looking Romans of the lowest class, in blue cloaks, russet cloaks and rags uncloaked, came and went, and talked together.

Women and children fluttered on the skirts of the scanty crowd. One large muddy spot was left quite bare, like a bald place on a man's head. A cigar merchant, with an earthen pot of charcoal ashes in one hand, went up and down crying his wares. A pastry-merchant divided his attention between the scaffold and his customers. Boys tried to climb up walls, and tumbled down again. Priests and monks elbowed a passage for themselves among the people, and stood on tiptoe for a sight of the knife, then went away. Artists in inconceivable hats of the middle-ages, and beards (thank Heaven!) of no age at all, flashed picturesque scowls about them from their stations in the throng. One gentleman, connected with the fine arts, I presume, went up and down in a pair of Hessian-boots, with a red beard hanging down on his breast, and his long and bright red hair plaited into two tails, one on either side of his head, which fell over his shoulders in front of him, very nearly to his waist, and were carefully entwined and braided!

Eleven o'clock struck: and still nothing happened. A rumour got about among the crowd, that the criminal would not confess; in which case, the priest would keep him until the Ave Maria (sunset); for it is their merciful custom never finally to turn the crucifix away from a man at that pass, as one refusing to be shriven and consequently a sinner abandoned of the Saviour, until then.

People began to drop off. The officers shrugged their shoulders and looked doubtful. The dragoons, who came riding up below our window every now and then, to order an unlucky hackney-coach or cart away, as soon as it had comfortably established itself, and was covered with exulting people (but never before), became imperious and quick-tempered. The bald place hadn't straggling hair upon it; and the corpulent officer, crowning the perspective, took a world of snuff.

Suddenly, there was a noise of trumpets. "Attention!" was among the foot-soldiers instantly. They were marched up to the scaffold and formed around it. The dragoons galloped to their nearer stations too. The guillotine became the centre of a wood of bristling bayonets and shining sabres. The people closed round nearer, on the flank of the soldiery. A long, straggling stream of men and boys, who had accompanied the procession from the prison, came pouring into the open space. The bald spot was scarcely distinguishable from the rest. The cigar and pastry-merchants resigned all thoughts of business, for the moment, and abandoning themselves wholly to pleasure, got good situations in the crowd. The perspective ended, now, in a troop of dragoons. And the corpulent officer, sword in hand, looked hard at a church close to him, which he could see, but we, the crowd could not.

After a short delay, some monks were seen approaching to the scaffold from this church and above their heads, coming on slowly and gloomily, the effigy of Christ upon the cross, canopied with black.

This was carried round the foot of the scaffold, to the front, and turned towards the criminal, that he might see it to the last. It was hardly in its place, when he appeared on the platform, bare-footed; his hands bound; and with the collar and neck of his shirt cut away, almost to the shoulder. A young man – six and twenty – vigorously made, and well-shaped. Face pale; small dark moustache, and dark brown hair.

He had refused to confess, it seemed, without first having his wife brought to see him; and they had sent an escort for her, which had occasioned the delay.

He immediately kneeled down below the knife. His neck was fitting into a hole, made for the purpose, in a cross plank, was shut down, by another plank above; exactly like the pillory. Immediately below him was a leathern bag. And into it his head rolled instantly.

The executioner was holding it by the hair, and walking with it round the scaffold, showing it to the people, before one quite knew that the knife had fallen heavily, and with a rattling sound.

When it had travelled round the four sides of the scaffold, it was set upon a pole in front, a little patch of black and white, for the long street to stare at, and the flies to settle on. The eyes were turned upward, as if he had avoided the sight of the leathern bag, and looked to the crucifix. Every tinge and hue of life had left it in that instant. It was dull, cold, livid, wax. The body also.

There was a great deal of blood. When we left the window, and went close up to the scaffold, it was very dirty; one of the two men who were throwing water over it, turning to help the other lift the body into a shell, picked his way as through mire. A strange appearance was the apparent annihilation of the neck. The head was taken off so close that it seemed as if the knife had narrowly escaped crushing the jaw or shaving the ear; and the body looked as if there was nothing left above the shoulder.

Nobody cared, or was at all affected. There was no manifestation of disgust, or pity, or indignation, or sorrow. My empty pockets were tried, several times, in the crowd immediately below the scaffold, as the corpse was being put into its coffin. It was an ugly, filthy, careless, sickening spectacle; meaning nothing but butchery beyond the momentary interest, to the one wretched actor. Yes! Such a sight had one meaning and one warning. Let me not forget it. The speculators in the lottery station themselves at favourable points for counting the gouts of blood that spurt out, here or there; and buy that number. It is pretty sure to have a run upon it.

The body was carted away in due time, the knife cleansed, the scaffold taken down, and all the hideous apparatus removed. The executioner: an outlaw ex officio (what a satire on the Punishment) who dare not, for his life, cross the Bridge of St Angelo but to do his work: retreated to his lair, and the show was over.

CHARLES DICKENS

A SLEEP TO STARTLE US

Household Words, 13 March 1852

Dickens was the social conscience of British Victorian journalism. "A Sleep to Startle Us" records a visit to the Ragged School in the City of London. *Household Words* was another journal of Dicken's own foundation.

At the top of Farringdon Street in the City of London, once adorned by the Fleet Prison and by a diabolical jumble of nuisances in the middle of the road called Fleet Market, is a broad new thoroughfare in a state of transition. A few years hence, and we of the present generation will find it not an easy task to recall, in the thriving street which will arise upon this spot, the wooden barriers and hoardings – the passages that lead to nothing – the glimpses of obscene Field Lane and Saffron Hill – the mounds of earth, old bricks, and oyster-shells – the arched foundations of unbuilt houses – the backs of miserable tenements with patched windows – the odds and ends of fever-stricken courts and alleys – which are the present features of the place. Not less perplexing do I find it now, to reckon how many years have passed since I traversed these byeways one night before they were laid bare, to find out the first Ragged School.

If I say it is ten years ago, I leave a handsome margin. The discovery was then newly made, that to talk soundingly in Parliament, and cheer for Church and State, or to consecrate and confirm without end, or to perorate to any extent in a thousand market-places about all the ordinary topics of patriotic songs and sentiments, was merely to embellish England on a great scale with whited sepulchres, while there was, in every corner of the land where its people were closely accumulated, profound ignorance and perfect barbarism. It was also newly discovered, that out of these noxious sinks where they were born to perish, and where the general ruin was hatching day and night, the people *would not come* to be improved. The gulf between them and all wholesome humanity had swollen to such a depth and breadth, that they were separated from it as by impassable seas or deserts; and so they lived, and so they died: an always-increasing band of outlaws in body and soul, against whom it were to suppose the reversal of all laws, human and divine, to believe that Society could at last prevail.

In this condition of things, a few unaccredited messengers of Christianity, whom no Bishop had ever heard of, and no Government-office Porter had ever seen, resolved to go to the miserable wretches who had lost the way to them: and to set up places of instruction in their own degraded haunts. I found my first Ragged School, in an obscure place called West Street, Saffron Hill, pitifully struggling for life, under every disadvantage. It had no means, it had no suitable rooms, it derived no power or protection from being recognised by any authority, it attracted within its wretched walls a fluctuating swarm of faces – young in years but youthful in nothing else – that scowled Hope out of countenance. It was held in a low-roofed den, in a sickening atmosphere, in the midst of taint and dirt and pestilence: with all the deadly sins let loose, howling and shrieking at the doors. Zeal did not supply the place of method and training; the teachers knew little of their office; the pupils, with an evil sharpness, found them out, got the better of them, derided them, made blasphemous answers to scriptural questions, sang, fought, danced, robbed each other; seemed possessed by legions of devils. The place was stormed and carried, over and over again; the lights were blown out, the books strewn in the gutters, and the female scholars carried off triumphantly to their old wickedness. With no strength in it but its purpose, the school stood it all out and made its way. Some two years since, I found it, one of many such, in a large convenient loft in this transition part of Farringdon Street quiet and orderly, full, lighted with gas, well whitewashed, numerously attended, and thoroughly established.

The number of houseless creatures who resorted to it, and who were necessarily turned out when it closed, to hide where they could in heaps of moral and physical pollution, filled the man-

agers with pity. To relieve some of the more constant and
deserving scholars, they rented a wretched house, where a few
common beds – a dozen or a dozen-and-a-half perhaps – were
made upon the floors. This was the Ragged School Dormitory;
and when I found the School in Farringdon Street, I found the
Dormitory in a court hard by, which in the time of the Cholera
had acquired a dismal fame. The Dormitory was, in all respects,
save as a small beginning, a very discouraging Institution. The
air was bad; the dark and ruinous building, with its small close
rooms, was quite unsuited to the purpose; and a general super-
vision of the scattered sleepers was impossible. I had great doubts
at the time whether, excepting that they found a crazy shelter for
their heads, they were better there than in the streets.

Having heard, in the course of last month, that this Dormitory (there are others elsewhere) had grown as the School had
grown, I went the other night to make another visit to it. I
found the School in the same place, still advancing. It was now
an Industrial School too; and besides the men and boys who
were learning – some, aptly enough; some, with painful difficulty; some, sluggishly and wearily; some, not at all – to read
and write and cipher; there were two groups, one of shoe-
makers, and one (in a gallery) of tailors, working with great
industry and satisfaction. Each was taught and superintended
by a regular workman engaged for the purpose, who delivered
out the necessary means and implements. All were employed in
mending, either their own, dilapidated clothes or shoes, or the
dilapidated clothes or shoes of some of the other pupils. They
were of all ages, from young boys to old men. They were quiet,
and intent upon their work. Some of them were almost as
unused to it as I should have shown myself to be if I had tried
my hand, but all were deeply interested and profoundly anxious to do it somehow or other. They presented a very
remarkable instance of the general desire there is, after all,
even in the vagabond breast, to know something useful. One
shock-headed man when he had mended his own scrap of a
coat, drew it on with such an air of satisfaction, and put himself
to so much inconvenience to look at the elbow he had darned,
that I thought a new coat (and the mind could not imagine a
period when that coat of his was new!) would not have pleased
him better. In the other part of the School, where each class

was partitioned off by screens adjusted like the boxes in a coffee-room, was some very good writing, and some singing of the multiplication table – the latter, on a principle much too juvenile and innocent for some of the singers. There was also a ciphering-class, where a young pupil teacher out of the streets, who refreshed himself by spitting every half-minute, had written a legible sum in compound addition, on a broken slate, and was walking backward and forward before it, as he worked it, for the instruction of his class, in this way:

Now then! Look here, all on you! Seven and five, how many?

SHARP BOY (in no particular clothes). Twelve.

PUPIL TEACHER. Twelve – and eight?

DULL YOUNG MAN (with water on the brain). Forty-five!

SHARP BOY. Twenty!

PUPIL TEACHER. Twenty. You're right. And nine?

DULL YOUNG MAN (after great consideration). Twenty-nine!

PUPIL TEACHER. Twenty-nine it is. And nine?

RECKLESS GUESSER. Seventy-four!

PUPIL TEACHER (drawing nine strokes). How can that be? Here's nine on 'em! Look! Twenty-nine, and one's thirty, and one's thirty-one, and one's thirty-two, and one's thirty-three, and one's thirty-four, and one's thirty-five, and one's thirty-six, and one's thirty-seven, and one's what?

RECKLESS GUESSER. Four-and-two-pence farden!

DULL YOUNG MAN (who has been absorbed in the demonstration). Thirty-eight!

PUPIL TEACHER (restraining sharp boy's ardour). Of course it is! Thirty-eight pence. There they are! (writing 38 in slate-corner). Now what do you make of thirty-eight pence? Thirty-eight pence, how much? (Dull young man slowly considers and gives it up, under a week.) How much, you? (to sleepy boy, who stares and says nothing). How much, *you*?

SHARP BOY. Three-and-twopence!

PUPIL TEACHER. Three-and-twopence. How do I put down three-and-twopence?

SHARP BOY. You puts down the two, and you carries the three.

PUPIL TEACHER. Very good. Where do I carry the three?

RECKLESS GUESSER. T' other side the slate!

SHARP BOY. You carries him to the next column on the left hand, and adds him on!

PUPIL TEACHER. And adds him on! and eight and three's
eleven, and eight's nineteen, and seven's what?
– And so on.

The best and most spirited teacher was a young man, himself
reclaimed through the agency of this School from the lowest
depths of misery and debasement, whom the Committee were
about to send out to Australia. He appeared quite to deserve the
interest they took in him, and his appearance and manner were a
strong testimony to the merits of the establishment.

All this was not the Dormitory, but it was the preparation for
it. No man or boy is admitted to the Dormitory, unless he is a
regular attendant at the school, and unless he has been in the
school two hours before the time of opening the Dormitory. If
there be reason to suppose that he can get any work to do and will
not do it, he is admitted no more, and his place is assigned to
some other candidate for the nightly refuge: of whom there are
always plenty. There is very little to tempt the idle and profligate.
A scanty supper and a scanty breakfast, each of six ounces of
bread and nothing else (this quantity is less than the present
penny-loaf), would scarcely be regarded by Mr Chadwick himself as a festive or uproarious entertainment.

I found the Dormitory below the School: with its bare walls
and rafters, and bare floor, the building looked rather like an
extensive coach-house, well lighted with gas. A wooden gallery
had been recently erected on three sides of it; and, abutting from
the centre of the wall on the fourth side, was a kind of glazed
meat-safe, accessible by a ladder; in which the presiding officer is
posted every night, and all night. In the centre of the room,
which was very cool, and perfectly sweet, stood a small fixed
stove; on two sides, there were windows; on all sides, simple
means of admitting fresh air, and releasing foul air. The ventila-
tion of the place, devised by Doctor Arnott, and particularly the
expedient for relieving the sleepers in the galleries from receiving
the breath of the sleepers below, is a wonder of simplicity,
cheapness, efficiency, and practical good sense. If it had cost
five or ten thousand pounds, it would have been famous.

The whole floor of the building, with the exception of a few
narrow pathways, was partitioned off into wooden troughs, or
shallow boxes without lids – not unlike the fittings in the shop of
a dealer in corn and flour, and seeds. The galleries were parcelled

out in the same way. Some of these berths were very short – for boys; some, longer – for men. The largest were of very contracted limits; all were composed of the bare boards; each was furnished only with one coarse rug, rolled up. In the brick pathways were iron gratings communicating with trapped drains, enabling the entire surface of these sleeping-places to be soused and flooded with water every morning. The floor of the galleries was cased with zinc, and fitted with gutters and escape-pipes, for the same reason. A supply of water, both for drinking and for washing, and some tin vessels for either purpose, were at hand. A little shed, used by one of the industrial classes, for the chopping up of firewood, did not occupy the whole of the spare space in that corner; and the remainder was devoted to some excellent baths, available also as washing troughs, in order that those who have any rags of linen may clean them once a-week. In aid of this object, a drying-closet, charged with hot-air, was about to be erected in the wood-chopping shed. All these appliances were constructed in the simplest manner, with the commonest means, in the narrowest space, at the lowest cost; but were perfectly adapted to their respective purposes.

I had scarcely made the round of the Dormitory, and looked at all these things, when a moving of feet overhead announced that the School was breaking up for the night. It was succeeded by profound silence, and then by a hymn, sung in a subdued tone, and in very good time and tune, by the learners we had lately seen. Separated from their miserable bodies, the effect of their voices, united in this strain, was infinitely solemn. It was as if their souls were singing – as if the outward differences that parted us had fallen away, and the time was come when all the perverted good that was in them, or that ever might have been in them, arose imploringly to Heaven.

The baker who had brought the bread, and who leaned against a pillar while the singing was in progress, meditating in his way, whatever his way was, now shouldered his basket and retired. The two half-starved attendants (rewarded with a double portion for their pains) heaped the six-ounce loaves into other baskets, and made ready to distribute them. The night-officer arrived, mounted to his meat-safe, unlocked it, hung up his hat, and prepared to spend the evening. I found him to be a very respectable-looking person in black, with a wife and family;

engaged in an office all day, and passing his spare time here, from
half-past nine every night to six every morning, for a pound a-
week. He had carried the post against two hundred competitors.

The door was now opened, and the men and boys who were to
pass that night in the Dormitory, in number one hundred and
sixty-seven (including a man for whom there was no trough, but
who was allowed to rest in the seat by the stove, once occupied by
the night-officer before the meat-safe was), came in. They passed
to their different sleeping-places, quietly and in good order.
Every one sat down in his own crib, where he became presented
in a curiously foreshortened manner; and those who had shoes
took them off, and placed them in the adjoining path. There
were, in the assembly, thieves, cadgers, trampers, vagrants,
common outcasts of all sorts. In casual wards and many other
Refuges, they would have been very difficult to deal with; but
they were restrained here by the law of kindness, and had long
since arrived at the knowledge that those who gave them that
shelter could have no possible inducement save to do them good.
Neighbours spoke little together – they were almost as uncom-
panionable as mad people – but everybody took his small loaf
when the baskets went round, with a thankfulness more or less
cheerful, and immediately ate it up.

There was some excitement in consequence of one man being
missing; "the lame old man". Everybody had seen the lame old
man upstairs asleep, but he had unaccountably disappeared.
What he had been doing with himself was a mystery, but, when
the inquiry was at its height, he came shuffling and tumbling in,
with his palsied head hanging on his breast – an emaciated
drunkard, once a compositor, dying of starvation and decay.
He was so near death, that he could not be kept there, lest he
should die in the night; and, while it was under deliberation what
to do with him, and while his dull lips tried to shape out answers
to what was said to him, he was held up by two men. Beside this
wreck, but all unconnected with it and with the whole world, was
an orphan boy with burning cheeks and great gaunt eager eyes,
who was in pressing peril of death too, and who had no possession
under the broad sky but a bottle of physic and a scrap of writing.
He brought both from the house-surgeon of a Hospital that was
too full to admit him, and stood, giddily staggering in one of the
little pathways, while the Chief Samaritan read, in hasty char-

acters underlined, how momentous his necessities were. He held the bottle of physic in his claw of a hand, and stood, apparently unconscious of it, staggering, and staring with his bright glazed eyes; a creature, surely, as forlorn and desolate as Mother Earth can have supported on her breast that night. He was gently taken away, along with the dying man, to the workhouse; and he passed into the darkness with his physic-bottle as if he were going into his grave.

The bread eaten to the last crumb; and some drinking of water and washing in water having taken place, with very little stir or noise indeed; preparations were made for passing the night. Some, took off their rags of smock frocks; some, their rags of coats or jackets, and spread them out within their narrow bounds for beds: designing to lie upon them, and use their rugs as a covering. Some, sat up, pondering, on the edges of their troughs; others, who were very tired, rested their unkempt heads upon their hands and their elbows on their knees, and dozed. When there were no more who desired to drink or wash, and all were in their places, the night officer, standing below the meat-safe, read a short evening service, including perhaps as inappropriate a prayer as could possibly be read (as though the Lord's Prayer stood in need of it by way of Rider), and a portion of a chapter from the New Testament. Then, they all sang the Evening Hymn, and then they all lay down to sleep.

It was an awful thing, looking round upon those one hundred and sixty-seven representatives of many thousands, to reflect that a Government, unable, with the least regard to truth, to plead ignorance of the existence of such a place, should proceed as if the sleepers never were to wake again. I do not hesitate to say – why should I, for I know it to be true! – that an annual sum of money, contemptible in amount as compared with any charges upon any list, freely granted in behalf of these Schools, and shackled with no preposterous Red Tape conditions, would relieve the prisons, diminish county rates, clear loads of shame and guilt out of the streets, recruit the army and navy, waft to new countries, Fleets full of useful labour, for which their inhabitants would be thankful and beholden to us. It is no deprecation of the devoted people whom I found presiding here, to add, that with such assistance as a trained knowledge of the business of instruction, and a sound system adjusted to the peculiar difficulties and conditions of this sphere of action, their usefulness could be increased fifty-fold in a few months.

My Lords and Gentlemen, can you, at the present time, consider this at last, and agree to do some little easy thing! Dearly beloved brethren elsewhere, do you know that between Gorham controversies, and Pusey controversies and Newman controversies, and twenty other edifying controversies, a certain large class of minds in the community is gradually being driven out of all religion! Would it be well, do you think, to come out of the controversies for a little while, and be simply Apostolic thus low down!

WILLIAM HOWARD RUSSELL

THE BATTLE OF BALACLAVA

The Times, 14 November 1854

An Irishman who fell into journalism by accident, Russell was employed
by the London *Times* to accompany the British army on its 1854 mission to
Crimea. The job appeared a pleasant jaunt – the army believed it had only
to rattle its sabres to deter Russia from spreading southwards – but turned
into a two-year tour of grinding journalistic duty, during which Russell's
accurate and clear dispatches made him the most famous war reporter of
the Victorian era. His criticisms of the army's system of command, its
unsuitable clothing and its poor food, led to sweeping reform. After the
Crimean War, Russell reported the Indian Mutiny, the American Civil
War (where his candid account of Union cowardice at Bull Run obliged
him to leave the country), the Franco-Prussian War and the Zulu War. He
was knighted for his services to journalism.

Russell pioneered the use of the telegraph, although many of his pieces
were written as long descriptive letters, including his celebrated account of
the Battle of Balaclava, 25 October 1854. This proved the major engagement of the Crimean War, and is forever remembered for its melancholic
"Charge of the Light Brigade".

If the exhibition of the most brilliant valour, of the excess of
courage, and of a daring which would have reflected lustre on
the best days of chivalry can afford full consolation for the
disaster of today, we can have no reason to regret the melancholy loss which we sustained in a contest with a savage and
barbarian enemy.

I shall proceed to describe, to the best of my power, what
occurred under my own eyes, and to state the facts which I have
heard from men whose veracity is unimpeachable, reserving to
myself the exercise of the right of private judgement in making

public and in suppressing the details of what occurred on this memorable day . . .

It will be remembered that in a letter sent by last mail from this place it was mentioned that eleven battalions of Russian infantry had crossed the Tchernaya, and that they threatened the rear of our position and our communication with Balaclava. Their bands could be heard playing at night by travellers along the Balaclava road to the camp, but they "showed" but little during the day and kept up among the gorges and mountain passes through which the roads to Inkermann, Simpheropol, and the south-east of the Crimea wind towards the interior. It will be recollected also that the position we occupied in reference to Balaclava was supposed by most people to be very strong – even impregnable. Our lines were formed by natural mountain slopes in the rear, along which the French had made very formidable intrenchments. Below those intrenchments, and very nearly in a right line across the valley beneath, are four conical hillocks, one rising above the other as they recede from our lines . . . On the top of each of these hills the Turks had thrown up earthen redoubts, defended by 250 men each, and armed with two or three guns – some heavy ship guns – lent by us to them, with one artilleryman in each redoubt to look after them. These hills cross the valley of Balaclava at the distance of about two and a half miles from the town. Supposing the spectator then to take his stand on one of the heights forming the rear of our camp before Sebastopol, he would see the town of Balaclava, with its scanty shipping, its narrow strip of water, and its old forts on his right hand; immediately below he would behold the valley and plain of coarse meadowland, occupied by our cavalry tents, and stretching from the base of the ridge on which he stood to the foot of the formidable heights on the other side; he would see the French trenches lined with Zouaves a few feet beneath, and distant from him, on the slope of the hill; a Turkish redoubt lower down, then another in the valley, then in a line with it some angular earthworks, then, in succession, the other two redoubts up Canrobert's Hill.

At the distance of two or two and a half miles across the valley there is an abrupt rocky mountain range of most irregular and picturesque formation, covered with scanty brushwood here and there, or rising into barren pinnacles and plateaux of rock. In outline and appearance, this position of the landscape is wonderfully like the Trossachs. A patch of blue sea is caught in between the overhanging cliffs of Balaclava as they close in the entrance to the harbour on the right. The camp of the Marines pitched on the hillsides more than one thousand feet above the level of the sea is opposite to you as your back is turned to Sebastopol and your right side towards Balaclava. On the road leading up the valley, close to the entrance of the town and beneath these hills, is the encampment of the 93rd Highlanders.

The cavalry lines are nearer to you below, and are some way in advance of the Highlanders, and nearer to the town than the Turkish redoubts. The valley is crossed here and there by small waves of land. On your left the hills and rocky mountain ranges gradually close in toward the course of the Tchernaya, till at three or four miles' distance from Balaclava the valley is swallowed up in a mountain gorge and deep ravines, above which rise tier after tier of desolate whitish rock garnished now and then by bits of scanty herbage, and spreading away towards the east and south, where they attain the alpine dimensions of Tschatir Dagh. It is very easy for an enemy at the Belbek, or in command of the road of Mackenzie's Farm, Inkermann, Simpheropol, or Bakhchisarai, to debouch through these gorges at any time upon this plain from the neck of the valley, or to march from Sebastopol by the Tchernaya and to advance along it towards Balaclava, till checked by the Turkish redoubts on the southern side or by the fire from the French works on the northern side, i.e., the side which in relation to the valley of Balaclava forms the rear of our position.

At half past seven o'clock this morning an orderly came galloping in to the headquarters camp from Balaclava, with the news that at dawn a strong corps of Russian horse supported by guns and battalions of infantry had marched into the valley, and had already nearly dispossessed the Turks of the redoubt No. 1 (that on Canrobert's Hill, which is farthest from our lines) and that they were opening fire on the redoubts Nos. 2, 3 and 4, which would speedily be in their hands unless the Turks offered a stouter resistance than they had done already.

Orders were dispatched to Sir George Cathcart and to HRH the Duke of Cambridge to put their respective divisions, the 4th and 1st, in motion for the scene of action, and intelligence of the advance of the Russians was also furnished to General Canrobert. Immediately on receipt of the news the General commanded

General Bosquet to get the Third Division under arms, and sent a strong body of artillery and some 200 Chasseurs d'Afrique to assist us in holding the valley. Sir Colin Campbell, who was in command of Balaclava, had drawn up the 93rd Highlanders a little in front of the road to the town at the first news of the advance of the enemy. The Marines on the heights got under arms; the seamen's batteries and Marines' batteries on the heights close to the town were manned, and the French artillery-men and the Zouaves prepared for action along their lines. Lord Lucan's little camp was the scene of great excitement. The men had not had time to water their horses; they had not broken their fast from the evening of the day before, and had barely saddled at the first blast of the trumpet, when they were drawn up on the slope behind the redoubts in front of the camp to operate on the enemy's squadrons. It was soon evident that no reliance was to be placed on the Turkish infantrymen or artillerymen. All the stories we had heard about their bravery behind stone walls and earthworks proved how differently the same or similar people fight under different circumstances. When the Russians advanced the Turks fired a few rounds at them, got frightened at the distance of their supports in the rear, looked round, received a few shots and shell, and then "bolted", and fled with an agility quite at variance with the commonplace notions of oriental deportment on the battlefield. But Turks on the Danube are very different beings from Turks in the Crimea, as it appears that the Russians of Sebastopol are not at all like the Russians of Silistria.

Soon after eight Lord Raglan and his staff turned out and cantered towards the rear of our position. The booming of artillery, the spattering roll of musketry, were heard rising from the valley, drowning the roar of the siege guns in front before Sebastopol. As I rode in the direction of the firing over the thistles and large stones which cover the undulating plain which stretches away towards Balaclava, on a level with the summit of the ridges above it, I observed a French light infantry regiment (the 27th, I think) advancing with admirable care and celerity from our right towards the ridge near the telegraph house, which was already lined with companies of French infantry, while mounted officers scampered along its broken outline in every direction.

General Bosquet, a stout soldierlike-looking man, who reminds one of the old *genre* of French generals as depicted at Versailles, followed, with his staff and small escort of Hussars, at a gallop. Faint white clouds rose here and there above the hill from the cannonade below. Never did the painter's eye rest upon a more beautiful scene than I beheld from the ridge. The fleecy vapours still hung around the mountain tops and mingled with the ascending volumes of smoke; the patch of sea sparkled freshly in the rays of the morning sun, but its light was eclipsed by the flashes which gleamed from the masses of armed men below.

Looking to the left towards the gorge we beheld six compact masses of Russian infantry which had just debouched from the mountain passes near the Tchernaya, and were slowly advancing with solemn stateliness up the valley. Immediately in their front was a regular line of artillery, of at least twenty pieces strong. Two batteries of light guns were already a mile in advance of them, and were playing with energy on the redoubts from which feeble puffs of smoke came at long intervals. Behind the guns, in front of the infantry, were enormous bodies of cavalry. They were in six compact squares, three on each flank, moving down *en échelon* towards us, and the valley was lit up with the blaze of their sabres and lance points and gay accoutrements. In their front, and extending along the intervals between each battery of guns, were clouds of mounted skirmishers, wheeling and whirling in the front of their march like autumn leaves tossed by the wind. The Zouaves close to us were lying like tigers at the spring, with ready rifles in hand, hidden chin deep by the earthworks which run along the line of these ridges on our rear, but the quick-eyed Russians were manoeuvring on the other side of the valley, and did not expose their columns to attack. Below the Zouaves we could see the Turkish gunners in the redoubts, all in confusion as the shells burst over them. Just as I came up the Russians had carried No. 1 redoubt, the farthest and most elevated of all, and their horsemen were chasing the Turks across the interval which lay between it and redoubt No. 2. At that moment the cavalry, under Lord Lucan, were formed in glittering masses – the Light Brigade, under Lord Cardigan, in advance of the Heavy Brigade, under Brigadier-General Scarlett, in reserve. They were drawn up just in front of their encampment, and were concealed from the view of the enemy by a slight "wave" in the plain. Considerably to the rear of their right, the 93rd Highlanders were drawn up in line, in front of the approach to Balaclava. Above and behind them on the heights, the Marines were visible through the glass, drawn up under arms, and the gunners could be seen ready in the earthworks, in which were placed the heavy ships' guns. The 93rd had originally been advanced somewhat more into the plain, but the instant the Russians got possession of the first redoubt they opened fire on them from our own guns, which inflicted some injury, and Sir Colin Campbell "retired" his men to a better position. Meantime the enemy advanced his cavalry rapidly. To our inexpressible disgust we saw the Turks in redoubt No. 2 fly at their approach. They ran in scattered groups across towards redoubt No. 3, and towards Balaclava, but the horse-hoof of the Cossacks was too quick for them, and sword and lance were busily plied among the retreating band. The yells of the pursuers and pursued were plainly audible. As the Lancers and Light Cavalry of the Russians advanced they gathered up their skirmishers with great speed and in excellent order – the shifting trails of men, which played all over the valley like moonlight on water, contracted, gathered up, and the little *peloton* in a few moments became a solid column. Then up came their guns, in rushed their gunners to the abandoned redoubt, and the guns of No. 2 redoubt soon played with deadly effect upon the dispirited defenders of No. 3 redoubt. Two or three shots in return from the earthworks, and all is silent. The Turks swarm over the earthworks and run in confusion towards the town, firing their muskets at the enemy as they run. Again the solid column of cavalry opens like a fan, and resolves itself into the "long spray" of skirmishers. It laps the flying Turks, steel flashes in the air, and down go the poor Muslim quivering on the plain, split through fez and musket-guard to the chin and breast-belt. There is no support for them. It is evident the Russians have been too quick for us. The Turks have been too quick also, for they have not held their redoubts long enough to enable us to bring them help. In vain the naval guns on the heights fire on the Russian cavalry, the distance is too great for shot or shell to reach. In vain the Turkish gunners in the earthen batteries which are placed along the French intrench-ments strive to protect their flying countrymen; their shots fly wide and short of the swarming masses. The Turks betake themselves towards the Highlanders, where they check their flight and form into companies on the flanks of the Highlanders.

As the Russian cavalry on the left of their line crown the hill, across the valley they perceive the Highlanders drawn up at the distance of some half-mile, calmly awaiting their approach. They halt, and squadron after squadron flies up from the rear, till they have a body of some 1500 men along the ridge – Lancers and Dragoons and Hussars. Then they move *en échelon* in two bodies, with another in reserve. The cavalry who have been pursuing the Turks on the right are coming up the ridge beneath us, which conceals our cavalry from view. The heavy brigade in advance is drawn up in two columns. The first column consists of the Scots Greys and of their old companions in glory, the Enniskillens; the second of the 4th Royal Irish, of the 5th Dragoon Guards, and of the 1st Royal Dragoons. The Light Cavalry Brigade is on their left in two lines also. The silence is oppressive; between the cannon bursts, one can hear the champing of bits and the clink of sabres in the valley below. The Russians on their left drew breath for a moment, and then in one grand line dashed at the Highlanders. The ground flies beneath their horses' feet – gathering speed at every stride they dash on towards that thin red streak topped with a line of steel. The Turks fire a volley at 800 yards, and run. As the Russians come within 600 yards, down goes that line of steel in front, and out rings a rolling volley of Minié musketry. The distance is too great. The Russians are not checked, but still sweep onwards with the whole force of horse and man, through the smoke, here and there knocked over by the shot of our batteries above. With breathless suspense everyone awaits the bursting of the wave upon the line of Gaelic rock; but ere they came within 150 yards, another deadly volley flashes from the levelled rifles, and carries death and terror into the Russians. They wheel about, open files right and left, and fly back faster than they came.

"Bravo Highlanders! Well done!" shout the excited spectators; but events thicken. The Highlanders and their splendid front are soon forgotten. Men scarcely have a moment to think of this fact that the 93rd never altered their formation to receive that tide of horsemen.

"No," said Sir Colin Campbell, "I did not think it worth while to form them even four deep!"

The ordinary British line, two deep, was quite sufficient to repel the attack of these Muscovite chevaliers. Our eyes were, however, turned in a moment on our own cavalry. We saw Brigadier-General Scarlett ride along in front of his massive squadrons. The Russians – evidently *corps d'élite* – their light-blue jackets embroidered with silver lace, were advancing on their left at an easy gallop, towards the brow of the hill. A forest of lances glistened in their rear, and several squadrons of grey-coated dragoons moved up quickly to support them as they reached the summit. The instant they came in sight the trumpets of our cavalry gave out the warning blast which told us all that in another moment we would see the shock of battle beneath our very eyes. Lord Raglan, all his staff and escort, and groups of officers, the Zouaves, the French generals and officers, and bodies of French infantry on the height, were spectators of the scene as though they were looking on the stage from the boxes of a theatre. Nearly everyone dismounted and sat down, and not a word was said.

The Russians advanced down the hill at a slow canter, which they changed to a trot and at last nearly halted. The first line was at least double the length of ours – it was three times as deep. Behind them was a similar line, equally strong and compact. They evidently despised their insignificant-looking enemy, but their time was come.

The trumpets rang out through the valley, and the Greys and Enniskillens went right at the centre of the Russian cavalry. The space between them was only a few hundred yards; it was scarce enough to let the horses "gather way", nor had the men quite space sufficient for the full play of their sword arms. The Russian line brings forward each wing as our cavalry advance and threaten to annihilate them as they pass on. Turning a little to their left, so as to meet the Russians' right, the Greys rush on with a cheer that thrills to every heart – the wild shout of the Enniskillens rises through the air at the same moment. As lightning flashes through a cloud the Greys and Enniskillens pierced through the dark masses of the Russians. The shock was but for a moment. There was a clash of steel and a light play of sword blades in the air, and then the Greys and the redcoats disappear in the midst of the shaken and quivering columns. In another moment we see them merging and dashing on with diminished numbers, and in broken order, against the second line, which is advancing against them to retrieve the fortune of the charge.

It was a terrible moment. "God help them! They are lost!" was the exclamation of more than one man, and the thought of many. With unabated fire the noble hearts dashed at their enemy – it was a fight of heroes. The first line of Russians which had been smashed utterly by our charge, and had fled off at one flank and towards the centre, were coming back to swallow up our handful of men. By sheer steel and sheer courage Enniskillen and Scot were winning their desperate way right through the enemy's squadrons, and already grey horses and redcoats had appeared right at the rear of the second mass, when, with irresistible force, like one bolt from a bow, the 1st Royals, the 4th Dragoon Guards, and the 5th Dragoon Guards rushed at the remnants of the first line of the enemy, went through it as though it were made of pasteboard, and dashing on the second body of Russians, as they were still disordered by the terrible assault of the Greys and their companions, put them to utter rout. This Russian horse in less than five minutes after it met our dragoons was flying with all its speed before a force certainly not half its strength.

A cheer burst from every lip – in the enthusiasm officers and men took off their caps and shouted with delight, and thus keeping up the scenic character of their position, they clapped their hands again and again . . .

And now occurred the melancholy catastrophe which fills us all with sorrow. It appears that the Quartermaster General, Brigadier Airey, thinking that the Light Cavalry had not gone far enough in front when the enemy's horse had fled, gave an order in writing to Captain Nolan, 15th Hussars, to take to Lord Lucan, directing His Lordship "to advance" his cavalry nearer to the enemy. A braver soldier than Captain Nolan the army did not possess. He was known to all his arm of the service for his entire devotion to his profession, and his name must be familiar to all who take interest in our cavalry for his excellent work published a year ago on our drill and system of remount and breaking horses. I had the pleasure of his acquaintance, and I know he entertained the most exalted opinions respecting the capabilities of the English horse soldier. Properly led, the British Hussar and Dragoon could in his mind break square, take batteries, ride over columns of infantry, and pierce any other cavalry in the world, as if they were made of straw. He thought they had not had the opportunity of doing all that was in their power, and that they had missed even such chances as they had offered to them – that, in fact, they were in some measure disgraced. A matchless rider and a first-rate swordsman, he held in contempt, I am afraid, even grape and canister. He rode off with his orders to Lord Lucan. He is now dead and gone.

God forbid I should cast a shade on the brightness of his honour, but I am bound to state what I am told occurred when he reached His Lordship. I should premise that, as the Russian cavalry retired, their infantry fell back towards the head of the valley, leaving men in three of the redoubts they had taken and abandoning the fourth. They had also placed some guns on the heights over their position, on the left of the gorge. Their cavalry joined the reserves, and drew up in six solid divisions, in an oblique line, across the entrance to the gorge. Six battalions of infantry were placed behind them, and about thirty guns were drawn up along their line, while masses of infantry were also collected on the hills behind the redoubts on our right. Our cavalry had moved up to the ridge across the valley, on our left, as the ground was broken in front, and had halted in the order I have already mentioned.

When Lord Lucan received the order from Captain Nolan and had read it, he asked, we are told, "Where are we to advance to?"

Captain Nolan pointed with his finger to the line of the Russians, and said, "There are the enemy, and there are the guns, sir, before them. It is your duty to take them," or words to that effect, according to the statements made since his death.

Lord Lucan with reluctance gave the order to Lord Cardigan to advance upon the guns, conceiving that his orders compelled him to do so. The noble Earl, though he did not shrink, also saw the fearful odds against him. Don Quixote in his tilt against the windmill was not near so rash and reckless as the gallant fellows who prepared without a thought to rush on almost certain death.

It is a maxim of war that "cavalry never act without support", that "infantry should be close at hand when cavalry carry guns, as the effect is only instantaneous", and that it is necessary to have on the flank of a line of cavalry some squadrons in column, the attack on the flank being most dangerous. The only support our Light Cavalry had was the reserve of Heavy Cavalry at a great distance behind them – the infantry and guns being far in the rear. There were no squadrons in column at all, and there was a plain to charge over before the enemy's guns were reached of a mile and a half in length.

At ten past eleven our Light Cavalry Brigade rushed to the front. They numbered as follows, as well as I could ascertain:

	MEN
4th Light Dragoons	118
8th Irish Hussars	104
11th Prince Albert's Hussars	110
13th Light Dragoons	130
17th Lancers	145
Total 607 sabres	

The whole brigade scarcely made one effective regiment, according to the numbers of continental armies; and yet it was more than we could spare. As they passed towards the front, the Russians opened on them from the guns in the redoubts on the right, with volleys of musketry and rifles.

They swept proudly past, glittering in the morning sun in all the pride and splendour of war. We could hardly believe the evidence of our senses! Surely that handful of men were not going to charge an army in position? Alas! it was but too true – their desperate valour knew no bounds, and far indeed was it removed from its so-called better part – discretion. They advanced in two lines, quickening their pace as they closed towards the enemy. A more fearful spectacle was never witnessed than by those who, without the power to aid, beheld their heroic countrymen rushing to the arms of death. At the distance of 1200 yards the whole line of the enemy belched forth, from thirty iron mouths, a flood of smoke and flame, through which hissed the deadly balls. Their flight was marked by instant gaps in our ranks, by dead men and horses, by steeds flying wounded or riderless across the plain. The first line was broken – it was joined by the second, they never halted or checked their speed an instant. With diminished ranks, thinned by those thirty guns, which the Russians had laid with the most deadly accuracy, with a halo of flashing steel above their heads, and with a cheer which was many a noble fellow's death cry, they flew into the smoke of the batteries; but ere they were lost from view, the plain was strewed with their bodies and with the carcasses of horses. They were exposed to an oblique fire from the batteries on the hills on both sides, as well as to a direct fire of musketry.

Through the clouds of smoke we could see their sabres flashing as they rode up to the guns and dashed between them, cutting down the gunners as they stood. The blaze of their steel, as an officer standing near me said, was "like the turn of a shoal of mackerel". We saw them riding through the guns, as I have said; to our delight we saw them returning, after breaking through a column of Russian infantry, and scattering them like chaff, when the flank fire of the battery on the hill swept them down, scattered and broken as they were. Wounded men and dismounted troopers flying towards us told the sad tale – demigods could not have done what they had failed to do. At the very moment when they were about to retreat, an enormous mass of lancers was hurled upon their flank. Colonel Shewell, of the 8th Hussars, saw the danger, and rode his few men straight at them, cutting his way through with fearful loss. The other regiments turned and engaged in a desperate encounter. With courage too great almost for credence, they were breaking their way through the columns which enveloped them, when there took place an act of atrocity without parallel in the modern warfare of civilized nations. The Russian gunners, when the storm of cavalry passed, returned to their guns. They saw their own cavalry mingled with the troopers who had just ridden over them, and to the eternal disgrace of the Russian name the miscreants poured a murderous volley of grape and canister on the mass of struggling men and horses, mingling friend and foe in one common ruin. It was as much as our Heavy Cavalry Brigade could do to cover the retreat of the miserable remnants of that band of heroes as they returned to the place they had so lately quitted in all the pride of life.

At twenty-five to twelve not a British soldier, except the dead and dying, was left in front of these bloody Muscovite guns. Our loss, as far as it could be ascertained in killed, wounded, and missing at two o'clock today, was as follows:

	Went into Action Strong	Returned from Action	Loss
4th Light Dragoons	118	39	79
8th Hussars	104	38	66
11th Hussars	110	25	85
13th Light Dragoons	130	61	69
17th Lancers	145	35	110
	607	198	409

WILLIAM HOWARD RUSSELL

MOSCOW GOES TO TOWN

The Times, 9 September 1856

Despite emancipating the serfs Czar Alexander II, whose coronation
Russell reports below, was assassinated by radicals in 1881.

There is nothing in the world like Moscow but itself. In Russia
nothing must be regarded as destroyed or lost for ever. When the
Winter Palace – a pile as large as Versailles – was burnt to the
ground, the autocrat of so many millions, with the force and
volition of a Cambyses or Xerxes in past ages, exclaimed, "On
the anniversary of this day I will give a ball in a new palace on that
very place", and at his word a mass of stone and marble rose by
the banks of the Neva till that promise was fulfilled to the very
letter. So when the blackened and shattered walls of the Kremlin,
a few stone houses, and the shells of desecrated churches, were all
that was left of Moscow, the popular will, guided by the Czar and
the nobility, resolved that a fairer and nobler city should spring
up in the midst of the waste, on the identical spot where
Napoleon imagined he had struck Russia to the heart. And thus,
with loftier spires and ampler cupolas, in larger proportions, and
more profuse elaboration, churches, palaces, Royal and princely
mansions – this miraculous capital, the centre of the Russian's
faith, of his devotion, of his patriotism, of his obedience, of his
history, again stood on the plain of the Moskva. Following their
instinct and their national characteristics, they scarcely sought to
improve on the ways of their ancestors, and the forms and
directions of the old streets were preserved almost intact; so that
the tortuous Tartar thoroughfares are still visible in their type in
the best quarters of the new city. All the eccentricities of the
Byzantine architecture are here developed and varied with tradi-

tionary skill. The wild Tartars, who could not perpetuate their faith, have given at least to the church of Russia some outward and visible signs of their religion, and the Mosque and the Greek chapel are here present, as it were, in perpetual silent conflict.

But there is no time left for me to try and describe the city, even if I had power for the task. It is three o'clock, and the long street with an unknown name, which phonically I believe to be the Nerskaia, is crowded by the people of the town and those of the country who have flocked for miles to witness the coronation. This street leads from the Kremlin to the Petrovsky Chateau, the boundary of the city being marked by a gate and triumphal arch, on the top of which there is a statue of Victory driving her chariot in a very excited way with unmanageable and runaway-looking horses. A dull heavy noise, like the single beat of a deep drum, is heard a long way off. It is the first *coup de canon* of the nine which announces that the Emperor is on his way to the entrance of his ancient capital. In a moment, far and wide the chimes of some 400 churches, scattered, as it were, broadcast all over the great city, ring out with stupendous clamour, which is musical in the depth of its tumult, and the crowd settles into an attitude of profound expectation and repose. The two lines formed by the soldiery are as strict and exact as those of the street itself, and the eye wanders down a long perspective of helmets, faces, red collars, green frocks, red cuffs, and white trousers, till they are diminished into mere streaks of colour in the distance. The officers dress the men within a hair's breadth, look along their chins and noses, till they are all in line, and then retire to their places in the ranks; again the careful sergeants and corporals go round and give their charges a last finishing touch, brush the dust off their shoes and crossbelts, and comb their moustaches. When the street has been made quite clear there are, of course, several dogs which run at full speed down the lines with their eyes staring and their tongues out in a manner quite worthy of Tattenham Corner, or the best race-courses in England, but these little incidents are not developed to their full extent for the interest and amusement of the public, inasmuch as there are no stoutish policemen to run after them, and these usually sagacious creatures are permitted to indulge in this folly of their race without let or hindrance. All this time a thousand church bells are ringing far and near with loyal vehemence, driving the rooks and pigeons in swarms out of their resting-places, to wheel and circle in the air. In a few moments more the flourishing of trumpets and the strains of martial music rise above all this tumult, and the trumpet band of the Rifles of the Guard, close at hand, commence a wild *alerte*, which is subdued after a time to the measure of a quick march. A few moments of suspense pass heavily, and at length there appears on the red path of sand, which looks like a carpet spread in the roadway, a small party of *Gendarmes-à-Cheval*, preceded by a *maître de police* in full uniform. This latter officer is not like the quiet gentlemen who administer justice in Bow Street or Guildhall, nor does he resemble the more formidable-looking personages who, in round hats and silver-bound collars, ride on whirlwind and direct the storm of popular enthusiasm in England. He is a soldier every inch, from plumed casque to spur, mounted on a prancing war horse, and clad in a rich uniform; two and two, one at each side of the way, his *gendarmes* follow him in light blue uniforms with white facings, and with helmets and plumes also. They are fine looking dragoons, and ride splendid horses. Behind them – but who shall describe these warlike figures which come on to their own music of clinking steel and jingling of armour? They fill up the whole roadway with a flood of colour. Such might have been the Crusaders, or rather such might have been the Knights of Saladin, when the Cross and the Crescent met in battle. Mounted on high-bred, spirited horses which are covered with rich trappings of an antique character, the escort of the Emperor comes by, and calls us at once back to the days of Ivan the Terrible. Their heads are covered with a fine chain armour – so fine, indeed, that some of them wear it as a veil before their faces. This mail falls over the neck and covers the back and chest, and beneath it glisten rich doublets of yellow silk. Some of the escort carry lances with bright pennons. All are armed with antique carabines, pistols, and curved swords. Their saddles are crusted with silver, and rich scarfs and sashes decorate their waists. Their handsome faces and slight sinewy frames indicate their origin. These are of that Circassian race which, mingling its blood with the Turks, have removed from them that stigma of excessive ugliness that once, according to old historians, affrighted Europe. Their influence on the old Muscovite type is said to be equally great, and the families which are allied with the Circassians,

Mingrelians, or Georgians exhibit, we are told, a marked difference from the pure and unmixed breed of Russian origin.

The whole breadth of the street was now occupied by a glittering mass of pennons, armour, plume, steel, and bright colours; the air was filled with the sounds of popular delight, the champing of bits and clinking of weapons, the flourishing of trumpets, and, above all, the loud voices of the bells. Close behind the Circassian escort and the wild Bashkirs comes a squadron of the Division of the Black Sea Cossacks of the Guard, in large flat black sheepskin caps, with red skull-pieces, long lances, the shafts painted red, and the pennons coloured blue, white, and red; their jackets of scarlet; their horses small, handsome, and full of spirit.

The forest of red lance shafts through which one looked gave a most curious aspect to the gay cavalcade. A squadron of the Regiment of Cossacks of the Guard, in blue, follows. Except in the shape of the head-dress, which is like one of our shakos in the olden time, and the colour of their uniform, these men resemble the Black Sea Cossacks.

Each squadron consists of about 200 men, and the men are by no means of that hairy, high-cheeked, *retroussé*-nosed, and small-eyed kind identified in the popular mind with their name; and far different are they from the long-coated, round-headed lancers on scraggy ponies who so long kept watch and ward over us from Canrobert's hill. These Cossacks are well mounted and well clad, and would afford to the stranger a very imperfect notion of what the Cossacks are who plunder and burn in the front of an advancing enemy, sweep away its supplies, and hover round it to do anything but fight, unless at some enormous vantage. Suggesting some strange likenesses and comparisons, there follows after these 400 Cossacks a large body of the *haute noblesse* on horseback and in uniform, two and two, headed by the Marshal of the Nobility for the district of Moscow. Nearly all of these nobles are in military uniforms, those who are not wear the old Russian boyard's dress, a tunic glistening with precious stones, golden belts studded with diamonds, and high caps with *aigrettes* of brilliants. On their breasts are orders, stars, crosses, ribands, innumerable. Menschikoffs, Rostopchins, Galitzins, Woronzoffs, Gortschakoffs, Strogonoffs, Cheremetieffs, Platoffs, Tolstoys, and the bearers of many another name unknown in Western Europe before the last century, are there carrying whole fortunes on their backs, the rulers and

masters of millions of their fellow men; but, brilliant as they are, the
interest they excite soon passes away when the next gorgeous
cavalcade approaches. This consists of the deputies of the various
Asiatic *peuplades* or race; which have submitted to Russia, all on
horseback, two and two. Here may be seen the costume of every age
at one view, and all as rich as wealth, old family treasures, hoarded
plunder, and modern taste can make it. Bashkirs and Circassians,
Tcherkess, Abassians, in coats of mail and surcoats of fine chain
armour, Calmucks, Tartars of Kazan and the Crimea, Mingrelians,
Karapapaks, Daghistanhis, Armenians, the people of Gouriel and
Georgia, the inhabitants of the borders of the Caspian, Kurds,
people of Astrakhan, Samoiedes, wild mountaineers from distant
ranges to which the speculations of even the "Hertfordshire Incumbent" have never wandered, Chinese from the Siberian frontiers, Mongols, and strange beings like Caliban in court-dress.
Some of them had their uncovered hair plaited curiously with gold
coins; others wore on the head only a small flat plate of precious
metal just over the forehead; others sheepskin head-dresses
studded with jewels; old matchlocks that might have rung on
the battlefields of Ivan Veliki, battle-axes, lances, and scimitars
and daggers of every form were borne by this gaudy throng, whose
mode of riding offered every possible variety of the way in which a
man can sit on a horse. Some rode without stirrups, loose and
graceful as the Greek warriors who live on the friezes of the
Parthenon; others sat in a sort of legless armchair, with their knees
drawn up after the manner of sartorial equestrians. Every sort of
bit, bridle, saddle, and horse-trapping which has been used since
horses were subjugated to man could be seen here. Some of the
saddlecloths and holsters were of surpassing richness and splendour. In the midst of all these cavaliers two attracted particular
notice. One was a majestic-looking old Turk with an enormous
beard and a towering turban, whose garments were of such a rich
material and strange cut that one was reminded immediately of the
figure of the High Priest in Rembrandt's picture, or of the old
engravings of the Sultan in old books of travel. The other was a
young deputy from Gouriel, with clustering hair flowing down in
curls from beneath a small patch of gold and jewels fixed on the top
of the head, whose face and figure were strikingly handsome, and
who was dressed in a magnificent suit of blue velvet *cramoisi*,
flashing with precious stones. He was a veritable Eastern Antinous,

and was well matched with his beautiful horse. This cavalcade of the *peuplades soumises à la Russie* was to strangers the most interesting part of the procession; but it passed too quickly by for the eye to decompose its ingredients. What stories of the greatness and magnificence of Russia will those people take back to their remote tribes! They went by, bright, shifting, and indistinct as a dream of the *Arabian Nights*. The only objection one could make to this part of the procession was that it was over too soon, and the eye wandered after it to the curve of the lines of soldiery which hid it from view. Already the *premier fourrier de la Cour*, in a uniform of green and gold, has passed us on a prancing charger, and then, two and two at each side of the street, comes an array of sixty valets of the Court, in cocked hats, gold and green liveries, breeches, and white silk stockings, shoes, and buckles. Alas! those shoes are often new and the buckles tight, for the four mile march on foot has much distressed these worthy gentlemen, and they walk gingerly over the red sand. After them in like order come six lacqueys of the chamber, then six Court runners, and finally, in gorgeous attire, eight negroes of the Court, grinning with all the dental abandon of their race. The ceremony is now becoming most exciting, for the carriages come in view round the turn of the street. They are preceded, however, by the *piqueur* of the Emperor on horseback, and twenty huntsmen in full livery, after whom rides in great grandeur the Head Huntsman – the master of the Emperor's hounds, or the *Chef de la Vénerie Imperiale*. The first vehicle is an open phaeton gilt richly from stem to stern, and lined with crimson velvet, drawn by six noble horses with the richest trappings; at the head of each horse there is a footman in cocked hat, green and gold livery, buckskins, and patent-leather jackboots, who holds his charge by a richly embossed rein; the driver, barring his livery, seems to have been abstracted from Buckingham Palace. In this gay vehicle are seated in uniforms of green and gold, two Masters of the Ceremonies of the Court, with huge wands of office. This description, bad as it is, must suffice for the next open phaeton and its paraphernalia, in which is seated the Grand Master of the Ceremonies. After this carriage comes a Master of the Ceremonies on horseback, followed by twenty-four Gentlemen of the Chamber, mounted on richly caparisoned horses, riding two and two. Another Master of the Ceremonies is next seen, preceding a cavalcade of twelve mounted chamberlains, who are stiff with gold lace, and covered with orders and ribands. Having got rid of an officer of the Imperial stables who looks very like a field-marshal, and two Palefreniers in uniforms too rich for an English General, we turn our attention to the following objects: The second *Charges de la Cour*, in gilt carriages, four and four, crimson velvet linings, green and gold footmen, and fine horses. Next the Marshal of the Court, in an open phaeton, gilt all over, with his grand baton of office flashing with gems. Next the Grand *Charges de la Cour*, by fours, in gilt and crimson carriages, all and each drawn like the first, with running footmen and rich trappings:

> All clinquant – all in gold like heathen gods;
> Every man that walked showed like a mine.

The members of the Imperial Council, in gilt carriages, followed the Grand *Charges* – all that is esteemed wise in Russia, skilful in diplomacy and venerated for past services, grave, astute, and polished nobles and gentlemen, whose lives have been spent in devoted efforts for the aggrandisement of their country and the promotion of the interests of their Imperial master, their breasts bear witness to the favour with which they have been regarded. It is with strange feelings one gazes on the representatives of a policy so crafty and so ambitious as that which is attributed to the Russian Court, and which in this nineteenth century is supported by no inconsiderable part of the learning and logic of the statesmen of Europe. As the last of the train of carriages passes a noise like distant thunder rolling along the street announces the approach of the Czar. But his presence is grandly heralded. Immediately after the members of the Council of the Empire the Grand Marshal of the Court rides in an open phaeton, gilt like the rest; but, bright as is he and all about him, there comes after that compared with the lustre of which he is as a mote in the sun. In gilt casques of beautiful form and workmanship surmounted by crest eagles of silver or gold, in milk-white coats and gilded cuirasses and back-plates, approach the giants of the first squadron of the *Chevaliers Gardes* of His Majesty the Emperor, each on a charger fit for a commander in battle. These are the picked men of 60,000,000 of the human race, and in stature they certainly exceed any troops I have ever seen. All their appointments are splendid, but it is said that they looked better in the

days of the late Emperor, when they wore white buckskins and
jack-boots, than they do now in their long trousers. The squadron was probably 200 strong, and the effect of the polished
helmets, crests, and armour was dazzling. Their officers could
scarcely be distinguished, except by their position and the extraordinary beauty and training of some of their horses, which
slowly beat time, as it were, with their hoofs to the strains of the
march. The First Squadron of the *Garde à Cheval* follows:

> . . . All furnished – all in arms,
> All plumed like estridges that wing the wind;
> Bated like eagles having lately bathed,
> Glittering in golden coats, like images.

So bright, so fine, that one is puzzled to decide which, they or the
chevaliers, are the bravest. But as we are debating the point the
tremendous cheering of the people and the measured hurrahs of
the soldiers, the doffed hats and the reverences of the crowd, the
waving of handkerchiefs, and the clash of presenting arms warn
us that the "Czar of All the Russians, of the Kingdom of Poland,
and of the Grand Duchy of Finland, which are inseparable from
them", is at hand, and Alexander Nicolaievitch is before us. His
Majesty is dressed in the uniform of a general officer, and seems
quite simply attired, after all the splendour which has gone past.
He wears a burnished casque with a long plume of white, orange,
and dark cock's feathers, a close fitting green tunic, with aiguill-
ettes and orders, and red trousers, and he guides his charger – a
perfect model of symmetry – with ease and gracefulness.

At the moment the Emperor entered the city of Moscow a salvo
of seventy-one guns was fired by the artillery outside the town; and
the Governor-General of the city, at the head of all the officers and
employés of the military departments, received His Majesty, and
afterwards joined the procession. The functionaries of the Hotel de
Ville and the city magistrates received him at the entry of the
Zemlenoy-Gorod Quarter, and the Marshal and the nobility of
Moscow at that of the Beloy-Gorod Quarter. Thence the procession moved on to the Gate of the Resurrection (Vosresenkie
Vovota), where the whole cortège, all save the Emperor and two
carriages, moving rapidly on, was lost to sight inside the Kremlin.

GEORGE AUGUSTUS SALA

EXPLOSION ABOARD
THE *GREAT EASTERN*

Daily Telegraph, 12 September 1859

The *Great Eastern* steamship was designed by I.K. Brunel for the Ceylon run. Her trial run is reported by the one-eyed Sala, one of the most accomplished and exotic of Victorian British journalists, whose usual beat was abroad but who in true professional style would "do" funerals and flower shows when there was "no war afoot".

On Board the *Great Eastern*, Portland Harbour,
Saturday, 10.30 a.m.

We had dined. It was six o'clock, and we were off Hastings, at about seven miles' distance from the shore. The majority of the passengers, having finished their repast, had gone on deck. The ladies had retired, and, as we conjectured, according to their usual custom, to their boudoir. The dining saloon was deserted, save by a small knot of joyous guests, all known to each other, who had gathered round the most popular of the directors, Mr Ingram. That gentleman, his hand on the shoulder of his young son, was listening, not apparently unpleased, to the eloquence of a friend, who was decanting on his merits while proposing his health. The glasses were charged; the orator's peroration had culminated; the revellers were upstanding; when – as if the fingers of a man's hand had come out against the cabin wall, and written, as in sand, that the Medes and Persians were at the gate, the verberation of a tremendous explosion was heard. The reverberation followed. Then came – to our ears, who were in the dining room – a tremendous crash, not hollow, as of thunder, but solid, as of objects that offered resistance. Then a sweeping, rolling, swooping, rumbling sound, as of cannon balls scudding along the deck above. Remember, I am only describing *now* my personal experience and sensations. The rumbling noise was followed by the smash of the dining saloon skylights, and the irruption of a mass of fragments of wood and iron, followed by a thick cloud of powdered glass, and then by coaldust. My garments are full of the first, my hair and eyebrows of the last, now. There was but one impulse, one question – to go on deck; to ask, "What can it be?" To me, the crash was greater than the explosion; and I thought more of a collision, or of the fall of one of the huge yards, than of an explosion; but my next neighbour cried out, "The boiler has burst!" On gaining the deck I could at first see nothing but billows of steam rolling towards us. Then along the deck I saw the engine hose rapidly drawn along, and in another moment dozens of men were seizing it and carrying it forward. The wind was blowing tolerably strong, and when the steam cleared away a little in my immediate vicinity, there came an eddying shower of splinters, fragments of gilt moulding, shreds of ornamental paper, and tatters of crimson curtains. Several gentlemen now exerted themselves in the most praiseworthy manner to get the passengers aft; the danger was evidently forward; a thick cloud of steam there concealed all objects; but there was smoke as well as vapour, and I thought the ship was on fire. As men and passengers came rushing by I heard ejaculations of "Fire", "The boilers", "The donkey engine has burst"; but these were more matters of question and answer than evidences of terror. There seemed to be amazement and curiosity, but – among the passengers at least – not the slightest panic. The Great Ship Company's guests requited the hospitality of the directors by rendering every assistance in their power to the officers by setting an example of quietude and cheerfulness, and by endeavouring to inspire confidence. It was a noble sight afterwards to see the young Marquis of Stafford, his sleeves tucked up, his hands and face grimed to the similitude of a chimneysweep, panting with his exertions in working at the hose and clearing away rubbish. There was another nobleman, who passed the ensuing night anointing the scarified limbs of tortured men with oil, and cheering them up with kindly words. There was *another*, who, the moment the accident occurred, derogated slightly from the dignity of his pilot coat and "Jack Tar" manners, wanted a boat to be lowered for his conveyance on shore, and vehemently expressed his opinion that the conduct of the Captain, in not making immediately for Dungeness, was "unjustifiable". But let this pass. I went forward and then had the first glimpse of the Ruin that had blasted a large portion of the ship. The "very forward" funnel and its flange, which last should have been dozens of feet below, were lying aslant on the raised centre of the foredeck; and forward of the grand saloon staircase the hoses were playing fast and furiously down through the cavity where the funnel should have been, down down into a hideous pit of Flame. The ship, thank God! was not on fire; but, by the abolition of the upward draught caused by the loss of the funnel – which had shot upwards through three tiers of deck like a skyrocket, and had been projected, some say ten, some say twenty, some say thirty feet into the air – the flames of the now unconfined furnace were spreading outwards below in a hundred myriad tongues of fire. Once for all, let me assure you that, although the danger was imminent, the *Great Eastern* was never on fire. Objects were blown up and away; but of the planks, and beams, and girders, I saw afterwards among the *debris*, I could not discern so much as a batten that, shattered and splintered as it may have been, was charred or even scorched.

The effects of the catastrophe soon became lamentably apparent. One by one, borne on the shoulders or in the arms of their comrades, or, in one or two cases, staggering past, came by the unfortunate men who had been scalded in the stokehole. The face of one was utterly without human semblance, and looked simply like a mass of raw beef-steak. Another was so horribly scalded about the groin, that the two hands might be laid in the raw cavity, and scraps of his woollen undergarment were mixed up with hanks of boiled flesh. Another I saw had his trousers scalded away from the mid-thigh; his two legs, bare from thigh to heel, were continuous scalds, the skin and flesh hanging here and there. As they raised another man, the flesh of his hands came away in the grasp of those who held him, and he looked as though he had two bloody gloves on. There were some cases of severe contusions, and cuts from fractured glass; but curiously enough, not one instance of broken limbs. Some of the sufferers were hysterical, laughing and crying in a pitiable manner. When in the hospital, or sick bay, the agony of some was so intolerable that – all gently and soothingly as it was done – they had to be held down. The remedies applied were linseed oil and cotton-wool, continuously renewed.

Descending to the lower deck, the scene irresistibly reminded one of the interior of the area of Covent Garden Theatre after the fire of 1856. The vast expanse between decks was one heap of fragments. You trod upon one vast sultry mass of ruin and desolation. The nests of sleeping berths, the corridors and staircases were all (save the main one) gone. The cabin which with two friends I had occupied no longer existed. With all in the same block it had been blown entirely away. A portmanteau belonging to your correspondent was subsequently recovered from the *débâcle*; but my two companions lost everything they possessed on board. Forward, in this lower deck, you saw the great, gaping pit, which had vomited forth the fruits of the "collapse". It was an infernal region, that horrible hole. The bed of the accursed "jacket", with torn and jagged ends, was still visible. In the hole, were beams and girders, planks and rails, and gigantic steampipes twisted double like disused speaking trumpets. The huge iron plates at the root of the funnel were torn or crumpled up like writing paper. The great wrought iron girders supporting the lower deck were curved and bent; the flooring of the deck itself was, in part, upheaved, and disclosed ominous gaps. The boilers had sustained no injury. Weeks' time and thousands of pounds in expenditure, must be consumed ere the *Great Eastern*'s proprietors will be able to repair the damage done to her "main cabin fittings".

Neither ship – as a ship – nor paddles, nor screw, were injured. At first there was an expressed intention to put into the nearest haven; but this idea was abandoned, and the *Great Eastern* proceeded on her voyage to Portland.

GEORGE W. SMALLEY

THE CONTEST IN MARYLAND

New York Tribune, 19 September 1862

The battle fought at Antietam Creek on 17 September 1862 was the bloodiest single-day engagement of the US Civil War. Although the casualties were near evenly split at 12,000 each for the North and the South, the battle crucially stemmed Robert E. Lee's invasion of the Union states. George Washburn Smalley, a Harvard attorney turned war correspondent, witnessed the contest at Antietam by posing as an aide-de-camp to General Hooker (correspondents, in 1862, were forbidden to accompany units in the field), a piece of cleverness he turned to even greater effect by being the first person to bring news of Antietam out of Maryland, sending a brief telegraphic report – intercepted by an anxious War Department in Washington DC – to the New York *Tribune* at 7 a.m. on the 18th, enabling it to be the only paper in the world to carry the story. His inspiration and determination not deserting him, Smalley then made a headlong dash for New York by train, writing a longer account of Antietam by the swinging oil lamp of the railroad coach, which the *Tribune* carried on the morning of Sunday, 19 September in a special edition. It was the journalistic feat of the nineteenth century. Most of his peers either missed the bloody game or were still becalmed in Maryland.

Fierce and desperate battle between 200,000 men has raged since daylight, yet night closes on an uncertain field. It is the greatest battle since Waterloo – all over the field contested with an obstinacy equal even to Waterloo. If not wholly a victory to-night, I believe it is the prelude to victory to-morrow. But what can be foretold of the future of a fight in which from five in the morning till seven at night the best troops of the continent have fought without decisive result?

I have no time for speculation – no time even to gather detail of the battle – only time to state its broadest features – then mount and spur for New York.

After the brilliant victory near Middletown, Gen. McClellan pushed forward his army rapidly, and reached Keedysville with three corps on Monday night. That march has already been described. On the day following the two armies faced each other idly, until night. Artillery was busy at intervals; once in the morning with spirit, and continuing for half an hour, with vigor, till the Rebel battery, as usual, was silenced.

McClellan was on the hill where Benjamin's battery was stationed and found himself suddenly under rather heavy fire. It was still uncertain whether the Rebels were retreating or re-enforcing – their batteries would remain in position in either case, and as they had withdrawn nearly all their troops from view, there was only the doubtful indication of columns of dust to the rear.

On the evening of Tuesday, Hooker was ordered to cross Antietam Creek with his corps, and feeling the left of the enemy, to be ready to attack next morning. During the day of apparent inactivity, McClellan and been maturing his plan of battle, of which Hooker's movement was one development.

The position on either side was peculiar. When Richardson advanced on Monday he found the enemy deployed and displayed in force on a crescent-shaped ridge, the outline of which followed more or less exactly the course of Antietam Creek. Their lines were then forming, and the revelation of force in front of the ground which they really intended to hold, was probably meant to delay our attack until their arrangements to receive it were complete.

During that day they kept their troops exposed and did not move them even to avoid the artillery fire, which must have been occasionally annoying. Next morning the lines and columns which had darkened cornfields and hill crests, had been withdrawn. Broken and wooded ground behind the sheltering hills concealed the Rebel masses. What from our front looked like only a narrow summit fringed with woods was a broad table-land of forest and ravine cover for troops everywhere, nowhere easy access for an enemy. The smoothly sloping surface in front and the sweeping crescent of slowly mingling lines was only a delusion. It was all a Rebel stronghold beyond.

Under the base of those hills runs the deep stream called Antietam Creek, fordable only at distant points. Three bridges cross it, one on the Hagerstown road, one on the Sharpsburg pike, one to the left in a deep recess of steeply falling hills. Hooker passed the first to reach the ford by which he crossed, and it was held by Pleasanton with a reserve of cavalry during the battle. The second was close under the Rebel center, and no way important to yesterday's fight. At the third, Burnside attacked and finally crossed. Between the first and third lay most of the battle lines. They stretched four miles from right to left.

Unaided attack in front was impossible. McClellan's forces lay behind low, disconnected ridges, in front of the Rebel summits, all or nearly all unwooded. They gave some cover for artillery, and guns were therefore massed on the center. The enemy had the Shepherdstown road and the Hagerstown and Williamsport road open to him in the rear for retreat. Along one or the other, if beaten, he must fly. This, among other reasons, determined, perhaps, the plan of battle which McClellan finally resolved on.

The plan was generally as follows: Hooker was to cross on the right, establish himself on the enemy's left if possible, flanking his position, and to open the fight. Sumner, Franklin and Mansfield were to send their forces also to the right, co-operating with and sustaining Hooker's attack while advancing also nearer the center. The heavy work in the center was left mostly to the batteries, Porter massing his infantry supports in the hollows. On the left Burnside was to carry the bridge already referred, advancing then by a road which enters the pike at Sharpsburg, turning at once the Rebel left flank and destroying his line of retreat. Porter and Sykes were held in reserve. It is obvious that the complete success of a plan contemplating widely divergent movements of separate corps, must largely depend on accurate timing, that the attacks should be simultaneous and not successive.

Hooker moved on Tuesday afternoon at four, crossing the creek at a ford above the bridge and well to the right, without opposition. Fronting south-west his line advanced not quite on the Rebel flank but over-lapping and threatening it. Turning off from the road after passing the stream, he sent forward cavalry skirmishers straight into the woods and over the fields beyond. Rebel pickets withdrew slowly before them, firing scattering and harmless shots. Turning again to the left, the cavalry went down on the Rebel flank, coming suddenly close to a battery which met them with unexpected grape shot. It being the nature of cavalry to retire before batteries, this company loyally followed the law of its being, and came swiftly back without pursuit.

Artillery was sent to the front, infantry was rapidly deployed, and skirmishers went out in front and on either flank. The corps moved forward compactly, Hooker as usual reconnoitering in person. They came at last to an open grass-sown field inclosed on two sides with woods, protected on the right by a hill, and entered through a cornfield in the rear. Skirmishers entering these woods were instantly met by Rebel shots, but held their ground, and as soon as supported advanced and cleared the timber. Beyond, on the left and in front, volleys of musketry opened heavily, and a battle seemed to have begun a little sooner than it was expected.

General Hooker formed his lines with precision and without hesitation. Rickett's Division went into the woods on the left in force. Meade, with the Pennsylvania Reserves, formed in the center. Doubleday was sent out on the right, planting his batteries on the hill, and opening at once on a Rebel battery that began to enfilade the central line. It was already dark, and the Rebel position could only be discovered by the flashes of their guns. They pushed forward boldly on the right, after losing ground on the other flank, but made no attempt to regain their first hold on the woods. The fight flashed; and glimmered, and faded, and finally went out in the dark.

Hooker had found out what he wanted to know. When the firing ceased the hostile lines lay close to each other – their pickets so near that six Rebels were captured during the night. It was inevitable that the fight should commence at daylight. Neither side had suffered considerable loss; it was a skirmish, not a battle. "We are through for to-night, gentlemen," remarked the General, "but to-morrow we fight the battle that will decide the fate of the Republic."

Not long after the firing ceased, it sprang up again on the left. General Hooker, who had taken up his headquarters in a barn, which had been nearly the focus of the Rebel artillery, was out at once. First came rapid and unusually frequent picket shots, then several heavy volleys. The General listened a moment and smiled grimly. "We have no troops there. The Rebels are shooting each other. It is Fair Oaks over again." So everybody lay down again, but all the night through there were frequent alarms.

McClellan had been informed of the night's work, and of the certainties awaiting the dawn. Sumner was ordered to move his corps at once, and was expected to be on the ground at daylight. From the extent of the Rebel lines developed in the evening, it was plain that they had gathered their whole army behind the heights and were waiting for the shock.

The battle began with the dawn. Morning found both armies just as they had slept, almost close enough to look into each other's eyes. The left of Meade's reserves and the right of Rickett's line became engaged at nearly the same moment, one with artillery, the other with infantry. A battery was almost immediately pushed forward beyond the central woods, over a plowed field, near the top of the slope where the cornfield began. On this open field, in the corn beyond, and in the woods which stretched forward into the broad-fields, like a promontory into the ocean, were the hardest and deadliest struggles of the day.

For half an hour after the battle had grown to its full strength, the line of fire swayed neither way. Hooker's men were fully up to their work. They saw their General everywhere in front, never away from the fire, and all the troops believed in their commander, and fought with a will. Two-thirds of them were the same men who under McDowall had broken at Manassas.

The half hour passed, the Rebels began to give way a little, only a little, but at the first indication of a receding fire, Forward, was the word, and on went the line with a cheer and a rush. Back across the cornfield, leaving dead and wounded behind them, over the fence, and across the road, and then back again into the dark woods, which closed around them, went the retreating Rebels.

Meade and his Pennsylvanians followed hard and fast – followed till they came within easy range of the woods, among which they saw their beaten enemy disappearing – followed still, with another cheer, and flung themselves against the cover.

But out of those gloomy woods came suddenly and heavily terrible volleys – volleys which smote, and bent, and broke in a moment that eager front, and hurled them swiftly back for half the distance they had won. Not swiftly, nor in panic, any further.

Closing up their shattered lines, they came slowly away – a regiment where a brigade had been, hardly a brigade where a whole division had been victorious. They had met from the woods the first volleys of musketry from fresh troops – had met them and returned them till their line had yielded and gone down before the might of fire, and till their ammunition was exhausted.

In ten minutes the fortune of the day seemed to have changed – it was the Rebels now who were advancing, pouring out of the woods in endless lines, sweeping through the cornfield from which their comrades had just fled. Hooker sent in his nearest brigade to meet them, but it could not do the work. He called for another. There was nothing close enough unless he took it from his right. His right might be in danger if it was weakened, but his center was already threatened with annihilation. Not hesitating one moment, he sent to Doubleday: "Give me your best brigade instantly."

The best brigade came down the hill on the run, went through the timber in front through a storm of shot and bursting shell and crashing limbs, over the open field beyond, and straight into the cornfield, passing as they went the fragments of three brigades shattered by the Rebel fire, and streaming to the rear. They passed by Hooker, whose eyes lighted as he saw these veteran troops led by a soldier whom he knew he could trust. "I think they will hold it," he said.

General Hartsuff took his troops very steadily, but now they they were under fire, not hurriedly, up the hill from which the cornfield begins to descend, and formed them on the crest. Not a man who was not in full view – not one who bent before the storm. Firing at first in volleys, they fired them at will with wonderful rapidity and effect. The whole line crowned the hill and stood out darkly against the sky, but lighted and shrouded ever in flame and smoke. There were the 12th and 18th Massachusetts and another regiment which I cannot remember – old troops all of them.

There for half an hour they held the ridge unyielding in purpose, exhaustless in courage. There were gaps in the line, but it nowhere quailed. Their General was wounded badly early in the fight, but they fought on. Their supports did not come – they were determined to win without them. They began to go down the hill and into the corn, they did not stop to think their ammunition was nearly gone; they were there to win the field and they won it. The Rebel line for the second time fled though the corn into the woods. I cannot tell how few of Hartsuff's brigade were left when the work was done, but it was done. There was no more gallant, determined heroic fighting in all this desperate day. General Hartsuff is very severely wounded, but I do not believe he counts his success too dearly purchased.

The crisis of the fight at this point had arrived: Rickett's division, vainly endeavoring to advance and exhausted by the effort had fallen back. Part of Mansfield's corps was ordered into their relief but Mansfield's troops came back again, and their General was mortally wounded. The left nevertheless was too extended to be turned, and too strong to be broken. Rickett sent word he could not advance, but could hold his ground. Doubleday had kept his guns at work on the right, and had finally silenced a Rebel battery that for half an hour had poured in a galling enfilading fire along Hooker's central line.

There were woods in front of Doubleday's hill which the Rebels held, but so long as those guns pointed that way they did not care to attack. With his left then able to take care of itself, with his right impregnable with two brigades of Mansfield still fresh and coming rapidly up, and with his center a second time victorious, General Hooker determined to advance. Orders were given to Crawford and Gordon – the two Mansfield brigades – to move directly forward at once, the batteries in the center were ordered on, the whole line was called on, and the General himself went forward.

To the right of the cornfield and beyond it was a point of woods. Once carried and firmly held, it was the key of the position. Hooker determined to take it. He rode out in front of his furthest troops on a hill to examine the ground for a battery. At the top he dismounted and went forward on foot, completed his reconnaissance, returned and remounted. The musketry fire from the point of woods was all the while extremely hot. As he put his foot in the stirrup a fresh volley of rifle bullets came whizzing by. The tall soldierly figure of the General, the white horse which he rode, the elevated place where he was – all made him a most dangerously conspicuous mark. So he had been all day, riding often without a staff officer or an orderly near him

– all sent off on urgent duty – visible everywhere on the field. The Rebel bullets had followed him all day, but they had not hit him, and he would not regard them. Remounting on this hill he had not ridden five steps when he was struck in the foot by a ball.

Three men were shot down at the same moment by his side. The air was alive with bullets. He kept on his horse for a few moments, though the wound was severe and excessively painful, and he would not dismount till he had given his last order to advance. He was himself in the very front. Swaying unsteadily on his horse, he turned in his seat to look about him. "There is a regiment to the right. Order it forward! Crawford and Gordon are coming up. Tell them to carry these woods and hold them – and it is our fight!"

It was found that the bullet had passed completely through his foot. The surgeon who examined it on the spot could give no opinion whether bones were broken, but it was afterward ascertained that though grazed they were not fractured. Of course the severity of the wound made it impossible for him to keep the field which he believed already won, so far as it belonged to him to win it. It was nine o'clock. The fight had been furious since five. A large part of his command was broken, but with his right still untouched and with Crawford's and Gordon's brigades just up, above all, with the advance of the whole central line which the men had heard ordered, with a regiment already on the edge of the woods he wanted, he might well leave the field, thinking the battle won – that *his* battle was won, for I am writing, of course, only about the attack on the Rebel left.

I see no reason why I should disguise my admiration of General Hooker's bravery and soldierly ability. Remaining nearly all the morning on the right, I could not help seeing the sagacity and promptness of his manoeuvres, how completely his troops were kept in hand, how devotedly they trusted to him, how keen was his insight into the battle; how every opportunity was seized and every reverse was checked and turned into another success. I say this the more unreservedly, because I have no personal relation whatever with him, never saw him till the day before the fight, and don't like his politics or opinions in general. But what are politics in such a battle?

Sumner arrived just as Hooker was leaving, and assumed command. Crawford and Gordon had gone into the woods, and were holding them stoutly against heavy odds. As I rode over toward the left I met Sumner at the head of his column advancing rapidly through the timber, opposite the point where Crawford was fighting. The veteran General was riding alone in the forest far ahead of his leading brigade, his hat off, his gray hair and beard contrasting strangely with the fire in his eyes and his martial air, as he hurried on to where the bullets were thickest.

Sedgwick's division was in advance, moving forward to support Crawford and Gordon. Rebel re-enforcements were approaching also, and the struggle for the roads was again to be renewed. Sumner sent forward two divisions, Richardson and French, on the left. Sedgwick moving in column of divisions through the woods in the rear, deployed and advanced in line over the cornfield. There was a broad interval between him and the nearest division, and he saw that if the Rebel line was complete his own division was in immediate danger of being flanked. But his orders were to advance, and those are the orders which a soldier – and Sedgwick is every inch a soldier – loves best to hear. To extend his own front as far as possible, he ordered the 34th New York to move by the left flank. The maneuver was attempted under a fire of the greatest intensity, and the regiment, broke. At the same moment the enemy, perceiving their advantage, came round on that flank. Crawford was obliged to give on the right, and his troops pouring in confusion through the ranks of Sedgwick's advance brigade, threw it into disorder and back on the second and third lines. The enemy advanced, their fire increasing.

General Sedgwick was three times wounded, in the shoulder, leg and wrist, but he persisted in remaining on the field so long as there was a chance of saving it. His Adjutant-General, Major Sedgwick, bravely rallying and trying to reform the troops, was shot through the body, the bullet lodging in the spine, and fell from his horse. Severe as the wound is it is probably not mortal. Lieutenant Howe of General Sedgwick's staff endeavored vainly to rally the 34th New York. They were badly cut up and would not stand. Half their officers were killed or wounded, their colours shot to pieces, the Colour-Sergeant killed, everyone of the colour-guard wounded. Only thirty-two were afterward got together.

The 15th Massachusetts went into action with 17 officers and nearly 600 men. Nine officers were killed or wounded, and some of the latter are prisoners. Captain Simons, Captain Saunders of the Sharpshooters, Lieutenant Derby and Lieutenant Berry are killed. Captain Bartlett and Captain Jocelyn, Lieutenant Sourr, Lieutenant Gale and Lieutenant Bradley are wounded. One hundred and thirty-four men were the only remnant that could be collected of this splendid regiment.

General Dans was wounded. General Howard, who took command of the division after General Sedgwick was disabled, exerted himself to restore order, but it could not be done there. General Sumner ordered the line to be reformed under fire. The test was too severe for volunteer troops under such fire. Sumner himself attempted to arrest the disorder, but to little purpose. Lieutenant-Colonel Revere and Captain Andenried of his staff were wounded severely, but not dangerously. It was impossible to hold the position. General Sumner withdrew the division to the rear, and once more the cornfield was abandoned to the enemy.

French sent word he would hold his ground. Richardson, while gallantly leading a regiment under heavy fire, was severely wounded in the shoulder. General Meagher was wounded at the head of his brigade. The loss in general officers was becoming frightful.

At one o'clock affairs on the right had a gloomy look. Hooker's troop were greatly exhausted, and their General away from the field. Mansfield's were no better. Sumner's command had lost heavily, but two of his divisions were still comparatively fresh. Artillery was yet playing vigorously in front, though the ammunition of many of the batteries was entirely exhausted, and they had been compelled to retire.

Doubleday held the right inflexibly. Sumner's headquarters were now in the narrow field where the night before, Hooker had begun the fight. All that had been gained in front had been lost! The enemy's batteries, which if advanced and served vigorously might have made sad work with the closely massed troops were fortunately either partially disabled or short of ammunition. Sumner was confident that he could hold his own; but another advance was out of the question. The enemy, on the other hand, seemed to be too much exhausted to attack.

At this crisis Franklin came up with fresh troops and formed on the left. Slocum, commanding one division of the corps, was sent forward along the slopes lying under the first range of rebel hills, while Smith, commanding the other division, was ordered to retake the cornfields and woods which all day had been so hotly contested. It was done in the handsomest style. His Maine and Vermont regiments and the rest went forward on the run, and cheering as they went, swept like an avalanche through the corn-fields, fell upon the woods, cleared them in ten minutes, and held them. They were not again retaken.

The field and its ghastly harvest which the reaper had gathered in those fatal hours remained finally with us. Four times it had been lost and won. The dead are strewn so thickly that as you ride over it you cannot guide your horse's steps too carefully. Pale and bloody faces are everywhere upturned. They are sad and terrible, but there is nothing which makes one's heart beat so quickly as the imploring look of sorely wounded men who beckon wearily for help which you cannot stay to give.

General Smith's attack was so sudden that his success was accomplished with no great loss. He had gained a point, however, which compelled him to expect every moment an attack, and to hold which, if the enemy again brought up reserves, would take his best energies and best troops. But the long strife, the heavy losses, incessant fighting over the same ground repeatedly lost and won inch by inch, and more than all, perhaps, the fear of Burnside on the left and Porter in front, held the enemy in check. For two or three hours there was a lull even in the cannonade on the right which hitherto had been incessant. McClellan had been over on the field after Sumner's repulse, but had speedily returned to his headquarters. Sumner again sent word that he was able to hold his position, but could not advance with his own corps.

Meanwhile where was Burnside, and what was he doing? On the right where I had spent the day until two o'clock, little was known of the general fortunes of the field. We had heard Porter's guns in the center, but nothing from Burnside on the left. The distance was too great to distinguish the sound of his artillery from Porter's left. There was no immediate prospect of more fighting on the right, and I left the field which all day long had seen the most obstinate contest of the war, and rode over to McClellan's headquarters. The different battle-fields were shut out from each other's view, but all partially visible from the central hill which General McClellan had occupied during the day. But I was more than ever impressed on returning with the completely deceitful appearance of the ground the Rebels had chosen when viewed from the front.

Hooker's and Sumner's struggle had been carried on over an uneven and wooded surface, their own line of battle extending in a semi-circle not less than a mile and a half. Perhaps a better notion of their position can be got by considering their right, center and left as forming three sides of a square. So long therefore as either wing was driven back, the centre became exposed to a dangerous enfilading fire, and the further the center was advanced the worse off it was, unless the lines on its side and rear were firmly held. This formation resulted originally from the efforts of the enemy to turn both flanks. Hooker at the very outset threw his column so far into the center of the Rebel lines that they were compelled to threaten him on the flank to secure their own center.

Nothing of all this was perceptible from the hills in front. Some directions of the Rebel lines had been disclosed by the smoke of their guns, but the whole interior formation of the country beyond the hills was completely concealed. When McClellan arranged his order of battle, it must have been upon information, or have been left to his corps and division commander to discover for themselves. Up to three o'clock Burnside had made little progress. His attack on the bridge had been successful, but the delay had been so great that to the observer it appeared as if McClellan's plans must have been seriously disarranged. It is impossible not to suppose that the attacks on the right and left were meant in a measure to correspond, for otherwise the enemy had only to repel Hooker on the one hand, then transfer his troops, and hurl them against Burnside.

Finally, at four o'clock, McClellan sent simultaneous orders to Burnside and Franklin; to the former to carry the batteries in his front at all hazards and at any cost; to the latter to carry the woods next in front of him to the right, which the rebels still held. The order to Franklin, however, was practically countermanded in consequence of a message from General Sumner that if Franklin went on and was repulsed, his own corps was not yet sufficiently reorganized to be depended on as a reserve.

Franklin, thereon, was directed to run no risk of losing his

present position, and, instead of sending his infantry into the
woods, contented himself with advancing his batteries over the
breadth of the fields in front, supporting them with heavy
columns of infantry, and attacking with energy the Rebel batteries immediately opposed to him. His movement was a success
so far as it went, the batteries maintaining their new ground and
sensibly affecting the steadiness of the Rebel fire. That being
accomplished, and all hazard of the right being again forced back
having been dispelled, the movement of Burnside became at once
the turning point of success and the fate of the day depended on
him.

How extraordinary the situation was may be judged from a
moment's consideration of the facts. It is understood that from
the outset Burnside's attack was expected to be decisive; it
certainly must have been if things went well elsewhere, and if
he succeeded in establishing himself on the Sharpsburg road in
the Rebel rear.

Yet Hooker, and Sumner, and Franklin, and Mansfield were
all sent to the right three miles away while Porter seems to have
done double duty with his single corps in front, both supporting
the batteries and holding himself in reserve. With all this immense force on the right, but 16,000 then were given to Burnside
for the decisive movement of the day.

Still more unfortunate in its results was the total failure of
these separate attacks on the right and left to sustain, or in any
manner co-operate with each other. Burnside hesitated for hours
in front of the bridge which should have been carried at once by a
coup de main. Meantime, Hooker had been fighting for four hours
with various fortune, but final success. Sumner had come up too
late to join in the decisive attack which his earlier arrival would
probably have converted into a complete success; and Franklin
reached the scene only when Sumner had been repulsed. Probably before his arrival the Rebels had transferred a considerable
number of troops to their right to meet the attack of Burnside, the
direction of which was then suspected or developed.

Attacking first with one regiment, then with two, and delaying
both for artillery, Burnside was not over the bridge before two
o'clock – perhaps not till three. He advanced slowly up the slope
in his front, his batteries in rear covering, to some extent, the
movements of the infantry. A desperate fight was going on in a

deep ravine on his right, the Rebel batteries were in full play and, apparently, very annoying and destructive, while heavy columns of Rebel troops were plainly visible, advancing as if careless of concealment, along the road and over the hills in the direction of Burnside's forces. It was at this point of time that McClellan sent him the order above given.

Burnside obeyed it most gallantly. Getting his troops well in hand, and sending a portion of his artillery to the front, he advanced them with rapidity and the most determined vigor, straight up the hill in front, on top of which the Rebels had maintained their most dangerous battery. The movement was in plain view of McClellan's position, and as Franklin, on the other side sent his batteries into the field about the same time, the battle seemed to open in all directions with greater severity than ever.

The fight in the ravine was in full progress, the batteries which Porter supported were firing with new vigour. Franklin was blaring away on the right, and every hill-top ridge and woods along the whole line was crested and veiled with clouds of smoke. All day had been clear and bright since the early cloudy morning, and now this whole magnificent, unequalled scene shone with the splendor of an afternoon September sun. Four miles of battle, its glory all visible, its horrors all veiled, the fate of the Republic hanging on the hour – could anyone be insensible of its grandeur.

There are two hills on the left of the road, the furthest the lowest. The Rebels have batteries on both. Burnside is ordered to carry the nearest to him, which is the furthest from the road. His guns opening first from this new position in front, soon entirely controlled and silenced the enemy's artillery. The infantry came on at once, moving rapidly and steadily up long dark lines, and broad, dark masses, being plainly visible without a glass as they moved over the green hill-side.

The next moment the road in which the Rebel battery was planted was canopied with clouds of dust swiftly descending into the valley. Underneath was a tumult of wagons, guns, horses, and men flying at speed down the road. Blue flashes of smoke burst now and then among them, a horse or a man or half a dozen went down, and then the whirlwind swept on.

The hill was carried, but could it be held? The Rebel columns, before seen moving to the left, increased their pace. The guns, on the hill above, sent an angry tempest of shell down among Burnside's guns and men. He had formed his columns apparently in the near angles of two fields bordering the road – high ground about them everywhere except in the rear.

In another moment a Rebel battle-line appears on the brow of the ridge above them, moves swiftly down in the most perfect order, and though met by incessant discharge of musketry, of which we plainly see the flashes, does not fire a gun. White spaces show where men are falling, but they close up instantly, and still the line advances. The brigades of Burnside are in heavy column; they will not give way before a bayonet charge in line. The Rebels think twice before they dash into those hostile masses.

There is a halt, the Rebel left gives way and scatters over the field, the rest stand fast and fire. More infantry comes up, Burnside is outnumbered; flanked, compelled to yield the hill he took so bravely. His position is no longer one of attack; he defends himself with unfaltering firmness, but he sends to McClellan for help. McClellan's glass for the last hour has seldom been turned away from the left.

He sees clearly enough that Burnside is pressed – he needs no messengers to tell him that. His face grows darker with anxious thought. Looking down into the valley where 15,000 troops are lying, he turns a half-questioning eye on Fitz John Porter, who stands by his side, gravely scanning the field. They are Porter's troops below, are fresh and only impatient to share in this fight. But Porter slowly shakes his head, and one may believe that the same thought is passing through the minds of both Generals: "They are the only reserves of the army; they cannot be spared."

McClellan remounts his horse, and with Porter and a dozen officers of his staff rides away to the left in Burnside's direction. Sykes meets them on the road – a good soldier, whose opinion is worth taking. The three Generals talk briefly together. It is easy to see that the moment has come when everything may turn on one order given or withheld, when the history of the battle is only to be written in thoughts and purposes and words of the General.

Burnside's messenger rides up. His message is "I want troops and guns. If you do not send them I cannot hold my position for half an hour." McClellan's only answer for the moment is a glance at the western sky. Then he turns and speaks very slowly, "Tell General Burnside that this is the battle of the war. He must hold his ground till dark at any cost. I will send him Miller's battery. I can do nothing more. I have no infantry." Then as the messenger was riding away he called him back. "Tell him if he *cannot* hold his ground, then the bridge, to the last man! – always the bridge! If the bridge is lost, all is lost."

The sun is already down; not half an hour of daylight is left. Till Burnside's message came, it had seemed plain to everyone that the battle could not be finished today. None suspected how near was the peril of defeat; of sudden attack on exhausted forces – how vital to the safety of the army and the nation were those 15,000 waiting troops of Fitz John Porter in the hollow. But the Rebels halted instead of pushing on, their vindictive cannonade died away as the light faded. Before it was quite dark, the battle was over. Only a solitary gun of Burnside's thundered against the enemy, and presently this also ceased, and the field was still.

The peril came very near, but it has passed, and in spite of the peril, at the close the day was partly a success – not a victory, but an advantage had been gained. Hooker, Sumner, and Franklin held all the ground they had gained, and Burnside still held the bridge and his position beyond. Everything was favourable for a renewal of the fight in the morning. If the plan of the battle is sound, there is every reason why McClellan should win it. He may choose to postpone the battle to await his reinforcements.

The Rebels may choose to retire while it is still possible. Fatigue on both sides might delay the deciding battle, yet, if the enemy means to fight at all, he cannot afford to delay. His reenforcements may be coming, his losses are enormous. His troops have been massed in woods and hollows, where artillery has its most terrific effect. Ours have been deployed and scattered. From infantry fire there is less difference.

It is hard to estimate losses on a field of such extent, but I think ours cannot be less than 6000 killed and wounded – it may be much greater. Prisoners have been taken from the enemy – I hear of a regiment captured entire, but I doubt it. All the prisoners whom I saw agree in saying that their whole army is there.

MARK TWAIN

THE AMERICAN
ASSAULT ON THE PYRAMIDS

Innocents Abroad, 1869

In 1867 Twain was hired by the *Daily Alta California* to accompany a
party of Americans on a grand tour of Europe and the Middle East. His
letters – the protypes of the humorous travel dispatches of P. J. O'Rourke
and Bill Bryson – to the *Daily Alta California* were subsequently ex-
panded into *Innocents Abroad.*

At the distance of a few miles the Pyramids, rising above the
palms, looked very clean-cut, very grand and imposing, and very
soft and filmy as well. They swam in a rich haze that took from
them all suggestions of unfeeling stone, and made them seem
only the airy nothings of a dream – structures which might
blossom into tiers of vague arches, or ornate colonnades, may
be, and change and change again into all graceful forms of
architecture, while we looked, and then melt deliciously away
and blend with the tremulous atmosphere.

At the end of the levee we left the mules and went in a sail-boat
across an arm of the Nile, or an overflow, and landed where the
sands of the Great Sahara left their embankment, as straight as a
wall, along the verge of the alluvial plain of the river. A laborious
walk in the flaming sun brought us to the foot of the great
Pyramid of Cheops. It was a fairy vision no longer. It was a
corrugated, unsightly mountain of stone. Each of its monstrous
sides was a wide stairway which rose upward, step above step,
narrowing as it went, till it tapered to a point far aloft in the air.
Insect men and women – pilgrims from the *Quaker City* – were
creeping about its dizzy perches, and one little black swarm were

waving postage stamps from the airy summit – handkerchiefs will be understood.

Of course we were besieged by a rabble of muscular Egyptians and Arabs who wanted the contract of dragging us to the top – all tourists are. Of course you could not hear your own voice for the din that was around you. Of course the Sheiks said *they* were the only responsible parties; that all contracts must be made with them, all moneys paid over to them, and none exacted from us by any but themselves alone. Of course they contracted that the varlets who dragged us up should not mention backsheesh once. For such is the usual routine. Of course we contracted with them, paid them, were delivered into the hands of the draggers, dragged up the Pyramids, and harried and be-devilled for backsheesh from the foundation clear to the summit. We paid it, too, for we were purposely spread very far apart over the vast side of the Pyramid. There was no help near if we called, and the Herculeses who dragged us had a way of asking sweetly and flatteringly for backsheesh, which was seductive, and of looking fierce and threatening to throw us down the precipice, which was persuasive and convincing.

Each step being full as high as a dinner-table; there being very, very many of the steps; an Arab having hold of each of our arms and springing upward from step to step and snatching us with them, forcing us to lift our feet as high as our breasts every time, and do it rapidly and keep it up till we were ready to faint – who shall say it is not lively, exhilarating, lacerating, muscle-straining, bone-wrenching and perfectly excruciating and exhausting pastime, climbing the Pyramids? I beseeched the varlets not to twist *all* my joints asunder; I iterated, reiterated, even *swore* to them that I did not wish to beat anybody to the top; did all I could to convince them that if I got there the last of all I would feel blessed above men and grateful to them for ever; I begged them, prayed them, pleaded with them to let me stop and rest a moment – only one little moment: and they only answered with some more frightful springs, and an unenlisted volunteer behind opened a bombardment of determined boosts with his head which threatened to batter my whole political economy to wreck and ruin.

Twice, for one minute, they let me rest while they extorted backsheesh, and then continued their maniac flight up the pyramid. They wished to beat the other parties. It was nothing to them that I, a stranger, must be sacrificed upon the altar of their unholy ambition. But in the midst of sorrow, joy blooms. Even in this dark hour I had a sweet consolation. For I knew that except these Mohammedans repented they would go straight to perdition some day. And *they* never repent – they never forsake their paganism. This thought calmed me, cheered me, and I sank down, limp and exhausted, upon the summit, but happy, *so* happy and serene within.

On the one hand, a mighty sea of yellow sand stretched away toward the ends of the earth, solemn, silent, shorn of vegetation, its solitude uncheered by any forms of creature life; on the other, the Eden of Egypt was spread below us – a broad green floor, cloven by the sinuous river, dotted with villages, its vast distances measured and marked by the diminishing stature of receding clusters of palms. It lay asleep in an enchanted atmosphere. There was no sound, no motion. Above the date-plumes in the middle distance swelled a domed and pinnacled mass, glimmering through a tinted, exquisite mist; away toward the horizon a dozen shapely pyramids watched over ruined Memphis; and at our feet the bland impassible Sphynx looked out upon the picture from her throne in the sands as placidly and pensively as she had looked upon its like full fifty lagging centuries ago.

We suffered torture no pen can describe from the hungry appeals for backsheesh that gleamed from Arab eyes and poured incessantly from Arab lips. Why try to call up the traditions of vanished Egyptian grandeur; why try to fancy Egypt following dead Rameses to his tomb in the Pyramid, or the long multitude of Israel departing over the desert yonder? Why try to think at all? The thing was impossible. One must bring his meditations cut and dried, or else cut and dry them afterward.

The traditional Arab proposed, in the traditional way, to run down Cheops, cross the eighth of a mile of sand intervening between it and the tall Pyramid of Cephron, ascend to Cephron's summit and return to us on the top of Cheops – all in nine minutes by the watch, and the whole service to be rendered for a single dollar. In the first flush of irritation, I said let the Arab and his exploits go to the mischief. But stay. The upper third of Cephron was coated with dressed marble, smooth as glass. A blessed thought entered my brain. He must infallibly break his neck. Close the contract with dispatch, I said, and let him go. He started. We watched. He went bounding down the vast broadside, spring after spring, like an ibex. He grew smaller and smaller till he became a bobbing pigmy, away down toward the bottom – then disappeared. We turned and peered over the other side – forty seconds – eighty seconds – a hundred – happiness, he is dead already; – two minutes – and a quarter – "There he goes!" Too true – it was too true. He was very small now. Gradually, but surely, he overcame the level ground. He began to spring and climb again. Up, up, up – at last he reached the smooth coating – now for it. But he clung to it with toes and fingers, like a fly. He crawled this way and that – away to the right, slanting upward – away to the left, still slanting upward – and stood at last, a black peg on the summit, and waved his pigmy scarf! Then he crept downward to the raw steps again, then picked up his agile heels and flew. We lost him presently. But presently again we saw him under us, mounting with undiminished energy. Shortly he bounded into our midst with a gallant war-whoop. Time, eight minutes, forty-one seconds. He had won. His bones were intact. I was a failure. I reflected. I said to myself, he is tired and must grow dizzy. I will risk another dollar on him.

He started again. Made the trip again. Slipped on the smooth coating – I almost had him. But an infamous crevice saved him. He was with us once more perfectly sound. Time, eight minutes, forty-six seconds.

I said to Dan, "Lend me a dollar – I can beat this game yet."

Worse and worse. He won again. Time, eight minutes, forty, eight seconds. I was out of all patience, now. I was desperate – Money was no longer of any consequence. I said, "Sirrah, I will give you a hundred dollars to jump off this pyramid head first. If you do not like the terms, name your bet. I scorn to stand on expenses now. I will stay right here and risk money on you as long as Dan has got a cent."

I was in a fair way to win, now, for it was a dazzling opportunity for an Arab. He pondered a moment, and would have done it. I think, but his mother arrived, then, and interfered. Her tears moved me – I never can look upon the tears of woman with indifference – and I said I would give her a hundred to jump off, too.

But it was a failure. The Arabs are too high-priced in Egypt.
They put on airs unbecoming to such savages.

We descended, hot and out of humour. The dragoman lit
candles, and we all entered a hole near the base of the pyramid,
attended by a crazy rabble of Arabs who thrust their services
upon us uninvited. They dragged us up a long inclined chute,
and dripped candle-grease all over us. This chute was not more
than twice as wide and high as a Saratoga trunk, and was walled,
roofed, and floored with solid blocks of Egyptian granite as wide
as a wardrobe, twice as thick and three times as long. We kept on
climbing, through the oppressive gloom, till I thought we ought
to be nearing the top of the pyramid again, and then came to the
"Queen's Chamber," and shortly to the Chamber of the King.
These large apartments were tombs. The walls were built of
monstrous masses of smoothed granite, neatly joined together.
Some of them were nearly as large square as an ordinary parlour.
A great stone sarcophagus like a bath-tub stood in the centre of
the King's Chamber. Around it were gathered a picturesque
group of Arab savages and soiled and tattered pilgrims, who held
their candles aloft in the gloom while they chattered, and the
winking blurs of light shed a dim glory down upon one of the
irrepressible memento-seekers who was pecking at the venerable
sarcophagus with his sacrilegious hammer.

We struggled out to the open air and the bright sunshine, and
for the space of thirty minutes received ragged Arabs by couples,
dozens and platoons, and paid them backsheesh for services they
swore and proved by each other that they had rendered, but
which we had not been aware of before – and as each party was
paid, they dropped into the rear of the procession and in due time
arrived again with a newly invented delinquent list for liquida-
tion.

We lunched in the shade of the pyramid, and in the midst of
this encroaching and unwelcome company, and then Dan and
Jack and I started away for a walk. A howling swarm of beggars
followed us – surrounded us – almost headed us off. A Sheik, in
flowing white bournous and gaudy head-gear, was with them. He
wanted more backsheesh. But we had adopted a new code – it was
millions for defence, but not a cent for backsheesh. I asked him if
he could persuade the others to depart if we paid him. He said yes
– for ten francs. We accepted the contract, and said –

"Now persuade your vassals to fall back."

He swung his long staff round his head and three Arabs bit the dust. He capered among the mob like a very maniac. His blows fell like hail, and wherever one fell a subject went down. We had to hurry to the rescue and tell him it was only necessary to damage them a little, he need not kill them. – In two minutes we were alone with the Sheik, and remained so. The persuasive powers of this illiterate savage were remarkable.

Each side of the Pyramid of Cheops is about as long as the Capitol at Washington, or the Sultan's new palace on the Bosporus, and is longer than the greatest depth of St Peter's at Rome – which is to say that each side of Cheops extends seven hundred and some odd feet. It is about seventy-five feet higher than the cross on St Peter's. The first time I ever went down the Mississippi, I thought the highest bluff on the river between St Louis and New Orleans – it was near Selma, Missouri – was probably the highest mountain in the world. It is four hundred and thirteen feet high. It still looms in my memory with undiminished grandeur. I can still see the trees and bushes growing smaller and smaller as I followed them up its huge slant with my eye, till they became a feathery fringe on the distant summit. This symmetrical Pyramid of Cheops – this solid mountain of stone reared by the patient hands of men – this mighty tomb of a forgotten monarch – dwarfs my cherished mountain. For it is four hundred and eighty feet high. In still earlier years than those I have been recalling, Holliday's Hill, in our town, was to me the noblest work of God. It appeared to pierce the skies. It was nearly three hundred feet high. In those days I pondered the subject much, but I never could understand why it did not swathe its summit with never-failing clouds, and crown its majestic brow with everlasting snows. I had heard that such was the custom of great mountains in other parts of the world. I remembered how I worked with another boy, at odd afternoons stolen from study and paid for with stripes, to undermine and start from its bed an immense boulder that rested upon the edge of that hill-top; I remembered how, one Saturday afternoon, we gave three hours of honest effort to the task, and saw at last that our reward was at hand; I remembered how we sat down, then, and wiped the perspiration away and waited to let a picnic party get out of the way in the road below – and then we started the boulder. It was

splendid. It went crashing down the hill-side, tearing up saplings, mowing bushes down like grass, ripping and crushing and
smashing everything in its path – eternally splintered and scattered a wood pile at the foot of the hill, and then sprang from the
high bank clear over a dray in the road – the negro glanced up
once and dodged – and the next second it made infinitesimal
mincemeat of a frame cooper shop, and the coopers swarmed out
like bees. Then we said it was perfectly magnificent, and left.
Because the coopers were starting up the hill to inquire.

Still, that mountain, prodigious as it was, was nothing to the
Pyramid of Cheops. I could conjure up no comparison that
would convey to my mind a satisfactory comprehension of the
magnitude of a pile of monstrous stones that covered thirteen
acres of ground and stretched upward four hundred and eighty
tiresome feet, and so I gave it up and walked down to the Sphynx.

THE SUPPRESSION OF THE PARIS COMMUNE

Daily News, 26 May 1871

In September 1870 the Third Republic of France was proclaimed, but surrender by its leaders in the Franco-Prussian War led working-class Parisians to rise in the famed 'Commune'. On 21 May troops loyal to the Royalist government at Versailles entered the French capital to suppress the rebellion. An estimated 20,000 Parisians lost their lives in the slaughter that followed.

Paris, Tuesday, 23 May, Five o'clock

The firing is furious and confusing all round. At the Opera House it is especially strong. I see troops and man after man skulking along the parapet of its roof. They have packs on, so I think they are Versaillists; but I cannot see their breeches and so cannot be certain. The *drapeau rouge* still waves from the statue on the summit of the New Opera House. The Federals are massed now at the top of the Rue Lafitte and firing down toward the boulevards. This must mean that the Versaillists are on the boulevards now. On account of the Versaillist fire the Federals cannot well come out into the Rue de Provence, and everywhere they seem between the devil and the deep sea. The people in the Porte Cochère are crying bravo and clapping their hands, because they think the Versaillists are winning.

Twenty Minutes Past Five

They were Versaillists that I saw on the parapet of the New Opera. There is a cheer; the people rush out into the fire and clap

their hands. The tricolor is waving on the hither end of the Opera
House. I saw the man stick it up. The red flag still waves at the
other end. A ladder is needed to remove it. Ha! you are a good
plucky one, if all the rest were cowards. You deserve to give the
army a good name. A little grig of a fellow in red breeches, he is
one of the old French linesman breed. He scuttles forward to the
corner of the Rue Halévy in the Boulevard Haussmann, takes up
his post behind a tree, and fires along the Boulevard Haussmann
towards the Rue Taitbout. When is a Frenchman not dramatic?
He fires with an air; he loads with an air; he fires again with a
flourish, and is greeted with cheering and clapping of hands.
Then he beckons us back dramatically, for he meditates firing up
the Rue de Lafayette, but changes his mind and blazes away
again up Haussmann. Then he turns and waves on his fellows as
if he were on the boards of a theatre, the Federal bullets cutting
the bark and leaves all around him. He is down. The woman and
I dart out from our corner and carry him in. He is dead, with a
bullet through the forehead.

Twenty-five Minutes to Six

The scene is intensely dramatic. A Versaillist has got a ladder and
is mounting the statue of Apollo on the front elevation of the New
Opera House. He tears down the *drapeau rouge* just as the
Versailles troops stream out of the Chaussée d'Antin across
the Boulevard Haussmann, and down the Rue Meyerbeer and
the continuation of the Chaussée d'Antin. The people rushed
from their houses with bottles of wine; money was showered into
the streets. The women fell on the necks of the sweaty, dusty men
in red breeches, and hugged them amid shouts of *Vive la ligne*.
The soldiers fraternized warmly; drank and pressed forward.
Their discipline was admirable. They formed in companies
behind the next barricade and obeyed the officer at once when
he called them from conviviality. Now the wave of Versaillists is
over us for good, and the red breeches are across the Great
Boulevard and going at the Place Vendôme. Everybody seems
wild with joy, and Communist cards of citizenship are being torn
up wholesale. It is not *citoyen* now under pain of suspicion. You
may say *monsieur* if you like.

Ten p.m.

Much has been done since the hour at which I last dated. The Versaillist soldiers, pouring down in one continuous stream by the Chaussée d'Antin, horse, foot, and artillery, crossed the Great Boulevard, taking the insurgents in flank, not without considerable fighting and a good deal of loss, for the Federals fought like wildcats wherever they could get the ghost of a cover. Anxious to ascertain whether there was any prospect of an Embassy bag to Versailles, I started up the now quiet Boulevard Haussmann, and by tacks and dodges got down into the Rue de Miromesnil, which debouches in the faubourg opposite the Palace of the Elysée. Shells were bursting very freely in the neighbourhood, but the matter was urgent, and I pressed on up to the Rue du Faubourg Saint-Honoré, and looked round the corner for a second. Had I looked a second longer, I should not have been writing these lines. A shell splinter whizzed past me as I drew back, close enough to blow my beard aside. The street was a pneumatic tube for shellfire. Nothing could have lived in it. I fell back, thinking I might get over to the Embassy as the firing died away, and waited in the entry of an ambulance for an hour. There were not a few ambulances about this spot. I saw, for a quarter of an hour, one wounded man carried into the one I was near every minute, for I timed the stretchers by my watch. Looking into others, I could see the courtyards littered with mattresses and groaning men. A few but not many corpses, chiefly of National Guards, lay in the streets, behind the barricades, and in the gutters.

As I returned to the Hôtel de la Chaussée d'Antin, I had to cross the line of artillery pouring southward from the Church of the Trinity, and so down the Rue Halévy, toward the quarter where the sound indicated hot fighting was still going on. The artillerymen received a wild ovation from the inhabitants of the Chaussée d'Antin. The men gave them money, the women tendered them bottles of wine. All was *gaudeamus*. Where, I wonder, had the people secreted the tricolor all these days of the Commune? It now waved from every window, and flapped in the still night air, as the shouts of *Vive la ligne* gave it a lazy throb.

Wednesday

And so evening wore into night, and night became morning. Ah! this morning! Its pale flush of aurora bloom was darkest, most sombre night for the once proud, now stricken and humiliated, city. When the sun rose, what saw he? Not a fair fight – on that within the last year Sol has looked down more than once. But black clouds flouted his rays – clouds that rose from the Palladium of France. Great God! that men should be so mad as to strive to make universal ruin because their puny course of factiousness is run! The flames from the Palace of the Tuileries, kindled by damnable petroleum, insulted the soft light of the morning and cast lurid rays on the grimy recreant Frenchmen who skulked from their dastardly incendiarism to pot at country-men from behind a barricade. How the place burned! The flames revelled in the historical palace, whipped up the rich furniture, burst out the plate-glass windows, brought down the fantastic roof. It was in the Prince Imperial's wing facing the Tuileries Gardens where the demon of fire first had his dismal sway. By eight o'clock the whole of the wing was nearly burned out. As I reached the end of the Rue Dauphine the red belches of flames were bursting out from the corner of the Tuileries facing the private gardens and the Rue de Rivoli: the rooms occupied by the King of Prussia and his suite on the visit to France the year of the Exhibition. There is a furious jet of flame pouring out of the window where Bismarck used to sit and smoke. Crash! Is it an explosion or a fall of flooring that causes this burst of black smoke and red sparks in our faces? God knows what fell devices may be within that burning pile; it were well surely to give it a wide berth.

And so eastward to the Place du Palais-Royal, which is still unsafe by reason of shot and shell from the neighbourhood of the Hôtel de Ville. And there is the great archway by which troops were wont to enter into the Place du Carrousel – is the fire there yet? Just there, and no more; could the archway be cut, the Louvre, with its artistic riches, might still be spared. But there are none to help. The troops are lounging supine in the rues; intent – and who shall blame weary, powder-grimed men? – on bread and wine. And so the devastator leaps from chimney to chimney, from window to window. He is over the archway now, and I would not give two hours' purchase for all the riches of the Louvre. In the name of modern vandalism, what means that burst of smoke and jet of fire? Alas for art; the Louvre is on fire independently. And so is the Palais-Royal and the Hôtel de Ville, where the rump of the Commune are cowering amidst their incendiarism; and the Ministry of Finance, and many another public and private building besides.

I turn from the spectacle sad and sick, to be sickened yet further by another spectacle. The Versaillist troops collected about the foot of the Rue Saint-Honoré were enjoying the fine game of Communist hunting. The Parisians of civil life are caitiffs to the last drop of their thin, sour, white blood. But yesterday they had cried *Vive la Commune!* and submitted to be governed by this said Commune. Today they rubbed their hands with livid currish joy to have it in their power to denounce a Communist and reveal his hiding place. Very eager at this work are the dear creatures of women. They know the rat-holes into which the poor devils have got, and they guide to them with a fiendish glee which is a phase of the many-sided sex. *Voilà!* the braves of France returned to a triumph after a shameful captivity! They have found him, the miserable! Yes, they drag him out from one of the purlieus which Haussmann had not time to sweep away, and a guard of six of them hem him round as they march him into the Rue Saint-Honoré. A tall, pale, hatless man, with something not ignoble in his carriage. His lower lip is trembling, but his brow is firm, and the eye of him has some pride and defiance in it. They yell – the crowd – "Shoot him; shoot him!" – the demon women most clamorous, of course. An arm goes into the air; there are on it the stripes of a non-commissioned officer, and there is a stick in the fist. The stick falls on the head of the pale man in black. Ha! the infection has caught; men club their rifles, and bring them down on that head, or clash them into splinters in their lust for murder. He is down; he is up again; he is down again; the thuds of the gunstocks on him sounding just as the sound when a man beats a cushion with a stick. A certain British impulse, stronger than consideration for self, prompts me to run forward. But it is useless. They are firing into the flaccid carcass now, thronging about it like blowflies on a piece of meat. His brains spurt on my boot and plash into the gutter, whither the carrion is bodily chucked, presently to be trodden on and rolled on by the feet of multitudes and wheels of gun carriages.

Womanhood, then, is not quite dead in that band of bedlamites who had clamoured "Shoot him." Here is one in hysterics; another, with wan, scared face, draws out of the press an embryo bedlamite, her offspring, and, let us hope, goes home. But surely all manhood is dead in the soldiery of France to do a deed like this. An officer – one with a bull throat and the eyes of Algiers – stood by and looked on at the sport, sucking a cigar meanwhile.

The merry game goes on. Denouncing becomes fashionable, and denouncing is followed in the French natural sequence by braining. Faugh! let us get away from the truculent cowards and the bloody gutters, and the yelling women, and the Algerian-eyed officers. Here is the Place Vendôme, held, as I learn on credible authority, by twenty-five Communists and a woman, against all that Versailles found it in its heart to do, for hours. In the shattered Central Place Versaillist sentries are stalking about the ruins of the column. They have accumulated, too, some forces in the rat-trap. There is one corpse in the gutter buffeted and besmirched – the corpse, as I learn, of the Communist captain of a barricade who held it for half an hour single-handed against the braves of France, and then shot himself. The braves have, seemingly, made sure of him by shooting him and the clay, which was once a man, over and over again.

And how about the chained wildcats in the Hôtel de Ville? Their backs are to the wall, and they are fighting now, not for life, but that they may do as much evil as they can before their hour comes – as come it will before the minute hand of my watch makes many more revolutions. The Versaillists do not dare to rush at the barricades around the Hôtel de Ville; they are at once afraid of their skins and explosions. But they are mining, circumventing, burrowing, and they will be inside the cordon soon. Meanwhile the holders of the Hôtel de Ville are pouring out death and destruction over Paris in miscellaneous wildness. Now it is a shell in the Champs-Elysées; now one in the already shattered Boulevard Haussmann; now one somewhere about the Avenue Reine Hortense. It is between the devil and the deep sea with the people in the Hôtel de Ville. One enemy with weapons in his hand is outside; another, fire, and fire kindled by themselves, is inside. Will they roast, or seek death on a bayonet point?

It is hard to breathe in an atmosphere mainly of petroleum smoke. There is a sun, but his heat is dominated by the heat of the conflagrations. His rays are obscured by the lurid, blue-black smoke that is rising with a greasy fatness everywhere into the air. Let us out of it, for goodness' sake. I take horse, and ride off by the river bank toward the Point-du-Jour, leaving at my back the still loud rattle of the firing and the smoke belches. I ride on to the Point-du-Jour through Dombrowski's "second line of defence" by the railway viaduct. Poor Dombrowski! a good servant to bad masters. I should like to know his fate for certain. Versaillists have told me that they saw him taken prisoner yesterday morning, dragged on to the Trocadéro, and there shot in cold blood in the face of day, looking dauntlessly into the muzzles of the chassepots. Others say he is wounded and a prisoner.

As I ride up the broad slope of the avenue between Viroflay and Versailles, I pass a very sorrowful and dejected company. In file after file of six each march the prisoners of the Commune – there are over two thousand of them together – patiently, and it seems to me with some consciousness of pride they march, linked closely arm in arm. Among them are many women, some of them the fierce barricade Hecates, others mere girls, soft and timid, who are here seemingly because a parent is here too. All are bareheaded and foul with dust, many powder-stained too, and the burning sun beats down on bald foreheads. Not the sun alone beats down, but the flats of sabres wielded by the dashing Chasseurs d'Afrique, who are the escort of these unfortunates. Their experiences might have taught them decency to the captives. No sabre blades had descended on their pates in that long, dreary march from Sedan to their German captivity; they were the prisoners of soldiers. But they are prisoners now no longer; as they caper on their wiry Arab stallions, and in their pride of cheap victory, they belabour unmercifully the miserable of the Commune. In front are three or four hundred prisoners, lashed together with ropes, and among these are not a few men in red breeches, deserters taken red-handed. I marvel that they are here at all, and not dead in the streets of Paris.

As I drive along the green margin of the placid Seine to Saint-Denis; the spectacle which the capital presents is one never to be forgotten. On its white houses the sun still smiles. But up through the sunbeams struggle and surge ghastly swart waves and folds and pillars of dense smoke; not one or two, but I reckon them on my fingers till I lose the count. Ha! there is a sharp crack, and then a dull thud on the air. No artillery that, surely some great explosion, which must have rocked Paris to its base. There rises a convolvulus-shaped volume of white smoke, with a jetlike spurt, such as men describe when Vesuvius bursts into eruption, and then it breaks into fleecy waves and eddies away to the horizon all round as the ripple of a stone thrown into a pool spreads to the margin of the water. The crowds of Germans who sit by the Seine, stolidly watching, are startled into a burst of excitement – the excitement might well be worldwide. "Paris the beautiful" is Paris the ghastly, Paris the battered, Paris the burning, Paris the blood-spattered, now. And this is the nineteenth century, and Europe professes civilization, and France boasts of culture, and Frenchmen are braining one another with the butt ends of muskets, and Paris is burning. We want but a Nero to fiddle.

EXTERMINATION OF THE KELLY GANG

The Age (Melbourne), 29 June 1880

The son of a transported Irish criminal, Ned Kelly (born 1885) was Australia's most notorious outlaw.

At last the Kelly gang and the police have come within shooting distance, and the adventure has been the most tragic of any in the bushranging annals of the colony. Most people will say that it is high time, too, for the murders of the police near Mansfield occurred as long ago as the 26th of October, 1878, the Euroa outrage on the 9th December of the same year, and the Jerilderie affair on the 8th and 9th of February, 1879. The lapse of time induced many to believe that the gang was no longer in the colony, but these sceptics must now be silent. The outlaws demonstrated their presence in a brutally effective manner by the murder of the unfortunate Aaron Sherritt at Sebastopol. Immediately on the news being spread the police were in activity. A special train was despatched from Melbourne at 10.15 on Sunday night. At Essendon Sub-inspector O'Connor and his five black trackers were picked up. They had come recently from Benalla, and were *en route* for Queensland again. Mr O'Connor, however, was fortunately staying with Mrs O'Connor's friends at Essendon for a few days before his departure. Mrs O'Connor and her sister came along thinking that they would be able to pay a visit to Beechworth. After leaving Essendon the train travelled at great speed, and before the passengers were aware of any accident having occurred, we had smashed through a gate about a mile beyond Craigieburn. All we noticed was a crack like a bullet striking the carriage. The brake of the engine had, however, been torn away, the footbridge of the carriage shattered, and the lamp on the guard's van destroyed. Guard Bell was looking out of the van at the time, and had a very narrow escape. The train had to be pulled up, but after a few minutes we started again, relying on the brake of the guard's van. Benalla was reached at half-past 1 o'clock, and there Superintendent Hare with eight troopers and their horses were taken on board. We were now about to enter the Kelly country, and caution was necessary. As the moon was shining brightly, a man was tied on upon the front of the engine to keep a lookout for any obstruction of the line. Just before starting, however, it occurred to the authorities that it would be advisable to send a pilot engine in advance, and the man on the front of our engine was relieved. A start was made from Benalla at 2 o'clock, and at 25 minutes to 3, when we were travelling at a rapid pace, we were stopped by the pilot engine. This stoppage occurred at Playford and Desoyre's paddocks, about a mile and a quarter from Glenrowan. A man had met the pilot and informed the driver that the rails were torn up about a mile and a half beyond Glenrowan, and that the Kellys were waiting for us near at hand. Superintendent Hare at once ordered the carriage doors on each side to be unlocked and his men to be in readiness. His orders were punctually obeyed, and the lights were extinguished. Mr Hare then mounted the pilot engine, along with a constable, and advanced. After some time he returned, and directions were given for the train to push on. Accordingly, we followed the pilot up to Glenrowan station, and disembarked.

No sooner were we out of the train, than Constable Bracken, the local policeman, rushed into our midst, and stated with an amount of excitement which was excusable under the circumstances, that he had just escaped from the Kellys, and that they were at that moment in possession of Jones's public house, about a hundred yards from the station. He called upon the police to surround the house, and his advice was followed without delay. Superintendent Hare with his men, and Sub-inspector O'Connor with his black trackers, at once advanced on the building. They were accompanied by Mr Rawlins, a volunteer from Benalla, who did good service. Mr Hare took the lead, and charged right up to the hotel. At the station were the reporters of the Melbourne press, Mr Carrington, of *The Sketcher*, and the two ladies who had accompanied us. The latter behaved with admirable courage, never betraying a symptom of fear, although bullets were whizzing about the station and striking the building and train. The first brush was exceedingly hot. The police and the gang blazed away at each other in the darkness furiously. It lasted for about a quarter of an hour, and during that time there was nothing but a succession of flashes and reports, the pinging of bullets in the air, and the shrieks of women who had been made prisoners in the hotel. Then there was a lull, but nothing could be seen for a minute or two in consequence of the smoke. In a few minutes Superintendent Hare returned to the railway-station with a shattered wrist. The first shot fired by the gang had passed through his left wrist. He bled profusely from the wound, but Mr Carrington, artist of *The Sketcher*, tied up the wound with his handkerchief, and checked the hemorrhage. Mr Hare then set out again for the fray, and cheered his men on as well as he could, but he gradually became so weak from loss of blood that he had reluctantly to retire and was soon afterwards conveyed to Benalla by a special engine. The bullet passed right through his wrist, and it is doubtful if he will ever recover the use of his left hand. On his departure Sub-inspector O'Connor and Senior-constable Kelly took charge, and kept pelting away at the outlaws all the morning. Mr O'Connor took up a position in a small creek in front of the hotel, and disposed his blackfellows one on each side, and stuck to this post gallantly throughout the whole encounter. The trackers also stood the baptism of fire with fortitude, never flinching for one instant.

At about 5 o'clock in the morning a heartrending wail of grief ascended from the hotel. The voice was easily distinguished as that of Mrs Jones, the landlady. Mrs Jones was lamenting the fate of her son, who had been shot in the back, as she supposed, fatally. She came out from the hotel crying bitterly and wandered into the bush on several occasions, and nature seemed to echo her grief. She always returned, however, to the hotel, until she succeeded, with the assistance of one of the prisoners, in removing her wounded boy from the building, and in sending him on to Wangaratta for medical treatment. The firing continued intermittently, as occasion served, and bullets were continually heard coursing through the air. Several lodged in the station building, and a few struck the train. By this time the hotel was completely surrounded by the police and the black trackers, and a vigilant watch of the hotel was kept up during the dark hours.

At daybreak police reinforcements arrived from Benalla, Beechworth, and Wangaratta. Superintendent Sadlier came from Benalla with nine more men, and Sergeant Steele, of Wangaratta, with six, thus augmenting the besieging force to about 30 men. Before daylight Senior-constable Kelly found a revolving rifle and a cap lying in the bush, about 100 yards from the hotel. The rifle was covered with blood, and a pool of blood lay near it. This was evidently the property of one of the bushrangers, and a suspicion therefore arose that they had escaped. That these articles not only belonged to one of the outlaws but to Ned Kelly himself was soon proved. When day was dawning the women and children who had been made prisoners in the hotel were allowed to depart. They were, however, challenged individually as they approached the police line, for it was thought that the outlaws might attempt to escape under some disguise.

At daylight the gang were expected to make a sally out so as to escape, if possible, to their native ranges, and the police were consequently on the alert. Close attention was paid to the hotel, as it was taken for granted that the whole gang were there. To the surprise of the police, however, they soon found themselves attacked from the rear by a man dressed in a long grey overcoat and wearing an iron mask. The appearance of the man presented an anomaly, but a little scrutiny of his appearance and behaviour soon showed that it was the veritable leader of the gang, Ned Kelly himself. On further observation it was seen that he was only armed with a revolver. He, however, walked coolly from tree to tree, and received the fire of the police with the utmost indifference, returning a shot from his revolver when a good opportunity presented itself. Three men went for him, viz., Sergeant Steele of Wangaratta, Senior-constable Kelly, and a railway guard named Dowsett. The latter, however, was only armed with a revolver. They fired at him persistently, but to their surprise with no effect. He seemed bullet-proof. It then occurred to Sergeant Steele that the fellow was encased in mail, and he then aimed at the outlaw's legs. His first shot of that kind made Ned Kelly stagger, and the second brought him to the ground with the cry, "I am done – I am done." Steele rushed up along with Senior-constable Kelly and others. The outlaw howled like a wild beast brought to bay, and swore at the police. He was first seized by Steele, and as that officer grappled with him he fired off another charge from his revolver. This shot was evidently intended for Steele, but from the smart way in which he secured the murderer the sergeant escaped. Kelly became gradually quiet, and it was soon found that he had been utterly disabled. He had been shot in the left foot, left leg, right hand, left arm, and twice in the region of the groin. But no bullet had penetrated his armour. Having been divested of his armour he was carried down to the railway station, and placed in a guard's van. Subsequently he was removed to the station-master's office, and his wounds were dressed there by Dr Nicholson, of Benalla. What statements he made are given below . . .

The siege was kept up all the forenoon and till nearly 3 o'clock in the afternoon. Some time before this the shooting from the hotel had ceased, and opinions were divided as to whether Dan Kelly and Hart were reserving their ammunition or were dead. The best part of the day having elapsed, the police, who were now acting under the direction of Superintendent Sadlier, determined that a decisive step should be taken. At 10 minutes to 3 o'clock another volley was fired into the hotel, and under cover of the fire Senior-constable Charles Johnson, of Violet Town, ran up to the house with a bundle of straw which (having set fire to) he placed on the ground at the west side of the building. This was a moment of intense excitement, and all hearts were relieved when Johnson was seen to regain uninjured the shelter he had left. All eyes were now fixed on the silent building, and the circle of besiegers began to close in rapidly on it, some dodging from tree to tree, and many, fully persuaded that everyone in the hotel must be *hors de combat*, coming out boldly into the open . . .

In the meantime the straw, which burned fiercely, had all been consumed, and at first doubts were entertained as to whether Senior-constable Johnson's exploit had been successful. Not very many minutes elapsed, however, before smoke was seen coming out of the roof, and flames were discerned through the front window on the western side. A light westerly wind was blowing at the time, and this carried the flames from the straw underneath the wall and into the house, and as the building was lined with calico, the fire spread rapidly. Still no sign of life appeared in the building.

When the house was seen to be fairly on fire, Father Gibney, who had previously started for it but had been stopped by the police, walked up to the front door and entered it. By this time the patience of the besiegers was exhausted, and they all, regardless of shelter, rushed to the building. Father Gibney, at much personal risk from the flames, hurried into a room to the left, and there saw two bodies lying side by side on their backs. He touched them, and found life was extinct in each. These were the bodies of Dan Kelly and Hart, and the rev. gentleman expressed the opinion, based on their position, that they must have killed one another. Whether they killed one another or whether both or one committed suicide, or whether both being mortally wounded by the besiegers, they determined to die side by side, will never be known. The priest had barely time to feel their bodies before the fire forced him to make a speedy exit from the room, and the flames had then made such rapid progress on the western side of the house that the few people who followed close on the rev. gentleman's heels dared not attempt to rescue the two bodies. It may be here stated that after the house had been burned down, the two bodies were removed from the embers. They presented a horrible spectacle, nothing but the trunk and skull being left, and these almost burnt to a cinder. Their armour was found near them. About the remains there was apparently nothing to lead to positive identification, but the discovery of the armour near them and other circumstances render it impossible to be doubted that they were those of Dan Kelly and Steve Hart. The latter was a much smaller man than the younger Kelly, and this difference in size was noticeable in their remains. Constable Dwyer, by-the-by, who followed Father Gibney into the hotel, states that he was near enough to the bodies to recognize Dan Kelly . . .

After the house had been burned Ned Kelly's three sisters and Tom Wright were allowed an interview with him. Tom Wright, as well as the sisters, kissed the wounded man, and a brief conversation ensued, Ned Kelly being to a certain extent recovered from the exhaustion consequent on his wounds. At times his eyes were quite bright, and, although he was of course excessively weak, his remarkably powerful physique enabled him to talk rather freely. During the interview he stated: "I was at last surrounded by the police, and only had a revolver, with which I fired four shots. But it was no good. I had half a mind to shoot myself. I loaded my rifle, but could not hold it after I was wounded. I had plenty of ammunition, but it was no good to me. I got shot in the arm, and told Byrne and Dan so. I could have got off, but when I saw them all pounding away, I told Dan I would see it over, and wait until morning."

"What on earth induced you to go to the hotel?" inquired a spectator.

"We could not do it anywhere else," replied Kelly, eyeing the spectators who were strangers to him suspiciously. "I would," he continued, "have fought them in the train, or else upset it if I had the chance. I didn't care a – who was in it, but I knew on Sunday morning there would be no usual passengers. I first tackled the line, and could not pull it up, and then came to Glenrowan station."

"Since the Jerilderie affair," remarked a spectator, "we thought you had gone to Queensland."

"It would not do for everyone to think the same way," was Kelly's reply. "If I were once right again," he continued, "I would go to the barracks, and shoot every one of the – traps, and not give one a chance."

Mrs Skillion (to her brother) – "It's a wonder you did not keep behind a tree."

Ned Kelly – "I had a chance at several policemen during the night, but declined to fire. My arm was broke the first fire. I got away into the bush, and found my mare, and could have rushed away, but wanted to see the thing out, and remained in the bush."

He is very reserved as to anything connected with his comrades, but answered questions freely when his individual case was alone concerned. He appeared to be suffering from a severe shock and exhaustion, and trembled in every limb. Now and again he fainted, but restoratives brought him round, and in his stronger moments he made the following statements:

"I was going down to meet the special train with some of my mates, and intended to rake it with shot; but it arrived before I expected, and I then returned to the hotel. I expected the train would go on, and I had the rails pulled up so that these – black-trackers might be settled. I do not say what brought me to Glenrowan, but it seems much. Anyhow I could have got away last night, for I got into the bush with my grey mare, and lay there all night. But I wanted to see the thing end. In the first volley the police fired I was wounded on the left foot; soon

afterwards I was shot through the left arm. I got these wounds in
front of the house. I do not care what people say about Sergeant
Kennedy's death. I have made my statement of the affair, and if
the public don't believe me I can't help it; but I am satisfied it is
not true that Scanlan was shot kneeling. He never got off his
horse. I fired three or four shots from the front of Jones's hotel,
but who I was firing at I do not know. I simply fired where I saw
police. I escaped to the bush, and remained there overnight. I
could have shot several constables if I liked. Two passed close to
me. I could have shot them before they could shoot. I was a good
distance away at one time, but came back. Why don't the police
use bullets instead of duck-shot? I have got one charge of duck-
shot in my leg. One policeman who was firing at me was a
splendid shot but I do not know his name. I daresay I would
have done well to have ridden away on my grey mare. The bullets
that struck my armour felt like blows from a man's fist. I wanted
to fire into the carriages, but the police started on us too quickly.
I expected the police to come."

Inspector Sadlier – "You wanted, then, to kill the people in the
train?"

Kelly – "Yes, of course I did. God help them, but they would
have got shot all the same. Would they not have tried to kill me?"

GEORGE WARRINGTON STEEVENS

THE ATTACK ON THE ATBARA

Daily Mail, 29 April 1898

The death of General Gordon at the hands of Pan-Islamic Mahdists at Khartoum in 1895 was viewed in Britain as an unmitigated national disgrace. Victorian pride and geo-politics (the threat posed to the Suez Canal, the empire's trade lifeline to India and the East) required the suppression of the Mahdi uprising and the reconquest of vast and barren Sudan. This was accomplished by Major-General Horatio Kitchener, whose campaign was covered by no fewer than sixteen London correspondents, among them the tyro Winston Churchill, but which was caught most authentically by the twenty-eight-year-old *Daily Mail* correspondent, George Warrington Steevens, an imperial voice for an imperial newspaper in time of imperialist endeavour. The action described below was part of Kitchener's drive on Omdurman and Khartoum.

Fort Atbara, 10 April

As the first rays of sunrise glinted on the desert pebbles, the army rose up and saw that it was in front of the enemy. All night it had moved blindly, in faith. At six in the evening the four brigades were black squares on the rising desert outside the bushes of Umdabea Camp, and they set out to march. Hard gravel underfoot, full moon overhead, about them a coy horizon that seemed immeasurable, yet revealed nothing. The squares tramped steadily for an hour. Then all lay down, so that the other brigades were swallowed up into the desert, and the faces of the British square were no more than shadows in the white moonbeams. The square was unlocked, and first the horses were taken down to water, then the men by half-battalions. We who had water ate some biscuits, put our heads on saddle-bags, rolled our bodies in blankets, and slept a little.

The next thing was a long rustle overhead; stealing in upon us, urgently whispering us to rise and mount and move. The moon had passed overhead. It was one o'clock. The square rustled into life and motion, bent forward, and started, half asleep. No man spoke, and no light showed, but the sand-muffled trampling and the moon-veiled figures forbade the fancy that it was all a dream. The shape of lines of men – now close, now broken, and closing up again as the ground broke or the direction changed – the mounted officers, and the hushed order, "Left shoulder forward," the scrambling Maxim mules, the lines of swaying camels, their pungent smell, and the rare neigh of a horse, the other three squares like it, which we knew of but could not see – it was just the same war machine as we had seen all these days on parade. Only this time it was in deadly earnest, moving stealthily but massively forward towards an event that none of us could quite certainly foretell.

We marched till something after four, then halted, and the men lay down again and slept. The rest walked up and down, talking to one and another, wondering in half-voices *were they there*, would they give us a fight or should we find their lines empty, how would the fight be fought, and, above all, how were we to get over their zariba. For Mahmud's zariba was pictured very high, and very thick and very prickly, which sounded awkward for the Cameron Highlanders, who were to assault it. Somebody had proposed burning it, either with war-rockets or paraffin and safety matches; somebody else suggested throwing blankets over it, though how you throw blankets over a ten by twenty feet hedge of camel-thorn, and what you do next when you have thrown them the inventor of the plan never explained; others favoured scaling ladders, apparently to take headers off on to the thorns and the enemy's spears, and even went so far as to make a few; most were for the simpler plan of just taking hold of it and pulling it apart. But how many of the men who pulled would ever get through the gap?

We could see their position quite well by now – the usual river fringe of grey-green palms meeting the usual desert fringe of yellow-grey mimosa. And the smoke-grey line in front of it all must be their famous zariba. Before its right centre fluttered half a dozen flags, white and pale blue, yellow and pale chocolate. The line went on till it was not half a mile from the flags. Then it halted.

Thud! went the first gun, and phutt! came faintly back, as its shell burst on the zariba into a wreathed round cloud of just the zariba's smoky grey. I looked at my watch, and it marked 6.20. The battle that had now menaced, now evaded us for a month – the battle had begun.

The bugle sang out the advance. The pipes screamed war, and the line started forward, like a ruler drawn over the tussock-broken sand. Up a low ridge they moved forward: when would the dervishes fire? The Camerons were to open from the top of the ridge, only 300 yards short of the zariba; up and up, forward and forward: when would they fire? Now the line crested the ridge; the men knelt down. "Volley-firing by sections" – and crash it came. It came from both sides, too, almost the same instant. Wht-t, wht-t, wht-t piped the bullets overhead: the line knelt very firm, and aimed very steady, and crash, crash, crash, they answered it.

Oh! A cry more of dismayed astonishment than of pain, and a man was upon his feet and over on his back and the bearers were dashing in from the rear. He was dead before they touched him, but already they found another for the stretcher. Then bugle again, and up and on: the bullets were swishing and lashing now like rain on the river. But the line of khaki and purple tartan never bent nor swayed; it just went slowly forward like a ruler. The officers at its head strode self-containedly; they might have been on the hill after grouse; only from their locked faces turned unswervingly towards the bullets could you see that they knew and had despised the danger. And the unkempt, unshaven Tammies, who in camp seemed little enough like covenanters or Ironsides, were now quite transformed. It was not so difficult to go on – the pipes picked you up and carried you on – but it was difficult not to hurry: yet whether they aimed or advanced they did it orderly, gravely, without speaking. The bullets had whispered to raw youngsters in one breath the secret of all the glories of the British Army.

Forward and forward, more swishing about them and more crashing from them. Now they were moving, always without hurry, down a gravelly incline. Three men went down without a

cry at the very foot of the Union Jack, and only one got to his feet
again; the flag shook itself and still blazed splendidly. Next, a
supremely furious gust of bullets, and suddenly the line stood
fast. Before it was a loose low hedge of dry camel-thorn – the
zariba, the redoubtable zariba. That it? A second they stood in
wonder, and then, "Pull it away," suggested somebody. Just
half-a-dozen tugs; and the impossible zariba was a gap and a
scattered heap of brushwood. Beyond is a low stockade and
trenches, but what of that? Over and in! Hurrah, hurrah, hurrah!

Now fall in, and back to the desert outside. And unless you are
congenitally amorous of horrors don't look too much about you.
Black spindle-legs curled up to meet red-gimbleted black faces,
donkeys headless and legless or sieves of shrapnel, camels with
necks writhed back on to their humps, rotting already in pools of
blood and bile-yellow water, heads without faces and faces
without anything below, cobwebbed arms and legs, and black
skins grilled to crackling on smouldering palm-leaf – don't look at
it. Here is the Sirdar's white star and crescent on red; here is the
Sirdar, who created this battle, this clean-jointed, well-oiled,
smooth-running clockwork-perfect masterpiece of a battle. Not a
flaw, not a check, not a jolt; and not a fleck on its shining success.
Once more, hurrah, hurrah, hurrah.

MARINES SIGNALLING
UNDER FIRE AT GUANTANAMO

McClure's, February 1899

Although Crane had written his great war novel *The Red Badge of Courage* (1895) without any personal experience of combat, he made good his education by reporting the Spanish-American War for the New York World and *McClure's* in 1898. Crane died two years later, of tuberculosis, aged twenty-eight.

I

They were four Guantanamo marines, officially known for the time as signalmen, and it was their duty to lie in the trenches of Camp McCalla, that faced the water, and, by day, signal the *Marblehead* with a flag and, by night, signal the *Marblehead* with lanterns. It was my good fortune – at that time I considered it my bad fortune, indeed – to be with them on two of the nights when a wild storm of fighting was pealing about the hill; and, of all the actions of the war, none were so hard on the nerves, none strained courage so near the panic point, as those swift nights in Camp McCalla. With a thousand rifles rattling; with the field-guns booming in your ears; with the diabolic Colt automatics clacking; with the roar of the *Marblehead* coming from the bay, and, last, with Mauser bullets sneering always in the air a few inches over one's head, and with this enduring from dusk to dawn, it is extremely doubtful if anyone who was there will be able to forget it easily. The noise; the impenetrable darkness; the knowledge from the sound of the bullets that the enemy was on three sides of the camp; the infrequent bloody stumbling and death of some man with whom, perhaps, one had messed two hours previous; the weariness of the body, and the more terrible weariness of the mind, at the endlessness of the thing, made it wonderful that at least some of the men did not come out of it with their nerves hopelessly in shreds.

But, as this interesting ceremony proceeded in the darkness, it was necessary for the signal squad to coolly take and send messages. Captain McCalla always participated in the defence of the camp by raking the woods on two of its sides with the guns of the *Marblehead*. Moreover, he was the senior officer present, and he wanted to know what was happening. All night long the crews of the ships in the bay would stare sleeplessly into the blackness toward the roaring hill.

The signal squad had an old cracker-box placed on top of the trench. When not signalling they hid the lanterns in this box; but as soon as an order to send a message was received, it became necessary for one of the men to stand up and expose the lights. And then – oh, my eye, how the guerillas hidden in the gulf of night would turn loose at those yellow gleams!

Signalling in this way is done by letting one lantern remain stationary – on top of the cracker-box, in this case – and moving the other over to the left and right and so on in the regular gestures of the wigwagging code. It is a very simple system of night communication, but one can see that it presents rare possibilities when used in front of an enemy who, a few hundred yards away, is overjoyed at sighting so definite a mark.

How, in the name of wonders, those four men at Camp McCalla were not riddled from head to foot and sent home more as repositories of Spanish ammunition than as marines is beyond all comprehension. To make a confession – when one of these men stood up to wave his lantern, I lying in the trench, invariably rolled a little to the right or left, in order that, when he was shot, he might not fall on me. But the squad came off scatheless, despite the best efforts of the most formidable corps in the Spanish army – the Escuadra de Guantanamo. That it was the most formidable corps in the Spanish army of occupation has been told me by many Spanish officers and also by General Menocal and other insurgent officers. General Menocal was Garcia's chief of staff when the latter was operating busily in Santiago province. The regiment was composed solely of practicos, or guides, who knew every shrub and tree on the ground over which they moved.

Whenever the adjutant, Lieutenant Draper, came plunging along through the darkness with an order – such as: "Ask the *Marblehead* to please shell the woods to the left" – my heart would come into my mouth, for I knew then that one of my pals was going to stand up behind the lanterns and have all Spain shoot at him.

The answer was always upon the instant: "Yes, sir."

Then the bullets began to snap, snap, snap, at his head, while all the woods began to crackle like burning straw. I could lie near and watch the face of the signalman, illumed as it was by the yellow shine of lantern-light, and the absence of excitement, fright, or any emotion at all on his countenance was something to astonish all theories out of one's mind. The face was in every instance merely that of a man intent upon his business, the business of wigwagging into the gulf of night where a light on the *Marblehead* was seen to move slowly.

These times on the hill resembled, in some ways, those terrible scenes on the stage – scenes of intense gloom, blinding lightning, with a cloaked devil or assassin or other appropriate character muttering deeply amid the awful roll of the thunder-drums. It was theatric beyond words: one felt like a leaf in this booming chaos, this prolonged tragedy of the night. Amid it all one could see from time to time the yellow light on the face of a preoccupied signalman.

Possibly no man who was there ever before understood the true eloquence of the breaking of the day. We would lie staring into the east, fairly ravenous for the dawn. Utterly worn to rags, with our nerves standing on end like so many bristles, we lay and watched the east – the unspeakably obdurate and slow east. It was a wonder that the eyes of some of us did not turn to glass balls from the fixity of our gaze.

Then there would come into the sky a patch of faint blue light. It was like a piece of moonshine. Some would say it was the beginning of daybreak; others would declare it was nothing of the kind. Men would get very disgusted with each other in these low-toned arguments held in the trenches. For my part, this development in the eastern sky destroyed many of my ideas and theories concerning the dawning of the day; but then, I had never before had occasion to give it such solemn attention.

This patch widened and whitened in about the speed of a man's accomplishment if he should be in the way of painting Madison Square Garden with a camel's-hair brush. The guerrillas always set out to whoop it up about this time, because they knew the occasion was approaching when it would be expedient for them to elope. I, at least, always grew furious with this wretched sunrise. I thought I could have walked around the world in the time required for the old thing to get up above the horizon.

One midnight, when an important message was to be sent to the *Marblehead*, Colonel Huntington came himself to the signal-place with Adjutant Draper and Captain McCauley, the quartermaster. When the man stood up to signal, the colonel stood beside him. At sight of the lights, the Spaniards performed as usual. They drove enough bullets into that immediate vicinity to kill all the marines in the corps.

Lieutenant Draper was agitated for his chief. "Colonel, won't you step down, sir?"

"Why, I guess not," said the grey old veteran in his slow, sad, always gentle way. "I am in no more danger than the man."

"But, sir –" began the adjutant.

"Oh, it's all right, Draper."

So the colonel and the private stood side to side and took the heavy fire without either moving a muscle.

Day was always obliged to come at last, punctuated by a final exchange of scattering shots. And the light shone on the marines, the dumb guns, the flag. Grimy yellow face looked into grimy yellow face, and grinned with weary satisfaction. Coffee!

Usually it was impossible for many of the men to sleep at once. It always took me, for instance, some hours to get my nerves combed down. But then it was great joy to lie in the trench with the four signalmen, and understand thoroughly that that night was fully over at last, and that, although the future might have in store other bad nights, that one could never escape from the prison-house which we call the past.

II

At the wild little fight at Cusco there were some splendid exhibitions of wigwagging under fire. Action began when an advanced detachment of marines under Lieutenant Lucas, with the Cuban guides, had reached the summit of a ridge overlooking a small valley where there was a house, a well, and a thicket of some kind of shrub with great broad oily leaves. This thicket, which was perhaps an acre in extent, contained the guerillas. The valley was open to the sea. The distance from the top of the ridge to the thicket was barely two hundred yards.

The *Dolphin* had sailed up the coast in line with the marine advance, ready with her guns to assist in any action. Captain Elliott, who commanded the two hundred marines in this fight, suddenly called out for a signalman. He wanted a man to tell the *Dolphin* to open fire on the house and the thicket. It was a blazing, bitter hot day on top of the ridge with its shrivelled chaparral and its straight, tall cactus-plants. The sky was bare and blue, and hurt like brass. In two minutes the prostrate marines were red and sweating like so many hull-buried stokers in the tropics.

Captain Elliott called out: "Where's a signalman? Who's a signalman here?"

A red-headed mick – I think his name was Clancy; at any rate, it will do to call him Clancy – twisted his head from where he lay on his stomach pumping his Lee, and, saluting, said that he was a signalman.

There was no regulation flag with the expedition, so Clancy was obliged to tie his blue polka-dot neckerchief on the end of his rifle. It did not make a very good flag. At first Clancy moved a way down the safe side of the ridge and wigwagged there very busily. But what with the flag being so poor for the purpose, and the background of ridge being so dark, those on the *Dolphin* did not see it. So Clancy had to return to the top of the ridge and outline himself and his flag against the sky.

The usual thing happened. As soon as the Spaniards caught sight of this silhouette, they let go like mad at it. To make things more comfortable for Clancy, the situation demanded that he face the sea and turn his back to the Spanish bullets. This was a hard game, mark you – to stand with the small of your back to volley firing. Clancy thought so. Everybody thought so. We all cleared out of his neighbourhood. If he wanted sole possession of any particular spot on that hill, he could have it for all we would interfere with him.

It cannot be denied that Clancy was in a hurry. I watched him. He was so occupied with the bullets that snarled close to his ears that he was obliged to repeat the letters of his message softly to himself. It seemed an intolerable time before the *Dolphin* answered the little signal. Meanwhile we gazed at him, marvelling every second that he had not yet pitched headlong. He swore at times.

Finally the *Dolphin* replied to his frantic gesticulation, and he delivered his message. As his part of the transaction was quite finished – whoop! – he dropped like a brick into the firing line and began to shoot; began to get "hunky" with all those people who had been plugging at him. The blue polka-dot neckerchief still fluttered from the barrel of his rifle. I am quite certain that he let it remain there until the end of the fight.

The shells of the *Dolphin* began to plough up the thicket, kicking the bushes, stones, and soil into the air as if somebody was blasting there.

Meanwhile, this force of two hundred marines and fifty Cubans and the force of – probably – six companies of Spanish guerillas were making such an awful din that the distant Camp McCalla was all alive with excitement. Colonel Huntington sent out strong parties to critical points on the road to facilitate, if necessary, a safe retreat, and also sent forty men under Lieutenant Magill to come up on the left flank of the two companies in action under Captain Elliott. Lieutenant Magill and his men had crowned a hill which covered entirely the flank of the fighting companies, but when the *Dolphin* opened fire, it happened that Magill was in the line of the shots. It became necessary to stop the *Dolphin* at once. Captain Elliott was not near Clancy at this time, and he called hurriedly for another signalman.

Sergeant Quick arose and announced that he was a signalman. He produced from somewhere a blue polka-dot neckerchief as large as a quilt. He tied it on a long, crooked stick. Then he went to the top of the ridge and, turning his back to the Spanish fire, began to signal to the *Dolphin*. Again we gave a man sole possession of a particular part of the ridge. We didn't want it. He could have it and welcome. If the young sergeant had had the smallpox, the cholera, and the yellow fever, we could not have slid out with more celerity.

As men have said often, it seemed as if there was in this war a

God of Battles who held His mighty hand before the Americans. As I looked at Sergeant Quick wigwagging there against the sky, I would not have given a tin tobacco tag for his life. Escape for him seemed impossible. It seemed absurd to hope that he would not be hit; I only hoped that he would be hit just a little, little, in the arm, the shoulder, or the leg.

I watched his face, and it was as grave and serene as that of a man writing in his own library. He was the very embodiment of tranquillity in occupation. He stood there amid the animal-like babble of the Cubans, the crack of rifles, and the whistling snarl of the bullets, and wigwagged whatever he had to wigwag without heeding anything but his business. There was not a single trace of nervousness or haste.

To say the least, a fight at close range is absorbing as a spectacle. No man wants to take his eyes from it until that time comes when he makes up his mind to run away. To deliberately stand up and turn your back to a battle is in itself hard work. To deliberately stand up and turn your back to a battle and hear immediate evidences of the boundless enthusiasm with which a large company of the enemy shoot at you from an adjacent thicket is, to my mind at least, a very great feat. One need not dwell upon the detail of keeping the mind carefully upon a slow spelling of an important code message.

I saw Quick betray only one sign of emotion. As he swung his clumsy flag to and fro, and end of it once caught on a cactus pillar, and he looked sharply over his shoulder to see what had it. He gave the flag an impatient jerk. He looked annoyed.

J.E. DILLON

"AH, YOU COWARDS": THE SECOND TRIAL OF DREYFUS

Daily Telegraph, 11 September 1899

Dreyfus, a French Jew, was unjustly convicted in 1894 of passing military secrets to Germany. After public protest, the Government ordered a retrial by court-martial at Rennes in September 1899. Again, the French Army perjured itself, and again Dreyfus was found guilty. Not until 1906 was Dreyfus pardoned.

Rennes, Saturday Night

Captain Alfred Dreyfus was once more condemned to degradation and imprisonment on Saturday, his day of fate, before an auditory trembling with emotion, a city nervous and passionate, and a world struck dumb with indignation. Five of his seven Judges have thus put themselves, in the eyes of most, beyond the pale of human reason and outside the reach of appeals to the moral sense. Their verdict is regarded as an outrage on what the bulk of mankind considers as truth and justice, and the contradictory terms in which it is couched destroy belief even in that simulacrum of sincerity which is afforded by a semi-hypnotized judgment and a wholly false conscience. Five officers deliberately closed their ears to unanswerable evidence, shut their eyes to solid facts, and opened their hearts to the most odious of human prejudices. Instead of adjudging the question put by the supreme tribunal – whether or not the prisoner was guilty of treason – they decided the issue illegally raised by Mercier whether they would save a full-blown general accused of a crime or a subordinate Jew who is proved to be innocent. And yet the popular cry for justice has not been stifled, but rather intensified, by the proceedings which have just culminated in the extraordinary verdict.

A misty, melancholy morning ushered in the memorable day known as Great Saturday by the followers of the Mosaic law, and the uncertain twilight lasted up to ten o'clock. Clouds lowered over the city, too dense for the rays of the sun to pierce, and the keen nip of autumnal air akin to the biting frost of winter winds stiffened the grey mist that wrapped the roofs of houses, hid the tops of trees, and hovered over the surface of the river. The sitting was an hour later than usual to-day, and it was seven o'clock as we crossed the bridge leading to that half of the city in which the now historic hall of judgment is situate. Before we reached the great square bounded by the quay, the post office, and the commercial exchange, a great rift in the grey mist revealed to our wondering eyes large bodies of dragoons split up into groups, sitting, standing or lying on the ground. Some were playing cards with a degree of passion which was tempered only by a feeling of the responsibility that was supposed to rest upon their shoulders on this last day of the great drama. Others were drinking coffee, or having the future foretold them with the help of the grounds; others, again, were chatting and joking, reading the morning journals, or looking after their horses, which stood in threes or fours around. The clatter of horses' hoofs was heard from all quarters of the city. Posses of mounted gendarmes came tearing along the cobble-paved streets, though several cordons were drawn around the Lycée. All the windows of the houses were black with human heads, the roofs were also crowded in some places, and Rennes wore the repellant look of a city garrisoned by the enemy. All the streets leading to the Lycée are guarded, and none of the ordinary tickets are recognized on this exceptional day before seven o'clock. The *camelots* who had been out forming a queue from a very early hour in the hope of finding purchasers for the places in the back of the court were driven from their positions and sent home by the police. No public is to be admitted to-day beyond a few detectives in plain clothes, gendarmes in uniforms, and a score or two of their well-behaved relatives. Troops continue to arrive from other cities, tramcars are forbidden to run, peasants on their way to the weekly market are stopped and told to make a long circuit. They refuse to turn back, and want to parley with the police, but are driven along like loudly-bleating sheep.

At seven o'clock, judges, witnesses, and pressmen provided with tickets are allowed to pass first one of the living barriers, then another, and, finally, the third. On entering the little courtyard leading to the Lycée my card is carefully examined, my name written down, and then, without a word of warning, two hard and heavy hands run down my back, across my chest, over all my pockets, and before I can realize what it means, I am literally pushed forward with a force strong enough to carry me several yards along. It was all over in a few seconds. There are two agents of the secret police to execute this precautionary work. Turning round to see how other comers were faring, I noticed my friend, Max Nordau, in the grip of the detectives, and a moment later heard a noise and hubbub. In one of Nordau's pockets an opera glass was found, seized, and retained by the police. The owner protested, but in vain. He was told to choose whether himself or his opera glass should remain without. Just as I was entering six of the members of the court martial drove up in a curiously shaped vehicle with a tarpaulin hood over it, shaped like the carts in which postmen are driven to their districts in Russia, and calves are conveyed to the slaughter-house in Austria. One of them jumped out, purchased a copy of the *Figaro* in a little tobacco shop, and then they all dispersed.

In the courtyard, in which we were wont to exchange ideas and compare notes, stood two batteries of artillery, and the sheen of drawn sabres and sharpened bayonets exerted a disagreeable fascination on the eye of the mere civilian. If on this historic Saturday the Army had resolved to abolish the Constitution, abrogate the laws, and change the form of government, no more elaborate or deterrent measures could have been adopted.

Lord Russell of Killowen enters attired in black, with a white waist-coat, and holding in his hand a silk hat and kid gloves, and takes his place near General Chamoin. Immediately after him enter the members of the court martial. Longer and louder than ever before were the echoes of the presenting of arms, and before they had died away the prisoner and his gaoler walked in. His face was unusually pale, his eyes dull, his gait slow, and his tread much less elastic than ever before. It might have been the gait of a brave man on his way to execution.

The discussion is exhaustive, elementary, and to us who are already convinced, wearisome. At nine the stream of argument is still flowing on as copiously as in the beginning. Occasionally the clatter of horses' hoofs is heard without. At ten o'clock there is a movement of impatience. People fear that the finding will be put off until Monday, which would be a terrible hardship for the poor prisoner. That he is certain to be released is an axiom accepted by all, and not open to discussion.

At last Colonel Jouaust adjourns for twenty minutes. We take our recreation in the familiar courtyard for the last time, questioning each other about our impressions. Optimism prevails among all. Jaures is extremely hopeful, Mathieu Dreyfus and Bernard Lazare likewise, and nobody feels or expresses any misgivings whatsoever. The weather, perhaps, contributed to dissipate any doubts one might have had. The mist had vanished, the clouds had drifted away, and the genial sun bathed the city in a flood of golden light. Will judgment be given in the forenoon, or will there be an afternoon sitting; will Captain Dreyfus accept the invitation given him by the Prince of Monaco or will he remain in France? Some have heard that a special train will take him to Switzerland to-night.

Suddenly the bell rings and we enter. For the last time, they say. The court fills up rapidly, the Judges return, and Maître Demange rises again. His moderation of tone has become disagreeable. He has honeyed words for all the generals, strictures for none. He keeps rigidly to the defensive, never once venturing to attack anyone. He admits that the prosecution have strung together suppositions which are this and nothing more, and, by way of answer, he imitates them, piling hypothesis upon hypothesis against Esterhazy. And at last he exclaims; "When you say to yourselves that on the other side of the Channel there is a man who could have . . . but it is not for us to declare him a traitor. Then your minds will be invaded by a doubt. This doubt, gentlemen, is enough for my purpose. This doubt is an acquittal." A moment later the Court and the prisoner had gone Pressmen prepared their urgent telegrams, one for each possibility – "Convicted", and "Acquitted".

At last the greffier, Coupors, entered, followed by Carriere, and everyone rushed to his place, while the Pressmen stood near the despatch boxes communicating with outside, so as to be able to throw in the proper telegram the moment the decisive word had been uttered. We all stood up with bated breath, but there was no sign of the coming of the Judges. We remained thus for fully ten minutes, but minutes of the kind which make up eternity, not time. Then there was a hushed murmur, the tinkling of a bell, a swaying of bodies, a creaking of desks, a scraping of boots on the floor. Nor did the noise subside until we were vaguely aware that it had somehow merged into the voice of the President uttering the awful words that were even now deciding the prisoner's fate. The multitude shuddered visibly as the glassy surface of an azure lake may curdle and darken when a storm-heralding wind passes over it. Everybody I saw was very pale, and many, like myself, were trembling. Colonel Jouaust's voice was unsteady, and seemed to have a funereal ring in it as he held up three sheets of paper in his left hand and read out the judgment. Was his voice loud enough for Captain Dreyfus in his little room away off the hall to hear? Few people knew what he was reading. An unerring instinct kept them on the watch for the essential words. Suddenly we heard; "Yes; the accused man is guilty," and a shudder convulsed the frames of the public. Thus hope mocks Dreyfus like a demon's laugh. But had we heard aright? I, for my part, could hear nothing further. I saw naught but Colonel Jouaust's bleached head and his thick white moustache. The speaking waxen face grew bigger and bigger, absorbing all things else in the hall, whirling round and round, swaying in a room of darkness, to the accompaniment of the sing-song sound which seemed inarticulate until the words, "Extenuating circumstances," "ten years seclusion" struck my ears. Then I noted the flood of golden light bathing the hall, the deep calm of the blue heaven visible through the open window, and the contrast between this tranquillizing frame and the blood-curdling picture made an everlasting impression on my soul.

Suddenly someone near to me shouted out to the Judges: "Ah! you cowards!"

WINSTON S. CHURCHILL

ESCAPE

Morning Post, 24 January 1900

Winston Churchill cut his teeth as a war correspondent during the Sudan campaign, where he employed family influence to wheedle a commission in the 21st Lancers, thus guaranteeing himself a front view of the action at Omdurman. He used a similar ploy when war broke out between Britain and uppity Dutch settlers in South Africa in 1899, persuading the army to grant him a commission in the South Africa Light Horse – at the same time as he enjoyed his £250 monthly wage from the *Morning Post*. This duality of occupation, however, almost cost Churchill his life when he was captured by Boer horsemen. General Joubert was inclined to shoot him because he was caught bearing arms, but in the event Churchill escaped from captivity in Pretoria and made his way to safety in Lourenço Marques, a colourful escapade which made his name.

How unhappy is that poor man who loses his liberty! What can the wide world give him in exchange? No degree of material comfort, no consciousness of correct behaviour, can balance the hateful degradation of imprisonment. Before I had been an hour in captivity I resolved to escape. Many plans suggested themselves, were examined and rejected. For a month I thought of nothing else. But the peril and difficulty restrained action. I think that it was the news of the British defeat at Stormberg that clinched the matter. All the news we heard in Pretoria was derived from Boer sources, and was hideously exaggerated and distorted. Every day we read in the *Volksstem* – probably the most amazing tissue of lies ever presented to the public under the name of a newspaper – of Boer victories and of the huge slaughters and shameful flights of the British. However much one might doubt and discount these tales they made a deep impression. A month's feeding on such literary garbage weakens the constitution of the mind. We wretched prisoners lost heart. Perhaps Great Britain would not persevere; perhaps foreign powers would intervene; perhaps there would be another disgraceful, cowardly peace. At the best the war and our confinement would be prolonged for many months. I do not pretend that impatience at being locked up was not the foundation of my determination; but I should never have screwed up my courage to make the attempt without the earnest desire to do something, however small, to help the British cause. Of course, I am a man of peace. I do not fight. But swords are not the only weapons in the world. Something may be done with a pen. So I determined to take all hazards; and, indeed, the affair was one of very great danger and difficulty.

The State Model Schools, the building in which we were confined, is a brick structure standing in the midst of a gravel quadrangle and surrounded on two sides by an iron grille and on two by a corrugated iron fence about ten feet high. These boundaries offered little obstacle to anyone who possessed the activity of youth, but the fact that they were guarded on the inside by sentries armed with rifle and revolver fifty yards apart made them a wellnigh insuperable barrier. No walls are so hard to pierce as living walls. I thought of the penetrating power of gold, and the sentries were sounded. They were incorruptible. I seek not to deprive them of the credit, but the truth is that the bribery market in this country has been spoiled by the millionaires. I could not afford with my slender resources to insult them heavily enough. So nothing remained but to break out in spite of them. With another officer who may for the present – since he is still a prisoner – remain nameless I formed a scheme.

After anxious reflection and continual watching, it was discovered that when the sentries near the offices walked about on their beats they were at certain moments unable to see the top of a few yards of the wall. The electric lights in the middle of the quadrangle brilliantly lighted the whole place, but cut off the sentries beyond them from looking at the eastern wall For behind the lights all seemed by contrast darkness. The first thing was therefore to pass the two sentries near the offices. It was necessary to hit off the exact moment when both their backs should be turned together. After the wall was scaled we should be in the garden of the villa next door. There our plan came to an end. Everything after this was vague and uncertain. How to get out of the garden, how to pass unnoticed through the streets, how to evade the patrols that surrounded the town and, above all, how to cover the two hundred and eighty miles to the Portuguese frontiers, were questions which would arise at a later stage. All attempts to communicate with friends outside had failed. We cherished the hope that with chocolate, a little Kaffir knowledge and a great deal of luck we might march the distance in a fortnight, buying mealies at the native kraals and lying hidden by day. But it did not look a very promising prospect.

We determined to try on the night of 11 December, making up our minds quite suddenly in the morning, for these things are best done on the spur of the moment. I passed the afternoon in positive terror. Nothing has ever disturbed me as much as this. There is something appalling in the idea of stealing secretly off in the night like a guilty thief. The fear of detection has a pang of its own. Besides, we knew quite well that on occasion, even on excuse, the sentries – they were armed police – would fire. Fifteen yards is a short range. And beyond the immediate danger lay a prospect of severe hardship and suffering, only faint hopes of success, and the probability at the best of five months in Pretoria Gaol.

The afternoon dragged tediously away. I tried to read Mr Lecky's *History of England*, but for the first time in my life that wise writer wearied me. I played chess and was hopelessly beaten. At last it grew dark. At seven o'clock the bell for dinner rang and the officers trooped off. Now was the time. But the sentries gave us no chance. They did not walk about. One of them stood exactly opposite the only practicable part of the wall. We waited for two hours, but the attempt was plainly impossible, and so with a most unsatisfactory feeling of relief to bed.

Tuesday, the 12th! Another day of fear, but fear crystallising more and more into desperation. Anything was better than further suspense. Night came again. Again the dinner bell sounded. Choosing my opportunity I strolled across the quadrangle and secreted myself in one of the offices. Through a chink I watched the sentries. For half an hour they remained stolid and obstructive. Then all of a sudden one turned and walked up to his comrade and they began to talk. Their backs were turned. Now or never. I darted out of my hiding-place and ran to the wall, seized the top with my hands and drew myself up. Twice I let myself down again in sickly hesitation, and then with a third resolve scrambled up. The top was flat. Lying on it I had one parting glimpse of the sentries, still talking, still with their backs turned; but, I repeat, fifteen yards away. Then I lowered myself silently down into the adjoining garden and crouched among the shrubs. I was free. The first step had been taken and it was irrevocable.

It now remained to await the arrival of my comrade. The bushes of the garden gave a good deal of cover, and in the moonlight their shadows lay black on the ground. Twenty yards away was the house, and I had not been five minutes in hiding before I perceived that it was full of people; the windows revealed brightly lighted rooms, and within I could see figures moving about. This was a fresh complication. We had always thought the house unoccupied. Presently – how long afterwards I do not know, for the ordinary measures of time, hours, minutes and seconds, are quite meaningless on such occasions – a man came out of the door and walked across the garden in my direction. Scarcely ten yards away he stopped and stood still, looking steadily towards me. I cannot describe the surge of panic which nearly overwhelmed me. I must be discovered. I dared not stir an inch. But amid a tumult of emotion, reason, seated firmly on her throne, whispered, "Trust to the dark background." I remained absolutely motionless. For a long time the man and I remained opposite each other, and every instant I expected him to spring forward. A vague idea crossed my mind that I might silence him. "Hush, I am a detective. We expect that an officer will break out here tonight. I am waiting to catch him." Reason – scornful this time – replied: "Surely a Transvaal detective would speak Dutch. Trust to the shadow." So I trusted, and after a spell another man came out of the house, lighted a cigar, and both he and the other walked off together. No sooner had they turned than a cat pursued by a dog rushed into the bushes and collided into me. The startled animal uttered a "miaul" of alarm and darted back again, making a horrible rustling. Both men stopped at once. But it was only the cat, and they passed out of the garden gate into the town.

I looked at my watch. An hour had passed since I climbed the wall. Where was my comrade? Suddenly I heard a voice from within the quadrangle say quite loud, "All up." I crawled back to the wall. Two officers were walking up and down the other side jabbering Latin words, laughing and talking all manner of nonsense – amid which I caught my name. I risked a cough. One of the officers immediately began to chatter alone. The other said slowly and clearly: ". . . cannot get out. The sentry suspects. It's all up. Can you get back again?" But now all my fears fell from me at once. To go back was impossible. I could not hope to climb the wall unnoticed. Fate pointed onwards. Besides, I said to myself, "Of course, I shall be recaptured, but I will at least have a run for my money." I said to the officers: "I shall go on alone."

Now, I was in the right mood for these undertakings – that is to say that, thinking failure almost certain, no odds against success affected me. All risks were less than the certainty. The gate which led into the road was only a few yards from another sentry. I said to myself, "*Toujours l'audace*": put my hat on my head, strode out into the middle of the garden, walked past the windows of the house without any attempt at concealment, and so went through the gate and turned to the left. I passed the sentry at less than five yards. Most of them knew me by sight. Whether he looked at me or not I do not know, for I never turned my head. But after walking a hundred yards I knew that the second obstacle had been surmounted. I was at large in Pretoria.

I walked on leisurely through the night humming a tune and choosing the middle of the road. The streets were full of burghers, but they paid no attention to me. Gradually I reached the suburbs, and on a little bridge I sat down to reflect and consider. I was in the heart of the enemy's country. I knew no one to whom I could apply for succour. Nearly three hundred miles stretched between me and Delagoa Bay. My escape must be known at dawn. Pursuit would be immediate. Yet all exits were barred. The town was picketed, the country was patrolled, the trains were searched, the line was guarded. I had £75 in my pocket and four slabs of chocolate, but the compass and the map which might have guided me, the opium tablets and meat lozenges which should have sustained me, were in my friend's pockets in the State Model School. Worst of all, I could not speak a word of Dutch or Kaffir, and how was I to get food or direction?

But when hope had departed, fear had gone as well. I formed a

plan. I would find the Delagoa Bay railway. Without map or
compass I must follow that in spite of the pickets. I looked at the
stars. Orion shone brightly. Scarcely a year ago he had guided me
when lost in the desert to the bank of the Nile. He had given me
water. Now he should lead me to freedom. I could not endure the
want of either.

After walking south for half a mile I struck the railroad. Was it
the line to Delagoa Bay or the Pietersburg branch? If it were the
former it should run east. But as far as I could see this line ran
northwards. Still, it might be only winding its way out among the
hills. I resolved to follow it. The night was delicious. A cool
breeze fanned my face and a wild feeling of exhilaration took hold
of me. At any rate I was free, if only for an hour. That was
something. The fascination of the adventure grew. Unless the
stars in their courses fought for me I could not escape. Where was
the need for caution? I marched briskly along the line. Here and
there the lights of a picket fire gleamed. Every bridge had its
watchers. But I passed them all, making very short detours at the
dangerous places, and really taking scarcely any precautions.

As I walked I extended my plan. I could not march three
hundred miles to the frontier. I would go by train. I would board
a train in motion and hide under the seats, on the roof, on the
couplings – anywhere. What train should I take? The first, of
course. After walking for two hours I perceived the signal lights
of a station. I left the line and, circling round it, hid in the ditch
by the track about two hundred yards beyond it. I argued that the
train would stop at the station and that it would not have got up
too much speed by the time it reached me. An hour passed. I
began to grow impatient. Suddenly I heard the whistle and the
approaching rattle. Then the great yellow headlights of the
engine flashed into view. The train waited five minutes at the
station and started again with much noise and steaming. I
crouched by the track. I rehearsed the act in my mind. I must
wait until the engine had passed, otherwise I should be seen.
Then I must make a dash for the carriages.

The train started slowly but gathered speed sooner than I had
expected. The flaring lights drew swiftly near. The rattle grew
into a roar. The dark mass hung for a second above me. The
engine driver silhouetted against his furnace glow, the black
profile of the engine, the clouds of steam rushed past. Then I

hurled myself on the trucks, clutched at something, missed, clutched again, missed again, grasped some sort of handhold, was swung off my feet – my toes bumping on the line, and with a struggle seated myself on the couplings of the fifth truck from the front of the train. It was a goods train, and the trucks were full of sacks, soft sacks covered with coal dust. I crawled on top and burrowed in among them. In five minutes I was completely buried. The sacks were warm and comfortable. Perhaps the engine driver had seen me rush up to the train and would give the alarm at the next station; on the other hand, perhaps not. Where was the train going to? Where would it be unloaded? Would it be searched? Was it on the Delagoa Bay line? What should I do in the morning? Ah, never mind that. Sufficient for the day was the luck thereof. Fresh plans for fresh contingencies. I resolved to sleep, nor can I imagine a more pleasing lullaby than the clatter of the train that carries you at twenty miles an hour away from the enemy's capital.

How long I slept I do not know, but I woke up suddenly with all feelings of exhilaration gone, and only the consciousness of oppressive difficulties heavy on me. I must leave the train before daybreak, so that I could drink at a pool and find some hiding-place while it was still dark. Another night I would board another train. I crawled from my cosy hiding-place among the sacks and sat again on the couplings. The train was running at a fair speed, but I felt it was time to leave it. I took hold of the iron handle at the back of the truck, pulled strongly with my left hand, and sprang. My feet struck the ground in two gigantic strides, and the next instant I was sprawling in the ditch, considerably shaken but unhurt. The train, my faithful ally of the night, hurried on its journey.

It was still dark. I was in the middle of a wide valley, surrounded by low hills and carpeted with high grass drenched in dew. I searched for water in the nearest gully and soon found a clear pool. I was very thirsty, but long after I had quenched my thirst I continued to drink that I might have sufficient for the whole day.

Presently the dawn began to break, and the sky to the east grew yellow and red, slashed across with heavy black clouds. I saw with relief that the railway ran steadily towards the sunrise. I had taken the right line after all.

Having drunk my fill, I set out for the hills, among which I hoped to find some hiding-place, and as it became broad daylight I entered a small group of trees which grew on the side of a deep ravine. Here I resolved to wait till dusk. I had one consolation: no one in the world knew where I was – I did not know myself. It was now four o'clock. Fourteen hours lay between me and the night. My impatience to proceed doubled their length. At first it was terribly cold, but by degrees the sun gained power, and by ten o'clock the heat was oppressive. My sole companion was a gigantic vulture, who manifested an extravagant interest in my condition, and made hideous and ominous gurglings from time to time. From my lofty position I commanded a view of the whole valley. A little tin-roofed town lay three miles to the westward. Scattered farmsteads, each with a clump of trees, relieved the monotony of the undulating ground. At the foot of the hill stood a Kaffir kraal, and the figures of its inhabitants dotted the patches of cultivation or surrounded the droves of goats and cows which fed on the pasture. The railway ran through the middle of the valley, and I could watch the passage of the various trains. I counted four passing each way, and from this I drew the conclusion that the same number would run at night. I marked a steep gradient up which they climbed very slowly, and determined at nightfall to make another attempt to board one of these. During the day I ate one slab of chocolate which, with the heat, produced a violent thirst. The pool was hardly half a mile away, but I dared not leave the shelter of the little wood, for I could see the figures of white men riding or walking occasionally across the valley, and once a Boer came and fired two shots at birds close to my hiding-place. But no one discovered me.

The elation and the excitement of the previous night had burned away, and a chilling reaction followed. I was very hungry, for I had had no dinner before starting, and chocolate though it sustains does not satisfy. I had scarcely slept, but yet my heart beat so fiercely and I was so nervous and perplexed about the future that I could not rest. I thought of all the chances that lay against me; I dreaded and detested more than words can express the prospect of being caught and dragged back to Pretoria. I do not mean that I would rather have died than have been retaken, but I have often feared death for much less. I found no comfort in any of the philosophical ideas that some men parade in their hours of ease and strength and safety. They seemed only fair weather friends. I realised with awful force that no exercise of my own feeble wit and strength could save me from my enemies, and that without the assistance of that High Power which interferes more often than we are always prone to admit in the eternal sequence of causes and effects, I could never succeed. I prayed long and earnestly for help and guidance. My prayer, as it seems to me, was swiftly and wonderfully answered. I cannot now relate the strange circumstances which followed, and which changed my nearly hopeless position into one of superior advantage. But after the war is over I shall hope to lengthen this account, and so remarkable will the addition be that I cannot believe the reader will complain.

The long day reached its close at last. The western clouds flushed into fire; the shadows of the hills stretched out across the valley. A ponderous Boer waggon, with its long team, crawled slowly along the track towards the town. The Kaffirs collected their herds and drew around their kraal. The daylight died, and soon it was quite dark. Then, and not till then, I set forth. I hurried to the railway line, pausing on my way to drink at a stream of sweet, cold water. I waited for some time at the top of the steep gradient in the hope of catching a train. But none came, and I gradually guessed, and I have since found out that I guessed right, that the train I had already travelled in was the only one that ran at night. At last I resolved to walk on and make, at any rate, twenty miles of my journey. I walked for about six hours. How far I travelled I do not know, but I do not expect it was very many miles in the direct line. Every bridge was guarded by armed men; every few miles were gangers' huts; at intervals there were stations with villages clustering round them. All the veldt was bathed in the bright rays of the full moon, and to avoid these dangerous places I had to make wide circuits and often to creep along the ground. Leaving the railroad I fell into bogs and swamps, and brushed through high grass dripping with dew, and so I was drenched to the waist. I had been able to take little exercise during my month's imprisonment, and I was soon tired out with walking, as well as from want of food and sleep. I felt very miserable when I looked around and saw here and there the lights of houses, and thought of the warmth and comfort within them, but knew that they only meant danger to me. After six or seven hours of walking I thought it unwise to go further lest I should exhaust myself, so I lay down in a ditch to sleep. I was nearly at the end of my tether. Nevertheless, by the will of God, I was enabled to sustain myself during the next few days, obtaining food at great risk here and there, resting in concealment by day and walking only at night. On the fifth day I was beyond Middleburg, as far as I could tell, for I dared not inquire nor as yet approach the stations near enough to read the names. In a secure hiding-place I waited for a suitable train, knowing that there is a through service between Middleburg and Lourenco Marques.

Meanwhile there had been excitement in the State Model Schools, temporarily converted into a military prison. Early on Wednesday morning – barely twelve hours after I had escaped – my absence was discovered – I think by Doctor Gunning, an amiable Hollander who used often to come and argue with me the rights and wrongs of the war. The alarm was given. Telegrams with my description at great length were despatched along all the railways. A warrant was issued for my immediate arrest. Every train was strictly searched. Everyone was on the watch. The newspapers made so much of the affair that my humble fortunes and my whereabouts were discussed in long columns of print, and even in the crash of the war I became to the Boers a topic all to myself. The rumours in part amused me. It was certain, said the *Standard and Digger's News*, that I had escaped disguised as a woman. The next day I was reported captured at Komati Poort dressed as a Transvaal policeman. There was great delight at this, which was only changed to doubt when other telegrams said that I had been arrested at Bragsbank, at Middleburg and at Bronkerspruit. But the captives proved to be harmless people after all. Finally it was agreed that I had never left Pretoria. I had – it appeared – changed clothes with a waiter, and was now in hiding at the house of some British sympathiser in the capital. On the strength of this all the houses of suspected persons were searched from top to bottom, and these unfortunate people were, I fear, put to a great deal of inconvenience. A special commission was also appointed to investigate "stringently" (a most hateful adjective in such a connection) the causes "which had rendered it possible for the war correspondent of the *Morning Post* to escape".

The *Volksstem* noticed as a significant fact that I had recently become a subscriber to the State Library, and had selected Mill's essay *On Liberty*. It apparently desired to gravely deprecate prisoners having access to such inflammatory literature. The idea will, perhaps, amuse those who have read the work in question.

All these things may provoke a smile of indifference; perhaps even of triumph after the danger is past; but during the days when I was lying up in holes and corners waiting for a good chance to board a train, the causes that had led to them preyed more than I knew on my nerves. To be an outcast, to be hunted, to be under a warrant for arrest, to fear every man, to have imprisonment – not necessarily military confinement either – hanging overhead, to fly the light, to doubt the shadows – all these things ate into my soul and have left an impression that will not perhaps be easily effaced.

On the sixth day the chance I had patiently waited for came. I found a convenient train duly labelled to Lourenço Marques standing in a siding. I withdrew to a suitable spot for boarding it – for I dared not make the attempt in the station – and, filling a bottle with water to drink on the way, I prepared for the last stage of my journey.

The truck in which I ensconced myself was laden with great sacks of some soft merchandise, and I found among them holes and crevices by means of which I managed to work my way into the inmost recess. The hard floor of the truck was littered with gritty coal dust, and made a most uncomfortable bed. The heat was almost stifling. I was resolved, however, that nothing should lure or compel me from my hiding-place until I reached Portuguese territory. I expected the journey to take thirty-six hours; it dragged out into two and a half days. I hardly dared sleep for fear of snoring.

I feared lest the trucks should be searched at Komati Poort, and my anxiety as the train approached this neighbourhood was very great. To prolong it we were shunted on to a siding for eighteen hours either at Komati Poort or the station beyond it. Once indeed they began to search my truck, but luckily did not search deep enough so that, providentially protected, I reached Delagoa Bay at last, and crawled forth from my place of refuge and of punishment, weary, dirty, hungry but free once more.

Thereafter everything smiled. I found my way to the British Consul, Mr Ross,* who at first mistook me for a fireman off one of the ships in the harbour, but soon welcomed me with enthusiasm. I bought clothes, I washed, I sat down to dinner with a real table-cloth and real glasses; and fortune, determined not to overlook the smallest detail, had arranged that the steamer *Induna* should leave that very night for Durban. It is from the cabin of this little vessel, as she coasts along the sandy shores of Africa, that I write these lines, and the reader who may persevere through this hurried account will perhaps understand why I write them with a feeling of triumph, and better than triumph, a feeling of pure joy.

* Alexander Carnegie Ross (1859–1940). Served as British Consul at Lourenço Marques 1898–1900. CB 1900.

JACK LONDON

THE STORY OF AN EYE-WITNESS: THE SAN FRANCISCO EARTHQUAKE

Collier's Weekly, 5 May 1906

To *Collier's* delight, the famous author of *The Call of the Wild* was an eye-witness to the earthquake which struck San Francisco on 17 April 1906. For London's subsequent 2500-word piece of *reportage, Collier's* paid him the then princely sum of 25 cents a word. It was to be the most money London earned from writing ever.

The earthquake shook down in San Francisco hundreds of thousands of dollars' worth of walls and chimneys. But the conflagration that followed burned up hundreds of millions of dollars' worth of property There is no estimating within hundreds of millions the actual damage wrought. Not in history has a modern imperial city been so completely destroyed. San Francisco is gone. Nothing remains of it but memories and a fringe of dwelling-houses on its outskirts. Its industrial section is wiped out. Its business section is wiped out. Its social and residential section is wiped out. The factories and warehouses, the great stores and newspaper buildings, the hotels and the palaces of the nabobs, are all gone. Remains only the fringe of dwelling houses on the outskirts of what was once San Francisco.

Within an hour after the earthquake shock the smoke of San Francisco's burning was a lurid tower visible a hundred miles away. And for three days and nights this lurid tower swayed in the sky, reddening the sun, darkening the day, and filling the land with smoke.

On Wednesday morning at a quarter past five came the earthquake. A minute later the flames were leaping upward. In a dozen different quarters south of Market Street, in the working-class ghetto, and in the factories, fires started. There was no opposing the flames. There was no organization, no communication. All the cunning adjustments of a 20th-century city had been smashed by the earthquake. The streets were humped into ridges and depressions, and piled with the debris of fallen walls. The steel rails were twisted into perpendicular and horizontal angles. The telephone and telegraph systems were disrupted. And the great water-mains had burst. All the shrewd contrivances and safe-guards of man had been thrown out of gear by thirty seconds' twitching of the earth-crust.

The Fire Made its Own Draught

By Wednesday afternoon, inside of twelve hours, half the heart of the city was gone. At that time I watched the vast conflagration from out on the bay. It was dead calm. Not a flicker of wind stirred. Yet from every side wind was pouring in upon the city. East, west, north, and south, strong winds were blowing upon the doomed city. The heated air rising made an enormous suck. Thus did the fire of itself build its own colossal chimney through the atmosphere. Day and night this dead calm continued, and yet, near to the flames, the wind was often half a gale, so mighty was the suck.

Wednesday night saw the destruction of the very heart of the city. Dynamite was lavishly used, and many of San Francisco's proudest structures were crumbled by man himself into ruins, but there was no withstanding the onrush of the flames. Time and again successful stands were made by the fire-fighters, and every time the flames flanked around on either side or came up from the rear, and turned to defeat the hard-won victory.

An enumeration of the buildings destroyed would be a direc-tory of San Francisco. An enumeration of the buildings undes-troyed would be a line and several addresses. An enumeration of the deeds of heroism would stock a library and bankrupt the Carnegie medal fund. An enumeration of the dead will never be made. All vestiges of them were destroyed by the flames. The number of the victims of the earthquake will never be known. South of Market Street, where the loss of life was particularly heavy, was the first to catch fire.

Remarkable as it may seem, Wednesday night while the whole city crashed and roared into ruin, was a quiet night. There were no crowds. There was no shouting and yelling. There was no hysteria, no disorder. I passed Wednesday night in the path of the advancing flames, and in all those terrible hours I saw not one woman who wept, not one man who was excited, not one person who was in the slightest degree panic-stricken.

Before the flames, throughout the night, fled tens of thousands of homeless ones. Some were wrapped in blankets. Others carried bundles of bedding and dear household treasures. Sometimes a whole family was harnessed to a carriage or delivery wagon that was weighted down with their possessions. Baby buggies, toy wagons, and go-carts were used as trucks, while every other person was dragging a trunk. Yet everybody was gracious. The most perfect courtesy obtained. Never in all San Francisco's history, were her people so kind and courteous as on this night of terror.

A Caravan of Trunks

All night these tens of thousands fled before the flames. Many of them, the poor people from the labour ghetto, had fled all day as well. They had left their homes burdened with possessions. Now and again they lightened up, flinging out upon the street clothing and treasures they had dragged for miles.

They held on longest to their trunks, and over these trunks many a strong man broke his heart that night. The hills of San Francisco are steep, and up these hills, mile after mile, were the trunks dragged. Everywhere were trunks with across them lying their exhausted owners, men and women. Before the march of the flames were flung picket lines of soldiers. And a block at a time, as the flames advanced, these pickets retreated. One of their tasks was to keep the trunk-pullers moving. The exhausted creatures, stirred on by the menace of bayonets, would arise and struggle up the steep pavements, pausing from weakness every five or ten feet.

Often, after surmounting a heart-breaking hill, they would find another wall of flame advancing upon them at right angles and be compelled to change anew the line of their retreat. In the end, completely played out, after toiling for a dozen hours like giants, thousands of them were compelled to abandon their trunks. Here the shopkeepers and soft members of the middle class were at a disadvantage. But the working-men dug holes in vacant lots and backyards and buried their trunks.

The Doomed City

At nine o'clock Wednesday evening I walked down through the very heart of the city. I walked through miles and miles of magnificent buildings and towering skyscrapers. Here was no fire. All was in perfect order. The police patrolled the streets. Every building had its watchman at the door. And yet it was doomed, all of it. There was no water. The dynamite was giving out. And at right angles two different conflagrations were sweeping down upon it.

At one o'clock in the morning I walked down through the same section. Everything still stood intact. There was no fire. And yet there was a change. A rain of ashes was falling. The watchmen at the doors were gone. The police had been withdrawn. There were no firemen, no fire-engines, no men fighting with dynamite. The district had been absolutely abandoned. I stood at the corner of Kearney and Market, in the very innermost heart of San Francisco. Kearny Street was deserted. Half a dozen blocks away it was burning on both sides. The street was a wall of flame. And against this wall of flame, silhouetted sharply, were two United States cavalrymen sitting their horses, calmly watching. That was all. Not another person was in sight. In the intact heart of the city two troopers sat their horses and watched.

Spread of the Conflagration

Surrender was complete. There was no water. The sewers had long since been pumped dry. There was no dynamite. Another fire had broken out further uptown, and now from three sides conflagrations were sweeping down. The fourth side had been burned earlier in the day. In that direction stood the tottering walls of the Examiner building, the burned-out Call building, the smouldering ruins of the Grand Hotel, and the gutted, devastated, dynamited Palace Hotel.

The following will illustrate the sweep of the flames and the inability of men to calculate their spread. At eight o'clock Wednesday evening I passed through Union Square. It was packed with refugees. Thousands of them had gone to bed on the grass. Government tents had been set up, supper was being cooked, and the refugees were lining up for free meals.

At half past one in the morning three sides of Union Square were in flames. The fourth side, where stood the great St Francis Hotel was still holding out. An hour later, ignited from top and sides, the St Francis was flaming heavenward. Union Square, heaped high with mountains of trunks, was deserted. Troops, refugees, and all had retreated.

A Fortune for a Horse!

It was at Union Square that I saw a man offering a thousand dollars for a team of horses. He was in charge of a truck piled high with trunks from some hotel. It had been hauled here into what was considered safety, and the horses had been taken out. The flames were on three sides of the Square and there were no horses.

Also, at this time, standing beside the truck, I urged a man to seek safety in flight. He was all but hemmed in by several conflagrations. He was an old man and he was on crutches. Said he: "Today is my birthday. Last night I was worth thirty thousand dollars. I bought five bottles of wine, some delicate fish and other things for my birthday dinner. I have had no dinner, and all I own are these crutches."

I convinced him of his danger and started him limping on his way. An hour later, from a distance, I saw the truck-load of trunks burning merrily in the middle of the street.

On Thursday morning at a quarter past five, just twenty-four hours after the earthquake, I sat on the steps of a small residence on Nob Hill. With me sat Japanese, Italians, Chinese, and negroes – a bit of the cosmopolitan flotsam of the wreck of the city. All about were the palaces of the nabob pioneers of Fortynine. To the east and south, at right angles, were advancing two mighty walls of flame.

I went inside with the owner of the house on the steps of which I sat. He was cool and cheerful and hospitable. "Yesterday morning," he said, "I was worth six hundred thousand dollars.

This morning this house is all I have left. It will go in fifteen minutes." He pointed to a large cabinet. "That is my wife's collection of china. This rug upon which we stand is a present. It cost fifteen hundred dollars. Try that piano. Listen to its tone. There are few like it. There are no horses. The flames will be here in fifteen minutes."

Outside the old Mark Hopkins residence a palace was just catching fire. The troops were falling back and driving the refugees before them. From every side came the roaring of flames, the crashing of walls, and the detonations of dynamite.

The Dawn of the Second Day

I passed out of the house. Day was trying to dawn through the smoke-pall. A sickly light was creeping over the face of things. Once only the sun broke through the smoke-pall, blood-red, and showing quarter its usual size. The smoke-pall itself, viewed from beneath, was a rose color that pulsed and fluttered with lavender shades. Then it turned to mauve and yellow and dun. There was no sun. And so dawned the second day on stricken San Francisco.

An hour later I was creeping past the shattered dome of the City Hall. Than it, there was no better exhibit of the destructive force of the earthquake. Most of the stone had been shaken from the great dome, leaving standing the naked framework of steel. Market Street was piled high with the wreckage, and across the wreckage lay the overthrown pillars of the City Hall shattered into short crosswise sections.

This section of the city, with the exception of the Mint and the Post-Office, was already a waste of smoking ruins. Here and there through the smoke, creeping warily under the shadows of tottering walls, emerged occasional men and women. It was like the meeting of the handful of survivors after the day of the end of the world.

Beeves Slaughtered and Roasted

On Mission Street lay a dozen steers, in a neat row stretching across the street just as they had been struck down by the flying ruins of the earthquake. The fire had passed through afterward and roasted them. The human dead had been carried away before the fire came. At another place on Mission Street I saw a milk wagon. A steel telegraph pole had smashed down sheer through the driver's seat and crushed the front wheels. The milk cans lay scattered around.

All day Thursday and all Thursday night, all day Friday and Friday night, the flames still raged on.

Friday night saw the flames finally conquered, through not until Russian Hill and Telegraph Hill had been swept and three-quarters of a mile of wharves and docks had been licked up.

The Last Stand

The great stand of the fire-fighters was made Thursday night on Van Ness Avenue. Had they failed here, the comparatively few remaining houses of the city would have been swept. Here were the magnificent residences of the second generation of San Francisco nabobs, and these, in a solid zone, were dynamited down across the path of the fire. Here and there the flames leaped the zone, but these fires were beaten out, principally by the use of wet blankets and rugs.

San Francisco, at the present time, is like the crater of a volcano, around which are camped tens of thousands of refugees. At the Presidio alone are at least twenty thousand. All the surrounding cities and towns are jammed with the homeless ones, where they are being cared for by the relief committees. The refugees were carried free by the railroads to any point they wished to go, and it is estimated that over one hundred thousand people have left the peninsula on which San Francisco stood. The Government has the situation in hand, and, thanks to the immediate relief given by the whole United States, there is not the slightest possibility of a famine. The bankers and business men hare already set about making preparations to rebuild San Francisco.

G. WARD-PRICE

MY ZEPPELIN CRASH

Daily Mail, 29 June 1910

The airships of Count von Zeppelin were the world's first commercial air liners.

Osnabrück (Germany), Tuesday

The *Deutschland*, the new Zeppelin airliner, in which I was today a passenger, lies a total wreck in the heart of the Teutoberger Wald, on the borders of Westphalia and Hanover. After a wild nine hours' struggle, waged high above the earth with a fierce gale, our petrol supply ran out. Caught in a sudden downward swirl of wind the great airship crashed helplessly down into a fir forest from the heart of a dense raincloud, fifteen hundred feet above, and was at once impaled in a dozen places upon the branches of the trees.

By wonderful good fortune not one of our complement of thirty-three persons was injured, though a broken jagged tree trunk drove itself through the floor of the cabin within six inches of where I stood.

All afternoon it had been a Titanic struggle between the great white airship and the rapidly rising gale, and even when, a hundred miles from our garage and with the petrol rapidly giving out, it became clear that an accident of some sort was humanly inevitable, we could not help watching the contest with fascination.

Now rocketing upwards, now plunging down to within a hundred feet of the earth, the *Deutschland*, like a sentient thing, sought in vain some level where she might find mitigation of the fury of the wind. And though the distorted bulk of the airship now lies among the swinging tree-tops, trailing the battered ruin of the after-third of her length like some huge crushed white worm, credit is due to the ship and her crew that she held out so long against a gale such as no airship has experienced before.

The sky was overcast as we motored out to Golzheimer Heide, Düsseldorf, at 7.30 this morning. A light breeze was blowing as the *Deutschland* was towed from her shed by groups of uniformed mechanics at the bow and stern. We clambered up the ladder to our seats in the car. We were twenty-three passengers in all.

The engines started with a surging roar, the propellers whirled themselves into black, shadowy discs against the sky, and we shot up smoothly, almost without knowing it, to a height of five hundred feet, and started out in a south-easterly direction, intending to make a three-hour circular flight and return to Düsseldorf at noon. For two hours we sailed smoothly on, high above the countryside. Horses and cattle jibbed and shied in all directions, startled by the whirring of our motors and uncertain which way to flee from this new monster of the air. Every town over which we passed poured out its entire population of tiny, black, gesticulating figures into the streets, and the sound of their cheering was borne faintly up to us on the breeze.

School children streamed out from their classrooms and scampered after us in companies along the roads. As a rule they were about two miles from their lessons when we lost sight of them, and still running gamely. Dense woods looked to us like clumps of ragged box hedging. The Rhine in the far distance was a narrow, curving ribbon of silver.

So, apparently masters of the upper air, we sped swiftly along the high levels traversed till now by the birds and the breezes alone. Over Elberfeld I made attempts at bomb dropping. My missiles contained, however, merely despatches to the *Daily Mail*. I had provided myself with cardboard tubes to which coloured tapes were attached to render their downward flight conspicuous. My first message was seized by the wind and deposited in a potato field. The second, which I aimed at the railway line at Elberfeld, found its billet, and I saw it retrieved by a group of platelayers.

Suddenly the port stern propellers stopped. There was a defect in the motor. The wind was freshening fast and with one propeller ineffective it was difficult to steer. We decided we should try to make Münster, where, with the help of the garrison, we could land on the military exercising ground and repair the motor. The wind grew stronger. We could not make Münster. We dare not now turn and fly before the wind, however, or the airship would lose steerage way.

So, doggedly, she was turned almost in the teeth of the gale to weather the storm in the air. "We might, perhaps, reach Osnabrück," said Dr Colsmann, a director of the airship company on board, "where are also military who could help us land." Telegrams warning them of our possible arrival were thrown from the ship.

And the swerving, diving, rain-beaten airship fought on inch by inch, sloping steeply first forward and then aft as we rose, and fell in the storm. It was very cold. Icy showers fell in torrents round us. Often we hung motionless for a quarter of an hour with the propellers revolving at full speed, powerless against the resistance of the wind.

Our petrol was now failing. We had been nearly nine hours in the air, instead of three. Just before five o'clock we saw dense black rain clouds ahead. A moment later we plunged into them and a white fog closed round us, shutting out everything from our eyes. So we continued for half an hour. Then the petrol gave out and the whirling propellers faltered and stood still. Almost simultaneously we broke through the floor of the cloud, and there, only a few feet below our bows, was a hill covered with a dense fir forest.

Our water ballast was exhausted. Some of us were ordered to run along the narrow gangway inside the keel of the airship to attempt to bring her to the ascending position. It was too late.

A downward eddy of the gale seized the swaying ship, and down we crashed into the tree-tops.

There was a rending, tearing sound. The airship shivered and struggled as if to rise. There was another crash, and the splintered tree trunks stabbed through the floor of the cabin and into the hinder part of the balloon, ripping the gas compartments in all directions.

There we stuck fast, held by the branches of the trees. Had we with the same force struck the open ground scarcely anyone in the airship could have escaped serious injury.

I clambered along the gangway to the forward engine car. Captain Kahlenberg, who was in command, had thrown out a grapnel rope-ladder, down which we clambered to the ground. "I have never been up in such a wind," said Captain Kahlenberg to me; "it is blowing twenty-five yards a second. It was impossible to steer the ship. Just as our power failed we got into a kind of whirlwind in which our steering planes were of no avail."

Soon the country people gathered at the scene. A landowner drove hurriedly up with a first-aid chest, having seen the accident from his house. We found we were two miles from Wellendorf and ten from Osnabrück. A motor-car passing on the road near by drove some of us to the station, where we telephoned to the Osnabrück Barracks, whence, less than two hours after the accident, a hundred soldiers were on the spot. They are guarding the wreck to-night.

The engines are uninjured, but the last third of the balloon, from the after engine-car, is torn and destroyed. The passengers' cabin and the after car are pierced and damaged by the trees. The airship will probably have to be dismantled in the wood.

Our flight in a direct line was one hundred miles, but the distance traversed was at least twice as great.

THE SIEGE OF SIDNEY STREET

Adventures in Journalism, 1923

The besieged were a group of jewel robbers thought to be anarchists. The place was 100 Sidney Street, in the East End of London. The date was 3 January 1911.

For some reason, which I have forgotten, I went very early that morning to the *Chronicle* office, and was greeted by the news editor with the statement that a hell of a battle was raging in Sidney Street. He advised me to go and look at it.

I took a taxi, and drove to the corner of that street, where I found a dense crowd observing the affair as far as they dared peer round the angle of the walls from adjoining streets. Heedless at the moment of danger, which seemed to me ridiculous, I stood boldly opposite Sidney Street and looked down its length of houses. Immediately in front of me four soldiers of one of the Guards' regiments lay on their stomachs, protected from the dirt of the road by newspaper "sandwich" boards, firing their rifles at a house halfway down the street. Another young Guardsman, leaning against a wall, took random shots at intervals while he smoked a Woodbine. As I stood near him, he winked and said, "What a game!"

It was something more than a game. Bullets were flicking off the wall like peas, plugging holes into the dirty yellow brick, and ricocheting fantastically. One of them took a neat chip out of a policeman's helmet, and he said, "Well, I'll be blowed!" and laughed in a foolish way. It was before the war, when we learned to know more about the meaning of bullets. Another struck a stick on which a journalistic friend of mine was leaning in an easy, graceful way. His support and his dignity suddenly departed from him.

"That's funny!" he said seriously, as he saw his stick neatly cut in half at his feet.

A cinematograph operator, standing well inside Sidney Street, was winding his handle vigorously, quite oblivious of the whiz of bullets, which were being fired at a slanting angle from the house, which seemed to be the target of the prostrate Guardsmen.

A large police inspector, of high authority, shouted a command to his men.

"What's all that nonsense? Clear the people back! Clear 'em right back! We don't want a lot of silly corpses lying round."

A cordon of police pushed back the dense crowd, treading on the toes of those who would not move fast enough.

I found myself in a group of journalists.

"Get back there!" shouted the police.

But we were determined to see the drama out. It was more sensational than any "movie" show. Immediately opposite was a tall gin palace – "The Rising Sun". Some strategist said, "That's the place for us!" We raced across before the police could out-flank us.

A Jew publican stood in the doorway, sullenly.

"Whatcher want?" he asked.

"Your roof," said one of the journalists.

"A quid each, and worth it," said the Jew.

At that time, before the era of paper money, some of us carried golden sovereigns in our pockets, one to a "quid". Most of the others did, but, as usual, I had not more than eighteenpence. A friend lent me the necessary coin, which the Jew slipped into his pocket as he let me pass. Twenty of us, at least, gained access to the roof of "The Rising Sun".

It was a good vantage point, or O.P., as we should have called it later in history. It looked right across to the house in Sidney Street in which Peter the Painter and his friends were defending themselves to the death – a tall, thin house of three storeys, with dirty window blinds. In the house immediately opposite were some more Guardsmen, with pillows and mattresses stuffed into the windows in the nature of sandbags as used in trench warfare. We could not see the soldiers, but we could see the effect of their intermittent fire, which had smashed every pane of glass and kept chipping off bits of brick in the anarchists' abode.

The street had been cleared of all onlookers, but a group of detectives slunk along the walls on the anarchists' side of the street at such an angle that they were safe from the slanting fire of the enemy. They had to keep very close to the wall, because Peter and his pals were dead shots and maintained something like a barrage fire with their automatics. Any detective or policeman who showed himself would have been sniped in a second, and these men were out to kill.

The thing became a bore as I watched it for an hour or more, during which time Mr Winston Churchill, who was then Home Secretary, came to take command of active operations, thereby causing an immense amount of ridicule in next day's papers. With a bowler hat pushed firmly down on his bulging brow, and one hand in his breast pocket, like Napoleon on the field of battle, he peered round the corner of the street, and afterwards, as we learned, ordered up some field guns to blow the house to bits.

That never happened for a reason which we on "The Rising Sun" were quick to see.

In the top-floor room of the anarchists' house we observed a gas jet burning, and presently some of us noticed the white ash of burnt paper fluttering out of a chimney pot.

"They're burning documents," said one of my friends.

They were burning more than that. They were setting fire to the house, upstairs and downstairs. The window curtains were first to catch alight, then volumes of black smoke, through which little tongues of flame licked up, poured through the empty window frames. They must have used paraffin to help the progress of the fire, for the whole house was burning with amazing rapidity.

"Did you ever see such a game in London!" exclaimed the man next to me on the roof of the public house.

For a moment I thought I saw one of the murderers standing on the window sill. But it was a blackened curtain which suddenly blew outside the window frame and dangled on the sill.

A moment later I had one quick glimpse of a man's arm with a pistol in his hand. He fired and there was a quick flash. At the same moment a volley of shots rang out from the Guardsmen opposite. It is certain that they killed the man who had shown himself, for afterwards they found his body (or a bit of it) with a bullet through the skull. It was not long afterwards that the roof fell in with an upward rush of flame and sparks. The inside of the house from top to bottom was a furnace.

The detectives, with revolvers ready, now advanced in Indian file. One of them ran forward and kicked at the front door. It fell in, and a sheet of flame leaped out. No other shot was fired from within. Peter the Painter and his fellow bandits were charred cinders in the bonfire they had made.

RICHARD HARDING DAVIS

SAW GERMAN ARMY ROLL ON LIKE FOG

New York Tribune, 23 August 1914

After years of enmity and sabre-rattling, the powers of Europe went to war on 4 August 1914 in a conflict that became most famous for its trench warfare on the Western Front, but spread around the world as the combatants – principally Germany and Austria on the Axis side, and Britain, France and Russia in the Allied camp – mauled over their colonial possessions.

The very day war was declared, the veteran American correspondent Richard Harding Davis sailed for Europe. He reached the epicentre of the conflict, luckless would-be neutral Belgium, just as the Germany army advanced through it towards the Channel.

Brussels, Friday, Aug. 21, 2 p.m.

The entrance of the German army into Brussels has lost the human quality. It was lost as soon as the three soldiers who led the army bicycled into the Boulevard du Regent and asked the way to the Gare du Nord. When they passed the human note passed with them.

What came after them, and twenty-four hours later is still coming, is not men marching, but a force of nature like a tidal wave, an avalanche or a river flooding its banks. At this moment it is rolling through Brussels as the swollen waters of the Con-cemaugh Valley swept through Johnstown.

At the sight of the first few regiments of the enemy we were thrilled with interest. After three hours they had passed in one unbroken steel gray column [and] we were bored. But when hour after hour passed and there was no halt, no breathing time, no open spaces in the ranks, the thing became uncanny, inhuman. You returned to watch it, fascinated. It held the mystery and menace of fog rolling toward you across the sea.

The gray of the uniforms worn by both officers and men helped this air of mystery. Only the sharpest eye could detect among the thousands that passed the slightest difference. All moved under a cloak of invisibility. Only after the most numerous and severe tests at all distances, with all materials and combinations of colours that give forth no colour could this gray have been discovered. That it was selected to clothe and disguise the German when he fights is typical of the German staff striving for efficiency to leave nothing to chance, to neglect no detail.

After you have seen this service uniform under conditions entirely opposite you are convinced that for the German soldier it is his strongest weapon. Even the most expert marksman cannot hit a target he cannot see. It is a grey green, not the blue grey of our Confederates. It is the grey of the hour just before daybreak, the grey of unpolished steel, of mist among green trees.

I saw it first in the Grand Place in front of the Hotel de Ville. It was impossible to tell if in that noble square there was a regiment or a brigade. You saw only a fog that melted into the stones, blended with the ancient house fronts, that shifted and drifted, but left you nothing at which you could point.

Later, as the army passed below my window, under the trees of the Botanical Park, it merged and was lost against the green leaves. It is no exaggeration to say that at a hundred yards you can see the horses on which the Uhlans ride, but cannot see the men who ride them.

If I appear to overemphasize this disguising uniform it, is because of all the details of the German outfit, it appealed to me as one of the most remarkable. The other day, when I was with the rear guard of the French Dragoons and Curassiers and they threw out pickets, we could distinguish them against the yellow wheat or green course at half a mile, while these men passing in the street, when they have reached the next crossing, become merged into the grey of the paving stones and the earth swallows them. In comparison the yellow khaki of our own American army is about as invisible as the flag of Spain.

Yesterday Major General von Jarotzky, the German Military Governor of Brussels, assured Burgomaster Max that the German army would not occupy the city, but would pass through it. It is still passing. I have followed in campaigns six armies, but, excepting not even our own, the Japanese or the British, I have not seen one so thoroughly equipped. I am not speaking of the fighting qualities of any army, only of the equipment and organization. The German army moved into this city as smoothly and as compactly as an Empire State Express. There were no halts, no open places, no stragglers.

This army has been on active service three weeks, and so far there is not apparently a chinstrap or a horseshoe missing. It came in with the smoke pouring from cookstoves on wheels, and in an hour had set up postoffice wagons, from which mounted messengers galloped along the line of column distributing letters and at which soldiers posted picture postcards.

The infantry came in in files of five, two hundred men to each company; the Lances in columns of four, with not a pennant missing. The quick fire guns and field pieces were one hour at a time in passing, each gun with its caisson and ammunition wagon taking twenty seconds in which to pass.

The men of the infantry sang "Fatherland, My Fatherland." Between each line of song they took three steps. At times two thousand men were singing together in absolute rhythm and beat. When the melody gave way the silence was broken only by the stamp of iron-shod boots, and then again the song rose. When the singing ceased the bands played marches. They were followed by the rumble of siege guns, the creaking of wheels and of chains clanking against the cobble stones and the sharp bell-like voices of the bugles.

For seven hours the army passed in such solid column that not once might a taxicab or trolley car pass through the city. Like a river of steel it flowed, gray and ghostlike. Then, as dusk came and as thousands of horses' hoofs and thousands of iron boots continued to tramp forward, they struck tiny sparks from the stones, but the horses and the men who beat out the sparks were invisible.

At midnight pack wagons and siege guns were still passing. At seven this morning I was awakened by the tramp of men and bando playing jauntily. Whether they marched all night or not I do not know; but now for twenty-six hours the grey army has rumbled by with the mystery of fog and the pertinacity of a steam roller.

HENRY G. WALES

DEATH COMES TO MATA HARI

International News Service, 19 October 1917

Mata Hari, born in 1876, was a beautiful double agent. Henry G. Wales was the Paris staff correspondent for the International News Service.

Mata Hari, which is Javanese for Eye-of-the-Morning, is dead. She was shot as a spy by a firing squad of Zouaves at the Vincennes Barracks. She died facing death literally, for she refused to be blindfolded.

Gertrud Margarete Zelle, for that was the real name of the beautiful Dutch-Javanese dancer, did appeal to President Poincare for a reprieve, but he refused to intervene.

The first intimation she received that her plea had been denied was when she was led at daybreak from her cell in the Saint-Lazare prison to a waiting automobile and then rushed to the barracks where the firing squad awaited her.

Never once had the iron will of the beautiful woman failed her. Father Arbaux, accompanied by two sisters of charity, Captain Bouchardon, and Maître Clunet, her lawyer, entered her cell, where she was still sleeping – a calm, untroubled sleep, it was remarked by the turnkeys and trusties.

The sisters gently shook her. She arose and was told that her hour had come.

"May I write two letters?" was all she asked.

Consent was given immediately by Captain Bouchardon, and pen, ink, paper, and envelopes were given to her.

She seated herself at the edge of the bed and wrote the letters with feverish haste. She handed them over to the custody of her lawyer.

Then she drew on her stockings, black, silken, filmy things, grotesque in the circumstances. She placed her high-heeled slippers on her feet and tied the silken ribbons over her insteps.

She arose and took the long black velvet cloak, edged around the bottom with fur and with a huge square fur collar hanging down the back, from a hook over the head of her bed. She placed this cloak over the heavy silk kimono which she had been wearing over her nightdress.

Her wealth of black hair was still coiled about her head in braids. She put on a large, flapping black felt hat with a black silk ribbon and bow. Slowly and indifferently, it seemed, she pulled on a pair of black kid gloves. Then she said calmly:

"I am ready."

The party slowly filed out of her cell to the waiting automobile.

The car sped through the heart of the sleeping city. It was scarcely half past five in the morning and the sun was not yet fully up.

Clear across Paris the car whirled to the Caserne de Vincennes, the barracks of the old fort which the Germans stormed in 1870.

The troops were already drawn up for the execution. The twelve Zouaves, forming the firing squad, stood in line, their rifles at ease. A subofficer stood behind them, sword drawn.

The automobile stopped, and the party descended, Mata Hari last. The party walked straight to the spot, where a little hummock of earth reared itself seven or eight feet high and afforded a background for such bullets as might miss the human target.

As Father Arbaux spoke with the condemned woman, a French officer approached, carrying a white cloth.

"The blindfold," he whispered to the nuns who stood there and handed it to them.

"Must I wear that?" asked Mata Hari, turning to her lawyer, as her eyes glimpsed the blindfold.

Maître Clunet turned interrogatively to the French officer.

"If Madame prefers not, it makes no difference," replied the officer, hurriedly turning away.

Mata Hari was not bound and she was not blindfolded. She stood gazing steadfastly at her executioners, when the priest, the nuns, and her lawyer stepped away from her.

The officer in command of the firing squad, who had been watching his men like a hawk that none might examine his rifle and try to find out whether he was destined to fire the blank cartridge which was in the breech of one rifle, seemed relieved that the business would soon be over.

A sharp, crackling command, and the file of twelve men assumed rigid positions at attention. Another command, and their rifles were at their shoulders; each man gazed down his barrel at the breast of the women which was the target.

She did not move a muscle.

The underofficer in charge had moved to a position where from the corners of their eyes they could see him. His sword was extended in the air.

It dropped. The sun – by this time up – flashed on the burnished blade as it described an are in falling. Simultaneously the sound of the volley rang out. Flame and a tiny puff of greyish smoke issued from the muzzle of each rifle. Automatically the men dropped their arms.

At the report Mata Hari fell. She did not die as actors and moving-picture stars would have us believe that people die when they are shot. She did not throw up her hands nor did she plunge straight forward or straight back.

Instead she seemed to collapse. Slowly, inertly, she settled to her knees, her head up always, and without the slightest change of expression on her face. For the fraction of a second it seemed she tottered there, on her knees, gazing directly at those who had taken her life. Then she fell backward, bending at the waist, with her legs doubled up beneath her. She lay prone, motionless, with her face turned towards the sky.

A non-commissioned officer, who accompanied a lieutenant, drew his revolver from the big, black holster strapped about his waist. Bending over, he placed the muzzle of the revolver almost – but not quite – against the left temple of the spy. He pulled the trigger, and the bullet tore into the brain of the woman.

Mata Hari was surely dead.

JOHN REED

A DAY THAT SHOOK THE WORLD

Ten Days That Shook the World, 1919

A radical American journalist, Reed covered the Russian Revolution of October 1917 for a number of periodicals, primarily the *Liberator*, and then rewrote his dispatches to produce perhaps the classic book of "instant" history, *Ten Days That Shook the World*. For once, as A. J. P. Taylor put it, "a great theme found the narrator it deserved". The extract below describes the Bolshevik-led occupation of the Winter Palace in St Petersburg (Petrograd), the seat of the moderate, provisional government, on 25 October. Like almost all the early acts of the Revolution, the "storming" was a curiously bloodless, almost symbolic, affair. Reed died of typhus in the Soviet Union in 1920. He was later immortalized in Warren Beatty's Hollywood bio-epic, *Reds*.

When we came into the chill night, all the front of Smolny* was one huge park of arriving and departing automobiles, above the sound of which could be heard the far-off slow beat of the cannon. A great motor-truck stood there, shaking to the roar of its engine. Men were tossing bundles into it, and others receiving them, with guns beside them.

"Where are you going?" I shouted.

"Down-town – all over – everywhere!" answered a little workman, grinning, with a large exultant gesture.

We showed our passes. "Come along!" they invited. "But there'll probably be shooting –" We climbed in: the clutch slid home with a raking jar, the great car jerked forward, we all toppled backward on top of those who were climbing in; past the

* Smolny Institute: the seat of the Petrograd Workers' and Soldiers' Council (Soviet)

huge fire by the gate, and then the fire by the outer gate, glowing red on the faces of the workmen with rifles who squatted around it, and went bumping at top speed down the Suvorovsky Prospect, swaying from side to side . . . One man tore the wrapping from a bundle and began to hurl handfuls of papers into the air. We imitated him, plunging down through the dark street with a tail of white papers floating and eddying out behind. The late passer-by stooped to pick them up; the patrols around bonfires on the corners ran out with uplifted arms to catch them. Sometimes armed men loomed up ahead, crying "*Stoi!*" and raising their guns, but our chauffeur only yelled something unintelligible and we hurtled on . . .

I picked up a copy of the paper, and under a fleeting streetlight read:

To the Citizens of Russia!

The Provisional Government is deposed. The State Power has passed into the hands of the organ of the Petrograd Soviet of Workers' and Soldiers' Deputies, the Military Revolutionary Committee, which stands at the head of the Petrograd proletariat and garrison.

The cause for which the people were fighting: immediate proposal of a democratic peace, abolition of landlord property-rights over the land, labour control over production, creation of a Soviet Government – that cause is securely achieved.

LONG LIVE THE REVOLUTION OF WORKMEN, SOLDIERS, AND PEASANTS!

Military Revolutionary Committee
Petrograd Soviet of Workers' and Soldiers' Deputies

A slant-eyed, Mongolian-faced man who sat beside me, dressed in a goatskin of Caucasian cape, snapped, "Look out! Here the provocators always shoot from the windows!" We turned into Znamensky Square, dark and almost deserted, careened around Trubetskoy's brutal statue and swung down the wide Nevsky, three men standing up with rifles ready, peering at the windows. Behind us the street was alive with people running and stooping. We could no longer hear the cannon, and the nearer we drew to the Winter Palace end of the city the quieter and more deserted were the streets. The City Duma was all brightly lighted. Beyond that we made out a dark mass of people, and a line of sailors, who yelled furiously at us to stop. The machine slowed down, and we climbed out.

It was an astonishing scene. Just at the corner of the Ekaterina Canal, under an arc-light, a cordon of armed sailors was drawn across the Nevsky, blocking the way to a crowd of people in column of fours. There were about three or four hundred of them, men in frock coats, well-dressed women, officers – all sorts and conditions of people. Among them we recognized many of the delegates from the Congress, leaders of the Mensheviki and Socialist Revolutionaries; Avksentiev, the lean, red-bearded president of the Peasants' Soviets, Sarokin, Kerensky's spokesman, Khinchuk, Abramovich; and at the head white-bearded old Schreider, Mayor of Petrograd, and Prokopovich, Minister of Supplies in the Provisional Government, arrested that morning and released. I caught sight of Malkin, reporter for the *Russian Daily News*. "Going to die in the Winter Palace," he shouted cheerfully. The procession stood still, but from the front of it came loud argument. Schreider and Prokopovich were bellowing at the big sailor who seemed in command.

"We demand to pass!" they cried. "See, these comrades come from the Congress of Soviets! Look at their tickets! We are going to the Winter Palace!"

The sailor was plainly puzzled. He scratched his head with an enormous hand, frowning. "I have orders from the Committee not to let anybody go to the Winter Palace," he grumbled. "But I will send a comrade to telephone to Smolny . . ."

"We insist upon passing! We are unarmed! We will march on whether you permit us or not!" cried old Schreider, very much excited.

"I have orders –" repeated the sailor sullenly.

"Shoot us if you want to! We will pass! Forward!" came from all sides. "We are ready to die, if you have the heart to fire on Russians and comrades! We bare our breasts to your guns!"

"No," said the sailor, looking stubborn, "I can't allow you to pass."

"What will you do if we go forward? Will you shoot?"

"No, I'm not going to shoot people who haven't any guns. We won't shoot unarmed Russian people . . ."

"We will go forward! What can you do?"

"We will do something!" replied the sailor, evidently at a loss. "We can't let you pass. We will do something."

"What will you do? What will you do?"

Another sailor came up, very much irritated. "We will spank you!" he cried energetically. "And if necessary we will shoot you too. Go home how, and leave us in peace!"

At this there was a great clamour of anger and resentment. Prokopovich had mounted some sort of box, and waving his umbrella, he made a speech:

"Comrades and citizens!" he said. "Force is being used against us! We cannot have our innocent blood upon the hands of these ignorant men! It is beneath our dignity to be shot down here in the streets by switchmen −" (What he meant by "switchmen" I never discovered.) "Let us return to the Duma and discuss the best means of saving the country and the Revolution!"

Whereupon, in dignified silence, the procession marched around and back up the Nevsky, always in column of fours. And taking advantage of the diversion we slipped past the guards and set off in the direction of the Winter Palace.

Here it was absolutely dark, and nothing moved but pickets of soldiers and Red Guards grimly intent. In front of the Kazan Cathedral a three-inch field-gun lay in the middle of the street, slewed sideways from the recoil of its last shot over the roofs. Soldiers were standing in every doorway talking in loud tones and peering down towards the Police Bridge. I heard one voice saying: "It is possible that we have done wrong . . ." At the corners patrols stopped all passers-by − and the composition of these patrols was interesting, for in command of the regular troops was invariably a Red Guard . . . The shooting had ceased.

Just as we came to the Morskaya somebody was shouting: "The *yunkers* have sent word that they want us to go and get them out!" Voices began to give commands, and in the thick gloom we made out a dark mass moving forward, silent but for the shuffle of feet and the clinking of arms. We fell in with the first ranks.

Like a black river, filling all the street, without song or cheer we poured through the Red Arch, where the man just ahead of me said in a low voice: "Look out, comrades! Don't trust them. They will fire, surely!" In the open we began to run, stooping low and bunching together, and jammed up suddenly behind the pedestal of the Alexander Column.

"How many of you did they kill?" I asked.

"I don't know. About ten . . ."

After a few minutes huddling there, some hundreds of men, the Army seemed reassured and without any orders suddenly began again to flow forward. By this time, in the light that streamed out of all the Winter Palace windows, I could see that the first two or three hundred men were Red Guards, with only a few scattered soldiers. Over the barricade of fire-wood we clambered, and leaping down inside gave a triumphant shout as we stumbled on a heap of rifles thrown down by the *yunkers* who had stood there. On both sides of the main gateway the doors stood wide open, light streamed out, and from the huge pile came not the slightest sound.

Carried along by the eager wave of men we were swept into the right-hand entrance, opening into a great bare vaulted room, the cellar of the east wing, from which issued a maze of corridors and staircases. A number of huge packing cases stood about, and upon these the Red Guards and soldiers fell furiously, battering them open with the butts of their rifles, and pulling out carpets, curtains, linen, porcelain, plates, glass-ware . . . One man went strutting around with a bronze clock perched on his shoulder; another found a plume of ostrich feathers, which he stuck in his hat. The looting was just beginning when somebody cried, "Comrades! Don't take anything. This is the property of the People!" Immediately twenty voices were crying, "Stop! Put everything back! Don't take anything! Property of the People!" Many hands dragged the spoilers down. Damask and tapestry were snatched from the arms of those who had them; two men took away the bronze clock. Roughly and hastily the things were crammed back in their cases, and self-appointed sentinels stood guard. It was all utterly spontaneous. Through corridors and up staircases the cry could be heard growing fainter and fainter in the distance, "Revolutionary discipline! Property of the People . . ."

We crossed back over to the left entrance, in the west wing. There order was also being established. "Clear the Palace!"

bawled a Red Guard, sticking his head through an inner door. "Come, comrades, let's show that we're not thieves and bandits. Everybody out of the Palace except the Commissars, until we get sentries posted."

Two Red Guards, a soldier and an officer, stood with revolvers in their hands. Another soldier sat at a table behind them, with pen and paper. Shouts of "All out! All out!" were heard far and near within, and the Army began to pour through the door, jostling, expostulating, arguing. As each man appeared he was seized by the self-appointed committee, who went through his pockets and looked under his coat. Everything that was plainly not his property was taken away, the man at the table noted it on his paper, and it was carried into a little room. The most amazing assortment of objects were thus confiscated; statuettes, bottles of ink, bed-spreads worked with the Imperial monogram, candles, a small oil-painting, desk blotters, gold-handled swords, cakes of soap, clothes of every description, blankets. One Red Guard carried three rifles, two of which he had taken away from *yunkers*; another had four portfolios bulging with written documents. The culprits either sullenly surrendered or pleaded like children. All talking at once the committee explained that stealing was not worthy of the people's champions; often those who had been caught turned around and began to help go through the rest of the comrades.

Yunkers came out in bunches of three or four. The committee seized upon them with an excess of zeal, accompanying the search with remarks like, "Ah, Provocators! Kornilovists! Counter-revolutionists! Murderers of the People!" But there was no violence done, although the *yunkers* were terrified. They too had their pockets full of small plunder. It was carefully noted down by the scribe, and piled in the little room . . . The *yunkers* were disarmed. "Now, will you take up arms against the People any more?" demanded clamouring voices.

"No," answered the *yunkers*, one by one. Whereupon they were allowed to go free.

We asked if we might go inside. The committee was doubtful, but the big Red Guard answered firmly that it was forbidden. "Who are you anyway?" he asked. "How do I know that you are not all Kerenskys?" (There were five of us, two women.)

"*Pazhal'st*", *tovarishchi!* Way, Comrades!" A soldier and a

Red Guard appeared in the door, waving the crowd aside, and other guards with fixed bayonets. After them followed single file half a dozen men in civilian dress – the members of the Provisional Government. First came Kishkin, his face drawn and pale, then Rutenberg, looking sullenly at the floor; Tereshchenko was next, glancing sharply around; he stared at us with cold fixity . . . They passed in silence; the victorious insurrectionists crowded to see, but there were only a few angry mutterings. It was only later that we learned how the people in the street wanted to lynch them, and shots were fired – but the sailors brought them safely to Peter-Paul . . .

In the meanwhile unrebuked we walked into the Palace. There was still a great deal of coming and going, of exploring new-found apartments in the vast edifice, of searching for hidden garrisons of *yunkers* which did not exist. We went upstairs and wandered through room after room. This part of the Palace had been entered also by other detachments from the side of the Neva. The paintings, statues, tapestries, and rugs of the great state apartments were unharmed; in the offices, however, every desk and cabinet had been ransacked, the papers scattered over the floor, and in the living-rooms beds had been stripped of their coverings and wardrobes wrenched open. The most highly prized loot was clothing, which the working people needed. In a room where furniture was stored we came upon two soldiers ripping the elaborate Spanish leather upholstery from chairs. They explained it was to make boots with . . .

The old Palace servants in their blue and red and gold uniforms stood nervously about, from force of habit repeating, "You can't go in there, *barin*! It is forbidden –" We penetrated at length to the gold and malachite chamber with crimson brocade hangings where the Ministers had been in session all that day and night, and where the *shveitzari* had betrayed them to the Red Guards. The long table covered with green baize was just as they had left it, under arrest. Before each empty seat was pen, ink, and paper; the papers were scribbled over with beginnings of plans of action, rough drafts of proclamations and manifestoes. Most of these were scratched out, as their futility became evident, and the rest of the sheet covered with absent-minded geometrical designs, as the writers sat despondently listening while Minister after Minister proposed chimerical schemes. I took one of these scribbled pages, in the handwriting of Konovalov, which read, "The Provisional Government appeals to all classes to support the Provisional Government –"

All this time, it must be remembered, although the Winter Palace was surrounded, the Government was in constant communication with the front and with provincial Russia. The Bolsheviki had captured the Ministry of War early in the morning, but they did not know of the military telegraph office in the attic, nor of the private telephone line connecting it with the Winter Palace. In that attic a young officer sat all day, pouring out over the country a flood of appeals and proclamations; and when he heard the Palace had fallen, put on his hat and walked calmly out of the building . . .

Interested as we were, for a considerable time we didn't notice a change in the attitude of the soldiers and Red Guards around us. As we strolled from room to room a small group followed us, until by the time we reached the great picture-gallery where we had spent the afternoon with the *yunkers*, about a hundred men surged in upon us. One giant of a soldier stood in our path, his face dark with sullen suspicion.

"Who are you?" he growled. "What are you doing here?" The others massed slowly around, staring and beginning to mutter. "*Provocatori!*" I heard somebody say, "Looters!" I produced our passes from the Military Revolutionary Committee. The soldier took them gingerly, turned them upside down and looked at them without comprehension. Evidently he could not read. He handed them back and spat on the floor. "*Bumagi!* Papers!" said he with contempt. The mass slowly began to close in, like wild cattle around a cow-puncher on foot. Over their heads I caught sight of an officer, looking helpless, and shouted to him. He made for us, shouldering his way through.

"I'm the Commissar," he said to me. "Who are you? What is it?" The others held back, waiting. I produced the papers.

"You are foreigners?" he rapidly asked in French. "It is very dangerous . . ." Then he turned to the mob, holding up our documents. "Comrades!" he cried, "These people are foreign comrades – from America. They have come here to be able to tell their countrymen about the bravery and the revolutionary discipline of the proletarian army!"

"How do you know that?" replied the big soldier. "I tell you

they are provocators! They say they came here to observe the
revolutionary discipline of the proletarian army, but they have
been wandering freely through the Palace, and how do we know
they haven't their pockets full of loot?"

"*Pravilno!*" snarled the others, pressing forward.

"Comrades! Comrades!" appealed the officer, sweat standing
out on his forehead. "I am Commissar of the Military Revolutionary Committee. Do you trust me? Well, I tell you that these
passes are signed with the same names that are signed to my
pass!"

He led us down through the Palace and out through a door
opening on to the Neva quay, before which stood the usual
committee going through pockets . . . "You have narrowly
escaped," he kept muttering, wiping his face.

"What happened to the Women's Battalion?" we asked.

"Oh – the women!" He laughed. "They were all huddled up in
a back room. We had a terrible time deciding what to do with
them – many were in hysterics, and so on. So finally we marched
them up to the Finland Station and put them on a train to
Levashovo, where they have a camp . . ."

We came out into the cold, nervous night, murmurous with
obscure armies on the move, electric with patrols. From across
the river, where loomed the darker mass of Peter-Paul came a
hoarse shout . . . Underfoot the sidewalk was littered with
broken stucco, from the cornice of the Palace where two shells
from the battleship *Avrora* had struck; that was the only damage
done by the bombardment.

It was now after three in the morning. On the Nevsky all the
street-lights were again shining, the cannon gone, and the only
signs of war were Red Guards and soldiers squatting around
fires. The city was quiet – probably never so quiet in its history;
on that night not a single hold-up occurred, not a single robbery.

RED TERROR IN BERLIN

Daily Express, 15 January 1919

Led by Rosa Luxembourg and Karl Liebknecht, the revolutionary Spar-
tacist League made an abortive bid for power in Berlin.

Berlin, 12 January (6.30 p.m.)

There has been another pitched battle in Berlin this afternoon.

The Spartacists obtained possession of the Russian Embassy in
Unter den Linden, and opened fire on the Government troops.
The latter installed themselves in the Hotel Bristol – which is
adjacent – and a battle royal began from the housetops. Government troops also occupied all the windows and doorways on the
opposite side of the street, and fighting went on for an hour and a
half. About seventy Government soldiers were killed or
wounded. All is quiet now.

Spartacus groups also occupied other spots in Berlin, notably
in the Friedrichstrasse and in the neighbourhood of the General
Post Office. There was a considerable amount of desultory
fighting all the afternoon, and the Government troops are still
trying to capture the beer-garden in the northern suburbs, where
I went to look for Eichorn the other day.

The ex-chief of police, by the way, is reported to be wounded,
but it is impossible to control these rumours. It is like the story
which got abroad this afternoon that the Spartacists had seized
some Russian prisoners and were using them as cannon fodder.

My car has returned from Spartacus captivity. These people
decreed that my chauffeur should drive them, and he had no
choice but to obey, as they threatened to shoot him if he refused.
This morning, when he was driving three of them, they stopped

for a drink. They drank a number of glasses of schnapps, and then the chauffeur suggested that he should pay for a round. He ordered the drinks, but when it came to payment he said that he had left all his money outside in the car. He "went to get it" – and the Spartacists are still looking for him.

Berlin, 13 January

The Government has moved at last.

I learn from a source which I consider to be well informed that 20,000 troops under officers are to enter the capital later in the afternoon.

It is pouring with rain, but that makes no difference; the battle of the housetops is unaffected by weather conditions. At eleven o'clock this morning the *Vorwärts* building fell into the hands of the Government troops. The battle began at eight. The Spartacists began the action with three machine-guns fired from the first-floor windows from behind barricades composed of rolls of paper. The Government troops replied with two pieces of field artillery. Fighting was maintained for three hours, and then the defenders surrendered.

There is a rumour in Berlin that Rosa Luxembourg was in the building, but the story is probably on a parallel with the rumour that Liebknecht has fled with Eichorn into Holland.

As an example of the confusion and the lack of knowledge of facts which prevail in Berlin one can cite the story of the surrender of the Spartacists defending the *Berliner Tageblatt* building. Notwithstanding that all the newspapers, as well as the Government, have said that the Spartacists have surrendered, this is utterly untrue.

What happened was that the defenders sent out a white flag, and a truce was called for the purpose of talking things over, but fighting was afterwards resumed and still continues. I only found this out by accident.

The Jerusalemstrasse, where the office of the *Berliner Tageblatt* is situated, is only a few minutes' walk from my hotel, and hearing continuous fighting, I went out to investigate. I found the battle proceeding, but one does not linger too long in these unhealthy neighbourhoods. Two passers-by were killed yesterday in the storming of the *Berliner Tageblatt* building. The casualties which have occurred this week must now number more than 1,500.

The most picturesque figure in the revolution is Erich Kuttner. He is a young man – he is under thirty – spectacled, blue-eyed, and he has a tuft of fair hair on his chin. He bears a charmed life. His adventures in one day are more than fall to the lot of most men in a lifetime.

Kuttner was a sub-editor of the staff of *Vorwärts* when the Spartacists captured the building. Instead of leaving the building he remained hidden in a cellar, and by means of a secret telephone kept in touch with the Government and told them all the Spartacists' plans.

He afterwards escaped from the *Vorwärts* building in the Lindenstrasse, and took over the command of a small body of men which was defending the Brandenburg Gate. Most of his men were killed or wounded in the first Spartacus rush, and he was driven from the gate. The Spartacists occupied it only for about half an hour. They were driven off by an attack that Kuttner organized. He held it again and repulsed other Spartacus attacks, killing twelve and wounding twenty-five. Kuttner is not acting under Government orders. He has got a body of men together who want to preserve order, so that the National Assembly may be held and peace signed as soon as possible.

Since the Brandenburg Gate has been better defended the Spartacists are not attacking. Kuttner goes off duty for a few hours, and with eleven men makes a search of houses for arms. Every day at about five o'clock he drops into the Hotel Adlon, drinks a cup of acorn coffee, and munches a slice of *ersatz* apple-cake, while he recounts the day's exploits. He said yesterday:

"I had to kill a man this morning. I went to search a room where I suspected that arms were hidden. I found them, and just when we were packing up the owner came into the room. He took a grenade from his pocket, and raised his arm to hurl it at us. I then shot him with my revolver."

Another extraordinary figure in the revolution came to see me this morning. He is Henry Burke, an ex-private of the 2nd Battalion Dublin Fusiliers, who was captured on 27 August 1914. Burke says that he used to live with his uncle in Russell Place, Dublin. He was wounded and taken prisoner, and then fell a victim to Casement's wiles. He was one of fifty-six men who joined the Irish Brigade.

Burke was released from prison in June 1917, and went to work at Danzig as a tailor's presser. Then he came to Berlin and worked in a furniture factory, but the workmen went on strike. This renegade was walking about when the street battle started. He saw an armed civilian fighting on the side of the Government throw away his rifle and run. Burke picked the weapon up, and since then he has been fighting for the Government. "An Irishman must fight somebody," he said.

This man now wants to go home, and is anxious to know whether he will be court-martialled. "I am willing to take my punishment," he said.

I took a walk this morning through the quarters of the city where the most severe fighting has taken place. Although Berlin has not been bombarded by the Allies' aeroplanes, the city shows more marks of damage than either London or Paris. The *Vorwärts* building is razed to the ground, and many houses adjacent are more or less severely damaged. There is hardly a street in the centre of the city that is untouched by rifle or machine-gun bullets. The ex-Kaiser's palace at the bottom of Unter den Linden has suffered more internally than it has externally, but the royal stables behind the palace are absolutely wrecked. The Reichstag is also damaged, as well as many famous monuments – and fighting is not yet over.

A TRIP UP THE VOLGA

Manchester Guardian, 13 October 1921

Ransome reported the Russian Civil War for the *Manchester Guardian* (later plain *The Guardian*), a happenstance that led to him meeting his second wife – Evgenia Shelepin, Trotsky's secretary. In 1930 he published the children's novel *Swallows and Amazons*, and the adventures of the Blacketts and the Walkers preoccupied him for the remainder of his writing life.

The question arose of how to get from Samara to Kazan. The Secretary of the Famine Committee at Samara telephoned down to the quay while I was going through his figures, and found that there was a boat going up the river in an hour's time. He asked what sort of a boat, but the telephone had been cut off. Telling him that we would go by whatever boat it might be, since we wished to reach Kazan in time to meet the American train, I rushed off to the hotel, found Ercole and his cameras, washed and shook out my clothes, splashed turpentine all over them, and hurried down to the river with our baggage in time to get on the steamer *Bogatyr*, after pushing our way through the crowd, the smell, and the curious persistent noise of the splitting of sunflower seeds and the expectoration of their husks.

Our good luck in falling on this boat was no stage management on the part of the Communists, for until I asked them to telephone they had no idea that we were leaving. But if they had wished to give us a feeling of renewed hope after the terrible sights we had seen in the morning they could not have done better. We found ourselves on a huge river steamer, launched in 1919, with clean-swept decks, very simply decorated, "a proletarian steamer", as one of the officers described her, a red banner across the saloon inscribed "*Bogatyr*, the best gift of Red work-men to the republic of Soviets". Even here, in the cabin, we found bugs, but outside we found the miracle of polished brass-work, engines properly kept, a certain amount of fresh paint, and a crew with something of the *esprit de corps* we know on English boats. We had a nice cabin, and as I was unpacking a stewardess came into wipe round the washing basin, where there was actually running water. I asked her how long she had been on the boat. She replied, like a true daughter of the Volga, not "two years" but "two navigations", for just as a sundial counts those hours only when the sun shines, so the river is the river only between ice and ice. She added, "I was working on him before he was launched. I have been with him since his birth." "Did you have much fun at his birth?" I asked. "Of course," she replied, "music and dancing; it was a great holiday." We could hardly show ourselves on deck without being begged by one of the crew to photograph some part of the ship, of course with himself in a prominent position.

We had had nothing to eat all day, and went into the buffet, where we had soup, sturgeon, and lemonade (very beastly lemon-ade), and were charged 15,000 roubles each. We offered the amount with a tip, and the waiter handed us back the tip. I nearly fell out of my chair. "I am myself the boss," he explained. "How is that?" I asked, and he told me. They have an artel, an institution known in Russia long before the revolution, in which all the members are jointly responsible for each one of their number. The artel delegates so many of its members to run the buffet on each steamer. "What were you before the revolution?" I asked. "I was a waiter," he replied, and added, "My old boss is working with me in this artel." The particular fellow who waited on us certainly deserved to be a "boss". He could not have done better if he had been the manager of a private hotel and we his first guests. We were lucky aboard the *Bogatyr*. We had a very different experience in another boat.

I suppose the trip up the Volga has been described a thousand times. But we made it in special circumstances. To stand on the deck of that comparatively clean steamer, looking up and down the immense river, after stepping hither and thither among people huddled together, crawling with vermin, none moving far from his belongings even for those purposes for which civilized humans usually seek some sort of seclusion; to look on the placid majesty of the river, to watch the green and gold of the autumn foliage on the high bank on one side, the gleaming sand on the other, after looking at scarcely human faces of misery and starvation; to hear the call of birds, the occasional splash of a fish, the pleasant purring of water under the prow instead of that incessant heartrending wailing of suffering children, was like stepping from hell to heaven. The contrast was so violent that it destroyed reality. Either those scenes of misery had never been, or this of quiet beauty was a cheating dream.

Yet the two were very near. On the steamer itself two small children had hidden themselves, hoping to go somewhere, to get something, anyhow to escape from the horror of the river bank. They were found, and the woman doctor on board washed them, and put them into clean rags of some kind, to hand them over to a relief station higher up the river. Both were ill. We stopped at a floating hospital barge, but it was full up, and the children had to be taken farther. At each river station at which we called the bank was crowded with refugees from the famine-stricken hinterland. In this country all roads lead to the river. But the river in this year of horror merely leads north and south between famine-stricken banks, and these who travel on it travel not from famine to plenty but from hunger to hunger. I remember particularly our stop at Tetiushy. Here a precipitous bank rises many hundred feet, like a brown wall, down which zig-zag tracks fall dangerously to the shore.

It was growing dusk. Half-dead horses were stumbling down the tracks bringing carts and more refugees to join the crowds already hopelessly camping. Little fires were burning all over the shores. Some of the campers had been there three weeks already. The nights were turning cold. They had fixed up little shelters against the wind, with old shawls, torn blankets, scraps of tinplate from some disintegrated steamer. Others had crawled under overturned boats and lay on their stomachs, just their heads showing, looking hopelessly out with passive eyes, like the dull eyes of bullocks expecting the slaughter. I felt the frost in the wind and knew that they would not have long to wait.

They made no attempt to board the steamer. They saw it come. They saw it go. It was going from one famine-stricken place to another and could do nothing for them. They scarcely moved.

Round the fires here and there a man or woman glanced round, but they turned instantly to their little pots. And in the pots? Horse-dung bread, the poisonous rind of the big green red-hearted pumpkins of Tsaritsin and Astrakhan, the gleanings of the road and the beach. They were peasants from up country. Often when we gave them chocolate they did not know what it was. The steamer gave its three whistles. A few turned for a moment. Those who lay watching went on watching, just masks under the gunwales of the overturned primitive boats (some of them hollowed from single tree trunks as by prehistoric man). But most of them had passed the stage of noticing anything, and crouched where they were, their backs to us, three loud hoots and the fuss of a departing steamer being incidents of a world to which they had already ceased to belong.

And then ropes were cast off, the wheels churned again, and in a moment or two of that ant-heap of human misery nothing was left but the great wall of the cliff, and below it the thousand tiny fires, which presently faded into the dusk, and we were alone once more with the quiet ceaseless murmur of the river, the changing cliffs cutting the evening sky, the low woods of the farther shore dim in the twilight, slipping up stream, higher and higher, watching the wind dust away the cobwebs of cloud, seeing the North Star peer out overhead, and at last the full glory of the moon pouring down over the enormous landscape.

KIRKE L. SIMPSON

BUGLES SOUND TAPS
FOR WARRIOR'S REQUIEM

Associated Press, 11 November 1921

Three years after the end of the Great War, the United States dedicated the Tomb of the Unknown Soldier at Arlington Cemetery. Simpson's account of the dedication was the first ever AP dispatch to earn a byline; it also gained him a 1922 Pulitzer Prize.

Under the wide and starry skies of his own homeland America's unknown dead from France sleeps tonight, a soldier home from the wars.

Alone, he lies in the narrow cell of stone that guards his body; but his soul has entered into the spirit that is America. Wherever liberty is held close in men's hearts, the honor and the glory and the pledge of high endeavor poured out over this nameless one of fame will be told and sung by Americans for all time.

Scrolled across the marble arch of the memorial raised to American soldier and sailor dead, everywhere, which stands like a monument behind his tomb, runs this legend: "We here highly resolve that these dead shall not have died in vain."

The words were spoken by the martyred Lincoln over the dead at Gettysburg. And today with voice strong with determination and ringing with deep emotion, another President echoed that high resolve over the coffin of the soldier who died for the flag in France.

Great men in the world's affairs heard that high purpose reiterated by the man who stands at the head of the American people. Tomorrow they will gather in the city that stands almost in the shadow of the new American shrine of liberty dedicated today. They will talk of peace; of the curbing of the havoc of war.

They will speak of the war in France, that robbed this soldier of life and name and brought death to comrades of all nations by the hundreds of thousands. And in their ears when they meet must ring President Harding's declaration today beside that flag-wrapped, honour-laden bier:

"There must be, there shall be, the commanding voice of a conscious civilization against armed warfare."

Far across the seas, other unknown dead, hallowed in memory by their countrymen, as this American soldier is enshrined in the heart of America, sleep their last. He, in whose veins ran the blood of British forebears, lies beneath a great stone in ancient Westminster Abbey; he of France, beneath the Arc de Triomphe, and he of Italy under the altar of the fatherland in Rome . . .

And it seemed today that they, too, must be here among the Potomac hills to greet an American comrade come to join their glorious company, to testify their approval of the high words of hope spoken by America's President. All day long the nation poured out its heart in pride and glory for the nameless American. Before the first crash of the minute guns roared its knell for the dead from the shadow of Washington Monument, the people who claim him as their own were trooping out to do him honour. They lined the long road from the Capitol to the hillside where he sleeps tonight; they flowed like a tide over the slopes about his burial place; they choked the bridges that lead across the river to the fields of the brave, in which he is the last comer . . .

As he was carried past through the banks of humanity that lined Pennsylvania Avenue a solemn, reverent hush held the living walls. Yet there was not so much of sorrow as of high pride in it all, a pride beyond the reach of shouting and the clamor that marks less sacred moments in life.

Out there in the broad avenue was a simpler soldier, dead for honor of the flag. He was nameless. No man knew what part in the great life of the nation he had died as Americans always have been ready to die, for the flag and what it means. They read the message of the pageant clear, these silent thousands along the way. They stood in almost holy awe to take their own part in what was theirs, the glory of the American people, honoured here in the honors showered on America's nameless son from France.

Soldiers, sailors, and marines – all played their part in the thrilling spectacles as the cortege rolled along. And just behind the casket, with its faded French flowers on the draped flag, walked the President, the chosen leader of a hundred million, in whose name he was chief mourner at his bier. Beside him strode the man under whom the fallen hero had lived and died in France, General Pershing, wearing only the single medal of Victory that every American soldier might wear as his only decoration.

Then, row on row, came the men who lead the nation today or have guided its destinies before. They were all there, walking proudly, with age and frailties of the flesh forgotten. Judges, Senators, Representatives, highest officers of every military arm of government, and a trudging little group of the nation's most valorous sons, the Medal of Honour men. Some were gray and bent and drooping with old wounds; some trim and erect as the day they won their way to fame. All walked gladly in this nameless comrade's last parade.

Behind these came the carriage in which rode Woodrow Wilson, also stricken down by infirmities as he served in the highest place in the nation, just as the humble private riding in such state ahead had gone down before a shell or bullet. For the dead man's sake, the former President had put aside his dread of seeming to parade his physical weakness and risked health, perhaps life, to appear among the mourners for the fallen.

There was handclapping and a cheer here and there for the man in the carriage, a tribute to the spirit that brought him to honour the nation's nameless hero, whose commander-in-chief he had been.

After President Harding and most of the high dignitaries of the government had turned aside at the White House, the procession, headed by its solid blocks of soldiery and the battalions of sailor comrades, moved on with Pershing, now flanked by secretaries Weeks and Denby, for the long road to the tomb. It marched on, always between the human borders of the way of victory the nation had made for itself of the great avenue; on over the old bridge that spans the Potomac, on up the long hill to Fort Myer, and at last to the great cemetery beyond, where soldier and sailor folk sleep by the thousands. There the lumbering guns of the artillery swung aside, the cavalry drew their horses out of the long line and left to the foot soldiers and the sailors and marines the last stage of the journey.

Ahead, the white marble of the amphitheater gleamed through the trees. It stands crowning the slope of the hills that sweep upward from the river, and just across was Washington, its clustered buildings and monuments to great dead who have gone before, a moving picture in the autumn haze.

People in thousands were moving about the great circle of the amphitheatre. The great ones to whom places had been given in the sacred enclosure and the plain folk who had trudged the long way just to glimpse the pageant from afar, were finding their places. Everywhere within the pillared enclosure bright uniforms of foreign soldiers appeared. They were laden with the jeweled order of rank to honor an American private soldier, great in the majesty of his sacrifices, in the tribute his honours paid to all Americans who died.

Down below the platform placed for the casket, in a stone vault, lay wreaths and garlands brought from England's King and guarded by British soldiers. To them came the British Ambassador in the full uniform of his rank to bid them keep safe against that hour.

Above the platform gathered men whose names ring through history – Briand, Foch, Beatty, Balfour, Jacques, Diaz, and others – in a brilliant array of place and power. They were followed by others, Baron Kato from Japan, the Italian statesmen and officers, by the notables from all countries gathered here for tomorrow's conference, and by some of the older figures in American life too old to walk beside the approaching funeral train.

Down around the circling pillars the marbled box filled with distinguished men and women, with a cluster of shattered men from army hospitals, accompanied by uniformed nurses. A surpliced choir took its place to wait the dead.

Faint and distant, the silvery strains of a military band stole into the big white bowl of the amphitheater. The slow cadences and mourning notes of a funeral march grew clearer amid the roll and mutter of the muffled drums.

At the arch where the choir awaited the heroic dead, comrades lifted his casket down and, followed by the generals and the admirals, who had walked beside him from the Capitol, he was carried to the place of honor. Ahead moved the white-robed singers, chanting solemnly. Carefully, the casket was placed above the banked flowers, and the Marine Band played sacred melodies until the moment the President and Mrs Harding stepped to their places beside the casket; then the crashing, triumphant chorus of "The Star Spangled Banner" swept the gathering to its feet again.

A prayer, carried out over the crowd over the amplifiers so that no word was missed, took a moment or two, then the sharp, clear call of the bugle rang "Attention!" and for two minutes the nation stood at pause for the dead, just at high noon. No sound broke the quiet as all stood with bowed heads. It was much as though a mighty hand had checked the world in full course. Then the band sounded, and in a mighty chorus rolled up in the words of America from the hosts within and without the great open hall of valor.

President Harding stepped forward beside the coffin to say for America the thing that today was nearest to the nation's heart, that sacrifices such as this nameless man, fallen in battle, might perhaps be made unnecessary down through the coming years. Every word that President Harding spoke reached every person through the amplifiers and reached other thousands upon thousands in New York and San Francisco.

Mr Harding showed strong emotion as his lips formed the last words of the address. He paused, then with raised hand and head bowed, went on in the measured, rolling periods of the Lord's Prayer. The response that came back to him from the thousands he faced, from the other thousands out over the slopes beyond, perhaps from still other thousands away near the Pacific, or close-packed in the heart of the nation's greatest city, arose like a chant. The marble arches hummed with a solemn sound.

Then the foreign officers who stand highest among the soldiers or sailors of their flags came one by one to the bier to place gold and jeweled emblems for the brave above the breast of the sleeper. Already, as the great prayer ended, the President had set the American seal of admiration for the valiant, the nation's love for brave deeds and the courage that defies death, upon the casket.

Side by side he laid the Medal of Honour and the Distinguished Service Cross. And below, set in place with reverent hands, grew the long line of foreign honours, the Victoria Cross, never before laid on the breast of any but those who had served the British flag; all the highest honours of France and Belgium and Italy and Rumania and Czechoslovakia and Poland.

To General Jacques of Belgium it remained to add his own touch to these honours. He tore from the breast of his own tunic the medal of valour pinned there by the Belgian King, tore it with a sweeping gesture, and tenderly bestowed it on the unknown American warrior.

Through the religious services that followed, and prayers, the swelling crowd sat motionless until it rose to join in the old, consoling Rock of Ages, and the last rite for the dead was at hand. Lifted by his hero-bearers from the stage, the unknown was carried in his flag-wrapped, simple coffin out to the wide sweep of the terrace. The bearers laid the sleeper down above the crypt, on which had been placed a little soil of France. The dust his blood helped redeem from alien hands will mingle with his dust as time marches by.

The simple words of the burial ritual were said by Bishop Brent; flowers from war mothers of America and England were laid in place.

For the Indians of America Chief Plenty Coos came to call upon the Great spirit of the Red Men, with gesture and chant and tribal tongue, that the dead should not have died in vain, that war might end, peace be purchased by such blood as this. Upon the casket he laid the coupstick of his tribal office and the feathered war bonnet from his own head. Then the casket, with its weight of honours, was lowered into the crypt.

A rocking blast of gunfire rang from the woods. The glittering circle of bayonets stiffened to a salute to the dead. Again the guns shouted their message of honor and farewell. Again they boomed out; a loyal comrade was being laid to his last, long rest.

High and clear and true in the echoes of the guns, a bugle lifted the old, old notes of taps, the lullaby for the living soldier, in death his requiem. Long ago some forgotten soldier-poet caught its meaning clear and set it down that soldiers everywhere might know its message as they sink to rest:

> Fades the light;
> And afar
> Goeth day, cometh night,
> And a star,
> Leadeth all, speedeth all,
> To their rest.

The guns roared out again in the national salute. He was home, The Unknown, to sleep forever among his own.

LANDRU IS EXECUTED

I Found No Peace, 1937

Henri Landru (a.k.a. "Bluebeard") was found guilty by a French court of the murder of ten women and duly sentenced to death by guillotine on 25 February 1922.

On the night of 24 February, together with half-a-dozen French reporters, I caught the electric train to Versailles. We went to the courthouse, obtained crudely mimeographed green *laissez-passers* for the execution and retired to the Hôtel des Réservoirs with five bottles of cognac to await dawn.

At 4 a.m. word came that M. Deibler, the famous executioner who performed all the executions throughout France, had arrived with his apparatus. Anatole Deibler, shy, wistful, goat-bearded, had performed more than 300 executions. His salary was 18,000 francs per year (a little over $1000 at the 1936 rate of exchange). He suffered from a weak heart and could not walk upstairs, but this did not seem to interfere with his gruesome vocation. He lived in a small house near Versailles under the name of M. Anatole, consorted very little with his neighbours, and led a retiring existence. He kept the guillotine in a shed outside his house. When performing an execution he wore white gloves and a long white "duster".

We hurried to the prison. Four hundred troops had drawn cordons at each end of the street and permitted only the possessors of the little green mimeographed tickets to pass. According to the French law, executions must occur in the open street in front of the prison door. On the damp, slippery cobblestones beside the streetcar tracks workmen were rapidly erecting the guillotine a dozen feet outside the towering gate of Versailles prison. It was still quite dark. The only light came from the workmen's old-fashioned lanterns with flickering candles and the few electric street lights. The workmen bolted the grisly machine together and adjusted its balance with a carpenter's level. Deibler hauled the heavy knife to the top of the uprights.

Nearly one hundred officials and newspapermen gathered in a circle around the guillotine; I stood about fifteen feet away. News arrived from inside the prison that Landru, whose long black beard had been cut previously, asked that he be shaved.

"It will please the ladies," he said to his gaolers.

His lawyer and a priest went into his cell. He refused the traditional cigarette and glass of rum always offered just before executions.

Landru wore a shirt from which the neck had been cut away, and a pair of cheap dark trousers. That was all – no shoes or socks. He would walk to the guillotine barefooted.

As his arms were strapped behind him his lawyer whispered, "Courage, Landru." "Thanks, Maître, I've always had that," he replied calmly.

Just as the first streaks of the chilly February dawn appeared, a large closed van drawn by horses arrived and backed up within a few feet of the right side of the guillotine. Deibler's assistants, wearing long smocks, pulled two wicker baskets from the van. They placed the small round basket carefully in front of the machine where the head would fall. Two assistants placed another basket about the size and shape of a coffin close beside the guillotine. Into that the headless body would roll.

The cordon of troops halted a streetcar full of workmen on their way to work. They decided to open the cordon to permit the car to proceed, and it slowly rumbled past within a few feet of the grim machine. Staring faces filled the windows.

The guillotine underwent a final test. Deibler raised the lunette, the half-moon-shaped wooden block which was to clamp down upon Landru's neck. Then he lowered it, and the heavy knife shot down from the top of the uprights with a crash which shook the machine. The lunette and knife were raised again. All was ready.

Suddenly the huge wooden gates of the prison swung open. The spectators became silent and tense. Three figures appeared, walking rapidly. On each side a gaoler held Landru by his arms, which were strapped behind him. They supported and pulled him forward as fast as they could walk. His bare feet pattered on the cold cobblestones, and his knees seemed not to be functioning. His face was pale and waxen, and as he caught sight of the ghastly machine, he went livid.

The two gaolers hastily pushed Landru face foremost against the upright board of the machine. It collapsed, and his body crumpled with it as they shoved him forward under the wooden block, which dropped down and clamped his neck beneath the suspended knife. In a split second the knife flicked down, and the head fell with a thud into the small basket. As an assistant lifted the hinged board and rolled the headless body into the big wicker basket, a hideous spurt of blood gushed out.

An attendant standing in front of the machine seized the basket containing the head, rolled it like a cabbage into the larger basket, and helped shove it hastily into the waiting van. The van doors slammed, and the horses were whipped into a gallop.

When Landru first appeared in the prison courtyard I had glanced at my wrist watch. Now I looked again. Only twenty-six seconds had elapsed.

NOTRE DAME'S "FOUR HORSEMEN"

New York Herald-Tribune, 19 October 1924

Born in 1880, Rice was the first sportswriter celebrity. He made celebrities, too: the senior backfield of Notre Dame's college football team were immortalized way above their ability courtesy of Rice's dispatch below.

Outlined against a blue-grey October sky, the Four Horsemen rode again. In dramatic lore they are known as Famine, Pestilence, Destruction and Death. These are only aliases. Their real names are Stuhldreher, Miller, Crowley and Layden. They formed the crest of the South Bend cyclone before which another fighting Army football team was swept over the precipice at the Polo Grounds yesterday afternoon as 55,000 spectators peered down on the bewildering panorama spread on the green plain below.

A cyclone can't be snared. It may be surrounded, but somewhere it breaks through to keep on going. When the cyclone starts from South Bend, where the candle lights still gleam through the Indiana sycamores, those in the way must take to storm cellars at top speed.

Yesterday the cyclone struck again as Notre Dame beat the Army, 13 to 7, with a set of backfield stars that ripped and crashed through a strong Army defence with more speed and power than the warring cadets could meet.

Notre Dame won its ninth game in twelve Army starts through the driving power of one of the greatest backfields that ever churned up the turf of any gridiron in any football age. Brilliant backfields may come and go, but in Stuhldreher, Miller, Crowley and Layden, covered by a fast and charging line, Notre Dame can take its place in front of the field.

Coach McEwan sent one of his finest teams into action, an aggressive organization that fought to the last play around the first rim of darkness, but when Rockne rushed his Four Horsemen to the track they rode down everything in sight. It was in vain that 1,400 grey-clad cadets pleaded for the Army line to hold. The Army line was giving all it had, but when a tank tears in with the speed of a motorcycle, what chance had flesh and blood to hold? The Army had its share of stars as Garbisch, Farwick, Wilson, Wood, Ellinger, and many others, but they were up against four whirlwind backs who picked up at top speed from the first step as they swept through scant openings to slip on by the secondary defence. The Army had great backs in Wilson and Wood, but the Army had no such quartet, who seemed to carry the mixed blood of the tiger and the antelope.

Rockne's light and tottering line was just about as tottering as the Rock of Gibraltar. It was something more than a match for the Army's great set of forwards, who had earned their fame before. Yet it was not until the second period that the first big thrill of the afternoon set the great crowd into a cheering whirl and brought about the wild flutter of flags that are thrown to the wind in exciting moments. At the game's start Rockne sent in almost entirely a second-string cast. The Army got the jump and began to play most of the football. It was the Army attack that made three first downs before Notre Dame had caught its stride. The South Bend cyclone opened like a zephyr.

And then, in the wake of a sudden cheer, out rushed Stuhldreher, Miller, Crowley and Layden, the four star backs who helped to beat Army a year ago. Things were to be a trifle different now. After a short opening flurry in the second period, Wood, of the Army, kicked out of bounds on Notre Dame's 20 yard line. There was no sign of a tornado starting. But it happened to be at just this spot that Stuhldreher decided to put on his attack and began the long and dusty hike.

On the first play the fleet Crowley peeled off fifteen yards and the cloud from the west was now beginning to show signs of lightning and thunder. The fleet, powerful Layden got six yards more and then Don Miller added ten. A forward pass from Stuhldreher to Crowley added twelve yards, and a moment later Don Miller ran twenty yards around Army's right wing. He was on his way to glory when Wilson, hurtling across the right of way, nailed him on the 10 yard line and threw him out of bounds. Crowley, Miller and Layden – Miller, Layden and Crowley – one or another, ripping and crashing through, as the Army defence threw everything it had in the way to stop this wild charge that had now come seventy yards. Crowley and Layden added five yards more and then, on a split play, Layden went ten yards across the line as if he had just been fired from the black mouth of a howitzer.

In that second period Notre Dame made eight first downs to the Army's none, which shows the unwavering power of the Western attack that hammered relentlessly and remorselessly without easing up for a second's breath. The Western line was going its full share, led by the crippled Walsh with a broken hand.

But there always was Miller or Crowley or Layden, directed through the right spot by the cool and crafty judgment of Stuhldreher, who picked his plays with the finest possible generalship. The South Bend cyclone had now roared eighty-five yards to a touchdown through one of the strongest defensive teams in the game. The cyclone had struck with too much speed and power to be stopped. It was the preponderance of Western speed that swept the Army back.

The next period was much like the second. The trouble began when the alert Layden intercepted an Army pass on the 48-yard line. Stuhldreher was ready for another march.

Once again the cheering cadets began to call for a rallying stand. They are never overwhelmed by any shadow of defeat as long as there is a minute of fighting left. But silence fell over the cadet sector for just a second as Crowley ran around the Army's right wing for 15 yards, where Wilson hauled him down on the 33 yard line. Walsh, the Western captain, was hurt in the play but soon resumed. Miller got 7 and Layden got 8 and then, with the ball on the Army's 20-yard line, the cadet defence rallied and threw Miller in his tracks. But the halt was only for the moment. On the next play Crowley swung out and around the Army's left wing, cut in and then crashed over the line for Notre Dame's second touchdown.

On two other occasions the Notre Dame attack almost scored. Yeomans saved one touchdown by intercepting a pass on his 5-yard line as he ran back 35 yards before he was nailed by two tacklers. It was a great play in the nick of time. On the next drive

Miller and Layden in two hurricane dashes took the ball 42 yards to the Army's 14-yard line, where the still game Army defence stopped four plunges on the 9-yard line and took the ball.

Up to this point the Army had been outplayed by a crushing margin. Notre Dame had put underway four long marches and two of these had yielded touchdowns. Even the stout and experienced Army line was meeting more than it could hold. Notre Dame's brilliant backs had been provided with the finest possible interference, usually led by Stuhldreher, who cut down tackler after tackler by diving at some rival's flying knees. Against this, each Army attack had been smothered almost before it got underway. Even the great Wilson, the star from Penn State, one of the great backfield runners of his day and time, rarely had a chance to make any headway through a massed wall of tacklers who were blocking every open route.

The sudden change came late in the third quarter, when Wilson, raging like a wild man, suddenly shot through a tackle opening to run 34 yards before he was finally collared and thrown with a jolt. A few minutes later Wood, one of the best of all punters, kicked out of bounds on Notre Dame's 5-yard line. Here was the chance. Layden was forced to kick from behind his own goal. The punt soared up the field as Yeomans called for a free catch on the 35-yard line. As he caught the ball he was nailed and spilled by a Western tackler, and the penalty gave the Army 15 yards, with the ball on Notre Dame's 20-yard line.

At this point Harding was rushed to quarter in place of Yeomans, who had been one of the leading Army stars. On the first three plays the Army reached the 12-yard line, but it was now fourth down, with two yards to go. Harding's next play was the feature of the game.

As the ball was passed, he faked a play to Wood, diving through the line, held the oval for just a half breath, then, tucking the same under his arm, swung out around Notre Dame's right end. The brilliant fake worked to perfection. The entire Notre Dame defence had charged forward in a surging mass to check the line attack and Harding, with open territory, sailed on for a touchdown. He travelled those last 12 yards after the manner of food shot from guns. He was over the line before the Westerners knew what had taken place. It was a fine bit of strategy, brilliantly carried over by every member of the cast.

The cadet sector had a chance to rip open the chilly atmosphere at last, and most of the 55,000 present joined in the tribute
to football art. But that was Army's last chance to score. From
that point on, it was seesaw, up and down, back and forth, with
the rivals fighting bitterly for every inch of ground. It was harder
now to make a foot than it had been to make ten yards. Even the
all-star South Bend cast could no longer continue to romp for any
set distances, as Army tacklers, inspired by the touchdown,
charged harder and faster than they had charged before.

The Army brought a fine football team into action, but it was
beaten by a faster and smoother team. Rockne's supposedly light,
green line was about as heavy as Army's, and every whit as
aggressive. What is even more important, it was faster on its feet,
faster in getting around.

It was Western speed and perfect interference that once more
brought the Army doom. The Army line couldn't get through
fast enough to break up the attacking plays; and once started, the
bewildering speed and power of the Western backs slashed along
for 8, 10, and 15 yards on play after play. And always in front of
these offensive drivers could be found the whirling form of
Stuhldreher, taking the first man out of the play as cleanly as
though he had used a hand grenade at close range. This Notre
Dame interference was a marvelous thing to look upon.

It formed quickly and came along in unbroken order, always at
terrific speed, carried by backs who were as hard to drag down as
African buffaloes. On receiving the kick-off, Notre Dame's
interference formed something after the manner of the ancient
flying wedge, and they drove back up the field with the runner
covered from 25 and 30 yards at almost every chance. And when a
back such as Harry Wilson finds few chances to get started, you
can figure upon the defensive strength that is barricading the
road. Wilson is one of the hardest backs in the game to suppress,
but he found few chances yesterday to show his broken-field
ability. You can't run through a broken field unless you get there.

One strong feature of the Army play was its headlong battle
against heavy odds. Even when Notre Dame had scored two
touchdowns and was well on its way to a third, the Army fought
on with fine spirit until the touchdown chance came at last. And
when the chance came, Coach McEwan had the play ready for the
final march across the line. The Army had a better team than it

had last year. So has Notre Dame. We doubt that any team in the country could have beaten Rockne's array yesterday afternoon, East or West. It was a great football team brilliantly directed, a team of speed, power and team play. The Army has no cause to gloom over its showing. It played first-class football against more speed than it could match.

Those who have tackled a cyclone can understand.

J. J. JONES

TOTAL ECLIPSE OF THE SUN

Evening News, 29 June 1927

As seen from Giggleswick, Yorkshire, in England. The eclipse occurred at 5.29 a.m. Jones – whose standard beat was crime – filed this dispatch in time for the paper's noon edition.

While Southern England, with rain falling and the sky filled with clouds, saw nothing of the eclipse, countless thousands of watchers at Giggleswick, Yorkshire, the centre of the totality belt, saw a wonderful spectacle.

Shortly before the eclipse began the clouds rolled away. The sunshine of the dawn broke and a second later total darkness descended on the earth.

The wind whined among the trees and an unnatural coldness made everyone shiver.

"One, two, three, four." A voice came from one of the observers ticking off those thrilling moments. He had called "twenty-three" when the darkness disappeared and the great light of the world was rekindled.

The divine beauty, terror and mystery of the sight left the watchers awed and shaken. The Astronomer Royal's observations were completely successful.

Beyond all that we had dreamed, beyond all that we had imagined of loveliness and unearthly beauty, was that spectacle in the darkened sky over the shadowed Pennine Hills today.

None of those countless thousands along the shadowed belt who saw that magnificent and terrible sight – that black disc in the deep purple sky, encircled with its halo of silvery light and red flame – will ever forget it.

Its divine beauty has left us all shaken.

It was the terror and mystery of the Universe revealed to us in twenty-three immortal seconds.

It came to us too when we were almost despairing.

Great battlemented clouds had piled themselves above the bleak height of Winskill Crag after a night of cloudless skies and glittering stars.

Then they opened, in rifts of blue sky, and the sun shone through in tantalizing glimpses – just enough to show the black rim of the moon biting further and further into its golden face.

Out of the south marched more clouds and still more clouds.

They passed in stately line across the dimming sun – great white clouds like galleons sailing.

Our hearts – the hearts of all of us up on the darkening hill where the great astronomers of England bent over their instruments – were torn with anxiety.

Would they pass in time?

Slowly they sailed by – just crept into the clouded western sky.

Pendle Hill, far away, grew dim and vanished in the gathering gloom.

Into the spread of the sky over our heads stole a strange ashen hue.

Would the clouds pass?

Surely, surely, they would pass.

The Astronomer Royal, cloth-capped Sir Frank Dyson, shouted "They will!", like an excited schoolboy.

A huge gap in the cloud line had come over the horizon and was advancing towards the hidden sun.

We were too racked with emotion to cheer but our hearts leaped.

The gap came closer, closer.

A golden light fringed the edge of the last cloud. And into the blue sky sailed the thin crescent of the sun – a crescent of burning gold.

England after 200 long years was to see the most magnificent spectacle in the Universe.

Someone counted out the minutes.

As his voice rang out in that cold silence, the crescent grew thinner and thinner, until it was just a line of intense gold.

The shadows had gathered thick. Dusk was already upon us.

Two blackbirds shrieked with alarm in the sky and flew

headlong to earth. The sheep in a field half a mile away bleated with terror.

"One minute to go," cried the counter.

The darkness – impalpable, uncanny, came heavier and heavier upon us.

A strange icy cold sprang at us. We shivered and turned out coat collars up round our ears. The ice was biting into our bones.

"One minute to go!"

And then the shadow rushed at us.

It came out of the west like a black wall.

It rushed at us with terrible speed.

It seemed to overwhelm us.

But suddenly we forgot the darkness. Our eyes turned back to that great drama which was being played out in the heavens.

The last gleam of sun went out and there flashed out around the thick black circle of the moon the unearthly radiance of the corona.

That halo of light was a of a silvery white of a loveliness we had never seen before in our lives – a halo of sheer beauty.

Round the black rim red flames glowed. They were the great mountains of fire which are roaring eternally from the surface of the sun.

Round that wonderful spectacle the sky was black.

The voice of the counter went on.

He told out the seconds. And as he shouted out "Twenty-three!" a tiny gleam of gold came to the edge of the sun and the corona disappeared in an instant.

The touch of gold grew into a crescent and the sun came back.

The great crowd standing on the hills had watched this tremendous drama in a silence which could be felt.

The only sound which came to my ears – a voice which came to me even through the cry of the counter – was an awed repetition of "My God, my God", from a man standing beside me.

And then, when the great sight had gone for generations to come, there came the most human thing about that drama of incomparable grandeur.

The rows of people lining the bleak slopes of the hills exploded into a cheer.

That pathetic sound seemed puny after those twenty-three seconds of mystery and terror, but the emotion which had held them all in its steel grip burst into expression.

What could they do but cheer?

Near me a woman stood transfigured. Her face was lit up with glory; down her cheeks the tears poured unheeded.

"It is terrible, terrible," she said brokenly.

They climbed down the hills talking with uncontrollable excitement.

"Did you see the shadows on the grass?" said one London man, shaken out of his metropolitan calm.

"They came at me in waves. And before the eclipse did you see how the light through the trees shone as little crescents?"

"Did you see how the shadow of your hands had all jagged edges? My fingers threw shadows like claws."

"I was terribly afraid."

That was the emotion which held every watcher who was privileged to see the total eclipse – a mingled emotion of fear and utter wonder.

As the great shadow leapt at us we were cowed.

The darkening of a golden morning filled us with terror which we tried to counter but could not.

It was a fear against which the will was powerless.

"The sun will never come back; the sun will never come back," sobbed a grey-haired woman.

A man who had watched the slow coming of the eclipse unmoved found himself repeating, "Something terrible will happen."

The moors are grim and strange enough even in sunlight – those severe lines of hills and the hard colour of them strike their own grim note.

No one who did not see them under the shadow of eclipse can envisage the eerie mystery of them on this golden morning of June.

It made the thousands of trippers, who had filled the little villages and towns of the shadow belt with laughter and jazz music all night, feel a little ashamed.

A BOOK OF GREAT SHORT STORIES

The New Yorker, 29 October 1927

A selection from "Constant Reader", Parker's book review column for *The New Yorker*. Parker (1893–1967) shone in public for her urbane wit and trenchant commentary, but had a disastrous private life and died alone and alcoholic in a Manhattan hotel.

Ernest Hemingway wrote a novel called *The Sun Also Rises*. Promptly upon its publication. Ernest Hemingway was discovered, the Stars and Stripes were reverentially raised over him, eight hundred and forty-seven book reviewers formed themselves into the word "welcome", and the band played "Hail to the Chief" in three concurrent keys. All of which, I should think, might have made Ernest Hemingway pretty reasonably sick.

For a year or so before *The Sun Also Rises*, he had published *In Our Time*, a collection of short pieces. The book caused about as much stir in literary circles as an incompleted dogfight on upper Riverside Drive. True, there were a few that went about quick and stirred with admiration for this clean, exciting prose, but most of the reviewers dismissed the volume with a tolerant smile and the word "stark". It was Mr. Mencken who slapped it down with "sketches in the bold, bad manner of the Café du Dôme," and the smaller boys, in their manner, took similar pokes at it. Well, you see, Ernest Hemingway was a young American living on the left bank of the Seine in Paris, France; he had been seen at the Dôme and the Rotonde and the Select and the Closerie des Lilas. He knew Pound, Joyce, and Gertrude Stein. There is something a little – well, a little *you*-know – in all of those things. You wouldn't catch Bruce Barton or Mary Roberts Rinehart doing them. No, sir.

And besides, *In Our Time* was a book of short stories. That's no way to start off. People don't like that; they feel cheated. Any bookseller will be glad to tell you, in his interesting *argot*, that "short stories don't go". People take up a book of short stories and say, "Oh, what's this? Just a lot of those short things?" and put it right down again. Only yesterday afternoon, at four o'clock sharp, I saw and heard a woman do that to Ernest Hemingway's new book, *Men Without Women*. She had been one of those most excited about his novel.

Literature, it appears, is here measured by a yard-stick. As soon as *The Sun Also Rises* came out, Ernest Hemingway was the white-haired boy. He was praised, adored, analyzed, best-sold, argued about, and banned in Boston; all the trimmings were accorded him. People got into feuds about whether or not his story was worth the telling. (You see this silver scar left by a bullet, right up here under my hair? I got that the night I said that any well-told story was worth the telling. An eighth of an inch nearer the temple, and I wouldn't be sitting here doing this sort of tripe.) They affirmed, and passionately, that the dissolute expatriates in this novel of "a lost generation" were not worth bothering about; and then they devoted most of their time to discussing them. There was a time, and it went on for weeks, when you could go nowhere without hearing of *The Sun Also Rises*. Some thought it without excuse; and some, they of the cool, tall foreheads, called it the greatest American novel, tossing *Huckleberry Finn* and *The Scarlet Letter* lightly out the window. They hated it or they revered it. I may say, with due respect to Mr Hemingway, that I was never so sick of a book in my life.

Now *The Sun Also Rises* was as "starkly" written as Mr. Hemingway's short stories; it dealt with subjects as "unpleasant". Why it should have been taken to the slightly damp bosom of the public while the (as it seems to me) superb *In Our Time* should have been disregarded will always be a puzzle to me. As I see it – I knew this conversation would get back to me sooner or later, preferably sooner – Mr Hemingway's style, this prose stripped to its firm young bones, is far more effective, far more moving, in the short story than in the novel. He is, to me, the greatest living writer of short stories; he is, also to me, not the greatest living novelist.

After all the high screaming about *The Sun Also Rises*, I feared for Mr Hemingway's next book. You know how it is – as soon as they all start acclaiming a writer, that writer is just about to slip downward. The little critics circle like literary buzzards above only the sick lions.

So it is a warm gratification to find the new Hemingway book, *Men Without Women*, a truly magnificent work. It is composed of thirteen short stories, most of which have been published before. They are sad and terrible stories; the author's enormous appetite for life seems to have been somehow appeased. You find here little of that peaceful ecstasy that marked the camping trip in *The Sun Also Rises* and the lone fisherman's days in "Big Two-Hearted River" in *In Our Time*. The stories include "The Killers", which seems to me one of the four great American short stories. (All you have to do is drop the nearest hat, and I'll tell you what I think the others are. They are Wilbur Daniel Steele's "Blue Murder", Sherwood Anderson's "I'm a Fool", and Ring Lardner's "Some Like Them Cold", that story which seems to me as shrewd a picture of every woman at some time as is Chekhov's "The Darling". Now what do *you* like best?) The book also includes "Fifty Grand", "In Another Country", and the delicate and tragic "Hills like White Elephants". I do not know where a greater collection of stories can be found.

Ford Madox Ford has said of this author, "Hemingway writes like an angel." I take issue (there is nothing better for that morning headache than taking a little issue.) Hemingway writes like a human being. I think it is impossible for him to write of any event at which he has not been present; his is, then, a reportorial talent, just as Sinclair Lewis's is. But, or so I think, Lewis remains a reporter and Hemingway stands a genius because Hemingway has an unerring sense of selection. He discards details with a magnificent lavishness; he keeps his words to their short path. His is, as any reader knows, a dangerous influence. The simple thing he does looks so easy to do. But look at the boys who try to do it.

ELLIOTT V. BELL

24 OCTOBER 1929 –
WALL STREET CRASHES!

We Saw It Happen, 1938

Bell was a pioneer of financial journalism, and fittingly served as the first president of The New York Financial Writers Association. When the stock-market fell through the floor in 1929, Bell was a staffer on *The New York Times*. Later in his career, he was editor and publisher of *Business Week*.

The day was overcast and cool. A light north-west wind blew down the canyons of Wall Street, and the temperature, in the low fifties, made bankers and brokers on their way to work button their topcoats around them. The crowds of market traders in the brokers' board rooms were nervous but hopeful as the ten o'clock hour for the start of trading approached. The general feeling was that the worst was over and a good many speculators who had prudently sold out earlier in the decline were congratulating themselves at having bought back their stocks a good deal cheaper. Seldom had the small trader had better or more uniform advice to go by.

The market opened steady with prices little changed from the previous day, though some rather large blocks, of 20,000 to 25,000 shares, came out at the start. It sagged easily for the first half-hour, and then around eleven o'clock the deluge broke.

It came with a speed and ferocity that left men dazed. The bottom simply fell out of the market. From all over the country a torrent of selling orders poured onto the floor of the Stock Exchange and there were no buying orders to meet it. Quotations of representative active issues, like Steel, Telephone, and Anaconda, began to fall two, three, five, and even ten points between sales. Less active stocks became unmarketable. Within a few moments the ticker service was hopelessly swamped and from then on no one knew what was really happening. By one-thirty the ticker tape was nearly two hours late; by two-thirty it was 147 minutes late. The last quotation was not printed on the tape until 7.08½ p.m., four hours, eight and one-half minutes after the close. In the meantime, Wall Street had lived through an incredible nightmare.

In the strange way that news of a disaster spreads, the word of the market collapse flashed through the city. By noon great crowds had gathered at the corner of Broad and Wall Streets where the Stock Exchange on one corner faces Morgan's across the way. On the steps of the Sub-Treasury Building, opposite Morgan's, a crowd of press photographers and newsreel men took up their stand. Traffic was pushed from the streets of the financial district by the crush.

It was in this wild setting that the leading bankers scurried into conference at Morgan's in a belated effort to save the day. Shortly after noon Mr Mitchell left the National City Bank and pushed his way west on Wall Street to Morgan's. No sooner had he entered than Albert H. Wiggin was seen to hurry down from the Chase National Bank, one block north. Hard on his heels came William C. Potter, head of the Guaranty Trust, followed by Seward Prosser of the Bankers Trust. Later George F. Baker, Jr, of the First National, joined the group.

The news of the bankers' meeting flashed through the streets and over the news tickers – stocks began to rally – but for many it was already too late. Thousands of traders, little and big, had gone "overboard" in that incredible hour between eleven and twelve. Confidence in the financial and political leaders of the country, faith in the "soundness" of economic conditions had received a shattering blow. The panic was on.

At Morgan's the heads of six banks formed a consortium – since known as the bankers' pool of October, 1929 – pledging a total of $240,000,000, or $40,000,000 each, to provide a "cushion" of buying power beneath the falling market. In addition, other financial institutions, including James Speyer and Company and Guggenheim Brothers, sent over to Morgan's unsolicited offers of funds aggregating $100,000,000. It was not only the first authenticated instance of a bankers' pool in stocks but by far the largest concentration of pool buying power ever brought to bear on the stock market – but in the face of the panic it was pitifully inadequate.

After the bankers had met, Thomas W. Lamont, Morgan partner, came out to the crowd of newspaper reporters who had gathered in the lobby of his bank. In an understatement that has since become a Wall Street classic, he remarked:

"It seems there has been some disturbed selling in the market."

It was at the same meeting that "T.W." gave to the financial community a new phrase – "air pockets", to describe the condition in stocks for which there were no bids, but only frantic offers. (Mr Lamont said he had it from his partner, George Whitney, and the latter said he had it from some broker.)

After the meeting, Mr Lamont walked across Broad Street to the Stock Exchange to meet with the governors of the Exchange. They had been called together quietly during trading hours and they held their meeting in the rooms of the Stock Clearing Corporation so as to avoid attracting attention. Mr Lamont sat on the corner of a desk and told them about the pool. Then he said:

"Gentlemen, there is no man nor group of men who can buy all the stocks that the American public can sell."

It seems a pretty obvious statement now, but it had a horrid sound to the assembled governors of the Exchange. It meant that the shrewdest member of the most powerful banking house in the country was telling them plainly that the assembled resources of Wall Street, mobilized on a scale never before attempted, could not stop this panic.

The bankers' pool, in fact, turned out a sorry fiasco. Without it, no doubt, the Exchange would have been forced to close, for it did supply bids at some price for the so-called pivotal stocks when, because of the panic and confusion in the market, there were no other bids available. It made a small profit, but it did not have a ghost of a chance of stemming the avalanche of selling that poured in from all over the country. The stock market had become too big. The days that followed are blurred in retrospect. Wall Street became a nightmarish spectacle.

The animal roar that rises from the floor of the Stock Exchange and which on active days is plainly audible in the Street outside, became louder, anguished, terrifying. The streets were crammed with a mixed crowd – agonized little speculators, walking aimlessly outdoors because they feared to face the ticker and the margin clerk; sold-out traders, morbidly impelled to visit the scene of their ruin; inquisitive individuals and tourists, seeking by gazing at the exteriors of the Exchange and the big banks to get a closer view of the national catastrophe; runners, frantically pushing their way through the throng of idle and curious in their effort to make deliveries of the unprecedented volume of securities which was being traded on the floor of the Exchange.

The ticker, hopelessly swamped, fell hours behind the actual trading and became completely meaningless. Far into the night, and often all night long, the lights blazed in the windows of the tall office buildings where margin clerks and bookkeepers struggled with the desperate task of trying to clear one day's business before the next began. They fainted at their desks; the weary runners fell exhausted on the marble floors of banks and slept. But within a few months they were to have ample time to rest up. By then thousands of them had been fired.

Agonizing scenes were enacted in the customers' rooms of the various brokers. There traders who a few short days before had luxuriated in delusions of wealth saw all their hopes smashed in a collapse so devastating, so far beyond their wildest fears, as to seem unreal. Seeking to save a little from the wreckage, they would order their stocks sold "at the market", in many cases to discover that they had not merely lost everything but were, in addition, in debt to the broker. And then, ironic twist, as like as not the next few hours' wild churning of the market would lift prices to levels where they might have sold out and had a substantial cash balance left over. Every move was wrong, in those days. The market seemed like an insensate thing that was wreaking a wild and pitiless revenge upon those who had thought to master it.

The excitement and sense of danger which imbued Wall Street was like that which grips men on a sinking ship. A camaraderie, a kind of gaiety of despair, sprang up. The Wall Street reporter found all doors open and everyone snatched at him for the latest news, for shreds of rumour. Who was in trouble? Who had gone under last? Where was it going to end?

I remember dropping in to see a vice-president of one of the larger banks. He was walking back and forth in his office.

"Well, Elliott," he said, "I thought I was a millionaire a few days ago. Now I find I'm looking through the wrong end of the telescope."

He laughed. Then he said: "We'll get those bastards that did this yet."

I never did find out whom he meant, but I learned later that he was not merely "busted" but hopelessly in debt.

CLAUD COCKBURN

INTERVIEW WITH AL CAPONE

I, Claud, 1956

Cockburn's interview with Prohibition gangster Al(phonse) Capone took place in 1930, when Cockburn was US correspondent for the London *Times*. Three years later Cockburn quit "The Thunderer" to found the muck-raking *The Week*, before becoming a staffer for the communist *Daily Worker*.

The Lexington Hotel [Chicago] had once, I think, been a rather grand family hotel, but now its large and gloomy lobby was deserted except for a couple of bulging Sicilians and a reception clerk who looked at one across the counter with the expression of a speakeasy proprietor looking through the grille at a potential detective. He checked on my appointment with some superior upstairs, and as I stepped into the elevator I felt my hips and sides being gently frisked by the tapping hands of one of the lounging Sicilians. There were a couple of ante-rooms to be passed before you got to Capone's office and in the first of them I had to wait for a quarter of an hour or so, drinking whisky poured by a man who used his left hand for the bottle and kept the other in his pocket.

Except that there was a sub-machine-gun, operated by a man called MacGurn – whom I later got to know and somewhat esteem – poking through the transom of a door behind the big desk, Capone's own room was nearly indistinguishable from that of, say, a "newly arrived" Texan oil millionaire. Apart from the jowly young murderer on the far side of the desk, what took the eye were a number of large, flattish, solid silver bowls upon the desk, each filled with roses. They were nice to look at, and they had another purpose too, for Capone when agitated stood up and dipped the tips of his fingers in the waters in which floated the roses.

I had been a little embarrassed as to how the interview was to be launched. Naturally the nub of all such interviews is somehow to get around to the question "What makes you tick?" but in the case of this millionaire killer the approach to this central question seemed mined with dangerous impediments. However, on the way down to the Lexington Hotel I had had the good fortune to see, in I think the *Chicago Daily News*, some statistics offered by an insurance company which dealt with the average expectation of life of gangsters in Chicago. I forget exactly what the average expectation was, and also what the exact age of Capone at that time was – I think he was in his early thirties. The point was, however, that in any case he was four years older than the upper limit considered by the insurance company to be the proper average expectation of life for a Chicago gangster. This seemed to offer a more or less neutral and academic line of approach, and after the ordinary greetings I asked Capone whether he had read this piece of statistics in the paper. He said that he had. I asked him whether he considered the estimate reasonably accurate. He said that he thought that the insurance companies and the newspaper boys probably knew their stuff. "In that case," I asked him, "how does it feel to be, say, four years over the age?"

He took the question quite seriously and spoke of the matter with neither more nor less excitement or agitation than a man would who, let us say, had been asked whether he, as the rear machine-gunner of a bomber, was aware of the average incidence of casualties in that occupation. He apparently assumed that sooner or later he would be shot despite the elaborate precautions which he regularly took. The idea that – as afterwards turned out to be the case – he would be arrested by the Federal authorities for income-tax evasion had not, I think, at that time so much as crossed his mind. And, after all, he said with a little bit of corn-and-ham somewhere at the back of his throat, supposing he had not gone into this racket? What would he have been doing? He would, he said, "have been selling newspapers barefoot on the street in Brooklyn."

He stood up as he spoke, cooling his finger-tips in the rose bowl in front of him. He sat down again, brooding and sighing. Despite the ham-and-corn, what he said was quite probably true and I said so, sympathetically. A little bit too sympathetically, as immediately emerged, for as I spoke I saw him looking at me suspiciously, not to say censoriously. My remarks about the harsh way the world treats barefoot boys in Brooklyn were interrupted by an urgent angry waggle of his podgy hand.

"Listen," he said, "don't get the idea I'm one of these goddam radicals. Don't get the idea I'm knocking the American system. The American system . . ." As though an invisible chairman had called upon him for a few words, he broke into an oration upon the theme. He praised freedom, enterprise and the pioneers. He spoke of "our heritage". He referred with contemptuous disgust to Socialism and Anarchism. "My rackets," he repeated several times, "are run on strictly American lines and they're going to stay that way." This turned out to be a reference to the fact that he had recently been elected the President of the Unione Siciliano, a slightly mysterious, partially criminal society which certainly had its roots in the Mafia. Its power and importance varied sharply from year to year. Sometimes there did seem to be evidence that it was a secret society of real power, and at other times it seemed more in the nature of a mutual benefit association not essentially much more menacing than, say, the Elks. Capone's complaint just now was that the Unione was what he called "lousy with black-hand stuff". "Can you imagine," he said, "people going in for what they call these blood feuds – some guy's grandfather was killed by some other guy's grandfather, and this guy thinks that's good enough reason to kill the other." It was, he said, entirely unbusinesslike. His vision of the American system began to excite him profoundly and now he was on his feet again, leaning across the desk like the chairman of a board meeting, his fingers plunged in the rose bowls.

"This American system of ours," he shouted, "call it Americanism, call it Capitalism, call it what you like, gives to each and every one of us a great opportunity if we only seize it with both hands and make the most of it." He held out his hand towards me, the fingers dripping a little, and stared at me sternly for a few seconds before reseating himself.

RED DAY ON CAPITOL HILL

The New Republic, 23 December 1931

Like many other novelists in the anti-capitalist 1930s, John Dos Passos frequently took up the journalist's typewriter in the cause of socialism. Here is his revolutionary view of the 1931 Hunger March on Washington D.C.

Washington has a drowsy look in the early December sunlight. The Greco-Roman porticoes loom among the bare trees, as vaguely portentous as phrases about democracy in the mouth of a Southern Senator. The Monument, a finger of light cut against a lavender sky, punctuates the antiquated rhetoric of the Treasury and the White House. On the hill, above its tall foundation banked with magnolia trees, the dome of the Capitol bulges smugly. At nine o'clock groups of sleepy-looking cops in well-brushed uniforms and shiny-visored caps are straggling up the hill. At the corner of Pennsylvania Avenue and John Marshall Place a few hunger marchers stand around the trucks they came in. They looked tired and frowzy from the long ride. Some of them are strolling up and down the avenue. That end of the avenue, with its gimcrack stores, boarded-up burlesque shows, Chinese restaurants and flophouses, still has a little of the jerk-water, out-in-the-sticks look it must have had when Lincoln drove up it in a barouche through the deep mud or Jefferson rode to his inauguration on his own quiet nag.

Two elderly labouring men are looking out of a cigar-store door at a bunch of Reds, young Jewish boys from New York or Chicago, with the white armbands of the hunger marchers. "Won't get nutten that a-way", one of them says. "Who's payin' for it anyway, hirin' them trucks and gasoline . . . Somebody's payin' for it," barks the clerk indignantly frox behind the cash register. "Better'd spent it on grub or to buy 'emselves over-coats," says the older man. The man who first spoke shakes his head sadly. "Never won't get nutten that a-way." Out along the avenue a few Washingtonians look at the trucks and old moving vans with *Daily Worker* cartoons pasted on their sides. They stand a good way off, as if they were afraid the trucks would explode; they are obviously swallowing their unfavourable com-ments for fear some of the marchers might hear them. Tough eggs, these Reds.

At ten o'clock the leaders start calling to their men to fall in. Some tall cops appear and bawl out drivers of cars that get into the streets reserved for the marchers to form up in. The marchers form in a column of fours. They don't look as if they'd had much of a night's rest. They look quiet and serious and anxious to do the right thing. Leaders, mostly bareheaded youngsters, run up and down, hoarse and nervous, keeping everybody in line. Most of them look like city dwellers, men and women from the needle trades, restaurant workers, bakery or laundry employees. There's a good sprinkling of Negroes among them. Here and there the thick shoulders and light hair of a truck driver or farm hand stand out. Motorcycle cops begin to cluster around the edges. The marchers are receiving as much attention as distinguished foreign officials.

Up on the hill, cordons of cops are everywhere, making a fine showing in the late-fall sunshine. There's a considerable crowd standing around; it's years since Washington has been interested in the opening of Congress. They are roping off the route for the hunger marchers. They stop a taxicab that is discovered to contain a small white-haired Senator. He curses the cops out roundly and is hurriedly escorted under the portals.

Inside the Capitol things are very different. The light is amber and greenish, as in an aquarium. Elderly clerks white as termites move sluggishly along the corridors, as if beginning to stir after a long hibernation. The elevator boy is very pale. "Here comes the army of the unfed," he says, pointing spitefully out of the window. "And they're carrying banners, though Charlie Curtis said they couldn't." A sound of music comes faintly in. Led by a band with silvery instruments like Christmas-tree ornaments that look cheerful in the bright sunlight, the hunger marchers have started up Capitol Hill. Just time to peep down into the Senate Chamber where elderly parties and pasty-faced pages are beginning to gather. Ever seen a section of a termite nest under glass?

There's a big crowd in the square between the Capitol and the Congressional Library. On the huge ramps of the steps that lead to the central portico the metropolitan police have placed some additional statuary; tastefully arranged groups of cops with rifles, riot guns and brand-new tear-gas pistols that look as if they'd just come from Sears, Roebuck. People whisper "machine-gun nests", but nobody seems to know where they are. There's a crowd on the roof around the base of the dome, faces are packed in all the windows. Everybody looks cheerful, as if a circus had come to town, anxious to be shown. The marchers fill the broad semicircle in front of the Capitol, each group taking up its position in perfect order, as if the show had been rehearsed. The band, playing "Solidarity Forever" (which a newspaper woman beside me recognizes as "Onward Christian Soldiers"), steps out in front. It's a curious little band, made up of martini-horns, drums, cymbals and a lyre that goes tinkle, tinkle. It plays cheerfully and well, led by a drum major with a red tasselled banner on the end of his staff, and repeats again and again. "The Red Flag", "Solidarity", and other tunes variously identified by people in the crowd. Above the heads of the marchers are banners with slogans printed out: IN THE LAST WAR WE FOUGHT FOR THE BOSSES: IN THE NEXT WAR WE'LL FIGHT FOR THE WORKERS . . . $150 CASH . . . FULL PAY FOR UNEMPLOYMENT RELIEF. The squad commanders stand out in front like cheerleaders at a football game and direct the chanting: "We Demand – Unemployed Insurance, We Demand – Unemployed Insurance, WE DEMAND – UNEMPLOYED INSURANCE."

A deep-throated echo comes back from the Capitol façade a few beats later than each shout. It's as if the statues and the classical-revival republican ornaments in the pediment were shouting too.

A small group leaves the ranks and advances across the open space towards the Senate side. All the tall cops drawn up in such fine order opposite the hunger marchers stick out their chests. Now it's coming. A tremor goes over the groups of statuary so tastefully arranged on the steps. The tear-gas pistols glint in the sun. The marchers stand in absolute silence.

Under the portal at the Senate entrance the swinging doors are protected by two solid walls of blue serge. Cameramen and reporters converge with a run. Three men are advancing with the demands of the hunger marchers written out. They are the centre of a big group of inspectors, sergeants, gold and silver braid of the Capitol and metropolitan police. A young fellow with a camera is hanging from the wall by the door. "Move the officer out of the way," he yells. "Thank you . . . A little back, please, lady, I can't see his face . . . Now hand him the petition."

"We're not handing petitions, we're making demands," says the leader of the hunger marchers. Considerable waiting around. The Sergeant at Arms sends word they can't be let in. Somebody starts to jostle, the cops get tough, cop voices snarl. The committee goes back to report while the band plays the "Internationale" on marini-horns and lyre . . .

D. SEFTON DELMER

REICHSTAG FIRE

Daily Express, 28 February 1933

The arson of the German parliament building was blamed by the Nazis on a communist Dutchman, van der Lubbe. As the *Daily Express'* man in Berlin subtly suggested, in his dispatch written as the flames still roared, the fire was started by the Nazis themselves to provide a pretext to introduce emergency dictatorship.

Monday, 27 February

"This is a God-given signal! If this fire, as I believe, turns out to be the handiwork of Communists, then there is nothing that shall stop us now crushing out this murder pest with an iron fist."

Adolf Hitler, Fascist Chancellor of Germany, made this dramatic declaration in my presence to-night in the hall of the burning Reichstag building.

The fire broke out at 9.45 tonight in the Assembly Hall of the Reichstag.

It had been laid in five different corners and there is no doubt whatever that it was the handiwork of incendiaries.

One of the incendiaries, a man aged thirty, was arrested by the police as he came rushing out of the building, clad only in shoes and trousers, without shirt or coat, despite the icy cold in Berlin tonight.

Five minutes after the fire had broken out I was outside the Reichstag watching the flames licking their way up the great dome into the tower.

A cordon had been flung round the building and no one was allowed to pass it.

After about twenty minutes of fascinated watching I suddenly saw the famous black motor-car of Adolf Hitler slide past, followed by another car containing his personal bodyguard.

I rushed after them and was just in time to attach myself to the fringe of Hitler's party as they entered the Reichstag.

Never have I seen Hitler with such a grim and determined expression. His eyes, always a little protuberant, were almost bulging out of his head.

Captain Goering, his right-hand man, who is the Prussian Minister of the Interior, and responsible for all police affairs, joined us in the Lobby. He had a very flushed and excited face.

"This is undoubtedly the work of Communists, Herr Chancellor," he said.

"A number of Communist deputies were present here in the Reichstag twenty minutes before the fire broke out. We have succeeded in arresting one of the incendiaries."

"Who is he?" Dr Goebbels, the propaganda chief of the Nazi Party, threw in.

"We do not know yet," Captain Goering answered, with an ominously determined look around his thin, sensitive mouth. "But we shall squeeze it out of him, have no doubt, doctor."

We went into a room. "Here you can see for yourself, Herr Chancellor, the way they started the fire," said Captain Goering, pointing out the charred remains of some beautiful oak panelling.

"They hung cloths soaked in petrol over the furniture here and set it alight."

We strode across another lobby filled with smoke. The police barred the way. "The candelabra may crash any moment, Herr Chancellor," said a captain of police, with his arms outstretched.

By a detour we next reached a part of the building which was actually in flames. Firemen were pouring water into the red mass.

Hitler watched them for a few moments, a savage fury blazing from his pale blue eyes.

Then we came upon Herr von Papen, urbane and debonair as ever.

Hitler stretched out his hand and uttered the threat against the Communists which I have already quoted. He then turned to Captain Goering. "Are all the other public buildings safe?" he questioned.

"I have taken every precaution," answered Captain Goering. "The police are in the highest state of alarm, and every public building has been specially garrisoned. We are waiting for anything."

It was then that Hitler turned to me. "God grant," he said, "that this is the work of the Communists. You are witnessing the beginning of a great new epoch in German history. This fire is the beginning."

And then something touched the rhetorical spring in his brain.

"You see this flaming building," he said, sweeping his hand dramatically around him. "If this Communist spirit got hold of Europe for but two months it would be all aflame like this building."

By 12.30 the fire had been got under control. Two Press rooms were still alight, but there was no danger of the fire spreading.

Although the glass of the dome has burst and crashed to the ground the dome still stands.

So far it has not been possible to disentangle the charred debris and see whether the bodies of any incendiaries, who may have been trapped in the building, are among it.

At the Prussian Ministry of the Interior a special meeting was called late tonight by Captain Goering to discuss measures to be taken as a consequence of the fire.

The entire district from the Brandenburg Gate, on the west, to the River Spree, on the east, is isolated to-night by numerous cordons of police.

ARE WRESTLERS PEOPLE?

Esquire, January 1934

Often, as I have sat at the ringside, watching great, hairy lumps of living meat spank, throttle and wring one another, it has occurred to me to wonder whether wrestlers love and are loved and whether they really suffer. Or are they, like the fishworm, incapable of emotion and insensible to pain?

Perhaps I am wrong in assuming that the fishworm has neither sentiments nor senses but I do assume as much because it spares my conscience on those rare occasions – the last one was in 1926 – when I string him on the hook. I did have a twinge of misgiving some time ago when I read in a sporting-goods catalogue of a device for luring the fishworm from his hole in the ground. This was an electrical apparatus, something like a tuning-fork, which, being jabbed in the ground near the worm-hole, uttered a faint mooing note and brought the male, or bull, worm charging out of the soil with his neck arched and his pulses pounding in his veins.

It suggested that the fishworm might have depths after all and that we might all be mistaken in our easy belief that because he does not quack, bark or snarl, he doesn't know he is being ill-treated. Maybe he is just reticent. There are New Englanders like that but we call them canny.

It would be very unchivalrous, I think, to impose upon the most beautiful sentiment of all in any of God's creatures with the siren call of love to seduce him to his doom. This, moreover, is quite aside from the moral aspect of the matter. Sex is something which Nature has implanted in all of us and in its proper relation to life is a very beautiful thing. But I would call it most immoral to inflame the fishworm's passion by artificial means even though we did not string him on a hook but merely left him there, bothered, bewildered and breathing hard.

The wrestler is a strange organism. It has certain characteristics which must test the conviction of the most confirmed Fundamentalist, suggesting that way, way back in some rocky cave all of us were wrestlers. It walks on its hind legs, it can be trained to speak and understand and Mr Jack Curley, the promoter of wrestling shows, once had one in his herd which could cook a good dinner. However it cooked only one dinner for Mr Curley.

He was entertaining a party of friends at his home in Great Neck, Long Island, that night and his wrestler had cooked pheasant for them. During the meal, Mr. Curley remarked to the lady sitting next to him that his cook was a wrestler.

"Oh, I would like to see it," the lady said and Mr. Curley, clapping his hands, cried, "Wrestler! Come heren sie!"

That was Mr Curley's way of addressing this wrestler. It was a German. When he wanted the wrestler to go downstairs he said, "Wrestler! Downstairsen sie" and when he wanted it to go upstairs he said, "Wrestler! Upstairsen sie." The ablative, you know.

So when the lady said she would like to see the wrestler which had cooked the dinner, Mr Curley clapped his hands and called, "Wrestler! Come heren sie!"

The kitchen door opened and the wrestler entered. It was wearing a pair of wool wrestling trunks and sneakers. Its hide and the fur on its chest were moist.

"Wrestler," said Mr Curley, "dinner is very good tonight."

"Jah?" said the wrestler, puckering its face in an appreciative grin and blinking its knobby ears. "Fine. But boy is it hot in that kitchen. Look how the sweat runs off of me."

Many a night at the ringside I have heard laymen sitting in the forward rows explain to their ladies that the punishment which wrestlers inflict on one another really does not hurt them as they are used to it and cannot feel, anyway. This is of a piece with the assumption that the fishworm cannot feel. I am not sure that it is true.

The fishworm wiggles and squirms when it is put upon the hook and the wrestler trumpets terribly and whooshes and writhes when it is being twisted in the ring. This may only mean that some vague intuition, such as turtles possess, is telling the wrestler not to go over on its back. Yet the wrestler is so amenable to training that it is comparatively easy to teach it to recognize a signal and, in violation of a strong natural instinct, to roll over on its back momentarily after thirty or forty minutes of wrestling, while the referee gives its adversary a slap on the shoulder signifying that it has won the contest.

The word contest, of course, is merely a trade term. Most of the minor politicians who constitute the various prizefight commissions and supervise wrestling do not authorize its use in connection with wrestling bouts. They insist upon calling them exhibitions and the newspaper boys who cover them call them mockeries or make-believes and refer to that thirty or forty minutes of action which precedes the fall as the squirm.

Wrestling is the one hazardous occupation in the sport department of journalism because wrestlers are vindictive in a dumb way and one never can tell when one of them will pick up another and throw it at a correspondent sitting at the ringside. Moreover, after one has seen a few squirms one has seen them all and consequently one is likely to doze off during that time when the wrestlers are putting on the squirm. One learns to gauge these catnaps and come out of it just in time for the signal.

But the wrestler may resent this as an affront to its art and retaliate by heaving two hundred fifty pounds of moist and rather smelly weight, usually foreign matter, into the journalist's lap. I have seen as many as six journalists mown down by one wrestler thrown in this manner and had a very exciting evening myself once when I made a mistake at the ringside.

One wrestler was sitting on top of another and, with the dumb concentration of a trick baboon untying a shoelace, was twisting a large, bare foot.

"Hey, wrestler!" I cried, in honest error, for they were badly tangled up, "you are twisting your own foot."

At that the wrestler let out a loud howl of "Ow-oo," thinking that if it was twisting its own foot it must be hurting itself, and let go. But it happened to be the other wrestler's foot after all and when the first one let go the other one jumped up.

This enraged the wrestler which had been twisting the foot and six times that evening it threw the other one at me with intent to inflict great bodily harm. But, fortunately, though it had plenty of swift, its control was bad. So nothing happened to me, although the New York *World-Telegram* was hit twice and the New York *Times's* typewriter was smashed.

The fact that wrestlers utter sounds of apparent anguish does not necessarily prove that they really feel pain. They are trained to that, too. In former times they wrestled without sound effects and these were introduced in recent years by Mr Curley who hired an expert in bird-calls and animal cries to instruct the members of his herd. At first the wrestlers made some ludicrous mistakes and one sometimes heard a wrestler twittering gayly when it was supposed to bleat piteously.

As to whether they love and are loved I just have no way of knowing. Maybe so, though. Hippopotamuses do.

H.R.S. PHILPOTT

THE GRESFORD COLLIERY DISASTER

Daily Herald, 24 September 1934

Gresford is near Wrexham, in North Wales.

Wrexham, Sunday

At regular intervals a bell clangs out dully three times and a hush, already unbearable, seems to become deeper still.

It is like the dreadful repetition of a funeral toll, and it has been going on for seemingly endless hours through the daylight and the darkness.

It is merely the signal that a cage is bringing up a rescue party for rest and food, but it gruesomely completes the knowledge that one is standing at the scene of a vast and terrible burial.

For two days and a night the one, two, three of the bell has been almost the only sound to break into a long and loaded silence.

Occasionally there is the low murmur of voices or the purring of the engine and a motor-ambulance. For the rest the silence continues.

The crowds stand hour after hour motionless, thinking neither of rest nor food, waiting, watching, and now hardly hoping.

There is no weeping, no fainting, no audible demonstration of the grief that has cruelly covered a whole community.

The people stand staring straight ahead, seeming to see nothing, but with a look of inexpressible hurt in their dry eyes – a dreadful look that makes one turn away and long never to see such a thing again.

I moved quietly about among them yesterday far into a bitterly cold night, and again today.

They told me heartbreaking little stories of why they were there, and their halting, simple sentences etched out and affrightened a picture of the smashed homes in which the echoes of the pit-head bell are being heard.

There was one little group I shall never forget – a group of three, two old men and a boy.

One was John Capper, of Pentre Broughton, a nearby village. He has given his own lifetime to the mine and now his son has given his life.

The old cloth-capped father had to cease work eighteen months ago because of nystagmus. He has tell-tale blue marks on his forehead and around his eyes.

He just looked vacantly ahead, his old eyes fixed on the winding gear, the twitching corners of his mouth giving the only sign of his suffering. This was at midnight.

"Waiting all day," he said. "My son is down there."

That was all, and so he continues his vigil, standing straight as a rod and still staring in that dreadful way at the winding gear.

By his side was a 14½-year-old boy, George Peters, of the neighbouring village of Llay. He told me he is one of a family of nine.

I asked him why he was among the watchers. "My father is down there," he said, and then broke down, making not a sound, but the tears streamed down his face. Young George himself works in another pit. On the other side of him was a little man in a bowler hat. "My son is down there," he said.

That is how they phrase it – "down there".

So I left them waiting there in the cold and the darkness – two old men thinking of their sons, and one young boy thinking of his father.

Before I tell you about the other watchers let me try to picture to you the surface scene.

The Gresford Colliery lies two or three miles outside Wrexham, just over a hedge from the main Chester Road. Smoke flows lazily from the top of a towering chimney stack, red brick buildings cluster round the pit-head.

The winding gear traces its familiar pattern on the sky.

The ambulance station is peopled with the nurses ready for anything – but as yet called on only to receive members of rescue gangs as they come to the surface.

Packed round a black yard are fleets of ambulances, which, like the watchers, just wait.

There are doctors, first aid men and ministers of religion all waiting.

That is the tragedy of it. There is nothing they can do but wait, because the men they are waiting for are still "down there".

The only men who can do anything, and they are working with noble heroism, are the rescue gangs.

They come from miles around. Many of them dashed off on their own account as soon as they heard of the disaster; others have been brought in organized gangs by neighbouring mine managers and other officials.

The rescue men are specially picked. Only half a dozen of them can go "down there" at a time. They wear respirators and are at the foremost point of danger.

They are the fire fighters, and I have talked with them before they had gone down and after they had come up.

To speak with one of them for even a moment or two is both an inspiration and a humiliation.

They do not realize they are doing anything remarkable, they put on their respirators, take their lamp and, wearing a pair of shorts, just go "down there".

They have to go two miles or more before they reach the scene of the fire.

Strung out behind them is a long line of volunteers passing up fire extinguishers and bags of sand, and taking back the empties from hand to hand, backwards and forwards along a great heroic human chain.

The work of rescue thus goes on, and when the respirators are nearing exhaustion the rescue men come up again, run across the yard to preserve their sweating bodies from chill, and into a room where a fire is burning, clothes await them and hot drinks and food are ready.

Two of the first rush rescue parties were killed on Saturday morning, and another is still missing

There is much wonderment here about why or how this should have been, but here is the story told by Price Beard, a member of the rescue team:

"Five of us went down," he said, "we had gone only about 200 yards off the main road, which is about a mile long, when we were faced with flames and fumes.

"In spite of our masks we began to choke. Dan Hughes, of Llay, and Ben Hughes, of Bradley, fell, and the rest of us were powerless to help them out.

"Captain Jack Williams went over, but I managed to pull him away. Later he was taken to hospital. Jack Lewis is still 'down there'."

Come back, like Price Beard, to the surface, and over there in a small building you will find a team of experts preparing and testing respirators.

They are working with the utmost precision and care for they know that the lives of the rescue men depend on what they are doing.

I asked one of them why rescue men had lost their lives.

"We weren't near them," he said, "I can't say anything."

I asked him if he had any idea. "Maybe I have," he said, "but I am keeping them to myself," and his friends carried on, testing and adjusting the stock of respirators.

The volunteer gangs going down to help them still contain scores of men who escaped from the pit at two o'clock on Saturday morning.

They have had little spells of rest, but back they come, insisting that they shall go again to meet the inferno they so narrowly missed.

Many of them are only sixteen or seventeen years old.

They will tell you little, not because they do not want to, but because they do not realize that they are doing anything heroic or dramatic.

Take two of them as examples. Both were as black as soot, when they came up. One of them told me he was only a volunteer. "Passing the stuff to the rescue teams," he said.

He did not get within a mile of the fire and he thought he had done nothing.

I found that his idea of doing nothing was that he was working while falls of coal were taking place round him, and props were bending and breaking.

The rescue team man was scorched and exhausted. He had been within a few yards of the wall of flame and had stayed the official time limit for his respirator.

All he had to say was that he was going down again presently.

*   *   *

Here are some of the stories of men who escaped alive.

One young man was flung by the explosion several feet along one of the pit roads, landing near an air shaft.

He and his companions were trapped by the tremendous fall on either side, and he knew that the only hope of escape was through the narrow air-shaft.

Vainly he tried to persuade his mates to make the attempt to climb the shaft with him, but they refused, as they feared they would become jammed in the shaft.

Alone he scrambled and climbed inch by inch up the shaft, which was barely wide enough to admit his body.

Finally, after nearly an hour's climb, he succeeded in reaching the top of the shaft and jumped to safety.

The shaft through which he made his perilous climb was about 200 feet high and just over 2 feet wide.

Cyril Challinor, aged twenty-one, of Windsor Road, New Broughton, one of the first to be brought out alive, said:

"There were about six of us, about 300 yards from the clutch, laughing and talking. Suddenly there was a gust of wind.

"An elderly fellow came running up and said: 'You had better get your clothes on and get out of here."

"About twenty other fellows joined us, and we started making our way to the pit bottom.

"We got to the end of the wind road and then we began to meet gas. All of us fanned hard with our shirts. The gas was getting in our eyes, but we had to face it.

"We took turns in leading so that everyone would have the same risk.

"We now began to meet falls, and we had to scramble over them. I thought the twenty fellows who joined us were following us. I looked round, but could not see them. I do not know what happened to them.

"The gas was getting thicker and choking us, but we kept on fanning, and we got through to the pit bottom, where we met the rescue party."

LOUISIANA'S KINGFISH LIES IN STATE

New York Post, 12 September 1935

Nicknamed "Kingfish", governor Huey Long (b. 1893) was notorious for
his corruption and for his politicking. He was assassinated.

Baton Rouge, Louisiana., 12 September

The Louisiana peasant who became Louisiana's king is on view
in his Capitol in his coffin today.

The face which in life never held the same expression for more
than two seconds is fixed in a studied smirk – an undertaker's idea
of how Huey Long should have looked.

Here, set forth in a dinner suit, is the man who sold lard
substitute to hook-wormed share croppers.

The shirt front is as smooth as a planed board, as white as a jail-
bird's face. The black tie flares with the nonchalant perfection of
a drawing in a fashion magazine.

You look down at it for the brief moment that the guards,
uniformed and plain clothed, permit. You can't believe that here
is anything but a bad wax sculpture of a super-humanly alive man
– and painted at that.

It is so much like one of those figures you see in store windows
which remind you of somebody, but you can't be quite sure of
just whom. Huey wouldn't have liked it, and his words wouldn't
have been fit to print.

The setting is superb. When Huey Long decreed the building
of a new State Capitol he specified it should have an entrance hall
that would impress people, all kinds of people.

It does impress. Brass doors with bas relief of such historical
happenings as the defeat of the British by Andrew Jackson; huge

Sèvres vases, the gift of France to its former possession, Louisiana; mural paintings in fine and subdued colours; a high and delicately tinted ceiling – don't let anybody tell you that it isn't an ornate rotunda.

Last night people flocked to see the genius the State has produced.

But it was a surprisingly small crowd. A fraction of the Long office-holders of this capital city would have made a larger one.

About 2,000 waited. True, it was drizzling, the hot, weakening drizzle of the Louisiana swamps, through the afternoon. But when, according to the widely spread information, the Kingfish was to be seen lying in state the crowd was still small.

This reporter became a part of the crowd. He wanted to know what was being said by the man in the street and the man on the dusty rural road.

This is what he heard:

"It sho' is hot heah with all these folks jammin' in thisaway."

"Do you heah that lil' baby, honey? What kind of a fool would be bringin' a baby to see this?"

"I do declare, we is getting closer all the time. Yoo hoo, Clairmont, how yu doin', chil?"

In short, this reporter didn't hear a single reference to Huey Long or his policies.

This reporter hazards no guess as to the meaning of last night's lack of enthusiasm.

He merely reports that the crowd was much more interested in the fact that movie men were taking a picture of the scene than in the fact that a great man of their State, the man who would make Louisiana the Empire State, was no more.

Some laughed and waved to friends, others pushed and shoved exactly as they would at a bargain sale.

The mourners' line curled into the front door and past the coffin.

As they departed they had to go past a half dozen carpenters who had opened their kits and spread their tools on the expensive marble floor of the rotunda. They were building two wooden fences to keep in line the crowds moving slowly past the coffin today.

Outside there was a clang of picks and spades. Grave diggers were hacking away at the turf in the sunken garden outside the Capitol.

"It's unlucky to leave a grave open at night," a man in the crowd muttered.

National Guardsmen, unarmed but straight and tall in their brown uniforms, stood guard at the coffin. The wall behind the casket was smothered with flowers, and they, too, were a sort of history of Huey Long's life.

"Eleventh Ward of New Orleans," read a gilt ribbon across a cluster of roses and asters.

"New Orleans Clearing House Association," proclaimed another one.

At dusk the 2,000 persons had drifted past the coffin, taking hurried looks at the body and turning to gape at the carpenters. One of the latter whistled softly as he sawed – a torch song called "When I Grow Too Old to Dream."

Earlier, Mrs Long, swathed to the chin in dark, melancholy blue, went to the funeral parlour and came out dabbing her eyes. Her daughter, Rose, twenty, and a younger son, Russell, walked by her side. Rose clenched her handkerchief in her right hand.

High officials of the State Government, including Governor O. K. Allen and Speaker Allen Ellender, visited the funeral parlor, too.

But the scene in the rotunda was for people who did not know Long – people who probably never saw him except in death. Farmers, red-necked from the sun and with the mud of bayous caked on their boots, stood in line in the rain for a two-second glimpse at the coffin.

The high French heels of young girls, going clickey-clack across the marble floor, challenged the din raised by the carpenters.

Generally, Long's enemies stayed away. Some of them were in the crowd outside the Capitol when the body was brought from the funeral parlour. They took off their straw hats, limp and drooping from the rain, as the coffin was carried up the sweeping flight of steps.

One of the first persons past the coffin was Mrs Josephine Fohn of New Orleans, an elderly woman in a shapeless brown dress. At the neck or her dress sparkled a pin – a gilt ornament in the shape of a fish. On the fish's head was a crown.

Rap, rap, rap, went the carpenters' hammers, and still Mrs Fohn talked.

"See," she said while waiting to pass the coffin, "See, a kingfish."

"I don't know whether he was right all the time," she said, "but I guess he was for poor folks. I'm poor folks. He said 'every man's a king,' and I guess he meant it.

"Maybe he was wrong some time, but when I read where he had died, I said to my two boys, 'You've got to take me up to Baton Rouge in your car so I can go to the funeral.' They couldn't get away. I came on the bus."

Now Mrs Fohn was abreast of the coffin. There was steam on the lenses of her horn-rimmed glasses, and she brushed at them angrily. Mrs Fohn took a quick look at the coffin and doddered out into the rain. The crowd swallowed her. Inside a carpenter whistled and pounded a nail.

JONATHAN MITCHELL

JOE LOUIS NEVER SMILES

The New Republic, 9 October 1935

These people are here, 95,000 of them, because they have money. Down there on the field, men have paid $150 and more for a pair of tickets. Twenty thousand seats were stamped "ringside", and the customers out beyond third base were bilked. They should have known that Mike Jacobs, who is running this fight, is a smart man. No one can do anything to him, because he has the support of Hearst.

It feels good to have money again. Everyone in this crowd has money. The people who were swindled by Jacobs can afford it. Happy days are here again. Of course, things aren't so good, with twenty millions on relief. A man can be fired, and next morning there are ten men in line waiting for his job. But the unemployed have been around for a long time. No one can expect us to sit home and be sympathetic indefinitely.

It is a cold, clear night. The Stadium rises steeply around one half of the field. The floodlights on its upper edge are directed on the field and the bleachers, and the Stadium itself is black except for a steady row of red exit signs. Almost the whole of the immense field is covered with chairs. Jacobs has pushed the customers so closely together that all that can be seen of them, under the floodlights, is their microscopic, bright faces. They form neat rows, divided into plots by the aisles, like commercial Dutch tulip beds. There are acres of them, shining pinkly. Men in white, with high cardboard signs in their caps, move gravely about selling pop, like gardeners. The ring is at second base, and the movie operators' metal cage, high on a pole, that you used to see at fights is missing. The only movement comes from white tobacco smoke, rising in heavy waves. Through it you can see the

American flags along the top of the Stadium, after the fashion of the opening verse of "The Star-Spangled Banner".

Near at hand the crowd is a respectable, bridge-playing one. About a fifth are Negroes, more carefully dressed and more mannerly than the whites. The little drunk with the long woollen muffler is certainly a Bronx dentist. He thinks correctly that the preliminary match now going on is poor, and keeps screaming, "Lousy". He brandishes a handful of crumpled bills and will give odds to anyone. There seems to be something painful in his past that he would like to explain, but the woollen muffler keeps blowing in his face, and communication between him and us is eternally frustrated.

There is a stirring in the aisles near the ring. The people who amount to something, and who are bowed through the police lines outside the Stadium, are entering. There are five state governors, the Republican National Committee, important business figures, and a large number of people whose press agents made them come so that their names would be in tomorrow's papers. Max Baer and his attendants are now at home plate. A dozen little pushing figures open up the crowd for him, and another dozen follow behind. Baer wears a white bathrobe, and has his hands on the shoulders of the state trooper in front of him. He nods to his many friends. Joe Louis, with another state trooper and other attendants, pushes in from third base. We learn afterwards that his bride, Marva Trotter, is in the first row in a bright green dress and orchids. Louis seems to see no one.

The floodlights are extinguished. Nothing exists except the brightly glowing ring. That is old Joe Humphries being lifted through the ropes, the man who announced fights before the depression. Since then he has been sick, and had a bad time. We have all been having a bad time, for that matter. Jack Dempsey squats in Baer's corner, but no one notices him. Humphries's assistant is bawling into the microphones: "Although Joe Louis is coloured, he is a great fighter, in the class of Jack Johnson and the giants of the past." His voice fades away, and returns. "American sportsmanship, without regard to race, creed or colour, is the talk of the world. Behave like gentlemen, whoever wins." Nearly two thousand police at the entrances of the Stadium are there to break up a possible race riot.

Baer has stripped. He has made a lot of money, Baer has. From all reports, he has spent a lot. He has played Broadway, Miami, and the other hot spots. Why shouldn't he have done so? Joe Louis takes off his flashing silk bathrobe, blue with a vermilion lining. It is the only extravagant gesture he makes. For all his youth, he is thick under the jaws, thick around the waist. His face is earnest, thoughtful, unsmiling.

Max Baer hasn't been, I suppose, what you would call a good boy. Joe Louis has, though. This is his greatest advantage. He once was taken to a night club, and it is reported that within ten minutes he wanted to go home. He said he was sleepy. He is supposed to have saved his money. Louis's father died when he was only two years old, down in Alabama. Until she married again, his mother had a hard struggle to support the children, and they were very dear to her. Louis is fond of his mother. She is a Lily of the Valley at her church in Detroit, where the family now lives. The Lilies are having a supper, or some such event, in a few days. She wants him there, and he is going with his new wife.

We are too far away to hear the gong. They are out in the middle of the ring, with a stubby little man in a white sweater moving softly around them. Baer holds both hands, open, clumsily in front of him. Look at Joe Louis. He is leading with a straight left arm, his right hand before his face ready to block, and his right elbow tucked in to his ribs. That is scientific. That is what they teach in correspondence courses, or the night gymnasium classes of the YMCA. In the first thirty seconds, you can tell that he reeks of study, practice, study. Any romantic white person who believes that the Negro possesses a distinctive quality ought to see Louis. He suggests a gorilla or a jungle lion about as much as would an assistant professor at the Massachusetts Institute of Technology.

Baer stands flat-footed, with his great death-dealing right fist doubled by his side. He swings, and you can almost count three while the fist sails through the air. Louis moves sidewise and back, because he has been taught that if you move with a blow it can never hurt you. Baer's glove slides up the side of Louis' head harmlessly. He swings again and again, and carefully and unhurriedly, Louis slips away. Look! Louis at last is going in. A left, a right and another left in close. Louis has pulled in his head, and with both arms up before him, he looks like a brown crayfish. All you can see is the twitching of his shoulders. So incredibly fast he is that the blows themselves are almost invisible. His hands cannot possibly move more than a few inches. Look! Baer is backing into a neutral corner. Louis is raining down blows. Baer's nose spurts blood, his lower lip bleeds, his face is red pulp.

Baer must have meant something to many people. He made wisecracks and went to parties and was a harbinger of the return of the old days. He was Broadway, he was California and Florida, he represented the possession of money once more and spending it. This saddle-coloured, dour-faced, tongue-tied, studious youth, who is punishing Baer, punishing him more cruelly than human flesh and bones can endure, what does he represent? Baer stands with his hands hanging at his sides. He is helpless. He cannot hit the dissolving form before him, and he has never learned to protect himself. He holds his fine head, with its sweep of tightly curled hair and its great, brooding nose, high above his torturer. Pride alone keeps his head up, pride that has no tangible justification whatever. It was the same pride that kept Colonel Baratieri at Adowa, twenty years before Joe Louis was born.

It is the first round, and the fight is as good as over. Maybe it was foolish to spend money going to a fight. There must be many people, even down there in the ringside seats, who couldn't afford to spend what they did on tickets. No one can be sure of his job with twenty million on relief. This is a crazy country, with people handing out a million dollars to Mike Jacobs and Hearst, while families right here in New York City are without enough to eat.

Round one is ended. Jack Dempsey vaults into the ring in a single, startling leap. Perhaps it is a trick. He must have vaulted from the ground to the edge of the ring platform, and from there into the ring itself. But from a distance, it seems one motion, and it is beautiful. Beside the man that Dempsey was, Baer and Louis and Schmeling are phonies. Nowadays everything, including men, is somehow different.

The next three rounds are slaughter. In the second, Baer makes a wild, swinging, purposeless attack. For probably fifteen seconds, he appears formidable, but his attack has no substance inside it. With the third round, he is beaten, but Louis does not rush in, as Dempsey would have, to kill. Deliberately he circles Baer, with his earnest, thoughtful face, seeking an opening through which to strike without possible risk of injury. He takes no chance of a last, desperate fling of Baer's prodigious right hand. He is a planner. He is a person who studies the basic aspects of a problem and formulates a programme. Apparently his studies are satisfactory, for he carefully steps up and knocks Baer down twice. Baer is on the canvas when time is called. Dempsey slides across the ring, picks Baer up like a mother, fusses over him until the fourth, and final, round. Baer once more is down. When the stubby referee, swinging his arm, reaches seven he tries to rouse himself. This turns out later to have been a fortunate gesture. The customers who suspected the honesty of the fight, and were unconvinced that a man could be half killed by fifty blows full on the jaw, were reassured as they watched Baer struggling to his feet. Had he been trying to throw the fight, they reasoned, he would have lain still. At the count of ten, Baer is on one knee, his swollen face wearing a comical expression of surprise.

The floodlights return us to time and space. Near at hand, there is remarkably little cheering, even from Negroes. They act as if, despite the police, they think it more prudent to restrain their feelings. There in the ring, placing his hand on Baer's shoulder in a stiff gesture, is the best fighter living, and the first Negro whose backers and trainer are men of his race. No white man shares in Louis' winnings. If the whites of the Boxing Commission will permit the match, he will be champion of the world.

All across the Stadium, the neat tulip beds are being broken up as tiny figures push into the aisles and towards the exits. A man with a small blond moustache is sobbing: "Maxie, why didn't you hit him?" Downtown in the Forties and Fifties, redecorated speakeasies will quickly be crammed to the doors and customers turned away. In Lenox Avenue in Harlem, Negroes will be tap-dancing from kerb to kerb, and singing: "The Baer goes over the mountain", and "Who won the fight?" Tomorrow the financial sections of the newspapers will report that business leaders regard the fight as final proof that the country's economic worries are past and a comfortable and prosperous future is assured.

DEATH IN THE DUST

San Francisco News, 21 October 1936

Three years before the publication of *The Grapes of Wrath*, Steinbeck visited "Okie" migrant camps in California on assignment for *San Francisco News*.

The squatters' camps are located all over California. Let us see what a typical one is like. It is located on the banks of a river, near an irrigation ditch or on a side road where a spring of water is available. From a distance it looks like a city dump, and well it may, for the city dumps are the sources for the material of which it is built. You can see a litter of dirty rags and scrap iron, of houses built of weeds, of flattened cans or of paper. It is only on close approach that it can be seen that these are homes.

Here is a house built by a family who have tried to maintain a neatness. The house is about 10 feet by 10 feet, and it is built completely of corrugated paper. The roof is peaked, the walls are tacked to a wooden frame. The dirt floor is swept clean, and along the irrigation ditch or in the muddy river the wife of the family scrubs clothes without soap and tries to rinse out the mud in muddy water.

The spirit of this family is not quite broken, for the children, three of them, still have clothes, and the family possesses three old quilts and a soggy, lumpy mattress. But the money so needed for food cannot be used for soap nor for clothes.

With the first rain the carefully built house will slop down into a brown, pulpy mush, in a few months the clothes will fray off the children's bodies, while the lack of nourishing food will subject the whole family to pneumonia when the first cold comes. Five years ago this family had 50 acres of land and $1,000 in the bank.

The wife belonged to a sewing circle and the man was a member of the Grange. They raised chickens, pigs, pigeons and vegetables and fruit for their own use; and their land produced the tall corn of the middle west. Now they have nothing.

If the husband hits every harvest without delay and works the maximum time, he may make $400 this year. But if anything happens, if his old car breaks down, if he is late and misses a harvest or two, he will have to feed his whole family on as little as $150. But there is still pride in this family. Wherever they stop they try to put the children in school. It may be that the children will be in a school for as much as a month before they are moved to another locality.

There is more filth here. The tent is full of flies clinging to the apple box that is the dinner table, buzzing about the foul clothes of the children, particularly the baby, who has not been bathed nor cleaned for several days. This family has been on the road longer than the builder of the paper house. There is no toilet here, but there is a clump of willows nearby where human faeces lie exposed to the flies – the same flies that are in the tent.

Two weeks ago there was another child, a four-year-old boy. For a few weeks they had noticed that he was kind of lackadaisical, that his eyes had been feverish. They had given him the best place in the bed, between father and mother. But one night he went into convulsions and died, and the next morning the coroner's wagon took him away. It was one step down.

They knew pretty well that it was a diet of fresh fruit, beans and little else that caused his death. He had had no milk for months. With this death there came a change of mind in this family. The father and mother now feel that paralysed dullness with which the mind protects itself against too much sorrow and too much pain.

Here, in the faces of the husband and his wife, you begin to see an expression you will notice on every face; not worry, but absolute terror of the starvation that crowds in against the borders of the camp. This man has tried to make a toilet by digging a hole in the ground near his house and surrounding it with an old piece of burlap. But he will only do things like that this year. He is a newcomer and his spirit and his decency and his sense of his own dignity have not been quite wiped out. Next year he will be like his next-door neighbour.

This is a family of six; a man, his wife and four children. They live in a tent the colour of the ground. Rot has set in on the canvas so that the flaps and the sides hang in tatters and are held together with bits of rusty bailing wire. There is one bed in the family and that is a big tick lying on the ground inside the tent. They have one quilt and a piece of canvas for bedding. The sleeping arrangement is clever. Mother and father lie down together and two children lie between them. Then, heading the other way, the other two children lie, the littler ones.

If the mother and father sleep with their legs spread wide, there is room for the legs of the children. And this father will not be able to make a maximum of $400 a year any more because he is no longer alert; he isn't quick at piecework, and he is not able to fight clear of the dullness that has settled on him.

The dullness shows in the faces of this family, and in addition there is a sullenness that makes them taciturn. Sometimes they still start the older children off to school, but the ragged little things will not go; they hide themselves in ditches or wander off by themselves until it is time to go back to the tent, because they are scorned in the school. The better-dressed children shout and jeer, the teachers are quite often impatient with these additions to their duties, and the parents of the "nice" children do not want to have disease carriers in the schools.

The father of this family once had a little grocery store and his family lived in back of it so that even the children could wait on the counter. When the drought set in there was no trade for the store any more. This is the middle class of the squatters' camp. In a few months this family will slip down to the lower class. Dignity is all gone, and spirit has turned to sullen anger before it dies.

The next-door-neighbour family, of man, wife and three children of from three to nine years of age, have built a house by driving willow branches into the ground and wattling weeds, tin, old paper and strips of carpet against them. A few branches are placed over the top to keep out the noonday sun. It would not turn water at all. There is no bed. Somewhere the family has found a big piece of old carpet. It is on the ground. To go to bed the members of the family lie on the ground and fold the carpet up over them.

The three-year-old child has a gunny sack tied about his middle for clothing. He has the swollen belly caused by malnutrition. He sits on the ground in the sun in front of the house, and the little black fruit flies buzz in circles and land on his closed eyes and crawl up his nose until he weakly brushes them away. They try to get at the mucus in the eye corners. This child seems to have the reactions of a baby much younger. The first year he had a little milk, but he has had none since. He will die in a very short time.

The older children may survive. Four nights ago the mother had a baby in the tent, on the dirt carpet. It was born dead, which was just as well because she could not have fed it at the breast; her own diet will not produce milk. After it was born and she had seen that it was dead, the mother rolled over and lay still for two days. She is up today, tottering around. The last baby, born less than a year ago, lived a week.

This woman's eyes have the glazed, faraway look of a sleep-walker's eyes. She does not wash clothes anymore. The drive that makes for cleanliness has been drained out of her and she hasn't the energy. The husband was a sharecropper once, but he couldn't make it go. Now he has lost even the desire to talk. He will not look directly at you, for that requires will, and will needs strength. He is a bad field worker for the same reason.

It takes him a long time to make up his mind, so he is always late in moving, and late in arriving in the fields. His top wage, when he can find work now, which isn't often, is $1 a day. The children do not even go to the willow clump any more. They squat where they are and kick a little dirt. The father is vaguely aware that there is a culture of hookworm, in the mud along the riverbank. He knows the children will get it on their bare feet. But he hasn't the will nor the energy to resist. Too many things have happened to him.

This is the lower class of the camp. This is what the man in the tent will be in six months; what the man in the paper house with its peaked roof will be in a year, after his house has washed down and his children have sickened or died, after the loss of dignity and spirit have cut him down to a kind of subhumanity.

Helpful strangers are not well received in this camp. The local sheriff makes a raid now and then for a wanted man, and if there is labour trouble the vigilantes may burn the poor houses. Social workers have taken case histories. They are filed and open for inspection. These families have been questioned over and over about their origins, number of children living and dead.

The information is taken down and filed. That is that. It has been done so often, and so little has come of it. And there is another way for them to get attention. Let an epidemic break out, say typhoid or scarlet fever, and the county doctor will come to the camp and hurry the infected cases to the pesthouse. But malnutrition is not infectious, nor is dysentery, which is almost the rule among the children.

The county hospital has no room for measles, mumps, whooping cough; and yet these are often deadly to hunger-weakened children. And although we hear much about the free clinics for the poor, these people do not know how to get the aid and they do not get it. Also, since most of their dealings with authority are painful to them, they prefer not to take the chance. This is the squatters' camp. Some are a little better, some much worse. I have described some typical families. In some of the camps there are as many as 300 families like these. Some are so far from water that it must be bought at five cents a bucket. And if these men steal, if there is developing among them a suspicion and hatred of well-dressed, satisfied people, the reason is not to be sought in their origin nor in any tendency to weakness in their character.

JUSTICE AT NIGHT

The Spectator, August 1936

A peace-time dispatch from Gellhorn (1908–98), whose greater fame was as a war correspondent. She was the wife of Ernest Hemingway for five years.

We got off the day coach at Trenton, New Jersey, and bought a car for $28.50. It was an eight-year-old Dodge open touring-car and the back seat was full of fallen leaves. A boy, who worked for the car dealer, drove us to the City Hall to get an automobile licence and he said: "The boss gypped the pants off you, you should of got his machine for $20 flat and it's not worth that." So we started out to tour across America, which is, roughly speaking, a distance of 3,000 miles.

I have to tell this because without the car, and without the peculiarly weak insides of that car, we should not have seen a lynching.

It was September, and as we drove south the days were dusty and hot and the sky was pale. We skidded in dust that was as moving and uncertain as sand, and when we stopped for the night we scraped it off our faces and shook it from our hair like powder. So, finally, we thought we'd drive at night, which would be cooler anyhow, and we wouldn't see the dust coming at us. The beauty of America is its desolation: once you leave New England and the industrial centres of the east you feel that no one lives in the country at all. In the south you see a few people, stationary in the fields, thinking or just standing, and broken shacks where people more or less live, thin people who are accustomed to semi-starvation and crops that never quite pay enough. The towns or villages give an impression of belonging to the flies; and it is impossible to imagine that on occasion these languid people move with a furious purpose.

We drove through Mississippi at night, trying to get to a town called Columbia, hoping that the hotel would be less slovenly than usual and that there would be some food available. The car broke down. We did everything we could think of doing, which wasn't much, and once or twice it panted wearily and then there was silence. We sat in it and cursed and wondered what to do. No one passed; there was no reason for anyone to pass. The roads are bad and mosquitoes sing too close the minute you stop moving. And the only reason to go to a small town in Mississippi is to sell something, or try to sell, and that doesn't happen late at night.

It was thirty miles or more to Columbia and we were tired. If it hadn't been for the mosquitoes we should simply have slept in the car and hoped that someone would drive past in the morning. As it was we smoked cigarettes and swatted at ourselves and swore and hated machinery and talked about the good old days when people got about in stage-coaches. It didn't make things better and we had fallen into a helpless silence when we heard a car coming. From some distance we could hear it banging over the ruts in the road. We climbed out and stood so the headlights would find us and presently a truck appeared, swaying crazily. It stopped and a man leaned out. As a matter of fact, he sagged out the side and he had a bottle in one hand, waving it at us.

"Anything wrong?" he said.

We explained about the car and asked for a lift. He pulled his head into the truck and consulted with the driver. Then he reappeared and said they'd give us a lift to Columbia later, but first they were going to a lynching and if we didn't mind the detour . . .

We climbed into the truck.

"Northerners?" the driver said. "Where did you all come from?"

We said that we had driven down from Trenton in New Jersey and he said, "In that old piece of tin?" referring to our car. The other man wiped the neck of the bottle by running his finger around inside it, and offered it to me. "Do you good," he said, "best corn outside Kentucky." It was no time to refuse hospitality. I drank some of the stuff which had a taste like gasoline, except that it was like gasoline on fire, and he handed it to my friend Joe, who also drank some and coughed, and they both laughed.

I said timidly, "Who's getting lynched?"

"Some goddam nigger, name of Hyacinth as I recollect."

"What did he do?"

"He got after a white woman." I began to think with doubt and disgust of this explanation. So I asked who the woman was.

"Some widow woman, owns land down towards Natchez."

"How old is she?" Joe asked. Joe was in doubt, too.

"Christ, she's so old she ought to of died. She's about forty or fifty."

"And the boy?"

"You mean that nigger Hyacinth?"

I said yes, and was told that Hyacinth was about nineteen, though you couldn't always tell with niggers; sometimes they looked older than they were and sometimes younger.

"What happened?" Joe said. "How do you know she got raped?"

"She says so," the driver said. "She's been screaming off her head about it ever since this afternoon. She run down to the next plantation and screamed and said hang that man; and she said it was Hyacinth. She ought to of knowed him anyhow; he was working for her sometime back."

"How do you mean; was he a servant?"

"No," the driver said, "he was working on her land on shares. Most of her croppers've moved off by now; she don't give them any keep and they can't make the crop if they don't get nothing to eat all winter. She sure is cruel hard on niggers, that woman; she's got a bad name for being a mean one."

"Well," Joe said, very gently, "it doesn't look likely to me that a boy of nineteen would go after a woman of forty or fifty. Unless she's very beautiful, of course."

"Beautiful," the man with the bottle said, "Jees, you ought to see her. They could stick her out in a field and she'd scare the crows to death."

We bumped in silence over the roads. I couldn't think of anything to say. These men were evidently going to the lynching, but I didn't see that they were blind with anger against the Negro, or burning to avenge the honour of the nameless widow. Joe whispered to me: "You know we can't just sit and take this. I don't believe the boy did anything to that woman. We can't just sit around and let a man get hung, you know." I began to feel hot and nervous and I decided I'd like a drink even if it was corn whiskey. But I couldn't think of anything to do.

"How many people will be coming? A big crowd?" I asked.

"Yeah. They been getting the word around all evening. Some of the boys gonna go down and spring the jail. That's easy. Sheriff don't plan on holding that nigger till trial time anyhow. There'll be a lot of folks driving in from all over the county. They been telephoning around this afternoon and visiting folks and it gets around if there's trouble with a nigger. There'll be plenty of folks there."

"But," Joe said, this time desperately, "you don't know that he did anything to that woman. You haven't any proof, have you?"

"She says he did," the driver said, "that's enough for us. You gotta take a white woman's word any time before you take a nigger's. Helluva place it'd be if you said white folks lied and niggers told the truth."

"But you said he worked for her," Joe went on. "You said she was mean and didn't give her share-croppers decent rations. He's so much younger than she is, too, and you said she wasn't any beauty. He may have been going to see her to ask for money for food and he may have gotten mad and raised his arm or something that made her think he was going to strike her . . ."

"Lissen, sonny," the man with the bottle said quietly, finally, "this here ain't none of your goddam business."

We drove in silence, lurching against each other, and the driver took a drink, steering with one hand, and then the other man drank. They were sore, I could see that. They'd come out to get drunk and have a good time and here we were, asking questions and spoiling their fun. They were getting a grim drunk, not a laughing one, and they were sore about it. They didn't offer us the bottle any more.

The road widened and ahead we could see tail-lights. The driver stepped on the gas and the truck rattled forward. We passed a touring car with six men in it; I saw some shot guns. "That you, Danny?" the driver shouted. "Hi, Luke, see you later."

We were evidently going to an appointed meeting place. I asked about this. "They'll bring him up from jail," the man with the bottle said. "We all are gonna get together at the Big Elm crossroads."

There were more cars now and the road was better. "Almost there," the driver said, and for no reason at all the man with the bottle said, "Attaboy", and laughed and slapped his leg.

There was no moon. I saw an enormous tree and, though there were no doubt others, it stood by itself and had a curious air of usefulness. The roads forked and there were shapeless dark cars sprawled in the dust and men waiting in groups, laughing, drinking, and looking down the road for something to appear; something that would give this party meaning. I couldn't judge the crowd but there must have been about fifty cars, and these cars travel full.

Presently a line of cars came up the road. They were going as fast as they could over the ruts. They stopped and men poured out of them, not making much noise, apparently knowing what they had to do as if it were a ritual, or something they had practised often before. Some of these men seemed to be the poorest of white farmers: tenants or share-croppers themselves. Tattered clothes, the usual thin unhinged bodies, that soiled look of people who live in little crowded places. There were one or two men who seemed to be there on principle, as one would go to a dinner party because it was an obligation, but a very boring one, and a few men, rather more compact than the others, who directed the show. It was hard to tell in this light, but they seemed men of middle age mostly, householders, heads of families, reliable people. Joe was saying now, "I'd like to kill somebody myself."

I couldn't think of anything at all. I kept wondering why we were here. I hadn't seen Hyacinth yet.

But Hyacinth was there, surrounded by men. He had been brought in one of the last cars. I heard a man say: "Hurry up before the bastard dies of fright." Hyacinth was walked across the road, through an open space, to the great tree. He had his hands tied and there was a rope around his waist. They were dragging him; his legs curled under him and his head seemed loose and heavy on his neck. He looked small and far too quiet. They had torn off his shirt.

The men gathered around; they came without any commands and stood at a distance to give the leaders room to work. There was not any decisive noise, no cheering or shouting, but just a steady threatening murmur of anger or determination. The action moved fast, with precision.

A sedan drove up and stopped under the tree. A man climbed on to the top quickly. Another. They stood black against the sky. From beneath, a group of men, shoving and pushing, got Hyacinth's limp thin body up to them. Hyacinth half-lay, half-squatted on the roof. From the ground a length of rope sailed up, hung in the air, curved and fell. A man tried again and the rope caught and hung down from a limb. The noosed end was thrown to one of the men standing on the car-roof. He held it and shook Hyacinth. There were no words now, only vague instructions, half-spoken. The crowd stood still; you could hear the mosquitoes whining.

The other man held something in his hand; it looked like a great jug. He held it over Hyacinth, who shivered suddenly, and came to life. His voice rose out of him like something apart, and it hurt one's ears to listen to it; it was higher than a voice can be, not human. "Boss," he said. "Boss, I didn't do nuthin, don't burn me Boss, Boss . . ." The crowd had trembled now, stirred by his voice, and there were orders to hurry, to kill the bastard, what the hell were they waiting for . . .

The two men held him up and put the noose around his neck, and now he was making a terrible sound, like a dog whimpering. The minute they let go, he slacked into a kneeling position and his whole body seemed to shrink and dwindle and there was this noise he made. The two men jumped down from the roof: the rope was taut now. The car started and the silly sound of the starter failing to work, then the hesitant acceleration of the motor were so important that nothing else was heard; there were no other sounds anywhere; just these, and a moment's waiting. The car moved forward, fast. Hyacinth skidded and fought an instant – less than an instant – to keep his footing or some hold, some safety. He snapped from the back of the car, hung suspended, twirling a little on the rope, with his head fallen sideways. I did not know whether he was dead. There was a choked sound beside me and it was Joe, crying, sitting there crying, with fury, with helplessness, and I kept looking at Hyacinth and thinking: it can't have happened. There had been a noise, a sudden guttural sound as of people breathing out a deep breath, when the rope carried

Hyacinth twisting into the air. Now a man came forward with a torch made of newspaper, burning. He reached up and the flames licked at Hyacinth's feet. He had been soaked in kerosene to make it easy, but the flames didn't take so well at first. Then they got on to his trousers and went well, shooting up, and there was a hissing sound and I thought a smell. I went away and was sick.

When I came back the cars were going off down the road quietly. And men were calling to each other saying: "So long, Jake . . ." "Hi there, Billy . . ." "See you t'morrow, Sam . . ." Just saying goodnight to each other and going home.

The driver and the man with the bottle came back to the truck and got in. They seemed in a good frame of mind. The driver said, "Well there won't be no more fresh niggers in these parts for a while. We'll get you to Columbia now. Sorry we hadta keep you waiting . . ."

THE BROOKERS

The Road to Wigan Pier, 1937

Orwell's exposé of the poverty of the industrial North of England was commissioned by the Left Book Club. Although not properly journalism – in the sense of being written for a periodical – Orwell's almost documentary-like social investigation was profoundly influential on British journalism.

The first sound in the mornings was the clumping of the mill-girls' clogs down the cobbled street. Earlier than that, I suppose, there were factory whistles which I was never awake to hear.

There were generally four of us in the bedroom, and a beastly place it was, with that defiled impermanent look of rooms that are not serving their rightful purpose. Years earlier the house had been an ordinary dwelling-house, and when the Brookers had taken it and fitted it out as a tripeshop and lodging-house, they had inherited some of the more useless pieces of furniture and had never had the energy to remove them. We were therefore sleeping in what was still recognizably a drawing-room. Hanging from the ceiling there was a heavy glass chandelier on which the dust was so thick that it was like fur. And covering most of one wall there was a huge hideous piece of junk, something between a sideboard and a hall-stand, with lots of carving and little drawers and strips of looking-glass, and there was a once-gaudy carpet ringed by the slop-pails of years, and two gilt chairs with burst seats, and one of those old-fashioned horsehair armchairs which you slide off when you try to sit on them. The room had been turned into a bedroom by thrusting four squalid beds in among this other wreckage.

My bed was in the right-hand corner on the side nearest the

door. There was another bed across the foot of it and jammed hard against it (it had to be in that position to allow the door to open) so that I had to sleep with my legs doubled up; if I straightened them out I kicked the occupant of the other bed in the small of the back. He was an elderly man named Mr Reilly, a mechanic of sorts and employed "on top" at one of the coal pits. Luckily he had to go to work at five in the morning, so I could uncoil my legs and have a couple of hours' proper sleep after he was gone. In the bed opposite there was a Scotch miner who had been injured in a pit accident (a huge chunk of stone pinned him to the ground and it was a couple of hours before they could lever it off), and had received five hundred pounds compensation. He was a big handsome man of forty, with grizzled hair and a clipped moustache, more like a sergeant-major than a miner, and he would lie in bed till late in the day, smoking a short pipe. The other bed was occupied by a succession of commercial travellers, newspaper-canvassers, and hire-purchase touts who generally stayed for a couple of nights. It was a double bed and much the best in the room. I had slept in it myself my first night there, but had been manoeuvred out of it to make room for another lodger. I believe all newcomers spent their first night in the double bed, which was used, so to speak, as bait. All the windows were kept tight shut, with a red sandbag jammed in the bottom, and in the morning the room stank like a ferret's cage. You did not notice it when you got up, but if you went out of the room and came back, the smell hit you in the face with a smack.

I never discovered how many bedrooms the house contained, but strange to say there was a bathroom, dating from before the Brookers' time. Downstairs there was the usual kitchen living-room with its huge open range burning night and day. It was lighted only by a skylight, for on one side of it was the shop and on the other the larder, which opened into some dark subterranean place where the tripe was stored. Partly blocking the door of the larder there was a shapeless sofa upon which Mrs Brooker, our landlady, lay permanently ill, festooned in grimy blankets. She had a big, pale yellow, anxious face. No one knew for certain what was the matter with her; I suspect that her only real trouble was over-eating. In front of the fire there was almost always a line of damp washing, and in the middle of the room was the big kitchen table at which the family and all the lodgers ate. I never saw this table completely uncovered, but I saw its various wrappings at different times. At the bottom there was a layer of old newspaper stained by Worcester Sauce; above that a sheet of sticky white oil-cloth; above that a green serge cloth; above that a coarse linen cloth, never changed and seldom taken off. Generally the crumbs from breakfast were still on the table at supper. I used to get to know individual crumbs by sight and watch their progress up and down the table from day to day.

The shop was a narrow, cold sort of room. On the outside of the window a few white letters, relics of ancient chocolate advertisements, were scattered like stars. Inside there was a slab upon which lay the great white folds of tripe, and the grey flocculent stuff known as "black tripe", and the ghostly translucent feet of pigs, ready boiled. It was the ordinary "tripe and pea" shop, and not much else was stocked except bread, cigarettes, and tinned stuff. "Teas" were advertised in the window, but if a customer demanded a cup of tea he was usually put off with excuses. Mr Brooker, though out of work for two years, was a miner by trade, but he and his wife had been keeping shops of various kinds as a side-line all their lives. At one time they had had a pub, but they had lost their licence for allowing gambling on the premises. I doubt whether any of their businesses had ever paid; they were the kind of people who run a business chiefly in order to have something to grumble about. Mr Brooker was a dark, small-boned, sour, Irish-looking man, and astonishingly dirty. I don't think I ever once saw his hands clean. As Mrs Brooker was now an invalid he prepared most of the food, and like all people with permanently dirty hands he had a peculiarly intimate, lingering manner of handling things. If he gave you a slice of bread-and-butter there was always a black thumb-print on it. Even in the early morning when he descended into the mysterious den behind Mrs Brooker's sofa and fished out the tripe, his hands were already black. I heard dreadful stories from the other lodgers about the place where the tripe was kept. Blackbeetles were said to swarm there. I do not know how often fresh consignments of tripe were ordered, but it was at long intervals, for Mrs Brooker used to date events by it. "Let me see now, I've had in three lots of froze (frozen tripe) since that happened," etc. We lodgers were never given tripe to eat. At the time I imagined that this was because tripe was too expensive; I have since thought that it was merely because we knew too much about it. The Brookers never ate tripe themselves, I noticed.

The only permanent lodgers were the Scotch miner, Mr Reilly, two old-age pensioners, and an unemployed man on the P.A.C. named Joe – he was the kind of person who has no surname. The Scotch miner was a bore when you got to know him. Like so many unemployed men he spent too much time reading newspapers, and if you did not head him off he would discourse for hours about such things as the Yellow Peril, trunk murders, astrology, and the conflict between religion and science. The old-age pensioners had, as usual, been driven from their homes by the Means Test. They handed their weekly ten shillings over to the Brookers and in return got the kind of accommodation you would expect for ten shillings; that is, a bed in the attic and meals chiefly of bread-and-butter. One of them was of "superior" type and was dying of some malignant disease – cancer, I believe. He only got out of bed on the days when he went to draw his pension. The other, called by everyone Old Jack, was an ex-miner aged seventy-eight who had worked well over fifty years in the pits. He was alert and intelligent, but curiously enough he seemed only to remember his boyhood experiences and to have forgotten all about the modern mining machinery and improvements. He used to tell me tales of fights with savage horses in the narrow galleries underground. When he heard that I was arranging to go down several coal mines he was contemptuous and declared that a man of my size (six feet two and a half) would never manage the "travelling"; it was no use telling him that the "travelling" was better than it used to be. But he was friendly to everyone and used to give us all a fine shout of "Good night, boys!" as he crawled up the stairs to his bed somewhere under the rafters. What I most admired about Old Jack was that he never cadged; he was generally out of tobacco towards the end of the week, but he always refused to smoke anyone else's. The Brookers had insured the lives of both old-age pensioners with one of the tanner-a-week companies. It was said that they were overheard anxiously asking the insurance-tout "how long people lives when they've got cancer."

Joe, like the Scotchman, was a great reader of newspapers and spent almost his entire day in the public library. He was the typical unmarried unemployed man, a derelict-looking, frankly ragged creature with a round, almost childish face on which there was a naively naughty expression. He looked more like a ne- glected little boy than a grown-up man. I suppose it is the complete lack of responsibility that makes so many of these men look younger than their ages. From Joe's appearance I took him to be about twenty-eight, and was amazed to learn that he was forty-three. He had a love of resounding phrases and was very proud of the astuteness with which he had avoided getting married. He often said to me, "Matrimonial chains is a big item," evidently feeling this to be a very subtle and portentous remark. His total income was fifteen shillings a week, and he paid out six or seven to the Brookers for his bed. I sometimes used to see him making himself a cup of tea over the kitchen fire, but for the rest he got his meals somewhere out of doors; it was mostly slices of bread-and-marg and packets of fish and chips, I suppose.

Besides these there was a floating clientele of commercial travellers of the poorer sort, travelling actors – always common in the North because most of the larger pubs hire variety artists at the week-ends – and newspaper-canvassers. The newspaper- canvassers were a type I had never met before. Their job seemed to me so hopeless, so appalling that I wondered how anyone could put up with such a thing when prison was a possible alternative. They were employed mostly by weekly or Sunday papers, and they were sent from town to town, provided with maps and given a list of streets which they had to "work" each day. If they failed to secure a minimum of twenty orders a day, they got the sack. So long as they kept up their twenty orders a day they received a small salary – two pounds a week, I think; on any order over the twenty they drew a tiny commission. The thing is not so impossible as it sounds, because in working-class districts every family takes in a twopenny weekly paper and changes it every few weeks; but I doubt whether anyone keeps a job of that kind long. The newspapers engage poor desperate wretches, out-of-work clerks and commercial travellers and the like, who for a while make frantic efforts and keep their sales up to the minimum; then as the deadly work wears them down they are sacked and fresh men are taken on. I got to know two who were employed by one of the more notorious weeklies. Both of them were middle-aged men with families to support, and one of them was a grandfather. They were on their feet ten hours a day, "working" their appointed streets, and then busy late into the night filling in blank forms for some swindle their paper was running – one of those schemes by which you are "given" a set of crockery if you take out a six weeks' subscription and send a two-shilling postal order as well. The fat one, the grandfather, used to fall asleep with his head on a pile of forms. Neither of them could afford the pound a week which the Brookers charged for full board. They used to pay a small sum for their beds and make shamefaced meals in a corner of the kitchen off bacon and bread-and-margarine which they stored in their suit-cases.

The Brookers had large numbers of sons and daughters, most of whom had long since fled from home. Some were in Canada "at Canada", as Mrs Brooker used to put it. There was only one son living near by, a large pig-like young man employed in a garage, who frequently came to the house for his meals. His wife was there all day with the two children, and most of the cooking and laundering was done by her and by Emmie, the fiancée of another son who was in London. Emmie was a fair-haired, sharp-nosed, unhappy-looking girl who worked at one of the mills for some starvation wage, but nevertheless spent all her evenings in bondage at the Brookers' house. I gathered that the marriage was constantly being postponed and would probably never take place, but Mrs Brooker had already appropriated Emmie as a daughter-in-law, and nagged her in that peculiar watchful, loving way that invalids have. The rest of the housework was done, or not done, by Mr Brooker. Mrs Brooker seldom rose from her sofa in the kitchen (she spent the night there as well as the day) and was too ill to do anything except eat stupendous meals. It was Mr Brooker who attended to the shop, gave the lodgers their food, and "did out" the bedrooms. He was always moving with incredible slowness from one hated job to another. Often the beds were still unmade at six in the evening, and at any hour of the day you were liable to meet Mr Brooker on the stairs, carrying a full chamber-pot which he gripped with his thumb well over the rim. In the mornings he sat by the fire with a tub of filthy water, peeling potatoes at the speed of a slow-motion picture. I never saw anyone who could peel potatoes with quite such an air of brooding resentment. You could see the hatred of this "bloody woman's work", as he called it, fermenting inside him, a kind of bitter juice. He was one of those people who can chew their grievances like a cud.

Of course, as I was indoors a good deal, I heard all about the Brookers' woes, and how everyone swindled them and was ungrateful to them, and how the shop did not pay and the lodging-house hardly paid. By local standards they were not so badly off, for, in some way I did not understand, Mr Brooker was dodging the Means Test and drawing an allowance from the P.A.C., but their chief pleasure was talking about their grievances to anyone who would listen. Mrs Brooker used to lament by the hour, lying on her sofa, a soft mound of fat and self-pity, saying the same things over and over again. "We don't seem to get no customers nowadays. I don't know 'ow it is. The tripe's just a-laying there day after day – such beautiful tripe it is, too! It does seem 'ard, don't it now?" etc., etc., etc. All Mrs Brookers' laments ended with "It does seem 'ard, don't it now?" like the refrain of a ballade. Certainly it was true that the shop did not pay. The whole place had the unmistakable dusty, flyblown air of a business that is going down. But it would have been quite useless to explain to them *why* nobody came to the shop, even if one had had the face to do it; neither was capable of understanding that last year's dead bluebottles supine in the shop window are not good for trade.

ERNEST HEMINGWAY

THE LOYALISTS

The New Republic, 1938

On leaving school, Ernest Hemingway took a job as cub reporter on the *Kansas City Star,* where he was given a style book that profoundly influenced his mature wordsmithcraft. In 1918 Hemingway quit the *Star* to serve as an ambulance driver on the Italian Front of the First World War. He found the taste of war hard to give up and in the 1930s reported the Civil War in Spain and a decade later would not be dissuaded from covering the Second World War. Below is a dispatch from Spain, where Hemingway's sympathies lay with the forces of the elected leftist Republic, the Loyalists.

On the Aragon Front

When we got up with the Americans they were lying under some olive trees along a little stream. The yellow dust of Aragon was blowing over them, over their blanketed machine guns, over their automatic rifles and their anti-aircraft guns. It blew in blinding clouds raised by the hooves of pack animals and the wheels of motor transports.

But in the lee of the stream-bank, the men were slouching fearful and grinning, their teeth flashing white slits in their yellow-powdered faces.

Since I had seen them last spring, they have become soldiers. The romantics have pulled out, the cowards have gone home along with the badly wounded. The dead, of course, aren't there. Those who are left are tough, with blackened matter-of-fact faces, and, after seven months, they know their trade.

They have fought with the first Spanish troops of the new government army, captured the strongly fortified heights and town of Quinto in a brilliantly conceived and executed fashion, and have taken part with three Spanish brigades in the final storming of Belchite after it had been surrounded by Spanish troops.

After the taking of Quinto, they had marched twenty miles across country to Belchite. They had lain in the woods outside the town and had worked their way forward with the Indian-fighting tactics that are still the most life-saving that any infantry can know. Covered by a heavy and accurate artillery barrage, they stormed the entry to the town. Then for three days they fought from house to house, from room to room, breaking walls with pickaxes, bombing their way forward as they exchanged shots with the retreating Fascists from street corners, windows, rooftops and holes in the walls.

Finally, they made a juncture with Spanish troops advancing from the other side and surrounded the cathedral, where 400 men of the town garrison still held out. These men fought desperately, bravely, and a Fascist officer worked a machine gun from the tower until a shell crumpled the masonry spire upon him and his gun. They fought all around the square, keeping up a covering fire with automatic rifles, and made a final rush on the tower. Then, after some fighting of the sort you never know whether to classify as hysterical or the ultimate in bravery, the garrison surrendered.

Robert Merriam, former California University professor and chief of staff of the Fifteenth Brigade, was the leader in the final assault. Unshaven, his face smoke-blackened, his men tell how he bombed his way forward, wounded six times slightly by hand-grenade splinters in his hands and face, but refusing to have his wounds dressed until the cathedral was taken. The American casualties were 23 killed and 60 wounded out of a total of 500 of all ranks who took part in the two operations.

The total government casualties given in the entire offensive were 2,000 killed and wounded. The entire garrison of 3,000 troops in Belchite was either captured or killed except for four officers who succeeded in escaping from the town during the last night before the final assault.

Madrid

They say you never hear the one that hits you. That's true of bullers, because, if you hear them, they are already past. But your correspondent heard the last shell that hit this hotel. He heard it start from the battery, then come with a whistling incoming roar like a subway train to crash against the cornice and shower the room with broken glass and plaster. And while the glass still tinkled down and you listened for the next one to start, you realized that now finally you were back in Madrid.

Madrid is quiet now. Aragon is the active front. There's little fighting around Madrid except mining, counter-mining, trench raiding, trench-mortar strafing and sniping, in a stalemate of constant siege warfare going on-in Carabanchel, Usera and University City. The cities are shelled very little. Some days there is no shelling and the weather is beautiful and the streets are crowded. The shops are full of clothing; jewelry stores, camera shops, picture dealers are all open and the bars are crowded.

Beer is scarce and whiskey is almost unobtainable. Store windows are full of Spanish imitations of all cordials, whiskies and vermouths. These are not recommended for internal use, although I am employing something called Milords Ecosses Whiskey on my face after shaving. It smarts a little, but I feel very hygienic. I believe it would be possible to cure athlete's foot with it, but one must be very careful not to spill it on one's clothes because it eats wool.

The crowds are cheerful and the sandbag-fronted cinemas are crowded every afternoon. The nearer one gets to the front, the more cheerful and optimistic the people are. At the front itself, optimism reaches such a point that your correspondent, very much against his good judgment, was induced to go swimming in a small river forming a no-man's land on the Cuenca front the day before yesterday.

The river was a fast-flowing stream, very chilly and completely dominated by Fascist positions, which made me even chillier. I became so chilly at the idea of swimming in the river at all under the circumstances that, when I actually entered the water, it felt rather pleasant. But it felt even pleasanter when I got out of the water and behind a tree.

At that moment, a government officer who was a member of the optimistic swimming party shot a watersnake with his pistol, hitting it on the third shot. This brought a reprimand from another, not so completely optimistic officer member, who asked what he wanted to do with that shooting – get machine guns turned on us?

We shot no more snakes that day, but I saw three trout in the stream which would weigh over four pounds apiece; heavy, solid, deep-sided ones that rolled up to take the grasshoppers I threw them, making swirls in the water as deep as though you had dropped a paving stone into the stream. All along the stream, where no road ever led until the war, you could see trout; small ones in the shallows and the biggest kind in the pools and in the shadow of the bank. It's a river worth fighting for, but just a little cold for swimming.

At this moment, a shell has just alighted on a house up the street from the hotel where I am typing this. A little boy is crying in the street. A Militiaman has picked him up and is comforting him. There was no one killed on our street, and the people who started to run slow down and grin nervously. The one who never started to run at all looks at the others in a very superior way, and the town we are living in now is called Madrid.

Brunete was not a last desperate effort by the government to relieve the siege of Madrid, but the first in a series of offensives launched on the realistic basis of regarding the war as of a possible duration of two years.

In order to understand the Spanish War, it is necessary to realize the Rebels are holding on to a single linked-up line of trenches on an 800-mile front. They are holding fortified towns, often unconnected by any defences; but those which dominate the country around them, much as castles did in the old feudal days, must be passed, turned, encircled and assaulted as the castles were in olden times.

Troops that had been on the defensive for nine months, waiting to attack, learned their first lessons in April in Casa del Campo, that frontal assaults in modern war against good machine-gun positions are suicidal. The only way an attack can overcome the superiority machine guns give defense, if the defenders are not panicked by aerial bombardment, is by surprise, obscurity or maneouvre.

The government first began to manoeuvre in a counter-offensive that beat the Italians at Guadalajara. At Brunete, the government troops were not yet experienced enough to turn and take their objectives on time so that the whole front could advance.

But they held and threw back a counter-offensive that cost the Rebels more men than they could afford to lose. The Loyalist casualties were estimated at 15,000. The Rebel counter-offensive across that bare terrain, lacking any element of surprise, must have cost them many more than that.

While Franco's troops have been advancing this week in the Asturias, the government troops have just completed another nibbling offensive in the extreme north of Aragon which brings them within striking distance of Jaca. Just now they are in striking distance of Huesca, Saragossa and Teruel. They can fight on in this way indefinitely, improving their positions in a series of small offensives, with limited objectives, designed to be carried out with a minimum of casualties, while teaching their army to manoeuvre in preparation for operations on a grand plan.

While this goes on, Franco is constantly forced to divert troops to meet these small offensives. He can continue to take "name" towns of no ultimate strategic importance, working along the coast and thus improving his international position with obvious cashable successes, or he can face the unavoidable, though postponable, necessity of again attacking Madrid and its lines of communication with Valencia.

Personally, I think Franco got himself into a fix when he advanced into Madrid and failed to take it, a situation from which he can never extricate himself. Sooner or later he must risk everything in a major offensive on the Castilian plateau.

Loyalist Army Headquarters, Teruel Front

For three days, all Teruel's communications had been cut and the government forces had taken successively Concud, Campillo and Villastar, important defensive towns guarding the city from the north, southwest and south.

Friday, while we watched from a hilltop above the town, crouching against boulders, hardly able to hold our field glasses in the fifty-mile gale which picked up the snow from the hillside and lashed it against our faces, government troops took the Muela de Teruel Hill, one of the odd thimble-shaped formations like extinct geyser cones which protect the city.

Fortified by concrete machine-gun emplacements, and surrounded by tank traps made of spikes forged from steel rails, it was considered impregnable, but four companies assaulted it as though they never had had explained to them by military experts what impregnable meant. Its defenders fell back into Teruel, and, a little later in the afternoon, as we watched, another battalion broke through the concrete emplacements of the cemetery, and the last defenses of Teruel itself were squashed or turned.

In zero weather, with a wind that made living a torture, and intermittent blizzards, the army of the Levante and part of the new army of manoeuvre, without the aid or presence of any International Brigades, had launched an offensive which was forcing the enemy to fight at Teruel when it was a matter of common knowledge that Franco had planned offensives against Guadalajara and in Aragon.

When we left the Teruel front last night for the all-night drive to Madrid to file this story, the presence of 1,000 Italian troops drawn from the Guadalajara front was signaled north of Teruel, where their troops, trains and transport had been bombed and machine-gunned by Loyalist aircraft. Authorities estimated that 30,000 Fascist troops were already massing on the Catalayud-Teruel road for a counter-offensive. So, regardless of whether Teruel is captured, the offensive has achieved its purpose of forcing Franco's hand and breaking up plans for simultaneous Guadalajara and Aragon offensives.

Across a country cold as a steel engraving, wild as a Wyoming blizzard or a hurricane mesa, we watched the battle which may be the decisive one of this war. In the Peninsular War, Teruel had been taken by the French in December and there was good precedent for an attack on it now. On the right were snowy mountains with timbered slopes, below was a winding pass which the Rebels held above Teruel on the Sagunto Road, from which many military authorities had expected a Franco attack to the sea to be launched. Below was the great yellow battleship-shaped natural fortification of Mansueto, the city's main protection, which the Loyalists had slipped past to the northwards, leaving it as hopeless as a stranded dreadnaught.

Close below were the spire and ocher-colored houses of Castralvo, which government troops entered as we watched. On the right, by the cemetery, there was fighting and shell bursts plumed up, while beyond, the city, neatly ordered against its fantastically eroded background of red sandstone, stood quiet as a tethered sheep too frightened to shiver when wolves are passing.

What Franco's Italians and Moors will do in the present situation of weather conditions in Teruel remains to be seen. Horses could never have stood up under the conditions of this offensive. Cars had their radiators frozen and their cylinder blocks cracked. But men could stand it, and did. One thing remains. You need infantry still to win battles, and impregnable positions are only as impregnable as the will of those who hold them.

A PORTRAIT OF HITLER

Inside Europe, 1940

A freelance American journalist abroad in Europe, Gunther wrote a series
of bestselling books entitled *Inside Europe*, giving the "real dope" on the
Continent's people and affairs. The following selection is Gunther's
portrait-in-words of Adolf Hitler.

Adolf Hitler, irrational, contradictory, complex, is an unpredictable character; therein lies his power and his menace. To millions
of honest Germans he is sublime, a figure of adoration; he fills
them with love, fear, and nationalist ecstasy. To many other
Germans he is meagre and ridiculous – a charlatan, a lucky
hysteric, and a lying demagogue. What are the reasons for this
paradox? What are the sources of his extraordinary power?

This paunchy, Charlie-Chaplin-moustached man, given to
insomnia and emotionalism, who is head of the Nazi party,
commander-in-chief of the German army and navy, Leader of
the German nation, creator, president, and chancellor of the
Third Reich, was born in Austria in 1889. He was not a German
by birth. This was a highly important point inflaming his early
nationalism. He developed the implacable patriotism of the
frontiersman, the exile. Only an Austrian could take Germanism
so seriously.

The inside story of Hitler includes many extraordinary and
bizarre episodes. Before discussing his birth and childhood and
outlining his career, it may be well to present a broad detailed
picture of his character and his daily routine and his attitudes and
habits, his personal characteristics and limitations.

Hitler the human being

His imagination is purely political. I have seen his early paintings, those which he submitted to the Vienna art academy as a boy. They are prosaic, utterly devoid of rhythm, colour, feeling, or spiritual imagination. They are architect's sketches: painful and precise draughtsmanship; nothing more. No wonder the Vienna professors told him to go to an architectural school and give up pure art as hopeless. Yet he still wants deeply to be an artist. In 1939 during the crisis leading to the Polish War, he told Sir Nevile Henderson, the British Ambassador, that his only ambition was to retire to the Berchtesgaden hills and paint.

His schooling was very brief, and by no stretch of generosity could he be called a person of genuine culture. He is not nearly so cultivated, so sophisticatedly interested in intellectual affairs as is, say, Mussolini. He reads almost nothing. The Treaty of Versailles was, probably, the most concrete single influence on his life; but it is doubtful if he ever read it in full. He dislikes intellectuals. He has never been outside Germany since his youth in Austria (if you except his War experiences in Flanders and two brief visits to Mussolini), and he speaks no foreign language, except a few words of French.

To many who meet him, Hitler seems awkward and ill at ease. This is because visitors, even among his subordinates, obtrude personal realities which interfere with his incessant fantasies. He has no poise. He finds it difficult to make quick decisions: capacity for quick decisions derives from inner harmony, which he lacks. He is no "strong, silent man".

Foreigners, especially interviewers from British or American papers, may find him cordial and even candid but they seldom have opportunity to question him, to participate in a give-and-take discussion. Hitler rants. He orates. He is extremely emotional. He seldom answers questions. He talks to you as if you were a public meeting, and nothing can stop the gush of words.

Years ago, before signing his short-lived friendship pact with Poland, he received a well-known American publicist and editor. He asked a question: What the American would think if, for example, Mexico were Poland and Texas were cut off from the United States by a "corridor" in Mexico. The American replied: "The answer to that is that Canada is not France." Hitler had intended the question rhetorically, and he was so shocked and upset by the little interruption that it took him some time to get in full voice again – on another point.

For a time it was said commonly that Hitler's best trait was loyalty. He would never, the sardonic joke put it, give up three things: the Jews, his friends, and Austria. Nobody would make that joke today, now that Captain Roehm is dead. Nor would anyone of knowledge and discernment have made it even before 30 June 1934, because the scroll of Hitler's disloyalties was written in giant words.

One after another he eliminated those who helped him to his career: Drexler, Feder, Gregor Strasser. It is true that he has been loyal to some colleagues – those who never disagreed with him, who gave him absolute obedience. This loyalty is not an unmixed virtue, considering the unsavouriness of such men as Streicher, the Nuremberg Jew-baiter. Nothing can persuade Hitler to give up Streicher and some other comrades. Unsavouriness alone is not enough to provoke his Draconian ingratitude.

His physical courage is doubtful. When his men were fired on in the Munich *Putsch* of 1923, he flung himself to the street with such violence that his shoulder was broken. Nazi explanations of this are two: (1) linked arm in arm with a man on his right who was shot and killed, he was jerked unwittingly to the pavement; (2) he behaved with the reflex action of the veteran front-line soldier, that is, sensibly fell flat when the bullets came.

Hitler has told an acquaintance his own story of the somewhat mysterious circumstances in which he won the Iron Cross. He was a dispatch bearer. He was carrying messages across a part of no-man's-land which was believed to be clear of enemy troops, when he heard French voices. He was alone, armed only with a revolver; so with great presence of mind he shouted imaginary orders to an imaginary column of men. The Frenchmen tumbled out of a deserted dug-out, seven in all, hands up. Hitler alone delivered all seven to the German lines. Recounting this story privately, he told his interlocutor that he knew the feat would have been impossible, had the seven men been American or English instead of French.

Like that of all fanatics, his capacity for self-belief, his ability to delude himself, is enormous. Thus he is quite "sincere" – he really believes it – when in an interview with the *Daily Mail* he says that the Nazi revolution cost only twenty-six lives. He believes absolutely in what he says – at the moment.

But his lies have been notorious. Heiden mentions some of the more recondite untruths, and others are known to every student. Hitler promised the authorities of Bavaria not to make a *Putsch*; and promptly made one. He promised to tolerate a Papen government; then fought it. He promised not to change the composition of his first cabinet; then changed it. He promised to kill himself if the Munich coup failed; it failed, and he is still alive.

The Man Without Habits

Hitler, nearing fifty-one, is not in first-rate physical condition. He has gained about twelve pounds in the past few years, and his neck and midriff show it. His physical presence has always been indifferent; the sloppiness with which he salutes is, for instance, notorious. The forearm barely moves above the elbow. He had lung trouble as a boy, and was blinded by poison gas in the War.

In August 1935, it was suddenly revealed that the Leader had suffered a minor operation some months before to remove a polyp on his vocal cords – penalty of years of tub-thumping. The operation was successful. The next month Hitler shocked his adherents at Nuremberg by alluding, in emotional and circumlocutory terms, to the possibility of his death. "I do not know when I shall finally close my eyes," he said, "but I do know that the party will continue and will rule. Leaders will come and Leaders will die, but Germany will live . . . The army must preserve the power given to Germany and watch over it." The speech led to rumours (quite unconfirmed) that the growth in Hitler's throat was malignant, and that he had cancer.

Nowadays Hitler broods and talks about death a good deal. One reason for his prodigious expansionist efforts in 1938 and 1939 was fear of death before his work was complete.

He takes no exercise, and his only important relaxation – though lately he began to like battleship cruises in the Baltic or North Sea – is music. He is deeply musical. Wagner is one of the cardinal influences on his life; he is obsessed by Wagner. He goes to opera as often as he can, and he was attending the Bayreuth Festival when, on 25 July 1934, Nazi putschists murdered Chancellor Dollfuss of Austria. Sessions of the Reichstag, which take place in the Kroll Opera House, sometimes end with whole performances of Wagner operas – to the boredom of non-musical deputies! When fatigued at night, in the old days, his friend Hanfstaengl was sometimes summoned to play him to sleep, occasionally with Schumann or Verdi, more often with Beethoven and Wagner, for Hitler needs music like dope.

Hitler cares nothing for books; nothing for clothes (he seldom wears anything but an ordinary brown-shirt uniform, or a double-breasted blue serge suit, with the inevitable raincoat and slouch hat); very little for friends; and nothing for food and drink. He neither smokes nor drinks, and he will not allow anyone to smoke near him. He is practically a vegetarian. At the banquet tendered him by Mussolini he would eat only a double portion of scrambled eggs. He drinks coffee occasionally, but not often. Once or twice a week he crosses from the Chancellery to the Kaiserhof Hotel (the GHQ of the Nazi party before he came to power), and sits there and sips – chocolate.

This has led many people to speak of Hitler's "asceticism", but asceticism is not quite the proper word. He is limited in æsthetic interests, but he is no flagellant or anchorite. There is very little of the *austere* in Hitler. He eats only vegetables – but they are prepared by an exquisitely competent chef. He lives "simply" – but his house in Berchtesgaden is the last word in modern sumptuousness.

He works, when in Berlin, in the palace of the Reichskanzler on the Wilhelmstrasse. He seldom uses the president's palace a hundred yards away on the same street, because when Hindenburg died he wanted to eliminate as much as possible the memory of Presidential Germany. The building is new, furnished in modern glass and metal, and Hitler helped design it. Murals of the life of Wotan adorn the walls. An improvised balcony has been built over the street, from which, on public occasions, the Leader may review his men. Beneath the hall – according to reports – is a comfortable bomb-proof cellar.

Hitler dislikes Berlin. He leaves the capital at any opportunity, preferring Munich or Berchtesgaden, a village in southern Bavaria, where he has an alpine establishment, Haus Wachenfeld. Perched on the side of a mountain, this retreat, dear to his heart, is not far from the former Austrian frontier, a psychological fact of great significance. From his front porch he could almost see the homeland which repudiated him, and for which he yearned for many years.

Above the Berchtesgaden house – where he came in 1938 and 1939 to spend more and more time, often neglecting Berlin for weeks on end – is an amazing lookout or eyrie his engineers have built on a mountain top, near Kehlstein. A special, heavily guarded, looping road leads to bronze gates cut into a sheer wall of rock; inside the solid mountain, an elevator shaft rises four hundred feet. Here, on top, is a large circular room walled with windows. And here, when he really wants to be alone, Hitler comes.

Another peculiar point about Hitler is his passionate interest in astrology. It is widely believed that he set the date for the Sudeten crisis by advice of astrologers.

Friends

By a man's friends may ye know him. But Hitler has very few.

The man who is probably closest to Hitler since Roehm's death is his chief bodyguard, Lieut. Brückner. Another close associate is Max Amman, who was his top-sergeant in the Great War. For a time his former captain, Fritz Wiedemann, now German consul-general in San Francisco, was also close. Politically his most intimate adviser is certainly the foreign minister, Herr von Ribbentrop, who is one of the very few people who can see him at any time, without previous arrangement. He is bewitched by Ribbentrop's "wisdom". His chief permanent officials, like Dietrich, his Press secretary, may see him daily, and so may Hess, the deputy leader of the party, but even Hess is not an *intimate* friend. Neither Goering nor Goebbels, as a rule, may see Hitler without appointment.

He is almost oblivious of ordinary personal contacts. A colleague of mine travelled with him, in the same aeroplane, day after day, for two months during the 1932 electoral campaigns. Hitler never talked to a soul, not even to his secretaries, in the long hours in the air; never stirred; never smiled. My friend remembers most vividly that, in order to sneak a cigarette when the plane stopped, he had to run out of sight of the *entourage*. He says that he saw Hitler a steady five or six hours a day during this trip, but that he is perfectly sure Hitler, meeting him by chance outside the aeroplane, would not have known his name or face.

He dams profession of emotion to the bursting point, then is apt to break out in crying fits. A torrent of feminine tears compensates for the months of uneasy struggles not to give himself away. For instance, when he spent a whole night trying to persuade a dissident leader, Otto Strasser, from leaving the party, he broke into tears three times. In the early days he often wept, when other methods to carry a point failed.

Hitler does not enjoy too great exposure of this weakness, and he tends to keep all subordinates at a distance. They worship him; but they do not know him well. They may see him every day, year in year out; but they would never dare to be familiar. A man quite close to him told me once that in all the years of their association he had never called Hitler anything except "Herr Hitler" (or "Herr Reichskanzler" after the Leader reached power); and that Hitler had never called him by first name or his diminutive. There is an inhumanity about the inner circle of the Nazi party that is scarcely credible.

An old-time party member, to-day, would address Hitler as "Mein Führer"; others as "Herr Reichskanzler". When greeted with the Nazi salute and the words "Heil Hitler", Hitler himself replies with "Heil Hitler". Speechmaking, the Leader addresses his followers as "My" German people. In posters for the ple-biscites he asks, "Dost thou, German man, and thou, German woman – etc." It is as if he feels closer to the German people in bulk than to any individual German, and this is indeed true. The German *people* are the chief emotional reality of his life.

Let us, now, examine Hitler's relation to the imperatives which dominate the lives of most men.

Attitude Towards Women

He is totally uninterested in women from any personal sexual point of view. He thinks of them as housewives and mothers or potential mothers, to provide sons for the battlefield – other people's sons.

"The life of our people must be freed from the asphyxiating perfume of modern eroticism," he says in *Mein Kampf*, his autobiography. His personal life embodies this precept to the fullest. He is not a woman-hater, but he avoids and evades women. His manners are those of the wary chevalier, given to hand-kissing – and nothing else. Many women are attracted to him sexually, but they have had to give up the chase. Frau Goebbels formerly had evening parties to which she asked pretty and distinguished women to meet him, but she was never able to arrange a match. Occasional rumours of the engagement of the coy Leader to various ladies are nonsense. It is quite possible that Hitler has never had anything to do with a woman in his life.

Occasionally young English or American girls, ardent Aryans, come to see him, and sometimes they are received, like Miss Unity Mitford. But Hitler does little but harangue them. At the top of his voice he talks politics and after a time subsides, as if limp and exhausted. Even these occasions are not tête-à-tête. For Hitler is very fond of the little daughter of Dr Goebbels, and, fantastic as it may seem, she is often in the room, sometimes on the Leader's knee.

Nor, as is so widely believed, is he homosexual. Several German journalists spent much time and energy, when such an investigation was possible, checking every lodging that Hitler, in Munich days, had slept in; they interviewed beer-hall proprietors, coffee-house waiters, landladies, porters. No evidence was discovered that Hitler had been intimate with anybody of any sex at any time. His sexual energies, at the beginning of his career, were obviously sublimated into oratory. The influence of his mother and childhood environment, contributed signally to his frustration. Most of those German writers and observers best equipped to know think that Hitler is a virgin.

Attitude Towards Money

Hitler has no use for money personally and therefore very little interest in it, except for political purposes. He has virtually no financial sophistication; his lack of knowledge of even the practical details of finance, as of economics, is profound.

Nowadays what would he need money for? The state furnishes him with servants, residences, motor-cars. One of his last personal purchases was a new raincoat for the visit to Mussolini in June 1934. Incidentally, members of his staff got into trouble over this, because on their advice he carried only civilian clothes;

when he stepped from his aeroplane and saw Mussolini and all the Italians in uniform, he was ashamed of his mufti nakedness, and even suspected his advisers of purposely embarrassing him.

Hitler takes no salary from the state; rather he donates it to a fund which supports workmen who have suffered from labour accidents; but his private fortune could be considerable, if he chose to save. He announced late in 1935 that he – alone among statesmen – had no bank account or stocks or shares. Previous to this, it had been thought that he was part owner of Franz Eher & Co., Munich, the publishers of the chief Nazi organs, *Völkische Beobachter, Angriff*, etc. one of the biggest publishing houses in Europe. Its director, Max Amman, Hitler's former sergeant, was for many years his business manager.

If Hitler has no personal fortune, he must have turned all his earnings from his autobiography, *Mein Kampf*, to the party. This book is obligatory reading for Germans and at a high price (RM 7.20 or about twelve shillings) it has sold 5,200,000 copies since its publication in 1925, now being in its 494th edition. If his royalty is fifteen per cent, a moderate estimate, Hitler's total proceeds from this source at the end of 1939 should have been at least £600,000.

Nothing is more difficult in Europe than discovering the facts of the private fortunes of leading men. It is sacrosanct and thus forbidden ground to questioners in all countries . . . Does any dictator, Hitler or Mussolini or Stalin, carry cash in his pocket, or make actual purchases in cash? It is unlikely.

Attitude Towards Religion

Hitler was born and brought up a Roman Catholic. But he lost faith early and he attends no religious services of any kind. His catholicism means nothing to him; he is impervious even to the solace of confession. On being formed, his government almost immediately began a fierce religious war against Catholics, Protestants, and Jews alike.

Why? Perhaps the reason was not religion fundamentally, but politics. To Hitler the overwhelming first business of the Nazi revolution was the "unification", the *Gleichschaltung* (co-ordination) of Germany. He had one driving passion, the removal from the Reich of any competition, of whatever kind. The Vatican, like

Judaism, was a profoundly international (thus non-German) organism. Therefore – out with it.

The basis of much of the early domestic madness of Hitlerism was his incredibly severe and drastic desire to purge Germany of non-German elements, to create a hundred per cent Germany for one hundred per cent Germans only. He disliked bankers and department stores – as Dorothy Thompson pointed out – because they represented non-German, international, financial and commercial forces. He detested socialists and communists because they were affiliated with world groups aiming to internationalize labour. He loathed, above all, pacifists, because pacifists, opposing war, were internationalists.

Catholicism he considered a particularly dangerous competitive force, because it demands two allegiances of a man, and double allegiance was something Hitler could not countenance. Thus the campaign against the "black moles", as Nazis call priests. Several times German relations with the Vatican have neared breaking point. Protestantism was – theoretically – a simpler matter to deal with because the Lutheran Church presumably was German and nationalist. Hitler thought that by the simple installation of an army chaplain, a ferocious Nazi named Müller, as Reichbishop, he could "co-ordinate" the Evangelical Church in Germany, and turn it to his service. The idea of a united Protestant Church appealed to his neat, architect's mind. He was wrong. The church question has been an itching pot of trouble ever since. All through 1937 and 1938 it raged.

It was quite natural, following the confused failure to Nazify Protestantism, that some of Hitler's followers should have turned to Paganism. The Norse myths are a first-class nationalist substitute. Carried to its logical extreme, Nazism in fact demands the creation of a new and nationalist religion. Hitler indicated this in a speech at Nuremberg in September 1935. "Christianity," he said, "succeeded for a time in uniting the old Teutonic tribes, but the Reformation destroyed this unity. Germany is now a united nation. National socialism has succeeded where Christianity failed." And Heiden has quoted Hitler's remark: "We do not want any other God than Germany itself." This is a vital point. *Germany* is Hitler's religion.

One of Hitler's grudges against God is the fact that Jesus was a Jew. He can't forgive either Christians or Jews for this. And many Nazis *deny* that Jesus was Jewish. Another grudge is nationalist in origin. The basis of the Nazi revolution was the defeat of Germany in the War. Thus religion had to be Nazified because no God who permitted the French and other "inferior" races to win the War could be a satisfactory God for Germany.

Hitler's attempt to unify religion in Germany may lead to one danger. He himself may become a God. And divinity entails difficulties. Gods have to perform miracles.

Vividly in *Mein Kampf* Hitler tells the story of his first encounter with a Jew. He was a boy of seventeen, alone in Vienna, and he had never seen a Jew in his life. The Jew, a visitor from Poland or the Ukraine, in native costume, outraged the tender susceptibilities of the youthful Hitler. "Can this creature be a Jew?" he asked himself. Then, bursting on him, came a second question: "Can he possibly be a *German*?"

This early experience had a profound influence on him, forming the emotional base of his perfervid anti-Semitism. He was provincially mortified that any such creature could be one with himself, a sharer in German nationality. Later he "rationalized" his fury on economic and political grounds. Jews, he said, took jobs away from "Germans"; Jews controlled the Press of Berlin, the theatre, the arts; there were too many Jewish lawyers, doctors, professors; the Jews were a "pestilence, worse than the Black Death".

No one can properly conceive the basic depth and breadth of Hitler's anti-Semitism who has not carefully read *Mein Kampf*. The book was written almost fifteen years ago. He has changed it as edition followed edition, in minor particulars, but in all editions his anti-Jewish prejudice remains implacable.

Long before he became chancellor, Hitler would not allow himself to speak to a Jew even on the telephone. A publicist as well known as Walter Lippmann, a statesman as eminent as Lord Reading, would not be received at the Brown House. An interesting point arises. Has Hitler, in maturity, actually ever been in the company of a Jew, ever once talked to one? Possibly not.

"Am I My Brother's Keeper?"

Extreme precautions are, naturally, taken to guard Hitler against assassination. When he rides out in Berlin, he travels in a

Mercedes-Benz as big as a locomotive. Lieut Brückner, his chief aide, usually sits beside him. SS men with rifles may stand on the running-boards. If the occasion is ceremonial and large crowds are present, the route is lined with SS men (Black Shirts) alternately facing inward and outward.

Brückner is of great importance politically because he serves to block Hitler off from normal contacts. The complaint frequently is heard that Hitler is badly informed on even vital matters, because Brückner so isolates him from wide acquaintance; even advisers with the best intentions may have little chance of seeing him.

Not long ago Hitler broke his new rule against social affairs by visiting informally a diplomat and his wife who had been useful to him in earlier days. The diplomat talked to Hitler frankly and told him some honest truths. Hitler was upset. Then, the story says, Brückner descended on the diplomat, warning him under no circumstances to dare talk frankly to Hitler again.

Insurance rates on Hitler's life are quoted in London. A man with important business in Germany, which might be ruined by the terror and revolution which would very likely follow Hitler's assassination, paid £10 10s. per month for each £200 of insurance against Hitler's death.

Personal Sources of Power

Now we may proceed to summarize what might be called Hitler's positive qualities.

First of all, consider his single-mindedness, his intent fixity of purpose. His tactics may change; his strategy may change; his *aim*, never. His aim is to create a strong national Germany, with himself atop it. No opportunistic device, no zigzag in polemics, is too great for him; but the aim, the goal, never varies.

Associated with his single-mindedness is the quality of stamina. All dictators have stamina; all need it. Despite Hitler's flabbiness and lack of vigorous gesture, his physical endurance is considerable. I know interviewers who have talked to him on the eve of an election, after he has made several speeches a day, all over Germany, week on end; they found him fresh and even calm. "When I have a mission to fulfil, I will have the strength for it," he said.

Unlike most dictators, he has no great capacity for hard work, for industry; he is not the sloghorse that, for instance, Stalin is. He is not a good executive; his desk is usually high with documents requiring his decision which he neglects. He hates to make up his mind. His orders are often vague and contradictory.

Yet he gets a good deal of work done. "Industry" in a dictator or head of a state means, as a rule, ability to read and listen. The major part of the work of Hitler or Mussolini is perusal of reports and attention to the advice of experts and subordinates. Half their working time they spend in receiving information. Therefore it is necessary for a dictator (*a*) to choose men intelligently – many of Hitler's best men he inherited from the old civil service, (*b*) to instil faith in himself in them. Hitler has succeeded in this double task amply. And when his men fail him, he murders them.

Hitler's political sense is highly developed and acute. His calculations are shrewd and penetrating to the smallest detail. For instance, his first three major acts in foreign policy, Germany's departure from the League of Nations, the introduction of conscription, and the occupation of the Rhineland, were all deliberately set for Saturday afternoon, to ease the shock to opinion abroad. When he has something unpleasant to explain, the events of June 30th for instance, he usually speaks well after eight p.m. so that foreign newspapers can carry only a hurried and perhaps garbled account of his words.

He made good practical use of his anti-Semitism. The Jewish terror was, indeed, an excellent campaign manœuvre. The Nazis surged into power in March 1933 with an immense series of electoral pledges. They promised to end unemployment, rescind the Versailles Treaty, regain the Polish corridor, assimilate Austria, abolish department stores, socialize industry, eliminate interest on capital, give the people land. These aims were more easily talked about than achieved. One thing the Nazis could do. One pledge they could redeem – beat the Jews.

Hitler bases most decisions on intuition. Twice, on supreme occasions, it served him well. In the spring of 1932 his most powerful supporters, chiefly Roehm, pressed him to make a *Putsch*. Hitler refused, *feeling* absolute certainty that he could come to power in a legal manner. Again, in the autumn of 1932, after the Nazis had lost heavily in the November elections, a strong section of the party, led by Gregor Strasser, urged him to

admit defeat and enter a coalition government on disadvanta-
geous terms. Hitler, with consummate perspicacity, refused. And
within three months he reached power such as the maddest of his
followers had not dreamed of.

Another source of Hitler's power is his impersonality, as
Frances Gunther has pointed out. His vanity is extreme, but
in an odd way it is not personal. He has no peacockery. Mussolini
must have given autographed photographs to thousands of admirers since 1922. Those which Hitler has bestowed on friends
may be counted on the fingers of two hands. His vanity is the
more effective, because it expresses itself in non-personal terms.
He is the vessel, the instrument, of the will of the German people;
or so he pretends. Thus his famous statement, after the June 30th
murders, that for twenty-four hours he had been the supreme
court of Germany.

Heiden says that Hitler's power is based on intellect, and his
intellect on logic. This would seem a dubious interpretation
because Hitler's mind is not ratiocinative in the least: he is a
man of passion, of instinct, not of reason. His "intellect" is that of
a chameleon who knows when to change his colour; his "logic"
that of a panther who is hungry, and thus seeks food. He himself
has said – proudly – that he is a "somnambulist". Strange
giveway!

His brain is small, limited, vulgar, sly, narrow, and suspicious.
But behind it is the lamp of passion, and this passion has such
quality that it is immediately discernible and recognizable, like a
diamond in the sand. The range of his interests is so slight that
any sort of stimulus provokes the identical reflex: music, religion,
economics, mean nothing to him except exercise in German
nationalism.

Anthony Eden, when he visited Berlin in the spring of 1935,
and talked with Hitler seven hours, was quoted as saying that he
showed "complete mastery" of foreign affairs. This is, of course,
nonsense. Hitler does not know one-tenth as much about foreign
affairs, as, say, H.R. Knickerbocker, or F.A. Voigt, or Hamilton
Fish Armstrong, or Dorothy Thompson, or Mr Eden himself.
What Eden meant was that Hitler showed unflagging mastery of
his own view of foreign affairs.

WILLIAM L. SHIRER

FRANCE SURRENDERS

Berlin Diary, 1941

Shirer arrived in Berlin in 1934 as the correspondent for Universal News Service (although he later switched to Columbia Broadcasting Service). Most of his broadcasts were heavily censored by the Nazi authorities, but he kept a secret journal containing his true thoughts and observations. This was published as the bestselling *Berlin Diary* shortly after his arrival back in the USA in December 1940. Here is his entry for 21 June 1940, the day France capitulated to Germany and signed a formal surrender. The signing took place in a railway carriage at Compiègne, France.

On the exact spot in the little clearing in the Forest of Compiègne where, at five a.m. on 11 November 1918, the armistice which ended the World War was signed, Adolf Hitler today handed *his* armistice terms to France. To make German revenge complete, the meeting of the German and French plenipotentiaries took place in Marshal Foch's private [railway] car, in which Foch laid down the armistice terms to Germany twenty-two years ago. Even the same table in the rickety old *wagon-lit* car was used. And through the windows we saw Hitler occupying the very seat on which Foch had sat at that table when he dictated the other armistice.

The humiliation of France, of the French, was complete. And yet in the preamble to the armistice terms Hitler told the French that he had not chosen this spot at Compiègne out of revenge; merely to right an old wrong. From the demeanour of the French delegates I gathered that they did not appreciate the difference . . .

The armistice negotiations began at three fifteen p.m. A warm June sun beat down on the great elm and pine trees, and cast pleasant shadows on the wooded avenues as Hitler, with the German plenipotentiaries at his side, appeared. He alighted from his car in front of the French monument to Alsace-Lorraine which stands at the end of an avenue about 200 yards from the clearing where the armistice car waited on exactly the same spot it occupied twenty-two years ago.

The Alsace-Lorraine statue, I noted, was covered with German war flags so that you could not see its sculptured work nor read its inscription. But I had seen it some years before – the large sword representing the sword of the Allies, and its point sticking into a large, limp eagle, representing the old Empire of the Kaiser. And the inscription underneath in French saying: "TO THE HEROIC SOLDIERS OF FRANCE . . . DEFENDERS OF THE COUNTRY AND OF RIGHT . . . GLORIOUS LIBERATORS OF ALSACE-LORRAINE."

Through my glasses I saw the Führer stop, glance at the monument, observe the Reich flags with their big swastikas in the centre. Then he strode slowly towards us, towards the little clearing in the woods. I observed his face. It was grave, solemn, yet brimming with revenge. There was also in it, as in his springy step, a note of the triumphant conqueror, the defier of the world. There was something else, difficult to describe, in his expression, a sort of scornful, inner joy at being present at this great reversal of fate – a reversal he himself had wrought.

Now he reaches the little opening in the woods. He pauses and looks slowly around. The clearing is in the form of a circle some 200 yards in diameter and laid out like a park. Cypress trees line it all round – and behind them, the great elms and oaks of the forest. This has been one of France's national shrines for twenty-two years. From a discreet position on the perimeter of the circle we watch.

Hitler pauses, and gazes slowly around. In a group just behind him are the other German plenipotentiaries: Göring, grasping his field-marshal's baton in one hand. He wears the sky-blue uniform of the air force. All the Germans are in uniform, Hitler in a double-breasted grey uniform, with the Iron Cross hanging from his left breast pocket. Next to Göring are the two German army chiefs – General Keitel, chief of the Supreme Command, and General von Brauchitsch, commander-in-chief of the German army. Both are just approaching sixty, but look younger, especially Keitel, who had a dapper appearance with his cap slightly cocked on one side.

242 BERLIN DIARY, *1941*

Then there is Erich Raeder, Grand Admiral of the German Fleet, in his blue naval uniform and the invariable upturned collar which German naval officers usually wear. There are two non-military men in Hitler's suite – his Foreign Minister, Joachim von Ribbentrop, in the field-grey uniform of the Foreign Office; and Rudolf Hess, Hitler's deputy, in a grey party uniform.

The time is now three eighteen p.m. Hitler's personal flag is run up on a small standard in the centre of the opening.

Also in the centre is a great granite block which stands some three feet above the ground. Hitler, followed by the others, walks slowly over to it, steps up, and reads the inscription engraved in great high letters on that block. It says: "HERE ON THE ELEVENTH OF NOVEMBER 1918 SUCCUMBED THE CRIMINAL PRIDE OF THE GERMAN EMPIRE . . . VANQUISHED BY THE FREE PEOPLES WHICH IT TRIED TO ENSLAVE."

Hitler reads it and Göring reads it. They all read it, standing there in the June sun and the silence. I look for the expression on Hitler's face. I am but fifty yards from him and see him through my glasses as though he were directly in front of me. I have seen that face many times at the great moments of his life. But today! It is afire with scorn, anger, hate, revenge, triumph. He steps off the monument and contrives to make even this gesture a masterpiece of contempt. He glances back at it, contemptuous, angry – angry, you almost feel, because he cannot wipe out the awful, provoking lettering with one sweep of his high Prussian boot. He glances slowly around the clearing, and now, as his eyes meet ours, you grasp the depth of his hatred. But there is triumph there too – revengeful, triumphant hate. Suddenly, as though his face were not giving quite complete expression to his feelings, he throws his whole body into harmony with his mood. He swiftly snaps his hands on his hips, arches his shoulders, plants his feet wide apart. It is a magnificent gesture of defiance, of burning contempt for this place now and all that it has stood for in the twenty-two years since it witnessed the humbling of the German Empire . . .

It is now three twenty-three p.m. and the Germans stride over to the armistice car. For a moment or two they stand in the sunlight outside the car, chatting. Then Hitler steps up into the car, followed by the others. We can see nicely through the car windows. Hitler takes the place occupied by Marshal Foch when the 1918 armistice terms were signed. The others spread themselves around him. Four chairs on the opposite side of the table from Hitler remain empty. The French have not yet appeared. But we do not wait long. Exactly at three thirty p.m. they alight from a car. They have flown up from Bordeaux to a nearby landing field. They too glance at the Alsace-Lorraine memorial but it's a swift glance. Then they walk down the avenue flanked by three German officers. We see them now as they come into the sunlight of the clearing.

General Huntziger, wearing a bleached khaki uniform, Air General Bergeret and Vice-Admiral Le Luc, both in dark blue uniforms, and then, almost buried in the uniforms, M Noël, French Ambassador to Poland. The German guard of honour, drawn up at the entrance to the clearing, snaps to attention for the French as they pass, but it does not present arms.

It is a grave hour in the life of France. The Frenchmen keep their eyes straight ahead. Their faces are solemn, drawn. They are the picture of tragic dignity.

They walk stiffly to the car, where they are met by two German officers, Lieutenant-General Tippelskirch, Quartermaster General, and Colonel Thomas, chief of the Führer's headquarters. The Germans salute. The French salute. The atmosphere is what Europeans call "correct". There are salutes, but no handshakes.

Now we get our picture through the dusty windows of that old *wagon-lit* car. Hitler and the other German leaders rise as the French enter the drawing-room. Hitler gives the Nazi salute, the arm raised. Ribbentrop and Hess do the same. I cannot see M Noël to notice whether he salutes or not.

Hitler, as far as we can see through the windows, does not say a word to the French or to anybody else. He nods to General Keitel at his side. We see General Keitel adjusting his papers. Then he starts to read. He is reading the preamble to the German armistice terms. The French sit there with marble-like faces and listen intently. Hitler and Göring glance at the green tabletop.

The reading of the preamble lasts but a few minutes. Hitler, we soon observe, has no intention of remaining very long, of listening to the reading of the armistice terms themselves. At three forty-two p.m., twelve minutes after the French arrive, we see

Hitler stand up, salute stiffly, and then stride out of the drawing-room, followed by Göring, Brauchitsch, Raeder, Hess, and Ribbentrop. The French, like figures of stone, remain at the green-topped table. General Keitel remains with them. He starts to read them the detailed conditions of the armistice.

Hitler and his aides stride down the avenue towards the Alsace-Lorraine monument, where their cars are waiting. As they pass the guard of honour, the German band strikes up the two national anthems, *Deutschland, Deutschland über Alles* and the *Horst Wessel* song. The whole ceremony in which Hitler has reached a new pinnacle in his meteoric career and Germany avenged the 1918 defeat is over in a quarter of an hour.

A REPORT DURING THE BLITZ

CBS Radio, 13 September 1940

Murrow was the European director for CBS. His radio dispatches during the Battle of Britain and the Blitz (with their trademark "This is London . . ." openings) were particularly resonant, and widely admired alike by his peers and the audience back home in the USA. The report below was broadcast shortly after the Luftwaffe began the Blitz, the mass bombing of London.

This is London at 3:30 in the morning. This has been what might be called a "routine night" – air-raid alarm at about 9 o'clock and intermittent bombing ever since. I had the impression that more high explosives and few incendiaries have been used tonight. Only two small fires can be seen on the horizon. Again the Germans have been sending their bombers in singly or in pairs. The antiaircraft barrage has been fierce but sometimes there have been periods of twenty minutes when London has been silent. Then the big red buses would start up and move on till the guns started working again. That silence is almost harder to bear. One becomes accustomed to rattling windows and the distant sound of bombs and then there comes a silence that can be felt. You know the sound will return – you wait, and then it starts again. That waiting is bad. It gives you a chance to imagine things. I have been walking tonight – there is a full moon, and the dirty-grey buildings appear white. The stars, the empty windows, are hidden. It's a beautiful and lonesome city where men and women and children are trying to snatch a few hours' sleep underground.

In the fashionable residential districts I could read the TO LET signs on the front of big houses in the light of the bright moon. Those houses have big basements underneath – good shelters, but they're not being used. Many people think they should be.

The scale of this air war is so great that the reporting is not easy. Often we spend hours traveling about this sprawling city, viewing damage, talking with people, and occasionally listening to the bombs coming down, and then more hours wondering what you'd like to hear about these people who are citizens of no mean city. We've told you about the bombs, the fires, the smashed houses, and the courage of the people. We've read you the communiqués and tried to give you an honest estimate of the wounds inflicted upon this, the best bombing target in the world. But the business of living and working in this city is very personal – the little incidents, the things the mind retains, are in themselves unimportant, but they somehow weld together to form the hard core of memories that will remain when the last "all-clear" has sounded. That's why I want to talk for just three or four minutes about the things we haven't talked about before; for many of these impressions it is necessary to reach back through only one long week. There was a rainbow bending over the battered and smoking East End of London just when the "all-clear" sounded one afternoon. One night I stood in front of a smashed grocery store and heard a dripping inside. It was the only sound in all London. Two cans of peaches had been drilled clean through by flying glass and the juice was dripping down onto the floor.

There was a flower shop in the East End. Nearly every other building in the block had been smashed. There was a funeral wreath in the window of the shop – price: three shillings and sixpence, less than a dollar. In front of Buckingham Palace there's a bed of red and white flowers – untouched – the reddest flowers I've ever seen.

Last night, or rather early this morning, I met a distinguished member of Parliament in a bar. He had been dining with Anthony Eden and had told the Secretary for War that he wouldn't walk through the streets with all that shrapnel falling about, and as a good host Eden should send him home in a tank. Another man came in and reported, on good authority, that the Prime Minister had a siren suit, one of those blue woollen coverall affairs with a zipper. Someone said the Prime Minister must resemble a barrage balloon when attired in his siren suit.

Things of that sort can still be said in this country. The fact that the noise – just the sound, not the blast – of bombs and guns can cause one to stagger while walking down the street came as a surprise. When I entered my office today, after bombs had fallen two blocks away, and was asked by my English secretary if I'd care for a cup of tea, that didn't come as much of a surprise.

Talking from a studio with a few bodies lying about on the floor, sleeping on mattresses, still produces a strange feeling but we'll probably get used to that. Today I went to buy a hat – my favourite shop had gone, blown to bits. The windows of my shoe store were blown out. I decided to have a haircut; the windows of the barbershop were gone, but the Italian barber was still doing business. Someday, he said, we smile again, but the food it doesn't taste so good since being bombed. I went on to another shop to buy flashlight batteries. I bought three. The clerk said: "You needn't buy so many. We'll have enough for the whole winter." But I said: "What if you aren't here?" There were buildings down in that street, and he replied: "Of course, we'll be here. We've been in business here for a hundred and fifty years."

But the sundown scene in London can never be forgotten – the time when people pick up their beds and walk to the shelter.

O.D. GALLAGHER

THE LOSS OF *REPULSE*

Daily Express, 12 December 1941

The principal cause of the extension of World War II to the Far East was Japan's decision to acquire a Pacific empire. She had invaded China in the 1930s but the jewels she truly coveted were the colonial possessions of the British, the French and the Dutch. This imperial desire also led directly to hostilities with the USA, which was zealously protective of her influence in the region. By 7 December 1941 the Pacific was aflame as Japanese units simultaneously attacked Pearl Harbor, Hong Kong, Wake Island, Guam and Midway. To protect the great naval base of Singapore, the British dispatched a surface fleet to intercept Japanese invasion forces while they were still at sea, but in the event the British were spotted first, and attacked by swarms of Japanese fighter-bombers. The British fleet had no fighter protection. The battleships HMS *Repulse* and HMS *Prince of Wales* were sunk within a single hour on 10 December. Two months later Singapore fell to the army of Nippon.

This is the simple story of a naval force which went into north-eastern Malayan waters on Monday. *Prince of Wales* and *Repulse* were the backbone of this force. I was in *Repulse*. The aim of the force was, in the words of the signal C-in-C Admiral Sir Tom Phillips sent to all ships: "The enemy has made several landings on the north coast of Malaya and has made local progress. Meanwhile fast transports lie off the coast. This is our opportunity before the enemy can establish himself.

"We have made a wide circuit to avoid air reconnaissance and hope to surprise the enemy shortly after sunrise to-morrow (Wednesday). We may have the luck to try our metal against the old Jap battle cruiser *Kongo* or against some Jap cruisers or destroyers in the Gulf of Siam.

"We are sure to get some useful practices with our high-angle armament, but whatever we meet I want to finish quickly and get well clear to eastward before the Japanese can mass a too formidable scale of air attack against us. So shoot to sink."

But at 5.20 that same evening a bugle sounded throughout my ship *Repulse* over the ship's loud-speakers, giving immediate orders to the whole ship's company and filling every space of engine room and wardroom with its urgent bugle notes, followed by the order: "Action stations. Enemy aircraft!"

I rushed on to the flag deck which was my action station. It was a single Nakajama Naka 93 twin-floated Jap reconnaissance plane. She kept almost on the horizon, too far for engagement, for a couple of hours.

A voice from the bridge came out of the loud-speakers: "We are being shadowed by enemy aircraft. Keep ready for immediate action to repel aircraft."

Two more Nakajama Naka 93s appeared. They kept a long relay watch on us. What an admiral most wishes to avoid has happened.

His ships were out at sea, sufficiently distant from shore to prevent him receiving air support before dawn the following morning, when a mass enemy air attack now seemed certain. We had not yet sighted any enemy naval force or received reports of an enemy transport convoy.

For dinner in our wardroom that night we had hot soup, cold beef, ham, meat pie, oranges, bananas, pineapples, and coffee. We discussed this unfortunate happening. We had travelled all day in good visibility without being spotted. Now, as the last hour of darkness fell, a lucky Jap had found us.

One of the *Repulse*'s Fleet Air Arm pilots who fly the ship's aircraft – this one a young New Zealander with a ginger beard – came in cursing: "My God! Someone's blacked the right eye of my air-gunner – the one he shoots with." The laughter ended. Everyone was fitted with a tight-fitting asbestos helmet which makes you look like a Disney drawing. We were all expecting action at dawn to-morrow, hoping to meet a Jap cruiser. At 9.05 p.m. came a voice from the loudspeakers: "Stand by for the Captain to speak to you."

Captain: "A signal has just been received from the Commander-in-Chief. We were shadowed by three planes. We were spotted after dodging them all day. Their troop convoy will now have dispersed. We will find enemy aircraft waiting for us now. We are now returning to Singapore."

Then followed a babble of voices and groans. A voice said: "This ship will never get into action. It's too lucky."

So it was. In the message from the Captain the previous day, in which he said: "We're going looking for trouble and I expect we shall find it," he noted that *Repulse* had travelled 53,000 miles in this war without action, although it trailed the *Bismarck* and was off northern Norway and has convoyed throughout the war.

I slept in the wardroom fully clothed that night and awoke to the call "Action stations" at 5 a.m. on Wednesday. It was a thin oriental dawn, when a cool breeze swept through the fuggy ship, which had been battened down all night as a result of the order to "darken ship".

The sky was luminous as pearl. We saw from the flag deck a string of black objects on the port bow. They turned out to be a line of landing barges, "like railway trucks", as a young signaller said. At 6.30 a.m. the loud-speaker voice announced: "Just received message saying enemy is making landing north of Singapore. We're going in."

We all rushed off to breakfast, which consisted of coffee, cold ham, bread, and marmalade. Back at action stations all the ship's company kept a look-out. We cruised in line-ahead formation, *Prince of Wales* leading, the *Repulse* second, and with our destroyer screen out.

Down the Malayan coast, examining with the help of terrier-like destroyers all coves for enemy landing parties.

At 7.55 a.m. *Prince of Wales* catapulted one of her planes on reconnaissance, with instructions not to return to the ship, but to land ashore after making a report to us on what she found.

We watched her become midget-size and drop out of sight behind two hummock-back islands, behind which was a beach invisible to us. We all thought that was where the enemy lay. But it reappeared and went on, still searching.

Meanwhile all the ship's company on deck had put on anti-flash helmets, elbow-length asbestos gloves, goggles and tin hats.

Prince of Wales looked magnificent. White-tipped waves rippled over her plunging bows. The waves shrouded them with watery lace, then they rose high again and once again dipped. She rose and fell so methodically that the effect of staring at her was hypnotic. The fresh breeze blew her White Ensign out stiff as a board.

I felt a surge of excited anticipation rise within me at the prospect of her and the rest of the force sailing into enemy landing parties and their escorting warships.

A young Royal Marines lieutenant who was my escort when first I went aboard the *Repulse* told me: "We've not had any action but we're a perfect team – the whole twelve hundred and sixty of us. We've been working together so long. We claim to have the Navy's best gunners."

My anticipatory reverie was broken by the voice from the loudspeakers again: "Hello, there. Well, we've sighted nothing yet, but we'll go down the coast having a look for them."

More exclamations of disappointment. The yeoman of signals said: "Don't say this one's off, too."

As we sped down-Malaya's changing coastline the wag of the flag-deck said travel-talkwise: "On the starboard beam, dear listeners, you see the beauty spots of Malaya, land of the orang-outang."

Again the loud-speaker announces: "Nothing sighted."

The *Repulse* sends off one of her aircraft. The pilot is not the ginger-bearded New Zealander, as he tossed a coin with another pilot and lost the toss, which means that he stays behind.

We drift to the wardroom again until 10.20 a.m. We are spotted again by a twin-engined snooper of the same type as attacked Singapore the first night of this new war.

We can do nothing about it, as she keeps well beyond range while her crew presumably studies our outlines and compares them with silhouettes in the Jap equivalent of *Jane's Fighting Ships*.

At 11 a.m. a twin-masted single funnel ship is sighted on the starboard bow. The force goes to investigate her. She carries no flag.

I was looking at her through my telescope when the shock of an explosion made me jump so that I nearly poked my right eye out. It was 11.15 a.m. The explosion came from the *Prince of Wales*'s portside secondary armament. She was firing at a single aircraft.

We open fire. There are about six aircraft.

A three-quarter-inch screw falls on my tin hat from the bridge deck above from the shock of explosion of the guns. "The old tub's falling to bits," observes the yeoman of signals.

That was the beginning of a superb air attack by the Japanese, whose air force was an unknown quantity.

Officers in the *Prince of Wales* whom I met in their wardroom when she arrived here last week said they expected some unorthodox flying from the Japs. "The great danger will be the possibility of these chaps flying their whole aircraft into a ship and committing hara-kiri."

It was nothing like that. It was most orthodox. They even came at us in formation, flying low and close.

Aboard the *Repulse*, I found observers as qualified as anyone to estimate Jap flying abilities. They know from first-hand experience what the RAF and the Luftwaffe are like. Their verdict was: "The Germans have never done anything like this in the North Sea, Atlantic or anywhere else we have been."

They concentrated on the two capital ships, taking the *Prince of Wales* first and the *Repulse* second. The destroyer screen they left completely alone except for damaged planes forced to fly low over them when they dropped bombs defensively.

At 11.18 the *Prince of Wales* opened a shattering barrage with all her multiple pom-poms, or Chicago Pianos as they call them. Red and blue flames poured from the eight-gun muzzles of each battery. I saw glowing tracer shells describe shallow curves as they went soaring skyward surrounding the enemy planes. Our Chicago Pianos opened fire; also our triple-gun four-inch high-angle turrets. The uproar was so tremendous I seemed to feel it.

From the starboard side of the flag-deck I could see two torpedo planes. No, they were bombers. Flying straight at us.

All our guns pour high-explosives at them, including shells so delicately fused that they explode if they merely graze cloth fabric.

But they swing away, carrying out a high-powered evasive action without dropping anything at all. I realize now what the purpose of the action was. It was a diversion to occupy all our guns and observers on the air defence platform at the summit of the mainmast.

There is a heavy explosion and the *Repulse* rocks. Great patches of paint fall from the funnel on to the flag-deck. We all gaze above our heads to see planes which during the action against the low fliers were unnoticed.

They are high-level bombers. Seventeen thousand feet. The

first bomb, the one that rocked us a moment ago, scored a direct hit on the catapult deck through the one hangar on the port side.

I am standing behind a multiple Vickers gun, one which fires 2,000 half-inch bullets per minute. It is at the after end of the flag-deck.

I see a cloud of smoke rising from the place where the final bomb hit. Another comes down bang again from 17,000 feet. It explodes in the sea, making a creamy blue and green patch ten feet across. The *Repulse* rocks again. It was three fathoms from the port side. It was a miss, so no one bothers.

Cooling fluid is spouting from one of the barrels of a Chicago Piano. I can see black paint on the funnel-shaped covers at the muzzles of the eight barrels actually rising in blisters big as fists.

The boys manning them – there are ten to each – are sweating, saturating their asbestos anti-flash helmets. The whole gun swings this way and that as spotters pick planes to be fired at.

Two planes can be seen coming at us. A spotter sees another at a different angle, but much closer.

He leans forward, his face tight with excitement, urgently pounding the back of the gun swiveller in front of him. He hits that back with his right hand and points with the left a stabbing forefinger at a single sneaker plane. Still blazing two-pounders the whole gun platform turns in a hail of death at the single plane. It is some 1,000 yards away.

I saw tracers rip into its fuselage dead in the centre. Its fabric opened up like a rapidly spreading sore with red edges. Fire . . .

It swept to the tail, and in a moment stabilizer and rudder became a framework skeleton. Her nose dipped down and she went waterward.

We cheered like madmen. I felt my larynx tearing in the effort to make myself heard above the hellish uproar of guns.

A plane smacked the sea on its belly and was immediately transformed into a gigantic shapeless mass of fire which shot over the waves fast as a snake's tongue. The *Repulse* had got the first raider.

For the first time since the action began we can hear a sound from the loud-speakers, which are on every deck at every action station. It is the sound of a bugle.

Its first notes are somewhat tortured. The young bugler's lips and throat are obviously dry with excitement. It is that most sinister alarm of all for seamen: "Fire!"

Smoke from our catapult deck is thick now. Men in overalls, their faces hidden by a coat of soot, man-handle hoses along decks. Water fountains delicately from a rough patch made in one section by binding it with a white shirt.

It sprays on the Vickers gunners, who, in a momentary lull, lift faces, open mouths and put out tongues to catch the cooling jets. They quickly avert faces to spit – the water is salt and it is warm. It is sea water.

The Chicago Piano opens up again with a suddenness that I am unable to refrain from flinching at, though once they get going with their erratic shell-pumping it is most reassuring.

All aboard have said the safest place in any battleship or cruiser or destroyer is behind a Chicago Piano. I believe them.

Empty brass cordite cases are tumbling out of the gun's scuttle-like exit so fast and so excitedly it reminds me of the forbidden fruit machine in Gibraltar on which I once played. It went amok on one occasion and ejected £8 in shillings in a frantic rush.

The cases bounce off the steel C deck, roll and dance down the sloping base into a channel for easy picking up later.

At 11.25 we see an enormous splash on the very edge of the horizon. The splash vanishes and a whitish cloud takes its place.

A damaged enemy plane jettisoning its bombs or another enemy destroyed? A rapid Gallup poll on the flag deck says: "Another duck down." Duck is a word they have rapidly taken from the Aussie Navy. It means enemy plane.

Hopping about the flag-deck from port to starboard, which-ever side is being attacked, is the plump figure of the naval photographer named Tubby Abrahams.

He was a Fleet Street agency pictureman now in the Navy. But all his pictures are lost. He had to throw them into the sea with his camera. He was saved. So was United States broadcaster Cecil Brown, of Columbia System.

Fire parties are still fighting the hangar outbreak, oblivious of any air attack used so far. Bomb splinters have torn three holes in the starboard side of the funnel on our flag-deck.

Gazing impotently with no more than fountain pen and note-book in my hands while gunners, signallers, surgeons and range-finders worked, I found emotional release in shouting rather stupidly, I suppose, at the Japanese.

I discovered depths of obscenity previously unknown, even to me.

One young signaller keeps passing me pieces of information in between running up flats. He has just said: "A couple of blokes are caught in the lift from galley to servery. They're trying to get them out."

The yeoman of signals interjected: "How the bloody hell they got there, God knows."

There is a short lull. The boys dig inside their overalls and pull out cigarettes. Then the loud-speaker voice: "Enemy aircraft ahead." Lighted ends are nipped off cigarettes. The ship's company goes into action again. "Twelve of them." The flag-deck boys whistle. Someone counts them aloud: "One, two, three, four, five, six, seven, eight, nine – yes, nine." The flag-deck wag, as he levels a signalling lamp at the *Prince of Wales*: "Any advance on nine? Anybody? No? Well, here they come."

It is 12.10 p.m. They are all concentrating on the *Prince of Wales*. They are after the big ships all right. A mass of water and smoke rises in a tree-like column from the *Prince of Wales*'s stern. They've got her with a torpedo.

A ragged-edged mass of flame from her Chicago Piano does not stop them, nor the heavy instant flashes from her high-angle secondary armament.

She is listing to port – a bad list. We are about six cables from her.

A snottie, or midshipman, runs past, calls as he goes: "*Prince of Wales*'s steering gear gone." It doesn't seem possible that those slight-looking planes could do that to her.

The planes leave us, having apparently dropped all their bombs and torpedoes. I don't believe it is over, though. "Look, look!" shouts someone, "there's a line in the water right under our bows, growing longer on the starboard side. A torpedo that missed us. Wonder where it'll stop."

The *Prince of Wales* signals us again asking if we've been torpedoed. Our Captain Tennant replies: "Not yet. We've dodged nineteen."

Six stokers arrive on the flag-deck. They are black with smoke and oil and are in need of first aid. They are ushered down to the armoured citadel at the base of the mainmast.

The *Prince of Wales*'s list is increasing. There is a great rattle of empty two-pounder cordite cases as Chicago Piano boys gather up the empties and stow them away and clear for further action.

12.20 p.m. . . . The end is near, although I didn't know it.

A new wave of planes appears, flying around us in formation and gradually coming nearer. The *Prince of Wales* lies about ten cables astern of our port side. She is helpless.

They are making for her. I don't know how many. They are splitting up our guns as they realize they are after her, knowing she can't dodge their torpedoes. So we fire at them to defend the *Prince of Wales* rather than attend to our own safety.

The only analogy I can think of to give an impression of the *Prince of Wales* in those last moments is of a mortally wounded tiger trying to beat off the *coup de grâce*.

Her outline is hardly distinguishable in smoke and flame from all her guns except the fourteen-inchers. I can see one plane release a torpedo. It drops nose heavy into the sea and churns up a small wake as it drives straight at the *Prince of Wales*. It explodes against her bows.

A couple of seconds later another explodes amidships and another astern. Gazing at her turning over on the port side with her stern going under and with dots of men leaping from her, I was thrown against the bulkhead by a tremendous shock as the *Repulse* takes a torpedo on her portside stern.

With all others on the flag-deck I am wondering where it came from, when the *Repulse* shudders gigantically. Another torpedo.

Now men cheering with more abandon than at a Cup Final. What the heck is this? I wonder. Then see it is another plane down. It hits the sea in flames also. There have been six so far as I know.

My notebook, which I have got before me, is stained with oil and is ink-blurred. It says: "Third torp."

The *Repulse* now listing badly to starboard. The loud-speakers speak for the last time: "Everybody on main deck."

We all troop down ladders, most orderly except for one lad who climbs the rail and is about to jump when an officer says: "Now then – come back – we are all going your way." The boy came back and joined the line.

It seemed slow going. Like all the others I suppose I was tempted to leap to the lower deck, but the calmness was catching. When we got to the main deck the list was so bad our shoes and feet could not grip the steel deck. I kicked off mine, and my damp stockinged feet made for sure movement.

Nervously opening my cigarette case I found I hadn't a match.

I offered a cigarette to a man beside me. He said: "Ta. Want a match?" We both lit up and puffed once or twice. He said: "I'll be seeing you, mate." To which I replied: "Hope so, cheerio."

We were all able to walk down the ship's starboard side, she lay so much over to port.

We all formed a line along a big protruding anti-torpedo blister, from where we had to jump some twelve feet into a sea which was black – I discovered it was oil.

I remember jamming my cap on my head, drawing a breath and leaping.

Oh, I forgot – the last entry in my notebook was: "Sank about 12.20 p.m." I made it before leaving the flag-deck. In the water I glimpsed the *Prince of Wales*'s bows disappearing.

Kicking with all my strength, I with hundreds of others tried to get away from the *Repulse* before she went under, being afraid of getting drawn under in the whirlpool.

I went in the wrong direction, straight into the still spreading oil patch, which felt almost as thick as velvet. A wave hit me and swung me round so that I saw the last of the *Repulse*.

Her underwater plates were painted a bright, light red. Her bows rose high as the air trapped inside tried to escape from underwater forward regions, and there she hung for a second or two and easily slid out of sight.

I had a tremendous feeling of loneliness, and could see nothing capable of carrying me. I kicked, lying on my back, and felt my eyes burning as the oil crept over me, in mouth, nostrils, and hair.

When swamped by the waves, I remember seeing the water I spurted from my mouth was black. I came across two men hanging on to a round lifebelt. They were black, and I told them they looked like a couple of Al Jolsons. They said: "Well, we must be a trio, 'cos you're the same."

We were joined by another, so we had an Al Jolson quarter on one lifebelt. It was too much for it and in the struggle to keep it lying flat on the sea we lost it.

We broke up, with the possibility of meeting again, but none of us would know the other, owing to the complete mask of oil.

I kicked, I must confess somewhat panicky, to escape from the oil, but all I achieved was a bumping into a floating paravane. Once again there were four black faces with red eyes gathered together in the sea.

Then we saw a small motor boat with two men in it. The engine was broken. I tried to organize our individual strength into a concerted drive to reach the idly floating boat. We tried to push or pull ourselves by hanging on the paravane, kicking our legs, but it was too awkward, and it overturned.

I lost my grip and went under. My underwater struggles happily took me nearer to the boat.

After about two hours in the water, two hours of oil-fuel poisoning, I reached a thin wire rope which hung from the boat's bows.

My fingers were numb and I was generally weak as the result of the poisoning, but I managed to hold on to the wire by clamping my arms around it. I called to the men aboard to help me climb the four feet to the deck.

They tried with a boat hook, but finally said: "You know, we are pretty done in, too. You've got to try to help yourself. We can't do it alone."

I said I could not hold anything. They put the boathook in my shirt collar, but it tore and finally they said: "Sorry pal, we can't lift you. Have you got that wire?"

"Yes," I said. They let me go and there I hung. Another man arrived and caught the wire. He was smaller than I was. I am thirteen stone. The men aboard said they would try to get him up. "He's lighter than you," they said.

They got him aboard during which operation I went under again when he put his foot on my shoulder. The mouth of one black face aboard opened and showed black-slimed teeth, red gums and tongue. It said: "To hell with this."

He dived through the oil into the sea, popped up beside me with a round lifebelt which he put over my head, saying: "Okay. Now let go the wire."

But I'm sorry to say I couldn't. I couldn't bear to part with it. It had kept me on the surface about fifteen minutes.

They separated us, however, and the next thing I was draped through the lifebelt like a dummy being hauled aboard at a rope's end, which they could grip as it was not oily or shiny.

Another oil casualty was dragged aboard, and later thirty of us were lifted aboard a destroyer. We were stripped, bathed and left naked on the fo'c'sle benches and tables to sweat the oil out of the pores in the great heat.

THE DEATH OF CAPTAIN WASKOW

Washington Daily News, 10 January 1944

Although Pyle despaired of the following column on the death of Captain Waskow ("This stuff stinks"), when the editors at the *Daily News* received it, they recognized its true value and devoted the day's entire front page to it. He won the Pulitzer Prize later in the same year. Pyle was killed reporting the war against Japan.

At the front lines in Italy. Jan. 10 (By Wireless) – In this war I have known a lot of officers who were loved and respected by the soldiers under them. But never have I crossed the trail of any man as beloved as Capt. Henry T. Waskow of Belton, Tex.

Capt. Waskow was a company commander in the 36th Division. He had been in this company since long before he left the States. He was very young, only in his middle twenties, but he carried in him a sincerity and gentleness that made people want to be guided by him.

"After my own father, he comes next," a sergeant told me.

"He always looked after us," a soldier said. "He'd go to bat for us every time."

"I've never known him to do anything unkind," another one said.

I was at the foot of the mule trail the night they brought Capt. Waskow down. The moon was nearly full, and you could see far up the trail, and even part way across the valley. Soldiers made shadows as they walked.

Dead men had been coming down the mountain all evening, lashed onto the backs of mules. They came lying belly down across the wooden packsaddle, their heads hanging down on the left side of the mule, their stiffened legs sticking awkwardly from the other side, bobbing up and down as the mule walked.

The Italian mule skinners were afraid to walk beside dead men, so Americans had to lead the mules down that night. Even the Americans were reluctant to unlash and lift off the bodies, when they got to the bottom, so an officer had to do it himself and ask others to help.

The first one came early in the morning. They slid him down from the mule, and stood him on his feet for a moment. In the half light he might have been merely a sick man standing there leaning on the other. Then they laid him on the ground in the shadow of the stone wall alongside the road.

I don't know who that first one was. You feel small in the presence of dead men, and you don't ask silly questions . . .

We left him there beside the road, that first one, and we all went back into the cowshed and sat on watercans or lay on the straw, waiting for the next batch of mules.

Somebody said the dead soldier had been dead for four days, and then nobody said anything more about him. We talked for an hour or more; the dead man lay all alone, outside in the shadow of the wall.

Then a soldier came into the cowshed and said there were some more bodies outside. We went out into the road. Four mules stood there in the moonlight, in the road where the trail came down off the mountain. The soldiers who led them stood there waiting.

"This one is Capt. Waskow," one of them said quickly.

Two men unlashed his body from the mule and lifted it off and laid it in the shadow beside the stone wall. Other men took the other bodies off. Finally, there were five lying end to end in a long row. You don't cover up dead men in the combat zones. They just lie there in the shadows until somebody else comes after them.

The uncertain mules moved off to their olive groves. The men in the road seemed reluctant to leave. They stood around, and gradually I could sense them moving, one by one, close to Capt. Waskow's body. Not so much to look, I think, as to say something in finality to him and to themselves. I stood close by and I could hear.

One soldier came and looked down, and he said our loud:
"God damn it!"

Another one came, and he said. "God damn it to hell anyway!"
He looked down for a few last moments and then turned and left.

Another man came. I think he was an officer. It was hard to tell
officers from men in the dim light, for everybody was grimy and
dirty. The man looked down into the dead captain's face and then
spoke directly to him, as tho he were alive:

"I'm sorry, old man."

Then a soldier came and stood beside the officer and bent over,
and he too spoke to his dead captain, not in a whisper but awfully
tender, and he said:

"I sure am sorry, sir."

Then the first man squatted down, and he reached down and
took the Captain's hand, and he sat there a full five minutes
holding the dead hand in his own and looking intently into the
dead face. And he never uttered a sound all the time he sat there.

Finally he put the hand down. He reached up and gently
straightened the points of the Captain's shirt collar, and then
he sort of rearranged the tattered edges of his uniform around the
wound, and then he got up and walked away down the road in the
moonlight, all alone.

The rest of us went back into the cowshed, leaving the five
dead men lying in a line, end to end, in the shadow of the low
stone wall. We lay down on the straw in the cowshed, and pretty
soon we were all asleep.

WILLIAM L. LAURENCE

A MUSHROOM CLOUD

New York Times, 3 September 1945

Nicknamed "Atomic Bill" for his interest in the development of the A-bomb, Laurence missed the Hiroshima mission but was aboard a B-29 on 9 August 1945 to see the destruction of Nagasaki. His account of the bombing won him his second Pulitzer Prize.

We flew southward down the channel and at 11:33 crossed the coastline and headed straight for Nagasaki, about one hundred miles to the west. Here we again circled until we found an opening in the clouds. It was 12:01 and the goal of our mission had arrived.

We heard the prearranged signal on our radio, put on our arc welder's glasses, and watched tensely the maneuverings of the strike ship about half a mile in front of us.

"There she goes!" someone said.

Out of the belly of *The Great Artiste* what looked like a black object went downward.

Captain Bock swung around to get out of range; but even though we were turning away in the opposite direction, and despite the fact that it was broad daylight in our cabin, all of us became aware of a giant flash that broke through the dark barrier of our arc welder's lenses and flooded our cabin with intense light.

We removed our glasses after the first flash, but the light still lingered on, a bluish-green light that illuminated the entire sky all around. A tremendous blast wave struck our ship and made it tremble from nose to tail. This was followed by four more blasts in rapid succession, each resounding like the boom of cannon fire hitting our plane from all directions.

Observers in the tail of our ship saw a giant ball of fire rise as though from the bowels of the earth, belching forth enormous white smoke rings. Next, they saw a giant pillar of purple fire, ten thousand feet high, shooting skyward with enormous speed.

By the time our ship had made another turn in the direction of the atomic explosion the pillar of purple fire had reached the level of our altitude. Only about forty-five seconds had passed. Awe-struck, we watched it shoot upward like a meteor coming from the earth instead of from outer space, becoming ever more alive as it climbed skyward through the white clouds. It was no longer smoke, or dust, or even a cloud of fire. It was a living thing, a new species of being, born right before our incredulous eyes.

At one stage of its evolution, covering millions of years in terms of seconds, the entity assumed the form of a giant square totem pole, with its base about three miles long, tapering off to about a mile at the top. Its bottom was brown, its center was amber, its top white. But it was a living totem pole, carved with many grotesque masks grimacing at the earth.

Then, just when it appeared as though the thing had settled down into a state of permanence, there came shooting out of the top a giant mushroom that increased the height of the pillar to a total of forty-five thousand feet. The mushroom top was even more alive than the pillar, seething and boiling in a white fury of creamy foam, sizzling upward and then descending earthward, a thousand Old Faithful geysers rolled into one.

It kept struggling in an elemental fury, like a creature in the act of breaking the bonds that held it down. In a few seconds it had freed itself from its gigantic stem and floated upward with tremendous speed, its momentum carrying it into the strato-sphere to a height of about sixty thousand feet.

But no sooner did this happen when another mushroom, smaller in size than the first one, began emerging out of the pillar. It was as though the decapitated monster was growing a new head.

As the first mushroom floated off into the blue it changed its shape into a flowerlike form, its giant petals curving downward, creamy white outside, rose-coloured inside. It still retained that shape when we last gazed at it from a distance of about two hundred miles. The boiling pillar of many colours could also be seen at that distance, a giant mountain of jumbled rainbows, in travail. Much living substance had gone into those rainbows. The quivering top of the pillar was protruding to a great height through the white clouds, giving the appearance of a monstrous prehistoric creature with a ruff around its neck, a fleecy ruff extending in all directions, as far as the eye could see.

HIROSHIMA

New Yorker, August 1946

In August 1946, the *New Yorker* gave over its entire space to John Hersey's reconstruction of the atomic bombing of Hirsohima. The print run sold out immediately, and *Hiroshima* the article became a story itself. An except follows.

At exactly fifteen minutes past eight in the morning, on 6 August, 1945, Japanese time, at the moment when the atomic bomb flashed above Hiroshima, Miss Toshiko Sasaki, a clerk in the personnel department at the East Asia Tin Works, had just sat down at her place in the plant office and was turning her head to speak to the girl at the next desk. At that same moment, Dr Masakazu Fujii was settling down cross-legged to read the Osaka *Asahi* on the porch of his private hospital, overhanging one of the seven deltaic rivers which divide Hiroshima; Mrs Hatsuyo Nakamura, a tailor's widow, stood by the window of her kitchen watching a neighbour tearing down his house because it lay in the path of an air-raid-defence fire lane; Father Wilhelm Kleinsorge, a German priest of the Society of Jesus, reclined in his underwear on a cot on the top floor of his order's three-storey mission house, reading a Jesuit magazine, *Stimmen der Zeit*; Dr Terufumi Sasaki, a young member of the surgical staff of the city's large, modern Red Cross Hospital, walked along one of the hospital corridors with a blood specimen for a Wassermann test in his hand; and the Reverend Mr Kiyoshi Tanimoto, pastor of the Hiroshima Methodist Church, paused at the door of a rich man's house in Koi, the city's western suburb, and prepared to unload a handcart full of things he had evacuated from town in fear of the massive B29 raid which everyone expected Hiroshima to suffer.

A hundred thousand people were killed by the atomic bomb, and these six were among the survivors. They still wonder why they lived when so many others died. Each of them counts many small items of chance or volition – a step taken in time, a decision to go indoors, catching one street-car instead of the next – that spared him. And now each knows that in the act of survival he lived a dozen lives and saw more death than he ever thought he would see. At the time none of them knew anything.

The Reverend Mr Tanimoto got up at five o'clock that morning. He was alone in the parsonage, because for some time his wife had been commuting with their year-old baby to spend nights with a friend in Ushida, a suburb to the north. Of all the important cities of Japan, only two, Kyoto and Hiroshima, had not been visited in strength by *B-san*, or Mr B, as the Japanese with a mixture of respect and unhappy familiarity, called the B-29; and Mr Tanimoto, like all his neighbours and friends, was almost sick with anxiety. He had heard uncomfortably detailed accounts of mass raids on Kure, Iwakuni, Tokuyama, and other nearby towns; he was sure Hiroshima's turn would come soon. He had slept badly the night before, because there had been several air-raid warnings. Hiroshima had been getting such warnings almost every night for weeks, for at that time the B-29s were using Lake Biwa, north-east of Hiroshima, as a rendezvous point, and no matter what city the Americans planned to hit, the Super-fortresses streamed in over the coast near Hiroshima. The frequency of the warnings and the continued abstinence of Mr B with respect to Hiroshima had made its citizens jittery; a rumour was going around that the Americans were saving something special for the city.

Mr Tanimoto is a small man, quick to talk, laugh, and cry. He wears his black hair parted in the middle and rather long; the prominence of the frontal bones just above his eyebrows and the smallness of his moustache, mouth, and chin give him a strange, old-young look, boyish and yet wise, weak and yet fiery. He moves nervously and fast, but with a restraint which suggests that he is a cautious, thoughtful man. He showed, indeed, just those qualities in the uneasy days before the bomb fell. Besides having his wife spend the nights in Ushida, Mr Tanimoto had been carrying all the portable things from his church, in the close-packed residential district called Nagaragawa, to a house that belonged to a rayon manufacturer in Koi, two miles from the centre of town. The rayon man, a Mr Matsui, had opened his then unoccupied estate to a large number of his friends and acquaintances, so that they might evacuate whatever they wished to a safe distance from the probable target area. Mr Tanimoto had no difficulty in moving chairs, hymnals, Bibles, altar gear, and church records by pushcart himself, but the organ console and an upright piano required some aid. A friend of his named Matsuo had, the day before, helped him get the piano out to Koi; in return, he had promised this day to assist Mr Matsuo in hauling out a daughter's belongings. That is why he had risen so early.

Mr Tanimoto cooked his own breakfast. He felt awfully tired. The effort of moving the piano the day before, a sleepless night, weeks of worry and unbalanced diet, the cares of his parish – all combined to make him feel hardly adequate to the new day's work. There was another thing, too: Mr Tanimoto had studied theology at Emory College, in Atlanta, Georgia; he had graduated in 1940; he spoke excellent English; he dressed in American clothes; he had corresponded with many American friends right up to the time the war began; and among a people obsessed with a fear of being spied upon – perhaps almost obsessed himself – he found himself growing increasingly uneasy. The police had questioned him several times, and just a few days before, he had heard that an influential acquaintance, a Mr Tanaka, a retired officer of the Toyo Kisen Kaisha steamship line, an anti-Christian, a man famous in Hiroshima for his showy philanthropies and notorious for his personal tyrannies, had been telling people that Tanimoto should not be trusted. In compensation, to show himself publicly a good Japanese, Mr Tanimoto had taken on the chairmanship of his local *tonarigumi*, or Neighbourhood Association, and to his other duties and concerns this position had added the business of organizing air-raid defence for about twenty families.

Before six o'clock that morning, Mr Tanimoto started for Mr Matsuo's house. There he found that their burden was to be a *tansu*, a large Japanese cabinet, full of clothing and household goods. The two men set out. The morning was perfectly clear and so warm that the day promised to be uncomfortable. A few minutes after they started, the air raid siren went off – a min-

ute-long blast that warned of approaching planes but indicated to
the people of Hiroshima only a slight degree of danger, since it
sounded every morning at this time, when an American weather
plane came over. The two men pulled and pushed the handcart
through the city streets. Hiroshima was a fan-shaped city, lying
mostly on the six islands formed by the seven estuarial rivers that
branch out from the Ota River; its main commercial and residential districts, covering about four square miles in the centre of
the city, contained three-quarters of its population, which had
been reduced by several evacuation programmes from a wartime
peak of 380,000 to about 245,000. Factories and other residential
districts, or suburbs, lay compactly around the edges of the city.
To the south were the docks, an airport, and an island-studded
Inland Sea. A rim of mountains runs around the other three sides
of the delta. Mr Tanimoto and Mr Matsuo took their way
through the shopping centre, already full of people, and across
two of the rivers to the sloping streets of Koi, and up them to the
outskirts and foothills. As they started up a valley away from the
tight-ranked houses, the all-clear sounded. (The Japanese radar
operators, detecting only three planes, supposed that they comprised a reconnaissance.) Pushing the handcart up to the rayon
man's house was tiring, and the men, after they had manoeuvred
their load into the driveway and to the front steps, paused to rest
awhile. They stood with a wing of the house between them and
the city. Like most homes in this part of Japan, the house
consisted of a wooden frame and wooden walls supporting a
heavy tile roof. Its front hall, packed with rolls of bedding and
clothing, looked like a cool cave full of fat cushions. Opposite the
house, to the right of the front door, there was a large, finicky
rock garden. There was no sound of planes. The morning was
still; the place was cool and pleasant.

Then a tremendous flash of light cut across the sky. Mr
Tanimoto has a distinct recollection that it travelled from east
to west, from the city toward the hills. It seemed a sheet of sun.
Both he and Mr Matsuo reacted in terror – and both had time to
react (for they were 3,500 yards, or two miles, from the centre of
the explosion). Mr Matsuo dashed up the front steps into the
house and dived among the bedrolls and buried himself there. Mr
Tanimoto took four or five steps and threw himself between two
big rocks in the garden. He bellied up very hard against one of

them. As his face was against the stone he did not see what happened. He felt a sudden pressure, and then splinters and pieces of board and fragments of tile fell on him. He heard no roar. (Almost no one in Hiroshima recalls hearing any noise of the bomb. But a fisherman in his sampan on the Inland Sea near Tsuzu, the man with whom Mr Tanimoto's mother-in-law and sister-in-law were living, saw the flash and heard a tremendous explosion; he was nearly twenty miles from Hiroshima, but the thunder was greater than when the B-29s hit Iwakuni, only five miles away.)

When he dared, Mr Tanimoto raised his head and saw that the rayon man's house had collapsed. He thought a bomb had fallen directly on it. Such clouds of dust had risen that there was a sort of twilight around. In panic, not thinking for the moment of Mr Matsuo under the ruins, he dashed out into the street. He noticed as he ran that the concrete wall of the estate had fallen over – toward the house rather than away from it. In the street, the first thing he saw was a squad of soldiers who had been burrowing into the hillside opposite, making one of the thousands of dugouts in which the Japanese apparently intended to resist invasion, hill by hill, life for life; the soldiers were coming out of the hole, where they should have been safe, and blood was running from their heads, chests and backs. They were silent and dazed.

Under what seemed to be a local dust cloud, the day grew darker and darker.

HOPE THIS IS THE LAST ONE, BABY

New York Herald Tribune, 16 August 1945

Japan agreed an unconditional surrender on 14 August. When the surrender came through a B-29 bombing mission was in mid-air, and it was too late to recall it. It was the last combat run of the Second World War. Aboard one of the B-29s was the *Herald Tribune*'s war correspondent, Homer Bigart, who was no stranger to bomber life and death, having ridden with the USAAF over Germany in 1943 as one of the group of eight warcos dubbed the "Flying Typewriters".

In a B-29 over Japan, Aug. 15

The radio tells us that the war is over but from where I sit it looks suspiciously like a rumour. A few minutes ago – at 1:32 a.m. – we fire-bombed Kumagaya, a small industrial city behind Tokyo near the northern edge of Kanto Plain. Peace was not official for the Japanese either, for they shot right back at us.

Other fires are raging at Isesaki, another city on the plain, and as we skirt the eastern base of Fujiyama Lieutenant General James Doolittle's B-29s, flying their first mission from the 8th Air Force base on Okinawa, arrive to put the finishing touches on Kumagaya.

I rode in the *City of Saco* (Maine), piloted by First Lieutenant Theodore J. Lamb, twenty-eight, of 103–21 Lefferts Blvd, Richmond Hill, Queens, NY. Like all the rest, Lamb's crew showed the strain of the last five days of the uneasy "truce" that kept Superforts grounded.

They had thought the war was over. They had passed most of the time around radios, hoping the President would make it official. They did not see that it made much difference whether

Emperor Hirohito stayed in power. Had our propaganda not portrayed him as a puppet? Well, then, we could use him just as the war lords had done.

The 314th Bombardment Wing was alerted yesterday morning. At 2:20 p.m., pilots, bombardiers, navigators, radio men, and gunners trooped into the briefing shack to learn that the war was still on. Their target was to be a pathetically small city of little obvious importance, and their commanding officer, Colonel Carl R. Storrie, of Denton, Texas, was at pains to convince them why Kumagaya, with a population of 49,000, had to be burned to the ground.

There were component parts factories of the Nakajima aircraft industry in the town, he said. Moreover, it was an important railway centre.

No one wants to die in the closing moments of a war. The wing chaplain, Captain Benjamin Schmidke, of Springfield, Mo., asked the men to pray, and then the group commander jumped on the platform and cried: "This is the last mission. Make it the best we ever ran."

Colonel Storrie was to ride in one of the lead planes, dropping four 1,000-pound high explosives in the hope that the defenders of the town would take cover in buildings or underground and then be trapped by a box pattern of fire bombs to be dumped by eighty planes directly behind.

"We've got 'em on the one yard line. Let's push the ball over," the colonel exhorted his men. "This should be the final knockout blow of the war. Put your bombs on the target so that tomorrow the world will have peace."

Even after they were briefed, most of the crewmen hoped and expected that an official armistice would come before the scheduled 5:30 take-off. They looked at their watches. Two and a half hours to go.

You might expect that the men would be in a sullen, almost mutinous, frame of mind. But morale was surprisingly high.

"Look at the sweat pour off me," cried Major William Marchesi, of 458 Baltic Street, Brooklyn. "I've never sweated out a mission like this one."

A few minutes earlier the Guam radio had interrupted its program with a flash and quoted the Japanese Domei Agency announcement that Emperor Hirohito had accepted the peace terms.

Instantly the whole camp was in an uproar. But then a voice snapped angrily over the squawk box: "What are you trying to do? Smash morale? It's only a rumour."

So the crews drew their equipment – parachutes, Mae Wests, and flak suits – and got on trucks to go out to the line. We reached the City of Saco at about 4:30 p.m., and there was still nearly an hour to go before our plane, which was to serve as a pathfinder for the raiders, would depart.

We were all very jittery. Radios were blaring in the camp area but they were half a mile from us and all we could catch were the words "Hirohito" and "Truman". For all we knew, the war was over.

Then a headquarters officer came by and told Lieutenant Lamb that the take-off had been postponed thirty minutes in expectation of some announcement from Washington.

By that time none of us expected to reach Japan, but we knew that unless confirmation came soon the mission would have to take off, and then very likely salvo its bombs and come home when the signal "Utah, Utah, Utah," came through. That was the code agreed upon for calling off operations in the event of an announcement of peace by President Truman.

Lamb's crew began turning the plane's props at 5:45, and we got aboard. "Boy, we're going to kill a lot of fish today," said Sergeant Karl L. Braley, of Saco, Maine.

To salvo the bombs at sea is an expensive method of killing fish.

We got San Francisco on the radio. "I hope all you boys out there are as happy as we are at this moment," an announcer was saying. "People are yelling and screaming and whistles are blowing."

"Yeah," said one of the crewmen disgustedly, "they're screaming and we're flying."

We took off at 6:07.

We saw no white flags when we reached Japanese territory. Back of the cockpit Radioman Staff Sergeant Rosendo D. Del Valle Jr., of El Paso, Texas, strained his ears for the message, "Utah, Utah, Utah." If it came on time, it might save a crew or two, and perhaps thousands of civilians at Kumagaya.

The message never came. Each hour brought us nearer the enemy coast. We caught every news broadcast, listening to hours of intolerable rot in the hope that the announcer would break in with the news that would send us home.

The empire coast was as dark and repellent as ever. Japan was still at war, and not one light showed in the thickly populated Tokyo plain.

Lamb's course was due north to the Kasumiga Lake, then a right angle, turning west for little Kumagaya. It was too late now. There would be bombs on Kumagaya in a few minutes.

Kumagaya is on featureless flats five miles south of the Tone River. It is terribly hard to pick up by radar. There were only two cues to Kumagaya. Directly north of the town was a wide span across the Tone, and a quarter of a mile south of it was a long bridge across the Ara River.

The radar observer, Lieutenant Harold W. Zeisler, of Kankakee, Ill, picked up both bridges in good time and we started the bomb run.

An undercast hid the city almost completely but through occasional rifts I could see a few small fires catching on from the bombs dropped by the two preceding pathfinders.

The Japanese were alert. Searchlights lit the clouds beneath us and two ack-ack guns sent up weak sporadic fire. Thirty miles to the north we saw Japanese searchlights and ack-ack groping for the bombers of another wing attacking Isesaki.

Leaving our target at the mercy of the eighty Superforts following us, we swerved sharply southward along the eastern base of Fujiyamaa and reached the sea. At one point we were within ten miles of Tokyo. The capital was dark.

Every one relaxed. We tried to pick up San Francisco on the radio but couldn't. The gunners took out photos of their wives and girl friends and said: "Hope this is the last, baby."

This postscript is written at Guam. It was the last raid of the war. We did not know it until we landed at North Field.

GEORGE ORWELL

"THE MOON UNDER WATER"

Evening Standard, 9 February 1946

This was an entirely inconsequential piece, penned by Orwell to fill allotted space. It is also a proof that Orwell was a genius in capturing the essence of Englishness and England on paper.

My favourite public house, "The Moon under Water", is only two minutes from a bus stop, but it is on a side-street, and drunks and rowdies never seem to find their way there, even on Saturday nights.

Its clientele, though fairly large, consists mostly of "regulars" who occupy the same chair every evening and go there for conversation as much as for the beer.

If you are asked why you favour a particular public house, it would seem natural to put the beer first, but the thing that most appeals to me about "The Moon under Water" is what people call its "atmosphere".

To begin with, its whole architecture and fittings are uncompromisingly Victorian. It has no glass-topped tables or other modern miseries, and, on the other hand, no sham roof-beams, ingle-nooks or plastic panels masquerading as oak. The grained woodwork, the ornamental mirrors behind the bar, the cast-iron fireplaces, the florid ceiling stained dark yellow by tobacco-smoke, the stuffed bull's head over the mantelpiece – everything has the solid comfortable ugliness of the nineteenth century.

In winter there is generally a good fire burning in at least two of the bars, and the Victorian lay-out of the place gives one plenty of elbow-room. There is a public bar, a saloon bar, a ladies' bar, a bottle-and-jug for those who are too bashful to buy their supper beer publicly, and upstairs, a dining-room.

Games are only played in the public, so that in the other bars you can walk about without constantly ducking to avoid flying darts.

In "The Moon under Water" it is always quiet enough to talk. The house possesses neither a radio nor a piano, and even on Christmas Eve and such occasions the singing that happens is of a decorous kind.

The barmaids know most of their customers by name, and take a personal interest in everyone. They are all middle-aged women – two of them have their hair dyed in quite surprising shades – and they call everyone "dear", irrespective of age or sex. ("Dear", not "Ducky": pubs where the barmaid calls you "Ducky" always have a disagreeable raffish atmosphere.)

Unlike most pubs, "The Moon under Water" sells tobacco as well as cigarettes, and it also sells aspirins and stamps, and is obliging about letting you use the telephone.

You cannot get dinner at "The Moon under Water", but there is always the snack counter where you can get liver-sausage sandwiches, mussels (a speciality of the house), cheese, pickles and those large biscuits with caraway seeds in them which only seem to exist in public houses.

Upstairs, six days a week, you can get a good, solid lunch – for example, a cut off the joint, two vegetables and boiled jam roll – for about three shillings.

The special pleasure of this lunch is that you can have draught stout with it. I doubt whether as many as ten percent of London pubs serve draught stout, but "The Moon under Water" is one of them. It is a soft, creamy sort of stout, and it goes better in a pewter pot.

They are particular about their drinking vessels at "The Moon under Water" and never, for example, make the mistake of serving a pint of beer in a handleless glass. Apart from glass and pewter mugs, they have some of those pleasant strawberry-pink china ones which are now seldom seen in London. China mugs went out about thirty years ago, because most people like their drink to be transparent, but in my opinion beer tastes better out of china.

The great surprise of "The Moon under Water" is its garden. You go through a narrow passage leading out of the saloon, and find yourself in a fairly large garden with plane trees under which there are little green tables with iron chairs round them. Up at one end of the garden there are swings and a chute for the children.

On summer evenings there are family parties, and you sit under the plane trees having beer or draught cider to the tune of delighted squeals from children going down the chute. The prams with the younger children are parked near the gate.

Many as are the virtues of "The Moon under Water" I think that the garden is its best feature, because it allows whole families to go there instead of Mum having to stay at home and mind the baby while Dad goes out alone.

And though, strictly speaking, they are only allowed in the garden, the children tend to seep into the pub and even to fetch drinks for their parents. This, I believe, is against the law, but it is a law that deserves to be broken, for it is the puritanical nonsense of excluding children – and therefore to some extent, women – from pubs that has turned these places into mere boozing-shops instead of the family gathering-places that they ought to be.

"The Moon under Water" is my ideal of what a pub should be – at any rate, in the London area. (The qualities one expects of a country pub are slightly different.)

But now is the time to reveal something which the discerning and disillusioned reader will probably have guessed already. There is no such place as "The Moon under Water".

That is to say, there may well be a pub of that name, but I don't know of it, nor do I know any pub with just that combination of qualities.

I know pubs where the beer is good but you can't get meals, others where you can get meals but which are noisy and crowded, and others which are quiet but where the beer is generally sour. As for gardens, offhand I can only think of three London pubs that possess them.

But, to be fair, I do know of a few pubs that almost come up to "The Moon under Water". I have mentioned above ten qualities that the perfect pub should have, and I know one pub that has eight of them. Even there, however, there is no draught stout and no china mugs.

And if anyone knows of a pub that has draught stout, open fires, cheap meals, a garden, motherly barmaids and no radio, I should be glad to hear of it, even though its name were something as prosaic as "The Red Lion" or "The Railway Arms".

MAURICE FAGENCE

SENTENCE DAY AT NUREMBERG

Daily Herald, 2 October 1946

At Nuremberg the surviving masters of Nazi Germany were tried for crimes relating to the breaking of peace treaties, the conduct of war and human rights.

When Goering came into court to hear the sentence – he was first – he play-acted in the most terrible few minutes of his life.

Maybe he meant to show the judges how superhumanly uninterested he was in anything they did to him.

Whatever the reason, this is the scene as we saw it. The judges had been the last people to take their seats in the packed court. Before a sliding walnut panel that serves as a door to the dock a teashop-size table had been placed. On it was a pair of earphones plugged to the wall near the floor.

Every guard in court, we noticed, including the two in the dock, appeared without a revolver for the first time.

Even Colonel Andrus, Court Marshal, had discarded his. The astonishing security proceedings had reached the point at which no risk was being taken of a condemned man seizing a gun from a soldier's holster.

I thought the court was without a gun till I saw one young officer with his hand firmly on a Colt in his belt, as he lurked in an alcove near the dock.

Noiselessly the panel slid aside at the touch of a remote electrical button. Two unarmed soldiers stepped through, and a second later, to stand between them at the table – Goering.

He had donned his lavender-coloured Air Marshal's uniform, discarded three months ago, for this occasion. No insignia on it now. There was not even room on the breast of this thinner Goering for the medals he used to wear.

His rarely still face was now almost cheekily composed. He donned the headphones casually as if testing somebody's set, stood at attention. When the words of Lord Justice Lawrence reached him "The tribunal sentences you," he waved the judge into silence.

By actions he conveyed to the judges that no sound was coming through.

What followed was unforgettable. Goering himself took turns at bending to the plug at floor level to see if there was good contact, always finishing by conveying that the earphones were not working.

Guards who had tested the earpieces and expressed themselves satisfied rushed into the dock. One vaulted a prisoner's seat. Goering handed them the earphones in turn, but although they were satisfied everything was working, he denied it with a faint smile.

They took turns at another pair of earphones, and Goering tested the floor contact again. And after two minutes he agreed all was well.

Lord Justice Lawrence read the sentence again – right up to "death by hanging". Goering, the man who ordered the bombing of London, and who now himself had to die, flashed a look of contempt on the court, turned ponderously on his heel and walked through the panel.

The guards maintain that never while they were listening through those two sets of earpieces did they fail to work.

We always knew Goering would take his sentence bravely. Did he prefer bravado?

Two minutes' hush – for each prisoner had to be brought up separately by lift from the prison tunnel – and Hess appeared.

With a savage swing of his arm he knocked down the earphones offered him, and faced the bench with legs far astride and hands clenched before him.

Imprisonment for life. He licked his lips and half goose-stepped out noisily in the boots he wore when he parachuted into Scotland.

Next Ribbentrop, pale and stooping when he appeared, but shaking himself into some sort of composure.

Death by hanging. He sagged, patted into place a bundle of papers that threatened to slide from under his arm, tried to walk out bravely, but drooped again as he reached the panel.

Then Keitel – rigid, erect, soldierly as he entered. A quick turn on his heels and he was out again.

Kaltenbrunner, the Gestapo chief, who killed in hundreds of thousands. Tall and impeccable in a new blue suit, with shirt and collar to match, he bowed on entering, bowed acceptance of those words, *"Death by hanging"*, and bowed himself out again. A brave show, but the muscles of that face were twitching and the eyes were haunted by fear.

Of the first five sentences four were death. Murmurs were breaking the silence of the court. Judge Biddle silenced a tittering woman with a glare.

Philosopher Rosenberg, the man who would have had us believe he was nothing more. *Death by hanging*. The small plumpish scholar recoils as if not expecting it, sways slightly and walks out, head bent.

Bald-headed Frank, who wiped out whole villages, and is now a convert to Roman Catholicism. "Thank you" he says to the guards who turn him to face the judges. "Thank you", to the judge who says: *Death by hanging*. And a final polite "Thank you" to the men who escorted him through the panel.

Frick, racy in a heavy tweed sports coat. *Death by hanging*. He continues to listen as if expecting more will follow. Guards turn him and he walks out uncomprehendingly.

Jew-baiter Streicher, the pervert whose pornographic library here in Nuremberg has been burnt by official order – whose eyes have never left a woman in his ten months in this dock. *Death by hanging*. He flung his earphones on the table with a crash, strutted out in a blaze of temper.

Funk, financial journalist turned fat banker, who stored the gold teeth of murdered millions in his vaults. *Imprisonment for life*. His eyes look slowly along the line of judges and he walks out, shaking his head.

Doenitz. *Ten years*. He walks out, as if still on the quarter deck.

Fellow Admiral Raeder. *Imprisonment for life*. He gulps hard, stands rooted for a full half-minute and droops away.

The most handsome man in the dock – and youngest – von Schirach, who, as leader of the Hitler Youth, taught the youth of

Germany Nazism and militarism – *Twenty years' imprisonment*. He pales, strives to whisper a word, and races through the panel.

Sauckel, who always impressed on the Court he was only a working man, but who sent five million people to slave labour in Germany – *Death by hanging*. He makes a whining noise. His every utterance in court has been a whine. He goes out helplessly.

Jodl, the General who ordered soldiers to butcher civilians – *Death by hanging*. He frowns as if a lance-corporal has cheeked him, glares, marches out.

Seyss-Inquart, the Austrian traitor who helped to put Austria under the German heel and then crushed Holland for his German masters – *Death by hanging*. He looks round the court anxiously, as if to see the effect, bows, leaves with swing.

Speer, the genius architect who used slave labour cruelly – *Twenty years' imprisonment*. He screws up his eyes and mumbles as if doing a sum in his head. Then bows, and walks away.

Grey, aristocratic von Neurath, one of the worst oppressors of occupied countries – *Fifteen years*. He puts the earphones down gently like a good butler, and almost tiptoes out.

And now sentence on an empty dock. As missing Martin Bormann is sentenced to death, spectators begin to trek to the doors.

THE GRAND NATIONAL:
THE VIEW FROM THE SADDLE

The Observer, 30 March 1947

Under the pen name "Phantom", Hislop was *The Observer*'s racing correspondent. In the 1947 Grand National he took a horseback's view of the action, riding Kami. Hislop, incidentally, was no stranger to danger, during World War II he had served with 2 SAS.

Aintree, 29 March

There were fifty-seven of us lined up at the start, like sardines in a tin, Kami's position was about one-third of the way from the inside, between Rearmament and Some Chicken. As usual, there was much restiveness and scrimmaging, with the starter shouting "Keep off the tapes!"

Then the gate went up and we jumped off, most of us as eagerly as if we had only five furlongs to go. Taking into consideration the heavy going after the morning's rain, the initial pace of the field as a whole was such that no horse could hope both to maintain it and complete the course.

Kami was squeezed when the field "broke", but settled into a swinging stride, which was not fast enough to keep anywhere near the solid wall of leaders, and we found ourselves going over the first fence well behind but clear of any interference.

Kami jumped it perfectly, in the style of a real Aintree horse, standing well back and landing without "pitching".

There were two or three other horses lying in the same area as Kami, with a loose horse or two in the vicinity. I went rather a long way round, towards the outside – for two reasons. In the first place the going there was less churned up. Second, I wanted Kami to be completely clear of any bumps or other mishap which would have put a horse of such frail build "on the floor".

He was still jumping perfectly. In fact, Kami never put a foot wrong all the way. His swinging, even gait gave me the greatest confidence and the consistency of his jumping – every fence measured off long before he got to it – made me feel certain that wherever he finished he would complete the course.

As we turned into the country for the last circuit, Kami gradually began to overtake the field. Jumping Becher's for the second time, our hopes of a possible victory became something more than the ambition of every steeplechase rider. There were, I suppose, some six or eight horses – that is, with their riders still on board – in front of me, but most of them were tiring, and as I passed them at least one rider threw me a word of encouragement that means so much in a race of this kind. "Well done, Johnny, keep going," someone said. As we crossed the road with only two more fences to jump I could see Prince Regent in front of me visibly tiring, and, still a good way ahead, the green jacket of Lough Conn and the green and blue of the eventual winner, of whose identity I was as ignorant as, I suppose, were the majority of spectators.

Coming into the last fence but one, there were two loose horses in front of me, and, on the inside, Prince Regent. I realized then that I had no hope of winning, as Kami was tiring; the heavy going had taken toll of his delicate frame and only his courage and innate stamina kept him going. But he jumped the fence perfectly, and went on towards the last with, I think, Prince Regent about level with us, but very tired.

We landed safely with the long stretch to the winning post spread out before us, both tired, but with Prince Regent beaten for sure. I got out my whip and kept swinging it without ever hitting Kami, and he answered nobly, gradually overhauling Mr Rank's gallant horse to take us into third place.

And so the placed jockeys rode back to the three unsaddling enclosures appointed for first, second, and third. Ahead of me went the winner, Caughoo, between two mounted policemen, surrounded by a crowd including owner, trainer, and friends, all running alongside to pat the winning mount and to congratulate his rider.

As for me, my feeling is of three-fold gratitude – to the horse for his courage and the way he carried me; to Tom Mason, the trainer, for Kami's wonderful condition; and to the gods for the luck which followed our journey.

CLUB FIGHTER

True, January 1948

Cannon began his journalistic career as a copy boy on the *New York Daily News*. Under the influence of Damon Runyon, he became one of the masters of sportwriting. Cannon died in 1975, aged 65.

I sat across from him at a table in the diner. He was a young guy with a pudgy body and a rum-hurt face. It was a very cold day, but he was moist with sweat. There was a wet rim around the collar of his blue shirt. I asked him to hand me the sugar bowl, and this started the conversation. He wanted to know what I did.

"I work on a paper," I said.

"Printer?" he asked.

"No," I said. "The editorial department."

"You write up the editorials," he said.

I said, "I write sports."

"Sports?" he said, as though this were a word seldom used and he was uncertain of its meaning. "What kind of sports?"

"General sports," I said. "All kinds."

"Boxing?" he asked.

"I do a lot of boxing," I said.

"I used to box myself," he said.

"Where?" I asked.

"Around Jersey," he said.

"What name did you box under?" I asked.

"You wouldn't know me," this guy said, getting shifty when I tried to nail him down. "I was just a ham-and-egger."

"What did you weigh?" I asked.

"One hundred and thirty-five," he answered, and then I was

reasonably certain he was a liar. Fighters usually say thirty-five or sixty and throw away the hundred.

"How many fights did you have?" I asked.

"Round thirty," the liar said. "I made a little money, and quit. I'm in the shirt business now."

The waiter brought my change, and I got away from him before he could give the lie any detail.

There are some men who believe that being a fighter makes you a special man. There are some fighters who believe that. One of them is Lew Perez. Once he was a semi-windup guy and he fought a few mains in his time. Now Perez boxes six-round preliminaries in neighborhood clubs in Brooklyn. He works in the daytime at odd jobs, but what he wants is to walk down the street in the slum where he lives and have the guys on the corner recognize him as a fighter. He walks by them, sharp in his zoot suit, the satchel in his hand, and if they say there goes the fighter, that is his reward.

Perez has been going eight years. There isn't anyone who will manage him. Matchmakers put him on a card because they like him. They know he doesn't quit or run and hide or stink out the other guy if he is hit on the chin. They give him fifty dollars for six rounds, and he cuts ten of it back to the second. He was born in the city of San Juan in Puerto Rico, and, after eight years of it, all he has is the right to say he's a prize fighter.

The club where he works most is the Ridgewood Grove. They have been fighting in this place for twenty-five years. Some of the young ones get good and leave it for the Garden and the other big arenas around the country. When they start going back, out of the Garden and the other important joints, they come back to the Ridgewood for a last shot. Perez has never fought in the Garden. The best he ever did was eight hundred fighting Wilfie Shanks in Albany, New York. By the time they cut him he didn't have much left, but it was one of the big nights of his life because it was a main event; he has had very few of those.

Guys like this live in a spectacular obscurity and enjoy a faceless celebrity. They are the guys who rebuke the sports pages and the fight racket of art and literature. They accept the poverty of their life, fascinated by the dubious ecstasy of hearing announcers shout their names in half empty arenas. They are always on the frontiers of starvation. They have no future in the cruelest of all sports. Winning doesn't help them. Losing doesn't tarnish their conception of themselves as anointed people.

They are the time-killers, the guys fighting as you come down the aisle to your seat. They are only half seen in their small moments of triumph, and their disgraces are vaguely remembered, like a joke told very late at night when everyone is drunk.

If they possess anything, it is the knowledge that a man once said there are no cowards in the ring. A fighter, said the unknown philosopher, must be game or he couldn't go through the ropes. Perez is typical of what he is. He is a preliminary fighter who will never do any better. Change the name, the birthplace, the weights, and each is alike, no matter where they are fighting. It is not an extraordinary story but a commonplace one.

At Ridgewood Grove, the fighters who work underneath sat in a slope-ceilinged room on this night as they waited to go into the ring.

If you go into rooms where athletes change their clothes as much as I do, you would be disgusted by the way this place smells. The customary odour of the locker room is a healthy one and is dominated by liniments, sweat and soap melting in the hot water of the showers. This room smelled of poverty.

It is a peculiar smell because these half-naked bodies are frequently cleansed by showers, and they are sound, young, muscular. The flaws of these bodies are minor. The noses are broken, and the breath creaks as it comes out of them. The ears are swollen and, in many cases, shapeless. There are usually clenched scars above the eyes, and the eyebrows are made bald in places by the marks of old wounds – the way a lawn might look if it were marred by a mower zigzagging across it after it had been neatly cropped by a gardener.

The room is a sanitary place, policed by health officers and sprayed frequently with disinfectant but the smell of that gets out of your nose if you stay there for any length of time. It is not a big smell, but you don't have to sniff to locate it. It is there, small and revolting, a mild smell of decay. It is the smell of old men sleeping in lodging houses, but not so strong. It confuses you because, in the lodging houses, these bodies have surrendered to death and wait for it with an eager hopelessness. But here in this fight club are young men who use their bodies to survive.

It is the smell you get from unmade beds in furnished rooms; from the impotent gas jets on the landings of tenement stairways which now use electricity; from socks which have been washed in the sink of a bus-station gents' room; from sandwiches wrapped in newspapers and carried in pockets; from clothes that dry on the body after being soaked by the rain; from the benches in parks where no flowers grow; from the overcoats panhandlers wear in the summertime. It is the old smell of poverty that follows the poor wherever they go. It is a smell you will recognize always if you were raised in the slums of a big city as I was.

Perez was sitting on a stool by himself, his street clothes hung on the pegs up above him. He is a dark man, firm-muscled, about twenty-four years old. His weight is 153 pounds, with the stomach wrinkled a little with furrows of fat but still flat. He wears a mustache, and he snorts occasionally to clear his nose. There is a scar on his head and one over his left eye.

"I was fighting with a guy", he said, pointing to the healed wound in his head.

Johnny Schwartz, the second, a monstrous man with a crushed face, who was dressed in a black sweater, black pants and a dark sport shirt, interrupted the fighter by holding up his soft right hand.

"In the street," Schwartz said. "It was a street fight."

"In the street I was fighting with a guy," Perez said. "His brother came and hit me on the head with a stick."

The second smiled contemptuously, pleased by his superior knowledge of the language.

"A bat, he means," the second said.

"All right," Perez said. "A bat."

The second shook with laughter, as though humour were an animal which frolicked inside his great body.

"A moustache he's got," the second said. "Lew Perez: next stop, Hollywood."

Perez said Buddy Bailey put the gash above his eye.

"The first round," Perez said. "The referee wanted to stop the fight. But I went the limit. I lost the decision. It never opened again. That is very good. It stays the way it is."

There is a theory that fighters with moustaches are the intellectuals of the ring. Hair on a man's lip is considered the mark of the scholar. The brown hand reached for the mustache as though it were an insect he was trying to brush off his face.

"I am a clown," he said proudly. "I am no cutie."

Perez, who came to New York when he was sixteen, first lived in the Spanish-speaking settlement in that part of Harlem which reaches to the northern end of Central Park.

"I have only one week in this country, and I not speak English so good," he explained. "One day I am fighting with a guy in the street. I am always fighting with a guy. Al King . . . a manager of fighters . . . is in an automobile and he sees this fight with a guy. He stopped the fight. He say to me: 'You want to make a couple of bucks?' I say: 'Sure. Why not?' He put me in the car, and he take me some place. I am fighting a guy in the street at five o'clock, and then in the ring that night. How do you like that?"

"Did you win it?" the second asked.

"I win it," Perez said. "The other guy quit."

"Why do you fight?" I asked him, because he knows as well as I do that this is as far as he will go and from now on it will get tougher.

"I like the sport of it," he said.

"You don't like being hit, do you?" I asked.

"No," the fighter said.

"Do you enjoy beating up the other guy?" I asked.

"No," he said. "I like the sport of it. I am working down the docks, on Pier 40. It's a good job. I make sixty-seven dollars a week. I get a fight. I quit. The sport appeals to me. I am a fighter. I work now in the daytime. I am a cashier in a carnival in the Bronx. My boss is good. He gives me a night to fight. I quit jobs all the time. In a laundry . . . dishwasher . . . porter . . . stevedore . . . delivery boy . . . racking up balls in a poolroom . . . bartender. I do not like this. I just like to fight."

The second wheezed. "He likes to give people a laugh. But they stopped him. The commission suspended him for clowning. Is that a bad thing? Making people laugh? But what can you do? They took his licence off him. He's got to be serious. A fine thing to do to a real clown!"

The fighter examined the knuckles of his hand while the second talked. The other fighters sat silently on their stools. They sat with the patience of men who turn up their suitcases and sit on them by the side of a highway, waiting for a hitch.

"It's rough," Perez said, talking about the fight racket as though it had just occurred to him that it was a dirty business.

"It's rough, but I like it. I don't feel bad when I am losing. I like to be a good winner. A good loser. I like to have the people enjoy themselves when I fight. Some guy will say to me: 'Lew, you are a bum.' I find the guy in the crowd. I pick out the guy who says I am a bum. I bow to him. I tell him it is not an insult. This is to make him laugh. I am not a champion. I know that. But I fight my best all the time. That is being a fighter. Fighting your best all the time. I am going to fight all I can. When I think I got enough, I quit. I will never be punch-drunk. I take care of myself. If I have the money, I eat good food. I sleep. I hit the road. I run over the Williamsburg Bridge. I exercise on my roof. I do not like to pay money to train in the gym. But I will never be punch-drunk. I am too smart for that. The sport will not appeal to me when I am being hurt."

The first six was on, and the second came over to Perez and ran his fat hand over the muscles of the stooped shoulders.

"Lew Perez," the second said, "you're on your way to Hollywood."

The second held up a green-trimmed, red-satin bathrobe. It was faded from many washings, but clean.

"By this they know Perez," the fighter said and began to move his arms in the old motions. The other people in the room did not notice his departure. They did not speak to him as he left the dressing room and walked into the dusk of the arena.

There was a girl with high-arched eyebrows, raised in perpetual astonishment on her plump, powder-white face. She stood up when Perez passed her. She shouted to him, and he waved back to her. This was the fighter's wife. She is always there when he works.

There were not many people in the place at this time although they sold out that night. There were more people up against the bar and in the lunchroom in the foyer. They demand a lot for their money in this club, but the second six didn't interest them much. There was little excitement as Joe Bostic introduced the two fighters in the angular language used for preliminary guys. They save the descriptive adjectives for the main event. Comedy is not good when it is associated with a fighter. The people in the seats shouted bantering jokes to Perez; their crude humour did not displease him.

The guy he drew that night was Henry Robinson, who seemed

embarrassed by appearing in public with only a pair of tights to cover him. He pulled them up as high as they would reach as he waited in his corner.

It was a bad fight. Robinson came cautiously from his corner, his right hand out in the pose of a left-hander. His advance turned into a sudden retreat when he discovered he was too close to Perez. Perez lunged at him, wildly, the offence without grace or pattern. Robinson cowered behind his raised arms, and a punch slipped through and grazed his chin. He fell down, writhing and moaning so loud you could hear him in the press row. The crowd laughed as he was counted out. Perez bowed with a stately humour. Bostic climbed into the ring and strolled over to the timekeeper.

"One oh six of the first round," the timekeeper yelled.

"Can you beat that," Bostic said. "Perez knocking someone out. Can you beat that?"

The people snickered as Perez came out of the ring. One of them rasped: "Atta boy, Lew." The voice was very big above the quiet savagery of the laughter. Perez searched through the audience, located the man who had saluted him and bowed again. He walked up the aisle to the dressing room, alone. The guys in his corner were working the next bout.

Perez went back to the dressing room, put his clothes on. He met his wife, and they went to the box office and collected the fifty, less the ten the second took. They ate a big, slow meal in a cafeteria near the club. They took the subway home.

They live in a tenement on Rivington Street, near the Bowery in a slum which is a disgrace to the city of New York. Wash hangs on clotheslines in the small, three-room apartment. The furniture is old but functional. There is a bed to sleep on, a crib for the baby, a table to eat off, a stove to cook on and enough chairs for them to sit in. The apartment is as bleak as despair, but there is steam in the pipes, which is unusual, for this is a neighborhood of cold-water flats. There was a pot of coffee on the stove, and it was good coffee, strong without being thick and hot without scalding your tongue. The baby was asleep in the bedroom, and they sat in the kitchen.

"He is a crowd-pleaser," said Mrs Perez, whose first name is Phyllis. "He fought mains, too. But now he takes anything they give him. Perez is a clown. I don't want anyone to take advantage of him just because he's Puerto Rican. I don't think that's fair. That's when I get mad. That's why I'm there every time he fights. I know the business. Just because he's only a preliminary boy I don't want him to come home with twenty dollars in his pocket. He can't express himself. He is good-natured. That's why I'm there."

The baby whimpered in his sleep.

"This apartment," Perez said, "I had two fights in one week so we could get this apartment."

The fighter's wife lit a cigarette. She inhaled deeply, gave it to the fighter. He took a drag.

"We do that all the time," he said.

The fighter's wife laughed.

"I used to go high after a fight," Perez said. "No more. I got the kid."

Memory caused her to frown, and her voice was thick with a remembered sorrow. "Many a time we don't have milk for the kid. He goes down to the trucking place in the store downstairs. He says to the guy: 'Put me on a truck so we can have what to eat.' He's good that way. He has a temper, but he is good to me. He knows I'm a friend, his mother as well as his wife. I leave it up to him the way he makes a dollar. If he wants to quit, let him quit. I'm not going to stand in his way. All I'm interested in is he knows he has a son and he has to support him."

Their son awakened and screamed. The mother went into the room and took him in her arms. He is a fat child with the features of his father. She came back to sit at the table, the child, wet-faced with tears, sleepy in her arms.

"Socks cost fifty-nine cents a pair," Mrs. Perez said. "The socks he wears in the ring, I mean. We had two pairs of them. But they were damp. We had to buy a pair for the fight last night. Fifty-nine cents a pair. It is a lot of money when you haven't got much. I could have married other fellows who would give me more. But Perez tries. He gives – he gives open. What he has. I knew him a month, and I married him. It's two years now. I met him at a dance, and he is the best rhumba dancer you ever saw. He is no fool. He knows toilet water. He knows perfume. They call him Killer Perez when he is dressed up."

The fighter's wife rose and handed the baby to the fighter, and the child wept as the mother poured the coffee.

"What was the other name you had?" she asked.

"Buttons," the fighter said. "Buttons is a comedy book in Puerto Rico."

The fighter said with a quiet bitterness, "I do a favour for a Spanish guy. I give him the pair of trunks. I have no trunks last night. They try to make me buy another pair of trunks. I borrow the trunks from another guy. It is too much money to spend. Five dollars. Too much."

The fighter's wife said spitefully, "They made him fight hungry one time."

"I fight hungry a lot of times," the fighter said.

"I mean the time when he wouldn't trust you," the fighter's wife said.

"Not Johnny Schwartz," the fighter explained. "Another one. I am hungry before the fight. I say to this guy: 'Give me a dollar to eat.' This guy say to me: 'I don't lend money to fighters.' I say: 'You are my second. You will make money with me tonight when I fight.' He say: 'I wouldn't lend a fighter a nickel if he dropped dead.' I fight that night hungry."

The dignity of the State Athletic Commission baffles them. They can't understand why the deputy commissioners warn Perez not to attempt comedy while he is in the ring.

"They don't know what he is going to do next when he is clowning," the wife said. "He comes out with a mouth full of water and spits it right in the guy's face. He is the Al Schacht of boxing. He is the Puerto Rican Max Baer."

"I do everything for a little laugh," the fighter said.

The fighter's wife is not troubled when he loses.

"I usually tell him his faults when he loses," she said. "I always tell him. 'Lew, the next time you'll do better.' I tell him: 'You shouldn't of done that.' I understand boxing. With him it is not a money proposition. He likes to do his best. He has no manager, so a lot of times they give the fight to the other guy. But he's never been hurt seriously. He is not afraid of anyone. He would get in there with Joe Louis to make a dollar."

"I will fight anyone to make a dollar," the fighter said.

The fighter's wife said, "It's been a real tough buck a lot of times. Like the time I was in the hospital. He's sick, too."

The fighter's wife nodded to him, and he started to tell the story.

"My hands hurt," the fighter said. "I had a high fever. I could hardly stand on my feet. But no money in the house."

The fighter's wife said, "I didn't want him to take that fight, but he said: 'It's a few dollars. We could use a few dollars. We got nothing.' He couldn't tell them how sick he was. The commission doctor wouldn't pass him."

The fighter winced with the ache of the past.

"Jimmy Mangia," the fighter said. "I lose the decision. I was in bed three days after the fight. I couldn't move."

"He's good," she said. "He's real good. Why don't someone bother with him? Why don't he get a manager? He never will be a champion. But he's Perez, the clown. He's a crowdpleaser everywhere he goes. The people in the Garden would love him. Just a break is all he needs. Just one little break."

The baby fell asleep. She walked into the other room and laid the infant in the crib.

"I never had any affection," she said, embracing the fighter. "I wanted affection. I never had any friends or nothing like that. But I got everything I want right here."

The fighter said, "Maybe we get lucky."

EVEREST CONQUERED

The Times, 8 June 1953

James Morris (later Jan Morris) was *The Times'* "special correspondent" with the 1953 British Everest Expedition.

Camp IV, Everest, 31 May

THE masters of Everest, Hillary and Tensing, returned to this camp (22,000 ft.) from the South Col yesterday afternoon in a blaze of sunshine and triumphant emotion, bringing their news with them.

It was a significantly beautiful day among the snows of the upper Western Cwm. All was crisp and sparkling, with the awful block of Nuptse only faintly shining with the curious greasy sheen of the melting surface snow. From the ridge of Lhotse a spiral of snow powder was driven upwards by the wind like a genie from a bottle. From down the Cwm came from time to time a sudden thrilling high-pitched whistle as a boulder screamed down from the heights. Everest itself, its rock ridge graceless against a blue sky, was as hard and enigmatical as ever.

It was a day for great news. Here in the camp on the north side of the Cwm there was already yesterday morning a tension, nerve-racking and yet deliciously exciting. At 9 a.m. on the previous day, 29 May, the two summit climbers had been seen by their support group, Gregory, Lowe, and a Sherpa, already crossing the South Summit at about 28,500 feet, and going strongly up the final ridge.

The weather had been perfect, the gales of the preceding days which had so ravaged Camp VII on the South Col had died down. Hillary and Tensing were known to be two of the most powerful climbers in the world, and were using the well-tested open circuit oxygen equipment. Reports brought down from the South Summit by Bourdillon and Evans, who had reached it on 26 May in the expedition's first assault, seemed to show that the unknown final ridge was not impassable, though undoubtedly difficult.

Because of these several encouraging factors, hopes at Camp IV were dangerously high, and the feeling of taut nerves and suppressed wild convictions was immeasurably strengthened when, just before lunch, five tiny figures were seen making their way across the traverse at the top of the face of Lhotse. They could only be the summit team and their supporters from the South Col. They were moving fast, and in three hours they would be in the Cwm. The camp was now alive with stinging expectation. Here in the camp Colonel Hunt sat on a wooden packing case, physically immobile, his waterproof hat jammed hard over his head, his face white with plastered glacier cream. Four or five of the climbers vacantly fingered newspapers in the big pyramid tent. One man sat outside with binoculars reporting the progress of the descending party.

"They must be getting to Camp VI," the watchers said. "They are hidden behind that serac [irregular-shaped pinnacle of ice on a glacier, formed by the intersection of crevasses] with the vertical crack in it – you know the one." "Two of them are sitting down; now they are up again." "Only another hour to wait. What are the odds?" At last, soon after 1.30, just as the radio was announcing the reported failure of the assault, the party emerged above a rise in the ground 300 yards or so above the camp, their blue windproof jackets, sharp and cheerful against the glistening snow. Hillary and Tensing were leading. All at once it was through the camp by the magic wireless of excitement that Everest had been climbed.

There was a sudden rush up the snow slope in the sunshine to meet the assault party. Hillary, looking extraordinarily fresh, raised his ice axe in greeting. Tensing slipped sideways in the snow and smiled, and in a twice they were surrounded. Hands were wrung ecstatically, photographs taken, there was the whirr of the ciné-camera, and laughter interrupted congratulations.

Hillary and Tensing, by now old climbing colleagues, posed with arms interlocked, Hillary's face aglow but controlled, Tensing's split with a brilliant smile of pleasure. As the group moved down the hill into the camp a band of Sherpas came diffidently forward to pay tribute to the greatest climber of them all. Like a modest monarch, Tensing received their greeting. Some bent their bodies forward, their hands clasped as in prayer. Some shook hands lightly and delicately, the fingers scarcely touching. One veteran, his pigtail flowing, bowed to touch Tensing's hand with his forehead.

"We so far forgot ourselves," wrote an English climber of an earlier generation, "as to shake hands on the summit." This expedition so far forgot itself that everywhere one fancied that sunglasses were steaming embarrassingly: and suddenly, as if spontaneously, each climber, Hillary and Tensing the first of them, turned to Colonel Hunt, reflective in the background, and shook his hand in recognition of the truth that in a team venture of great happiness and success his has been the friendly hand which inexorably as it seems has led the expedition to success.

In the pyramid tent, over an omelet served on an aluminium plate, Hillary told the story of the final climb. The tent was uncomfortably crowded. Newspapers were all over the floor, and in one corner the discredited radio lay scornfully tilted on a cardboard box. The climbers sat around on packing-cases, groundsheets, and bedding rolls. From time to time the flushed face of an excited Sherpa would appear through the tent door with a word of delight.

Hillary's account began with the events of 28 May, when he, Tensing and the support party – Gregory, Lowe, and a tough young Sherpa, Ang Nima – left South Col to establish Camp VIII on the ridge below the South Summit. Colonel Hunt had already dumped most of the necessary stores at about 27,500 feet during the first "reconnaissance-assault". Now the camp was to be established at a point as high as possible so that the next day Hillary and Tensing, relying in large measure on their limited oxygen, would not have so far to climb. It had been planned that two Sherpas would accompany the party, but one was sick and as a result the amount of oxygen carried had to be reduced.

The party left Camp VII on the South Col, about seven, and set off up the back-breaking steepness of the ridge to find a suitable camp site for climbers carrying 50 lb. to 65 lb. each and Sherpas 40 lb. to 45 lb. It was a difficult climb. For what seemed hours no possible site showed itself, and the ridge was covered with difficult snow. Oxygen began to run short, and Gregory and Ang Nima had to use some from the assault cylinders. Tensing remembered a possible tent site just below Lambert's Point. Successive ridges in the rock proved impracticable, but at last the place was found at an estimated 27,800 feet. Camp VIII was established – incomparably the highest camp ever put up on a mountain – and Gregory and Lowe, their mission brilliantly accomplished, returned to the South Col.

Hillary and Tensing were left alone in their eyrie. They spent the next two hours pitching a tent on the snow-covered rock, but were handicapped by the lack of rock pitons. The tent platform was on two levels, with a step in the middle. Tensing sat in the lower half, Hillary in the top.

As darkness gathered they took a little sleeping oxygen, but throughout the night they sustained themselves with sardines and biscuits – "paradise" is Tensing's word for them. It was a calm night though a cold one – the temperature at one time was minus 27 deg. Centigrade. At four in the morning they thawed their boots over the Primus stove, and half an hour later looked out of the tent. It was a glorious clear morning, calm and peaceful. They could see far down the valley to the monastery of Thyangboche, the expedition's original rear base, on its lofty wooded hill.

They were away from camp by six o'clock on 29 May, and started up through deep, crusty, powdered snow towards the South Summit. There were no signs of tracks left by Bourdillon and Evans and they had to cut steps constantly, taking it in turns to break the trail. They kept going steadily, but Hillary describes this climb to the South Summit as the hardest part of the day. At nine they were on the South Summit, the little knoll of snow-capped rock about half a mile from the summit proper, and were seen by the exhilarated watchers on the South Col. They spent ten minutes there, and took off their oxygen masks without any sudden reaction. Nevertheless their main worry was their short-age of oxygen supplies. To economize, when they moved off again they reduced their flow of oxygen from the normal four litres a minute to three.

They were now on the final ridge of Everest, never reached before. Hillary describes it as "technically good, interesting

Alpine work". They moved along the west side of the ridge, characterized by difficult cornices, with occasional glimpses of this camp, an infinity below. They crossed safely the one major obstacle on the ridge, a difficult rock step almost vertical. At every moment they expected to see the summit, but time and again minor elevations deceived them. It was at 11.30 a.m., 29 May 1953, that they stepped at last on to the snow-covered final eminence of Everest.

Hillary describes this as "a symmetrical, beautiful snow cone summit" – very different from the harsh rock ridge which is all that can be seen from below. The view was not spectacular. They were too high for good landscape, and all below looked flat and monotonous.

To the north the route to the summit on which pre-war Everest expeditions pinned their hopes looked in its upper reaches prohibitively steep. Tensing spent the fifteen minutes on the summit eating mint cake and taking photographs, for which purpose Hillary removed his oxygen mask without ill effects. Tensing produced a string of miscellaneous flags and held them high, while Hillary photographed them. They included the Union Jack, the Nepal flag, and that of the United Nations. Tensing, who is a devout Buddhist, also laid on the ground in offering some sweets, bars of chocolate, and packets of biscuits.

At 11.45 they left the summit on the return climb, keeping a careful check on the oxygen gauges. Because of the shortage of oxygen supplies they dare not stay at the ridge camp, and they moved straight down towards the South Col, the going being reasonably good. Above the South Col they met Lowe and Noyce. Noyce was the leader of a rescue or reinforcement party which had come up from Camp IV; it was Noyce's second climb to the South Col. By 4.30 all four were back at Camp VII, and yesterday morning, 30 May, they made their way down the face of Lhotse to the Cwm.

Hillary and Tensing seem in astonishingly good form, with none of the desperate fatigue that has overcome Everest summit parties in the past. Nor have they any other than modest pride in their achievements, and more still in the wonderful success of the expedition as a whole. The heroic quality is undoubtedly in them, as it is in most of this fine team, but yesterday afternoon, after the first flood of emotion, it was agreeably shielded by the aura of not very good omelets (eaten indigestibly fast), untidy tents, high spirits, and home thoughts from abroad.

For within a day or two the expedition will be down at the base camp at Khumbu Glacier on its way home. One obstacle remains before it – the icefall has now changed beyond recognition since the centre of operations moved into the Western Cwm. Three weeks ago it had a certain stark and nasty grandeur; now, under the pressure of the thaw, it resembles nothing so much as a gigantic squashed meringue. It is as if the mountain, thwarted of its isolation, has prepared one last hazard for the climbers, and there is certainly no member of the expedition who will not feel a deep relief when this danger is passed.

Setting foot on the base camp again will be a symbol, undramatic perhaps but vivid, that implacable Everest's sting has been drawn at last. It has been drawn, if one may descend for a moment into the personal, by as good a company of adventurers under as skilful a captain as your Correspondent can ever expect to meet.

BILLY GRAHAM IN NEW YORK

Manchester Guardian, 7 March 1955

The veteran English correspondent Cooke (1908–) has reported on US affairs for several British newspapers; his radio "Letter from America", meanwhile, is the longest running solo programme on BBC wireless. It was first broadcast in 1946.

New York, 4 March

Billy Graham is a deeply modest man. He never minded his obscurity in his native land. He had to wrestle with the devil all over Europe, draw crowds he never dreamed of, and received the blessing of the Archbishop of Canterbury before it occurred to him that the Lord might be reserving the main bout for Madison Square Garden.

Last night he made it. He came for the first time into the arena of the immortals and took his place with them, with Joe Louis, and Al Smith, with the rodeo and Thomas Edmund Dewey, and the Ringling circus. His debut was held under the tested auspices of The Word of Life Hour, a network radio programme, a weekly offshoot of an established holy enterprise known as The Word of Life Fellowship, Inc. Fifteen years ago this now booming salvation industry had a kitty of only three hundred dollars, and its original investors were a young couple who felt burdened to claim verses like Jeremiah, xxxiii. 3: "Call unto me, and I will answer thee, and shew thee great and mighty things." Today the weekly budget is a mighty six thousand dollars, and last night's rally was the eighth the Fellowship has been prosperous enough to hold in Madison Square Garden.

So in a sense Billy Graham has not yet met the challenge of our town, of the neon-lit Babylon he longs to claim for the Lord. His audience was built in. And there was no exact way of knowing how many of the sailors from the Eighth Avenue saloons, the curious cab-drivers, the penitent delicatessen-owners would have slipped in there if they had not been fairly sure of fusing their identity with a solid nucleus of the saved. It was apparent at once that the multitude was made up of anything but hungry heathens and vagrant Runyonites. They were smartly dressed, as our English idiom has it, meaning they looked clean and tasteless in a respectable way. Some of the old men had an owlish earnestness, and many of the young men were bridled colts, sweating with the guilt of delinquent fantasies they were here to prohibit. They all sat so prim and orderly under three limp Old Glories and a white flag with a red cross, that the curving rows of seats and the dividing aisles were just as they appear in the seating plan. Unsmeared by foul tobacco smoke or any of the fumes of sin, the air was crystalline, clear enough to count the faithful. The *New York Times* counted 22,000, the *Herald Tribune* 19,000, an Irish cop with his sights on Rome charitably guessed that the assembly of heretics ran to no more than 15,000.

But however many there were, the great bulk of them, it seemed to one sinner, were joyless matrons and their lumpish daughters. Not a smitch or smear of lipstick violated their well pursed lips. Not a pretty girl or a roguish buck in the lot. But neither were they drab. There is something in the full-time practice of virtue that inclines the female of the species especially to hydrangea blue. It would take a complexion as blooded as Santa Claus and a skin tone as flashing as a Hawaiian to rescue the human face from such an ocean of ghastly blue. Ava Gardner herself would drown incognito in it. Not one, alas, of the greyfaced angels who sported it salvaged her features. They sat, row upon serried row, in a faceless sea, until the music started. Only the smiling ushers, all enrolled servants of The Word of Life Fellowship Inc., exercised that occupational cordiality they share with insurance agents and airline hostesses. It was they, and their similarly radiant brothers on the platform, who – as they say in secular circles only two blocks away – "had the joint jumpin'".

Came first Cliff Barrows, the song leader, a friendly professional greeter type with no more diffidence than a radio announcer. His conducting was a mere bow to custom, for the true believers had known these tunes since the day they saw the light and they took off on the upbeat and bellowed in remarkable unison and tunefulness through one majestic hymn by Haydn and two awful caterwaulings by Anon. Then we had "your favourite and mine", Beverly Shea, the Graham team's travelling baritone, who modulates a voice of pleasing timbre with a breathing trick or two learned from Crosby. The show moved on as slickly as a Republican rally, the Word of Life quarter next gliding to the microphone. Four slim young men in blue coats and light slacks chanting "I'm redeemed" in the oldtime gospel tempo with crooning overtones. They were accompanied by a girl at an electric organ, and ever afterwards its throbbing tremolo hung on the air to soften the hard-hearted and sicken the musical.

Just before the great man stood up, a very pretty girl walked in, wearing a fitted grey silk blouse and a flaring black skirt that were mated by a twenty-inch waist. She had a Grace Kelly hair-do and a fetching pout, and the cop who piloted her in was as nonplussed as the scowling rows of angels. But she was some relative, evidently, of the radio technician supervising a tape-recorder and she naturally gravitated to the neutral compound of the press. She had no sort of connexion with the official goings-on and was plainly so baffled by it all that she could be instantly discounted as non-union competition. She was joined a few minutes later by a second houri, a strawberry blonde in a black sheath. But by then Billy was in full cry, and if this couple had been hired as decoys of the Devil to test and strengthen the flock, it was a wasted effort. No one paid them any kind of attention, except three long-haired scribblers from the British press.

By Billy's express command there was no clap or salute when he rose. He welcomed them all to Jesus. He declared that Churchill and Eisenhower had both said that the only salvation of the Western world lay in a religious revival, "and if our intellectual and political leaders say so we as Christians better be about it". A stalwart coloured man in a port-side gallery let out a resonant "Yeah!" But Billy turned his pained Apollonine profile, and the ushers dashed to smoke the man out. He never did it again; it was the one and only echo from the crowd all evening of the honest orgies by the levees and the Mississippi baptisms long ago.

They showed no sign of trance, but maybe they knew that this was only the teaser. Billy would be back. For the present he wanted to say why he was here. New York might not be wickeder than any other place, but it was no better: "Crime is rampant, juvenile delinquency is out of hand, church attendance is below the national average." He stood at a big redwood lectern (he called it a podium), a gift from the president of International Business Machines. It was, said Billy, equipped with "all sorts of buttons and controls" that timed the speaker and flashed warning lights. The red light glowed, and Billy shrugged an admission that his time was up. At the barest flutter of applause he thundered:

"Every time I see my name up in lights, every time I am patted on the back . . . it makes me sick at heart . . . for God said He will share His glory with no man. So if you want to stop my ministry, pat *me* on the back."

No one breathed. His lilting Southern voice rode the steady, well-tempered hum of the air conditioning. He was going to collect the expenses of his coming Scottish campaign. He was going, he said heartrendingly, to help to save Glasgow. There was a rustle and a clinking as many bodies leaned over to reach in their pockets, to dig deep for the unshriven souls of Glasgow.

The Word of Life quartet came back again, ripe now with a barber-shop pathos. And again the electric organ spilled its treacly glissandos. It set the tone for a confessional by a former all-American football star, who wanted to know, "Who's coaching you in this great game of life?" The vast audience heaved in again with a mournful melody, wobbling over a wailing counterpoint, to the effect that "On Christ, the solid rock, I stand; all other ground is sinking sand."

At last it was time. Time for "the message". Time for Billy to give his all. Time, he said for "absolute silence, for thirty minutes, there must be no talking, no applause, no whispering, no movement anywhere, time that we have this like a sanctuary and a church service without a sound." He must be the only modern performer who can demand silence and get it.

He took from Luke xiv. the 18th verse: "And they all with one consent began to make excuse." It was a perfect text for his method, which is not, like the old Salvationists, to threaten hellfire and palpitate the audience with pictures of the brimstone sins, of lust and greed and lust especially; but to sympathize with the modern confusion of the ordinary decent man, to chide with a muscular paternal understanding the twentieth-century sinner, the lie abed, the procrastinator, the fretted business man, the preoccupied breadwinner, the city dweller fearful of the hydrogen bomb.

"Sure, Billy," he hears them whine, "I'll come to Jesus, but not just now." Meanwhile they go about their pestiferous "business", they get "ulcers and all the other diseases". To what end? "Every fourth person here" – he intoned it like a curse – "will be dead in ten years, if the law of averages works out. Dead!"

So how do we mortals spend our precious time? Yearning for "the riches of Wall Street, the gold of Fort Knox, all the pleasures of Hollywood?" Maybe not, but "You've sold your soul for a little bit of it. You don't deny Christ in the flesh, but you won't stand up and accept Him." And you know why? Because "with one consent they all began to make excuse". And for why, what are you afraid of? What will the boys at the office say, the men on the football team, the girls in the block? "What'll the crowd I run with think? isn't that it?"

He knew there were "hundreds of people here who have their names on a church list. On Sundays you have a halo around your head, and Monday morning the horns begin to grow." Well, he was going to tell them, he was going to put it on the line. He had a man come to him and say, "Billy, I'd have to give up my job. I can't become a Christian." His job? A bartender." "You surely can't, Brother," I said to him. And this man earned forty-five dollars a week. Well, the Devil couldn't buy *my soul* for forty-five lousy dollars a week." He was going to tell them right now, tonight, because now was the time. He rocked with the accented syllables: "You-can't-be-a-Christian-and-live-any-way-you-want-to."

Amen, breathed a man down front, and a pink-cheeked usher fixed him with his eye. None of that, he seemed to say, none of that old-time vulgar gospel stuff. Where do you think you are, Little Rock, Arkansas? Well, sure enough, we were in Madison Square Garden, spacious and metropolitan, glistening with high floodlights, uniquely clean. We had a pulpit fashioned by International Business Machines, and a switch-board with lights clocking the schedule, and burring tape recorders, and a shepherd in double-breasted blue gaberdine. But as he gets into his stride, he is seen to be treading out the vintage with the original God of Wrath. For though his Jesus is no black-browed, bearded Old Testament avenger, he is also not the "weak, frail, effeminate" hero of the calendars. Billy routs the myth of the Pale Galilean, who he implies could conquer nothing and nobody in this vitamin-packed age. No, he must be put in training and brought up to date. Why, shouts Billy, angry that the news is not yet an axiom, "He was a real he-man; talk about your football players . . . He was physically the strongest man on earth."

Billy is full of surprising information of this sort, and of free-ranging quotations of the words of Christ, of rescued admonitions and snappy warnings and rousing pep talks that must have got lost in all versions of the New Testament later than the Aramaic. It is this bulging image that excites him into something bordering on ecstasy. And now as he talks, and begins to crouch and gesture like a Friday-night football coach, his tenor voice hardens and he falls into a metrical sob. For all his microphone suavity and the gorgeous contour of his hair-do, he is one at last with the grizzled rustics who bark damnation over the hill-billies down by the river. And it is in his voice and tone and phrasing that the old Bible-thumping South claims its own.

"He was a man like you, but He was God. If the chisel should slip in the carpenter's shop, His blood was warm and red, warm like yours, brother, red like yours." The unmistakable repetitions come in ("I married a wife and therefore I cannot come. I married a wife. Brother, you got the best excuse right there.") The same over-and-over, syncopated phrasing of the blues. He threw his arms high to mime Christ on the Cross. And in the panting apostrophe of "Je-sus!", phrased as three syllables, he was not far away from the strain of the Reverend Heck Mosby of Beale Street, Memphis, who used to stump up to his pulpit on a wooden leg, throw his arms high and chant "O Lord, O Boss Man".

What is modern and superior in his cunning, and it could be wholly unconscious, is the prohibition of all applause. He cages up his audience for thirty minutes and dangles red meat from outside. And when he finally braces his splendid biceps and bends the bars apart, where else can the sprung prisoners go but to him? They are demonstrably free to scatter, but they are just as visibly transfixed by the fear of the Saviour, who has been recreated in the image, however glamorous and cleanlimbed, of Big Brother. This Jesus is a snooping, darting detective, spotting you in your mirror, riding in the Underground, watching at the foot of your bed, anticipating the waking excuse, posted at every exit of the Garden if you should dare to bolt for it. The jig is up, the sinners are told.

And when Billy cools off and drops his voice to a whisper, and begs the organ start up its artful gurgle, and says he will stand and pray and wait for the brave to come forward, there is only a momentary pause. And they burst the unbearable silence and shuffle up: the halt and the lame in spirit, surely, but also the pasty-faced, the mean, the care-worn, a hangdog sailor, "teen-agers" in desperation, a mountainous mother and her huge sullen daughters, regiments of the awkward and the unloved; and possibly somewhere in here a few humble souls holding fast, against all the foregoing seductions, to the mild Man of the New Testament, to that gentle Jesus, no athlete, who "best to love is and most meek". But how many have responded to "the strongest man in the world", the clean-limbed Superman, something not unlike the 6 ft. 4 in. Billy himself?

Decency will not stay for an answer. It is our time now, time to leave quietly, to exchange the electric organ and its gargling vox humana for the comparative wholesomeness of Eighth Avenue, with its movie houses and pawnshops, drugstores and bars, and cops on clanking horses. For the converted there will be hours, perhaps days or months, of peace. For the others there was one flawless jewel to take away: Billy's grateful recollection of Cecil B. deMille standing last summer on Mount Sinai and crying aloud to his minions – "Cut out two tablets of stone and carve on them the Ten Commandments and give them to Billy Graham. And they carved out two stones and gave me the Ten Commandments." Moses did no better.

THE WEDDING OF GRACE KELLY AND PRINCE RAINIER

Express '56, 1957

Kelly's wedding to the Prince of Monaco took place on 19 April 1956. Edgar was the London *Daily Express*' man at the scene.

It was a sparkling morning on Thursday as I got into my stiff shirt, tied my white tie and put on my tail-coat for the final act of the Monte Carlo spectacular – the nuptial mass in the Cathedral which would add the blessing of the Church to the marriage of Grace and Rainier. There had been much discussion – even passionate at times – among the British and American male guests whether to wear morning coats or to conform to the European custom and appear in what we know as evening dress. I did not trouble to argue. If they wanted me to wear evening dress at a morning ceremony, well and good, for by this time I would have been quite willing to hire the full-dress uniform of Napoleon's Old Guard.

Helen Hamer arrived in the *Express* Rolls to pick me up. She looked delightful and as stylish as any of the daughters of the rich and famous. The Rolls idea did not turn out too good, except for the photographers, for we had to walk most of the way up the hill to the Cathedral.

It was certainly an impressive sight! There was a carefully swept red carpet and on either side were naval detachments from the visiting warships – American, French and Italian sailors and a party of Royal Marines from HMS *Dalrymple*. There were squads of photographers, TV camera crews and a film unit. I noted some new names to add to my list – Somerset Maugham looking absolutely immaculate, a credit to his tailor and valet, Lady Diana Cooper, the widow of Duff Cooper who after the war had been a renowned ambassador to France, and the enormously tall Conrad Hilton, who was there as President Eisenhower's representative, not as the immensely rich hotel proprietor whose hotels now proclaim American influence, if not elegance, throughout the world.

I took Helen's arm and we found our places in the Cathedral. There was a long wait and I had time to look around and admire the efficiency of the MGM technicians. Everything had been organized to make a great film sequence. Finally, to solemn organ music Grace came up the aisle on the arm of her father. Once more one could not but admire her loveliness. Rainier followed, beetle-browed as ever, once more laden with medals and decorations. The arc-lamps came on; the photographers and cameramen behind and on each side of the altar began their work.

Even in that theatrical setting, even with that sort of a congregation, the beauty of the nuptial mass with noble music, well-rehearsed choir and the ritual Latin phrases of the priests wove its spell. They say that in the film, which I did not see, tears fell down Grace's cheeks as she knelt before the altar. Were they sincere? Were they the final proof of professionalism? I incline to the former.

After the ceremony I guided Helen along a narrow, picturesque lane to the courtyard of the Palace where tables were laden with salmon, chicken and every sort of delicacy and where champagne flowed bountifully. The wedding-cake was an enormous work of art.

The now indubitable Princess Grace of Monaco showed herself with her husband to the crowds lining the streets of the town in an open Rolls, loaned by the millionaire Scottish draper, Hugh Fraser. She prayed, according to the tradition of newly wed Princesses of Monaco, at the shrine of the local patron saint, Dévote, in the tiny church dedicated to her.

Grace appeared on the Palace balcony in all her splendour, smiling and waving. Rainier, by her side, managed an uneasy grin. I think our Helen enjoyed it all though she only nervously sipped her champagne and nibbled at a sandwich. I delivered her back safely to the yacht and Eve Perrick and went back to the hotel to get out of my stiff collar and think about the story I would be writing.

In the afternoon Grace and Rainier embarked on the *Deo Juvante* for their honeymoon cruise and sailed out of the harbour with crowds waving and ships and yachts sounding their sirens.

It was over! It was finally over! The bar of the Hôtel de Paris filled up with men and women journalists stretching themselves at ease, even smiling at each other as the consciousness grew that the struggle was over – even with Rainier's officials. In the evening there was dancing in the streets, wine flowed and rockets soared once more in the sky – no doubt, once more at the expense of Mr Onassis.

D. SEFTON DELMER

THE REVOLUTION IN HUNGARY

Daily Express, 24 October 1956

The Communists – with Russian backing – had taken power in Hungary in 1947, and made the country a one-party Stalinist state. Throughout the 1950s discontent with the regime grew, causing dissension within the Communists' ranks themselves, with a popular, liberal wing growing up around prime minister Imre Nagy. On 23 October an anti-Stalinist insurrection broke out in Budapest.

Budapest 23 October 1956

I have been the witness today of one of the great events of history. I have seen the people of Budapest catch the fire lit in Poznan and Warsaw and come out into the streets in open rebellion against their Soviet overlords. I have marched with them and almost wept for joy with them as the Soviet emblems in the Hungarian flags were torn out by the angry and exalted crowds. And the great point about the rebellion is that it looks like being successful.

As I telephone this dispatch I can hear the roar of delirious crowds made up of student girls and boys, of Hungarian soldiers still wearing their Russian-type uniforms, and overalled factory workers marching through Budapest and shouting defiance against Russia. "Send the Red Army home," they roar. "We want free and secret elections." And then comes the ominous cry which one always seems to hear on these occasions. "Death to Rakosi." Death to the former Soviet puppet dictator – now taking a "cure" on the Russian Black Sea Riviera – whom the crowds blame for all the ills that have befallen their country in eleven years of Soviet puppet rule.

Leaflets demanding the instant withdrawal of the Red Army and the sacking of the present Government are being showered among the street crowds from trams. The leaflets have been printed secretly by students who "managed to get access", as they put it, to a printing shop when newspapers refused to publish their political programme. On house walls all over the city primitively stencilled sheets have been pasted up listing the sixteen demands of the rebels.

But the fantastic and, to my mind, really superingenious feature of this national rising against the Hammer and Sickle, is that it is being carried on under the protective red mantle of pretended Communist orthodoxy. Gigantic portraits of Lenin are being carried at the head of the marchers. The purged ex-Premier Imre Nagy, who only in the last couple of weeks has been readmitted to the Hungarian Communist Party, is the rebels" chosen champion and the leader whom they demand must be given charge of a new free and independent Hungary. Indeed, the Socialism of this ex-Premier and – this is my bet – Premier-soon-to-be-again, is no doubt genuine enough. But the youths in the crowd, to my mind, were in the vast majority as anti-Communist as they were anti-Soviet – that is if you agree with me that calling for the removal of the Red Army is anti-Soviet.

In fact there was one tricky moment when they almost came to blows on this point. The main body of students and marchers had already assembled outside their university in front of the monument to the poet-patriot Petofi who led the 1848 rebellion against the Austrians. Suddenly a new group of students carrying red banners approached from a side street. The banners showed them to be the students of the Leninist-Marxist Institute, which trains young teachers of Communist ideology and supplies many of the puppet rulers' civil servants.

The immediate reaction of the main body, I noticed, was to shout defiance and disapproval of the oncoming ideologists. But they were quickly hushed into silence and the ideologists joined in the march with the rest of them, happily singing the *Marseillaise*.

PICASSO, 75, GETS A SURPRISE PRESENT

Evening Standard, 26 October 1956

White was Paris correspondent for the London *Evening Standard for* forty years.

I came here to see Pablo Picasso on his seventy-fifth birthday bearing a gift from a former mistress of his. She is Dora Maar, who lived with him during the thirties.

Mlle Maar is a Roman Catholic and the present she sent this gnarled old atheist was a devotional book by a Dominican priest.

I had a moment of apprehension on delivering it, fearing that Picasso might receive it with a touch of facetiousness – some joking reference to her efforts at converting him. Not a bit of it. His eyes positively gleamed with pleasure as he handled this paper-backed book.

The next moment there was uproar. Picasso seemed to be in half a dozen different rooms at once as he shouted for his present companion, Jacqueline Roque. "Come at once, where are you? I have just had a present from Dora."

I looked round the room during his absence. Chaos. A birthday chaos superimposed on the normal chaos. There were mounds of paper from unwrapped parcels everywhere, piles of telegrams and letters.

The room was uncarpeted, barely furnished. There were litters of newspapers, magazines, books, and canvases everywhere.

There was a similar chaos about the birthday preparations. No invitations had been sent out.

"I expect those of my friends who can make it to just drop in," said Picasso. As a result about half a dozen people were already camped in the villa.

The house itself is a three-storeyed wedding-cake affair, built by a Victorian champagne millionaire.

Picasso bought it recently for £15,000, leaving the villa in the nearby pottery town of Vallauris, in which he had lived since the war, in the possession of a former mistress, Françoise Gilot, in whose name it had been bought.

The house remains in exactly the same state of neglect as when Picasso bought it, and this, combined with a neglected garden, gives the house an unlived-in look.

Picasso cares nothing for appearances, and simply does not see the ugliness of the house.

He likes to tease friends to comment on it by saying: "Ah, good taste, what a dreadful thing. Taste is the enemy of creativeness."

Apart from Mlle Roque and Picasso only two other people live in it, an elderly couple, the woman doing the cooking, and her husband the odd jobs and butlery.

Paul, Picasso's son by his only marriage, chauffeurs his father in a large American car which has replaced the now decrepit Hispano, which he used before the war.

Mlle Roque is a strikingly handsome woman, approaching middle-age, bosomy, short, with a beautifully cut profile, which is seen in a great deal of Picasso's latest work.

She is a native of Vallauris, and was formerly the wife of a minor French colonial official. She is a woman of superb poise. coupled with a very attractive directness of manner.

She dresses almost dowdily, in French provincial fashion, and her only affectation is a black handkerchief which she wears as a hat in something of the shape of a Spanish mantilla.

Picasso himself is an astonishingly dashing figure, with a peasant's rude health and vitality.

See him as I saw him yesterday dressed up to receive a civic welcome from the town council of Vallauris and he looks like an Andalusian rancher (he is, of course, an Andalusian) dressed in his swaggering Sunday best.

He was wearing a beautifully cut, almost skin-tight, pair of black trousers, a delicately knit black matador's jacket which shone like silk, and a string tie.

All that was missing were the high-heeled boots.

That was only one of the day's functions, for in the evening he was received by the pottery workers at Vallauris, where he blew out the seventy-five candles on his birthday cake in three lusty gusts.

He was still going strong late into the night, when everyone else was wilting in the over-crowded, over-heated room.

This boundless good health of Picasso's is no accident. He takes great care of himself. He eats sparingly and simply, drinks nothing apart from an occasional glass of champagne, or white wine.

He appears to smoke heavily – about thirty black tobacco cigarettes a day – but in fact he does not inhale. He sleeps late, rarely rising before twelve, and goes to bed well after midnight.

His eating habits remain Spanish – late afternoon lunches and near-midnight dinners. He is much shorter than his head-and-shoulder photographs suggest. He is, in fact, a small-boned little man with delicate hands, small feet and somewhat spindly legs.

Picasso is a strangely uncomplex character. He is superstitious and sentimental, hates old age and has a horror of death.

Part of the reason why his home is so cluttered up is that he loathes to part with anything, no matter how slight, which has a sentimental or symbolic value for him.

A friend summed up this aspect of his character to me:

"Picasso does not throw away things or people that have become part of him."

His relations with the women who have played a part in his life is one of close friendship.

Similarly, both his art dealer, Daniel Kahnweiller, and his financial adviser are people he has known for nearly fifty years.

His loyalty to friends remains untouched, even by meanness or silliness on their part.

As to his membership of the Communist Party, that, too, is now encased in the hard shell of his loyalty.

There remains the question of his fortune which technically ought to be immense.

A Picasso sketch is worth about £700 and recently a small painting from his "Blue" period was sold for £20,000.

His own tastes are simple, and all the women who have figured in his life have been similarly indifferent to money or developed extravagant tastes.

Only one man knows how Picasso's money is disposed of, and that is an old friend, a retired French banker, Max Pellequer.

BOB ADIE

THE SPORTSWRITER

Washington Post and Times Herald, 13 August 1957

Adie knew of what he wrote; he was a sports columnist for the *Post and Times Herald*.

He affects sports shirts, sports jackets, sports overcoats, and sports shoes. He would like to affect a sports car, but he can only afford the sports cap. But, as you can see, he is a sport all the way.

He usually has had very little sports experience on the playing field. In high school and college, he was the official scorer, the waterboy, the equipment man, the team manager. When anyone asks him if he played college football, he says: "I was too light."

He's a frustrated foreign correspondent (who is a frustrated sportswriter). He would like to wear a trenchcoat, smoke a pipe, wear a fuzzy hat with a feather in it, speak nine foreign languages, and escort mysterious Swedish beauties out of the country a step ahead of the Russian spy ring which is trying to steal the secret on how to wear seersucker suits without wrinkling the cloth.

He's also a political seer and thinks he never misses picking a presidential race. After all, he figures, he picks sixteen teams in the major leagues in baseball and then picks the No. One football team in the country out of hundreds of aspirants; so how hard can it be to pick between two candidates?

He can never leave his work because people won't let him. After all, he's in sports and sports to most people are recreation and relaxation. People like to relax talking about sports.

If he marries – and he usually does to pick up a reader – his wife generally knows nothing about sports and couldn't care less. If he has any kids they must be in the mould of the champions he has admired.

If people look down their nose at his occupation, the sportswriter is quick to remind you that some of our most respected pundits were once sportswriters – people like Westbrook Pegler, Paul Gallico, the late Heywood Broun, Scotty Reston, Drew Middleton, Eddy Gilmore, George Dixon, and Winston Churchill. (Churchill covered cricket during the Boer War.)

He's proud of his profession and points to such giants in his business as the late Damon Runyon, the late Ring Lardner, the late W.O. McGeehan, the late Grantland Rice, and the late O. B. Keeler. The reason he admires all the late sportswriters is that our hero will never admit anyone alive is better than he is. But still he's proud of his integrity and points to the famous line of W. O. McGeehan, who was once offered a sum of money for a story. "If it's a bribe, it's not enough," W. O. said. "If it's a gift, it's too much."

He always brings up the story of John Kieran, the erudite, onetime sportswriter of the New York *Times*. John was asked to speak at Yale but some students objected to the compromise with intellectualism in allowing a sportswriter to address a group of old Eli's sons. So Kieran made his entire address in Latin.

He's proud, too, of the "characters" in his business – fellows who have become legends with their flights of whimsey. There was the old sportswriter, for instance, who was asked by a cub: "Is that the west where the sun is setting?" And the veteran replied: "If it isn't you have one helluva story, son." Then there were the two New York sportswriters in Texas covering the Giants spring training years ago. They got homesick while "tapping the tea" and decided to take a taxi all the way back to New York. As they got in the cab, one said: "You'd better get in first because I'm getting out on 34th Street."

He is, after all, a newspaperman so he's proud of his scoops. But the day he writes a story which beats everybody else, people will forget where they read about it.

He is quick to defend and slow to offend. He can count on the fingers of one hand the number of athletes who have ever thanked him for a story but if he had a dime for every guy who threatened him when he wrote a critical story, he'd be too rich to write sports.

He can pontificate on the strategy of a football coach who has something like one hundred intricate plays at his command and usually has them executed with the precision of a machine. But that doesn't awe the sportswriter, who figures all coaches are managing editors with their brains knocked out. (Or maybe it's the other way around.)

He lives in a beautiful world where it's always game time and yesterday's tragedies fade like the ripples on a lake. He's the eternal juvenile who would not change places with a king. He's Pagliacci, the Pied Piper, Walter Mitty, Peter Pan, and Jack Armstrong, the All-American Boy.

LITTLE ROCK –
VIOLENCE AT CENTRAL HIGH

Associated Press, 4 September 1957

For his accounts of the Little Rock, Arkansas, School integration crisis, Relman "Pat" Morin won the Pulitzer for national reporting in 1958. He has previously won the Pulitzer for international reporting (with Don Whithead, also of AP) for dispatches from the Korean War.

It was exactly like an explosion, a human explosion.

At 8.35 a.m., the people standing in front of the high school looked like the ones you see every day in a shopping center.

A pretty, sweet-faced woman with auburn hair and a jewel-green jacket. Another holding a white portable radio to her ear. "I'm getting the news of what's going on at the high school," she said. People laughed. A grey-haired man, tall and spare, leaned over the wooden barricade. "If they're coming," he said, quietly, "they'll be here soon." "They better," said another, "I got to get to work."

Ordinary people – mostly curious, you would have said – watching a high school on a bright blue-and-gold morning.

Five minutes later, at 8.40, they were a mob.

The terrifying spectacle of 200-odd individuals, suddenly welded together into a single body, took place in the barest fraction of a second. It was an explosion, savagery chain-reacting from person to person, fusing them into a white-hot mass.

There are three glass windowed telephone booths across the street from the south end of the high school.

At 8.35, I was inside one of them, dictating.

I saw four Negroes coming down the center of the street, in

twos. One was tall and big shouldered. One was tall and thin. The other two were short. The big man had a card in this hat and was carrying a Speed Graphic, a camera for taking news pictures.

A strange, animal; growl rose from the crowd.

"Here come the Negroes."

Instantly, people turned their backs on the high school and ran toward the four men. They hesitated. Then they turned to run.

I saw the white men catch them on the sidewalk and the lawn of a home, a quarter-block away. There was a furious, struggling knot. You could see a man kicking at the big Negro. Then another jumped on his back and rode him to the ground, forearms deep in the Negro's throat.

They kicked him and beat him on the ground and they smashed his camera to splinters. The other three ran down the street with one white man chasing them. When the white man saw he was alone, he turned and fled back toward the crowd.

Meanwhile, five policemen had rescued the big man.

I had just finished saying, "Police escorted the big man away –"

At that instant, a man shouted, "Look, the niggers are going in."

Directly across from me, three Negro boys and five girls were walking toward the side door at the south end of the school.

It was an unforgettable tableau.

They were carrying books. White bobby-sox, part of the high school uniform, glinted on the girls' ankles. They were all neatly dressed. The boys wore open-throat shirts and the girls ordinary frocks.

They weren't hurrying. They simply strolled across perhaps fifteen yards from the sidewalk to the school steps. They glanced at the people and the police as though none of this concerned them.

You can never forget a scene like that.

Nor the one that followed.

Like a wave, the people who had run toward the four Negro men, now swept back toward the police and the barricades.

"Oh, God, the niggers are in the school," a man yelled.

A woman – the one with the auburn hair and green jacket – rushed up to him. Her face was working with fury now.

Her lips drew back in a snarl and she was screaming, "Did they go in?"

"The niggers are in the school," the man said.

"Oh, God," she said. She covered her face with her hands. Then she tore her hair, still screaming.

She looked exactly like the women who cluster around a mine head when there has been an explosion and men are trapped below.

The tall, lean man jumped up on one of the barricades. He was holding on to the shoulders of others nearby.

"Who's going through?" he roared.

"We all are," the people shrieked.

They surged over and around the barricades, breaking for the police.

About a dozen policemen, in short-sleeved blue shirts, swinging billy clubs, were in front of them.

Men and women raced toward them and the policemen raised their clubs, moving this way and that as people tried to dodge around them.

A man went down, pole-axed when a policeman clubbed him.

Another, with crisp curly black hair, was quick as a rat. He dodged between two policemen and got as far as the schoolyard. There the others caught him.

With swift, professional skill, they pulled his coat half-way down his back, pinning his arms. In a flash they were hustling him back toward the barricades.

A burly, thick-bodied man wearing a construction worker's "hard hat" charged a policeman. Suddenly, he stopped and held both hands high above his head.

I couldn't see it, but I assume the officer jammed a pistol in his ribs.

Meanwhile, the women – the auburn-haired one, the woman with the radio, and other – were swirling around the police commanding officers.

Tears were streaming down their faces. They acted completely distraught.

It was pure hysteria.

And they kept crying, "The niggers are in our school. Oh, God, are you going to stand there and let the niggers stay in school?"

Then, swiftly, a line of cars filled with state troopers rolled toward the school from two directions. The flasher-signals on the tops of the cars were spurting red warnings.

WOMAN STONED TO DEATH

Daily Express, 11 February 1958

A scene from Jeddah, Saudi Arabia.

The unending procession of brand new giant American cars nosed slowly along the dusty street.

The shop windows near by were crammed with glittering goods – refrigerators and air-conditioners from America, cameras from Germany, electrical fittings from Italy.

Round the corner plasterers were hard at work putting the finishing touches to a 12-storey modernistic office building, one of scores that are being rushed to a finish all over the bursting, bustling seaport of Jeddah.

But the big and silent crowd had eyes for none of this.

A prince, a nephew of the king, sat stern-faced on a chair. Before him was a strip of carpet. From a lorry a man was led forward by two khaki-clad policemen. He was in his late twenties and was completely composed.

His hands were chained together behind him and he walked awkwardly because of the chains festooned about his ankles.

Arrived at the edge of the carpet he knelt and was told by the police to keep his eyes fixed on the prince's face.

At his side an official unrolled a scroll and started to read aloud the man's misdeeds and the punishment decreed by the court. The crowd was now utterly hushed.

Suddenly the line of police parted and the executioner appeared, sword in hand. He approached the victim from behind and on tiptoe. As the reading stopped the executioner bent and touched the kneeling man lightly on the back with his finger.

Instinctively the man started, and in so doing raised his head.

On the instant, with a swift and expert blow, the executioner decapitated him.

A long, slow sigh came from the onlookers.

Now a woman was dragged forward. She and the man had together murdered her former husband. She, too, was under thirty, and slender.

The recital of her crime too was read out as she knelt, and then the executioner stepped forward with a wooden stave and dealt a hundred blows with all his strength upon her shoulder.

As the flogging ended the woman sagged over on her side.

Next, a lorry loaded with rocks and stones was backed up and its cargo deposited in a pile. At a signal from the prince the crowd leaped on the stones and started pelting the woman to death.

It was difficult to determine how she was facing her last and awful ordeal, since she was veiled in Moslem fashion and her mouth was gagged to muffle her cries.

Had this scene been taking place in the middle of the desert it would have been grim enough, but that it should have been enacted in the heart of modern Jeddah's business neighbourhood lent it a dismally macabre quality.

The sun shone down from a glorious blue sky. A familiar American soft drink advertisement showed its gentle blandishments. "Come to the Middle East" pleaded an air lines travel poster in a nearby window. "Savour its romance, its colour, its quaint traditions . . ."

The crowd were no longer silent. The men snarled and shouted as they flung their stones, their faces transformed into masks of sadism.

The execution of the man? Well, let us not forget that it was as recently as 1936 that the French held their last public execution. And the beheading was at least humanly and quickly carried out.

But the doing to death of the woman is something which the handful of horrified Europeans in the crowd will not quickly forget.

It took just over an hour before the doctor in attendance, who halted the stoning periodically to feel the victim's pulse, announced her dead.

This double execution took place just the other day.

Savage, barbaric? By our standards, of course, yes. But to the Arabians – who have leaped from the eighth to the twentieth century in less than a decade, thanks to the discovery of an immense lake of oil beneath their sands, this was altogether seemly.

This was execution according to Koranic law. A few weeks earlier, in this same spot, fourteen men, convicted of theft, had their right hands chopped off.

This is the stern and automatic penalty for thievery in Saudi Arabia. No appeal – and if you should be so imprudent as to steal a second time, off comes your left hand.

Again, let us not be too sweeping in our condemnation. Within the last century and a half, men were hanged in England for petty theft – and these Saudi Arabians, in spite of their Cadillacs, air-conditioners, and gold wrist-watches, have been flung from the desert to the penthouse by one of the most gigantic flukes of modern times.

And as I was proudly assured more than once, Saudi Arabia is the most honest country in the Middle East. If a would-be thief knows that if he is caught he loses his right hand, well, he pauses.

There is no drinking of alcohol and no smoking (a Frenchman strolling through the bazaars of Riyadh with me, unthinkingly, lit a cigarette. Instantly, a passer-by stepped up and gravely but firmly told him to throw it away).

No profit-making on the lending of money is allowed. Horse-racing? Oh yes, at the race-track in Riyadh some splendid racing with fine Arabian horses takes place.

But never a bet is placed, for betting and gambling are totally illegal. Baked mud, from which Saudi houses were fashioned through many centuries, is to-day terribly non-U. Cement is all the thing – although much of it is of poor quality and cracks badly.

However, who cares? "We have the money – we want to do things well." This was a phrase I heard repeatedly.

Throw up the new buildings. Install the air-conditioners (never mind if they break down from time to time).

Lay down the new four-and-six-lane motor roads. (Pavements? Never mind them. No one walks, anyway.)

Get on to Detroit and order 700 more Cadillacs (at £5,000 a time).

But why is the telephone service so bad? Why is the automatic system not made available? Why are so few private homes on the telephone?

"Well," I was told in whispers, "you know, we could have an automatic system in every home tomorrow. But at the last moment someone thought of a dreadful possibility. With the telephone handy – the women might start gossiping among themselves. And that would never do!"

EDWIN TETLOW

INSIDE THE CUBAN REVOLUTION

As It Happened, 1990

The luckiest break I ever had came on New Year's Eve, 1958. This was after somebody in the Foreign News Room of the *Daily Telegraph* in London had an idea as he was reading some skimpy new bulletins broadcast by Fidel Castro from somewhere in the wilds of Cuba. since very different bulletins were emanating from the headquarters of President Fulgencio Batista in the Presidential Palace in Havana, my benefactor made this suggestion: Why don't we get Tetlow to fly down to Havana to do us a feature story on how the city celebrates the coming of the New Year with Castro apparently closing in on it?

The proposal appealed to me as I read the service message outlining it in the New York office of the newspaper, even though its final sentence ran rather forbiddingly: "Don't write too much as space is tight." (I was to enjoy rereading that admonition later!) This sounded like a pleasant compact assignment: a two-hour flight into the Caribbean sunshine in the middle of winter, a day and an evening spent roaming the cafes, clubs and casinos of Havana, the next morning spent in writing the story, then back to New York, with everything finished in seventy-two hours at most. There would be novelty, too, for I had never been closer to Havana than its airport. I should enjoy observing the most notorious center of naughty gaiety in Latin America, even if the wings of the purveyors of gaiety were being clipped closer and closer by a tatterdemalion mob of bearded revolutionaries led by an unpredictable young man who might very well be a troublesome Communist, for all anybody really knew.

Cubana Airlines ran a daily plane to Havana from New York. And when I reached Idlewild Airport, as it was then called, and tried to board the daily plane on 31 December, I had my first indication that everything was not quite normal this day. For one thing, only three passengers were waiting to make the trip. For another, we three had to sit around for some hours while the airline staff, seemingly obeying strict orders from the Presidential Palace, went to lengths to ensure that all three of us were above suspicion. We were rigorously questioned to establish exactly who we were and every piece of our luggage was thoroughly searched before it was taken aboard. But at last everything was cleared, and the plane took off in mid-afternoon. I was happy to note that it was a Britannia. The other two passengers were a young American of playboy aspect going to join friends in Havana for a New Year party, and a taciturn Cuban who may have been a diplomat if not something more mysterious. We had all the in-flight attention we could desire. The attractive stewardess served us delightful rum cocktails and a hearty repast, and she assured us with almost convincing earnestness how much we were going to enjoy being in Havana for the New Year.

The approaches to the city from the airport seemed normal enough as viewed from a big old Buick taxi which I shared with the young American, who confided to me that he expected to find "a lovely young thing" among those welcoming him to Cuba. The dark-complexioned driver hummed softly to the music from his radio as he piloted us skilfully through the turbulent traffic. The Hotel Nacional, a great oblong block of a place, had a few rooms available, at a hefty rate for those days. I settled in and had a leisurely dinner from an expansive menu in the hotel restaurant, which was filled with well-dressed, and obviously well-heeled, Cubans and a minority of foreigners. Feeling comfortable, I set out to stroll in the warm evening air, dropping in on some of the tourist haunts of suburban Vedado and upper midtown Havana, amassing material for the feature article I should be writing the following morning.

Eventually, around 11 p.m., I strolled into the Casino at the Hotel Nacional to await midnight. I noted that the bar was being heavily patronized. A four-piece band was playing in one corner of the ornate salon, accompanying a lusty and busty Cuban contralto who was singing at full strength to make herself heard above the band and the hubbub from the bar, and the softer, sleeker noises from the casino itself, so different from the rattle, slap and clap made by dice-players as they thumped down their leathern cups on tables in the humbler haunts of the city. As the time passed towards midnight the noise became unbelievably piercing. How Cubans love noise! Eventually neither band nor contralto could be heard as separate entities.

Around the gaming tables, under glittering chandeliers bigger and more fanciful than any I had seen for years, guests both Cuban and foreign gambled with deep concentration. Only occasionally did heads turn and envious smiles appear round tight-lipped mouths when somebody shrieked in ecstasy after hitting the jackpot at one of the fruit machines lining the walls of the casino. Also along the walls were several armed policemen stationed like sentries. I asked once or twice of seemingly knowledgeable guests why they were there. One man just shrugged and said languidly: "Who knows?" One other man told me they had appeared for the first time only a few evenings earlier.

At midnight there came a token acknowledgment that 1959 had arrived. The intense proceedings at the gaming tables and the fruit machines was halted for but a few moments. A few men and women kissed and some people shook hands and smiled at each other before resuming the serious business of the night. At about 12.30 a.m. the members of the band quietly packed their instruments, the singer folded up her microphone stand, and she and the musicians walked off into the night. Only the bar and the gaming tables continued operations, the former being sustained mainly by a party of American and other foreigners, who, growing more disarrayed almost by the minute, still managed to keep the tiring bartenders busy. At that hour I decided I had seen enough. I wanted to go to bed. Once there, I spent a few minutes jotting down facts and reminders for the writing I expected to be doing next morning. Satisfied that I had my assignment under control, I settled down and went to sleep.

I was awakened before 8 a.m. by an excited phone call from Robert Perez, my local correspondent, an energetic Puerto Rican who had lived for some years in Havana. "He's gone," he spluttered into the phone. "Who's gone?" I asked, still half-asleep. "Batista! Batista!" came the galvanizing answer from Perez. "He went in the night."

So he had. At about the time I was setting down to sleep he and a party of about forty, including many members of his family,

had motored over to a military airfield at Camp Columbia on the
fringe of Havana, and – excessively heavily laden with baggage –
had boarded an Army plane for a short hop eastwards across the
water to the Dominican Republic, then still in the grip of
Batista's fellow-dictator, Generalissimo Rafael Trujillo, later
assassinated.

Pure luck had landed me in the very centre of a revolution
while it was happening and being won. No hasty packing of a
suitcase this time, no mad rush to catch the first plane to the
scene of action, no hectic chase after news which was already
growing old! This was a foreign correspondent's dream come
true, and I was determined to make the most of it. First, on the
sound recommendation of Robert Perez, I moved out of the
lordly but isolated Hotel National and into the Hotel Colina, a
small and well-placed observation-post giving a view from my
third-floor window of the approaches to the University of Havana, where Fidel Castro had been educated and where he was
said to have substantial secret support.

The city was eerily quiet at about 8.45 a.m. as Perez and I made
our cautious way to the Colina, not at all sure what might happen
as we did so. Weren't revolutions affairs of wild shooting and
melodramatic action? Not this one – yet. I felt as if I were in the
eye of a hurricane, the centre where everything is still while
furious winds whirl all around. Hardly anybody was moving.
Perez told me as we inched our way towards the Colina that
Cubans in the capital had done exactly what people in most
countries of the Caribbean did when, as happens all too often in
that steamy region, trouble threatened. They closed and locked
their shutters, bolted all their doors, and holed up.

Once installed in my new strategic headquarters I implemen-
ted my plan of campaign. I despatched Perez on a mission of
news-gathering in the city, asking him to phone me as often as
seemed necessary with any information he had. I calculated that
because of his intimate knowledge of the city, contacts he had,
plus his command of his native Spanish, he would have no
trouble about keeping me in touch with what was happening.
And he did so with great efficiency. As for myself, I stayed as a
willing prisoner in my hotel room. I put in a telephone call to my
newspaper after having been told by the local exchange that there
was, predictably, "long delay" in calls to the outside world,

including distant London. While I waited I began assembling the story I would telephone as soon as the call came through. I listened to Radio Havana as it broadcast messages from Fidel Castro telling the populace to keep calm while it waited for him to take control of the nation. "Don't worry, I shall come to you," he said. I took messages from the assiduous Perez and as best I could I kept an eye on what was happening in the streets leading to the University.

In fact, very little happened all that morning. Only a very few people were to be seen hurrying along in order to carry out missions which presumably could not be put off. I noticed that almost all these scurrying pedestrians kept as close as possible to any nearby wall or other cover they were afforded. However, my heaven-sent story was shaping up well. It was helped greatly by word from Robert Perez that Fidel Castro had sent an amplified message to the people of Havana. Speaking from his field camp near Santa Clara, the last sizeable city between him and the capital, he said he did not accept as a bargaining agent a three-man junta of "so-called neutrals" whom Batista had left behind to represent him. "I shall be coming into Havana soon," Castro promised. "Keep the peace until then. I am sending a company of Barbudos [bearded ones] to administer Havana until I get there. They will preserve Havana – and you."

This message galvanized the nervous population of the city. Reassured, thousands of them opened their shutters and doors and got into their cars, to celebrate their unexpected liberation. They staged a fantastic crawl-around of the city streets. They draped their vehicles, almost all of them American-made, with Cuban flags. If the car was a convertible, they wound down the top and then joined the follow-my-leader procession of their neighbourhood. As they did so, more and more people climbed up on and into the cars until, as I counted from my observation-point in the Hotel Colina, there were often as many as ten persons in one car. As each individual procession made its slow progress along the old, narrow streets, the ecstatic celebrants chanted the word *Li-ber-tad* and most of them added emphasis by pounding with their fists their car's side or roof in rhythm with the three syllables of the word for liberty. Very soon the din became hard to stand. I was staggered by the intensity, emotion and, I must add, childlike character of the manifestation of happy relief.

Nobody could possibly foresee the tribulations in store for Cuba for the next forty years . . .

My telephone call to London came through at last in the early afternoon, in time for me to dictate over fifteen hundred words, many of them forming impromptu sentences, as thoughts occurred to me, across the bed of the Atlantic Ocean. Even my vigil the previous evening in the casino of the Hotel Nacional was not wasted; indeed, the languid scene around the gaming tables and the jollity in the bar on the eve of one of the most startling and profound revolutionary upheavals of the century in Latin America added to the impact of the story I was able to tell. This was by far the most vivid first-hand report I had written in fifty years, during war as well as peace; and now that it was safely in the hands of my editors in Fleet Street, I was free to leave my bedroom at the Hotel Colina. I could spend the next couple of hours before my second phone call seeing for myself what was going on in the liberated city.

I permitted myself one substantial tot of Bacardi rum before I set out on the long walk from Vedado to midtown Havana. I had to thrust my way though the thick ranks of people watching, some with tears of joy coursing down their faces, the motorized crawl-around. But just as I was making the last turn into the Prado, which roughly marks the boundary between respectable bourgeois Havana and the livelier but sleazy downtown, I saw that something had happened to cut short the touching celebration. Panic was spreading among both Cubans in their cars and the onlookers who had been cheering them on. Vehicles were peeling off from the processions, screeching away into side-streets, and the crowds were scurrying for cover as quickly as their feet would race. In a matter of minutes I found myself uncomfortably alone in the mid-section of the broad Prado. What had happened?

The answer was forthcoming almost as soon as I asked myself the question. The underworld was taking over. One by one a party of dirty and ruffianly looking young Cubans emerged from Calle Neptuno and other side-streets. Each was carrying a rifle or shotgun across his chest. They walked warily along the street, their gaze darting everywhere as they made sure that nobody was going to challenge them. Nobody did. Batista's hated armed policemen had fled into hiding once they heard that their protector had gone. (It transpired that by no means all of them escaped vengeance. Stories of beatings and murders of these men abounded during the next twenty-four hours.) The small-time gangsters now taking over central Havana were organized and ingenious. Some took up positions as watchdogs at strategic points, ordering away at gunpoint people such as myself, while their comrades went on a rampage of looting. Their first targets were parking-meters. These were smashed apart so that their contents could be rattled out and pocketed. Then came the turn of pinball machines and other gaming devices in arcades and deserted casinos which could easily be entered, including an especially lucrative one close to the Sevilla Biltmore Hotel. Here, from a discreet distance, I watched one gang of looters drag a slot-machine into the street and batter it open with jagged pieces of metal from a destroyed parking-meter. It struck me as a remarkable and possibly unique confirmation of the validity of the old saying that money makes money.

The physical hazards of remaining outdoors grew as the bandits got their hands on rum. They started shooting. Mostly it was the wildest kind of exhibitionism, but even so it claimed victims. Ambulances soon began making screaming runs through the streets on journeys to and from hospitals – and mortuaries. Late in the afternoon I went into one hospital and found it in chaos, overflowing with wounded persons and roughly bandaged out-patients. "Some have been in street accidents, but mostly they seem to have been hit by flying bullets," said one nurse to me.

There appeared to be no reason for most of the shooting. Indeed, one series of incidents which I ran into on my way back to the Colina tended to show that Cubans just weren't to be trusted with weapons. A man's rifle would go off either because it was defective or because he had forgotten his finger was on the trigger, or even because of a need – common in Latin America – to show off. The trouble was that very often a haphazard shot would start a chain reaction. Men who heard the shot would start firing their own weapons, with the result that shotgun pellets and bullets began flying around an area, ricocheting off walls, smashing windows and occasionally hitting an unlucky pedestrian. Rarely did there seem to be a justifiable target. Alas, this kind of irresponsibility seemed to be occurring mostly near the University, and I was disturbed to deduce that the perpetrators were not underworld bandits of the kind I had met in the Prado but students who were supporters of Fidel Castro and were apparently obeying his broadcast admonitions to preserve the peace in Havana until he arrived. They were probably earnest enough in their devotion to his cause, but they wouldn't be much use if Batista's police and troops rallied. I reasoned that Fidel Castro would be well advised to get his trained Barbudos into Havana as quickly as he could. If they didn't come soon, there would probably be a confrontation between his amateur followers and the downtown bandits, and if the latter won, which seemed likely, unimaginable bloody chaos would follow.

The most senseless shooting spree of all happened on the afternoon of 2 January, the second day of the revolution. I was standing in the shelter of a shopping arcade near the Parque Centrale, in the centre of Havana, and was looking at the debris of splintered windows and doors and ransacked shelves left by yesterday's looters when I became aware of a noisy commotion on a street corner close to the Sevilla Biltmore. The cracks made by ragged rounds of gunshots were coming from somewhere close at hand. I crept cautiously forward to investigate. A squad of about half a dozen young men wearing armbands to show that they were members of a pro-Castro group which had come out of hiding during the past forty-eight hours were firing rifles and automatic pistols from the west side of the Prado at an upper window of a building on the opposite side of the wide thoroughfare. Their collective aim was atrocious. I could see bullets squelching into stonework far above, below and around the window, and only one or two were flying through it into the room beyond. The attack lasted at least half an hour, without, as I noted most carefully, a single shot coming back in reply. This one-sided "battle" was happening so close to the Sevilla Biltmore that a party of American tourists, wisely obeying a recommendation from the US Embassy not to venture outdoors, could hear all the shooting but had no more idea of what it all meant than, it emerged, did the men involved.

The facts came to me eventually. Word had reached a volunteer unit of Castro supporters that some fugitives of the Batista regime were hiding in a room on the top floor of the building now being attacked. There were said to be at least a dozen armed followers of Rolando Masferrer, a notorious henchman of Batista, locked inside the room. When the shooting ended, one militiaman said gloatingly to me: "We got the lot." In truth, as I was able to confirm for myself a little later, there had been nobody at all in the whole building.

This crazy little episode served as a warning to me for years. On each of the fourteen visits I paid to Havana between 1959 and 1965 I always made a point of looking up at the pockmarked outer wall of that building. Nobody ever did anything to clear away the telltale signs of the "battle" of 2 January 1959. The same old tattered blind remained flapping forlornly from the top of the unrepaired window every time I went to the spot, and the recurring sight reminded me always to be slow to believe anything told to me by a Cuban (including Fidel Castro) unless it was either obviously true or until it could be confirmed. There is a fey quality in the Cuban temperament, often beguiling but sometimes irritating, which prompts many Cubans to promote drama by exaggerating facts, ignoring inconvenient ones, or simply inventing a few. The delivery is usually accompanied by a wide smile, an expansive sweep of the arm, or an expressive flash of the eye. I learned to beware.

I never got back at night to my cosy bed at the Colina at the end of this eventful day. I hasten to mention that this was not at all because I yielded to the allure of one of the painted ladies who, although very much subdued and clearly worried about their future, still plied their trade in bars and other haunts in downtown Havana; they had heard like everybody else that the bearded revolutionary who now ruled Cuba was something of a social reformer. They had nothing to do with my enforced absence from my bed. It happened because I was taken into what is comfortingly called protective custody by a group of young men, mostly students, trying ever so hard to do what Fidel Castro had asked them.

I had been writing in the evening at the one secure haven I knew in the downtown labyrinth of Havana. This was the office of the *Havana Post*, an English-language newspaper for which Robert Perez worked, near the waterfront at the junction of Animas and Lealtad. Around 9 p.m. I joined a small party of other correspondents, all Americans, for the rather long walk of something like a mile and a half to our hotels in Vedado. There was no alternative to walking on this second day of revolution. Buses and taxis had vanished from the streets. We had covered about half the distance when we ran into trouble. A voice called out suddenly in grating Spanish from somewhere in the darkness a few feet ahead of us: "Halt. Hands up!" Peering ahead, I could see three men with rifles pointed straight at us. Two of them were kneeling side by side on the pavement while the third, their leader, stood barring the way directly ahead. He had a revolver in his right hand – and an armed Cuban was not a man to be trifled with. His gun might very well go off by chance.

But I have never had much time for amateur warriors anywhere. Tonight, also, I was tired, hungry and consequently bad-tempered and of fallible judgement. I was tempted to bluff my way through and I was slow to comply with the orders of our interceptors. My American companions were perhaps wiser. They all raised their hands and one of them muttered impatiently to me as he did so: "Come on, man. You'll get us all shot!" Unwillingly, I complied.

Our captors motioned us into the passageway of an apartment house. There, blocking the way, sat an unshaven young fellow at a desk. We were in the unit's rough-and-ready headquarters. The man at the desk started questioning the two Americans nearest to him. I was very hot indeed in that passageway. I sidled back into the street, leaving it to others who spoke far better Spanish than I to argue and protest against this unwarranted interference with the free movement of foreign civilians pursuing their daily task in extremely difficult circumstances, and so on. As I breathed the welcome fresh air I mentally assessed the odds about being able to make a dash for it and go up the hill to my hotel. I decided against trying to do so. Several of these amateur gunmen were still around, for I could hear them talking close to me. Even though there was a good chance that if they fired after me as I ran away they might very well miss me, I considered the risk not worth taking. If I were wounded or killed, my newspaper would be the innocent loser.

Meanwhile our negotiators were making no impression whatever on the man at the desk. He told them he was chief of one of the paramilitary units which had been ordered by Fidel Castro to keep the city peaceful, and he couldn't in good conscience let us go on our way. "My authority doesn't extend very far," he confessed. "There are a lot of bandits still roaming around out there. You might get robbed – or worse – if I let you go off into the night." It availed nothing that our spokesman told him we were well able to take care of ourselves and anyway intended to hole up in our hotels as soon as we got there. "Sorry, you'll have to spend tonight under our protection," the man insisted.

We were bundled into two cars and driven to a dingy-looking house in one of the streets running diagonally off the Malecon boulevard on the sea front. It turned out to have been a "safe" house used by revolutionary agents and couriers as well as by fugitives from Batista's police. I was shown to a small and none-too-savoury bedroom immediately underneath a rooftop water cistern. Dumping my typewriter, my only luggage, resignedly in a corner of the room, I obeyed my captors' order to go down to the desk, sign my name in a register and claim a key.

As I did so, the good fortune which had sent me to Havana in the first place and had attended me for forty-eight hours there-after worked again. I was walking away from the hotel desk when I noticed a big utility truck standing in the street outside the hotel entrance. Half a dozen laughing soldiers – real soldiers this time – were unloading their kit and other baggage from it. I was astonished to observe that two of them standing with their backs facing me had black hair hanging down so long below their shoulders that I should have said they were girls if they obviously had not been blessed with thick black beards. I walked forward and began talking with them. They were, they said, the very first detachment of Barbudos which Castro had promised to send into Havana.

So the seeming ill-luck that had landed me into being arrested had also brought me another lively segment for the morrow's story. This is yet another example of how compensations have so frequently offset what seemed initially to be setbacks in my profession as a journalist. A missed train or plane, failure to establish contact by phone or cable with London, somebody's refusal to tell me something, were irritating when encountered, but so often were followed by a piece of unexpected good fortune. Perhaps this helps to explain my perennial optimism.

The Barbudos were among the fittest and happiest young warriors I have ever seen. They had good reason for being so. They had had very little serious fighting and, as the never-robust morale had seeped away from Batista's conscripts during the past few months in the Sierra Maestra, an astonishingly easy victory had fallen to them. They told me that they had enjoyed a leisurely, unchallenged, advance upon the capital from the eastern province of Oriente, through Camagüey and Las Villas. The peasants in these mostly rural areas had welcomed them with increasing ardour as the reality of Castro's total victory had become manifest. People had been eager to give them anything they wanted. One Barbudo told me he couldn't remember when he had been last paid. "The one thing we didn't need was money," he said. "People couldn't do enough for us. They lavished everything, especially food, on us."

Proof of this was forthcoming as some of the contents of the truck were arrayed on the counter of the hotel reception desk. There were hams, strings of sausages, cottage-made bread, butter, beer and many other such good provender. We were all invited to tuck into a midnight feast – rebel soldiers, our captors, American reporters, including one lone Englishman, and anybody else who happened to be about. Good fellowship bloomed with every mouthful. There was much hearty back-slapping, joking, talk and toasting of international understanding, and some glowing forecasts from the Barbudos of the future Cuba once Fidel Castro took charge. The devotion of the young warriors, none of whom was much more than eighteen or nineteen years old, for their leader was awesome.

As I talked, watched and listened, my mind went back in memory to another such occasion in 1944. I had flown in as a passenger in a Flying Fortress of the United States Air Force from Foggia, in southern Italy, over German-occupied Yugoslavia to Bucharest, which had just been captured by the Soviet Army. The mission of a squadron of Fortresses was to pick up several hundred American and British airmen who had been shot down over the Ploiesti oilfields and then captured. But the real significance of the occasion for me was that it represented the link-up of Soviet forces surging into Europe from the east and Anglo-American forces advancing at last from the west. The first soldiers in the Soviet Army I met were two young motorcyclists leaning on the handlebars of their machines, each with a light rifle slung across his back, awaiting the landing of my Fortress on the runway of the military airport at Bucharest. We managed to bridge the language gap by using my imperfect German and their even less able command of the same tongue. They told me they were an advance patrol of the main army now taking over the Romanian capital. In Bucharest, as later in Havana, there had been back-slapping, smiles, good fellowship and expressions of faith in international goodwill. Alas, both meetings were to become sterile. As with the Russians, Cubans were to become isolated for decades by political misunderstandings, blunders and prejudices. The Soviet Union was to be betrayed by Joseph Stalin and the Cuban revolution was doomed to lose the happy spontaneity of that first encounter with the Barbudos. Fidel Castro and a succession of American presidents and State Department planners were, between them, to frustrate the impulse of the common man of both nations to offer comradeship and cooperation with his opposite number. National leaders seem determined never to learn.

HUMPHREY TYLER

EYE-WITNESS AT SHARPEVILLE

The Observer, 27 March 1960

On 21 March 1060 a demonstration by black South Africans against Apartheid pass laws in the township of Sharpeville was fired upon by police. Fifty-six demonstrators were killed. Tyler's account of the massacre first appeared in the South African magazine *Drum*.

We went into Sharpeville the back way, around lunch time last Monday, driving along behind a big grey police car and three Saracen armoured cars.

As we went through the fringes of the township many people were shouting the Pan Africanist slogan "*Izwe Lethu*" (Our Land). They were grinning and cheerful. Some kids waved to the policemen sitting on the Saracens and two of the policemen waved back.

It was like a Sunday outing – except that Major A.T.T. Spengler, head of the Witwatersrand Security Branch, was in the front car and there were bullets in the Saracens' guns.

At the main gates of the fenced-off location, policemen were stopping all cars coming in from the outside. Spengler and the Saracens headed for the police station which is deep inside the settlement, and we followed. The policemen were by now all inside the Saracens, with the hatches battened down, looking at Sharpeville through chinks of armour plating. Yet the Africans did not appear to be alarmed by the cars. Some looked interested and some just grinned.

There were crowds in the streets as we approached the police station. There were plenty of police, too, well armed.

A constable shoved the butt of his rifle against my windshield. Another pointed his rifle at my chest. Another leaned into the car, shouting: "Have you got a permit to be in this location?"

I said no, whereupon he bellowed: "Then get out, get out, get out! or I will arrest you on the spot. Understand?"

He had a police gun in his holster and a black pistol tucked into his belt. We decided to go around the other side of the police station, where we parked in a big field.

We could see a couple of the Saracens, their tops poking starkly above the heads of the crowd, just over 100 yards away from us. This was about seven minutes before the police opened fire.

The crowd seemed to be loosely gathered around them and on the fringes people were walking in and out. The kids were playing. In all there were about 3,000 people. They seemed amiable.

I said to Ian Berry, *Drum*'s chief photographer: "This is going to go on all day." He replied: "Let's hang on for a bit."

Suddenly there was a sharp report from the direction of the police station.

"That's a shot," Berry said.

There were shrill cries of *Izwe Lethu* – women's voices, I thought. The cries came from the police station and I could see a small section of the crowd swirl around the Saracens. Hands went up in the Africanist salute.

Then the shooting started. We heard the chatter of a machine-gun, then another, then another.

"Here it comes," said Berry. He leaped out of the car with two cameras and crouched in the grass, taking pictures.

The first rush was on us, then past.

There were hundreds of women, some of them laughing. They must have thought that the police were firing blanks.

One woman was hit about ten yards from our car. Her companion, a young man, went back when she fell. He thought she had stumbled.

Then he turned her over and saw that her chest had been shot away. He looked at the blood on his hand and said: "My God, she's gone!"

Hundreds of kids were running, too. One little boy had on an old black coat which he held up behind his head, thinking perhaps that it might save him from the bullets. Some of the children, hardly as tall as the grass, were leaping like rabbits. Some of them were shot, too.

Still the shooting went on. One of the policemen was standing on top of a Saracen, and it looked as though he was firing his sten gun into the crowd. He was swinging it around in a wide arc from his hip as though he were panning a movie camera. Two other police officers were on the truck with him, and it looked as though they were firing pistols.

Most of the bodies were strewn in the road running through the field in which we were. One man who had been lying still, dazedly got to his feet, staggered a few yards then fell in a heap. A woman sat with her head cupped in her hands.

One by one the guns stopped. Nobody was moving in our field except Berry. The rest were wounded – or dead. There was no longer a crowd and it was very quiet.

Berry ran back to the car, saying: "Let's go before they get my film." We drove out through the main gate, looking straight ahead.

Before the shooting, I heard no warning to the crowd to disperse. There was no warning volley. When the shooting started, it did not stop until there was no living thing on the huge compound in front of the police station.

The police have claimed they were in desperate danger because the crowd was stoning them. Yet only three policemen were reported to have been hit by stones – and more than 200 Africans were shot down.

The police also have said that the crowd was armed with "ferocious weapons" which littered the compound after they fled.

I saw no weapons, although I looked very carefully, and afterwards studied the photographs of the death scene. While I was there I saw only shoes, hats and a few bicycles left among the bodies.

It seemed to me that tough stuff was behind the killings at Sharpeville. The crowd gave me no reason to feel scared, though I moved among them without any distinguishing mark to protect me, quite obvious with my white skin.

I think the police were scared, though, and I think the crowd knew it.

That final shrill cry from the women before the shooting started certainly sounded much more like a jeer than a battle-cry. And the first Africans who fled past me after the shooting started were still laughing.

MARK ARNOLD-FORSTER

THE BERLIN WALL

The Observer, 26 November 1961

In August 1961 the Soviet authorities began the building of a massive concrete wall to divide off their sector of conquered Berlin from those occupied by the Western powers. Ostensibly, the wall was to prevent spying by the West; more truthfully, it was to prevent the mass escape to the West of East Germans disaffected with Stalinism.

The wall starts in a bird sanctuary on the banks of a stream called the Tegeler Fliess. It flows through a marshy valley 200 yards from the village of Lubars, which has four big farms, a policeman, a duck pond – now frozen – and an inn called The Merry Finch. The village is reputed to be the coldest place in Berlin. It might have been moved here from Wiltshire.

It belongs, all the same, to the French sector of the city and the high road leading out of it leads only to the Russian sector. The barrier is seven minutes from The Merry Finch, but the East German People's Police can see you sooner. Here, as everywhere along the wall, they operate in pairs, one man with field glasses, the other with a gun.

At this point the barrier consists of three barbed-wire fences supported on concrete posts seven feet high and six inches thick. The first fence is on the border itself; the second is ten feet behind the first; the third is 150 yards behind the second. Each fence has up to ten strands of barbed wire and the ground between the first and second is obstructed with more barbed wire coiled over wooden supports consisting of two crosses linked together and resembling, but for the wire, gigantic devices for keeping carving knives off table-cloths.

The ground between the second and third fences has been

cleared and can be lit at night. A line of poles thirty feet high, spaced thirty yards apart, carries a power line; each pole has a cluster of electric lights. There is a line of watchtowers twenty feet high spaced 600 yards apart which has been manned throughout this week.

Farther south, where the suburbs become denser, the border is marked by a railway embankment. In Berlin, as in Surrey, railway lines in leafy suburbs tend to be flanked by gardens. By this week the People's Police had managed to get rid of most of the gardens that were in their way on the east side of the tracks. On Wednesday they were burning the rubbish, the tool sheds along with cherry trees, at the Bornholmerstrasse Station, four and three-quarter miles south of the point at which the railway becomes the frontier.

Five hundred yards further south, at the back of the Hertha football stadium, the wall itself begins.

For most of its length it is eight feet high. It is made of pink prefabricated concrete slabs measuring three feet four inches by three feet eight inches. They are one foot thick. Smaller prefabricated concrete blocks, the size of four English bricks, have been used to fill in awkward corners.

In most places the wall has now been capped with one or two rows of grey cement posts, eleven feet eight inches long and a foot square and laid on their sides. Cemented into them are Y-shaped welded rods carrying seven strands of barbed wire, two of which overhang the wall on the Western side and two on the other. In the city the People's Police have cleared as much ground as they can on their side of the wall and have, in places, reinforced it with fences.

At one point in the south-eastern borough of Neukolln they have planted two seven-foot fences on the Western side of the wall – the first four feet from it and the second four feet from the first – and a third fence, only five feet high, 100 feet behind the wall. The power line and the lights run down the middle of the open ground.

This kind of clearance is neither necessary nor possible in most places. A mile south of the Hertha football stadium is the Bernauerstrase, in the borough of Wedding, where the sector boundary runs east and west and coincides with the building line on the south side of the street. Here, as in other places, the

People's Police have made their wall out of houses. At first they bricked up the front door and the ground-floor windows: people who lived on the south side of the street were talking to people who lived on the north side.

Some of them were doing more than that. At a bus stop opposite No. 44 neighbours have put a cross in memory of a student called Bernd Lunser who, pursued by the People's Police, jumped off the roof on 4 October. The West Berlin Fire department tried, but failed, to catch him in a jumping sheet. No. 44 is five storeys high. This week, all the roofs on the southern side of the Bernauerstrasse have been fenced with barbed wire.

Two hundred yards down the road from No. 44 the wall has been heightened to ten feet. Behind it, at this point, is the graveyard of the Church of Reconciliation, Wedding. Farther west again the graveyard of the Church of St Sophia has also been walled in to a height of ten feet. Neither section carries the usual barbed wire superstructure. Churchyards get broken glass instead.

The new wall round the French cemetery in the Lisenstrasse has barbed wire, but is even higher. It was the highest section of wall I saw.

Round the corner in the Invalidesstrase is a crossing point for the 500-odd West Berliners still allowed to visit East Berlin. A poster across the road says: THE STRONGER THE GERMAN DEMO-CRATIC REPUBLIC GETS THE GREATER IS THE CERTAINTY OF PEACE IN GERMANY. It was here that an East German railway policeman shot and killed an unknown man who had dived into the neigh-bouring Humboldt Dock from the grounds of the Charite Hospital.

From the Humboldt Dock the wall follows the bank of the Spree to skirt the Reichstag building (at present occupied, in part, by the Durham Light Infantry) and to join this week's new works at the Brandenburg Gate. Here the wall is now thicker than anywhere else and its construction is more solid.

When they built it the East Germans began by sinking a row of steel posts into the roadway and cementing them in. They then laid slotted prefabricated concrete slabs over the posts, which projected through the slabs and held them steady. They then poured wet cement over the slabs and laid another layer on top, repeating the process until they had made a multi-decker sandwich in which slabs of concrete had been substituted for bread, the wet cement for butter.

The wall follows to the inch the western boundary of East Berlin which, in front of the Gate, bulges out into the roadway in a segment of a circle 100 yards wide and fifty deep. The East German construction workers – few, so it is said, come from Berlin – began the job at half-past five last Sunday evening and finished at half past ten on Tuesday night. They were heavily guarded by People's Police, dressed for the most part in camouflaged combat uniforms. They ate at a field kitchen parked beneath the Gate.

From the gate down the Ebertstrasse to the Potsdamerplatz they added, in the same period, two rows of heavy welded steel tripods, fixed in the roadway with cement. These have been camouflaged, ineffectively, with the sort of netting used round tennis courts. Their military purpose seems to be to deter the Western Powers from attacking with tanks the site of the Wertheim department store, an undertaking once regarded here as Germany's answer to Harrods.

From the Potsdamerplatz the wall runs south to include the ruins of the Potsdam Station, then north again, then east towards the Spree. It bisects the Wilhelmstrasse immediately south of what used to be Göring's Air Ministry. This week, early on Tuesday morning, about 200 young West Berliners gathered here to protest against the reinforcement of the wall. Some of them threw burning torches into the Russian sector. The People's Police replied with a jet of water and ninety-seven tear-gas bombs. The West Berlin replied, in turn, with 107.

The next street east is Friedrichstrasse where foreigners may cross the border. It is a narrow place of tension where only one tank can operate at a time. Here, for a day and two nights last month, the United States and Russia faced each other with their guns loaded. The whole might and purpose of Nato was represented by the gunner of a single Patton tank, Private Baker, aged twenty, of Michigan.

The next gap in the wall is at the Heinrich Heine Strasse. Coffins are exchanged here on Wednesdays. The Wall runs thence along the northern boundary of the borough of Kreuzberg round the back of the Bethany Hospital to the banks of the River Spree.

From the Spree for rather more than half a mile the border follows the Landwehrkanal, forty yards wide and a once-useful waterway.

In Neukolln, the wall twists between blocks of flats, shops, houses, gardens. In two streets the boundary follows the building line, but here the situation that obtains in the Bernauerstrasse is reversed. The houses belong to the West, the pavement to the East.

Where this happens the People's Police have built their wall in the gutter. A notice at the end of one such street reads: CITIZENS OF SEBASTIANSTRASSE! WE DRAW YOUR ATTENTION TO THE FACT THAT THE PAVEMENT YOU USE BELONGS TO THE TERRITORY OF THE GERMAN DEMOCRATIC REPUBLIC AND THAT THE BUILDING LINE IS THE STATE FRONTIER. WE EXPECT YOU TO REFRAIN FROM ANY PROVOCATION ON THE TERRITORY BECAUSE OTHERWISE WE WILL TAKE THE SECURITY MEASURES THAT ARE NECESSARY.

There is an artificial mound in a children's playground in the courtyard between the two blocks of flats in the Wildenbruchstrasse in Neukolln which provides a better view across the wall than any other eminence in the borough. The People's Police across the way have once or twice reacted angrily to sightseers watching from its grassy summit. The people in the flats complain that the gas still lingers in their children's sandpit.

The wire ends four miles on in Rudow, a distant, pleasant southern suburb on State Highway 179, the road that leads to East Berlin Airport and to the site of Hitler's most powerful broadcasting station. Under its local name, Waltersdorfer Chaussee, the road now ends in two rows of barbed wire and a slit-trench.

The last house in West Berlin is No. 197: small, neat and loved. What must have been No. 199 has been bulldozed away. It was, by all accounts, as neat and modest as 197. In the place where it used to stand the earth has been cleared away and flattened. The cherry trees have been flung aside to make way for the wire.

I WAS A PLAYBOY BUNNY

Show Magazine, 1963

Steinem's infiltrating of the Playboy Club and resultant exposè caused Hugh Hefner to cease the physical examination given prospective "Bunnies". Steinem posed as "Marie Ochs".

Thursday 31st January
[The Playboy Club at 5 East 59th Street, New York]

I now have two bunny costumes – one orange satin and one electric blue. The colour choice and the quality of satin are about the same as those in athletic-supply catalogues. Costume bodies, precut to body and bra-cup size, are fitted while you wait. I waited, standing on the cement floor in bare feet and bikini pants. The wardrobe mistress gave me a small bathroom rug to stand on. "Can't have brand new Bunnies catching cold," she said. I asked if she could follow the line of my bikini pants in fitting the bottom; the costume I had tried the day before was cut up higher than any I had seen in photographs. She chuckled. "Listen, baby, you think that was high, you should see *some*." The whole costume was darted and seamed until it was two inches smaller than any of my measurements everywhere except the bust. "You got to have room in there to stuff," she said. "Just about everybody stuffs. And you keep your tips in there. The 'vault' they call it."

A girl with jet black hair, chalky makeup, and a green costume stopped at the door. "My tail droops," she said, pushing it into position with one finger. "Those damn customers always yank it."

The wardrobe mistress handed her a safety pin. "You better

get a cleaner tail too, baby. You get demerits running around with a scruffy old tail like that." More girls began calling for their costumers, checking them out in a notebook chained to the counter. I learned that costumes were not allowed out of the building and that each girl paid $2.50 a day to cover the cost of her costume's upkeep and cleaning. Bunnies also paid $5.00 a pair for their thin black nylon tights and could be given demerits if they wore tights with runs in them. The wardrobe mistress gave me swatches from my two costumes and told me to have shoes dyed to match. I asked if the club allowed us any money for shoes. "You crazy or something, baby?" she said. "This place don't allow you no money for nothing. Make sure you get three-inch heels. You get demerits, you wear 'em any lower."

I dressed and went to the Bunny Mother's room. Sheralee was at the desk. With her long hair pinned back she looked about eighteen. She gave me a large, shocking pink form marked "Bunny Application" and a brown plastic briefcase with a miniature nude girl and THE PLAYBOY CLUB printed on it in orange. "This is your Bunny bible," she said seriously, "and I want you to promise me you'll study it all weekend."

The application form was four pages long. I had already made up most of the answers for my biography, but some questions were new. Was I dating any Playboy Club keyholders, and what were their names? None. Did I plan to date a particular key-holder? No. Did I have a police record? No. The space for social security number I left blank.

Up one flight in the main office, I delivered the form to Miss Shay. The cement-floored room was chequered with desks, but, as personnel director, Miss Shay rated a corner position. She scanned the form and began taking more Polaroid pictures of me. "Be sure and bring your Social Security card tomorrow," she said, and I wondered what to do about the fact that Marie Ochs had none. A stout man in a blue suit, black shirt, and white tie approached and gestured toward a chubby girl standing behind him. "Mr Roma told me to bring her over, and I'd sure appreciate anything you can do for her," he said, and winked.

"In cases of extreme personal recommendation," said Miss Shay coolly, "we do schedule a girl's interview right away." She signalled to Sheralee, who took the girl downstairs. The stout man looked relieved.

A red-haired woman and two men came over, but Miss Shay asked them to wait. The younger man tapped the redhead's chin with his fist and grinned. 'You ain't got a thing to worry about, baby." She gave him a look of utter scorn and lit a cigarette.

I signed an income-tax form, a meal ticket, a receipt for the meal ticket, an application form, an insurance form, and a release of all photographs for any purpose – publicity, editorial, or otherwise – deemed fit by Playboy Clubs International. A harried-looking young man in shirt sleeves came to tell Miss Shay that two men working in the basement were going to quit. They had expected to work six days for seventy-five dollars and were working only five days for sixty dollars. They were upset about it because they had families to support. "I can't make changes," she said crisply. "I can only implement Mr Roma's decisions."

Miss Shay stapled a set of Polaroid pictures to my employment form and gave me my schedule. "Tomorrow, you'll have makeup guidance at Larry Mathews's, this weekend is Bunny-bible study, and Monday I've made an appointment for you to see our doctor for a physical exam." She leaned forward confidentially. "A *complete* physical," she said. "Monday afternoon is the Bunny Mother lecture and Bunny Father lecture. Tuesday you'll have Bunny school, and Wednesday you'll train on the floor." I asked if I could go to my own doctor. "No," she said, "you must go to our doctor for a special physical. All Bunnies have to."

Miss Shay gave me one last form to sign, a request that Marie Ochs's birth record be sent to the Playboy Club. I signed it, hoping that the state of Michigan would take a while to discover that she did not exist. "In the meantime, I'll need your birth certificate," she said. "We can't let you work without it." I agreed to send a special-delivery letter home for it.

Of course I won't be allowed to serve liquor or work late hours without proof of age. Why didn't I think of that?

Well, Marie's future may be short, but she can still try to make it through Bunny school.

Friday, February 1st

I was fitted for false eyelashes today at Larry Mathews's, a twenty-four-hour-a-day beauty salon in a West Side hotel. As a makeup expert feathered the eyelashes with a manicure scissors, she pointed out a girl who had just been fired from the club "because she wouldn't go out with a Number One keyholder". I said I thought we were forbidden to go out with customers. "You can go out with them if they've got Number One keys," the makeup girl explained. "They're for club management and reporters and big shots like that." I explained that being fired for *not* going seemed like a very different thing. "Well," she said thoughtfully. "I guess it was the way she said it. She told him to go screw himself."

I paid the bill. $8.14 for the eyelashes and a cake of rouge, even after the 25-percent Bunny discount. I had refused to invest in darker lipstick even though "girls get fired for looking pale"! I wondered how much the Bunny beauty concession was worth to Mr Mathews. Had beauty salons sent in sealed bids for this lucrative business?

I am home now, and I have measured the lashes. Maybe I don't have to worry so much about being recognized in the club. They are three quarters of an inch long at their shortest point.

Sunday 3rd

I've spent an informative Sunday with the Bunny bible, or the *Playboy Club Bunny Manual*, as it is officially called. From introduction ("You are holding the top job in the country for a young girl") to appendix ("Sidecar: Rim glass with lime and frost with sugar"), it is a model of clarity.

Some dozen supplements accompany the bible. Altogether, they give a vivid picture of a Bunny's function. For instance:

> . . . You . . . are the only direct contact most of the readers will ever have with *Playboy* personnel. . . . We depend on our Bunnies to express the personality of the magazine.
> . . . Bunnies will be expected to contribute a fair share of personal appearances as part of their regular duties for the Club.
> . . . Bunnies are reminded that there are many pleasing means they can employ to stimulate the club's liquor volume, thereby increasing their earnings significantly.
> . . . The key to selling more drinks is *Customer Contact*
> . . . they will respond particularly to your efforts to be

friendly. . . . You should make it seem that [the customer's] opinions are very important. . . .

The Incentive System is a method devised to reward those table Bunnies who put forth an extra effort. . . . The Bunny whose [drink] average per person is highest will be the winner. . . . Prize money . . . will likewise be determined by over-all drink income.

There is a problem in being "friendly" and "pampering" the customer while refusing to go out with him or even give him your last name. The manual makes it abundantly clear that Bunnies must never go out with anyone met in the club – customer or employee – and adds that a detective agency called Willmark Service Systems, Inc., has been employed to make sure that they don't. ("Of course, you can never tell when you are being checked out by a Willmark Service representative.") The explanation written for the Bunnies is simple: "Men are very excited about being in the company of Elizabeth Taylor, but they know they can't paw or proposition her. The moment they felt they could become familiar with her, she would not have the aura of glamour that now surrounds her. The same must be true of our Bunnies." In an accompanying letter from Hugh Hefner to Willmark, the explanation is still simpler. "Our licences are laid on the line any time any of our employees in any way engages, aids, or abets traffic in prostitution. . . ." Willmark is therefore instructed to "Use your most attractive and personable male representatives to proposition the Bunnies, and even offer . . . as high as $200 on this, 'right now', for a promise of meeting you outside the Club later." Willmark representatives are told to ask a barman or other male employee "if any of the girls are available on a cash basis for a 'friendly evening'. . . . Tell him you will pay the girls well or will pay him for the girls." If the employee does act 'as a procurer'", Willmark is to notify the club immediately. "We naturally do not tolerate any merchandising of the Bunnies," writes Mr Hefner, "and are most anxious to know if any such thing is occurring."

If the idea of being merchandised isn't enough to unnerve a prospective Bunny, there are other directives that may. Willmark representatives are to check girls for heels that are too low, runs in their hose, jewelry, underwear that shows, crooked or unmatched ears, dirty costumes, absence of name tags, and "tails in

good order". Further: "When a show is on, check to see if the
Bunnies are reacting to the performers. When a comic is on, they
are supposed to laugh." Big Brother Willmark is watching you.

In fact, Bunnies must *always* appear gay and cheerful. (". . .
Think about something happy or funny . . . your most important
commodity is personality") in spite of all worries, including the
demerit system. Messy hair, bad nails, and bad makeup cost five
demerits each. So does calling the room director by his first name,
failing to keep a makeup appointment, or eating food in the Bunny
Room. Chewing gum or eating while on duty is ten demerits for the
first offence, twenty for the second, and dismissal for the third. A
three-time loser for "failure to report for work without replace-
ment" is not only dismissed but blacklisted from all other Playboy
Clubs. Showing up late for work or after a break costs a demerit a
minute, failure to follow a room director's instructions costs
fifteen. "The dollar value of demerits," notes the Bunny bible,
"shall be determined by the general manager of each club."

Once the system is mastered, there are still instructions for
specific jobs. Door Bunnies greet customers and check their keys.
Camera Bunnies must operate Polaroids. Cigarette Bunnies explain why a pack of cigarettes can't be bought without a Playboy
lighter; hat-check Bunnies learn the checking system; gift-shop
Bunnies sell Playboy products; mobile-gift-shop Bunnies carry
Playboy products around in baskets, and table Bunnies memorize
thirteen pages of drinks.

There's more to Bunnyhood than stuffing bosoms.

Note: Section 523 says: "Employees may enter and enjoy the
facilities of the club as bona fide guests of 1 [Number One]
keyholders." Are these the big shots my makeup expert had in
mind?

Morning, Monday 4th

At 11:00 a.m. I went to see the Playboy doctor ('Failure to keep
doctor's appointment, twenty demerits") at his office in a nearby
hotel. The nurse gave me a medical-history form to fill out. "Do
you know this includes an internal physical? I've been trying to
get Miss Shay to warn the girls." I said I knew, but that I didn't
understand why it was required. "It's for your own good," she
said, and led me into a narrow examining room containing a

medicine chest, a scale, and a gynecological table. I put on a hospital robe and waited. It seemed I had spent a good deal of time lately either taking off clothes, waiting, or both.

The nurse came back with the doctor, a stout, sixtyish man with the pink and white skin of a baby. "So you're going to be a Bunny," he said heartily. "Just came back from Miami myself. Beautiful club down there. Beautiful Bunnies." I started to ask him if he had the coast-to-coast franchise, but he interrupted to ask how I liked Bunnyhood.

"Well, it's livelier than being a secretary," I said, and he told me to sit on the edge of the table. As he pounded my back and listened to me breathe, the thought crossed my mind that every Bunny in the New York club had rested on the same spot. "This is the part all the girls hate," said the doctor, and took blood from my arm for a Wassermann test. I told him that testing for venereal disease seemed a little ominous. "Don't be silly," he said, "all the employees have to do it. You'll know everyone in the club is clean." I said that their being clean didn't really affect me and that I objected to being put through these tests. Silence. He asked me to stand to "see if your legs are straight." "Okay," I said, "I have to have a Wassermann. But what about an internal examination? Is that required of waitresses in New York State?"

"What do you care?" he said. "It's free, and it's for everybody's good."

"How?" I asked.

"Look," he said impatiently, "we usually find that girls who object to it strenuously have some reason . . ." He paused significantly. I paused, too. I could either go through with it or I could march out in protest. But in protest of what?

Back in the reception room, the nurse gave me a note to show Miss Shay that I had, according to preliminary tests at least, passed. As I put on my coat, she phoned a laboratory to pick up "a blood sample and a smear." I asked why those tests and no urine sample? Wasn't that the most common laboratory test of all? "It's for your own protection," she said firmly, "and anyway, the club pays."

Down in the lobby, I stopped in a telephone booth to call the board of health. I asked if a Wassermann test was required of waitresses in New York City? "No." Then what kind of physical examination *was* required? "None at all," they said.

KENNEDY ASSASSINATED

UPI, 23 November 1963

Smith's dispatch recording the assassination of JFK earned him a 1964 Pulitzer.

It was a balmy, sunny noon as we motored through downtown Dallas behind President Kennedy. The procession cleared the centre of the business district and turned into a handsome highway that wound through what appeared to be a park.

I was riding in the so-called White House press "pool" car, a telephone company vehicle equipped with a mobile radio-telephone. I was in the front seat between a driver from the telephone company and Malcom Kilduff, acting White House press secretary for the President's Texas tour. Three other pool reporters were wedged in the back seat.

Suddenly we heard three loud, almost painfully loud cracks. The first sounded as if it might have been a large firecracker. But the second and the third blasts were unmistakable. Gunfire.

The President's car, possibly as much as 150 or 200 yards ahead; seemed to falter briefly. We saw a flurry of activity in the secret service follow-up car behind the chief executive's bubble-top limousine.

Next in line was the car bearing Vice-President Lyndon B. Johnson. Behind that, another follow-up car bearing agents assigned to the vice-president's protection. We were behind that car.

Our car stood still for probably only a few seconds, but it seemed like a lifetime. One sees history explode before one's eyes and, for even the most trained observer, there is a limit to what one can comprehend.

I looked ahead at the President's car but could not see him or his companion, Gov. John Connally. Both had been riding on the right side of the limousine. I thought I saw a flash of pink that would have been Mrs Jacqueline Kennedy.

Everybody in our car began shouting at the driver to pull up closer to the President's car. But at this moment, we saw the big bubbletop and a motorcycle escort roar away at high speed.

We screamed at our driver, "get going, get going". We careened around the Johnson car and its escort and set out down the highway, barely able to keep in sight of the President's car and the accompanying secret service car.

They vanished around a curve. When we cleared the same curve we could see where we were heading – Parkland Hospital. We spilled out of the pool car as it entered the hospital driveway.

I ran to the side of the bubbletop.

The President was face down on the back seat. Mrs Kennedy made a cradle of her arms around the President's head and bent over him as if she were whispering to him.

Gov. Connally was on his back on the floor of the car, his head and shoulders resting in the arms of his wife, Nellie, who shook with dry sobs. Blood oozed from the front of the governor's suit. I could not see the President's wound. But I could see blood spattered around the interior of the rear seat and a dark stain spreading down the right side of the President's dark grey suit.

From the telephone car, I had radioed the Dallas UPI Bureau that three shots had been fired at the Kennedy motorcade.

Clint Hill, the secret service agent in charge of the detail assigned to Mrs Kennedy, was leaning over into the rear of the car.

"How badly was he hit, Clint?" I asked.

"He's dead," Hill replied curtly.

THE MAGIC BUS

The Electric Kool-Aid Acid Test, 1968

Sometime reporter for the *Springfield Union* and *New York Herald-Tribune*, Dr Wolfe (1931–) was the pioneer of the narcissistic New Journalism of the sixties. For which there was no more fitting subject than Ken Kesey's "Merry Pranksters". Initially Wolfe reported the "Merry Pranksters" drug-fuelled and mind-bended exploits for the *World Tribune Journal*, before writing up the dispatches into the iconic *The Electric Kool-Aid Acid Test*.

I couldn't tell you for sure which of the Merry Pranksters got the idea for the bus, but it had the Babbs touch. It was a superprank, in any case. The original fantasy, here in the spring of 1964, had been that Kesey and four or five others would get a station wagon and drive to New York for the New York World's Fair. On the way they could shoot some film, make some tape, freak out on the Fair and see what happened. They would also be on hand, in New York, for the publication of Kesey's second novel, *Sometimes a Great Notion*, early in July. So went the original fantasy.

Then somebody – Babbs? – saw a classified ad for a 1939 International Harvester school bus. The bus belonged to a man in Menlo Park. He had a big house and a lot of grounds and a nice set of tweeds and flannels and eleven children. He had rigged out the bus for the children. It had bunks and benches and a refrigerator and a sink for washing dishes and cabinets and shelves and a lot of other nice features for living on the road. Kesey bought it for $1,500 – in the name of Intrepid Trips, Inc.

Kesey gave the word and the Pranksters set upon it one afternoon. They started painting it and wiring it for sound and cutting a hole in the roof and fixing up the top of the bus so you could sit up there in the open air and play music, even a set of drums and electric guitars and electric bass and so forth, or just ride. Sandy went to work on the wiring and rigged up a system with which they could broadcast from inside the bus, with tapes or over microphones, and it would blast outside over powerful speakers on top of the bus. There were also microphones outside that would pick up sounds along the road and broadcast them inside the bus. There was also a sound system inside the bus so you could broadcast to one another over the roar of the engine and the road. You could also broadcast over a tape mechanism so that you said something, then heard your own voice a second later in variable lag and could rap off of that if you wanted to. Or you could put on earphones and rap simultaneously off sounds from outside, coming in one ear, and sounds from inside, your own sounds, coming in the other ear. There was going to be no goddamn sound on that whole trip, outside the bus, inside the bus, or inside your own freaking larynx, that you couldn't tune in on and rap off of.

The painting job, meanwhile, with everybody pitching in in a frenzy of primary colors, yellow, oranges, blues, reds, was sloppy as hell, except for the parts Roy Seburn did, which were nice manic mandalas. Well, it was sloppy, but one thing you had to say for it; it was freaking lurid. The manifest, the destination sign in the front, read: "Furthur," with two *u*'s.

They took a test run up into northern California and right away this wild-looking thing with the wild-looking people was great for stirring up consternation and vague befuddling resentment among the citizens. The Pranksters were now out among them, and it was exhilarating – look at the mothers staring! – and there was going to be holy terror in the land. But there would also be people who would look up out of their poor work-a-daddy lives in some town, some old guy, somebody's stenographer, and see this bus and register . . . delight, or just pure open-invitation wonder. Either way, the Intrepid Travelers figured, there was hope for these people. They weren't totally turned off. The bus also had great possibilities for altering the usual order of things. For example, there were the cops.

One afternoon the Pranksters were on a test run in the bus going through the woods up north and a forest fire had started.

There was smoke beginning to pour out of the woods and everything. Everybody on the bus had taken acid and they were zonked. The acid was in some orange juice in the refrigerator and you drank a paper cup full of it and you were zonked. Cassady was driving and barrelling through the burning woods wrenching the steering wheel this way and that way to his innerwired beat, with a siren wailing and sailing through the rhythm.

A *siren?* It's a highway patrolman, which immediately seems like the funniest thing in the history of the world. Smoke is pouring out of the woods and they are all sailing through leaf explosions in the sky, but the cop is bugged about this freaking bus. The cop yanks the bus over to the side and he starts going through a kind of traffic-safety inspection of the big gross bus, while more and more of the smoke is billowing out of the woods. Man, the licence plate is on wrong and there's no light over the licence plate and this turn signal looks bad and how about the brakes, let's see that hand brake there. Cassady, the driver, is already into a long monologue for the guy, only he is throwing in all kinds of sirs: "Well, yes sir, this is a Hammond bi-valve serrated brake, you understand, sir, had it put on in a truck ro-de-o in Springfield, Oregon, had to back through a slalom course of baby's bottles and yellow nappies, in the existential culmination of Oregon, lots of outhouse freaks up there, you understand, sir, a punctual sort of a state, sir, yes sir, holds to 28,000 pounds, 28,000 pounds, you just look right here, sir, tested by a pure-blooded Shell Station attendant in Springfield, Oregon, winter of '62, his gumball boots never froze, you understand, sir, 28,000 pounds hold, right here –" Whereupon he yanks back on the hand-brake as if it's attached to something, which it isn't, it is just dangling there, and jams his foot on the regular brake, and the bus shudders as if the hand brake has a hell of a bite, but the cop is thoroughly befuddled now, anyway, because Cassady's monologue has confused him, for one thing, and what the hell are these . . . *people* doing. By this time everybody is off the bus rolling in the brown grass by the shoulder, laughing, giggling, yahooing, zonked to the skies on acid, because, mon, the woods are burning, the whole world is on fire, and a Cassady monologue on auto-motive safety is rising up from out of his throat like weenie smoke, as if the great god Speed were frying in his innards, and the cop, representative of the people of California in this total freaking situation, is all hung up on a hand brake that doesn't exist in the first place. And the cop, all he can see is a bunch of crazies in screaming orange and green costumes, masks, boys and girls, men and women, twelve or fourteen of them, lying in the grass and making hideously crazy sounds – Christ almighty, why the hell does he have to contend with . . . So he wheels around and says, "What are you, uh – show people?"

"That's right, officer," Kesey says. "We're show people. It's been a long row to hoe, I can tell you, and it's *gonna* be a long row to hoe, but that's the business."

"Well," says the cop, "you fix up those things and . . ." He starts backing off toward his car, cutting one last look at the crazies. ". . . And watch it next time . . ." And he guns on off.

That was it! How can you give a traffic ticket to a bunch of people rolling in the brown grass wearing Day-Glo masks, practically Greek masques, only with Rat phosphorescent *élan*, giggling, keening in their costumes and private world while the god Speed sizzles like a short-order French fry in the gut of some guy who doesn't even stop talking to breathe. A traffic ticket? The Pranksters felt more immune than ever. There was no more reason for them to remain in isolation while the ovoid eyes of La Honda supurated. They could go through the face of America muddling people's minds, but it's a momentary high, and the bus would be gone, and all the Fab foam in their heads would settle back down into their brain pans.

So the Hieronymus Bosch bus headed out of Kesey's place with the destination sign in front reading "Furthur" and a sign in the back saying "Caution: Weird Load." It was weird, all right, but it was euphoria on board, barreling through all that warm California sun in July, on the road, and everything they had been working on at Kesey's was on board and heading on Furthur. Besides, the joints were going around, and it was nice and high out here on the road in America. As they headed out, Cassady was at the wheel, and there was Kesey, Babbs, Page Browning, George Walker, Sandy, Jane Burton, Mike Hagen, Hassler, Kesey's brother Chuck and his cousin Dale, a guy known as Brother John, and three newcomers who were just along for the ride or just wanted to go to New York.

One of them was a young, quite handsome kid – looked sort of like the early, thin Michael Caine in *Zulu* – named Steve Lambrecht. He was the brother-in-law of Kesey's lawyer, Paul Robertson, and he was just riding to New York to see a girl he knew named Kathy. Another was a girl named Paula Sundsten. She was young, plump, ebullient, and very sexy. Kesey knew her from Oregon. Another one was some girl Hagen of the Screw Shack had picked up in San Francisco, on North Beach. She was the opposite of Paula Sundsten. She was thin, had long dark hair, and would be moody and silent one minute and nervous and carrying on the next. She was good-looking like a TV witch.

By the time they hit San Jose, barely 30 miles down the road, a lot of the atmosphere of the trip was already established. It was nighttime and many souls were high and the bus had broken down. They pulled into a service station and pretty soon one of the help has his nose down in under the hood looking at the engine while Cassady races the motor and the fluorescent stanchion lights around the station hit the bus in weird phosphorescent splashes, the car lights stream by on the highway, Cassady guns the engine some more, and from out of the bus comes a lot of weird wailing, over the speakers or just out the windows. Paula Sundsten has gotten hold of a microphone with the variable-lag setup and has found out she can make weird radio-spook laughing ghoul sounds with it, wailing like a banshee and screaming "How was your stay-ay-ay-ay . . . in San Ho-zay-ay-ay-ay-ay," with the variable lag picking up the ay-ay-ay-ays and doubling them, quadrupling them, octupling them. An endless ricocheting echo – and all the while this weird, slightly hysterical laugh and a desperate little plunking mandolin sail through it all, coming from Hagen's girl friend, who is lying back on a bench inside, plunking a mandolin and laughing – in what way. . .

Outside, some character, some local, has come over to the bus, but the trouble is, he is not at all impressed with the bus, he just has to do the American Man thing of when somebody's car is broken down you got to come over and make your diagnosis.

And he is saying to Kesey and Cassady, "You know what I'd say you need? I'd say you need a good mechanic. Now, I'm not a good mechanic, but I – " And naturally he proceeds to give his diagnosis, while Paula wails, making spook-house effects, and the Beauty Witch keens and goons – and – "– like I say, what you need is a good mechanic, and I'm not a good mechanic, but –"

And – of course! – the Non-people. The whole freaking world was full of people who were bound to tell you they weren't qualified to do this or that but they were determined to go ahead and do just that thing anyway. Kesey decided he was the Non-navigator. Babbs was the Non-doctor. The bus trip was already becoming an allegory of life.

NORMAN MAILER'S NIGHT OUT

The Sunday Times, 25 April 1965

When Norman Mailer flew into London last week he took up residence very discreetly with his fourth wife, Beverley, in Room 776 at the Savoy Hotel. Discreetly, that is, as far as such a word can ever be applied to a man whose private life has attracted headlines for a decade and whose reputation will probably now always travel at least two jumps ahead of him.

Mailer is in London to launch – "that's what you call it here, in America we just say hustle" – his fourth novel, *An American Dream* which André Deutsch publishes tomorrow. Not that any further publicity, even if constructed on the most massive Hollywood scale, could add to the Mailer myth of anarchic egomania, which is so contagious that one spent the first part of an evening with America's high priest of sensation nervously waiting a cataclysm.

But none came. In the event it was almost a shock to see such a very quiet American in an unmistakably English suit (made in Dover Street, he said) treading his way diffidently across the Savoy carpet and then mildly wondering if he could get a Bourbon and orange juice without disturbing any of the waiters too much. It was an undramatic introduction.

Mailer is short, wide and heavy – he has the humped build of the classic stand-off half – and his physical presence is palpable. Later, over dinner with a group of people, it was noticeable that when conversation passed him by for any length of time the others tended to keep throwing looks at him as if to reassure themselves that he hadn't been up to anything in the last thirty seconds. His face is Celtic rather than Jewish and very kind – he has a faun look, with deep-set eyes, a lot of curly hair getting a bit grizzled about the sideboards he wears long, and a way of looking shrewdly sideways to see if some point has been taken, followed by a big grin. Althogether he has the air of someone who has got used to charming people over the years.

One of the resemblances he shares with Sergius O'Shaughnessy, the hero of his second novel, *The Deer Park*, and Stephen Rojack, who in the new book takes the anti-hero about as far as he will go, is that despite the deliquencies people go on liking him. And his hero's peccadilloes are not the kind that get shrugged off lightly – in the first chapter of *An American Dream*, for example, Rojack manages to get drunk, almost commit suicide, take a lot of pleasure in strangling his wife Deborah; and find the time for acrobatic sex with a German maid before pitching his wife's body ten storeys down in front of a car.

Over his orange juice and Bourbon Mailer was talking mildly and politely, in a voice with more Massachusetts than Brooklyn in it, about how much he likes London. The only note of criticism came when he denied a Sunday newspaper story that he was contemplating settling down here. "One thing, though, I think your papers are very much worse than ours. In your popular Press most of the stories are so short, and a lot of things just can't be written about shortly. There are also the lies, like this story about me – it's complete invention."

But he likes it here. "It's funny, but in a way I grew up in Brooklyn with an English father – he was a South African and came from a Johannesburg Jewish family to Brooklyn in 1920. He's a small, very elegant man who looks like a banker He used to play the role of an Englishman, he used to wear spats and talk with an English accent – say 'vanilly' instead of 'vanilla'? this kind of affectation. When I come here I feel at home – say, like a Colonial."

He carried on the family tradition and stood up when his wife, formerly the actress Beverley Bentley, came in. (All through the evening he got to his feet whenever a woman joined the party and was highly punctilious about going through doors last.) On the way out of the Savoy he wondered whether the doorman should have been tipped and demanded a rundown on the local habits. "That's the kind of thing that gets you nervous in a foreign country."

Later he elaborated on what he liked about London, mainly in terms of its differences from New York. One wondered how accurate it was, but Mailer at least was deeply convinced. "Here there must be maybe 5,000 street corners that have been the same for a hundred years. People who grow up there, a clerk or someone, they're like spirits of the place, they see every little change and they do something to the mood. New York is different. We waste everything in America, we waste our substance. I suppose we just get more so we waste more. We don't allow our tree stumps to hang around, we blow them up or bulldoze them. You don't have modern architecture where in the same way – it depends on sensation, which is electric rather then sensuous, and shatters all mood. Most modern architecture induces a sense of shivering and awe, it doesn't give you relaxation or pleasure."

New York, he thought, was getting like Berlin in the twenties. "Everyone is looking for something to break that awful bleak tension of the city which comes down on you like a smog and gets into your nerves. Everyone's crazy for abrupt sensation. Say a man thinks in the morning he wants to go to bed with his wife that night – well, he realizes that something is sure to go wrong so the best thing to do is to have a row in the early evening and hope it will somehow get patched up later on. That's why 'camp' has run right through New York, so people will break into a conversation say about the Yankees and come up with something completely disrupting just for a laugh – 'I like mustard on my Rocquefort', something crazy like that. It came originally from the upper East Side, where you'd find a painter firing bullets at balloons with pigments in them so they'd explode on the canvas – that's the last child of Dada."

The fragmentation and tension of the city he kept talking about is reflected in the way he wrote his new novel. Towards the end of dinner he started to talk about it. "I knew I wanted to write a novel about a man who was violent," he said. "You know it first came out in eight instalments in *Esquire*. Ten days before the first deadline I still had the idea in my mind of a completely different book, and even when I'd got going there were times in the first two or three instalments when I felt scared I'd dry up – but then it was all right." The whole method is typical of Mailer (though not one he intends to try again; now he is working on a big novel that "might take two or might take five years"). It was a kind of literary gamble, the only kind he really takes seriously.

He does a bit of the other kind of gambling. "Personally, the biggest bet I've ever had was $500 at evens on the Torres–Pastramo Fight. Torres is a friend of mine and I know what a good fighter he is. I was sure he was going to win. I thought of betting a thousand dollars, but then I got scared and didn't want to be too greedy and maybe wreck the whole thing." (Mailer won his $500; Torres beat Pastrano in nine.)

True to the Hemingway–James Jones tradition Mailer likes to fight and constantly feels a need to prove his physical courage. "Just before I came here I sparred three rounds with Torres. It was like fighting a puma – a very kind puma who gave me a couple of jabs now and then to make me feel remotely honest."

And the violence, of course, is reflected in his books.

"I don't think anyone ever condemns murder *really*. Society may be founded on Kant's categorical imperative, but individual murder gives a sense of life to those around the event. Take newspaper readers – doesn't the suburban commuter get a moment of pleasure on the subway reading about murder? Is he perverse or is it really something life-giving? I prefer the second view of Man, the less bleak one."

By this time they had brought coffee. The conversation got round to Vietnam. Mailer thought that Johnson was using it as a substitute for what he called a "national myth". "I think the politicians have it in their minds that the Civil Rights movement will go on more easily if there's a war somewhere." Gesturing with his surprisingly small and plump hands he talked about gas and the new Lazy Dog weapon in Vietnam. He agreed that it probably wasn't any worse than napalm. "Napalm, yes, but napalm's been used up aesthetically – you have to have a new weapon to get a new psychic release. Every time a new weapon is produced every cadet gets a free ride."

And about the outraged reactions in the States to his hero Rojack's pleasurable sensations after murdering his wife and the social consequences of this kind of writing, Mailer said, "I don't know about the consequences; all I know is that a man feels good when he commits a murder – immediately after, that is. Have you ever seen soldiers coming back from a killing spree? They're happy. If I wrote any other way about it, it would be meretricious."

But eventually we finished up at Annie's Room, an after-hours jazz club. There Mailer drank brandy and champagne for an hour and then decided the only way to finish this interview was in his hotel.

It was 2.25 when we got back to the Savoy's grey carpets and white bedspreads, and Mailer celebrated the homecoming by ordering chicken sandwiches and six glasses of Pimm's from room service. Against an un-Maileresque background of tastefully arranged flowers he started to talk about the bad period which comes to almost every novelist who has an infant prodigy success, as he did almost exactly twenty years ago when *The Naked and the Dead* became an overnight best-seller. The next two novels, *Barbary Shore* and *The Deer Park*, were both attacked and in certain cases virtually dismissed by the critics. "It's hard, there's something in the seed of American culture that throws up writers all the time and then destroys them. Yes, it happened to Fitzgerald, but he had it a lot easier than me all the way up, and I think of myself being about five times tougher than he was."

With interruptions (mainly for Beverley to ring New York to find out how their thirteen-month-old son Michael was getting on) we moved to the more cheerful subject of what Mailer has made out of his writing. From *An American Dream* alone (for which Warner Bros, have taken up their option) he has so far netted something approaching the equivalent of £170,000.

"Of course, it's a lot of money," said Mailer, looking suitably modest as he attacked a chicken sandwich, "but my situation is I have to make $30,000 – say a good £10,000 – a year after tax before I can spend a cent." (There are four children from his three previous marriages.)

"I'll go on record on one thing in the advice to young writers department – I was too greedy: either get married once or not at all. Though I suppose you learn one thing: by the time you've been through the four stages of women – courtship, marriage, motherhood and divorce – you may be gentlemanly enough *not* to talk about it, but if you do then you certainly know in your heart that you're well qualified to speak." He seemed to muse on his former marriages. "After a divorce all I can say is at best there's a dead reserve and at worst an active bitchery back and forth."

He started on another Pimms (it was 3.15) and talked about the death of Kennedy – "For a time we felt the country was ours, now it's theirs again, – and then about the Mailer whose personal life once created melodrama for the New York newspapers. 'Yes, maybe in the first instance I used to create situations myself, but then they started to come on at me when I didn't expect them. That's not funny at all. And I'm not at all happy with many of the slogans I coined years ago – there's still a lot to be done with the novel, a lot of reality no one dares to write about, a whole new area of perception on the other side of writing – think of what Lawrence did in 1912. But it's hard, you've got to destroy something in your readers, their unwillingness to open their mood, and if you do it too many times it's at your peril because they either get shocked or don't understand and either way they don't read your books any more. That's the disadvantage of my reputation, it's helped in the sense that I get talked about perhaps, but readers also tighten up in advance.'

3.45. The hotel corridor deserted except for a grey ghost with a vacuum cleaner, and Mailer, finally ready to sleep, having the last word. "Say, how would you feel being interviewed at this time in the morning?" Grinning disreputably round the door he finally went to bed.

A VOTE FOR BOBBY K.

Village Voice, 1965

K for Kennedy. Bobby was the younger brother of the assassinated JFK.

When there first began to be talk, back last winter, of Bobby Kennedy going in against Kenneth Keating, I had the reaction of a prize-fight manager who has seen better days: Put down no bets, they're a couple of bums. Keating never did a thing to me. He had a face like the plastic dough children play with. Smells like a bottle of moistened saccharine, sticks to the fingers, fails to hold its shape. I disliked the rhetoric with which he strutted into discussions of Cuba; the righteousness was enough to make you throw up. For righteous politicians, like bullies, have their greatest test of character when they've got you on the ground – can they keep from kicking you in the ear? At his best, Keating seemed a passable if unctuous assistant to a hard worker like Javits – at his worst he was errand boy for Rockefeller plus every special interest there to be discovered. So Keating lit the kind of fire in my political heart which a turkey gobbler would light on the table if you developed the suspicion he was still alive. If one had to vote for Keating, there was no vote. The choice was left with Bobby. Bobby! – whom everybody I know called Raul Castro. Bobby! – the Irish equivalent of Roy Cohn on the good old McCarthy team; Bobby! – with the face of a Widmark gunsel, that prep-school arrogance which makes good manual labourers think of smashing a fist through a wall; Bobby! who wrote books called *The Enemy Within,* about Come-you-Nism and crooked unions, Bobby who wrote in a style so bad that (to repeat from something just written) he had a dead stick's prose; Bobby, who had always had it break the right way for him; Bobby, who played the game down the center, so had no sense at all of how it felt to be outside, try to get in. Who could vote for Bobby?

But we've had a couple of months of the campaign, and a liberal hogshead of much ado about almost no difference. Since each of the candidates was considerably farther to the right even a few years ago, their protestations of liberalism now, about which Hentoff, I. F. Stone, and Arthur Schlesinger have given us copious documentation back and forth, are not finally convincing, or even important to the vote. If Keating and Kennedy were both cons up before a parole board and were debating who had prayed his way back closer to Jesus, and each was buttressed in his arguments by impossible-to-follow allegations, and by disputes over microscopic facts delivered by lawyers altogether skillful at working the grit from a detail, one would have a natural suspicion that when a con claims he is close to Jesus it is to get parole – which con is actually the closest would have little to do with allegations, facts, or details. Or, in this case, issues. It would take a constitutional lawyer to decide on the issues whether Keating or Kennedy is now more liberal. When it comes to being more liberal in this hour, in this election, you could not get a short curled hair between them. They're so liberal you don't have to vote, not for liberalism – you got a liberal either way. Of course, if the country turns right, you got a conservative either way. Have you? Well, you know you have with Ken Keating. He doesn't have a face like plastic dough for nothing. But we are with Bobby. Here the difference begins to appear. I don't know. I wouldn't pretend to say Bobby Kennedy is not capable of marching at the front of a Right Wing movement. But the Right is not likely to suffer from a lack of leaders. Goldwater may be no more than the cork out of the bottle. The appeal of the Right, since it is emotional, will attract demagogues. I think Bobby Kennedy may be the only liberal about, early or late, who could be a popular general in a defense against the future powers of the Right Wing. For there's no one else around. The Democratic Party is bankrupt, bankrupt of charisma; the Right Wing has just begun. Anyone who was at the Democratic Convention in Atlantic City must confess – if they can afford to – that the mood was equal to a yellow jaundice ward on the banks of a swamp.

By this logic, it comes to this: we are in the absence of real and immediate political issues. So we must vote for one candidate because he is a neutron, or must vote for the other because he is an active principle who will grow and change and become – odds are – a powerful leader of the Left or the Right. Posed that way, I take the second alternative. I vote for the active principle. To vote for a man who is neuter is to vote for the plague. I would rather vote for a man on the assumption he is a hero and have him turn into a monster than vote for a man who can never be a hero. For follow it through: a hero, even a failed-hero, or a hero-as-monster, is more likely to create other heroes, by his example or by opposition to him, than a man who gains power and has never been anything at all. A forceful political structure with a great number of particular heroes is a way to describe the Renaissance; a powerful political structure governed by faceless men is a way to describe the Mafia. The vote goes then to Bobby Kennedy. He has finally a face.

Say one thing more. Few vote by logic alone. Sentiment enters. I have affection for Bobby Kennedy. I think something came into him with the death of his brother. I think Bobby Kennedy has come a pilgrim's distance from that punk who used to play Junior D. A. for Joe McCarthy and grabbed headlines by riding Jimmy Hoffa's back. Something compassionate, something witty, has come into the face. Something of sinew. So I think. I could be wrong, but I'd rather go this way and be wrong, than vote the other way trying to stop a possibility with a nonentity. When the issues at stake are small, it is natural to vote for the man who has the more arresting personality, as once before, when issues were small, America elected Jack Kennedy. Of course, if you remember, Jack Kennedy was not then enormously popular in New York. He had a dubious liberal record and seemed unpredictable. New York voted for him but did not like him. In New York we prefer to vote to stop things. So New Yorkers know nonentity. They know durance sufficiently vile to have endured for twelve years a nonentity for Mayor and a nonentity, these last six years, for Senator. My vote goes therefore to establishing a new face in the Senate. Is that not half the welfare of a liberal society – to have something new to discuss at the dinner table? Consider: six more years of Ken Keating with Brussels sprouts or six with Bobby K. and some red snapper.

LONDON, THE MOST EXCITING CITY IN THE WORLD

Weekend Telegraph, 16 April 1965

Crosby, an American journalist living in London, has claimed to have invented the phrase "Swinging London".

> *Fly me to the moon and let me play among the stars*
> *Let me know what spring is like on Jupiter and Mars*

An American girl from Natchez, Mississippi, singing at the new Cool Elephant. Blue walls. Cigarette smoke. The gleam of a trombone through the nightclub blackness.

At Annabel's in Berkeley Square are the elegant crowd – the Duchess of Northumberland. Frank Sinatra when he's in town, King Constantine dancing with his young queen, Anne-Marie, Aristotle Onassis, a sprinkling of Saudi Arabians, perhaps Princess Margaret. In Soho, at the Ad Lib, the hottest and swingingest spot in town the noise is deafening, the beat group is pounding out *I Just Don't Know What to Do with Myself*, on the floor, under the red and green and blue lights, a frenzy of the prettiest legs in the whole world belonging to models, au pair girls or just ordinary English girls, a gleam of pure joy on their pretty faces, dancing with the young bloods, the scruffy very hotshot photographers like David Bailey or Terry Donovan, or a new pop singer – all vibrating with youth. At the corner table more or less permanently reserved for the Beatles (you'll always find at least one of them there when they're in town) Ringo proposes to Maureen (that's where he did it).

These are for the rich and famous. But London's throbbing

nightlife has room for everyone. At the Marquee, a jazz club, non-alcoholic, on Wardour Street, you'll find the young kids from the offices. The Scene on Great Windmill Street brings in the Mods. Ronnie Scotts in Soho is a classless place – the sons of dukes and working men rubbing elbows in mutual appreciation of jazz; the Flamingo, a beat spot, caters to the West Indians.

Diana Vreeland, who as editor of *Vogue* is almost supreme arbiter of taste in America, has said simply, "London is the most swinging city in the world at the moment" – putting into words what a lot of us Americans living here have long felt. The young bloods from Madrid and Rome – for reasons they only dimly understand – suddenly converge on London. London is where the action is, as New York and then Paris were right after the war, as Rome was in the mid-Fifties. Now it's London – the gayest, most uninhibited, and – in a wholly new, very modern sense – most wholly elegant city in the world. It seems to me that the last people to find it out are the Londoners themselves, under whose nose these changes in mood and tone have taken place, almost imperceptibly over the past four or five years.

Fill my heart with song, let me sing for ever more
You are all I long for, all I worship and adore

There's a quality of eager innocence in that old song and that's exactly the tone of London's nightlife. In an English girl's eyes is a starry innocence only possible in an island that has not been invaded for 1,000 years. Behind the dark-eyed invitation in a French girl, a Spanish girl, an Italian girl, there always lies a hint of wariness, a tiny veil of distrust, the ancient memory of ancient rapes, forgotten pillage.

I asked Leslie Linder, proprietor of those Elephants, The White Elephant (restaurant), and the Crazy and Cool Elephants, both night-clubs, what made London a swinging town. He answered simply and immediately. "It's the girls. Italian and Spanish men are kinky for English girls. When I opened The White Elephant we had the prettiest girls I ever saw."

Mark Birley, the immensely tall and coolly elegant owner of the coolly elegant Anabel's says the same thing. "The girls are prettier here than anywhere else – much more so than in Rome or Paris."

They're more than pretty; they're young, appreciative, sharp-tongued, glowingly alive. Even the sex orgies among the sex-and-pot set in Chelsea and Kensington have youth and eagerness and, in a strange way, a quality of innocence about them. In Rome and Paris, the sex orgies are for the old, the jaded, the disgusting and disgusted. Young English girls take to sex as if it's candy and it's delicious.

England, in fact, is getting something of a corner on all the pretty girls who are flying in from all the other capitals of Europe. "The au pair girls started all that," says Leslie Linder. "All these pretty young chicks from Sweden and Denmark. London is getting very Continental. We've got all these French chicks. Spanish chicks, German chicks. Of course, Rome has a lot of foreign chicks, too, but it seems to me the girls are nicer here and more natural: In Rome, all the chicks are grabbing – they want to be film stars or they want to marry a millionaire. Here, they're just students or au pair girls. They don't want anything except to be girls. It's a healthier atmosphere than either Rome or Paris."

The deluge of pretty girls is on all levels. Betty Kenward, who writes the social column under the name of Jennifer for *Queen* magazine, points out, "The young King and Queen of Greece may fly in for a ball and that brings in all those young princesses from Holland or Denmark. Then there are so many international marriages. Tina Onassis, a Greek, married to the Marquess of Blandford. Lord Bessborough is married to a chic American girl. So is Kenneth Keith. Young David Montagu has a charming young French wife. We have charming young Italian wives, charming Spanish wives – and they all bring in their friends from their countries of birth."

The nightlife is just a symptom, the outer and visible froth, of an inner, far deeper turbulence that boiled up in Britain around – if we must date it – 1958, though some astounded at what is happening. Why – they say – is this happening here and not in America, and they go right home and start young men's shops in their own stores.

There's a revolution in men's clothes here that is very much part of the London swinging scene, partly because it's adding so much dash and colour and glamour to the London street scene, but also as a sign of deeper social turmoil that is transforming England, especially among the young. English men's clothes were once almost uniform: staid, sober and, above all, correct, advertising your precise rung on the social ladder and even your bank account. Today the working-class boys – many of them fresh out of the Army or Navy and in full revolt against con- formity of dress – their pockets full of money, are splurging on suede jackets, skin-like tweed trousers, double-breasted pin- striped suits (the very latest mode) with two buttons – or perhaps six. The impact of Carnaby Street is becoming worldwide. Tony Curtis wears Carnaby Street clothes. So do Peter Sellers and the Beatles.

The same thing on a different social and income level can be seen at Blades in Dover Street where the custom-made suits cost £52. At Blades the clothes have an elegance and a sort of look-at- me dash not seen since Edwardian times. On the racks I found, just as an example of what goes on there, a jet black velvet dinner jacket – trousers the same material – with a mandarin collar and buttons that I would never have the courage to wear.

A typical customer of Blades is Hercules Bellville, not long out of Oxford, who swathes himself in brown corduroy of velvety texture, long skirted, with waspish pants, which he tops with a short fur-collared coat. Fully assembled, with his flowing blond hair and almost classical good English looks, Hercules looks like something straight out of Max Beerbohm.

The proprietor of Blades is Rupert Lycett-Green, and both he and Bellville typify the revolt of the upper-class young. Bellville toiled in advertising a while, a socially acceptable occupation, then threw the whole thing up to get into movie-making. He's an assistant-assistant director now, frequently out of work, but he's doing what he wants.

Lycett-Green worked for a bit in the family engineering firm in the north of France. Two years ago, he quit and started Blades with his own money. After a shaky start it is doing quite well.

"Twenty-five years ago," says Lycett-Green, "young people would be almost afraid to speak out and do something like this with their money. They'd have followed their fathers into the City, or estate management. Now the young people want to see what they can do on their own. Some of my friends have started their own insurance companies, their own restaurants or their own nightclubs. They're all doing what they want to do, not what's expected of them."

Another case is Noel Picarda, another Oxonian, who comes from a long line of lawyers. His father and brothers are barristers and they wanted Noel in the law firm, too. But he's in love with show business and he's performing at the Establishment, writing and appearing in sketches at the Poor Millionaire and has started a talent agency.

Richard de la Mare, grandson of Walter de la Mare, declined a nice safe job in the publishing house of Faber & Faber, where his father is chairman, to undertake the extremely precarious and not at all lucrative task of making *avant garde* films like *Carousella* about the life of stripteasers.

The caste system, in short, is breaking down at both ends. The working-class young are busting out of the lower depths and invading fields where they can make more money and the upper-class is breaking down walls to get into the lower levels where they can have more fun. Caroline Charles says: "Here they're so much more democratic than America – everybody mixes!" It's the bounce and vitality of these youngsters, both upper and lower class, that contributes most of the fizz to London.

De La Mare observed also, "My mother told me that, after she and my father were married for about five years, they settled down. But she says that my wife and I have been married five years and haven't settled down. By settling down, they mean moving to the country, playing golf and raising roses and children. The young marrieds don't settle down like that any more. They keep right on swinging right here in London."

This has changed the nature of their entertaining much for the better, according to *Queen*'s Mrs Kenward. English upper-class dinner parties used to be renowned for the quantities of servants and the tastelessness of the food. Now, the servants have disappeared and the food is much better. Mrs Kenward credits the late Constance Spry who taught many of the young brides how to cook. "Cooking is much better than it was," she said, "Young married couples know how to entertain much better – without staff or with temporary staff."

Much of the stuffiness, in fact, has been knocked out of the Royal entertaining. The Queen's party for Princess Alexandra and Angus Ogilvy was a really swinging affair that went on to the wee hours, my American friends who attended it told me. Those used to be dreary affairs. Not long ago, Prince Charles and

Princess Anne gave a twist and shake party for their young friends at Windsor Castle. Princess Margaret is usually found with actors, writers or painters rather than Guards officers.

London, says Leslie Linder – and everyone else – has lost its reputation as a bad food city. Largely, I suspect, because the English are travelling abroad more, they are demanding and getting better food in the restaurants. The young swingers prefer the little restaurants – places like Trattoria Terrazza in Soho, Pavillon or Au Pere de Nico in Chelsea, or Chanterelle on Old Brompton Road – rather than the stuffier big places like the Savoy Grill which used to get the play. The White Tower on Percy Street has magnificent food and superb wines for the well-heeled. Tiberio's Italian food is marvellous. Even the penniless young ones eat better – at Buzzy's Bistro under the footpath on King's Road, Chelsea, or at Hades in Exhibition Road, South Kensington, where the girls are beautiful, the prices rock bottom and the food not at all bad.

The most astonishing change of all to me is the muscular virility of England's writers and dramatists and actors and artists – this from an island we'd mostly thought of in terms of Noel Coward and drawing-room comedy. English plays used to be jaded, fey, rococo – and so were the actors. Now, it's all anger, sweat and the working classes, and expresses the vitality and energy and virility among the young people I meet.

Vitality was the keynote of *Tom Jones* which made a fortune (for the Americans because the British film companies didn't have the sense to invest in it) and was also one of the principal ingredients of the James Bond film *Goldfinger* which has already earned £7,800,000 and of *Lawrence of Arabia* and the Beatles film – all British-written, directed and acted. (And all of them American-owned. Why haven't you British any faith in your own writers and directors and actors?)

Talent is getting to be Britain's greatest export commodity. Not long ago, the New York film critics made their nominations for the year's best acting and every last actor was English (and two of the actresses were English, too.) In Paris, at New Jimmy's or at Kastel's, they dance now to the records of the Beatles or Cilla Black or the Rolling Stones where only a year ago the music came from Frank Sinatra, Tony Bennett and Dean Martin – all Americans.

The new National Theatre has presented almost casually one masterpiece after another, from *Uncle Vanya*, which was described as the supreme achievement of the English stage, to *Othello*, a somewhat more controversial masterpiece. To a theatregoer, the variety to pick from is sumptuous. And in that great pile of red plush and crystal chandeliered elegance, Covent Garden, Kenneth Macmillan has unveiled a wholly new, very renaissance, very masculine version of Prokofiev's *Romeo and Juliet*. The theatres themselves with their 19th-century opulence and curves and charm are a perennial lure to visitors.

This explosion of creative vitality, a sort of English renaissance, has occurred on the very highest levels, as well as the more frivolous ones. On the topmost sphere of pure thought. Fred Hoyle, the Cambridge astronomer, has just advanced a theory about the physical nature of the universe as sweeping in its implications as those of Copernicus, Newton or Einstein.

Several theories have been suggested as to why all this is happening, where all this explosion of creative energy came from. It has been suggested that England, shorn of its worldwide responsibilities for keeping the peace, has turned its energies, previously dissipated in running the colonies, inward toward personal self-expression.

I think this is quite true but there's another factor. The English, I think, had a long Dark Age which started in the depression of the Thirties, continued through the long and terrible war and culminated in a long period of austerity, much longer than anyone else's. Longer even than Germany's, that didn't end really until about 1958. After any prolonged darkness, the Middle Ages, or the Napoleonic Wars, there's a renaissance, a flowering, a release of pent-up energy – and London is right in the middle of it.

Or perhaps just at the beginning. Most of these kids, who are starting dress shops or writing songs or making films, are in their twenties or early thirties. The best years, several decades of them, might well lie ahead when these talents mature.

MAUREEN CLEAVE

JOHN LENNON: "WE'RE MORE POPULAR THAN JESUS NOW"

Evening Standard, 4 March 1966

When Cleave's article was reprinted in American fanzines in May 1966, Lennon's claim that the Beatles were bigger than Jesus excited furious anger in the Southern Bible Belt. Lennon was forced into an humiliating recantation, which he never quite forgot or forgave. It was the beginning of the end for the "Fab Four". They never played on a public stage after 1966.

The Beatles are now the most famous people in the English speaking world. They are famous in the way the Queen is famous. When John Lennon's Rolls-Royce, with its black wheels and its black windows, goes past, people say "It's the Queen" or "It's the Beatles". With her they share the security of a stable life at the top. They all tick over in the public esteem – she in Buckingham Palace, they in the Weybridge–Esher area. Only Paul remains in London.

The Weybridge community consists of the three married Beatles; they live there among the wooded hills and the stockbrokers. They have not worked since Christmas and their existence is secluded and curiously timeless. "What day is it?" John Lennon asks with interest when you ring up with news from outside. The fans are still at the gates but the Beatles see only each other. They are better friends than ever before.

Ringo and his wife, Maureen, may drop in on John and Cyn; John may drop in on Ringo; George and Patti may drop in on John and Cyn and they might all go round to Ringo's – by car, of course. Outdoors is for holidays.

They watch films, they play rowdy games of Buccaneer; they watch television till it goes off, often playing records at the same time. They while away the small hours of the morning making mad tapes. Bedtimes and mealtimes have no meaning as such. "We've never had time before to do anything but just be Beatles," John Lennon said.

He is much the same as he was before. He still peers down his nose, arrogant as an eagle, although contact lenses have righted the short sight that originally caused the expression. He looks more like Henry VIII than ever now that his face has filled out – he is just as imperious, just as unpredictable, indolent, disorganized, childish, vague, charming and quick-witted. He is still easy-going, still tough as hell. "You never asked after Fred Lennon," he says, disappointed. (Fred is his father; he emerged after they got famous.) "He was here a few weeks ago. It was only the second time in my life I'd seen him – I showed him the door." He went on cheerfully, "I wasn't having him in the house."

His enthusiasm is undiminished and he insists on its being shared. George has put him on to this Indian music. "You're not listening, are you?" he shouts after twenty minutes of the record. "It's amazing this – so cool. Don't the Indians appear cool to you? Are you listening? This music is thousands of years old; it makes me laugh, the British going over there and telling them what to do. Quite amazing." And he switched on the television set.

Experience has sown few seeds of doubt in him; not that his mind is closed, but it's closed round whatever he believes at the time. "Christianity will go," he said. "It will vanish and shrink. I needn't argue about that; I'm right and I will be proved right. We're more popular than Jesus now; I don't know which will go first – rock 'n' roll or Christianity. Jesus was all right but his disciples were thick and ordinary. It's them twisting it that ruins it for me." He is reading extensively about religion.

He shops in lightning swoops on Asprey's these days and there is some fine wine in his cellar, but he is still quite unselfconscious. He is far too lazy to keep up appearances, even if he had worked out what the appearances should be – which he has not.

He is now twenty-five. he lives in a large, heavily panelled, heavily carpeted mock Tudor house set on a hill with his wife Cynthia and his son Julian. There is a cat called after his aunt

Mimi and a purple dining room. Julian is three; he may be sent to the Lycee in London. "Seems the only place for him in his position," said his father, surveying him dispassionately. "I feel sorry for him, though. I couldn't stand ugly people even when I was five. Lots of the ugly ones are foreign, aren't they?"

We did a speedy tour of the house, Julian panting along behind clutching a large porcelain Siamese cat. John swept past the objects in which he had lost interest; "That's Sidney" (a suit of armour); "That's a hobby I had for a week" (a room full of model racing cars); "Cyn won't let me get rid of that" (a fruit machine). In the sitting room are eight little green boxes with winking red lights; he bought them as Christmas presents but never got round to giving them away. They wink for a year; one imagines him sitting there till next Christmas surrounded by the little winking boxes.

He paused over objects he still fancies: a huge altar crucifix of a Roman Catholic nature with IHS on it; a pair of crutches, a present from George; an enormous Bible he bought in Chester; his gorilla suit.

"I thought I might need a gorilla suit," he said; he seemed sad about it. "I've only worn it twice. I thought I might pop it on in the summer and drive round in the Ferrari. We were all going to get them and drive round in them but I was the only one who did. I've been thinking about it and if I didn't wear the head it would make an amazing fur coat – with legs, you see. I would like a fur coat but I've never run into any."

One feels that his possessions – to which he adds daily – have got the upper hand; all the tape recorders, the five television sets, the cars, the telephones of which he knows not a single number. The moment he approaches a switch it fuses; six of the winking boxes, guaranteed to last till next Christmas, have gone funny already. His cars – the Rolls, the Mini-Cooper (black wheels, black windows), the Ferrari (being painted black) – puzzle him. Then there's the swimming pool, the trees sloping away beneath it. "Nothing like what I ordered," he said resignedly. He wanted the bottom to be a mirror.

"It's an amazing household," he said. "None of my gadgets really work except the gorilla suit – that's the only suit that fits me."

He is very keen on books, will always ask what is good to read.

He buys quantities of books and these are kept tidily in a special room. He has Swift, Tennyson, Huxley, Orwell, costly leather-bound editions of Tolstoy, Oscar Wilde. Then there's *Little Women*, all the William books from his childhood; and some unexpected volumes such as *Forty-One Years In India*, by Field Marshal Lord Roberts, and *Curiosities of Natural History*, by Francis T. Buckland.

This last with its chapter headings – Ear-less Cats, Wooden-Legged People, The Immortal Harvey's Mother – is right up his street.

He approaches reading with a lively interest untempered by too much formal education. "I've read millions of books," he said, "that's why I seem to know things." He is obsessed by Celts. "I have decided that I am a Celt," he said. "I am on Boadicea's side – all those bloody, blue-eyed blonds chopping people up. I have an awful feeling wishing I was there – not there with scabs and sores but there through *reading* about it. The books don't give you more than a paragraph about how they *lived*; I have to imagine that."

He can sleep almost indefinitely, is probably the laziest person in England. "*Physically* lazy," he said. "I don't mind writing or reading or watching or speaking, but sex is the only physical thing I can be bothered with any more."

Occasionally he is driven to London in the Rolls by an ex-Welsh guardsman called Anthony; Anthony has a moustache that intrigues him.

The day I visited him he had been invited to lunch in London, about which he was rather excited. "Do you know how long lunch lasts?" he asked. "I've never been to lunch before. I went to a Lyons the other day and had egg and chips and a cup of tea. The waiters kept looking and saying: 'No, it *isn't* him, it *can't be* him'."

He settled himself into the car and demonstrated the television, the folding bed, the refrigerator, the writing desk, the telephone. He has spent many fruitless hours on that telephone. "I only once got through to a person," he said, "and they were out."

Anthony had spent the weekend in Wales. John asked if they'd kept a welcome for him in the hillside and Anthony said they had. They discussed the possibility of an extension for the telephone. We had to call at the doctor's because John had a bit of sea urchin in his toe. "Don't want to be like Dorothy Dandridge," he said, "dying of a splinter fifty years later." He added reassuringly that he had washed the foot in question.

We bowled in a costly fashion through the countryside. "Famous and loaded" is how he describes himself now. "They keep telling me I'm all right for money but then I think I may have spent it all by the time I'm forty so I keep going. That's why I started selling my cars; then I changed my mind and got them all back and a new one, too.

"I want the money just to *be rich*. The only other way of getting it is to be born rich. If you have money, that's power without having to be powerful. I often think that it's all a big conspiracy, that the winners are the Government and people like us who've got the money. That joke about keeping the workers ignorant is still true; that's what they said about the Tories and the land-owners and that; then Labour were meant to educate the workers but they don't seem to be doing that any more."

He has a morbid horror of stupid people: "Famous and loaded as I am I still have to meet soft people. It often comes into my mind that I'm not really rich. There are *really* rich people but I don't know where they are."

He finds being famous quite easy, confirming one's suspicion that the Beatles had been leading up to this all their lives. "Everybody thinks they *would* have been famous if only they'd had the Latin and that. So when it happens it comes naturally.

"You remember your old grannie saying soft things like: 'You'll make it with that voice.'" Not, he added, that he had any old grannies.

He got to the doctor two and three quarter hours early and to lunch on time but in the wrong place. He bought a giant compendium of games from Asprey's but having opened it he could not, of course, shut it again. He wondered what else he should buy. He went to Brian Epstein's office. "Any presents?" he asked eagerly; he observed that there was nothing like getting things free. He tried on the attractive Miss Hanson's spectacles.

The rumour came through that a Beatle had been sighted walking down Oxford Street. He brightened. "One of the others must be out," he said, as though speaking of an escaped bear. "We only let them out one at a time," said the attractive Miss Hanson firmly.

He said that to live and have a laugh were the things to do; but was that enough for the restless spirit?

"Weybridge," he said, "won't do at all. I'm just stopping at it, like a bus stop. Bankers and stockbrokers live there; they can add figures and Weybridge is what they live in and they think it's the end, they really do. I think of it every day – me in my Hansel and Gretel house. I'll take my time; I'll get my *real* house when I know what I want.

"You see there's something else I'm going to do, something I must do – only I don't know what it is. That's why I go found painting and taping and drawing and writing and that, because it may be one of them.

"All I know is, this isn't it for me."

Anthony got him and the compendium into the car and drove him home with the television flickering in the soothing darkness while the Londoners outside rushed home from work.

ENGLAND WIN THE WORLD CUP

Daily Telegraph, 31 July 1966

They had fetched him, three and a half years ago, from quiet Ipswich, a taciturn, shy, deeply reserved man, and calmly leading with his chin, as they say, he had promised to win them the World Cup. There were those who laughed, and some were still laughing when the tournament began. Yet by the finish, with a relentless inflexibility of will, with sterling courage, with efficiency that brought unbounded admiration, his team, England's team, helped to keep that promise.

They did it, Alf Ramsey and England, after just about the worst psychological reverse possible on an unforgettable afternoon. With victory dashed from their grasp, cruelly only seconds from the final whistle, they came again in extra time, driving weary limbs across the patterned turf beyond the point of exhaustion, and crowned the ultimate achievement with a memorable goal with the last kick of all by Hurst, making him the first player to score a hat-trick in the World Cup Final.

We had all often talked of the thoroughness of preparation of the deposed champions, Brazil, but England's glory this day, to be engraved on that glinting, golden trophy, was the result of the most patient, logical, painstaking, almost scientific assault on the trophy there had perhaps ever been – and primarily the work and imagination of one man.

For those close to him through the past three exciting seasons, Ramsey's management had been something for unending admiration, and the unison cry of the 93,000 crowd, "Ram-sey, Ram-sey" as his side mounted the steps to collect Jules Rimet's statuette from the Queen was the final rewarding vindication for one who had unwaveringly pursued his own, often lonely, convictions.

As the crowd stood in ovation, Greaves looked on wistfully. Injury had cost him his place, and though he recovered, Ramsey had resisted the almost overpowering temptation to change a winning side. This, too, was vindication, his whole aim since 1963 having been to prepare not a team but a squad, so that at any moment he might replace an out of form or injured man without noticeable deterioration in the side. When the time came, the luckless Greaves's omission caused hardly a stir of pessimism.

At the start of the tournament, I had written that if England were to win, it would be with the resolution, physical fitness and cohesion of West Germany in 1954, rather than with the flair of Brazil in the two succeeding competitions. And so it proved, with the added coincidence that it was the Germans themselves, as usual bristling with all these same characteristics in profusion, who were the unlucky and brave victims of England's methodical rather than brilliant football. Before the semi-finals I said that the deciding factor of this World Cup, when all others had cancelled out in the modern proficiency of defensive systems, would be character, and now the character of every England player burned with a flame that warmed all those who saw it. The slightest weakening, mentally or physically, in any position, could have lost this match a hundred times over, but the way in which Ball, undoubtedly the man of the afternoon, Wilson, Stiles, Peters, Bobby Charlton and above all Moore, impelled themselves on, was something one would remember long after the tumult of excitement and the profusion of incidents had faded. Justifiably, Moore was voted the outstanding player of the competition; his sudden, surging return to form on tour beforehand had helped cement the castle at the critical hour.

All assessments of great events should be measured by absolute standards along with the quality of contemporaries, and therefore one had to say that England were not a great team, probably not even at that moment the best team in the world, depending on what you mean by best.

What matters is that they were the best there at Wembley in July, on that sunny, showery afternoon, best when the chips were down in open combat, and that, after all, is what counts – the result, rather than its manner, goes into the record books. Besides, Ramsey had not set about producing the most entertaining but the most successful team. Could he afford to be the one romantic in a world of hard-headed, win-at-all-costs efficiency? Could he favour conventional wingers who promised much and produced little? A manager is ultimately only as good as the players at his disposal; handicapped by a shortage of world class, instinctive players of the calibre of the South Americans, Italians, Hungarians, or his own Bobby Charlton, and by an over-abundance of average competence, Ramsey had slowly eliminated all those who lacked what he needed for cohesion. What greater demonstration of unity of purpose could there have been than the insistence of the winners, for all the emotion of the moment, that the eleven reserves join them on the lap of honour, and after share equally the £22,000 bonus.

Some complained England were helped by playing all their matches at Wembley, yet certainly in that mood and form they could and would have won anywhere in the country. Besides, under Ramsey, England had had more success abroad than ever before. If nothing else, this World Cup, penetrating almost every home in the land, should have persuaded the doubters, the detractors and the cynics that this is the greatest spectator sport there is, and the Final was a fitting climax.

At the start England asserted themselves – Bobby Charlton exerting a telling influence in midfield, even though closely watched by Beckenbauer sent Peters streaming through with fine anticipation, into spaces behind the German midfield trio. Suddenly, however, in the thirteenth minute, England found themselves a goal down for the first time in the competition. It was not an error under pressure, it was unforced. As a centre from the left came over, Wilson stood alone, eyes riveted on the dropping ball. He made to head it down to Moore, but his judgement betrayed him, sending it instead straight to Haller, who whipped in a low skidding shot past an unsighted, helpless Banks.

The strapping Germans and their flag-waving supporters bounced with joy, but within six minutes England were level. Midway inside the German half, on the left, Overath tripped Moore, and even before the referee had finished wagging his finger at Overath, Moore had spotted a gaping hole in the German rearguard. He placed the ball and took the kick almost in one move, a dipping floater that carried thirty-five yards and was met by Hurst, streaking in from the right, with

another graceful, expertly-timed header like that which beat
Argentina.

The pattern swung once more in the ten minutes before half-
time. The three German strikers, nosing in and out like carni-
vorous fish, began to create havoc that was only averted after
extreme anxiety. In between, Hunt, from a glorious pass by
Bobby Charlton, hammered a thundering shot, a difficult one
running away to his left, straight at Tilkowski. On the stroke of
half-time, it was England who were desperately lucky, when a
fast dipper by Seeler was tipped over by Banks, arched in mid-air
like a stalling buzzard.

Little happened for nearly twenty-five minutes after halftime,
the lull punctuated only by "Oh, oh, what a referee," as Mr
Dienst went fussily about his business. Then, with twenty
minutes to go, England's rhythm began to build up again, Bobby
Charlton, Ball and Peters stretching the Germans to the extreme
of their physical endurance with passes that again and again
almost saw Hurst and Hunt clear. With eleven minutes to go, Ball
won a corner, put it across, the ball was headed out, and hit back
first-time by Hurst. It struck a defender, fell free, and Peters
swooped to lash it home.

England, sensing victory, played it slow, slow, but Hunt
wasted a priceless chance when it was three red England shirts
to one white German on the edge of the penalty area, by mis-
judging his pass. With a minute left, all was disaster as Jack
Charlton was most harshly penalized for "climbing" over the top
of Held. Emmerich blasted the free kick. A German in the
penalty area unquestionably pulled the ball down with his hand,
and after a tremendous scramble, Weber squeezed the ball home
to level the match.

You could see England's spirits sink as the teams changed over
for extra time but, quickly calmed and reassured by the emotion-
less Ramsey, they rallied themselves instantly. Ball, still unbelievably dynamic, going like the wind right to the finish, had a
shot tipped over, Bobby Charlton hit a post and with twelve
minutes gone, England were once more in front as Stiles slipped
the ball up the wing to Ball, whose cross was thumped hard by
Hurst. The ball hit the bar, bounced down and came out, and
after consultation with the Russian linesman, Bakhramov, a goal
was given. I had my doubts, doubled after later seeing television,

but that surely had to be the winner, for now, socks rolled down, both teams were physically in distress. Again England sought economy with gentle passes, keeping precious possession, wearing the Germans down yet further, Poor Wilson hardly knew where he was after a blow on the head. Slowly the minutes ticked away, agonisingly, until with the referee looking at his watch, Hurst staggered on alone from yet one more of Moore's perceptive passes, to hit the ball into the roof of the net with what, little strength he had left, and make England's victory, like their football, solid and respectable. Whether Ramscy, as silent in victory as defeat, could achieve the impossible and adapt these same characteristics to win in Mexico in 1970 was a chapter that would unfold over the next four years.

ENGLAND: – Banks (*Leicester*); Cohen (*Fulham*), Charlton J. (*Leeds*), Moore (*W. Ham*), Wilson (*Everton*); Stiles (*Manchester United*), Charlton R. (*Manchester United*), Peters (*W. Ham*); Ball (*Blackpool*), Hunt (*Liverpool*), Hurst (*W. Ham*).

WEST GERMANY: – Tilkowski; Hoettges, Schulz, Weber, Schnellinger; Beckenbauer, Haller, Overath; Seeler, Held, Emmerich.

Referee: – G. Dienst (Switzerland).

Linesmen: – K. Galba (Czechoslovakia), T. Bakhramov (USSR).

WILLIAM REES-MOGG

WHO BREAKS A
BUTTERFLY ON A WHEEL?

The Times, 1 July 1967

When the Rolling Stones' Mick Jagger was sentenced to jail for minor drug offences in the Summer of '67 there was public unease in Britain over the severity of the punishmen. Even such an Establishment organ as *The Times* was moved to join the protest with a leader by editor Rees-Mogg which, with a literary flourish, borrowed a line from Alexander Pope for its header.

A month after Rees-Mogg's famed leader Jagger's conviction was quashed by the court of appeal.

Rees-Mogg retired as editor of *The Times* in 1981.

Mr Jagger has been sentenced to imprisonment for three months. He is appealing against conviction and sentence, and has been granted bail until the hearing of the appeal later in the year. In the meantime, the sentence of imprisonment is bound to be widely discussed by the public. And the circumstances are sufficiently unusual to warrant such discussion in the public interest.

Mr Jagger was charged with being in possession of four tablets containing amphetamine sulphate and methyl amphetamine hydrochloride; these tablets had been bought, perfectly legally, in Italy, and brought back to this country. They are not a highly dangerous drug, or in proper dosage a dangerous drug at all. They are of the benzedrine type and the Italian manufacturers recommend them both as a stimulant and as a remedy for travel sickness.

In Britain it is an offence to possess these drugs without a doctor's prescription. Mr Jagger's doctor says that he knew and had authorized their use, but he did not give a prescription for them as indeed they had already been purchased. His evidence was not challenged. This was therefore an offence of a technical character, which before this case drew the point to public attention any honest man might have been liable to commit. If, after his visit to the Pope, the Archbishop of Canterbury had bought proprietary airsickness pills on Rome airport, and imported the unused tablets into Britain on his return, he would have risked committing precisely the same offence. No one who has ever travelled and bought proprietary drugs abroad can be sure that he has not broken the law.

Judge Block directed the jury that the approval of a doctor was not a defence in law to the charge of possessing drugs without a prescription, and the jury convicted. Mr Jagger was not charged with complicity in any other drug offence that occurred in the same house. They were separate cases, and no evidence was produced to suggest that he knew that Mr Fraser had heroin tablets or that the vanishing Mr Sneidermann had cannabis resin. It is indeed no offence to be in the same building or the same company as people possessing or even using drugs, nor could it reasonably be made an offence. The drugs which Mr Jagger had in his possession must therefore be treated on their own, as a separate issue from the other drugs that other people may have had in their possession at the same time. It may be difficult for lay opinion to make this distinction clearly, but obviously justice cannot be done if one man is to be punished for a purely contingent association with someone else's offence.

We have, therefore, a conviction against Mr Jagger purely on the ground that he possessed four Italian pep pills, quite legally bought but not legally imported without a prescription. Four is not a large number. This is not the quantity which a pusher of drugs would have on him, nor even the quantity one would expect in an addict. In any case Mr Jagger's career is obviously one that does involve great personal strain and exhaustion: his doctor says that he approved the occasional use of these drugs, and it seems likely that similar drugs would have been prescribed if there was a need for them. Millions of similar drugs are prescribed in Britain every year, and for a variety of conditions.

One has to ask, therefore, how it is that this technical offence,

divorced as it must be from other people's offences, was thought
to deserve the penalty of imprisonment. In the courts at large it is
most uncommon for imprisonment to be imposed on first offen-
ders where the drugs are not major drugs of addiction and there is
no question of drug traffic. The normal penalty is probation, and
the purpose of probation is to encourage the offender to develop
his career and to avoid the drug risks in the future. It is surprising
therefore that Judge Block should have decided to sentence Mr
Jagger to imprisonment, and particularly surprising as Mr Jagger's is about as mild a drug case as can ever have been brought
before the Courts.

It would be wrong to speculate on the Judge's reasons, which
we do not know. It is, however, possible to consider the public
reaction. There are many people who take a primitive view of the
matter, what one might call a pre-legal view of the matter. They
consider that Mr Jagger has "got what was coming to him". They
resent the anarchic quality of the Rolling Stones' performances,
dislike their songs, dislike their influence on teenagers and
broadly suspect them of decadence, a word used by Miss Monica
Furlong in the *Daily Mail*.

As a sociological concern this may be reasonable enough, and
at an emotional level it is very understandable, but it has nothing
at all to do with the case. One has to ask a different question: has
Mr Jagger received the same treatment as he would have received
if he had not been a famous figure, with all the criticism and
resentment his celebrity has aroused? If a promising under-
graduate had come back from a summer visit to Italy with four
pep pills in his pocket would it have been thought right to ruin his
career by sending him to prison for three months? Would it also
have been thought necessary to display him handcuffed to the
public?

There are cases in which a single figure becomes the focus for
public concern about some aspect of public morality. The Stephen Ward case, with its dubious evidence and questionable
verdict, was one of them, and that verdict killed Stephen Ward.
There are elements of the same emotions in the reactions to this
case. If we are going to make any case a symbol of the conflict
between the sound traditional values of Britain and the new
hedonism, then we must be sure that the sound traditional values
include those of tolerance and equity. It should be the particular

quality of British justice to ensure that Mr Jagger is treated exactly the same as anyone else, no better and no worse. There must remain a suspicion in this case that Mr Jagger received a more severe sentence than would have been thought proper for any purely anonymous young man.

AIRMOBILITY, DIG IT

Dispatches, 1977

Herr covered the war in Vietnam for *Esquire* and *Rolling Stone* in 1967 and 1968. He later wrote the screenplay for *Apocalypse Now*, which leaned heavily on the 'Nam reports he had collected together as *Dispatches*.

"Hey what're you guys, with the USO? Aw, we thought you was with the USO 'cause your hair's so long." Page took the kid's picture, I got the words down and Flynn laughed and told him we were the Rolling Stones. The three of us travelled around together for about a month that summer. At one LZ the brigade chopper came in with a real foxtail hanging off the aerial, when the commander walked by us he almost took an infarction.

"Don't you men salute officers?"

"We're not men," Page said. "We're correspondents."

When the commander heard that, he wanted to throw a spontaneous operation for us, crank up his whole brigade and get some people killed. We had to get out on the next chopper to keep him from going ahead with it, amazing what some of them would do for a little ink. Page liked to augment his field gear with freak paraphernalia, scarves and beads, plus he was English, guys would stare at him like he'd just come down off a wall on Mars. Sean Flynn could look more incredibly beautiful than even his father, Errol, had thirty years before as Captain Blood, but sometimes he looked more like Artaud coming out of some heavy heart-of-darkness trip, overloaded on the information, the input! The input! He'd give off a bad sweat and sit for hours, combing his moustache through with the saw blade of his Swiss Army knife. We packed grass and tape: "Have You Seen Your Mother Baby Standing in the Shadows", "Best of the Animals",

"Strange Days", "Purple Haze", "Archie Bell and the Drells", "C'mon now everybody, do the Tighten Up . . ." Once in a while we'd catch a chopper straight into one of the lower hells, but it was a quiet time in the war, mostly it was LZ's and camps, grunts hanging around, faces, stories.

"Best way's to just keep moving," one of them told us. "Just keep moving, stay in motion, you know what I'm saying?"

We knew. He was a moving-target-survivor subscriber, a true child of the war, because except for the rare times when you were pinned or stranded the system was geared to keep you mobile, if that was what you thought you wanted. As a technique for staying alive it seemed to make as much sense as anything, given naturally that you were there to begin with and wanted to see it close; it started out sound and straight but it formed a cone as it progressed, because the more you moved the more you saw, the more you saw the more besides death and mutilation you risked, and the more you risked of that the more you would have to let go of one day as a "survivor". Some of us moved around the war like crazy people until we couldn't see which way the run was even taking us any more, only the war all over its surface with occasional, unexpected penetration. As long as we could have choppers like taxis it took real exhaustion or depression near shock or a dozen pipes of opium to keep us even apparently quiet, we'd still be running around inside our skins like something was after us, ha ha, La Vida Loca.

In the months after I got back the hundreds of helicopters I'd flown in began to draw together until they'd formed a collective meta-chopper, and in my mind it was the sexiest thing going; saver-destroyer, provider-waster, right hand-left hand, nimble, fluent, canny and human; hot steel, grease, jungle-saturated canvas webbing, sweat cooling and warming up again, cassette rock and roll in one ear and door-gun fire in the other, fuel, heat, vitality and death, death itself, hardly an intruder. Men on the crews would say that once you'd carried a dead person he would always be there, riding with you. Like all combat people they were incredibly superstitious and invariably self-dramatic, but it was (I knew) unbearably true and close exposure to the dead sensitized you to the force of their presence and made for long reverberations; long. Some people were so delicate that one look was enough to wipe them away, but even bone-dumb grunts seemed to feel that something weird and extra was happening to them.

Helicopters and people jumping out of helicopters, people so in love they'd run to get on even when there wasn't any pressure. Choppers rising straight out of small cleared jungle spaces, wobbling down on to city rooftops, cartons of rations and ammunition thrown off, dead and wounded loaded on. Sometimes they were so plentiful and loose that you could touch down at five or six places in a day, look around, hear the talk, catch the next one out. There were installations as big as cities with 30,000 citizens, once we dropped in to feed supply to one man. God knows what kind of Lord Jim phoenix numbers he was doing in there, all he said to me was, "You didn't see a thing, right Chief? You weren't even here." There were posh fat airconditioned camps like comfortable middle-class scenes with the violence tacit, "far away"; camps named for commanders' wives, LZ Thelma, LZ Betty Lou; number-named hilltops in trouble where I didn't want to stay; trail, paddy, swamp, deep hairy bush, scrub, swale, village, even city, where the ground couldn't drink up what the action spilled, it made you careful where you walked.

Sometimes the chopper you were riding in would top a hill and all the ground in front of you as far as the next hill would be charred and pitted and still smoking, and something between your chest and your stomach would turn over. Frail grey smoke where they'd burned off the rice fields around a free-strike zone, brilliant white smoke from phosphorus ("Willy Peter/Make you a buh liever"), deep black smoke from 'palm, they said that if you stood at the base of a column of napalm smoke it would suck the air right out of your lungs. Once we fanned over a little ville that had just been airstruck and the words of a song by Wingy Manone that I'd heard when I was a few years old snapped into my head, "Stop the War, These Cats Is Killing Themselves". Then we dropped, hovered, settled down into purple LZ smoke, dozens of children broke from their hootches to run in towards the focus of our landing, the pilot laughing and saying, "Vietnam, man. Bomb 'em and feed 'em, bomb 'em and feed 'em."

Flying over jungle was almost pure pleasure, doing it on foot was nearly all pain. I never belonged in there. Maybe it really was what its people had always called it, Beyond; at the very least it was serious, I gave up things to it I probably never got back.

("Aw, jungle's okay. If you know her you can live in her real good, if you don't she'll take you down in an hour. Under.") Once in some thick jungle corner with some grunts standing around, a correspondent said, "Gee, you must really see some beautiful sunsets in here," and they almost pissed themselves laughing. But you could fly up and into hot tropic sunsets that would change the way you thought about light forever. You could also fly out of places that were so grim they turned to black and white in your head five minutes after you'd gone.

That could be the coldest one in the world, standing at the edge of a clearing watching the chopper you'd just come in on taking off again, leaving you there to think about what it was going to be for you now: if this was a bad place, the wrong place, maybe even the last place, and whether you'd made a terrible mistake this time.

There was a camp at Soc Trang where a man at the LZ said, "If you come looking for a story this is your lucky day, we got Condition Red here," and before the sound of the chopper had faded out, I knew I had it too.

"That's affirmative," the camp commander said, "we are *definitely* expecting rain. Glad to see you." He was a young captain, he was laughing and taping a bunch of sixteen clips together bottom to bottom for faster reloading, "grease". Everyone there was busy at it, cracking crates, squirrelling away grenades, checking mortar pieces, piling rounds, clicking banana clips into automatic weapons that I'd never even seen before. They were wired into their listening posts out around the camp, into each other, into themselves, and when it got dark it got worse. The moon came up nasty and full, a fat moist piece of decadent fruit. It was soft and saffron-misted when you looked up at it, but its light over the sandbags and into the jungle was harsh and bright. We were all rubbing Army-issue nightfighter cosmetic under our eyes to cut the glare and the terrible things it made you see. (Around midnight, just for something to do, I crossed to the other perimeter and looked at the road running engineer-straight towards Route 4 like a yellow frozen ribbon out of sight and I saw it move, the whole road.) There were a few sharp arguments about who the light really favoured, attackers or defenders, men were sitting around with Cinemascope eyes and jaws stuck out like they could shoot bullets, moving and antsing and shifting around inside their fatigues. "No sense us getting too relaxed, Charlie don't relax, just when you get good and comfortable is when he comes over and takes a giant shit on you." That was the level until morning, I smoked a pack an hour all night long, and nothing happened. Ten minutes after daybreak I was down at the LZ asking about choppers.

A few days later Sean Flynn and I went up to a big firebase in the American TAOR that took it all the way over to another extreme, National Guard weekend. The colonel in command was so drunk that day that he could barely get his words out, and when he did, it was to say things like, "We aim to make good and goddammit sure that if *those guys* try *anything cute* they won't catch us with our pants down." The main mission there was to fire H&I, but one man told us that their record was the worst in the whole Corps, probably the whole country, they'd harassed and interdicted a lot of sleeping civilians and Korean Marines, even a couple of Americal patrols, but hardly any Viet Cong. (The colonel kept calling it "artillerary". The first time he said it Flynn and I looked away from each other, the second time we blew beer through our noses, but the colonel fell in laughing right away and more than covered us.) No sandbags, exposed shells, dirty pieces, guys going around giving us that look, "We're cool, how come you're not?" At the strip Sean was talking to the operator about it and the man got angry. "Oh *yeah*? Well fuck *you*, how tight do you think you want it? There ain't been any veecees around here in three months."

"So far so good," Sean said. "Hear anything on that chopper yet?"

But sometimes everything stopped, nothing flew, you couldn't even find out why. I got stuck for a chopper once in some lost patrol outpost in the Delta where the sergeant chain-ate candy bars and played country-and-western tapes twenty hours a day until I heard it in my sleep, some sleep, "Up on Wolverton Mountain" and "Lonesome as the bats and the bears in Miller's Cave" and "I fell into a burning ring of fire", surrounded by strungout rednecks who weren't getting much sleep either because they couldn't trust one of their 400 mercenary troopers or their own hand-picked perimeter guards or anybody else except maybe Baby Ruth and Johnny Cash, they'd been waiting for it so long now they were afraid they wouldn't know it when they finally got it, *and it burns burns* . . . Finally on the fourth day a helicopter came in to deliver meat and movies to the camp and I went out on it, so happy to get back to Saigon that I didn't crash for two days.

Airmobility, dig it, you weren't going anywhere. It made you feel safe, it made you feel Omni, but it was only a stunt, technology. Mobility was just mobility, it saved lives or took them all the time (saved mine I don't know how many times, maybe dozens, maybe none), what you really needed was a flexibility far greater than anything the technology could provide, some generous, spontaneous gift for accepting surprises, and I didn't have it. I got to hate surprises, control freak at the crossroads, if you were one of those people who always thought they had to know what was coming next, the war could cream you. It was the same with your ongoing attempts at getting used to the jungle or the blow-you-out climate or the saturating strangeness of the place which didn't lessen with exposure so often as it fattened and darkened in accumulating alienation. It was great if you could adapt, you had to try, but it wasn't the same as making a discipline, going into your own reserves and developing a real war metabolism, slow yourself down when your heart tried to punch its way through your chest, get swift when everything went to stop and all you could feel of your whole life was the entropy whipping through it. Unlovable terms.

The ground was always in play, always being swept. Under the ground was his, above it was ours. We had the air, we could get up in it but not disappear in *to* it, we could run but we couldn't hide, and he could do each so well that sometimes it looked like he was doing them both at once, while our finder just went limp. All the same, one place or another it was always going on, rock around the clock, we had the days and he had the nights. You could be in the most protected space in Vietnam and still know that your safety was provisional, that early death, blindness, loss of legs, arms or balls, major and lasting disfigurement – the whole rotten deal – could come in on the freakyfluky as easily as in the so-called expected ways, you heard so many of those stories it was a wonder anyone was left alive to die in firefights and mortar-rocket attacks. After a few weeks, when the nickel had jarred loose and dropped and I saw that everyone around me was carrying a gun, I also saw that any one of them could go off at any time, putting you where it wouldn't matter whether it had been an accident or not. The roads were mined, the trails booby-trapped, satchel charges and grenades blew up jeeps and movie theatres, the VC got work inside all the camps as shoeshine boys and laundresses and honey-dippers, they'd starch your fatigues and burn your shit and then go home and mortar your area. Saigon and Cholon and Danang held such hostile vibes that you felt you were being dry-sniped every time someone looked at you, and choppers fell out of the sky like fat poisoned birds a hundred times a day. After a while I couldn't get on one without thinking that I must be out of my fucking mind.

Fear and motion, fear and standstill, no preferred cut there, no way even to be clear about which was really worse, the wait or the delivery. Combat spared far more men than it wasted, but everyone suffered the time between contact, especially when they were going out every day looking for it; bad going on foot, terrible in trucks and APCs, awful in helicopters, the worst, travelling so fast towards something so frightening. I can remember times when I went half dead with my fear of the motion, the speed and direction already fixed and pointed one way. It was painful enough just flying "safe" hops between firebases and LZ's; if you were ever on a helicopter that had been hit by ground fire your deep, perpetual chopper anxiety was guaranteed. At least actual contact when it was happening would draw long raggedy strands of energy out of you, it was juicy, fast and refining, and travelling towards it was hollow, dry, cold and steady, it never let you alone. All you could do was look around at the other people on board and see if they were as scared and numbed out as you were. If it looked like they weren't you thought they were insane, if it looked like they were it made you feel a lot worse.

RICHARD GOTT

US INTELLIGENCE AGENT IN AT CHE GUEVARA'S DEATH

Guardian, 11 October 1967

After playing a leading role in the Cuban Revolution, the Argentine-born Guevara departed Cuba in 1965 to forment guerrilla warfare in Bolivia. Within months he was captured and executed by Bolivian troops and the CIA.

Gott, a self-proclaimed Marxist, was sacked by the *Guardian* in 1994 after allegations he had been taking the KGB's rouble.

The body of Che Guevara was flown into this small hill town in south-eastern Bolivia at five o'clock last night.

From the moment the helicopter landed bearing the small figure strapped in a stretcher to the landing rails, the succeeding operation was to a large extent left in the hands of a man in battledress, who, all the correspondents here agree, was unquestionably a representative of one of the United States intelligence agencies.

He was probably a Cuban exile and so Che Guevara, who in life had declared war almost singlehanded on the United States, found himself in death face to face with his major enemy.

The helicopter purposely landed far from where a crowd had gathered and the body of the dead guerrilla leader was hastily transferred to a van. We commandeered a jeep to follow it and the driver managed to get through the gates of the hospital grounds where the body was taken to a small colour-washed hut that served as a mortuary.

The doors of the van burst open and the American agent leapt out, emitting a war cry of "Let's get the hell out of here." One of the correspondents asked him where he came from. "Nowhere," was the surly response.

The body, dressed in olive green fatigues with a zippered jacket, was carried into the hut. It was undoubtedly that of Che Guevara. Ever since I first reported in January that Che was probably in Bolivia I have not shared the general scepticism about his whereabouts.

I am probably one of the few people here who have seen him alive. I saw him in Cuba at an Embassy reception in 1963 and there is no doubt in my mind that this body was that of Che. It had a black wispy beard, long matted hair, and the shadow of a scar on the right temple, probably the result of an accident in July when he was grazed by a rifle shot.

On his feet he wore moccasins as though he had been shot down while running fleet-footed through the jungle. He had two wounds in the lower part of the neck and possibly one in the stomach. It is believed that he was captured when seriously wounded, but died before a helicopter could arrive to take him out of the battle zone.

My only doubts about the identity arose because Che was much thinner and smaller than I had recalled, but it is hardly surprising that after months in the jungle he had lost his former heavy appearance.

As soon as the body reached the mortuary the doctors began to pump preservative into it, and the American agent made desperate efforts to keep off the crowds. He was a very nervous man and looked furious whenever cameras were pointed in his direction. He knew that I knew who he was and he also knew that I knew that he should not be there, for this is a war in which the Americans are not supposed to be taking part. Yet here was this man, who has been with the troops in Vallegrande, talking to the senior officers on familiar terms.

One can hardly say that this was the factor with which Che failed to reckon, for it was his very purpose to provoke United States intervention in Latin America as a way of bringing help and succour to the embattled Vietnamese. But he certainly did fail to estimate correctly the strength and pervasiveness of the US intelligence agencies in this continent, and this more than anything else has been the cause of his downfall and that of the Bolivian guerrillas.

And so he is dead. As they pumped preservative into his half-naked, dirty body and as the crowd shouted to be allowed to see, it was difficult to recall that this man had once been one of the great figures of Latin America.

It was not just that he was a great guerrilla leader, he had been a friend of Presidents as well as revolutionaries. His voice had been heard and appreciated in inter-American councils as well as in the jungle. He was a doctor, an amateur economist, once Minister of Industries in revolutionary Cuba, and Fidel Castro's right-hand man. He may well go down in history as the greatest continental figure since Bolivar. Legends will be created around his name.

He was a Marxist but impatient of the doctrinal struggles between the Russians and the Chinese. He was perhaps the last person who tried to find a middle way between the two and attempted to unite radical forces everywhere in a concerted campaign against the US. He is now dead, but it is difficult to feel that his ideas will die with him.

A MULE CORTEGE FOR
THE APOSTLE OF THE POOR

Guardian, 9 April 1968

The Civil Rights leader Dr Martin Luther King was assassinated in
Memphis, Tennessee, on 4 April 1968.

Once before, the ninth of April was memorial day throughout the
South. One hundred and three years ago today Robert E. Lee
tendered his sword to General Grant and was granted in return
the release of "your men and their mules to assist in the spring
ploughing". Today, on a flaming spring day, with the magnolias
blooming and the white dogwood and the red sprinkling the land,
they brought a farm wagon and its mules to stand outside the
church on the street where Martin Luther King was born and,
after the funeral service to carry his body four miles to his college
and lay it to rest. The "mule train" is the oldest and still most
dependable form of transport of the rural poor in the Southland.
And somebody had the graceful idea that a mule train would be
the aptest cortege for the man who was the apostle of the poor.

From the warm dawn into the blazing noon, the black bodies
wearing more suits and ties than they would put on for a
coronation, moved through the Negro sections of the town
towards the street of comfortable, two-storey frame houses where
the coloured business and professional men live and where,
across from Cox's Funeral Home, the Rev. Martin Luther King
lived and preached, in the Ebenezer Baptist Church, a red-
bricked nondescript tabernacle.

Thousands of college students had volunteered to act as
marshals to hold the crowds; but though there was a tremendous

push and jostle of people before the service began, there were enough police on hand to stem the crush and hand the visiting celebrities through like very pregnant women.

The bell tolled out the tune of "We Shall Overcome" and big cars slid up to the entrance, and out of them climbed the Attorney General, Ramsey Clark, and Mrs. John E. Kennedy, and Richard Nixon and Senator Eugene McCarthy, Governor and Mrs. Romney of Michigan, and Governor Rockefeller and John Lindsay of New York, the new Roman Catholic Archbishop Terence Cooke, Sidney Poitier, the Metropolitan Opera's Leontryne Price, Eartha Kitt, Sammy Davis Jr., Bobby and Ethel Kennedy and brother Edward, and Dr Ralph Bunche, U. Thant's man and Dr King's friend.

Over the breaking waves of street noise and the tolling bell, the strong baritone of the Rev. Ralph Abernathy, Dr King's heir, chanted from time to time: "We will please be orderly now . . . let us have dignity . . . please . . . there are no more seats in the church." Somebody lifted a squalling baby and passed it out over the tossing heads to safety.

It is a small church, and shortly after 10.30 the last cars and the last mourners were slotted in their places. First, Mrs King and her four children and the dead man's brother, and Harry Belafonte. Then at last an alert squad of aides and Secret Service men surrounding Vice-President Humphrey. The conspicuous absentee was Lester Maddox, the Governor of Georgia, a segregationist whose presence could upset a coloured funeral any place North or South.

The inside of the church impressively belies its outside. It is a plesantly modern room with a single oriel window, above a white cross over the choir and the pulpit. The flanking walls have two simple Gothic windows decorated alike with a single shield bearing a cross and surmounted with the crown of Christ. Tiny spotlights embedded in the ceiling threw little pools of light on the famous and the obscure equally. The warm shadows these shafts encouraged gave an extraordinary chiaroscuro to the congregation, making Bobby Kennedy at one point look like the captain of Rembrandt's "Night Guard" amid his lieutenants slumbering in the shade.

It was a normal Baptist service with Southern overtones of gospel singing and solos, by black girls in white surplices, of Dr

King's favourite hymns sung with impassioned locking of the hands and closed eyes. Through it all, Mrs King sat back at a sideways angle with the carved, sad fixity of an African idol. Dr King's brother covered his face with a handkerchief once and others dabbed at their eyes: and the youngest King daughter sagged over in deep sleep like a rag doll. But Mrs King was as impassive as Buddha behind her thin veil while the prayers were given, the hymns, the eulogy by a New York dean as white as Siegfried, who had taught theology to Dr King. Once there was a suspicion of a glitter in her eyes when the Rev. Abernathy told of the last meal he had with Dr King, an anecdote as simple as a parable.

"On that Thursday noon in the Lorraine Motel, in Memphis. Tennessee, the maid served up only one salad, and Martin took a small portion of it and left the rest. Then someone reminded the girl that she had brought up one order of fish instead of two. And Martin said, 'Don't worry about it, Ralph and I can eat from the same plate', and I ate my last meal that Thursday noon. And I will not eat bread or meat or anything until I am thoroughly satisfied that I am ready for the task at hand."

There was one innovation that was nearly forgotten at the end. Both the casket and the family were ready to go, but there was a quick whisper in the Rev. Abernathy's ear and he announced that Mrs King had requested a playback of one of Dr King's last sermons.

It was the premonitory vision of his inevitable end, and is voice resounded through the hushed church: "I think about my own death, and I think about my own funeral . . . and every now and then I ask myself what it is that I would want said and I leave the word to this morning . . . I don't want a long funeral, and if you get somebody to deliver the eulogy, tell him not to talk too long . . . tell him not to mention that I have a Nobel peace prize – that isn't important. Tell him not to mention that I have 300 or 400 awards – that's not important . . . I'd like somebody to mention that day that Martin Luther King tried to give his life serving others. I want you to say that day that I tried to be right and to walk with them. I want you to be able to say that day that I did try to feed the hungry. I want you to be able to say that day that I did try in my life to clothe the naked . . . I want you to say that I tried to love and serve humanity."

Then the doors were opened and the family went out and all the parsons, and the mule team bore its flowered casket and moved towards the many, many thousands that had gone on before to Morehouse College.

JOHN FETTERMAN

P.F.C. GIBSON COMES HOME

Louisville Times, July 1968

Fetterman's story on the return home of the body of "Little Duck" Gibson won a Pulitzer Prize for local news reporting.

It was late on a Wednesday night and most of the people were asleep in Hindman, the county seat of Knott County, when the body of Private First Class James Thurman (Little Duck) Gibson came home from Vietnam.

It was hot. But as the grey hearse arrived bearing the gray Army coffin, a summer rain began to fall. The fat raindrops glistened on the polished hearse and steamed on the street. Hindman was dark and silent. In the distance down the town's main street the red sign on the Square Deal Motor Co. flashed on and off.

Private Gibson's body had been flown from Oakland, California, to Cincinnati and was accompanied by Army Staff Sgt Raymond A. Ritter, assigned to escort it home. The body was picked up in Cincinnati by John Everage, a partner in the local funeral home, and from that point on it was in the care of people who had known the 24-year-old soldier all his life.

At Hindman, the coffin was lifted out while Sgt Ritter, who wore a black mourning band on his arm, snapped a salute. One funeral home employee whispered to another: "It's Little Duck. They brought him back."

Most of his life he had been called Little Duck for so long that many people who knew him well had to pause and reflect to recall his full name.

By Thursday morning there were few people who did not know that Little Duck was home – or almost home. During the morning the family came; his older brother, Herschel, whom they call Big Duck; his sister Betty Jo; and his wife Carolyn.

They stood over the glass-shielded body and let their tears fall upon the glass, and people spoke softly in the filling station next door and on the street outside.

The soldier's parents, Mr and Mrs Norman Gibson, waited at home, a neat white house up the hollow which shelters Flax Patch Creek, several miles away. Mrs Gibson had been ill for months, and the family did not let her take the trip to Hindman. Later in the morning, they took Little Duck home.

Sweltering heat choked the hills and valleys as Little Duck was placed back in the hearse and taken home. The cortege had been joined by Maj. Lyle Haldeman, a survival assistance officer, sent, like Sgt Ritter, to assist the family. It was a long, slow trip – over a high ridge to the south, along Irishman Creek and past the small community of Amburgey.

At Amburgey, the people stood in the sun, women wept and men removed their hats as the hearse went past. Mrs Nora Amburgey, the postmistress, lowered the flag of the tiny fourth-class post office to half-mast and said, "We all thought a lot of Little Duck."

At the point where Flax Patch Creek empties into Irishman Creek, the hearse turned, crossed a small wooden bridge and drove the final mile up Flax Patch Creek to the Gibson home. The parents and other relatives waited in a darkened, silent home.

As the coffin was lifted upon the front porch and through the door into the front living room, the silence was broken by cries of grief. The sounds of anguish swelled and rolled along the hollow. Little Duck was home.

All afternoon and all night they came, some walking, some driving up the dusty road in cars and trucks. They brought flowers and food until the living room was filled with floral tributes and the kitchen was crammed with food. The people filled the house and yard. They talked in small groups, and members of the family clasped to each other in grief.

They went, time and time again, to look down into the coffin and weep.

The mother, a sweet-faced mountain woman, her gray hair brushed back and fastened behind her head, forced back the pangs of her illness and moved, as in a trance, among the crowd as she said:

"His will will be done no matter what we say or do."

The father, a tall, tanned man, his eyes wide and red from weeping, said:

"He didn't want to go to the Army, but he knew it was the right thing to do; so he did his best. He gave all he had. I'm as proud of him as I can be. Now they bring him home like this."

Around midnight the rain returned and the mourners gathered in the house, on the porch and backed against the side of the house under the eaves.

The father talked softly of his son.

"I suppose you wonder why we called him Little Duck. Well, when the boys were little they would go over and play in the creek every chance they got. Somebody said they were like ducks.

"Ever since then Herschel was 'Big Duck' and James was 'Little Duck'.

"You worked hard all your life to raise your family. I worked in 32-inch seam of coal, on my hands and knees, loading coal to give my family what I could.

"There was never a closer family. Little Duck was born here in this house and never wanted to leave."

Other mourners stepped up to volunteer tributes to Little Duck.

"He never was one to drink and run up and down the road at night."

"He took care of his family. He was a good boy."

Little Duck was a big boy. He was 6 feet 5½ inches tall and weighed 205 pounds. His size led him to the basketball team at Combs High School where he met and courted the girl he married last January.

Little Duck was home recently on furlough. Within a month after he went down Flax Patch Creek to return to the Army, he was back home to be buried. He had been married six months, a soldier for seven.

The Army said he was hit by mortar fragments near Saigon, but there were few details of his death.

The father, there in the stillness of the early morning, was remembering the day his son went back to the Army.

"He had walked around the place, looking at everything. He told me, 'Lord, it's good to be home.' "

"Then he went down the road. He said, 'Daddy, take care of yourself and don' work too hard.' "

"He said, 'I'll be seeing you,' But he can't see me now."

An elderly man, walking with great dignity, approached and said, "Nobody can ever say anything against Little Duck. He was as good a boy as you'll ever see."

Inside the living room, the air heavy with the scent of flowers, Little Duck's mother sat with her son and her grief.

Her hand went out gently, as to comfort a stranger, and she talked as though to herself.

"Why my boy? Why my baby?"

She looked toward the casket, draped in an American flag, and when she turned back she said:

"You'll never know what a flag means until you see one on your own boy."

Then she went back to weep over the casket.

On Friday afternoon Little Duck was taken over to the Providence Regular Baptist Church and placed behind the pulpit. All that night the church lights burned and the people stayed and prayed. The parents spent the night at the church.

"This is his last night," Little Duck's mother explained.

The funeral was at 10 o'clock Saturday morning, and the people began to arrive early. They came from the dozens of hollows and small communities in Letcher, Knot, and Perry counties. Some came back from other states. They filled the pews and then filled the aisle with folding chairs. Those who could not crowd inside gathered outside the door or listened beneath the windows.

The sermon was delivered by the Rev. Archie Everage, pastor at Montgomery Baptist Church, which is on Montgomery Creek near Hindman. On the last Sunday that he was home alive, Little Duck attended services there.

The service began with a solo, "Beneath the Sunset," sung by a young girl with a clear bell-like voice; then there were hymns from the church choir.

Mr Everage, who had been a friend of Little Duck, had difficulty in keeping his voice from breaking as he got into his final tribute. He spoke of the honour Little Duck had brought to his family, his courage and his dedication. He spoke of Little Duck "following the colours of his country". He said Little Duck died "for a cause for which many of our forefathers fought and died".

The phrase touched off a fresh wail of sobs to fill the church. Many mountain people take great pride in their men who "follow the colours". It is a tradition that goes back to October 1780, when a lightly regarded band of mountaineers handed disciplined British troops a historic defeat at Kings Mountain in South Carolina and turned the tide of the Revolutionary war.

Shortly before Little Duck was hit in Vietnam, he had written two letters intended for his wife. Actually the soldier was writing a part of his own funeral. Mr Everage read from one letter:

Honey, they put me in a company right down on the Delta. From what everybody says that is a rough place, but I've been praying hard for the Lord to help me and take care of me so really I'm not too scared or worried. I think if He wants it to be my time to go that I'm prepared for it. Honey, you don't know really when you are going to face something like this, but I want you to be a good girl and try to live a good life. For if I had things to do over I would have already been prepared for something like this. I guess you are wondering why I'm telling you this, but you don't know how hard it's been on me in just a short time. But listen here, if anything happens to me, all I want is for you to live right, and then I'll get to see you again.

And from another letter:

Honey, listen, if anything happens to me I want you to know that I love you very very much and I want you to keep seeing my family the rest of their lives and I want you to know you are a wonderful wife and that I'm very proud of you. If anything happens I want Big Duck and Betty Jo to know I loved them very much. If anything happens also tell them not to worry, that I'm prepared for it.

The service lasted two hours and ended only after scores of people, of all ages, filed past the coffin.

Then they took Little Duck to Resthaven Cemetery up on a hill in Perry County. The Army provided six pallbearers, five of whom had served in Vietnam. There was a seven-man firing squad to fire the traditional three volleys over the grave and bugle to sound taps.

The pallbearers, crisp and polished in summer tans, folded the flag from the coffin and Sgt Ritter handed it to the young widow, who had wept so much, but spoken so little, during the past three days.

Then the soldier's widow knelt beside the casket and said softly, "Oh, Little Duck."

Then they buried Little Duck beneath a bit of the land he died for.

WOODSTOCK

Rolling Stone, September 1969

Friday was the first day of the Woodstock Music and Arts Fair, now moved to White Lake near Bethel, New York, a hundred miles from New York City and fifty miles from Woodstock proper. The intrepid *Rolling Stone* crew thought it would be bright to beat the traffic, so we left the city early in the morning and headed up. When we got to Monticello, a little town eight miles from the festival, the traffic was light. Then we hit it. Eight miles of two-lane road jammed with thousands of cars that barely moved. Engines boiling over, people collapsed on the side of the road, everyone smiling in common bewilderment.

Automotive casualties looked like the skeletons of horses that died on the Oregon Trail. People began to improvize, driving on soft shoulders until they hit the few thousand who'd thought of the same thing, then stopping again. Finally the two lanes were transformed into four and still nothing moved. Bulbous vacationers (for this was the Catskills, laden with chopped liver and bad comedians) stared at the cars and the freaks and the nice kids, their stomachs sticking out into the road. Here we were, trying to get to the land of Hendrix and the Grateful Dead, all the while under the beady eyes of Mantovani fans.

There wasn't any traffic control. We sat still in our car and figured out all sorts of brilliant solutions to the transportation problem, everything from one-way roads to hired buses (a plan that failed at the last minute), but we still weren't getting anywhere, and it had been four hours now. This was the road on the map, right? No other way to get there? A lot of kids were pulling over and starting to walk through the fields. We had six miles to go. It was a cosmic traffic jam, where all the cars fall into place like pieces in a jigsaw puzzle and stay there for ever.

The police estimated that there were a million people on the road that day trying to get to the festival. A million people; 186,000 tickets had been sold; the promoters figured that maybe 200,000, tops, would show. That seemed outlandish, if believable. But no one was prepared for what happened, and no one could have been.

Perhaps a quarter of a million never made it. They gave up and turned back, or parked on the highway and set up tents on the divider strip and stuck it out. Shit, they'd come to camp out for three days, and they were gonna do it. Many had walked fifteen miles in the rain and the mud, only to give up a mile or so before the festival and turn back, but they were having fun. Camped on the highway with no idea where White Lake was or what was going on, they were making friends, dancing to car radios and making their own music on their own guitars.

"Isn't it pretty here, all the trees and the meadows? And whenever it gets too hot, it rains and cools everyone off. Wow." "Yeah, but you paid eighteen dollars and drove all the way from Ohio and you can't even get to the festival. Aren't you disappointed? Or pissed off?" "No, man. Everyone is so friendly, it's like being stuck in an elevator with people when the power goes off. But it's much nicer here than in an elevator."

It was an amazing sight, the highway to White Lake: it looked, as someone said, like Napoleon's army retreating from Moscow. It looked like that for three days. Everywhere one looked one saw tents and campfires, cars rolled into ditches, people walking, lying down, drinking, eating, reading, singing. Kids were sleeping, making love, wading in the marshes, trying to milk the local cows and trying to cook the local corn. The army of New York State Quickway 17B was on manoeuvres.

Thinking back to Saturday, one image sticks in my mind, an image that I doubt is shared by many but one that I will never forget. Friday night, folk music had been played – Joan Baez, Arlo Guthrie, Sweetwater and Ravi Shankar. But by the next morning the future was unclear, and rumours that the area had been declared an official disaster seemed quite credible. Many left Saturday morning, oppressed by water shortages, ninety-degree heat, ninety-nine percent humidity and the crush of bodies.

"I love all these people," said a young girl, "they're all beautiful, and I never thought I'd be hassled by so many beautiful people, but I am, and I'm going home." Faces were drawn and tired, eyes blank, legs moving slowly on blistered and sore feet. The lack of water, food and toilets was becoming difficult, though everyone shared, and many simply roamed the area with provisions with the sole purpose of giving them away. But it got hotter and hotter, and a boy was running toward the lake in a panic, cradling his little puppy in his arms. The dog was unconscious, its tongue out of its mouth but not moving. The boy thought the dog was going to die, and he was scared. He kept running, and I stared after him, and then I left the festival and decided to go home. I couldn't get a plane, and I was lucky to stay, but that scene was real, and it too was part of the festival at White Lake.

Everyone in the country has seen pictures of the crowd. Was it bigger than it looked? Whoever saw so many people in the same spot, all with the same idea? Well, Hitler did, and General MacArthur, and Mao, but this was a somewhat better occasion. They came to hear the music, and they stayed to dig the scene and the people and the countryside. Any time, no matter who was playing, one could see thousands moving in every direction and more camped on every hill and all through the woods. The magnificent sound system was clear and audible long past the point at which one could no longer see the bands.

The outstanding thing was the unthinkable weight of the groups that played. Take Saturday night and Sunday morning (the music was scheduled to begin at one in the afternoon and run for twelve hours, but it began at three or four and went until the middle of the next morning). Here's the line-up: Joe Cocker, Country Joe and the Fish, Ten Years After, the Band, Johnny Winter, Blood, Sweat and Tears, Crosby, Stills, Nash and Young, the Paul Butterfield Blues Band, Sha Na Na and Jimi Hendrix. It's like watching God perform the Creation. "And for My next number   "

Sometime around four in the morning the stage crew began to assemble the apparatus for the festival's most unknown quantity, Crosby, Stills, Nash and Young. This was not exactly their debut – they'd played once or twice before – but this was a national audience, both in terms of the composition of the crowd and the press and because of the amazing musical competition with which they were faced.

It took a very long time to get everything ready, and the people onstage crowded around the amplifiers and the nine or ten guitars and the chairs and mikes and organ, more excited in anticipation than they'd been for any other group that night. A large semi-circle of equipment protected the musicians from the rest of the people. The band was very nervous. Neil Young was stalking around, kissing his wife, trying to tune his guitar off in a corner, kissing her wife again, staring off away from the crowd. Stills and Nash paced back and forth and tested the organ and the mikes, and drummer Dallas Taylor fiddled with his kit and kept trying to make it more than perfect. Finally, they went on.

They opened with "Suite Judy Blue Eyes", stretching it out for a long time, exploring the figures of the song for the crowd, making their quiet music and flashing grimaces at each other when something went wrong. They strummed and picked their way through other numbers, and then began to shift around, Crosby singing with Stills, then Nash and Crosby, back and forth. They had the crowd all the way. They seemed like several bands rather than one.

Then they hit it. Right into "Long Time Gone", a song for a season if there ever was one: Stills on organ, shouting out the choruses; Neil snapping out lead; Crosby aiming his electric twelve-string out over the edge of the stage, biting off his words and stretching them out – lyrics as strong as any we are likely to hear.

> There's something, something, something
> Goin' on around here
> That surely, surely, surely
> Won't stand
> The light of day
> Ooooooohhh!
> And it appears to be a long time . . .

I have never seen a musician more involved in this music. At one point Crosby nearly fell off the stage in his excitement.

Deep into the New York night they were, early Sunday

morning in the dark after three days of chaos and order, and it seemed like the last of a thousand and one American nights. Two hundred thousand people covered the hills of a great natural amphitheatre, campfires burning in the distance, the lights shining down from the enormous towers on to the faces of the band. Crosby, Stills, Nash and Young were just one of the many acts at this festival, and perhaps they wouldn't top the bill if paired with Hendrix or the Airplane or Creedence Clearwater or the Who or the Band, but this was their night. Their performance was scary, brilliant proof of the magnificence of music, and I don't believe it could have happened with such power anywhere else. This was a festival that had triumphed over itself, as Crosby and his band led the way toward the end of it.

SEYMOUR M. HERSH

MY LAI: LIEUTENANT ACCUSED OF MURDERING 109 CIVILIANS

St Louis Dispatch, 13 November 1969

Hersh's investigation of the My Lai atrocity, and its subsequent cover-up by the US military, won him a Pulitzer Prize. His book *My Lai 4* was published in 1970.

Fort Benning, Ga., Nov. 13 – Lt William L. Calley Jr, 26 years old, is a mild-mannered, boyish-looking Vietnam combat veteran with the nickname "Rusty". The Army is completing an investigation of charges that he deliberately murdered at least 109 Vietnamese civilians in a search-and-destroy mission in March 1968 in a Viet Cong stronghold known as "Pinkville".

Calley has formally been charged with six specifications of mass murder. Each specification cites a number of dead, adding up to the 109 total, and charges that Calley did "with premeditation murder . . . Oriental human beings, whose names and sex are unknown, by shooting them with a rifle".

The Army calls it murder; Calley, his counsel and others associated with the incident describe it as a case of carrying out orders.

"Pinkville" has become a widely known code word among the military in a case that many officers and some Congressmen believe will become far more controversial than the recent murder charges against eight Green Berets.

One man who took part in the mission with Calley said that in the earlier two attacks "we were really shot up".

"Every time we got hit it was from the rear," he said. "So the third time in there the order came down to go in and make sure no one was behind.

"We were told to just clear the area. It was a typical combat assault formation. We came in hot, with a cover of artillery in front of us, came down the line and destroyed the village.

"There are always some civilian casualties in a combat operation. He isn't guilty of murder."

The order to clear the area was relayed from the battalion commander to the company commander to Calley, the source said.

Calley's attorney said in an interview: "This is one case that should never have been brought. Whatever killing there was was in a firefight in connection with the operation.

"You can't afford to guess whether a civilian is a Viet Cong or not. Either they shoot you or you shoot them.

"This case is going to be important – to what standard do you hold a combat officer in carrying out a mission?

"There are two instances where murder is acceptable to anybody: where it is excusable and where it is justified; if Calley did shoot anybody because of the tactical situation or while in a firefight, it was either excusable or justifiable."

Adding to the complexity of the case is the fact that investigators from the Army inspector general's office, which conducted the bulk of the investigation, considered filing charges against at least six other men involved in the action 16 March.

A Fort Benning infantry officer has found that the facts of the case justify Calley's trial by general court-martial on charges of premeditated murder.

Pentagon officials said that the next steps are for the case to go to Calley's brigade commander and finally to the Fort Benning post commander for findings on whether there should be a court-martial. If they so hold, final charges and specifications will be drawn up and made public at that time, the officials said.

Calley's friends in the officer corps at Fort Benning, many of them West Point graduates, are indignant. However, knowing the high stakes of the case, they express their outrage in private.

"They're using this as a Goddamned example," one officer complained. "He's a good soldier. He followed orders.

"There weren't any friendlies in the village. The orders were to shoot anything that moved."

Another officer said: "It could happen to any of us. He has

killed and has seen a lot of killing . . . Killing becomes nothing in Vietnam. He knew that there were civilians there, but he also knew that there were VC among them."

A third officer, also familiar with the case, said: "There's this question – I think anyone who goes to [Viet] Nam asks it. What's a civilian? Someone who works for us at day and puts on Viet Cong pajamas at night?"

There is another side of the Calley case – one that the Army cannot yet disclose. Interviews have brought out the fact that the investigation into the Pinkville affair was initiated six months after the incident, only after some of the men who served under Calley complained.

The Army has photographs purported to be of the incident, although these have not been introduced as evidence in the case, and may not be.

"They simply shot up this village and [Calley] was the leader of it," said one Washington source. "When one guy refused to do it, Calley took the rifle away and did the shooting himself."

Asked about this, Calley refused to comment.

One Pentagon officer discussing the case tapped his knee with his hand and remarked. "Some of those kids he shot were this high. I don't think they were Viet Cong. Do you?"

None of the men interviewed about the incident denied that women and children were shot.

A source of amazement among all those interviewed was that the story had yet to reach the press.

"Pinkville has been a word among GIs for a year," one official said. "I'll never cease to be amazed that it hasn't been written about before."

A high-ranking officer commented that he first heard talk of the Pinkville incident soon after it happened; the officer was on duty in Saigon at the time.

Why did the Army choose to prosecute this case? On what is it basing the charge that Calley acted with premeditation before killing? The court-martial should supply the answers to these questions, but some of the men already have their opinions.

"The Army knew it was going to get clobbered on this at some point," one military source commented. "If they don't prosecute somebody, if this stuff comes out without the Army taking some action, it could be even worse."

Another view that many held was that the top level of the military was concerned about possible war crime tribunals after the Vietnam war.

As for Calley – he is smoking four packs of cigarettes daily and getting out of shape. He is 5-foot-3, slender, with expressionless grey eyes and thinning brown hair. He seems slightly bewildered and hurt by the charges against him. He says he wants nothing more than to be cleared and return to the Army.

"I know this sounds funny," he said in an interview, "but I like the Army . . . and I don't want to do anything to hurt it."

Friends described Calley as a "gung-ho Army man . . . Army all the way". Ironically, even his stanchest supporters admit, his enthusiasm may be somewhat to blame.

"Maybe he did take some order to clear out the village a little bit too literally," one friend said, "but he's a fine boy."

Calley had been shipped home early from Vietnam, after the Army refused his request to extend his tour of duty. Until the incident at Pinkville, he had received nothing but high ratings from his superior officers. He was scheduled to be awarded the Bronze and Silver Stars for his combat efforts, he said. He has heard nothing about the medals since arriving at Fort Benning.

Calley was born in Miami, Fla, and flunked out of the Palm Beach Junior College before enlisting in the Army. He became a second lieutenant in September 1967, shortly after going to Vietnam. The Army, lists his home of record as Waynesville, NC.

An information sheet put out by the public affairs officer of the Americal Division the day after the 16 March engagement contained this terse mention of the incident: "The swiftness with which the units moved into the area surprised the enemy. After the battle the Eleventh Brigade moved into the village searching each hut and tunnel."

SALLY BEAUMAN

BUT THE PEOPLE ARE BEAUTIFUL

Telegraph Magazine, 5 February 1971

Andy Warhol sits in the corner of this Paris apartment like a small silver seraph. His neat little feet are laced up in black shoes and he sits, knees together, just so, behind the day's edition of the *New York Herald Tribune.* Every so often one of his small pink hands covered in a soft fur of snow white hairs emerges from behind the paper and turns a page, very precise, folding it back so there are no nasty rumples. Over the top of the page his head is just visible: the famous shock of silver hair, looking as if it had been cut with nail scissors on a dark night, and his pale pink, curiously old-looking face. How old *is* Warhol? He admits to 40, but a number of his friends say he's nearer 50. Looking at him he could be any age – 35, 45, 55: the face is old but the hair is young.

That hair . . . even from a distance over the top of a newspaper it has a haphazard disconnected look, the silver tufts sprouting from a pinkly plastic parting. Could it be . . . ? But no, one puts the thought aside immediately. Andy Warhol wear a toupee? Impossible. Frank Sinatra, John Wayne, Prince Philip – I mean even Abbie Hoffman, any of them, but Warhol? Somehow the idea has a rich absurdity, an ultimate incongruity, like some successful lavatory graffiti: Mary Poppins Smokes Pot – *Andy Warhol Wears a Toupee.*

Such a careful, middle-class kind of an action: it does not go with making silkscreens of Jackie and Marilyn and Campbell's soup cans. It does not go with his novel *a* – 24 hours of transcribed tape recordings of Andy and friends, some of the friends being bombed out of their skulls on amphetamines. It does not go with the Factory, his downtown loft headquarters in New York and its much publicised assemblage of freaks, acid heads, lesbians, transvestites – it does not go at all, *and yet . . .* if ever a hair-parting was hand stitched, this is it.

Warhol blinks and turns a page. He looks vulnerable and soft, a less officious version of Alice's White Rabbit. Even to think of toupees seems uncharitable. *And yet . . .* how many of his ex-Superstars, finding themselves dropped from the Warhol entourage as suddenly as they were picked up, have testified to his peculiar ruthlessness: Valerie Solanas, who shot him in the summer of 1968, was obsessed by the influence he had over others, particularly women. The way Valerie Solanas wrote about him, Andy Warhol sounded like Svengali . . . Yet now he sits in his chair and fiddles with his newspaper, and it is clear that he is shy. He is going to sit behind the pages of the *New York Herald Tribune* for just as long as is necessary, and anything so rude as the prod of a direct question will, quite obviously, put him to immediate flight.

Around him is a mild form of chaos, which he studiously ignores. He, or rather Andy Warhol Productions, which is a group name for Paul Morrissey, Fred Hughes and Jed Johnson the sound man, all of whom filmed *Flesh*, and more recently *Trash*, are in Paris to make their first European movie to be entitled *Les Beautés – a French Farce*. Alternative title: *The Pissoirs of Paris*.

By movie-making standards their equipment is fairly minimal: a couple of lights; a 16 mm camera mounted on a tripod in one corner; one microphone; the sound recording equipment. But the apartment is small, and the equipment (flown over specially from America, and promptly confiscated by the French Customs, who – unaware of Warhol's filming techniques – refused at first to believe that anyone needed 40 hours of film to make a single movie and thought they were going to sell it) . . . the equipment is not attuned to French electrical circuits. For the first three days, shooting had been delayed while the lights continually blew. Now the lights do not blow, they merely smoke ominously, filling the tiny room with a dry acrid smell.

But even with lights, tapes, cannisters, flex snaking around tables, scattered on the carpets, this apartment is chic! Studiously chic. It is in the Rue Bonaparte in St Germain, a few yards from the Seine, but such considerations, once inside, are irrelevant: for this apartment exists not in space but in time. The outside world is hidden behind mirrored shutters: inside we are back in the past, it is 1930. Everything is white and beige like a Jean Harlow set. The lamps are elegant chrome mushrooms, the mica and marble tables have those beautiful Odeon edges . . . it is a room that could only have been created by an interior decorator, and the interior decorator/ designer – Karl Lagerfeld – is, in this case, also acting in the movie. Now he is having a busy time pointing out the niceties of his interior decoration to Morrissey and Johnson and Hughes as they swarm all over the room throwing switches, checking lights, testing camera angles.

There is a sofa/bed covered in soft beige wool that looks like suede but is not – "I can't *stand* leather, so vulgar," says Karl. And the sofa/bed is piled high with cushions. "The cushions have original lamé covers, of course – that modern lamé can look so trashy don't you think?"

Scattered with largesse on tables and shelves are an assortment of Fouquet cigarette cases (for decoration, you understand, not cigarettes), exquisitely enamelled. "Hmmm," says Paul Morrissey, picking one up approvingly, "Fouquet? Signed, of course?" and Karl Lagerfeld inclines his handsome head in assent. Of course. Of course.

And suddenly one begins to get the feeling . . . what is going *on* here? Remember all those early Warhol films in ratty old West Side apartments with Brigid Polk bulging out of tatty jeans, and all those Press stories about those *freaks*? If that kind of scene does not seem to go with Warhol-in-a-toupee, it does not seem to go with this apartment, which is pure *Vogue*, either. And Morrissey with his nice clean jeans and his short short hair, and his voice like a Brooklyn version of Truman Capote, has moved on to a vase which is all silvery and shimmery and extremely beautiful and he is holding it *reverently* for all the world like an auctioneer, a valuer at Sotheby's . . . and Karl Lagerfeld strokes it lovingly too, and pronounces the name of its august French creator, and then Andy Warhol surfaces from the *Herald Tribune* for the first time that afternoon. "Wow," he says, "in New York that would fetch around $15,000!"

And he is *interested*. Warhol, you understand, is not animated. His conversation is usually limited to a sweet, "Yeah", or an, "Oh really?" as he walks around like a shy somnambulist. But now he puts the paper down and looks at the vase in question for a good half minute:

Fif-teen thou-sand dollars.

Things have certainly changed.

Andy Warhol was born Andrew Warhola, the second of three sons of two Polish immigrants in Chicago – Ondrej and Julia Warhola. His two brothers still live in Chicago where they are manual workers. The poverty of the family throughout Warhol's childhood was intense: he was a child of the Depression years. His father died in 1942, in West Virginia, where he had gone in search of work in the mines. Warhol left high school at 16, attended the Carnegie Institute of Technology in Pittsburgh where he studied pictorial design and immediately he graduated went to New York; it was then the beginning of the Fifties. Little is known about the ten years before he began to become celebrated in the early Sixties. He worked as a commercial artist designing shoe advertisements for expensive shoe stores like I. Miller. His earliest serious work, aside from professional graphics (at which he was extremely successful), was a series of oil paintings which were reproductions of mass media advertisements, occasionally slightly altered or arranged as a collage. He reproduced fragments of comic strips, drew the original Campbell's soup cans, and at first received a very negative response from galleries. In 1962, he discovered the medium which was perfectly suited to his art – the silk screen, and embarked on the now famous series of portraits – Troy Donahue, Liz Taylor, Jackie Kennedy.

And somewhere round about 1963 he became famous: New York's rich cultural élite queued up to have Warhol portraits of them: it became difficult to open an American magazine without reading about him: Warhol turned out to have the same flair for manipulating the media as for reproducing it. "It's easier," an American journalist once told me, "to get photographs and publicity material from the Factory, than it is from 20th Century Fox."

In 1965 Warhol gave up painting because he wanted to concentrate on making films. The early movies were as subversive to people's nice settled ideas about what was cinema as his Campbell's soup can silkscreens had been to their nice settled ideas about what was painting. He made *Sleep* ("six hours of a friend who slept a lot, asleep") and *Kiss* which was Baby Jane Holtzer and Gerard Malanga kissing in close up for a long time, not very passionately. There was *Empire*, eight hours from a static camera of the Empire State Building. Next came a whole series of wild, zany films, many based on screen plays by the writer Ronald Travel – like *Screen Tests One and Two*, and *Life of Juanita Castro*, and a series of spoofs like *Batman Dracula* and *Horse* – a send-up of the traditional Western that foreshadowed his later *Lonesome Cowboys*. But increasingly the films became an extraordinary kind of *cinema vérité*, depending for their often spasmodic effect on the static unedited recording of people like Ondine and Brigid Polk and Viva, who sat in front of the camera and did and said exactly whatever they felt like. Occasionally, as in *Bike Boy*, people were put into situations (a homosexual menswear shop; on a couch with a half-naked Viva) which were designed to elicit some sort of response from them, but apart from that Warhol's adherence to his artistic unities was firm: no plot; no script; no takes; no editing. "I like making movies," Warhol said, "because it's easier than painting paintings." He said some other rather engaging things too – like the famous, "The camera-work is lousy, the lighting's lousy, the sound is lousy, but the people are beautiful." He was known to walk out of the room during the filming and just let the camera go on running. In his *Chelsea Girls*, two films shown simultaneously on a split screen ("So," Warhol said, "the audience could look at the other if they got bored with the first"), Ondine, a Warhol Superstar of the time, got bored with talking. He announced on camera that he wanted to stop. Impervious, Warhol's camera went on running and Ondine resumed his monologue until the film ran out.

Chelsea Girls was, of course, a commercial success. MGM was reputed to have made an offer of a million dollars for distribution rights: they were turned down and in the end the film probably grossed that much anyway. And since then there have been signs that Warhol's films have been taking into account the possibility of a mass audience; maybe even seeking it . . . it began to look as if Warhol, the man who portrayed so brilliantly in his paintings the products of society – whether they were Brillo boxes or film stars – was beginning to want a few products himself.

After all both *Flesh* and *Trash* were fairly radical departures from his earlier work in that they depended on a fairly rigid plot line, and were carefully edited. And now *Les Beautés* too has a plot, a large budget, ($200,000, provided by Peter Brandt, a rich New York collector of Warhol's paintings) and an amazing shooting ratio of around 30 to one – that 40 hours of film coming down to a movie an hour and a half long that they hope to have distributed all over Europe. Why, on this movie they are even doing takes. I ask Paul Morrissey about this. He smiles. "It's quite simple," he says. "What we're interested in doing now is making commercial entertainments."

Things have certainly changed. There is everyone in Hollywood falling over themselves trying to make Films of Integrity that will appeal to a youthful audience, films like *Strawberry Statement* and *Getting Straight*, and here is Andy Warhol Productions coming right out and laying it on the line. *What we want to do is make commercial entertainments*. The only thing which is unclear is how much Warhol himself agrees with his new emphasis: after all, during the filming of most of *Flesh* he was in hospital recovering from the Valerie Solanas shooting. And *Trash* is being referred to as "Paul's film", although it will be distributed as an Andy Warhol production. I beard Warhol behind his newspaper and he smiles seraphically. "Oh, that's right," he says, "it's so nice to be entertaining. You know shooting in Europe is really like taking a paid vacation."

It is certainly fairly peaceful in the apartment now: Fred Hughes is on the phone, Karl Lagerfeld is looking in the mirror, the lights are smoking, Paul Morrissey lounges on the Thirties lamé. The only trouble is that – apart from Karl – there is no sign of the other actors. On the phone Fred Hughes's voice takes on a plaintive note:

"What d'you mean you can't come over, Patti, we're supposed to be shooting. Well, there's a bathroom here if that worries you. What, you won't? Patti, what were you *doing last night*?" He pauses to give the room a thumbs down signal. "Well, how about tomorrow? You're going to *Venice* tomorrow? But Patti, we're shooting a *picture*." He hangs up. There is a silence. "Why not get Max," squeaks Paul Morrissey. "We could shoot a scene between Karl and Max. Max could tell Karl he's been having an affair with Patti."

"Has he been having an affair with Patti?"

"No, but he could do."

Andy Warhol makes his first suggestion.

"We could get Jane and Donna over," he says mildly.

"Jane and Donna are at the hairdressers having their hair dyed again."

Fred Hughes gets on the phone once more. It is now 3.30.

"Hello, Max, can you come over now? What, you just woke up? Well, that doesn't matter, come anyway."

"The thing about the film is," Michael Sklar, the leading actor, had told me earlier, "that it has a rather complicated sort of a plot. Because French farces always do, of course. You see there's me, and I play a character with the same name as me, Michael, and I'm a rich American – the son of a man who made a fortune out of bathroom supplies, and I come to Paris to see if I can promote lavatory deodorants for use in the pissoirs of Paris, right? Well, then I meet this young Frenchman, Max, and he comes to live with me. But it also happens that I'm writing a musical and one night we have a blind date with two girls and it turns out that they'd be perfect to play the leads in my musical, and then it occurs to me that if we got married, I mean if I married Donna who's the blonde and he married Jane who's the brunette then we could all live together but people wouldn't talk. And so we plan all that and then I fall really in love with Donna and I want to get her on to the cover of *Vogue* because she's a model." He pauses for breath, "*Meanwhile*, we have this friend Peter who's a ski champion who's married to Carole but he's trying to have an affair with Patti, who's married to Karl. Get it?"

I said it wasn't exactly Feydeau but it certainly had a lot of possibilities. "Well, the nice thing is, you see," he explained, "it's all like real life, because Donna *is* on the cover of this month's French *Vogue*, and Peter is a pretty good skier and and . . ."

His voice trails off. It seems tactful not to ask what other similarities there are between the cast's factual and fictional existences.

I am desperately trying to remember all this when Max arrives to shoot the scene with Karl. Max is French but lives in Rome where he has done some film work: he speaks a kind of heavily-accented Maurice Chevalier English. He and Karl sit down on armchairs at the corner of the room, the crew adjust the light, Andy Warhol gets behind the camera, it is all about to start . . .

"One moment," says Karl. "I think I look better in beige, no?"

At present he is wearing green trousers, a pink shirt and the kind of working men's sleeveless pullover that costs a minimum of 500 NF at Ted Lapidus. "The room is beige, you see," he says, "so I think maybe . . ." He disappears for some minutes and reappears looking even more beautiful than before in beige trousers, a beige silk shirt decorated with swallows, and beige canvas boots. His complexion has been suitably darkened with a bronzer and the whole ravishing effect is completed with pale pink lipstick and a necklace of tiny seed pearls.

"Right," says Paul Morrissey to Max, "now how about you say something like what a nice room this is, then Karl can tell you all about it and then you can say, 'I've been having trouble with my affairs.'" Clearly there is going to be no nonsense about Motivation on this picture: Warhol switches on the camera, the tapes start recording the sound.

"What a beyootiful room zis ees," says Max obligingly, and he and Karl improvise their scene. Every time they seem in danger of drying up, or saying something that will throw the plot haywire, they stop the cameras, stop the sound, and Paul Morrissey suggests some more lines to them. Whenever anyone says anything in the least lively, and natural, so artificial is the atmosphere, it seems extremely funny.

"Now how about you tell him you've been having a little affair with his wife," says Paul.

Max clears his throat, the camera rolls. "Er, Karl," he says, "I zink maybe you should know, I make a leetle zing with Patti."

Karl makes a delighted moue. "I think *I* should know," he says, "what is a little thing?"

They improvise a few more sentences, then Warhol cuts off the camera. Everyone falls about. "Did you hear that, hey that was great! 'Make a little thing.' Did you *hear* that, Andy?" But Andy is invisible behind the camera. It makes almost as good a shield as the *New York Herald Tribune*.

"This'll be a good scene," chortles Paul Morrissey. "You'll like this scene. This is the one where Michael takes the girls around the *pissoirs* of Paris distributing his company's lavatory deodorants, and Donna poses outside each *pissoir* with a deodorant cake for the cover of *Vogue*." (*Is nothing sacred*? I hear them cry at

Condé Nast.) Anyway, here we all are assembled at two o'clock waiting to assault the *pissoirs* of Paris. We wait in the apartment in the Boulevard St Germain lent to Andy by a friend. Warhol sits on a rococo sofa and crochets. Michael Sklar fills a bag with dubiously scented deodorant cakes. The two girl stars adjust their make-up and fill in time by reading *Le Semaine à Paris*. They are, as Michael Sklar had promised, a twosome out of Hans Christian Andersen – Snow White and Rose Red. Jane Forth's hair is raven black and her eyebrows are shaved; Donna Jordan's eyebrows are bleached and her hair is platinum.

They are both dressed in a spectacular assemblage of forties' clothes – wedgie shoes and fox fur capes and mid-calf skirts, with make-up to match – authentic cakey crimson lipstick, orange eyeshadow, brilliant rouge; the effect is spectacularly *kitsch*: they are a walking, talking exercise in sartorial camp. And their voices! These come from deep inside the nasal region, and filter audibly through the adenoids, bursting upon the room with the relentless power of a New York pneumatic drill.

"I feel so *nawseus*," says Jane once, and then again, and again at five minute intervals. But Donna is ecstatic: are they not this very week, showing *Gentlemens Prefer Blonde* at the Cinemathcquc? "*Gentlemen Prefer Blondes*," someone murmurs. "Right," drills Donna blithely, "*Gentlemens Prefer Blonde*. And *Gilda* tooo! Think of tha-at. You know I never saw a Rita Hayworth movie."

Jane and Donna are young: 18 years old, they reiterate. "I'm 18," Jane says in *Trash*, to Joe Dellesandro. "How old are you?" "Eighteen too," mumbles Joe. "Oooh," says Jane, freaking them all from Bolton to San Francisco, "with those bags under your eyes I thought you must be pushin' 25 or sumpin'."

"Yes, they're young," says Michael Sklar, not a little grimly, as we finally go outside to start shooting, "and frankly they're a bit brattish. I mean Warhol's people are strong on personality, but they're not so hot on technique." Michael is an actor (unusual in a Warhol film). He was trained at UCLA and by Stella Adler, and he had a small part in *Trash*, as the social worker. "Careerwise, my agent asked me after *Trash*, is it wise to make another Warhol movie? But then when the reviews came out and they were good, I mean they all recognised it was serious social commentary, I thought why not? I mean professionally things haven't come all that easy, that's what the girls can't understand. For me this is gravy."

We have arrived at the *pissoir* and are waiting for the van to materialize bringing the equipment, Andy and the girls. Fred Hughes tells Michael Sklar how they will be filming. It appears this does not correspond with how Paul Morrissey had said they would be filming. Michael puts up a fight: "But I've prepared this whole scene in my head and now you're telling me it's all *different*. I mean that throws out all my *motivation*."

Fred Hughes stands tight-lipped. Michael stands tight-lipped. "The trouble with this picture is," he says to me, "there are too many people making Artistic Decisions." We all stare at the *pissoir* for want of anything else: all you can see is feet, but if you stay there long enough you can make some interesting sociological observations. "Time and motion study," says Michael Sklar as the cameras arrive. The camera, with Warhol operating it, is well hidden inside the van, which backs up on the pavement so it can focus most effectively on the starring *pissoir*. French workers continue trucking on in and out, all unaware of the *scene* about to descend upon them . . . Donna and Jane and Michael line up further down the street. Paul Morrissey tells them to do one thing: Fred Hughes tells them to do another.

Michael protests. "What's the matter, Michael?" asks Jane Forth, "isn't your face enough on camera?" Paul Morrissey is soothing. "Oh, come on Paul," says Fred Hughes. "Don't prima donna him . . ."

It is all getting a little temperamental; the leading actresses are glowering; clearly there are some considerable ego trips involved in this picture . . . in the midst of all the fracas, Andy Warhol, hand on the camera button, gives a gentle sigh. "Oh, come on," he says in his sweet way, "do anything. It doesn't matter *what* they do . . ." And it works like magic.

The three stars converge on the *pissoir*; the pneumatic drill voices come into action – useful at last, with live sound and the roar of the Paris traffic. Donna cosies up to the *pissoir*, and, deodorant cake in hand, goes into a series of gummy pin-up smiles, of lightning cheesecake postures.

A little old lady, passing, stops in wonderment. What are these crazies doing . . . ? The last pair of male feet shuffles out from the *pissoir*, and before you can say "gendarme" Donna and Jane are inside, you can see their wedgie shoes teetering round and round in a circle, and clear across the Paris traffic comes Jane's voice, tinnily echoing, "Oooh my Gawd, it smells awful. I feel *nawseus* in here!"

It is the first *pissoir* of many. There is then the St Germain *pissoir*. The Arc de Triomphe *pissoir*. The Pigalle *pissoir*. In each they do several takes until they have one that is good, or the police arrive – whichever happens first. On one particularly good take Andy forgets to press the button, and only when they are finished realises the camera did not roll. Occasionally Jed Johnson, who mostly sits quietly in the van recording sound, suggests some shots. It is he, after all, who is going to have the job of editing this picture. "If we did so and so," he points out, "we'd have a matching shot, so when we edited . . ."

"Right!" says everyone. "Right!" And they shoot it just the way he says.

Later the same day we watch some rushes. The movie screen is set up in Andy's apartment, and everyone sits on the floor squinting at the flickering images. All the outdoor shots are over-exposed, so the actors and actresses appear to float around Paris in a ghostly white mist.

"Oh," says Fred Hughes, "what did we do wrong? Didn't we check the exposure on the meter?"

"Never mind," says Paul Morrissey. "It looks kind of pretty like that. Anyway, they can always print it darker . . ."

There are several takes of Donna on the telephone; some takes of Donna and Jane walking around Paris with their friends Jay and Corey; there is a jealous scene between Max and Michael in bed, during which Max – who is naked – firmly keeps a pillow between his legs: clearly this is not going to be as explicit as *Flesh* or *Trash* – but maybe that is all part of being a Hollywood-style commercial entertainment. Except, of course, that it obviously is not going to be that either: a cast of mostly amateurs improvising lines to one 16mm camera is not Hollywood; it is also, as becomes increasingly clear, not Warhol either. The freshness and exciting haphazardness of his early films has gone. One begins to wonder – just what is the point of having actors improvise scenes which are strictly plot links? Warhol freed the cinema from heavy narrative necessity – how come he is going backwards?

But no one but me is bothered by such considerations. The

vital question is, what do the stars look like? Never mind what they say or do, are their clothes fashionable; is their hair set just right? It is a bit like sitting among the Press at a Paris fashion show: there is a constant background coo of compliments . . . "Oh wow, doesn't Jane look *pretty!*" "Donna's hair is great like that isn't it – just great." "Oooh – look at Jay – was he wearing make-up in this sequence?" And Andy sits curled up on the carpet, his arms clasped around his knees, like a small child mesmerised by the TV screen. And every once in a while he joins in the murmur: "Oh that's so pretty, doesn't she look cute?"

Easy to see why Valerie Solanas saw the gentle Warhol as a Svengali: it is clear he desperately wants to turn his actors into stars. "I'd like everyone to be famous for 15 minutes," he once said. Fame is, for him, a part of the artistic process; because fame is the active creation and dissemination of an image; a second identity more acceptable to you than the one with which you were born. It is for this reason – his obsession with people's image as their more real self – that his portraits have almost always been of the famous, and have been from photographs, not from real life. Now with his films you feel that the actors, the hype, the film and the reactions to it are all part of one giant creative process, harnessed to him.

The light from the screen reflects back on his near-white hair: it no longer seems surprising that he should wear a toupee. Maybe in Warhol's private movie he sees himself a star: forever young with fairy silver hair.

"You know, the funny thing is," says Michael Sklar, "that everywhere we go in Paris we attract so much attention. Just the other night we went to see a Buster Keaton film, and there we were, just waiting in the queue, and everyone came by and stared at us. Paul says it's my personal magnetism. He says I'm their new Superstar, but I don't take any notice of that." He smiles modestly. It is clear the idea fascinates him.

It fascinates Jane and Donna too: "Who's the star of this picture?" they demand constantly, only half joking, turning perfect profiles to the camera. The long line of discarded Warhol Superstars before them – Edie Sedgewick, Taylor Mead, Ondine, Mario Montez, Ultra Violet, Viva . . . Donna Jordan shrugs off their memory with nonchalant 18-year-old shoulders. What should she care? She is going to be in Andy's next movie,

"And the next movie is goin' to be like a million dollar movie," she says. "You know, real Hollywood."

Meanwhile it is a *bit* like Hollywood here in the Blvd St Germain. After all there is a famous director, a camera, adulation – pastiche Hollywood make-up and pastiche Hollywood clothes. They may not begin filming at dawn and they may not have a script, and there may be only one camera – but still they have glossily chic sets, and a plot of sorts, and when it is finished it will be distributed all over the United States, and maybe Europe, and there they will all be, super life size, stretched up in the dark on the cinema screens.

And meanwhile the media pays them almost as much attention as real stars: hasn't Jane, as she tells me, been a *personality* on television talk shows coast to coast? And there is Andy's coffee table loaded with magazines full of their images – Donna in French *Vogue*, Patti (who has still not appeared and is rumoured to have fled to Venice in pursuit of Helmut Berger) with pert naked breasts on the cover of *Lui*. There are pictures of them all in the latest edition of *Stern* – and even now right here in this apartment the photographers are clustered: a man from *Vingt Ans* who wants a fashion cover; *The Daily Telegraph Magazine* photographer; a man from the French film glossy magazine, *Zoom*; two or three freelancers . . . And on top of this Fred Hughes and Andy have a Polaroid! They are taking lots of pictures – everyone ogles for the lens . . .

"Take my picture, Andy," Jane Forth begs. "Quick, quick, I want to see how I look!"

And Andy turns the Polaroid on her: she angles her perfectly manufactured face with her dyed black hair, the eyebrows she has almost erased, the lids she has painted scarlet, the cheekbones she has reshaped with Leichner rouge . . . the camera clicks: Andy pauses, then peels off a damp square of film.

"Oh give it to me, Andy, give it me!"

And he gives it her – a blurry out-of-focus version of her features, but she is rapt.

It is as if Warhol were handing over her identity smelling of chemicals, on a film of plastic, two by four.

HUNTER S. THOMPSON

FEAR AND LOATHING AT THE 1972 REPUBLICAN CONVENTION

Fear and Loathing on the Campaign Trail '72, 1973

The creator of "Gonzo" journalism covered the '72 presidential campaign for *Rolling Stone.*

What happened, in a nut, was that I got lost in a maze of hallways in the back reaches of the convention hall on Tuesday night about an hour or so before the roll-call vote on Nixon's chances of winning the GOP nomination again this year . . . I had just come off the convention floor, after the Secret Service lads chased me away from the First Family box where I was trying to hear what Charlton Heston was saying to Nelson Rockefeller, and in the nervous wake of an experience like that I felt a great thirst rising . . . so I tried to take a shortcut to the Railroad Lounge, where free beer was available to the press; but I blew it somewhere along the way and ended up in a big room jammed with Nixon Youth workers, getting themselves ready for a "spontaneous demonstration" at the moment of climax out there on the floor . . . I was just idling around in the hallway, trying to go north for a beer, when I got swept up in a fast-moving mob of about two thousand people heading south at good speed, so instead of fighting the tide I let myself be carried along to wherever they were going . . .

Which turned out to be the "Ready Room," in a far corner of the hall, where a dozen or so people wearing red hats and looking like small-town high-school football coaches were yelling into bull-horns and trying to whip this herd of screaming sheep into shape for the spontaneous demonstration, scheduled for 10:33 p.m.

It was a very disciplined scene. The red-hatted men with the bullhorns did all the talking. Huge green plastic "refuse" sacks full of helium balloons were distributed, along with handfuls of New Year's Eve party noisemakers and hundreds of big cardboard signs that said things like: "NIXON NOW!" . . . "FOUR MORE YEARS!" . . . "NO COMPROMISE!"

Most of the signs were freshly printed. They looked exactly like the "WE LOVE MAYOR DALEY" signs that Daley distributed to his sewer workers in Chicago in 1968: red and blue ink on a white background . . . but a few, here and there were hand-lettered, and mine happened to be one of these. It said, "GARBAGE MEN DEMAND EQUAL TIME." I had several choices but this one seemed right for the occasion.

Actually, there was a long and active time lag between the moment when I was swept into the Ready Room and my decision to carry a sign in the spontaneous demonstration. I have a lot of on-the-spot notes about this, somewhere in my suitcase, but I can't find them now and it's 3:15 a.m. in Miami and I have to catch a plane for Chicago at noon – then change planes for Denver, then change again in Denver for the last plane to Aspen – so I'll try to put some flesh on this scene when I get to Woody Creek and my own typewriter; this one is far too slow for good dialogue or fast-moving behaviour.

Just to put a fast and tentative ending on it, however, what happened in that time lag was that they discovered me early on, and tried to throw me out – but I refused to go, and that's when the dialogue started. For the first ten minutes or so I was getting very ominous Hells Angels flashbacks – all alone in a big crowd of hostile, cranked-up geeks in a mood to stomp somebody – but it soon became evident that these Nixon Youth people weren't ready for that kind of madness.

Our first clash erupted when I looked up from where I was sitting on the floor against a wall in the back of the room and saw Ron Rosenbaum from the *Village Voice* coming at me in a knot of shouting Nixon Youth wranglers. 'No press allowed!" they were screaming. "Get out of here! You can't stay!"

They had nailed Rosenbaum at the door – but, instead of turning back and giving up, he plunged into the crowded room and made a beeline for the back wall, where he'd already spotted me sitting in peaceful anonymity. By the time he reached me he was gasping for breath and about six fraternity/jock types were clawing at his arms. "They're trying to throw me out!" he shouted.

I looked up and shuddered, knowing my cover was blown. Within seconds, they were screaming at me, too. "You crazy bastard," I shouted at Rosenbaum. "You *fingered* me! Look what you've done!"

"No press!" they were shouting. "OUT! Both of you!"

I stood up quickly and put my back to the wall, still cursing Rosenbaum. "That's right!" I yelled. "Get that bastard out of here! No press allowed!"

Rosenbaum stared at me. There was shock and repugnance in his eyes – as if he had just recognized me as a lineal descendant of Judas Iscariot. As they muscled him away, I began explaining to my accusers that I was really more of a political observer than a journalist. "Have *you* run for office?" I snapped at one of them. "No! I thought not, goddamnit! You don't have the look of a man who's been to the well. I can see it in your face!"

He was taken aback by this charge. His mouth flapped for a few seconds, then he blurted out: "What about *you?* What office did *you* run for?"

I smiled gently. "Sheriff, my friend. I ran for Sheriff, out in Colorado – and I lost by just a hair. Because the *liberals* put the screws to me! Right! Are you surprised?"

He was definitely off balance.

That's why I came here as an *observer*," I continued. "I wanted to see what it was like on the inside of a *winning* campaign."

It was just about then that somebody noticed my "press" tag was attached to my shirt by a blue and white McGOVERN button. I'd been wearing it for three days, provoking occasional rude comments from hotheads on the convention floor and in various hotel lobbies – but this was the first time I'd felt called upon to explain myself. It was, after all, the only visible McGOVERN button in Miami Beach that week – in Flamingo Park or anywhere else – and now I was trying to join a spontaneous Nixon Youth demonstration that was about to spill out onto the floor of the very convention that had just nominated Richard Nixon for re-election, against McGovern.

They seemed to feel I was mocking their efforts in some way

. . . and at that point the argument became so complex and disjointed that I can't possibly run it all down here. It is enough, for now, to say that we finally compromised: if I refused to leave without violence, then I was damn well going to have to carry a sign in the spontaneous demonstration – and also wear a plastic red, white, and blue Nixon hat. They never came right out and said it, but I could see they were uncomfortable at the prospect of all three network TV cameras looking down on their spontaneous Nixon Youth demonstration and zeroing in – for their own perverse reasons – on a weird-looking, 35-year-old speed freak with half his hair burned off from overindulgence, wearing a big blue McGOVERN button on his chest, carrying a tall cup of "Old Milwaukee" and shaking his fist at John Chancellor up in the NBC booth – screaming: "You dirty bastard! You'll *pay* for this, by God! We'll rip your goddamn teeth out! KILL! KILL! Your number just came up, you communist son of a bitch!"

I politely dismissed all suggestions that I remove my McGOVERN button, but I agreed to carry a sign and wear a plastic hat like everybody else. "Don't worry," I assured them. "You'll be proud of me. There's a lot of bad blood between me and John Chancellor. He put acid in my drink last month at the Democratic Convention, then he tried to humiliate me in public."

"Acid? Golly, that's terrible! What kind of acid?"

"It felt like Sunshine," I said.

"Sunshine?"

"Yeah. He denied it, of course – But hell, he *always* denies it."

"Why?" a girl asked.

"Would *you* admit a thing like that?"

She shook her head emphatically. "But I wouldn't do it either," she said. "You could *kill* somebody by making them drink acid – why would he want to kill *you*?"

I shrugged, "Who knows? He eats a lot of it himself." I paused, sensing confusion . . . "Actually I doubt if he really wanted to kill me. It was a hell of a dose, but not *that* strong." I smiled. "All I remember is the first rush: It came up my spine like nine tarantulas . . . drilled me right to the bar stool for two hours; I couldn't speak, couldn't even blink my eyes."

"Boy, what kind of acid does that?" somebody asked.

"Sunshine," I said. "Every time."

By now several others had picked up on the conversation. A bright-looking kid in a blue gabardine suit interrupted: "Sunshine acid? Are you talking about LSD?"

"Right," I said.

Now the others understood. A few laughed, but others muttered darkly, "You mean John Chancellor goes around putting LSD in people's drinks? He takes it himself? . . . He's a dope addict . . . ?"

"Golly," said the girl. "That explains a lot, doesn't it?"

By this time I was having a hard time keeping a straight face. These poor, ignorant young waterheads. Would they pass this weird revelation on to their parents when they got back home to Middletown, Shaker Heights, and Orange County? Probably so, I thought. And then their parents would write letters to NBC, saying they'd learned from reliable sources that Chancellor was addicted to LSD-25 – supplied to him in great quantities, no doubt, by Communist agents – and demanding that he be jerked off the air immediately and locked up.

I was tempted to start babbling crazily about Walter Cronkite: that he was heavy into the white slavery trade – sending agents to South Vietnam to adopt orphan girls, then shipping them back to his farm in Quebec to be lobotomized and sold into brothels up and down the Eastern seaboard . . .

But before I could get into this one, the men in the red hats began shouting that the magic moment was on us. The Ready Room crackled with tension; we were into the countdown. They divided us into four groups of about five hundred each and gave the final instructions. We were to rush onto the floor and begin chanting, cheering, waving our signs at the TV cameras, and generally whooping it up. Every other person was given a big garbage bag full of twenty-five or thirty helium balloons, which they were instructed to release just as soon as we reached the floor. Our entrance was timed precisely to coincide with the release of the thousands of non-helium balloons from the huge cages attached to the ceiling of the hall . . . so that our balloons would be *rising* while the others were *falling*, creating a sense of mass euphoria and perhaps even weightlessness for the prime-time TV audience.

DRAINED CRYSTALS

The Observer, 16 September 1973

The antipodean James was TV critic of the London *Observer* between 1972–82, before becoming a fixture on the medium he had once written about. His TV criticism was collected in *Visions before Midnight* and *The Crystal Bucket.*

On *Star Trek* (BBC1) our galaxy got itself invaded from a parallel universe by an alien *Doppelgänger* toting mysterioso weaponry. These bad vibes in the time-warp inspired the line of the week. "Whatever that phenomenon was," piped Kirk's dishy new black lieutenant, "it drained our crystals almost completely. Could mean trouble."

In our house for the past few years it's been a straight swap between two series: if my wife is allowed to watch *Ironside* I'm allowed to watch *Star Trek*, and so, by a bloodless compromise possible only between adults, we get to watch one unspeakable show per week each. (My regular and solitary viewing of *It's a Knock-Out* and *Mission Impossible* counts as professional dedication.)

How, you might ask, can anyone harbour a passion for such a crystal-draining pile of barbiturates as *Star Trek*? The answer, I think, lies in the classical inevitability of its repetitions. As surely as Brünnhilde's big moments are accompanied by a few bars of the Valkyries' ride, Spock will say that the conclusion would appear to be logical, captain. Uhura will turn leggily from her console to transmit information conveying either (a) that all contact with Star Fleet has been lost, or (b) that it has been regained. Chekhov will act badly. Bones ("Jim, it may seem unbelievable, but my readings indicate that this man has . . . *two hearts*") will act extremely badly. Kirk, employing a thespian technique picked up from someone who once worked with somebody who knew Lee Strasberg's sister, will lead a team consisting of Spock and Bones into the *Enterprise*'s transporter room and so on down to the alien planet on which the Federation's will is about to be imposed in the name of freedom.

The planet always turns out to be the same square mile of rocky Californian scrubland long ago overexposed in the Sam Katzman serials: Brick Bradford was there, and Captain Video – not to mention Batman, Superman, Jungle Jim and the Black Commando. I mean like this place has been *worn smooth*, friends. But the futuristic trio flip open their communicators, whip out their phasers, and peer alertly into the hinterland, just as if the whole lay-out were as threateningly pristine as the Seven Cities of Cibola. *Star Trek* has the innocence of belief.

It also has competition. On the home patch, an all-British rival has just started up. Called *Moonbase 3* (BBC1), it's a near-future space opera plainly fated to run as a serial, like *Dr Who*, rather than as a series. In this way it will avoid the anomalies – which I find endearing – that crop up when one self-contained *Star Trek* episode succeeds another. In a given episode of the *Enterprise's* voyages (Its Mission: To Explore Strange New Worlds) the concept of parallel universes will be taken for granted. In the next episode, the possibility will be gravely discussed. Such inconsistencies are not for *Moonbase 3*, which after one instalment has already turned out to possess the standard plot of the bluff new commander setting out to restore the morale of a shattered unit: i.e., *Angels One Five* or *Yangize Incident* plus liquid oxygen.

Moonbases 1 and 2 belong to the United States and the U.S.S.R. Moonbase 3 belongs to Europe, so it looks like ELDO got into orbit after all. Being European, the base's budget is low, but its crew can supply zest and colour when aroused. The ambitious second-in-command, Lebrun, says things like "Zoot" to prove that he is French. The in-house quack, Dr Smith, is a lushly upholstered young lady with a grape-pulp mouth who is surely destined to drain the new commander's crystals, at an early date.

In the revived *Softly*, *Softly* (BBC1), Harry the Hawk leapt back to form by cocking up within the first ten minutes, thereby opening the way for a sequence of pithy sermons from Frank Windsor. The Hawk externalized his frustrations in the usual manner, opening and closing every door in sight. Evans has lost two stone and Snow has now reached the final stage of *angst*-ridden taciturnity, staring at his superiors like Diogenes when Alexander blocked the sun. The dirigible-sized question hanging over the series is whether Barlow will return.

Spy Trap (BBC1) is back, but Commander Anderson has moved on, being replaced by a narrow-eyed wonder-boy called Sullivan, who in the first episode successively penetrated HQ's security, uncovered Commander Ryan's secret, tortured a heavy and ripped off the cap of a ball-point with his teeth.

One of those BBC2 link-men, specially chosen for their inability to get through a typewritten line of the English language without fluffing, announced "another in this series of nothing ventured, nothing win adventures starring noo, nah, George Plimpton."

The male voice-over on the new Make-a-Meal commercial said: "If you're a woman you're a meal-maker for someone." Keep a hand over your crystals, brother: if a women's libber catches you they'll be drained for sure. One of the art directors on the old Vincent Price movie *The Fly* (ITV) bore the name Theobold Holsopple. Beat that.

MISS WOODS PUTS HER FOOT IN IT

The Guardian, 28 November 1973

Filed from Washington during the last days of the reign of President Nixon.

For eighteen minutes and fifteen seconds – it seemed like hours – we listened this morning to an electronic buzz. At first the excited courtroom listened with rapt attention; then, as the noise droned unpleasantly on, people began to fidget. About halfway through, Judge John Sirica looked at his watch. It was an historic courtroom moment and undoubtedly the most unremittingly boring in the history of criminal jurisprudence.

The noise oscillated gently but with no more emotion for the inexpert ear than a soliloquy in a Japanese Noh drama. For the layman it had only one possible significant characteristic: that for the first four minutes or so it was louder and of higher pitch. Then it ascended into not much better than a buzz. Finally, in reprise, it momentarily gained its original volume and tone.

This presented the possibility that there were two noises, not one; two acts of obliteration, not one, committed against the tape recording of President Nixon's conversation with Mr H. R. Haldeman between 11.26 a.m. and 12.45 p.m. on 20 June 1972. Miss Rose Mary Woods, the president's confidential secretary, had testified that she might have been responsible for erasing the tape while speaking on the telephone during transcribing it on 1 October this year, but she cannot recall speaking on the phone for as long as eighteen minutes.

However that may be, the story that she accidentally obliterated the tape was wearing thinner and thinner as the case moved on today. For her to have done so would have required her not only to press the record button in mistake for the stop button when she turned to answer her telephone (which she says she did), but also to keep her foot on the control pedal of the machine for eighteen minutes, fifteen seconds while talking on the telephone and making shorthand notes.

In a scene that had Perry Mason beat she was asked to rehearse the incident on the witness stand. The recorder was in front of her, where it would have been at right angles to her desk. The machine was running. Her imaginary telephone rang at the far left-hand side of her desk.

"Show us what you did," asked prosecuting counsel Jill Vollmer. Her colleague, Richard Ben-Veniste, was positioned behind Miss Woods. She removed her headphones, pressed a button on the machine, turned half in her chair and stretched way to the left for her telephone and – as the lawyers triumphantly spotted – removed her left foot from the control pedal. It was hard to see how she could have done otherwise. It would have been physically uncomfortable, to say the least, to have kept her foot on the pedal. It was a big metal pedal, like the accelerator in a car; it made a loud click every time it was used. Moreover, as had been established yesterday, all that was necessary for her to do in order to stop the playback while answering the telephone was to remove the foot from the control; there was no need to press any buttons at all.

Poor Miss Woods. The Perry Mason trick destroyed her. Perhaps not so much her as her masters at the White House, and above all the man she has called "the boss" for twenty-two years, serving him with unquestioning devotion. For this morning, when the explanation offered for the obliterated tape (whatever Miss Woods's role in the matter) became finally and totally implausible, the atmosphere in the courtroom heightened and everyone there must have felt that they were attending the trial of President Richard Nixon.

The lawyers of the special Watergate prosecuting force, who are helping to conduct what is supposed to be no more than a fact-finding inquiry concerning the tapes, began to look and sound like prosecutors smelling conviction: Judge Sirica's face registered his disbelief and irritation more openly even than yesterday; and the White House lawyers at the other table revealed their distress with stagey nonchalance. The whole feel of that courtroom this morning was that the future of the president of the United States could be effectively decided before this week is out.

The credibility of the White House position drained away as the long-awaited moment came for the first public performance of one of the celebrated White House tapes. Never was there such a premiere. We were to hear the tail-end of a conversation between Mr Nixon and his ex-second advisor Mr John Ehrlichman. Then we were to hear Mr Ehrlichman leave and Mr Haldeman enter the room. Then we were to hear the noise. Miss Woods, acting as disc jockey, turned on the machine. The tape, the extant portion of the tape, was almost wholly inaudible. It sounded like somebody vacuum-cleaning at a cocktail party. It was a huge, insulting practical joke. People giggled nervously. One reporter said to another: "Is this the bit she erased?" He replied: "No, this is the good part." The first reporter said: "Good God!"

We were listening to one of the tapes the president had made for history. Testimony has been given that the system was of the highest quality, periodically checked. The tape we were hearing was virtually worthless for any purpose.

You could just recognize the president's voice. Occasionally, phrases came through: "Go ahead": "Oh, sure"; "Okay"; "Appreciate it". The clearest moment, just about the only intact sentence audible in the courtroom, was: "I'd like a little of that consommé." But we already knew that the president was going to say something of the kind to the White House steward. We also heard the president whistling.

At least history will know that three days after the Watergate burglary the president whistled and drank consommé.

SIMON WINCHESTER

RATTLE OF A BROKEN MAN

The Guardian, 10 August 1974

The last that we saw of him as president was his limp right hand flapping occasionally like a dying fish, trying to wave a laconic farewell through the bullet-proof glass of the shiny green heli-copter. A few moments before, as he turned at the top of the helicopter's steps, he gave a more typical Nixonian valedictory, his arm crossing his head with the sign of finale that a conductor gives at the finish of the 1812. But the flapping hand we saw through the glass more aptly expressed the utter dejection and humiliation of the man who now passes into the most public kind of obscurity; it was a kind of political and personal death shudder.

At 10.15 a.m. Richard and Patricia Nixon, still technically "President and First Lady", swished away westward in the glittering blue and silver flagship of the US Air Force fleet. One hour and twenty minutes later, when the couple were somewhere over the Mississippi river, near the quintessentially Middle American town of Carbondale, Illinois, a stiff white envelope was taken by Haig to the small office in the White House used by the secretary of state. Dr Kissinger opened the note which read starkly: "Dear Mr Secretary, I hereby resign the office of President of the United States. Sincerely, Richard Nixon." And as Air Force One crossed into the State of Mis-souri, so the thirty-seventh president officially laid down the mantle, and the thirty-eighth, the recently obscure lawyer from Michigan, took over. The manner of the passing may have been exquisitely hurtful for Mr and Mrs Nixon, as they must now be known, but the world, six miles beneath the shiny belly of the great jet, would never know exactly how it felt.

His last hours at the White House must have been agonizing. Official photographs released today show him hugging his weeping daughter Julie in the wake of taking his decision. The press were locked inside the room – the one Mr Nixon had designed specially for their comfort – when he walked the paths to his last dinner at the official mansion last night. We were not allowed to see how terrible he looked.

The telephone calls from his supporters that came in after his television speech can only slightly have mollified the hurt of the baying crowds that gathered on Pennsylvania Avenue as the night wore on. The mob there was huge – 5,000 people, mostly young, many of them drunk, nearly all giggling, laughing, shouting derision at the policemen at the White House. A sign, "under new management", was hung briefly on the mansion fences, before being torn away by the guards.

A slight figure in a pink dress pushed aside the curtains in an upstairs room in the White House to peer out at the crowds, which turned to jeer even louder until the window darkened again. Probably it was Tricia, who is said to be the president's favourite child. The sight outside could not have been a pleasant one for her.

And then this morning, after we had seen the near incredible headlines; in which the *New York Times* looked for once in its life like the *Daily Express* and when the never-to-be-read supplement, in easily disposable sections, had been discarded by the ton, Mr Nixon and his stiffly sad family trooped into the East Room for the final indignity – a bitter, grotesque public farewell to the staff of the Executive Mansion.

If Mr Nixon had been at his best last night, then he was at his worst this morning. Sometimes one wished that his agonized wife would take this wretched, slobbering, spluttering man away by the arm and propel him into some windowless vehicle for transport to obscurity. But Pat Nixon, with Julie and Tricia and their grey-faced husbands beside them, allowed the man to proceed. It would have been worse, perhaps, if they had tried to stop him.

"I remember my old man. They would have called him a common man . . . he was a street car motorman at first . . . my mother" – at this point he sobbed violently, his tears somehow eluding the gravitational pull and remaining shining in his eyes – "a saint. She will have no books written about her." That was the measure of the address – Checkers revisited, only far, far more painful for everyone who had to suffer hearing it.

Once more, there was not a spark of contrition in the man. "Sure, we have done some things wrong in this administration. And the top man always takes the responsibility. And I've never ducked it . . . but no man and no woman came into this administration and left it with more than he came in, no man or woman ever profited at the public expense or the public till. Mistakes, yes. But not for personal gain, ever. You did what you believed in, sometimes right, sometimes wrong."

A viewer at this point breathed "How dare he?"; his staff and cabinet in the East Room, though, looked stony-faced through it all. None of them seeming concerned, but even at the end Mr Nixon was not coming clean as he had this final opportunity to do.

And so, asking for help for President Ford, and thanking the staff for their loyalty, Mr Nixon and his small loyal troupe walked quickly out to the south lawn. Mr and Mrs Ford shook hands with them. Then, without further ceremony, the Nixons went to the helicopter. The blades began to whirl, women in the crowd became immediately more concerned that their skirts stayed put than that the president was leaving, and the lone machine climbed into the grey sky.

It passed over the mudflats of the Potomac river, the Jefferson Memorial to the right, Washington Monument ahead, Lincoln behind, the White House itself below to the left. Twelve minutes later it landed at Andrews Air Force Base, Maryland; five minutes later still, Air Force One was airborne, and Mr Nixon was carried out of Washington for the last time as chief executive. But almost certainly he will be back. Unless President Ford offers immunity, a wealth of trials, to which Mr Nixon could be witness for the accused, are due to open here. Mr Jaworski left open last night the possibility that, for alleged tax frauds and for alleged conspiracy to obstruct justice, Richard Nixon could soon be back in the dock.

Americans are divided on the need for such a final public vengeance; some think that, for the guardian of the public trust, some retribution, over and above giving up that trust, is required. Others say that all should be forgotten and that the "nightmare", as President Ford called it today, should be permitted to conclude. But debate on that issue is the business of next week. For the time being, all one can say is that after 2,027 days and 2,026 nights, Richard Nixon has taken the counsel of his people and has left the city where he was wanted no longer.

SYDNEY H. SCHANBERG

AN AMERICAN REPORTER'S BRIEF BRUSH WITH ARREST AND DEATH

New York Times, 9 May 1975

The Cambodian capital, Phnom Penh, fell to the Khmer Rouge on 17 April 1975. Schanberg served as South-East Asia correspondent for the *New York Times* for the last two years of Cambodia's civil war. His articles about Dith Pran, a Cambodian employed by the *New York Times*, formed the basis for the 1984 film *The Killing Fields*.

Bangkok, Thailand, May 8

Some of the foreigners who stayed behind after the American evacuation of Phnom Penh learned quickly and at first hand that the Communist-led forces were not the happy-go-lucky troops we had seen in the initial stage of the Communist take-over.

I had my first experience with the tough Khmer Rouge troops early in the afternoon of the first day of the take-over.

With Dith Pran, a local employee of the *New York Times*, Jon Swain of the *Sunday Times* of London, Alan Rockoff, a freelance American photographer, and our driver, Sarun, we had gone to look at conditions in the largest civilian hospital, Preah Keth Mealea. Doctors and surgeons, out of fear, had failed to come to work and the wounded were bleeding to death in the corridors.

As we emerged from the operating block at 1 p.m. and started driving toward the front gate, we were confronted by a band of heavily armed troops just then coming into the grounds. They put guns to our heads and, shouting angrily, threatened us with execution. They took everything – cameras, radio, money, typewriters, the car – and ordered us into an armoured personnel carrier, slamming the hatch and rear door shut. We thought we were finished.

But Mr Dith Pran saved our lives, first by getting into the personnel carrier with us and then by talking soothingly to our captors for two and a half hours and finally convincing them that we were not their enemy but merely foreign newsmen covering their victory.

We are still not clear why they were so angry, but we believe it might have been because they were entering the hospital at that time to remove the patients and were startled to find us, for they wanted no foreign witnesses.

At one point they asked if any of us were Americans, and we said no, speaking French all the time and letting Mr Dith Pran translate into Khmer. But if they had looked into the bags they had confiscated, which they did not, they would have found my passport and Mr Rockoff's.

We spent a very frightened half-hour sweating in the baking personnel carrier, during a journey on which two more prisoners were picked up – Cambodians in civilian clothes who were high military officers and who were, if that is possible, even more frightened than we.

Then followed two hours in the open under guard at the northern edge of town while Mr Dith Pran pulled off his miracle negotiation with our captors as we watched giddy soldiers passing with truckloads of looted cloth, wine, liquor, cigarettes and soft drinks, scattering some of the booty to soldiers along the roadside.

We were finally released at 3:30 p.m., but the two Cambodian military men were held. One was praying softly.

GEORGE FRANK

A MEMBER OF THE MANSON GANG TRIES TO KILL PRESIDENT FORD

UPI, 6 September 1975

The place was California. Charles Manson was a psychotic killer whose gang had killed actress Sharon Tate (wife of Roman Polanski) in the "Helter Skelter Murder".

The day was sunny and beautiful, and the tiny woman in red waited with other spectators for President Ford to walk by.

Most of the well-wishers wanted to shake Ford's hand.

The woman in red had a gun.

Lynette Alice Fromme, 27, known as "Squeaky" in the terrorist Charles Manson family to which she belongs, stood quietly behind the spectators on the grounds of the state capitol, eyewitnesses said.

"Oh, what a beautiful day," she told a girl in the crowd, Karen Skelton, 14.

"She looked like a gypsy," Karen said later.

Squeaky wore a long red gown and red turban, and carried a large, red purse. They matched her red hair.

On her forehead was a red "X" carved during the 1971 Los Angeles trial in which Manson and three women followers were convicted of murder.

Squeaky, who had moved to Sacramento in northern California to be closer to the imprisoned Manson, 41, waited patiently for President Ford.

In her purse was a loaded .45 calibre automatic.

The sun beat down. The spectators squirmed in the 90-plus-degree morning heat.

Then, suddenly, the crowd perked up. Ford had emerged from the Senator Hotel and was coming up a sidewalk through the park of the Capitol grounds. Secret Service agents accompanied him.

He stopped to return greetings from the crowd.

The spectators, restrained by a rope, pressed forward to say hello.

He faced to his left and reached out for the extended hands.

"Good morning," he said to the well-wishers, one after the other.

Squeaky made her move.

She lunged forward from the rear of the spectators, splitting them away on both sides.

Now she was only two feet from the President and, said police, aimed the gun at him.

Ford saw the revolver and "the colour went out of his face," said Karen Skelton.

He looked "alarmed, frightened, and he hunched over," said another spectator, Roy Miller, 50.

At that moment Secret Service Agent Larry Buendorf took the action that may have saved the President's life. Risking his own life, he lunged forward and threw himself between Squeaky and Ford.

He wrestled Squeaky to the ground, and he and police disarmed her.

Squeaky screamed, "He's not your servant."

Then she told police, "Easy, guys, don't batter me. The gun didn't go off."

Four or five agents threw themselves around the President and pushed him away from the crowd.

Ford's knees, troubled in the past, buckled in the crush, and he almost stumbled. But he stood up quickly.

"The country is in a mess," shouted Squeaky as officers handcuffed her. "The man is not your President."

Moments later, as a police car drove her away, she had a faint smile on her face and appeared calm.

LETTER FROM
A FAINTHEARTED FEMINIST

The Guardian, 21 January 1981

From the regular correspondence of "Martha" to her younger "sister"-in-arms.

Dear Mary,

Sorry I haven't written for a while, but back here in Persil Country the festive season lasts from 1 November (make plum pudding) to 31 January (lose hope and write husband's thank-you letters). I got some lovely presents. Your useful *Spare Rib Diary*. A book called *The Implications of Urban Women's Image in Early American Literature*. A Marks and Sparks rape alarm. A canvas Backa-Pak so that the baby can come with me wherever I go (a sort of DIY rape alarm). Things I did not get for Christmas: a Janet Reger nightie, a feather boa, a pair of glittery tights.

Looking back, what with "God Rest Ye Merry Gentlemen", "Good King Wenceslas", "Unto Us a Son is Born", "We Three Kings", Father Christmas ho-hoing all over the place and the house full of tired and emotional males, I feel like I'm just tidying up after a marathon stag party. Our Lady popped up now and again but who remembers the words to her songs once they've left school? We learnt them but, then, ours was an all-girl school, in the business of turning out Virgin Mother replicas. If I ever get to heaven, I'll be stuck making manna in the Holy Kitchens and putti-sitting fat, feathered babies quicker than I can say Saint Peter. Josh, on the other hand, will get a celestial club chair and a stiff drink. If God is a woman, why is She so short of thunderbolts?

I went to a fair number of parties dressed up as Wife of Josh but, to tell you the shameful truth, it was my Women's Collective beanfeast that finally broke my nerve. One wouldn't think one could work up a cold sweat about going as oneself to an all-woman party, would one? One can. I had six acute panic attacks about what to wear, for a start. Half my clothes are sackclothes, due to what Josh still calls my menopausal baby (come to me, my menopausal baby) and the other half are ashes, cold embers of the woman I once was. Fashion may well be a tool of women's oppression but having to guess is worse. In the end I went make-up-less in old flared jeans and saw, too late, that Liberation equals Calvin Klein and Lip Gloss or Swanky Modes and Toyah hair but not, repeat not, Conservative Association jumble. Misery brought on tunnel vision, I swooned like a Victorian lady and had to be woman-handled into a taxi home. Quelle fiasco.

That same evening, the blood back in my cheeks, I complained to Josh that I was cooking the 360th meal of 1980 and he said move aside, I'll take over. Coming to, I found myself, family and carry-cot in a taxi driving to a posh restaurant. Very nice, too, but Josh was so smug afterwards that I felt it incumbent upon me, in the name of Wages for Housework, to point out that his solution to the domestic chore-sharing problem had just cost us fifty quid, and if he intended to keep that up, he'd have to apply for funding to the IMF. Bickered for the rest of the evening, Josh wittily intoning his Battle of Britain speech – you can please some of the women all of the time and all of the women . . . but you know the rest, ha ha.

I had hardly recovered from these two blows to the system when Mother arrived to administer her weekly dose of alarm and despondency. How can I *think*, she said eighteen times, of letting my Daughter drive a van, alone, to Spain? Do I *want* her to be raped, mutilated and left for dead in foreign parts? It is my duty to insist that a *man* goes with her. I point out that Jane is a large, tough, twenty-year-old rather more competent than me. Mother and Mother's Husband put together and Mother leaves room in huff. I then had a panic attack about Jane being raped, mutilated and left for dead in foreign parts and insisted she took a man with her. Like the Yorkshire Ripper, for instance, shouted Jane and left room in huff.

Myself, I blame British Rail. Does Sir Peter Parker realise the mayhem caused to family units all over Britain by pound-a-trip Grans intent on injecting overdue guilt into long-unvisited daughters? Josh's Ma trained over, too, apparently to make sure I wouldn't grass on Josh if he turned out to be the Yorkshire Ripper. Ma, I said, what alternative would I have? Even the sacred marriage bonds might snap, given that one's spouse was a mass murderer. Marriage bonds maybe, she said, but I am his Mother. Then she said would I give Ben away, I said what else could I do and she said I could stop his pocket money. She did. Ben, I said, glaring at the stick of celery that is my son, if I hear you've murdered *one more woman*, no sixpence for you next Friday. Well, now they've arrested someone who's got a wife and a mother. Keep your ears pinned back for the feminine connection.

Ben's friend Flanagan stayed most of the holiday. He explained that he had left home because his mother had this new boyfriend. How difficult it must be, I thought, for adolescent boys in the midst of the Oedipal Dilemma to have alien males vying for their love-object's favours. Flanagan said he couldn't stand the way his Mum bullied her boyfriends and now she had chucked them both out because of her women's meetings. You're as bad as the NFers, he told her. I can't help being a boy, can I, any more than if I was black? But you are black, I said, and black is beautiful. Yeah, except I'm white, he said. Flanagan's Dad is white, said Ben, so why shouldn't Flanagan choose? What am I, anyway, a racist or something? With that, they both pulled on jackets covered with swastikas and went out. At times like this, I am so grateful for the baby. Dear thing, he's hardly a boy yet at all.

You probably won't read this letter until mid-January – I read in the papers that your lot had gone to Rome to picket

Nativity Scenes. My goings-on here on the home front must seem very trivial to you. Ah well, we also serve who only stand and whine. – Yours from a hot stove.
Martha

MAX HASTINGS LEADS THE WAY: THE FIRST MAN INTO PORT STANLEY

London Evening Standard, 15 June 1982

The war between Britain and Argentina for the Falklands/Malvinas ended on 14 June 1982, with the surrender of the Argentine forces under General Menendez. It had been a "good war" for the *Evening Standard*'s astute and athletic Max Hastings, who put the cherry on his reputation by becoming the first Briton to enter Port Stanley, the Falklands' capital. Hastings was later the editor of *The Telegraph* and *Evening Standard*.

British forces are in Port Stanley. At 2.45 p.m. British time today [14 June], men of the 2nd Parachute Regiment halted on the outskirts at the end of their magnificent drive on the capital pending negotiations.

There, we sat on the racecourse until, after about twenty minutes I was looking at the road ahead and there seemed to be no movement. I thought, well I'm a civilian so why shouldn't I go and see what's going on because there didn't seem to be much resistance.

So I stripped off all my combat clothes and walked into Stanley in a blue civilian anorak with my hands in the air and my handkerchief in my hand.

The Argentinians made no hostile movement as I went by the apparently undamaged but heavily bunkered Government House.

I sort of grinned at them in the hope that if there were any Argentinian soldiers manning the position they wouldn't shoot at me.

Nobody took any notice so I walked on and after a few minutes

I saw a group of people all looking like civilians a hundred yards ahead and I shouted at them.

I shouted: "Are you British?" and they shouted back: "Yes, are you?" I said "Yes."

They were a group of civilians who had just come out of the civil administration building where they had been told that it looked as if there was going to be a ceasefire.

We chatted for a few moments and then I walked up to the building and I talked to the senior Argentinian colonel who was standing on the steps. He didn't show any evident hostility.

They were obviously pretty depressed. They looked like men who had just lost a war but I talked to them for a few moments and I said: "Are you prepared to surrender West Falkland as well as East?"

The colonel said: "Well, maybe, but you must wait until four o'clock when General Menendez meets your general."

I said: "May I go into the town and talk to civilians?" He said: "Yes," so I started to walk down the main street past Falklanders who were all standing outside their houses.

They all shouted and cheered and the first person I ran into was the Catholic priest, Monsignor Daniel Spraggon, who said: "My God, it's marvellous to see you."

That wasn't directed at me personally but it was the first communication he had had with the British forces.

I walked on and there were hundreds, maybe thousands, of Argentinian troops milling around, marching in columns through the streets, some of them clutching very badly wounded men and looking completely like an army in defeat with blankets wrapped around themselves.

There were bits of weapons and equipment all over the place and they were all moving to central collection points before the surrender or ceasefire.

Eventually I reached the famous Falklands hotel, the Upland Goose. We had been dreaming for about three months about walking into the Upland Goose and having a drink, and I walked in and again it was marvellous that they all clapped and cheered.

They offered me gin on the assumption that this is the traditional drink of British journalists, but I asked if they could make it whisky instead and I gratefully raised my glass to them all.

Owner of the Upland Goose, Desmond King said: "We never

doubted for a moment that the British would turn up. We have just been waiting for the moment for everybody to come."

The last few days had been the worst, he said, because Argentinian guns had been operating from among the houses of Stanley and they had heard this terrific, continuous battle going on in the hills.

They were afraid that it was going to end up with a house-to-house fight in Stanley itself. The previous night when I had been with the Paras we were getting a lot of shell fire coming in on us and eventually we sorted out the coordinates from which it was firing. Our observation officer tried to call down to fire on the enemy batteries and the word came back that you could not fire on them because they are in the middle of Stanley.

So the battalion simply had to take it and suffer some casualties.

Anyway, there we were in the middle of the Upland Goose with about twenty or thirty delighted civilians who said that the Argentinians hadn't done anything appalling. It depends what one means by appalling, but they hadn't shot anybody or hung anybody up by their thumbs or whatever.

They had looted a lot of houses that they had taken over. At times they got very nervous and started pushing people around with submachine guns in their backs and the atmosphere had been pretty unpleasant.

Robin Pitaleyn described how he had been under house arrest in the hotel for six weeks, since he made contact by radio with the *Hermes*. He dismissed criticism of the Falkland Island Company representatives who had sold goods to the occupiers.

"We were all selling stuff," he said. "You had a simple choice – either you sold it or they took it. I rented my house to their air force people. They said – either you take rent or we take the house. What would you have done?"

Adrian Monk described how he had been compulsorily evicted from his own house to make way for Argentinian soldiers who had then totally looted it. There appears to have been widespread looting in all the houses of Stanley to which the Argentinians had access.

The houses on the outskirts of the town in which the Argentinians had been living were an appalling mess full of everything from human excrement all over the place to just property lying all over the place where soldiers had ransacked through it. But they were all alive and they all had plenty of food and plenty to drink and they were all in tremendous spirits.

It wasn't in the least like being abroad. One talks about the Falklanders and yet it was as if one had liberated a hotel in the middle of Surrey or Kent or somewhere.

It was an extraordinary feeling just sitting there with all these girls and cheerful middle-age men and everybody chatting in the way they might chat at a suburban golf club after something like this had happened.

I think everybody did feel a tremendous sense of exhilaration and achievement. I think the Paras through all their tiredness knew they had won a tremendous battle.

It was the Paras' hour and, after their heavy losses and Goose Green and some of the fierce battles they had fought, they had made it all the way to Stanley and they were enjoying every moment of their triumph.

A question that has to be answered is how the Argentinian troops managed to maintain their supplies of food and ammunition.

I think it's one of the most remarkable things. I think intelligence hasn't been one of our strong points throughout the campaign.

Even our commanders and people in London agree that we have misjudged the Argentinians at several critical points in the campaign.

Our soldiers have been saying in the last couple of days how astonished they were when they overran enemy positions. We have been hearing a great deal about how short of food and ammunition they were supposed to be but whatever else they lacked it certainly was not either of those.

They had hundreds of rounds of ammunition, masses of weapons and plenty of food.

The civilians told me they had been running Hercules on to the runway at Port Stanley despite all our efforts with Naval gunnery, with Vulcans, with Harriers up to and including last night and, above all, at the beginning of May they ran a very big container ship called the *Formosa* through the blockade and got her back to Buenos Aires again afterwards. She delivered an enormous consignment of ammunition which really relieved the

Argentinians' serious problems on that front for the rest of the campaign.

I think in that sense we have been incredibly lucky. The British forces have been incredibly lucky.

Considering the amount of stuff the Argentinians got in, we have done incredibly well in being able to smash them when they certainly had the ammunition and equipment left to keep fighting for a long time.

So why did they surrender? I think their soldiers had simply decided that they had had enough. Nobody likes being shelled and even well-trained troops find it an ordeal.

Even the Paras freely admit that it's very, very unpleasant being heavily shelled.

The last two nights, the Argentinian positions had been enormously heavily shelled by our guns. They gave them a tremendous pounding and when an Army starts to crumble and collapse it's very, very difficult to stop it.

I think that the Argentinian generals simply had to recognize that their men no longer had the will to carry on the fight.

This story of the fall of Port Stanley begins last night, when men of the Guards and the Gurkhas and the Parachute Regiment launched a major attack supported by an overwhelming British bombardment on the last line of enemy, positions on the high ground above the capital.

Three civilians died in British counter-battery fire the night before last, as far as we know the only civilian casualties of the war. Mrs Doreen Burns, Mrs Sue Whitney and 82-year-old Mrs Mary Godwin were all sheltering together in a house hit by a single shell. Altogether only four or five houses in Stanley have been seriously damaged in the battle.

At first light the Paras were preparing to renew their attack in a few hours after seizing all their objectives on Wireless Ridge under fierce shell and mortar fire. Suddenly, word came that enemy troops could be seen fleeing for their lives in all directions around Port Stanley. They had evidently had enough. The decision was taken to press on immediately to complete their collapse.

Spearheaded by a company of the Parachute Regiment commanded by Major Dare Farrar-Hockley, son of the regiment's colonel, British forces began a headlong dash down the rocky hills for the honour of being first into Stanley.

I marched at breakneck speed with Major Farrar-Hockley through the ruins of the former Royal Marine base at Moody Brook, then past the smoking remains of buildings and strongpoints destroyed by our shelling and bombing.

Our route was littered with the debris of the enemy's utter defeat.

We were already past the first houses of the town, indeed up to the War Memorial beside the sea, when the order came through to halt pending negotiations and to fire only in self-defence.

The men, desperately tired after three nights without sleep, exulted like schoolboys in this great moment of victory.

The Parachute Regiment officer with whom I was walking had been delighted with the prospect that his men who had fought so hard all through this campaign were going to be the first British troops into Stanley. But they were heart-broken when, just as we reached the racecourse the order came to halt.

Major Farrar-Hockley ordered off helmets, on red berets. Some men showed their sadness for those who hadn't made it all the way, who had died even during the last night of bitter fighting.

The Regiment moved on to the racecourse and they tore down the Argentinian flag flying from the flagpole. Afterwards they posed for a group photograph . . . exhausted, unshaven but exhilarated at being alive and having survived a very, very bitter struggle.

After half an hour with the civilians I began to walk back to the British lines. Scores of enemy were still moving through the town, many assisting badly wounded comrades, all looking at the end of their tether.

Damaged enemy helicopters were parked everywhere among the houses and on the racecourse. Argentine officers still looked clean and soldierly, but they made no pretence of having any interest in continuing the struggle.

Each one spoke only of "four o'clock", the magic moment at which General Moore was scheduled to meet General Menendez and the war presumably come to a halt.

Back in the British lines, Union Jacks had been hoisted and Brigadier Julian Thompson and many of his senior officers had hastened to the scene to be on hand for the entry into the capital.

Men asked eagerly about the centre of Stanley as if it was on the other side of the moon.

By tomorrow, I imagine, when everyone has seen what little there is of this little provincial town to be seen, we shall all be asking ourselves why so many brave men had to die because a whimsical dictator, in a land of which we knew so little, determined that his nation had at all costs to possess it.

ROBERT FISK

"IT WAS THE CHRISTIANS": MASSACRE AT CHATILA REFUGEE CAMP

The Times, 20 September 1982

After the Israeli army invaded South Lebanon in June 1982, PLO (Palestine Liberation Organization) fighters were evacuated to Syria. Many Palestinian refugees and non-combatants, however, remained behind in their Lebanese camps, which passed into the control of the local Christian militia.

They were everywhere, in the road, in laneways, in backyards and broken rooms, beneath crumpled masonry and across the top of garbage tips. The murderers – the Christian militiamen whom Israel had let into the camp to "flush out terrorists" fourteen hours before – had only just left. In some cases the blood was still wet on the ground. When we had seen a hundred bodies, we stopped counting.

Even twenty-four hours after the massacre of the Palestinians at Chatila had ended, no one was sure how many had been killed there. Down every alleyway there were corpses – women, young men, babies and grandparents – lying together in lazy and terrible profusion where they had been knifed or machine-gunned to death. Each corridor through the rubble produced more bodies. The patients at a Palestine hospital simply disappeared after gunmen ordered the doctors to leave. There were signs of hastily dug mass graves. Perhaps a thousand people were butchered here, perhaps half that number again.

The full story of what happened in Chatila on Friday night and Saturday morning may never be known, for most of the witnesses are either dead or would never wish to reveal their guilt.

What is quite certain is that at six o'clock on Friday night, truckloads of gunmen in the uniform – and wearing the badges – of the right-wing Christian Phalange militia and Major Saad Haddad's renegade army from Southern Lebanon were seen by reporters entering the southern gate of the camp.

There were bonfires inside and the sound of heavy gunfire. Israeli troops and armour were standing round the perimeter of the camp and made no attempt to stop the gunmen – who have been their allies since their invasion of Lebanon – going in.

A spokesman for the Israeli foreign ministry was to say later that the militias had been sent into Chatila to hunt down some of the 2000 Palestinian "terrorists" whom the Israelis alleged were still in the camp. Correspondents were forbidden to enter.

What we found inside the camps at ten o'clock next morning did not quite beggar description, although it would perhaps be easier to retell in a work of fiction or in the cold prose of a medical report.

But the details should be told for – this being Lebanon – the facts will change over the coming weeks as militias and armies and governments blame each other for the horrors committed upon the Palestinian civilians.

Just inside the southern gates of the camp, there used to be a number of single-storey concrete-walled houses. When we walked across the muddy entrance of Chatila, we found that these buildings had all been dynamited to the ground. There were cartridge cases across the main road and clouds of flies swarmed across the rubble. Down a laneway to our right, not more than fifty yards from the entrance, there lay a pile of corpses.

There were more than a dozen of them, young men whose arms and legs had become entangled with each other in the agony of death. All had been shot at point-blank range through the right or left cheek, the bullet tearing away a line of flesh up to the ear and entering the brain. Some had vivid crimson scars down the left side of their throats. One had been castrated. Their eyes were open, and the flies had only begun to gather. The youngest was perhaps only twelve or thirteen years old.

On the other side of the main road, up a track through the rubble, we found the bodies of five women and several children. The women were middle-aged, and their corpses lay draped over a pile of rubble. One lay on her back, her dress torn open, and the head of a little girl emèrging from behind her. The girl had short, dark curly hair and her eyes were staring at us and there was a frown on her face. She was dead.

Another child lay on the roadway like a discarded flower, her white dress stained with mud and dust. She could have been no more than three years old. The back of her head had been blown away by a bullet fired into her brain. One of the women also held a tiny baby to her body. The bullet that had passed through her breast had killed the baby too.

To the right of us there was what appeared to be a small barricade of concrete and mud. But as we approached it we found a human elbow visible on the surface. A large stone turned out to be part of a torso. It was as if the bodies had been bulldozed to the side of the laneway, as indeed they had. A bulldozer – its driver's seat empty – stood guiltily just down the road.

Beyond this rampart of earth and bodies there was a pile of what might have been sacks in front of a low redstone wall. We had to cross the barricade to reach it and tried hard not to step on the bodies buried beneath.

Below the low wall a line of young men and boys lay prostrated. They had been shot in the back against the wall in a ritual execution, and they lay, at once pathetic and terrible, where they had fallen. The execution wall and its huddle of corpses was somehow reminiscent of something seen before, and only afterwards did we realize how similar it all was to those old photographs of executions in Occupied Europe during the Second World War. There may have been twelve or twenty bodies there. Some lay beneath others . . .

It was always the same. I found a small undamaged house with a brown metal gate leading to a small courtyard. Something instinctive made me push it open. The murderers had just left. On the ground there lay a young woman. She lay on her back as if she was sunbathing in the heat and the blood running from her back was still wet. She lay, feet together, arms outspread, as if she had seen her saviour in her last moments. Her face was peaceful, eyes closed, almost like a madonna. Only the small hole in her chest and the stain across the yard told of her death . . .

There had been fighting inside the camp. The road was slippery with cartridge cases and ammunition clips near the

Sabra mosque and some of the equipment was of the Soviet type used by the Palestinians.

There have clearly been guerrillas here. In the middle of this part of the road, however, there lay – incredibly – a perfectly carved scale-model wooden Kalashnikov rifle, its barrel snapped in two. It had been a toy . . .

Across Chatila came the disembodied voice of an Israeli officer broadcasting through a Tannoy from atop an armoured personnel carrier. "Stay off the streets," he shouted. "We are only looking for terrorists. Stay off the streets. We will shoot."

An hour later, at Galerie Semaan – far from Chatila – someone did open fire at the soldiers and I threw myself into a ditch beside an Israeli Major. The Israelis fired shoals of bullets into a ruined building beside the road, blowing pieces of it into the air like confetti. The Major and I lay huddled in our ditch for fifteen minutes. He asked about Chatila and I told him all I had seen.

Then he said, "I tell you this. The Haddad men were supposed to go in with us. We had to shoot two of them yesterday. We killed one and wounded another. Two more we took away. They were doing a bad thing. That is all I will tell you." Was this at Chatila? I asked. Had he been there himself? He would say no more.

Then his young radio operator, who had been lying behind us in the mud, crawled up next to me. He was a young man. He pointed to his chest. "We Israelis don't do that sort of thing," he said. "It was the Christians."

A YANKEE IN OUTER MONGOLIA

The Observer, 14 November 1982

"Rowan berries in August mean a hard winter," said the literary critic, as he showed me the view from the Kremlin terrace. "But after the hard winter," I said, sententious as Mao, "there will come the spring." He nodded, "How true!", as we pondered the insignificance of what neither had said.

The critic asked, "Have you read 'Gorky Park'?" I said that I had not because I have made it a rule only to read novels by Nobel Prize winners. That way one will never read a bad book.

As we chatted, two Russian soldiers walked by us. One was in uniform; the other wore blue jeans and a T-shirt emblazoned with the words "The United States Military Academy, West Point". The literary critic smiled, "Could an American soldier wear a Kremlin T-shirt?" I explained to him, patiently I hope, the difference between the free and the unfree world. Abashed, he changed the subject: where was I going next? When I said, "Ulan Bator," he laughed. When I wanted to know what was so funny, he said, "I thought you said you were going to Ulan Bator." When I told him that that was exactly where I was going, to the capital of the Mongolian People's Republic (sometimes known as Outer Mongolia), he looked very grave indeed.

At midnight the plane leaves Moscow for Ulan Bator, with stops at Omsk and Irkutsk (in Siberia). The trip takes 10 hours; there is a five-hour time difference between Moscow and Ulan Bator – UB to us fans. Moscow Aeroflot planes have a tendency to be on time; but the ceilings are too low for claustrophobes and there is a curious smell of sour cream throughout the aircraft. Contrary to legend, the stewardesses are agreeable, at least on the Siberian run.

Our little group was being hurtled through the Siberian skies
to a part of Outer Mongolia where no white – or for that matter
black – westerner had ever been before – or as one of our men at
the American embassy put it: "You will be the first American
ever to set foot in that part of the Gobi desert." When I suggested
that I might destabilize the Mongolian government while I was
there, one of our men was slightly rattled. "Actually," he said,
"no American has ever been there because there isn't anything
there." My fierce patriotism was seriously tried by this insou-
ciance. "Then why," I asked, "am I going?" He said he hadn't a
clue. Why was I going?

It all came back to me on the night flight to Ulan Bator. The
World Wildlife Fund has taken to sending writers around the
world to record places where the ecology is out of joint. My task
was a bit the reverse. I was to report on the national park that the
Mongolian government is creating in the Gobi in order to keep
pristine the environment so that flora and fauna can proliferate in
a perfect balance with the environment.

As I stared out of the porthole window at my own reflection
(or was it Graham Greene's? – the vodka bottle seemed
familiar) – my mind was awhirl with the intense briefings
that I had been submitted to. For instance, is the People's
Republic of Mongolia part of the Soviet Union? No. It is an
independent socialist nation, grateful for the "disinterested"
aid that it gets from the other socialist nations. When did it
come into being? Sixty years ago when the Chinese were
ejected and their puppet, the Living Buddha, was shorn of
his powers and the 28-year-old Damdiny Sükh known as Ulan
Bator ("Red Hero" in Mongolian) took charge of the state,
with disinterested Soviet aid.

The people were nomadic. Every now and then, in an offhand
way, they'd conquer the world. Genghis Khan ruled from the
Danube to the Pacific Ocean while some 1,200 years ago, according to one account, Mongol tribes crossed from Asia to North
America via the Bering Sea, making the Western hemisphere a
sort of Mongol colony.

In 60 years, an illiterate population has become totally literate;
life expectancies have increased; industries and mining have
taken the place of the old nomadic way of life; and there is a
boom in population. "Sixty per cent of the population," said

Boris Petrovich, "is under 16 years of age." Then he asked me, changing the subject, "Should I buy Lauren Bacall's book?"

Although Mongolia smells of mutton fat, the Mongols smell not at all, even though the Russians go on about the great trouble they have getting them to bathe. Men and women are equally handsome: tall, narrow-waisted, with strong white teeth. Some wear the national tunic with sash and boots; others wear the international uniform of blue jeans. "Why," I asked one of our Mongolian colleagues, "are there no bald men here?" He was startled by the question. "The old men shave their heads," he said as if this was an answer. Yet there are no bald men to be seen anywhere. Our group came to the conclusion that over the millennia bald babies were exposed at birth.

The next day there was rain in the Gobi. Something unheard of, we were told. In fact, there had been a flood a few days before and many people were said to have been drowned. Due to bad weather, the plane would not take us to the encampment. So we set out on a grey afternoon in jeeps and Land-Rovers. There is no road, only a more or less agreed-upon trail.

As we left Altai, we saw a bit of the town that we were not allowed to see earlier that morning, where real-life Mongols live in what the Russians call "yurtas" and the owners call "gers": round tents, ingeniously made of felt, with a removable flap across the top to let out smoke. In winter the fire is lit in the morning for cooking; then it goes out until sundown, when it is lit again for the evening meal. Apparently, the yurtas retain warmth in winter; are cool in summer. At Altai, every hundred or so yurtas are surrounded by wooden fences, "to hold back the drifts of snow in winter," said a Russian or, "to keep them in their particular collective," said a cynical non-Russian. Whatever, the wooden fences have curious binary devices on them: "King's ring" and "Queen's ring," I was told by a Mongol; and no more.

Every time we were close to penetrating one of the enclosures, a policeman would indicate that we should go back to the hotel. Meanwhile, the children would gather around until we took a picture; then they would shriek "nyet" and scamper off, only to return a moment later, with many giggles. The older people quite liked being photographed, particularly the men on their ponies whose faces – the ponies' – are out of prehistory, pendulous-lipped with sly, slanted eye. In costume, women wear boots; out of costume, they wear high heels as they stride over the dusty gravelled plain, simulating the camel's gait.

We are in a jeep, lurching over rough terrain. The driver is young, wears a denim jacket, grins as he crashes over boulders. Picture now a grey-streaked sky. In the distance a dun-coloured mountain range, smooth and rounded the way old earth is. We are not yet in the Gobi proper. There is water. Herds of yaks and camels cross the horizon. But once past this watered plain, the Gobi desert begins – only it is not a proper desert. Sand is the exception not the rule. Black and brown gravel is strewn across the plain. Occasional white salt-slicks vary the monotony. All sorts of shy plants grow after a rain or near one of the rare springs. Actually, there is water under a lot of the Gobi; in some places, only a few feet beneath the surface. For those who missed out on the journeys to the moon, the Gobi is the next best thing.

On a high hill with dark mountains behind, the Gobi stretches as far as anyone could wish, the flatness broken by the odd mountain, set island-like in the surrounding gravel. I got out of the jeep to commune with the silence. The driver started to pluck at small dark green clumps of what turned out to be chives. We ate chives and looked at the view and I proceeded to exercise the historical imagination and conjured up Genghis Khan on that famous day when he set his standard of nine yak-tails high atop Gupta, and the Golden Horde began its conquest of Europe.

"Hey," I heard the Americanized voice of Boris Petrovich, "did any of you guys see 'The Little Foxes' with Elizabeth Taylor?"

We stopped at an oasis – a bright strip of ragged green in the dark shining gravel. Water bubbles up from the earth and makes a deep narrow stream down a low hill to a fenced-in place where a Mongol grows vegetables for the camp. The water is cool and pure and the Mongols with us stare at it for a time and smile; then they lie down on their bellies and drink deeply. We all do. In fact, it is hard to get enough water in Gobi. Is this psychological or physiological? The Mongol gardener showed me his plantation. "The melons don't grow very large," he apologized, holding up a golfball of a melon. "It is Gobi, you see." I tried to explain to him that if he were to weed his patch, the vegetables would grow larger, but in that lunar landscape I suspect that the weeds are as much a delight to him as the melons.

At the deserted village, each jeep took a different route towards the dark mountains in the distance. En route, the jeep that I was travelling in broke down four times. Long after the others had arrived at camp, our group was comfortably seated on a malachite-green rock, sipping whisky from the bottle and watching the sun pull itself together for a Gobi Special Sunset, never to be forgotten. For once, Mother Nature was the soul of discreet good taste. Particularly the northern sky, where clouds like so many plumes of Navarre had been dipped in the most subtle shade of Dubarry grey while the pale orange of the southern sky did not cloy. True, there was a *pink* after-glow in the east. But then perfection has never been Mother Nature's bag.

We were told that close to camp there is a famous watering hole, where, at sundown, the snow leopard lies down, as it were, with the wild ass. But we had missed sundown. Nevertheless, ever game, our party walked half-way to the hole before settling among rocks on a ridge to fortify ourselves with alien spirits against the black desert night that had fallen with a crash about us. As we drank, we were joined by a large friendly goat. Overhead, the stars shone dully: rain clouds were interfering with the Gobi's usual sure-fire light show. I found the Dipper; it was in the wrong place. There was a sharp difference of agreement on the position of Orion's Belt. Shooting stars made me think, comfortably, of war. I showed Boris Petrovich what looked to be one of the Great Republic's newest satellites. "Keeping watch over the Soviet Union," I said. "Unless," he said, "it is one of our missiles on its way to Washington. But, seriously," he added, "don't you agree that Elizabeth Taylor was a first-rate *movie* actress? You know, like Susan Hayward."

First light seized us from our pup-tents where we had slept upon the desert floor, inhaling the dust of millennia. As I prepared for a new day of adventure, sinuses aflame, there was a terrible cry; then a sob; a gasp – silence. Our friend of the evening before, the goat, was now to be our dinner.

We checked out the watering hole, which turned out to be a muddy place in the rocks: there were no signs of beasts. Again, we were on the move; this time south easterly toward the Mount Mother system. The heat was intense. We glimpsed a wild ass, wildly running up ahead of us. Some gazelles skittered in the distance. The countryside was almost always horizontal but never pleasingly flat. To drive over such terrain is like riding a Wild West bronco.

Halfway up the red mountain, we made camp at the mouth of a ravine lined with huge smooth red rocks – glacial? – remains of a sea that had long since gone away? No geologist was at hand to tell us but in the heights above the ravine there were the Seven Cauldrons of Khatan Khairkhan where, amongst saxaul groves and elm trees, the waters have made seven rock basins in which most of our group disported themselves. The author, winded halfway up, returned to camp and read Mme de La Fayette's "La Princesse de Clèves".

That night our friend the goat was served in the famous Mongolian hot pot. Red-hot rocks are dropped into metal pots containing whatever animal has been sacrificed to man's need. The result is baked to a T. As usual, I ate tomatoes, cucumbers and bread. We drank to the Golden Horde, now divided in three parts: Outer Mongolia, which is autonomous, thanks to the "disinterested" Soviet Union's presence; Inner Mongolia, which is part of China and filling up with highly interested Chinese; and Siberia, which contains a large Mongolian population. Since functioning monasteries are not allowed in China or Siberia, practising Buddhists come to Ulan Bator where there is a large school, a lamasary, and the Living Buddha – although this particular avatar is not the result of the usual search for the exact incarnation as in ancient times. He was simply selected to carry on.

Even rarer than a functioning lamasary in Mongolia is the Przewalski horse. They exist in zoos around the world but whether or not they are still to be found in Gobi is a subject of much discussion. Some think that there are a few in the Chinese part of the Gobi; some think that they are extinct. In any case, the Great Gobi National Park plans to reintroduce – from the zoos – the Przewalski horse to its original habitat. We drank to the Przewalski horse. We drank to the plane that was to pick us up the next morning when we returned to base. "Would it really be there?" I asked. "No problem."

At dawn we lurched across the desert beneath a lowering sky. At Tsogt, there was no plane. "No problem." We would drive four or five hours to Altai. Along the way we saw the marks that our tyres had made on the way down. "In Gobi, tracks may last 50 years," one of the Russians said.

At the Altai airport low-level anxiety went swiftly to high: the plane for Ulan Bator might not take off. Bad weather. The Deputy Minister of Forestry made a ministerial scene and the plane left on time. There was not a cloud on the route. We arrived at dusk. The road from the airport to the city passes beneath not one but two huge painted arches. From the second arch, Ulan Bator in its plain circled by mountains looks very large indeed. Four hundred thousand people live and have their being beneath a comforting industrial smog. As well as the usual fenced-off yurtas, there are high-rise apartment houses, an opera house, a movie palace, functioning street-lamps and rather more neon than one sees in, say, Rome. Although our mood was gala as we settled in at the Ulan Bator Hotel, low-level anxiety never ceased entirely to hum. Would the visas for the Soviet Union be ready in time? Had the plane reservations for Moscow and the West been confirmed? Would we get back the passports that we had surrendered upon arrival?

The next day, our questions all answered with "No problem", we saw the sights of Ulan Bator. A museum with a room devoted to oddly-shaped dinosaur eggs, not to mention the skeletons of the dinosaurs that had laid them. Every public place was crowded. A convention of Mongol experts was in town; there was also a delegation of Buddhists, paying their respects to the Living Buddha who would be, his secretary told me, too busy with the faithful to receive us that day. Undaunted, we made our way to the Buddhist enclosure where we found several temples packed with aged priests and youthful acolytes with shaved heads. As the priests read aloud from strips of paper on which are printed Sanskrit and Tibetan texts, their voices blend together like so many bees in a hive while incense makes blue the air and bells tinkle at odd intervals to punctuate the still-living texts. In a golden robe, the Living Buddha sat on a dais. As the faithful circled him in an unending stream, he maintained a costive frown. Outside, aged costumed Mongols of both sexes sat about the enclosure, at a millennium's remove from cement-block and Aeroflot

Your man in Ulan Bator, James Paterson, received us at the British Embassy. Outside, a suspicious policeman stands guard with a walkie-talkie, keeping close watch not only on the ambassador and his visitors but on the various Mongols who pause in front of the embassy to look at the colour photographs, under glass, of the wedding of the Prince and Princess of Wales. The Mongols would study the pictures carefully; and then, suddenly, smile beatifically. How very like, I could practically hear them say to themselves, our own imperial family – the Khans of yesteryear!

At Moscow airport on our way home Boris Petrovich made a small speech about the necessity of good Soviet-American relations, the importance of world peace, the necessity of world co-operation on environmental matters. Then he lowered his voice. "I have a question to ask you." He looked about to see if we were being overheard. Thus, I thought to myself, Philby was recruited. Swiftly, I made my decision. If I were to sell out the Free World, I must be well-paid. I would want a dacha on the Baltic, near Riga. I would . . . "How tall," asked Boris Petrovich, "is Paul Newman, really?"

THE WORLD ACCORDING TO SPIELBERG

The Observer, 21 November 1982

Steven Spielberg's films have grossed approximately $1,500 million. He is 34, and well on his way to becoming the most effective popular artist of all time . . . What's he got? How do you do it? Can *I* have some?

"Super-intensity" is Spielberg's word for what he comes up with on the screen. His films beam down on an emotion and then subject it to two hours of muscular titillation. In "Jaws" ($410 million) the emotion was terror; in "Close Encounters" ($250 million) it was wonder; in "Raiders of the Lost Ark" ($310 million) it was exhilaration; in "Poltergeist" ($80 million and climbing) it was anxiety; and now in "E.T." – which looks set to outdo them all – it is love.

Towards the end of "E.T.", barely able to support my own grief and bewilderment, I turned and looked down the aisle at my fellow sufferers: executive, black dude, Japanese businessman, punk, hippie, mother, teenager, child. Each face was a mask of tears. Staggering out, through a tundra of sodden hankies, I felt drained, pooped, squeezed dry; I felt as though I had lived out a year-long love affair – complete with desire and despair, passion and prostration – in the space of 120 minutes.

By now a billion Earthlings have seen Spielberg's films. They have only one thing in common. They have all, at some stage, been children.

It is pretty irresistible to look for Spielberg's "secret" in the very blandness of his suburban origins – a peripatetic but untroubled childhood spent mostly in the Southwest. As I entered his offices in Warner Boulevard, Burbank Studios, I wondered if he had ever really left the chain-line, ranch-style embryos of his youth. The Spielberg bungalow resembles a dormitory cottage or beach-house – sliding windows, palm-strewn backyard. The only *outré* touch is an adjacent office door marked TWILIGHT ZONE ACCOUNTING: perhaps it is into this fiscal warp that the millions are eventually fed, passing on to a plane beyond time and substance . . .

Within, all is feminine good humour. Spielberg has always surrounded himself with women – surrogate aunts, mothers, kid sisters. These gently wisecracking ladies give you coffee and idly shoot the breeze as you wait to see the great man. That girl might be a secretary; this girl might be an executive producer, sitting on a few million of her own. Suddenly a tousled, shrugging figure lopes into the anteroom. You assume he has come to fix the Coke-dispenser. But no. It is Mr Spielberg.

His demeanour is uncoordinated, itchy, boyish: five foot nine or so, 150 pounds, baggy T-shirt, jeans, running-shoes. The beard, in particular, looks like a stick-on after-thought, a bid for adulthood and anonymity. Early photographs show the shaven Spielberg as craggy and distinctive; with the beard, he could be anyone. "Some people look at the ground when they walk," he said later. "Others look straight ahead. I always look upward, at the sky. This means that when you walk into things, you don't cut your forehead, you cut your chin. I've had plenty of cuts on my chin." Perhaps this explains the beard. Perhaps this explains the whole phenomenon.

Spielberg sank on to a sofa in his gadget-crammed den, a wide, low room whose walls bear the usual mementoes of movie art-work and framed magazine covers. "I had three younger sisters," he began. "I was isolated, left alone with my thoughts. I ima-gined the very best things that could happen and the very worst, simply to relieve the tedium. The most frightening thing, the most uplifting thing." He stared round the room, seemingly flustered by the obligation to explain himself for the thousandth time – weighed down, indeed, by the burden of all these mega-hits, these blockbusters and smasheroos. "I was the weird skinny kid with the acne. I was a wimp."

His mother, Leah, has confirmed that Steven "was not a cuddly child". Evidently he kept a flock of parakeets flapping around wild in his room. Leah never liked birds, and only reached a hand through the door once a week to grope for the laundry bag. She didn't go in there for years. Steven also kept an 8 mm camera. According to his sister Anne, big brother would systematically "dole out punishment" while forcing the three girls to participate in his home movies. This technique is well-tried in Hollywood: it is known as *directing*.

Spielberg's films deal in hells and heavens. Against the bullying and bedevilled tyke, we can set the adolescent dreamer, the boy who tenderly nursed his apocalyptic hopes. One night, when he was six, Steven was woken by his father and bundled into the car. He was driven to a nearby field, where hundreds of suburbanites stood staring in wonder (this is probably the dominant image in his films). The night sky was full of portents. "My father was a computer scientist," said Spielberg. "He gave me a technical explanation of what was happening. 'These meteors are space debris attracted by the gravitational . . .' But I didn't want to hear that. I wanted to think of them as falling stars."

All his life Spielberg has believed in things: vengeful 10-yard sharks, whooping ghosts, beautiful beings from other worlds. "Comics and TV always portrayed aliens as malevolent. I *never* believed that. If they had the technology to get here, they could only be benign . . . I know they're out there." The conviction, and desire, lead in a straight line from "Firelight" (one of his SF home movies) to the consummation of "E.T.". "Just before I made 'Close Encounters' I went outside one night, looked up at the sky and started crying. I thought I was falling apart."

In "Poltergeist" a suburban family is terrorised by demons that emerge from the household television set. When Spielberg describes the film as "my revenge on TV", he isn't referring to his own apprenticeship on the small-screen networks. "TV was my third parent." His father used to barricade and boobytrap the set, leaving a strand of hair on the aperture, to keep tabs on Steven's illegal viewing. "I always found the hair, memorized its position, and replaced it when I was through."

Rather to the alarm of his girl friend, Kathleen Carey, Spielberg still soaks up a great deal of nightly trivia. "All I see is junk," she says, "but he looks for ideas." It is clear from the annuals and potboilers on his office shelves that Spielberg is no bookworm (this is Hollywood after all, where high culture means an after-dinner game of Botticelli). TV is popular art: Spielberg is a popular artist who has outstripped but not outgrown the medium that shaped him. Like Disney – and, more remotely, like Dickens – his approach is entirely non-intellectual, heading straight for the heart, the spine, the guts.

"All right," conceded Spielberg, shifting up a gear in his own defence. "I do not paint in the strong browns and greens of Francis [Coppola], or in Marty's [Martin Scorsese's] sombre greys and whites. Francis makes films about power and loyalty, Marty makes films about paranoia and rage. I use primary colours, pastel colours. But these colours make strange squiggles when they run together on the palette . . . I'm coming out of my pyrotechnic stage now. I'm going in for close-ups. Maybe I will move on to explore the darker side of my make-up."

In all his major films, the context has not varied. It places ordinary people, of average resources, in situations of extraordinary crisis. How would *you* shape up to a shark? Would *you* enter that cathedral-organ of a mother-ship and journey to the heavens, never to return? Accordingly, as the strength of his bargaining position has increased, Spielberg has been less and less inclined to use star actors in his films. One scans the cast-lists of "Poltergeist" and "E.T." in search of a familiar name. Craig T. Nelson? Dee Williams? Peter Coyote? These are useful performers, but they are not headliners and never will be. He casts his actors for their *anti*-charismatic qualities. "The play's the thing," he says. "In every movie I have made, the movie is the star." He is the first director with the nerve to capitalise on something very obvious: audiences are comprised of ordinary people.

"E.T." is all Spielberg, essential Spielberg, and far away his most personal film. "Throughout, 'E.T.' was conceived by me as a love story – the love between a 10-year-old and a 900-year-old alien. In a way I was terrified. I didn't think I was ready to make this movie – I had never taken my shirt off in public before. But I think the result is a very intimate, seductive meeting of minds."

Intimacy is certainly the keynote of "E.T.". Using a predominantly female production team, Spielberg effectively recreated the tremulous warmth of his own childhood: a ranch-style suburban home, full of women and kids, with Spielberg the dreaming nucleus of the action. His well-attested empathy with children is tied to a precise understanding of how they have changed since he was a boy. "The years of childhood have been subject to a kind of inflation. At 16, I was the equivalent of a 10-year-old today." In the movie, the kids have a wised-up naivety, a callow. TV-fed sophistication. Reared on video games and Spielberg movies, with their Space-Invader T-shirts, robot toys and electronic gizmos, they are in a way exhaustively well-prepared for the intrusion of the supernatural, the superevolved.

Despite his new-deal self-discipline, Spielberg decided to "wing 'E.T.'", to play it by ear and instinct. (He brought the movie in on the nail anyway, at $10 million.) "If you over-rehearse kids, you risk a bad case of the cutes. We shot 'E.T.' chronologically, with plenty of improvization. I let the kids feel their way into the scenes. An extraordinary atmosphere developed on the set." E.T. is, after all, only an elaborate special effect (costing $1.5 million – "Brando would cost three times that," as Spielberg points out); but "a very intense relationship" developed between E.T. and his young co-star, Henry Thomas. "The emotion of the last scene was genuine. The final days of shooting were the saddest I've ever experienced on a film set." Little Henry agrees, and still pines for his vanished friend. "E.T. was a person," he insists.

Later, while scoring the film, Spielberg's regular composer John Williams shied away from what he considered to be an over-ripe modulation on the soundtrack. "It's shameless," said Williams, "will we get away with it?" "*Movies* are shameless," was Spielberg's reply. "E.T." is shameless all right, but there is nothing meretricious about it. Its purity is utopian, and quite unfakeable.

You can ask around Los Angeles – around the smoggy pool-sides, the oak and Formica rumpus-rooms, the squeaky-clean bars and restaurants – in search of damaging gossip about Steven Spielberg, and come away sorely disappointed. There isn't any. No, he does not "do" 10 grand's worth of cocaine a day. No, he does not consort with heavily set young men. In this Capitol of ambition, trivia and perversity, you hear only mild or neutral things about Spielberg, spiced with many examples of his generosity and diffidence.

He has walked out with starlets, notably Amy Irving. He blows a lot of money on gadgets, computers, video games. He owns a mansion, a beach-house; he has just spent $4 million on a four-acre hillock in Bel Air. He seldom goes to parties: "When I do go, I'm the guy in the corner eating all the dip." Spielberg, it appears, is a pretty regular guy. Apart from his genius, his technique, his energy, his millions, his burgeoning empire, he sometimes seems almost ordinary.

Towards the end of the interview, I asked him why he had never dealt with "adult relationships", with sex, in his movies. After all, in "Raiders" he de-eroticized Indiana Jones, who was originally conceived as a playboy, and he excised the adultery from "Jaws" (the sex-interest in the novel Spielberg attributes to "bad editorial advice"; actually the culprit was bad writing – but this is California). For the first time Spielberg grew indignant. "I think I have an *incredibly* erotic imagination. It's one of my ambitions to make everyone in an 800-seat theatre come at the same time." Well, we'll have to wait until he has completed "Raiders II", "E.T. II" and – "if George Lucas doesn't want to do it" – "Star Wars IV", as well as the host of minor projects he is currently supervising. But if Spielberg does for sex what he has done for dread and yearning, he can expect a prompt visit from the Vice Squad.

"I just make the kind of films that I would like to see." This flat remark explains a great deal. Film-makers today – with their target boys and marketing gurus – tie themselves up in knots trying to divine the Lowest Common Denominator of the American public. The rule is: no one ever lost money underestimating the intelligence of the audience. Spielberg doesn't need to do this because in a sense he is there already, uncynically. As an artist, Spielberg is a mirror, not a lamp. His line to the common heart is so direct that he unmans you with the frailty of your own defences, and the transparency of your most intimate fears and hopes.

JAMES CAMERON

SACRED BLUES

The Guardian, 23 November 1982

A column from the twilight of Cameron's fifty-year career on Fleet Street, when his days as roving exposer of poverty and military atrocities – captured in his autobiography *Point of Departure* – were just behind him. He died in 1985, aged 74.

Another bunch of slickers is monkeying about with Holy Writ, and I deplore it. The Bible is too Good a Book to need trendifying. Thou hadst not thought to read such words from me, but there thou ist.

I do not go to the kirk, and I am one of little faith. I am what my late Wee Free grandad, of whom I brag continually (and who himself wrote a Doric translation of the Psalms) would have called a flawed Christian. Yet I read, or dip into, the Bible more than I bet most of thee, my brethren; it is one of my bedroom books, along with the papist E. Waugh and the impious Orwell. I do this not for spiritual comfort or moral reassurance, since I am reckoned to be now beyond the reach of either. I read it to help me in my job, the only one I know: I read it to learn how to write.

Now another group of saboteurs ("more than 130 scholars from eight countries working for seven years") has just published another rejig of the Authorized Version. That seems to me to be a lot of time and manpower to corrupt and devalue an antiquated manuscript that, even from a sensitive pagan point of view, needs no improvement. It reminds me of a well-to-do acquaintance of mine who, to conform with his ghastly decor, painted a Sheraton sideboard white.

According to my revered colleague Martyn Halsall, the *Guardian's* Churches Correspondent (now there is a daunting job), the scholars decided that more non-stop and reverent activity was required, and commissioned the new version. Literature in their view must not be left to the literate; it is time that the Philistines got in on the act. This indeed may be right in the case of railway timetables or daily newspapers; I question if the judgment holds in works of, however minor, art.

For me, in this case, the medium *is* the message. Why else should heretics read the Testaments unasked, but that they value the words more than lessons? The religious do not have to be cajoled or convinced by poetry, though poetry must make it more persuasive. The unbeliever will not be seduced by words, however graceful, but he will read them with pleasure, to which even agnostics are entitled from time to time.

Of course crude parsons can corrupt the words into liturgical parody, and that is their fault, not their script's. My namesake, the late Scottish turncoat King James VI (I) in the 17th century commissioned a better pride of poetry than did the editor of this anodyne version, Dr Raymond Brown of Spurgeon Theological College, whoever he may be. He is far from the first to know better than his betters. Only last year the Gideons International, purveyors of Holy Writ to the world's hotels, put out their own Bible Mark XV, which is less abrasive than the new one, but still a mockery of the old dignities. Why do they do this?

Can it be the churchmen are running scared? Today we also have a revamped *Hymns for Today's Church* from Hodder's, a work of crushing banality that even attracted the derision of the well-known iconoclasts' journal *Private Eye*. Even that does not make it acceptable.

Always one to get in on an act, I am in process of preparing an updated *Works of Shakespeare*, or the *Moron's Bard*. I have not yet got very far, but I submit these examples of how all that Elizabethan waffle can be fined down to a reasonable economy.

Hath not old custom made this life more sweet
Than that of painted pomp?
Revised Version: Weren't you better off the way you were?

W.S.: Weariness can snore upon the flint.
When rested sloth finds the down pillow hard.
R.V.: A certain physical tiredness can doze off in a third-

class railway carriage, while the unemployed man
has difficulty dozing in the Ritz.

W.S.: Give thy thoughts no tongue,
Nor any unproportioned thought his act;
Be thou familiar, but no means vulgar.

R.V.: Keep your mouth shut. Give them a chance, but
play it straight.

W.S.: To be or not to be, that is the question.
Whether 'tis nobler in the mind to suffer
The slings and arrows of outrageous fortune
Or to take arms against a sea of troubles
And by opposing end them.

R.V.: It's a matter of priorities. Either put up with your
bad luck, or you do something about it.

I am in good company. In last week's *Guardian* a Yorkshire
vicar, Peter Mullen, was sounding off in angry criticism of this
new hymnal, too. To be sure, much of the old one was doggerel,
but it was fairly decent doggerel, even accepting that it had a few
superfluous thees and thous. Poor old Cranmer and Newman and
Wesley would writhe at all the "can'ts" and "won'ts" and pidgin
poetry, as though they had been adapted for the *Sun* newspaper.

This is not of much importance, since it is unlikely that anyone
will take this 1982 hymnbook seriously. Many youngsters, however, may well come upon this Dr Brown's new Patent Bible and
take it to be the thing their elders have been for years telling them
to read for style and will take us to be crazy. As I see it,
"testament" means "covenant". That means you do not break
faith. Whatever that may be.

SIMON HOGGART

BRITANNIA RUNS THE SHOP

The Observer, 2 January 1983

The Observer's political sketch-writer profiles British Prime Minister Margaret Thatcher at the zenith of her power.

Mrs Thatcher's morning generally begins the previous night. One of her Ministers describes a typical encounter. "It's 1 a.m. and you've had a hell of a day, so you're tottering down a Commons corridor with a whole bottle of claret swilling around inside you wondering when on earth you can go to bed, when you see this vision in blue drifting along looking as if she's just emerged from the beauty parlour. 'Ah,' she says. 'How are you, dear? Now tell me what you think about these new statistics! And *what* do you propose to do about them?' It is absolutely terrifying."

Sometimes she is weaving her way around the late-night committees bolstering the morale of her troops, like Henry V on St Crispin's Eve. With her (before his elevation) was Ian Gow, then her devoted parliamentary private secretary, and as she roamed the corridors he whispered in her ear, telling her who was of the True Faith and who had been heard to take her name in vain over buttered crumpets in the Tea Room. Then the Rover sweeps her back to Downing Street, where there is just time to squeeze in another hour's work on the Red Boxes, those urgent governmental papers on which every Prime Minister must spend hours of each day.

Or rather, on which this Prime Minister spends hours every day. Probably no Premier in history has devoted so long to the Boxes. She is the living refutation of Parkinson's Law, proof that time expands to accommodate the work available for it. She is obsessively industrious, a source of much resentment to those who work with her. "I regard it as quite unwholesome," another Minister says. A senior colleague says: "I went for a short holiday last summer. It had been a rough year, and my wife and I needed the break. But she never let me forget it. 'Of course, *you'll* be on holiday,' she would say sniffily, as if I was going for a fortnight in a brothel. She is quite incapable of distinguishing between leisure and idleness."

At 2 a.m. or even later, she is in the flat at the top of 10 Downing Street, tucked up in her bed. She dislikes going to bed because it means she has to stop work. She might read a page or two of a book: Kipling, perhaps, of whose writing she can quote great chunks by heart, or someone like John le Carré. Or it might be an Improving Work by a right-wing thinker. "If she sees a thought she likes, such as 'You cannot abolish poverty by first abolishing wealth,' she will underline it twice and show it to you," according to one MP.

She is not between the sheets for long. Whenever she went to bed, she will be up around 6.30 (or even earlier; startled staff have sometimes been asked if they heard an item on "Farming To-day," which begins at 6.10). Leaving Denis to sleep, she makes her own breakfast of toast or grapefruit while she listens to the BBC "Today" programme. Downing Street is really London's most elegant office block, and downstairs the staff are beginning to clock in.

From 8 to 9 she will finish off the last of the night's Boxes. "She thinks that she must know everything that is going on, every single detail," a Cabinet Minister says. "It can be infuriating. She just will not allow you to get on with it." She might spare a moment to glance through the newspapers, but certainly no longer. She flips through the pop papers as well as the heavy ones, and will give as much weight to a headline in *The Sun* as to a learned pundit's paragraph in *The Times* or *The Guardian*. She hardly ever reads articles about herself, and she never watches herself on television. Every day a digest of the Press is prepared for her, and this is brief, even curt. For example. "The Foreign Secretary's speech is widely reported. It is being interpreted as an attack on your economic policy."

Meetings begin at 9 o'clock, and on Tuesday and Thursdays the first session is devoted to plotting Prime Minister's Questions. This 15-minute session is regarded as of crucial importance, partly because she permits any topic at all to be raised.

"She thinks that Questions are her hotline to the British people," a close associate says. "She's the woman under the dryer chatting to her friends, and there they are on about the judge who gave a short sentence to a rapist. She says 'Tut, tut, isn't it shocking, if I was Prime Minister I'd do something about it,' and a fairy godmother turns up and says. 'But you *are* Prime Minister and you can do something about it!' "

She knows exactly, instinctively, to whom she is talking. She often calls them "Our People": thrifty, hard-working middle-class English folk, such as populate the Conservative Associations in Grantham and Finchley. They are for hanging and against immigration, for the British nuclear deterrent and against high taxes. They are suspicious of both the wealthy and the poor. Unlike many Cabinet "wets", they do not have thousands of acres to protect them from inflation.

"Her upbringing as a grocer's daughter is absolutely central to her outlook," says a Minister who knows her well. "Her belief in sound money has got nothing to do with hi-falutin' Chicago economists. She just knows that you cannot spend more than you take in at the till. She often refers to her father's shop as if it had lessons for running an industrialized economy. I would bet she has never been in debt in her life." She has little time for the City. "During the Falklands a lot of bankers told her that the Argentines might default and wreck the world banking system. She just ignored them, despised them," an admirer claimed later.

For these reasons, she has always preferred to make up her own mind without troubling her colleagues for their views. She often likes to give the impression that her Ministers are actually nothing to do with her. "You half expect her to say, 'If you ask me, I blame the Government,'" an MP says. "I remember one session in the Tea Room when she was hammering on about the nationalized industries, and how disgraceful they were, putting up prices and so on, as if she had no part in it at all. We sat there with our jaws hanging open, but nobody dared to say anything."

Most of her day is spent in meetings, sometimes of a distinctly argumentative nature. Gordon Richardson, the departing Governor of the Bank, now consoled with a peerage, was perhaps the worst sufferer. "He would hardly be in the door when she would loose off at him floods of abuse. Then he would say: 'Err, Prime Minister, if I might . . .' but he would be silenced by another salvo," a witness reports. Nor are her most senior colleagues spared. "There was a magnificent clash of personalities between her and Francis Pym," another Minister says. "He thought she was impetuous. She thought he was a terrible ditherer. They were both right really."

She loves a good argument and will shout, "That's absolute nonsense, don't be so wet" at someone. This angers quite a few people, and they hint darkly that she will one day pay for her disloyalty. Her admirers claim it is her way of testing the strength of her own case, a dress rehearsal for the arguments she will face later.

Probably without knowing it, she can make people's brains freeze. "I was in Downing Street with a Cabinet Minister she got on well with, and during the discussion she made two important factual errors," an MP recalls. "Nobody, including the senior Minister, corrected her. I suddenly realized he was afraid." Worse than her occasional shouts and crisp put-downs is the way she can look at people. "I'd made some bad mistake which caused her a lot of trouble," one of her staff says. "I expected a real dressing-down. Instead she gave me this *look* which meant: 'Nanny is not cross. She is just very, very sad.' It was ghastly."

In the evening there might be a reception at Downing Street. Whisked between official residences in official cars, Prime Ministers soon become sealed off from the real world and begin to place exaggerated store by their meetings with ordinary people, whether across a factory bench or over a gin-and-tonic. But nobody, introduced to the Prime Minister, is going to start by attacking her. Reality soon begins to disappear, like a shape half-glimpsed in the mist, discerned only through short, haphazard and misleading encounters. "You see, they all go mad, they all start hearing voices," says an MP who has studied several Prime Ministers. "They are cut off from the world, so they rely on their gut instinct, and of course it is very often wrong."

If she has no official dinner, she will return to the Commons to chat to Conservative MPs. She is much better at this than Ted Heath ever was. Sometimes she will take a quick snack in the cafeteria, the only Prime Minister to make a habit of this. She invariably has buck rarebit, toasted cheese with an egg on top. Sometimes she decides to eat in the Members' Dining Room, in which case an aide is sent before her, to prepare The Way.

As she arrives, the gossip and the small talk, the rumble of half-sozzled conversation is suddenly silenced. She distributes quick and searching questions about the state of the economy or the world. Eager sycophants praise her last speech, her dazzling parliamentary barbs. Members who had hoped to order another bottle of House of Commons Red think better of it. Those who were about to leave remain glued to their green leather chairs. "You can tell her mood from her clothes," one says. "Shimmery in blue means she's confident, on top of things. Red, speckly clothes mean she has problems, she's fussed."

Sometimes someone will get it horribly wrong. "Robin Maxwell-Hyslop had done something to please her, and when she sat down she said: 'Ah, dear Robin!' So, emboldened, he launched into a long and risqué anecdote he'd read in *Private Eye*. Nothing could stop him. He went on and on. She sat there, frozen and po-faced. It was awful, unimaginable."

Some people say she has no sense of humour whatever, though it's apparent that these are political opponents with whom she is probably not at ease. People she likes better credit her with a line in mocking irony, though no one suggests she is a source of belly laughs.

Her rudeness to many colleagues coexists with a remarkable memory for, and concern about, people's private lives and problems. She can always recall the names of MPs' children, or whose wife has been poorly. If colleagues go to hospital, an aide will materialize by the grapes with a cleverly chosen gift. "She always wants to know if you've had enough to eat, and if you haven't, she'll be in the kitchen cutting sandwiches," an MP says.

Apart from occasional visits to the opera (when she has usually read the score beforehand) her own family are her only real interest outside politics. In particular, she worries about Mark who, it must be said, is far from loved by his mother's circle of acquaintance. "She was only ever in a bad mood when he failed his accountancy exams," a former colleague says, "so that was pretty often." The one time she has cracked in Downing Street was when he seemed lost in the Sahara. "That upset her more than anything, much more than the strain of the Falklands," a close colleague says.

Unlike, say, Harold Wilson, she does not try to fix her Cabinets beforehand. There are no sessions with old pals swigging brandy at Number 10. "This is not a late-night drinking club," says one official, severely. She might occasionally see a recalcitrant MP if the whips ask her, but this is rare. "She demands complete loyalty from everyone – party, Government and civil service," a colleague says. "She is a bit more cavalier about returning it, but then all Prime Ministers are much the same."

For a crusader, she spends a lot of time watching her back. For some time she believed (wrongly) that there was a plot between Francis Pym and Jim Prior to usurp her job. She doesn't like people she thinks she can't trust. "She loves old Willie because he wouldn't do anything against her, and she liked Peter Carrington because, as a peer, he couldn't," a colleague says. Persons who made critical remarks during the leadership campaign found themselves without preferment after her assumption. This frame of mind she shared with Harold Wilson, but not a great deal else. "Wilson was concerned with what he could get away with, whereas she likes to give the impression that she is driven by the need to do what destiny demands," a sceptical Minister says.

"The point about Denis Thatcher is that he is exactly like the *Private Eye* letters," says a friend. He himself hates them, and particularly the stage show "Anyone for Denis", because they depict him as an incompetent ninny and, as he often points out, he was the managing director of a large firm. He is also very rich.

But the social style: the drinks, golf in the Algarve with William Deedes, editor of the *Daily Telegraph*, the vocabulary, the attitudes – all these are pure "Dear Bill". He does have strong views about the Bolshies who run the unions, he does say "just time for a tincture", he does call her "The Boss" and he firmly believes that the BBC is run by a crowd of pinkoes. George Howard, chairman of the BBC, once told him "Thatcher, you're so far to the Right you're barely visible," and it is Denis who tells the story against Howard. He is engagingly frank about his opinions, which is one reason why it was decided early that he should not give interviews to the Press. On foreign trips he tends to judge each country by the quality of its golf courses.

Some people think that he is in awe of her, but it seems more likely that he has simply learned to live with the bossiness of the average self-assured British middle-class woman. A friend tells the story of a Downing Street reception where Denis was drinking gin and tonic. A Special Branch detective hove up and whispered in his ear: "The Boss is back, Sir." As Denis's left hand poured the gin into a convenient pot plant, his right hand stretched out to greet his wife. On another occasion, however, they were flying to Scotland in the morning and Denis ordered a drink from the stewardess. "Isn't it a bit early for gin and tonic?" his wife asked. "It is never too early for a gin and tonic," he said crisply.

"He is marvellous when she's down," says someone who knows them both well. "He's a great backslapper and very encouraging. But I think he is more worrying when she's up. He sweeps her along, and reinforces her instinct when a little caution would help."

"He admires her like mad," says another friend. "He really is her greatest fan, and he's terribly good at formal do's, though his opinions might make your hair curl. But what he really likes doing is playing golf and having too much to drink with his chums."

It is an article of faith among some Tories that the Prime Minister gets on badly with the Queen. Given Her Majesty's long practised social skills this seems unlikely, but it is true that Mrs Thatcher gets fussed. She is not at her ease in the Royal Presence. One insider tells the story of last year's annual Prime Ministerial visit to Balmoral. The Royal Family usually has a barbecue on the estate, lighting their own fire, grilling their own sausages, and so forth. "She was terribly agitato, and can you blame her? All those Hanoverians on horseback. Afterwards the Queen insisted on washing up, in a little hut. Margaret was appalled and wanted to do it herself, but the Queen wouldn't let her, because it was the one day of the year she can pretend to be a real person." One is left with this vivid image of Britain's two leading women locked in genteel combat over the Fairy Liquid.

She doesn't really have friends in the sense that most people do, because friends imply, leisure, which she doesn't believe in.

But she sees people she admires and who can help her: Sir Hector Laing, the chairman of United Biscuits; Lord (Hugh) Thomas, the right-wing historian, is particularly esteemed; Ronnie Millar, a playwright who has written more forgotten dramas than Ernie Wise, helps her with her speeches – he coined the phrase "The lady's not for turning." She likes men who treat her with a certain insouciant gallantry. "It's a kind of hearty pink ginnery," a friend says. "People who say 'Margaret, you're looking perfectly splendid!' She loves it, and not many men dare try it. Humphrey Atkins did. So does Robin Leigh-Pemberton. So does Marcus Sieff. In a platonic way, of course, she fancies them."

Few gain access to the innermost sanctum, the sitting-room in the flat above Downing Street. One is Norman Tebbit, the Employment Secretary, probably the man she most admires in her Cabinet. "Basically she thinks that everyone is useless except Norman," says a backbencher who knows her well. Tebbit shares her gut right-wing instincts; like her he comes from a lower middle-class background and has got where he is through hard work and determination. He identifies entirely with her cause and he believes that if she has a fault it is that she is not sufficiently ruthless. He could be heard complaining some time ago that she should have sacked more people, earlier. She tells him almost everything and he never ever leaks it, to anyone.

I asked one of her Chosen Few whether, as she finally turns out the light in her Downing Street bedroom, she might ever be troubled by the fear that she had got it all wrong: that, far from saving Britain, she might be wrecking it. He thought for a moment, then shook his head. "You see, we believe very strongly that we are actually right and that we have to keep on going. We cannot afford to indulge in needless self-doubt. Some politicians doubt themselves and they fall into vacillation. She will never do that."

IAN JACK

MODERN LIFE IS RUBBISH

Sunday Times, 19 May 1985

In which Jack records a day in the life of Merseyside men and women as they scavenged through the local tip in the poverty-stricken mid 80s.

The sight of miners and miners' children scrambling for coal over a colliery waste heap is probably the most striking visual metaphor for poverty and desperation that Britain has produced in the 20th century. Documentary film-makers first filmed it in south Wales in the 1930s, and it received fresh life last year at the height of the pit strike in television pictures from the coalfields of Yorkshire and the northeast.

We may now forget it. We can wipe it from the tape and consign it to folk history, with the poor match girl and Mr Bumble's wretched establishment for orphans. Proceed instead, fast-forward, to the metropolitan county of Merseyside and a rubbish tip on the outskirts of Birkenhead in the spring of 1985. Here unemployed men – and sometimes their womenfolk and children – are snatching a living of sorts by scavenging among thousands of tons of waste matter that Merseyside council dumps each week in 23 acres of barren ground surrounded by a railway line, an old dock and a steelworks and known as Bidston Moss.

"Waste matter" is the careful and correct phrase. These are not people who go out at dead of night to retrieve pine chests from skips in gentrifying zones. These are people up to their shins every day in old tea bags, cat-food tins and onion skins, sliding and falling on slopes of polythene bags and bacon rind, scrambling to get to the copper wire before the next man, seizing a pair of discarded shoes, unearthing a bicycle pump, shouting warnings when the municipal bulldozer bursts forward again and threatens to bury half a dozen of them in a grave of discarded stockings and fish-finger cartons. A visitor to Bidston Moss has some difficulty in believing what he is seeing. Later, he is not sure whether he has witnessed scenes in Birkenhead, England, or in the nastier slums of Bombay.

But no, it must have been Birkenhead. Untouchables in Bombay do not scramble as energetically or dangerously as these men. Instead they squat on their haunches and sift through the filth: old newsprint in this pile, cardboard in the next, tin cans in a third. Everything is recyclable in India. In Birkenhead, so far, they are more selective.

Rubbish tips, of course, have always attracted "totters" – professional scrap gatherers – and in the 1970s Bidston Moss had one or two of those. But over the past few years a new kind of scavenger has crossed the railway line and slipped through the high wire fence. The unemployment rate in Birkenhead now runs – officially – at 20%, In the tip, however, it is much higher. According to Frank Field, the local MP, nearly one person in every two cannot find work. Quite crudely, unemployment is creating a new scavenging class. Every week Bidston Moss gathers new recruits. Old hands at the tip borrow the National Coal Board's terminology for strike-breakers and refer to them, with no detectable irony, as "new faces".

At Bidston Moss I talked to a man, formerly a labourer with a decorating firm, who was burning the plastic sheathing from a few rolls of copper wire which, if he collected a hundredweight, would fetch him £30. He said he had been coming to the tip most days for the past two years. In front of us a dozen men were slithering around on the tip trying to take up strategic positions behind a waste lorry which had just arrived. The lorry's back reared up, rubbish spewed out, while the men beneath, rubbish cascading onto them, went poking into the plastic bags. Fresh lorries arrived every few minutes. Always there was the same scramble.

"I couldn't believe it when I came here at first," said the man with the wire. "I stood here and looked at them. I'd never been out of work before and never seen anything like it. But there's not much else you can do. Just now, the kids' bedroom needs redecorating. I could never afford the paper and paint on social security. This way you earn a bit extra, but I still can't stand the shite and dogs. You get half a dozen dead dogs here every day. And cats. People put them into plastic bags. Even now if I come across shite or a dead dog, that's it. I walk down the road and go home for the day."

In fact, the tip does not smell too badly. Anyone who has had their head stuck in their own dustbin for an hour or two, the result of some unfortunate prank, could tolerate Bidston Moss. Many of its scavengers say theirs is a fine, healthy life. The wind, they say, comes straight off the Irish Sea. Only a few cuts have turned septic, and the most serious accident in the living memory of Bidston Moss has been the matter of a few fingers. A youth lost them recently when his over-eager hand got caught in the machinery which was still cranking a skip to the ground. His friends, eyes sharpened by months of peering into waste, found his fingers easily enough and quickly bagged them; but it was too late for surgical repairs.

Some scavengers at Bidston Moss go further. Mick, who was once a charge hand at Cammell Laird's shipyard, said that coming to the tip every day had saved his marriage. Max insisted that it had helped him recover from a nervous breakdown. Several said that the tip and the money they made from it were a better alternative to "mugging old ladies in Wallasey". One man said: "It keeps me outta jail." Another: "You come every day and meet your mates. It's like a proper job." And another: "I eat, breathe and sleep tip. I'd still come if I won the pools."

The day I went in March, about 50 men were picking their way over the tip, searching for anything sellable, repairable, wearable, or even eatable, provided it was sealed inside a tin. According to Merseyside council, the same phenomenon can be observed at other tips in the county, though on a smaller scale. The scavengers said they thought it was happening not just in the county but throughout the country. "Or it will be soon," said Gerry, unscrewing a brass door fitting.

The weekend is the most rewarding time. "That's when the poshies come," Gerry explained. "They drive up from Hoylake and New Brighton in their Mercs and Granadas and they dump some lovely stuff." To cater for this influex, the scavengers at Bidston employ their wives and children. They bring flasks and sandwiches and make a day of it. Gerry said he could make £80 or £90 a week. Add that to his social security and the money his officially unemployed wife made "on the fiddle" and his family were approaching a decent weekly wage. Most men do not do nearly so well; perhaps enough to get decently drunk twice a week. One man said, stretching and yawning: "Oh, a great life. I go home, have a shower, sit down, watch the video."

As we talked, the scavengers displayed that day's catch: old bicycle handlebars, books, vintage postcards, a TV set that could be easily made to work, a new pair of ladies' shoes from Taiwan, an old pair of men's shoes that were still wearable. "It's disgusting: what people throw away," said Max, and presented me with a Durabeam torch, still in its manufacturer's packet. Max was wearing stuff he'd found on the tip: good boots but of different sizes and a plastic baseball cap. From behind, he kept up a sombre political counterpoint, the Greek chorus of Bidston Moss. This being Merseyside, everybody talked vividly, knowledgably, and at once.

Jim: "These postcards are that old, I bet Fox Talbot took them. You can get threepence each for these in Liverpool . . ."

Max: "She's a murderess, that woman. People on the dole are killing themselves. It's going to get worse . . ."

Frank: "Sometimes you get tinned food. When somebody passes away, they clear out their kitchens and dump it. Nothing wrong with it, like."

Mick: "A fella got married in a suit he found on this tip. A proper pinstripe. Married in his tip suit . . ."

Old man in woollen hat: "These shoes'd cost me 18 quid in a shop . . ."

Max: "She's a murderess, a murderess, a murderess . . ."

Jim: "Who's that, Max?"

Max: "Her, she's a murderess."

Jim: "Oh, her. Right, right."

Times have changed. Twenty-odd years ago Samuel Beckett placed two of his characters in dustbins and filled their dialogue with incoherent melancholy and anger, and audiences in Paris and London applauded the result as a piece of outré (if profound) symbolism. Today, should the same play be staged in Bidston, it would pass merely as a humdrum work of documentary realism. An irrelevant and pretentious thought to have on Bidston Moss, but it struck me all the same, listening to men who had so quickly learnt to rationalise what they did to make money. Frank said that he knew scavenging was "the lowest form of life", and in the next breath added. "But I'm proud to work here on the tip. We're giving work to scrap yards and putting antiques back into the system, aren't we?"

Anger is mainly confined to the newcomers. One man, trembling with a violent rage, threatened to give Peter Marlow, the photographer, a "proper doing over" if he ever saw him and his bloody cameras on the tip again. But it was explained to us that he was a "new face", fresh that month. Older hands at Bidston Moss have already featured in a film made for Granada Television's current affairs programme World in Action, and talk about it a lot. They complain that the film made their work harder because it popularized the tip as a source of income, increased the labour force and lowered individual profit. They do not complain that the film intruded into areas of private shame; they have long since stopped worrying about how other people see them.

"I've got it on the video," said Frank. "Come home and watch it." We followed him over the level crossing and into council-estate Britain, where it is dangerous to leave a car unattended for half an hour because of the price of heroin.

His flat was immaculate: well carpeted and well furnished, with trophies from the tip hung on the walls. Two Victorian watercolour prints. A photograph of the Blue Funnel freighter SS Nestor at the Liverpool landing stage around 1920. Shelves beneath contained a salvaged set of Arthur Mee's Children's Encyclopaedia and The Oxford Companion to Law. "Yes," said Frank, "the tip has been good to us."

He added, however, that he and his family intended to move out quite soon. "We want to get somewhere decent," he said. A pair of heroin dealers lived upstairs; there were recurrent visits from the police, interminable rows and outbreaks of drugged madness. He has saved enough from the tip to put down the deposit on a house, and trusts the social security to look after the mortgage repayments.

Of course, the social security agents could find out about Frank's income from the tip and cut his benefit. The police could prosecute him for trespassing on the railway line. Merseyside council could get him for disturbing rubbish and endangering health (his own, in this case) under section 28 of the Control of Pollution Act, 1974. But officialdom in Merseyside, one senses, has been visited by shame and impotence as well as realism. There are moral and practical difficulties in taking legal action against hard-pressed men who are merely removing goods which someone else has thrown away.

And so Bidston Moss will probably outlive Cammell Laird's shipyard as a source of local employment, though even Bidston Moss will not survive for ever. By the 1990s it should have reached its planned growth height of 100 ft, when it will be nicely contoured, covered with topsoil and planted with grass and saplings. By that time too, North Sea oil should be running out and we shall have the opportunity to find out if, as the more pessimistic futurologists insist, Britain will finally slide into the Third World.

The only question about that prognosis, after a visit to Bidston Moss, concerns the use of the future tense.

I. VEDENEEVA

THE ULTIMATE STEP

Ogonyok, January 1989

Under editor Vitaly Korotich, *Ogonyok* was the journalistic flagship of *glasnost* in the late Soviet Union, when its blend of investigative reporting – eptomized by Vedeneeva's account of the work of the Moscow hospital for attempted suicides – and defence of political freedom garnered it sales in excess of 3 million per issue.

'*Nobody could endure what I've been through these last three years. I can't take any more. I'm taking my life . . .*"

"*Thanks for the 'help', Mum. It made me a laughing-stock at school. I'll never forgive you and Dad for putting me through that . . .*"

"*I'm forty-four. I can't go on with this pointless, humiliating existence . . .*"

"*Tell Victor he's got what he wanted. He's free now. Let him get on with his life and enjoy himself . . .*"

"*Yury darling, I've no more strength. My illness has made us all suffer so much. I can't stand any more. I'm very tired. Please don't be sad. This is the best way. Kiss my little Nadya for me, and say Granny's staying with friends . .*"

These are all suicide notes. Thousands of such notes are written every year. Thousands more don't write anything. What impels someone to take their own life? The burdens and

humiliations of life, or a surfeit of joy? Friends who betray, or
wasted talents? Unattainable desires, or the lack of desires?

We are at Moscow's Sklifosvsky Institute, the only hospital in the capital to treat attempted suicides. People arrive here poisoned or cut down from the noose, but still alive. The ones who die go elsewhere.

They're taken straight to the resuscitation rooms. Pressure chambers, stomach pumps, blood transfusions, sutures. Hundreds of people, men and women, married and divorced, the old and the young, the sick, the healthy, and the homeless – all are equal as they lie lifeless under the white sheet of the operating table. It's not the doctors' job to go into the details of their personal dramas. The doctors' job is to resuscitate them. And they're especially busy in the evening, when the suicide rate shoots up.

Dr Ivan Diky, the institute's director, is up to his eyes in work. Some patients are waiting to be discharged, others need to be examined, the telephone never stops ringing, the ward-round is about to start, and now he has to talk to a journalist . . . Diky answers my questions briskly and without emotion. He has worked here for a long time and he has got used to people who don't want to live. His responsibility is to get them on their feet as quickly as he can. A sheet of paper on the wall above him shows the number of people admitted to the hospital, and the percentage of those who don't survive. It's up to him to make sure this percentage remains as low as possible.

He hands me a white coat, shouts out some instructions to someone, and dashes off to the wards, with me tagging along behind. He takes me to various beds, and I listen in some embarrassment as he tells me matter-of-factly that this one is Vasya. He was no good at work, his wife left, he decided to hang himself – look, there's the scar on his neck. These people wouldn't have had a chance in the past, he says, but these days we can save them with pressure chambers . . . Now here is Olya. Her husband was an alcoholic and beat her, and she had nowhere to go, so she took an overdose . . . And this one is Nikolai, he was bullied by his workmates . . .

Olya, Vasya, Nikolai, and the rest lie there with their bandaged throats, faces, and hands, eyes closed, faces turned to the wall, paying us absolutely no attention, indifferent to whatever the doctor cares to say about them. These are the observation wards, and they are the most difficult ones of all. Here are the patients who have just been brought out of the resuscitation room and need to be closely monitored.

As we move on to new wards and new patients, the doctor continues his running commentary. This poor chap from the back of beyond came to the capital thinking things would be easier here. Little did he know! Couldn't get a job, no one wanted him, couldn't get registered, driven from pillar to post, nothing worked out, so in desperation he decided to throw himself under a train. But even that didn't work out. The train just cut his legs off and left him alive to face a new problem – how to get invalidity benefit without a residence permit. So now he's staying here while the doctors sort things out for him.

Dr Diky waves his arm, and on we go.

"You wouldn't believe how many desperate, messed-up people we've got here," he says. "We have to give a lot of them their bus fare when they go, otherwise they'd be stranded here. The problem for most of these people, though, is that they don't have anywhere to go. Meet Nikolai here. He used to sleep in railway stations. When they moved him on he lived rough on the streets. He slept out in the snow and got such a bad case of pneumonia the doctors were amazed it hadn't killed him. How did you manage it, eh, old boy?"

The "old boy" has evidently long since lost the habit of being addressed as a human being, let alone being taken care of. Terribly thin, with sunken cheeks, a yellow face, and a gaping wound in his chest, he gazes devotedly into the doctor's eyes, nodding his head at him after he leaves . . .

"We also get a fair number of students, many of them from the top universities," says the doctor, continuing on his round. "Humanities, arts, technical sciences, the lot. Problem is they're spoilt! Take Marina, that nice-looking young girl over there. She'd almost graduated and her handsome boyfriend had just arrived. What more could you want? But no, she had to put a rope round her neck. She was terrified of living, you see. Afraid to live, but not afraid to hang herself . . ."

The girl with the brushed-back hair and a deep, blue weal on her neck stares silently ahead of her . . .

"There's a professor who recently discharged himself from here. Another doctor, a colleague. It was depression, you see, he just couldn't go on. And take that granny over there. Why would an old lady like her want to die? OK, the young ones don't know anything about life, but her . . . There are a lot of soldiers here too. Can't take their military service. Lot of teenagers, too. Take Olechka here, intelligent girl, doing well at school, played the violin, then invented some high-flier for herself instead of making do with a real-life boy . . ."

We go on. The nurses talk on the telephone. Their resuscitated patients sleep, lie quietly, read, look out of the window, and play chess. Meanwhile new patients keep arriving, with closed eyes and darkened faces. Life goes on as usual in the hospital for those who want to die . . .

Tens of thousands of people kill themselves every year in our country. The figures are appalling, equivalent to the disappearance of whole towns.

For a long time all our suicide statistics were suppressed. In the developed countries in the West and some socialist ones, the figures are regularly published and carefully analysed, to permit the best possible programme to help those who have fallen on hard times. The last time official suicide data were published here, however, was in the 1920s, by the Department of Moral Statistics. This department was closed down in the thirties, and it was only literally a few weeks ago that the information was made available again. Now at last we can see the true picture of events.

Lydia Postovalova, a candidate of philosophy who works at the All-Union Scientific-Methodological Suicidology Centre, helped to explain these figures to me with some data provided by the Ministry of Statistics.

In 1965, 39,550 people killed themselves. The worst year was 1984, when the figure rose to 81,417. The number then declined: in 1985 it was 68,073; in 1986, 52,830; and in 1987, 45,105. Suicide figures for 1987, by sex and age:

Women		Men	
Under 20	522	Under 20	1,672
20–30	1,260	20–30	6,791
30–50	3,436	30–50	16,594
50–70	5,050	50–70	11,725
70 +	3,648	70 +	3,399
Total	13,916	Total	40,181

"The 1984 peak was followed by a marked decline," says Postovalova, "which we attribute to the recent anti-alcohol campaign, since so many suicides are committed under the influence of drink. On the other hand, the suicide rate amongst adolescents and the old has risen dramatically.

"Statistics fail to convey the full picture. Let's say there are 1,275 suicides in Moscow in 1987, 660 in Leningrad, and 210 in Izhevsk. Now it may appear that things are very much better in Izhevsk, but in fact the situation is far more alarming there than in Leningrad, where the rate is 15 per 100,000 of the population, whereas in Izhevsk it's as many as 33 in every 100,000.

"Because the statistics have been concealed for so long and scientists haven't had access to them, there's a lot that's hard to explain, and we have no available data on people's social status, family situation, ethnic origins, state of health, or possible motivations for killing themselves. Take the 1986 statistics for the Latvian Republic, for instance, where more than seventeen times more twenty- to twenty-four-year-old men commit suicide than women. Women of the same age in Tadjikistan in the same year, however, are 1.6 times more likely than men to commit suicide. Why is this? Or consider Udmurtia, which leads the autonomous republics with 41.1 suicides for every 100,000 of the population, almost the same rate as in Hungary, which has the highest suicide rate in the world. But why Udmurtia? Why not neighbouring Mordovia, where the figures for 1986 were just 16.9?

"Then the suicide rate in the countryside has now started to exceed that in the towns. Why is this? Which social groups are most likely to commit suicide in the cities? Only when we have the full picture and can study it as thoroughly as do our Western counterparts can we begin to give effective help to those who need it."

Lydia Postovalova's Suicidology Centre is attempting to find answers to these and other questions. I asked the Centre's director, Honoured Scientist of the USSR Aina Ambrumova, to tell me about its work.

"We're the centre of a complex of social and psychological welfare offices, a telephone help-line, and the Soviet Union's first crisis clinic. This clinic is very different from the usual psychiatric hospital. We try here to identify people with suicidal tendencies, and to work with those who have already attempted suicide. We have already had some success. Repeated suicide attempts have sharply declined in Moscow thanks to us, and all the evidence points to the high probability of these second attempts, especially in the first year.

"But we still have a lot of problems. The telephone help-line, for instance. For a long time it was referred to very grudgingly as a bourgeois invention, of no possible use to any Soviet citizen, so it's hardly surprising if not as many people know about it as we would like. It operates twenty-four hours a day, seven days a week, and we very much hope that Moscow's example will be followed by other towns, especially places like Sverdlovsk and Arkhangelsk, where the situation is especially worrying.

"But the clinic is our proudest achievement. People in psychological distress come here voluntarily and talk to experienced psychiatrists, and they leave feeling quite different about things . . ."

The clinic is indeed very cosy, with comfortable furniture, discreet lighting, nice curtains, and none of the doctors wearing white coats. It has only thirty beds, and when you consider all the thousands of people trying to kill themselves, thirty beds does seem an awfully small number, even with nice curtains and comfortable furniture. But thank goodness even for them.

It is seven o'clock. Psychiatrists Poleev and Starshenbaum have spent the day teaching their patients to live, and now their working day is over and we sit talking over glasses of tea.

"You think people commit suicide because they don't want to live?" Alexander Poleev asks me. "Nothing of the sort! Many of them want to live more than you or I. But they can't.

"Take a man we had here recently. He was healthy, good-looking, and enormously strong-willed. Everything had seemed to be going his way. Happily married, two lovely children, interesting job. Then all of a sudden he falls head-over-heels in love with another woman. Forgive me, he says to his wife, I'm off. He gives her everything – flat, furniture, the lot – and moves in with this new woman, with whom he lives happily for a year. Then suddenly she says: 'I love you, but I need more out of life,' and tells him she's leaving him to marry a diplomat and settle abroad. When our patient walks back that evening to the flat they've shared for a year and sees her and a man silhouetted against the window, he takes several packets of strong sleeping powder and gulps them down with snow. It's only thanks to his strong constitution that he survived at all.

"People kill themselves when they return from the local soviet office, or the shops, or the endless queues, because of the utter frustration and humiliation of it all. This is the grey, mindless, unendurable routine of our everyday lives, from which the more sensitive and emotional of us can see no escape . . .

"For many years doctors in the Soviet Union considered everyone who committed suicide to be mentally ill. The normal, healthy person wants to live, our doctors informed us, and the rest of us went along with them. But the suicide rate is now reaching such epic proportions that if we continue to regard such people as sick we must regard our entire society as sick.

"Things are especially hard nowadays for children and teenagers, and the suicide rate in this age group has recently increased much faster than among adults. Generally neither parents nor teachers can explain why a child killed itself. Everything seemed fine, they say, she was healthy, well-adjusted, well-fed and clothed . . .

"Take Olya K. At three in the afternoon she came home from school as usual, ate the meal that had been left for her, washed her plate, did her maths homework, tidied her folder, opened the window . . . and jumped from the fourteenth floor. A good, quiet little girl, said her parents. Obedient and well-brought-up, said her teachers. A happy child, they all said. But happy children don't throw themselves out of windows! Only later did we learn about her parents' violent rows, the endless shouting at home, her teacher's roughness . . ."

"Teenagers, like the old, are suffering increasingly from loneliness," says Valery Khaikin, the Centre's specialist in adolescent problems. "Family misunderstandings are exacerbated by housing problems. Most teenagers don't have a room of their own or any chance of privacy, and even if they do, their parents tend to spy on them, demanding to know who they're going around with and so on. Things are often no better at school. With such huge classes, a teacher rarely gets the chance to establish a proper personal relationship with every teenager in her class . . ."

I recalled a Baltic documentary film I saw at a recent festival, about an eleven-year-old boy who took his own life. He lived in a remote little town somewhere, and at first there didn't seem to be anything particularly wrong. He and his little sister had no father. Their mother slaved away all day at a farm, and when she returned home exhausted she would shout at them and sometimes even hit them, as do many mothers in these benighted little towns.

The film-makers didn't seek to prove anything. They didn't blame the mother, half-dead with grief, or go looking for culprits in the school. They simply tried to see through the little boy's eyes the sort of life he had led.

We see the squalid little town, the slush and the washed-away roads. We see his mother getting up at dawn and setting off for the farm. We see the bus, the sleepy, exhausted passengers in their boots, and the dirty farm. We see the phone ringing in the flat as the mother wakes up her daughter. We see the food on the stove, the radio blaring out its usual monotonous news, the walk to school and the walk back home again. We see the mother, cold and tired, an unappetising meal on the table, hands rough with work, ugly clothes, the occasional unloving boyfriend, the mother weeping, shouting, exhausted . . . Homework, the dreary landscape outside the window, then television and sleep. And tomorrow will be exactly the same, and so will the day after, and the day after that . . .

It could have been the mother herself, but she's resigned to her life. The little boy refused to resign himself to it and killed himself.

"To take one's life under the influence of some unbearable inner crisis is something of which only the very rare, exceptionally noble soul is capable," Einstein wrote.

Yet suicide is also something none of us has the right to judge. To try to help and understand is another matter. We are only just beginning to realize how little we understand human psychology.

Our country, despite the promise of its slogan "All in the name of the People!", appears in fact to have done very little for its people. No amount of achievements in science and technology, agriculture and industry, the ballet and space travel, can help someone to understand themselves and others. None of these things can help us to live, and to find solutions to the emotional crises which beset us.

We must look after our people. Otherwise a new night will fall, and hundreds will decide that they no longer want to live . . .

MARY ANN GWINN

A DEADLY CALL OF THE WILD

Seattle Times, 4 April 1989

The 1990 Pulitzer for National Reporting was awarded to Ross Anderson, Bill Dietrich, Mary Ann Gwinn and Eric Nalder of the *Seattle Times* for their coverage of the Exxon Valdez oil spill. Here is Gwinn's account of a visit to the scene of the environmental crime, Prince William Sound in Alaska.

Valdez, Alaska

I had tried to prepare myself for Green Island, but nothing can prepare you for the havoc wreaked on the creatures of Prince William Sound.

From the helicopter that took me there, the 987-foot tanker Exxon Valdez, stuck like a toy boat on Bligh Reef, was dwarfed by the immensity of the sound. It was hard to believe that we could fly 60 miles, land and walk right into the ruination of a landscape, so far from that broken boat.

The helicopter landed on the beach of Green Island. Its beaches are broad and slope gently, in contrast to the rocky, vertical shores of many of the other islands in the sound. For that reason, Green Island is favoured by wildlife. Now the oil has turned the gentle beach into a death trap.

No sooner had the Alaska National Guard helicopter roared away than a black lump detached itself from three or four others bobbing in the oil-streaked water. It was an old squaw, a sea bird normally recognizable by its stark black-and-white plumage. The tuxedo plumage had turned a muddy brown and orange.

It staggered up the beach, its head compulsively jerking back and forth, as if trying to escape the thing that was strangling it.

Tony Dawson, a photographer for Audubon magazine, and I watched it climb a snowbank and flap into the still centre of the woods. "They move up into the grass, along the creek beds and into the woods, where they die," Dawson said. "It's like they're fleeing an invisible enemy."

Dawson used to be a veterinarian. He said documenting the oil spill makes him feel like a photographer in Vietnam: "Every day, a new body count." As in that war, helicopters drone across the sky, boats beach on shore, men land, size up the situation and depart.

Eleven days into the spill, scientists are trying to decide which beaches to clean and which to leave alone, reasoning that disruption would hurt some more than it would help. Very little actual beach cleanup is taking place. Most of the animals are going to die, a few dozen or hundred every day, by degrees.

I walked along the beach, which in some places was glutted with oil like brown pudding; in others, streaked and puddled with oil the consistency of chocolate syrup. The only sounds came from a few gulls and the old squaw's mate, which drifted down the polluted channel toward its fate. Far away, a cormorant spread its wings and stretched in a vain attempt to fluff its oil-soaked feathers. A bald eagle passed overhead.

It was then that I heard a sound so strange, for a brief moment all my 20th-century rationality dropped away.

Something was crying in the vicinity of the woods, a sound not quite human. I looked into the trees.

Whooooooh. Whooooh. Whoooh. Up and down a mournful scale. Something is coming out of those woods, I thought, and is going to take vengeance for this horror on the first human being it sees.

Then I saw a movement in the grass at the end of the beach. It was a loon.

Loons have become something of a cause célèbre to bird lovers. They are beautiful birds, almost as large as geese, with long, sharp beaks, striking black-and-white striped wings and a graceful, streamlined head. They are a threatened species in the United States because they need large bodies of water to fish in and undeveloped, marshy shorelines to nest on, and most shoreline in this country has been landscaped and pruned.

The most compelling thing about the loon is its call – something between a cry, a whistle and a sob, a sound so mournful and chilling it provoked the word "loony", a term for someone wild with sorrow, out of their head.

This was an artic loon in its winter plumage, brown instead of the striking black and white of summer. It had ruby-red eyes, which blinked in terror because it could barely move. It was lightly oiled all over – breast, feet, wings, head – destroying its power of flight. Its sinuous head darted here and there as we approached. It flapped and stumbled, trying to avoid us, and then it came to rest between two large rocks.

As Dawson photographed it, it intermittently called its mournful call. Its mate swam back and forth, calling back, a few yards offshore.

I could see it tremble, a sign that the bird was freezing. Most oiled birds die because the oil destroys their insulation.

"It's like someone with a down coat falling into a lake," Dawson explained. The breeze ruffled its stiffening feathers. As Dawson moved closer with the camera, it uttered a low quivering cry.

After 10 minutes or so, I just couldn't watch anymore. It was so beautiful, and so helpless and so doomed. We had nothing like a bag, sack or cloth to hold it in. I walked around the point.

Then I heard Dawson calling. He walked into view holding the furious, flapping loon by its upper wings, set it down on the grass and said, "Come here and help me. He won't hurt you."

I was stunned by the rough handling of such a wild thing, but it developed that Dawson, the former veterinarian, knew his birds. He had grasped the loon exactly in the place where his wings would not break. He would tell me later that most bird rescuers are too tender-hearted or frightened of birds to contain them, and let a lot of salvageable birds get away.

We had to wait for the helicopter, and Dawson had to take more pictures, so I grasped the loon behind the upper wings, pinning them together, and took up the loon watch. The bird rose, struggled and fell back to earth, then was still.

I was as afraid of the loon as it was of me in a way that touching a totally wild thing can provoke. But I began to feel its strength. It was warm, it had energy, and it could still struggle. I could hear it breathing, and could feel its pulse. It turned its red eye steadily on me. We breathed, and waited, together.

Dawson returned, took a black cord from a lens case and neatly looped it around the bird's wings. The helicopter dropped out of the sky and settled on the beach. I held the string as the loon, unblinking, faced the terrific wind kicked up by the machine. Then Dawson neatly scooped up the bird and settled into the helicopter. The loon lashed out with its needle beak until David Grimes, a fisherman working with the state on the spill, enveloped it in a wool knit bag he carried with him. The bird stilled.

Dawson and I were both streaked with oil and blood from the loon's feet, lacerated by barnacles on the beach. He gave me a small black and white feather that had fallen from the bird's wing.

We took the loon to the bird-rescue center in Valdez. I don't know if it will live. Dawson thought it had a good chance. I thought of the mate we had left behind in the water.

Afterward, we talked about whom bird rescues help more, the rescued or the rescuer. Most rescued birds don't make it. And tens of thousands more from the Valdez spill will die before they even get a chance.

I know only that the loon told me something that no one other thing about this tragedy could. If only we could learn to value such stubborn, determined life. If only we could hold safe in our hands the heart of the loon.

ONE MAN'S SUN-BAKED THEORY
ON ATHLETIC SUPREMACY

Los Angeles Times, 30 April 1989

Sports columnist for the *Los Angeles Times*, Murray won the 1990 Pulitzer for Commentary.

A few days ago, NBC, which should have known better, presented a one-hour seminar-type TV programme that undertook to show that blacks are better athletes than whites. Next week, presumably, they're going to have one to show the earth is round. Water is wet.

But it's when they got into the reasons for blacks being superior that they got into water they couldn't tread. They brought in grave scientists to give learned discourses. And when they traced it to physiological racial differences, they raised the hackles on large segments of the populace.

Any sportswriter could have told them that would happen.

You see, none of us likes to be told we're different. Even if the differences are advantageous. With the exception of a few Anglo-Saxon eccentrics who despise the rest of mankind, we're a conformist lot.

If we're good at something, we don't like to be told it's because we have this twitch muscle not given to the rest of human beings. It's like being able to see better because you've got three eyes.

Great athletes, like great musicians, of course, have some gift the rest of mankind doesn't. Sam Snead, the great golfer, is double-jointed. Ted Williams, in his prime, had the eyesight of a hungry hawk. But these were hardly group legacies.

Do black athletes have some edge that accounts for their

preponderance of representation in all sports they undertake? Well, of course they do. There's an old saying that when a thing happens once, it can be an accident. Twice, it can be a coincidence. But if it keeps happening, it's a trend.

The poor doctors on the network, a physiologist and an anthropologist who stuck their test tubes into this liquid dynamite of an issue, appeared on television to be politically and sociologically naive.

They seemed startled that their innocent research could arouse such vehement passions as when the Berkeley sociologist, Harry Edwards, with whom few dare to cross adjectives and prepositions, thundered that their study was racist. You learn never to cross points of view with Harry. He's bigger than you are. Also louder.

The scientists are not only naive, they were a little unscientific. To understand why American blacks were succeeding in such boggling numbers, they studied *West Africans*. Figure that one out.

It didn't take Harry Edwards long to point out – correctly – that American blacks are a long way genetically from any African blacks. The American black, like the American anything, is a mixture of races, cultures and pigments. Sherman's army has descendants in every ghetto in America, you can bet me. Edwards himself reminded the panel that he had great, great grandparents who were Irish. So did I but I never had a good jump shot.

Harry likes to think racism and segregation drove the young blacks into the one avenue open to them in a closed society – sports. They got good at them because they were desperate.

I can buy that. Up to a point. Deprivation is a powerful motivating force. So is hatred. There's very little doubt raging hatred made Ty Cobb excel after the day he came home and found that his mother had shot and killed his father by "accident". Cobb set out to make the world pay.

But I would like to offer my own theory of athletic supremacy.

Unweighted by any scientific gobbledygook, not bogged down by any documented research, not even cluttered by facts, Murray's Law of Athletic Supremacy is beautiful in its simplicity, based on a longtime non-balancing of the issues, a resolute refusal to entertain any other points of view. Charles Darwin, I'm not. I base my findings on that most incontrovertible of stances – total ignorance. Compared to me, Darwin was equivocal.

First of all, I don't think it is twitch muscles or long tendons or larger lungs or even that old standby, rhythm, that contrives to make African-Americans superior athletes.

In the second place, I have never been able to understand the convoluted scientific efforts to explain away the darker pigment on some human beings. To me, it is a simple matter of geography. The closer you get to the Equator, the darker the skin.

I mean, aren't southern Italians darker than Swedes? Skin colouring is a function of climate. I will cling to this notion until a blond, blue-eyed baby is born to natives in Zimbabwe or a black-skinned child emerges in Scandinavia.

I am absolutely positive that if you had put a colony of Irishmen in the Sudan in, say, 5000 BC, their descendants would be black today. If you had put a Sudanese population in Dublin in 5000 BC, their descendants would have red hair.

Now, we come to athletic prowess. Murray's Law is simple: athletic prowess is bestowed on that part of the population that is closer to the soil, deals with a harshness of existence, asks no quarter of life and gets none.

Nothing in my business, journalism, makes me laugh louder than to pick up a paper and find some story, marvelling wide-eyed, at how some deprived youngster from a tar paper shack in Arkansas, one of 26 children, rose to become heavyweight champion of the world, all-world centre in the NBA, home run champion or Super Bowl quarter-back. Well, of course he did. That's dog-bites-man stuff.

A much bigger, more astonishing story would be if a youngster came out of a silk-sheets, chauffeur-to-school, governess-at-home atmosphere in the mansions of Long Island to become heavyweight champion of the world, or even left fielder for the Yankees.

You always get great athletes from the bottom of the economic order. That goes back to the days of ancient Rome, when the gladiators were all slaves (later Christians, and we all know the early Christians were the poor).

In this country, the lineups of professional teams were always filled with the names of farm boys or the sons of the waves of immigrants who came over here from the farmlands of Ireland or

Germany or Italy or Poland. How do you think Shoeless Joe got his nickname? Why do you think he couldn't read or write?

The African-Americans are simply taking up where the Irish-Americans, German-Americans, Jewish-Americans, Italian-Americans and the home-grown farm boys left off. Like their predecessors, they come from a long line of people who worked long, hot hours in the sun, growing grapes, chopping cotton, cutting cane. This makes the belly hard, the muscles sinewy, the will stubborn but accustomed to hardship. This is the edge the black athlete has. The same edge the boys from the cornfield, the boys who came from a long line of Bavarian stump-clearers, had in another era.

And what happened to them may happen to the American black. Already, as blacks migrate from the levees and cotton fields of the Old South and get more than one generation away from it to the metropolises of the North and East and live their lives by radiators and soft beds and eat junk food instead of soul food, they are losing their places, increasingly, to the hardy breeds from Central America and the Caribbean. That's the way it goes.

Don't ask me to explain any of this. Trust me. I'm fresh out of test tubes. Don't burden me with facts. Or twitch muscles. As Harry Edwards and I could tell you, Irishmen don't have twitch muscles.

JONATHAN STEELE

MCDONALD'S IN MOSCOW

The Guardian, 1 February 1990

A quarter of an hour to closing time, the queue outside the first Soviet McDonald's was down to 300.

"We'll go on to midnight if necessary to serve all these good people," Mr George Godden, the operations manager, promised as he stood at the front of the line in Moscow last night, letting batches of thirty or forty people in every five minutes.

On the first day of its opening more than 20,000 people streamed into the fantasy-land restaurant, which is not only bigger than any other in the world but also more lavish in its decor. Most of the customers had never had a hamburger in their lives. Natalya Kaltshekh, a doctor in her early forties, gazed at the huge plate-glass windows behind which happy Russians were tucking into food twice as fast as anything else Moscow has ever offered.

She had only been queuing for fifteen minutes and was already at the front of the line. In her hand she held a copy of the multicoloured menu given out to people in the queue. "I have never eaten this kind of food," she confessed. She had heard about McDonald's on Soviet television.

People did not stay inside as long as the management had feared. They had worried that customers would be much slower than the food. "Not a bit of it," said Mr Godden. "They've stayed on average just the same time as anywhere else in the world." Many people had bought several portions to take home, he said. "They're feeding their families on this."

A couple of young computer science undergraduates, Volodya and Natasha Leshinsky, emerged smiling after about forty minutes inside. Asked how it compared with typical Soviet cafés,

Natasha said: "The service is so good." They had eaten hamburgers before at one of the new co-operative cafés, Volodya said. "But the meat is poor quality, and it was relatively more expensive, at least for what you were getting for your money. This place is world class."

Half a dozen policemen stood around near stacks of crash barriers. Earlier in the day the queue had been up to 2,000, snaking back through a zig-zag of barriers on the edge of Pushkin Square, Moscow's Piccadilly Circus, a favourite spot for strollers, except that it has been remarkably devoid of neon until today. Now it is lit up by McDonald's trademark golden yellow arch.

The restaurant is a joint venture between the Moscow City Council and McDonald's Canadian subsidiary. It has taken fourteen years to get McDonald's to Moscow. The first overtures were made at the Montreal Olympics in 1976. Unlike most other joint ventures in the service field, this one only takes roubles. Westerners in Moscow are surrounded by joint venture hotels, restaurants, Xeroxing offices, film processing kiosks, and food shops. None of them caters for the vast majority of Russians who have no access to hard currency.

McDonald's has done it differently. Its vice-president, George Cohon, remembers the moment when one Russian looked at the plaque outside the door which says that service is for roubles only. "This is *perestroika*," he beamed.

THE BOMBING OF BAGHDAD

The Observer, 20 January 1991

Operation Desert Storm, the Allied attempt to drive Iraq from its illegal occupation of Kuwait, began with an aerial armageddon comprising 110,000 air sorties in two weeks. Targets included the Iraqi capital city of Baghdad, first bombed in the early morning of 17 January 1991. John Simpson, the Foreign Affairs Editor of the BBC, was among the Western journalists in Baghdad when the heavens opened with bombs.

It had taken us much too long to get our gear together. I was angry with myself as we ran across the marble floor of the hotel lobby, scattering the security men and Ministry of Information minders.

A voice wailed after us in the darkness: "But where are you going?" "There's a driver here somewhere," said Anthony Wood, the freelance cameraman we had just hired. When I saw which driver it was, I swore. He was the most cowardly of them all. The calmer, more rational voice of Eamonn Matthews, our producer, cut in: "We'll have to use him. There's no one else." It was true. The other drivers knew there was going to be an attack, and had vanished.

We had no idea where we wanted to go. There was no high ground, to give us a good shot of the city. We argued as the car screeched out of the hotel gate and down into the underpass. "No bridges," I said. "He's heading for 14 July Bridge. If they bomb that we'll never get back."

The driver swerved alarmingly, tyres squealing. At that moment, all round us, the anti-aircraft guns started up. Brilliant red and white tracers arched into the sky, then died and fell away. There was the ugly rumble of bombs. I looked at my watch: 2.37

a.m. The bombing of Baghdad had begun twenty-three minutes earlier than we had been told to expect. For us, those minutes would have made all the difference.

The sweat shone on the driver's face in the light of the flashes. "Where's he going now?" He did a wild U-turn, just as the sirens started their belated wailing. Anthony wrestled with the unaccustomed camera. "I'm getting this," he grunted. The lens was pointing at a ludicrous angle into the sky as another immense burst of fireworks went off beside us. It was hard not to flinch at the noise.

"The bloody idiot – he's heading straight back to the hotel." The driver had had enough. He shot in through the gates and stopped. We had failed ignominiously in our effort to escape the control of the authorities and now we were back.

I had become obsessed with getting out of the Al Rasheed Hotel. It smelled of decay, and it lay between five major targets: the presidential palace, the television station, an airfield, several Ministries. I had no desire to be trapped with 300 people in the underground shelters there, and I wanted to get away from the government watchers. Television requires freedom of action, and yet we were trapped again.

In the darkness of the lobby angry hands grabbed us and pushed us downstairs into the shelter. The smell of frightened people in a confined space was already starting to take over. Anthony held the camera over his head to get past the sobbing women who ran against us in the corridor. Children cried. Then the lights went out, and there was more screaming until the emergency power took over. Most of the Western journalists were hanging round the big shelter. I was surprised to see one of the cameramen there: he had a reputation for courage and independence, but now he was just looking at the waves of frightened people with empty red eyes. Anthony, by contrast, was neither worried nor elated. He was mostly worried about getting his equipment together.

Not that it *was* his equipment. Anthony had stepped in to help us because our own cameramen had to leave. It had been a difficult evening. As more and more warnings came in from New York, Paris and London, about the likelihood of an attack, almost every news organization with people in Baghdad was instructing them to leave. The personal warnings President Bush had given to American editors suggested that the coming onslaught would be the worst since the Second World War.

I remembered my grandfather's stories of men going mad under the bombardment at the Somme and Passchendaele. This would be the first high-tech war in history and most newspapers and television companies were reluctant to expose their employees to it. The BBC, too, had ordered us out. Some wanted to; others didn't. In the end it came to a four-three split: Bob Simpson, the radio correspondent and a good friend of mine for years, decided to stay; so did Eamonn Matthews. I was the third. In our cases the BBC, that most civilized of British institutions, came up with a sensible formula: it was instructing us to leave, but promised to take no action against us if we refused.

We still needed a cameraman. But by now there were several people whose colleagues had decided to move out, but who were determined to stay themselves. We found two who were prepared to work with us: Nick Della Casa and Anthony Wood.

There seemed to be no getting out of the shelter. Guards, some of them armed with Kalashnikovs, stood at each of the exits from the basement. They had orders to stop anyone leaving. The main shelter was now almost too full to sit or lie down. Some people seemed cheerful enough, and clapped and sang or watched Iraqi television. Children were crying, and guests and hotel staff were still arriving all the time from the upper floors.

In the general panic, the normal patterns of behaviour were forgotten. A woman in her thirties arrived in a coat and bath towel, and slowly undressed and put on more clothes in front of everyone. Nobody paid her the slightest attention. The heavy metal doors with their rubber linings and the wheel for opening and closing them, as in a submarine, stayed open.

Even so, I felt pretty bad. From time to time it seemed to me that the structure of the hotel swayed a little as if bombs were landing around us. Perhaps it was my imagination. To be stuck here, unable to film anything except a group of anxious people, was the worst thing I could imagine. Anthony and I got through the submarine door and tried to work our way up the staircase that led to the outside world. A guard tried to stop us, but I waited till the next latecomer arrived and forced my way through. Anthony followed.

The upper floors were in darkness. We laboured along the corridor, trying to work out by feel which was our office. Listening at one door, I heard the murmur of voices and we were let in. The sky was lit up by red, yellow and white flashes, and there was no need for us to light torches or candles. Every explosion had us cowering and ducking. I wandered round a little and asked a friendly cameraman to film what's called in the trade "a piece to camera" for me.

Despite the crash and the whine of bombs and artillery outside we whispered to each other. By now, though, I was acclimatizing to the conditions, and sorted out the words in my head before I started. You are not popular with cameramen if you need too many takes under such circumstances.

Back in the corridor there was a flash from a torch, and an Iraqi called out my name. A security man had followed me up from the shelter. In order to protect the others I walked down towards him in the yellow torchlight. I had no idea what I was going to do, but I saw a partly open door to my left and slipped inside. I was lucky. The vivid flashes through the window showed I was in a suite of rooms which someone was using as an office.

I worked my way past the furniture and locked myself in the bedroom at the end. Lying on the floor, I could see the handle turning slowly in the light from the battle outside. When the security man found the door was locked he started banging on it and calling out my name, but these doors were built to withstand rocket attacks; a mere security man had no chance.

Close by, a 2,000-pound penetration bomb landed, but contrary to the gossip in the hotel neither my eyeballs nor the fillings in my teeth came out. I switched on the radio I found by the bed and listened to President Bush explaining what was going on. It was 5.45, and I was soon asleep.

At nine o'clock there was more banging on the door, and more calling of my name. It was Eamonn, who had tracked me down to tell me he had got our satellite telephone to work. Smuggling the equipment through the airport two weeks before had been a smart piece of work, and in a city without power and without communications we now had both a generator and the means to broadcast to the outside world.

Eamonn moved the delicate white parasol of the dish around until it locked on to the satellite. It was hard to think that something so complex could be achieved so easily. We dialled up the BBC and spoke to the pleasant, cool voice of the traffic manager. It was just as if we were somewhere sensible, and not sheltering against a brick wall from the air raids. I gave a brief account to the interviewer at the other end about the damage that the raids had caused in the night: the telecommunications tower damaged, power stations destroyed. I had less idea what was happening on the streets. Directly the broadcast was over, I headed out with Anthony for a drive around. "Not good take picture now, Mr John," said the driver. He was an elderly crook but I had an affection for him all the same. "Got to work, I'm afraid, Ali." He groaned.

It was extraordinary: the city was in the process of being deprived of power and communications, and yet the only sign of damage I could see was a broken window at the Ministry of Trade. The streets were almost empty, except for soldiers trying to hitch a lift. "Going Kuwait, Basra," said Ali. Some were slightly wounded, and their faces seemed completely empty.

Iraqis are normally animated and sociable, but there was no talking now, even in the bigger groups. A woman dragged her child along by its arm. A few old men squatted with a pile of oranges or a few boxes of cigarettes in front of them. An occasional food shop or a tea-house was open; that was all.

"Allah." A white car was following us. "He see you take picture." I told Ali to take a sudden right turn, but he lacked the courage. The security policeman waved us down. "Just looking round," I said, as disarmingly as I could. "He say you come with him." "Maybe," said Anthony.

We got back into the car, and followed the white car for a little. The Al Rasheed Hotel was in the distance. "Go there," I said loudly, and Ali for once obeyed. The policeman waved and shouted, but by now the sirens were wailing again and the Ministry of Defence, on the left bank of the river, went up in a column of brown and grey smoke.

Ali put his foot down, and made it to the hotel. The policeman in his white car arrived thirty seconds after us, but obediently searched for a place in the public car park while the three of us ran into the hotel and lost ourselves in the crowd which filled the lobby.

In a windowless side office, where our minders sat for safety, I spotted a face I knew: Jana Schneider, an American war photographer, completely fearless. Throughout the night she had wandered through Baghdad filming the falling missiles. Near the Sheraton she had watched a "smart" bomb take out a Security Ministry building while leaving the houses on either side of it undamaged.

I found it hard to believe, and yet it tied in with my own observation. This extraordinary precision was something new in warfare. As the day wore on, Baghdad seemed to me to be suffering from an arteriosclerosis – it appeared unchanged, and yet its vital functions were atrophying with each new air raid. It was without water, power and communication.

I was putting together an edited report for our departing colleagues to smuggle out when someone shouted that a cruise missile had just passed the window. Following the line of the main road beside the hotel and travelling from south-west to north-east, it flashed across at 500 miles an hour, making little noise and leaving no exhaust. It was twenty feet long, and was a good hundred yards from our window. It undulated a little as it went, following the contours of the road. It was like the sighting of a UFO.

Another air raid began, and I ran down the darkened corridor to report over our satellite phone. Lacking the navigational sophistication of the cruise missile, I slammed into a heavy mahogany desk where the hotel security staff sometimes stationed themselves. I took the corner in the lower ribs and lay there for a little.

When I reported soon after that I was the only known casualty of the day's attacks among the Al Rasheed's population and explained that I had cracked a couple of ribs, this was taken in London to be a coded message that I had been beaten up.

I was deeply embarrassed. Having long disliked the journalist-as-hero school of reporting, I found myself a mild celebrity for something which emphatically hadn't taken place. An entire country's economic and military power was being dismantled, its people were dying, and I was broadcasting about cracked ribs. Each time they hurt I felt it was a punishment for breaking the basic rule: don't talk about yourself.

In the coffee shop, a neat but exhausted figure was reading

from a thick sheaf of papers. Naji Al-Hadithi was a figure of power for the foreign journalists in Baghdad, since he was Director-General of the Information Ministry. Some found him sinister: a *New York Times* reporter took refuge in the US embassy for four nights after talking to him. I thought he was splendid company, a considerable Anglophile, and possessed of an excellent sense of humour. Once I took a colleague of mine to see him, and he asked where we'd been. "We went to Babylon, to see what the whole country will look like in a fortnight's time," I said. For a moment I thought I'd gone much too far, then I saw Al-Hadithi was rocking with silent laughter.

Now he looked close to exhaustion, and his clothes were rumpled. He read out some communiques and a long, scarcely coherent letter from Saddam Hussein to President Bush. Afterwards we talked about the censorship the Ministry planned to impose. In the darkened lobby of the hotel, with the candlelight glinting on glasses and rings and the buttons of jackets, we argued amicably about the new rules. It seemed to me that it was the Security Ministry, not his own, that was insisting on them.

That evening Brent Sadler, the ITN correspondent, rang me. CNN had warned him that our hotel was to be a target that evening. I told the others. No one wanted to go down to the shelter. We decided instead to do what Jana Schneider had done the previous night, and roam the streets.

I cleared out my safety deposit box, and gathered the necessities of my new life: identification in case of arrest, money for bribes, a hairbrush in case I had to appear on television, a notebook and pen. No razor, since without water shaving was impossible. But we were unlucky again. The sirens wailed early, at eight o'clock, and the automatic doors of the hotel were jammed shut. Once again, we were taken down into the shelter.

The whole cast of characters who inhabited our strange new world was there: Sadoun Jenabi, Al-Hadithi's deputy, a large, easy going man who had spent years in Britain and stayed in the shelter most of the time now; and English peace campaigner, Edward Poore, who was a genuine eccentric, carried a cricket bat everywhere and had knotted a Romanian flag round his neck to remind himself of the time he spent there in the revolution; most of our minders and security men; just about all the journalists; and a large number of the hotel staff and their families, settling down nervously for the night. It was cold. I put a flak-jacket over me for warmth and used my bag as a pillow.

MARK FRITZ

BACK WITH A VENGEANCE: REFUGEE REBELS BATTLE TO CONQUER HELL

Associated Press, 17 May 1994

Fritz won the Pulitzer Prize for his dispatches from the African state of Rawanda, torn apart by ethnic conflict between the minority Tutsi tribe and the majority Hutus.

Rugende, Rwanda (AP)

Francois Rwagansana once took well-off Westerners on exotic but safe safaris throughout Africa. But he came home for the ultimate adventure tour: guerrilla warfare.

"It was exciting," said Rwagansana, 33, who plies his new trade at a rebel base here, five miles north of the divided capital. He has learned how to survive sickness, carry weeks of food on his back – and break the proper bones of rigid dead enemies to better remove their coveted clothing.

And he has learned how to kill.

"Sometimes I ask myself: what am I doing here?" said the tall, lanky Rwagansana, a university graduate in sociology smartly dressed in jungle fatigues and Adidas high-top sneakers.

What Rwagansana and others like him are doing is fighting a war against a government they believe has carefully orchestrated the slaughter of what the United Nations estimates is 100,000 to 200,000 people in the past five weeks.

The mind-boggling killing spree broke out after the Hutu president died in a mysterious plane crash. Government soldiers and civilian militias began massacring Tutsis and Hutus perceived as their allies.

At the time, the rebel Rwandan Patriotic Front had brokered a truce with the government. When the killings began, however, it mobilized its troops and launched a new offensive. It now controls most of this blood-drenched nation of 8 million people.

The complex ethnic and social tensions date to colonial days and the 1959 rebellion by the majority Hutus against the repressive minority Tutsi government.

Thousands of Tutsis field to Uganda, Zaire, Kenya and Burundi to escape the reprisals that followed, and they raised a lost generation of Rwandan children who formed the core of the rebel army that launched the RPF invasion from Uganda in 1990.

"These young men hardly know their country, hardly know the difference between a Hutu and a Tutsi," said Tito Rutaremara, 49, a RPF political leader.

"Yet there they are, in the bush, fighting the war," he said, gesturing to the lovely green hills filled with thousands of corpses.

To their supporters, the rebels are seen as the cavalry coming to the rescue of a country hemorrhaging rivers of blood.

Human rights organizations and aid workers have uniformly held the Hutu-led militias responsible for most of the carnage in Rwanda. The vast majority of victims have been Tutsis, most of them hacked to death with clubs and machetes.

The Tutsi-dominated rebel movement, which includes many Hutus and professes a platform of national unity, has ordered troops to refrain from seeking retribution against Hutu soldiers and civilian militias.

Revenge is officially prohibited, and there have been only scattered, isolated and unconfirmed reports of reprisals.

But Rwagansana, 33, admits the anti-vengeance edict is a hard code to live by.

"You see all those people dead because they were Tutsi, and you make them want to pay," said Rwagansana, who left Rwanda as a child and came home from Kenya three years ago. "Why don't they fight us instead of innocent peasants?"

Guerrilla Eric Ruhumuriza – a 16-year-old, baby-faced kid who looks closer to 12 – struggles with the same emotion. His parents were killed during a massacre in early April. The orphan was quickly adopted by the rebels, who gave him a small uniform and a big AK-47.

"I have a feeling of revenge, but the code prevents it," he said as he sat at the rebel base here on Sunday.

Mortar shells boomed in the background as the rebels fired on a government base on the outskirts of Kigali, the capital where large units of government soldiers are based.

The smell of rotting massacre victims in the surrounding fields wafted through the base as the soldiers drank tea and ate rice and beans.

Suddenly a new song came on the radio, its lyrics urging people to kill RPF sympathizers.

"They're still killing innocent people," said Capt. Mark Sebaganji, a rebel commander.

Rwagansana says the worst problems he faced with his old job as a tour guide with the US-based Overseas Adventure Travel were quarreling tourists and broken-down safari vehicles.

"Imagine coming from a city like Nairobi [Kenya] and you find yourself in the bush," he said. "Suddenly, you're just there, and you're attacking people and they're attacking you.

"You sleep outside, there's mosquitoes – I've had malaria twice," he said. "You got a gun, people are shooting and bombs are falling."

Shortly after he joined the rebels in 1991, Rwagansana said he realized he was in a grim new world when he and a more seasoned rebel approached the body of a dead government soldier.

He found out it was time to resupply.

"He broke the bones at the elbow and took the shirt, then he took the pants and the boots," he said. "I asked myself: Could I do that?"

DEATH AT THE TOP OF THE WORLD

Into Thin Air, 1997

A contributing editor to *Outside* magazine, Krakauer went to Everest in 1996 to report on the popularity of guided ascents of the mountain. He got more story than he expected, when a killer storm descended on Everest on 10 May, leaving many climbers stranded, among them the New Zealander Rob Hall.

Around 9:30 a.m. [11 May], Ang Dorje and Lhakpa Chhiri left Camp Four and started climbing toward the South Summit with a thermos of hot tea and two extra canisters of oxygen, intending to rescue Hall. They faced an exceedingly formidable task. As astounding and courageous as Boukreev's rescue of Sandy Pittman and Charlotte Fox had been the night before, it paled in comparison to what the two Sherpas were proposing to do now: Pittman and Fox had been a twenty-minute walk from the tents over relatively flat ground; Hall was 3,000 vertical feet above Camp Four – an exhausting eight- or nine-hour climb in the best of circumstances.

And these were surely not the best of circumstances. The wind was blowing, in excess of 40 knots. Both Ang Dorje and Lhakpa were cold and wasted from climbing to the summit and back just the day before. If they did somehow manage to reach Hall, moreover, it would be late afternoon before they got there, leaving only one or two hours of daylight in which to begin the even more difficult ordeal of bringing him down. Yet their loyalty to Hall was such that the two men ignored the over-whelming odds and set out toward the South Summit as fast as they could climb.

Shortly thereafter, two Sherpas from the Mountain Madness

team – Tashi Tshering and Ngawang Sya Kya (a small, trim man, greying at the temples, who is Lopsang's father) – and one Sherpa from the Taiwanese team headed up to bring down Scott Fischer and Makalu Gau. Twelve hundred feet above the South Col the trio of Sherpas found the incapacitated climbers on the ledge where Lopsang had left them. Although they tried to give Fischer oxygen, he was unresponsive. Scott was still breathing, barely, but his eyes were fixed in their sockets, and his teeth were tightly clenched. Concluding that he was beyond hope, they left him on the ledge and started descending with Gau, who, after receiving hot tea and oxygen, and with considerable assistance from the three Sherpas, was able to move down to the tents on a short-rope under his own power.

The day had started out sunny and clear, but the wind remained fierce, and by late morning the upper mountain was wrapped in thick clouds. Down at Camp Two the IMAX team reported that the wind over the summit sounded like a squadron of 747s, even from 7,000 feet below. Meanwhile, high on the Southeast Ridge, Ang Dorje and Lhakpa Chhiri pressed on resolutely through the intensifying storm toward Hall. At 3:00 p.m., however, still 700 feet below the South Summit, the wind and subzero cold proved to be too much for them, and the Sherpas could go no higher. It was a valiant effort, but it had failed – and as they turned around to descend, Hall's chances for survival all but vanished.

Throughout the day on 11 May, his friends and teammates incessantly begged him to make an effort to come down under his own power. Several times Hall announced that he was preparing to descend, only to change his mind and remain immobile at the South Summit. At 3:20 p.m., Cotter – who by now had walked over from his own camp beneath Pumori to the Everest Base Camp – scolded over the radio, "Rob, get moving down the ridge."

Sounding annoyed, Hall fired back, "Look, if I thought I could manage the knots on the fixed ropes with me frostbitten hands, I would have gone down six hours ago, pal. Just send a couple of the boys up with a big thermos of something hot – then I'll be fine."

"Thing is, mate, the lads who went up today encountered some high winds and had to turn around," Cotter replied, trying to convey as delicately as possible that the rescue attempt had been abandoned, "so we think your best shot is to move lower."

"I can last another night here if you send up a couple of boys with some Sherpa tea, first thing in the morning, no later than nine-thirty or ten," Rob answered.

"You're a tough man, Big Guy," said Cotter, his voice quavering. "We'll send some boys up to you in the morning."

At 6:20 p.m., Cotter contacted Hall to tell him that Jan Arnold was on the satellite phone from Christchurch and was waiting to be patched through. "Give me a minute," Rob said. "Me mouth's dry. I want to eat a bit of snow before I talk to her." A little later he came back on and rasped in a slow, horribly distorted voice, "Hi, my sweet-heart. I hope you're tucked up in a nice warm bed. How are you doing?"

"I can't tell you how much I'm thinking about you!" Arnold replied. "You sound so much better than I expected . . . Are you warm, my darling?"

"In the context of the altitude, the setting, I'm reasonably comfortable." Hall answered, doing his best not to alarm her.

"How are your feet?"

"I haven't taken me boots off to check, but I think I may have a bit of frostbite. . . ."

"I'm looking forward to making you completely better when you come home," said Arnold. "I just know you're going to be rescued. Don't feel that you're alone. I'm sending all my positive energy your way!"

Before signing off, Hall told his wife, "I love you. Sleep well, my sweetheart. Please don't worry too much."

These would be the last words anyone would hear him speak. Attempts to make radio contact with Hall later that night and the next day went unanswered. Twelve days later, when Breashears and Viesturs climbed over the South Summit on their way to the top, they found Hall lying on his right side in a shallow ice hollow, his upper body buried beneath a drift of snow.

JONATHAN FREEDLAND

THE HOMECOMING

The Guardian, 1 September 1997

The popular icon of the latter part of the 20th century, Diana Spencer, ex-wife of the Prince of Wales, was killed in a car crash in Paris, 30 August 1997.

In the end, they let her go quietly. No drum, no funeral note – only a dumb silence as the body of Diana, Princess of Wales, returned to the land she might have ruled as queen.

There was no crowd to meet her, none of the hordes of flag-wavers she so delighted in life. Instead the flat, grey tarmac of RAF Northolt, windy as a prairie, a line-up of dignitaries – and a hearse.

She had made the journey from Paris by plane, on an RAF BAe 146. They kept the coffin in the passenger cabin, within sight of her two sisters, Lady Jane Fellows and Lady Sarah McCorquodale, and her former husband, the Prince of Wales.

The skies themselves seemed to make way for her arrival, the clouds parting like an honour guard. Once the plane had landed, it nudged toward the welcoming party hesitantly, as if weighed down by its tragic cargo. Waiting there was the kind of receiving line Diana met every day. In the middle, arms by his sides, fists clenched tight, the prime minister. A cleric stood close by, bright in scarlet cassock. None of them said a word.

Eventually the plane door opened, and the prince appeared head down, hands clasped behind his back. He was guided by the Lord Chamberlain, the Earl of Airlie. In another context it might have been a standard royal visit: Charles shown round a new factory or hospital wing. But he had come on a more baleful duty. He took his place in line – as he has done so often.

By now, the team of coffin bearers, each one in the crisp uniform of the Queen's Colour Squadron, had completed its precise march toward the other side of the aircraft. At the stroke of seven o'clock, the hatch opened revealing a glimpse of colour, the Royal Standard clinging to the hard, square outline of the coffin. It seemed an unforgiving shape: just a box, with none of the curve or sparkle of the woman whose body lay within. The silence of the air was cut, and not just by the sound of distant traffic – which rumbled on, as if to prove that the clocks never stop, even for the death of a princess.

The air was filled with the *chickageev, chickageev* of the thousand camera lenses pointed at the scene ahead. Even now the world's telephoto eye was still staring at her, more focused than ever. Despite everything, everyone still wanted a piece of Diana. The cameras kept up their din, but there was an eerie silence from the men who held them. Once they would cry out, "Diana! Diana!" – urging her to look their way or to flash just one more of those million-dollar smiles. But there was no shouting yesterday. And no smiles either.

The bearers of the body inched their way to the hearse. They stood, swivelled on their heels, and clasping tight with their white-gloved hands, lowered the coffin as smoothly as a hydraulic pump. They were about to turn away, but a bit of the flag was still spilling out; it had to be tucked in, just like the train of one of Diana's more lavish ball gowns.

The sisters stepped forward, each one turning to curtsy for the man whom Diana had once loved. Charles kissed each one before they stepped into the royal Daimler. The next car was filled with bouquets.

The prince himself did his duty, talking to each one of the VIPs who had stood beside him. Tony Blair clasped both royal hands in a double handshake, nodding intently. Charles made a gesture with upturned palms, as if to say "What can I do?" He thanked the RAF guard and disappeared back inside the plane, heading for Balmoral and his newly bereaved young sons. "He's going back to the boys," said his spokesman.

And then, on the final day of August, the sky darkened, and the wind whipped harder. It felt like the last day of summer, and the beginning of a long winter.

AN AFGHAN VILLAGE, DESTROYED AT THE HANDS OF MAN WHO VOWED PEACE

New York Times, 27 October 1997

John F. Burns won the 1997 Pulitzer Prize for his dispatches recounting the fundamentalist Taliban insurrection in Afghanistan.

Sar Cheshma, Afghanistan – In a country where at least 10,000 villages have been bombed, shelled and burned into rubble, the razing of one more hamlet can pass almost unnoticed. For hundreds of thousands of Afghan families who have lost their homes, the anonymity of the loss only adds to the pain.

So when a battered Kabul taxi arrived here Thursday morning, smoke still rising and the smell of torched ruins heavy in the air, villagers clamored to tell outsiders how Sar Cheshma had died.

Hastening down narrow lanes between fire-blackened houses, the handful of people remaining in the village abandoned for a moment their rush to board trucks waiting to carry them away as refugees.

The villagers' story has been a familiar one in the 18 years that Afghanistan has been at war. The twist this time was that the men who destroyed Sar Cheshma were the turbaned warriors of the Taliban, the ultra-conservative Muslims who have imposed a medieval social order across much of Afghanistan.

Two years ago, the Taliban sprang from religious schools with a promise to suppress the carnage that has killed an estimated 1.5 million Afghans and driven millions of others from their homes.

The villagers of Sar Cheshma say 30 Taliban fighters swept in at dawn on Tuesday, then spent several hours pouring canisters of gasoline into the 120 courtyard houses and setting them on fire.

Sar Cheshma lies barely five miles from the northern outskirts of Kabul, the capital, where the Taliban forces are fighting a village-by-village battle with the forces of Ahmad Shah Massoud, a less conservative Muslim leader whose troops used Sar Cheshma briefly on Monday as a base to fire on the Taliban.

A young mother and her three sons were killed by a Taliban rocket fired when the Massound forces were in the village.

There were no further deaths in the torching that nearly obliterated the village. But in one mud-walled courtyard after another, where hundreds of people lived, little remains but buckled bed frames, melted kitchen utensils and charred piles of grain.

"Are we not humans?" sobbed a 45-year-old woman named Narwaz, rushing forward with others to greet visitors who had slipped past Taliban checkpoints posted to keep outsiders away.

Beside her, a villager named Khairuddin, 55, waved a bloodied burqa, the head-to-toe shroud that the Taliban force all women to wear outside their homes. The garment was all that remained of his daughter, the woman killed with her sons in the Taliban rocket attack.

In a home up one of the village's dusty pathways, another man, Najmuddin, 30, broke away from sifting through his blackened grain supply, hoping to find enough uncharred bits to carry away.

Suddenly, the grain forgotten, his face contorted, he rushed to fetch a metal bowl piled high with ashes that had been balanced on a section of broken wall. It was all that remained of a copy of the Koran that he said had been in his family for generations.

"Tyrants! Tyrants!" he shouted, referring to the Taliban. "This is the book of God. Kill us if you must, but don't burn our holy book!"

Their attention attracted by his cries, several neighbors rushed forward, one with a large metal plate sitting among the utensils that Najmuddin had saved from the fire. Reverentially, Najmuddin placed the bowl with the ashes onto the plate and carried it away.

"We honor these ashes," he said, weeping. "The Koran is the book of God."

The shock of what happened here appeared to be all the greater among the villagers because the perpetrators were the Taliban.

When they emerged as a fighting force in 1994, the Taliban presented themselves as the harbingers of a new Afghanistan, modeled on the teachings of the Koran and inspired by a burning zeal to reunify the country.

From their original base in the southern city of Kandahar, they swept east and west, suppressing local militias that had reduced much of the country to anarchy. The Muslim clerics who led the Taliban promised that their forces would set new standards of decency in the fighting.

Taliban units appear to have avoided raping and pillaging in the manner of most of the other Afghan forces that have fought in the civil war. But they have become widely hated for the draconian social order laid down by the Taliban leaders, which bans women from working outside the home and girls from going to school, requires men to grow beards and forbids children to fly kites or play soccer.

Since Kabul fell to the Taliban four weeks ago, there has been a series of uprisings against them in towns and villages north of the capital. Now the Taliban have gone a step further, using tactics indistinguishable from those of other forces that have contributed to the country's destruction.

Today, two days after the attack on Sar Cheshma, Taliban jets bombed Kalakan, a village under the control of the Massoud forces about 10 miles further north.

According to an account by a reporter for the BBC who visited the village, the bombing killed 20 civilians.

Scene of Fighting Against Russians

In the case of Sar Cheshma, the Taliban attack was the latest in a series of disasters. The residents have repeatedly found themselves in the middle of the fighting because of the village's strategic position, hard up against the Ghoza mountain range, which runs like a shield across the northwestern flank of Kabul.

In the decade that Soviet forces were here, Sar Cheshma

became a stronghold for the Muslim guerrillas who ultimately drove out the Soviet troops.

Soviet bombers pounded the village more than once, leaving jagged ruins where mudwalled homes once stood and forcing many villagers to flee to Pakistan and Iran as refugees. Some returned after the Russians left, but barely a third of the village's 300 homes were occupied this week.

In the atmosphere of panic that gripped Sar Cheshma Thursday, many villagers said the Taliban were worse than the Russians.

"We killed more than 40 Russian soldiers in this village, but they never burned our houses," said Nizamuddin, 35, who like most others here had supported his family by raising livestock and working a small plot of land.

Again and again the villagers voiced special loathing for the Taliban because of the religious movement's claim to be the true upholders of the Koran.

"Didn't they do a wonderful job here, these Muslims?" said Nizamuddin, leading the visitors on a house-by-house tour. "Wasn't this burning of our village a true act of faith? We should applaud them – they are surely the best Muslims in the world."

If razing the village showed how none of the armies fighting for control of Afghanistan shows much mercy for civilians, it also demonstrated that the war has gone beyond a competition between faiths and ideologies and become little more than an ethnic struggle.

One reason the Taliban have been driven back so quickly from the northward advances they made after overrunning Kabul is that many villages dotting the dusty plain between Kabul and the Hindu Kush mountains 60 miles to the north are inhabited by ethnic Tajiks, the second-largest population group in Afghanistan.

All but a tiny minority of Taliban fighters are from the Pathan ethnic group, which is the largest in Afghanistan, accounting for about half the country's 16 million people.

As a Tajik village, Sar Cheshma was a natural attraction for Massoud's forces, and a natural target for Taliban suspicion. The villagers say Taliban fighters arrived last weekend, summoned them and ordered them to surrender all of their weapons. This done, the Taliban departed with a warning that any attempt by Massoud forces to enter the village should be reported immediately to a nearby Taliban post.

"We gave them our Kalashnikovs, and they said they would protect us," said the villager named Khairuddin.

On Monday, the villagers said, they awoke to find that a group of Massoud fighters under the command of a Muslim cleric from the village, Mullah Taj Mohammed, had slipped into Sar Cheshma overnight.

The Massoud fighters ordered the villagers to stay in their homes, making any warning to the Taliban impossible, the villagers said. A brief battle followed, they said, in which Khairuddin's family members were killed, then the Massoud fighters slipped away to the mountains, leaving the villagers to face the Taliban's wrath at first light on Tuesday.

For most of the villagers, the immediate future appears to lie in joining hundreds of thousands of refugees in Kabul, many of them so destitute that they wander the streets begging.

But one Sar Cheshma resident said she was finished with fleeing. Sajida, 40, a widow, clutched her son, Abdullah, 12, and said she would stay amid the ruins of her home.

Six years ago, her husband, an officer in the Communist army that disintegrated in 1992, was killed by a guerrilla rocket in Kabul. "I left Kabul to escape from the fighting," she said, "but the fighting has followed me wherever I have gone. Now, if I must, I will stay and die here."

THE CLOCK SAID 7.55 – PRECISELY THE TIME THE MISSLE STRUCK

The Independent, 24 March 2003

The great veteran and humanist of war correspondents, Fisk reported Gulf War II from behind Iraqi lines. The dispatch below was sent from Baghdad.

In the smashed concrete and mud, there was a set of Batwoman comics. On page 17, where the dirt had splashed on to the paper, Batwoman was, oddly, rescuing Americans from a burning tower block.

Not far from the crater, I found a history book recording the fate of old King Faisal and the armed opposition to British rule in Iraq. The cruise missile had flipped this book open to a page honouring "the martyr Mahmoud Bajat".

On the wall of the sitting room, and the floor was missing, the clock still hung on its nail. It had stopped at exactly 7.55, which was when the cruise missile smashed into numbers 10 and 10A of the laneway in the Zukah district of Baghdad on Saturday night.

Zukah is a slightly down-at-heel middle-class suburb with old orange trees and half-dead bougainvillaea and two-storey villas that need many coats of paint. There is a school at one end of the lane and, round the corner, a building site, but no obvious military target that I could see.

Amr Ahmed al-Dulaimi is a family man, 11 children and his wife were in number 10A when the missile crashed into the house of his neighbour, Abdul-Bari Samuriya, burying Mr Samuriya's wife and two children and punching a crater 20 feet into the ground. He managed to dig them out, both wounded children were still in hospital yesterday, but his home has gone. All that was left of the front room was a wooden sofa almost buried under six feet of earth, a table chopped neatly in half by the blast and a totally undamaged vase of bright red plastic flowers

So why the missile? Why should the Americans target with their supposedly precision ordnance this little middle-class ghetto? Mr Dulaimi runs a small engineering plant, Mr Sumuriya is a buisnessman. Could it be that the black curtains of oil smoke shrouding Baghdad in the attempt to mislead the guidance system of missiles had done its work all too well?

Crunching yesterday through the glass and powdered concrete of the road outside, I discovered a neighbour, as usual, it was a case of no names, who admitted he had sent his family away because "on Friday night, we had 15 missiles here". Fifteen? On little old, harmless Zukah? What did this mean? The missile fragments had scattered across dozens of houses and the Iraqi security men had turned up at dawn to collect them.

Down the road, another villa had been damaged, its walls cracked, its windows smashed. "This has always been a quiet district," its owner said to me. "Never ever have we experienced anything like this. Why, why, why?" How many times have I heard these words from the innocent? After every bombing, confronted by journalists, they say this to us. Always the same words.

Then I remembered what Iraqi radio said 24 hours before, and what the Iraqi Vice-President would tell us an hour later. "They are trying to assassinate President Hussein." Taha Yassin Ramadan. said. "What kind of state tries to assassinate another country's leader then says it is fighting a war on terror?"

The inhabitants of this little laneway in Zukah are none too happy about the way they have been targeted and I wasn't so certain that they were as keen to be "liberated" as the Americans might like to think.

ACKNOWLEDGMENTS

The editor has made every effort to locate all persons having rights in the selections appearing in this anthology and to secure permission for usage from the holders of such rights. Any queries regarding the use of material should be addressed to the editor c/o the publishers.

Adie, Bob. "The Sportswriter", Washington *Post and Times Herald* 13 August 1957. Copyright © 1957 *Washington Post*.

Amis, Martin. "The World According to Spielberg", *The Observer* 21 November 1982.

Arnold-Forster, Mark. "The Berlin Wall", *The Observer* 26 November 1961. Copyright © *The Observer* 1961.

Beauman, Sally. "But the People Are Beautiful", *Telegraph* magazine 5 February 1971. Copyright © 1971 Sally Beauman.

Bell, Elliott V. *We Saw It Happen*, Simon & Schuster Inc, 1938. Copyright © 1938 Simon & Schuster Inc.

Bigart, Homer. "Hope This is the Last One, Baby", New York *Herald Tribune* 16 August 1945. Copyright © 1945 New York *Herald Tribune*.

Burns, John F., "An Afghan Village, Destroyed at the Hands of Men who Vowed Peace": *New York Times*, 27 October 1997.

Cameron, James. "Sacred Blues", *Guardian* 23 November 1982. Copyright © 1985 the Estate of James Cameron.

Cannon, Jimmy. "Club Fighter", *True* January 1948. Copyright © 1948, 1951 Jimmy Cannon.

Cleave, Maureen. "John Lennon: We're More Popular Than Jesus Now", *Evening Standard* 4 March 1966. Copyright © 1966 the *Evening Standard*.

Cockburn, Claud. *I, Claud*, Penguin Books, 1967.

Cooke, Alistair. "Billy Graham in New York", Manchester *Guardian* 7 March 1955. Copyright © 1955 the *Guardian*.

Cooke, Alistair. "A Mule Cortege for the Apostle of the Poor", *Guardian* 9 April 1968. Copyright © 1968 the *Guardian*.

Cookman, Joseph. "Louisiana's Kingfish Lies in State", *New York Post* 12 September 1935.

Crosby, John. "London, The Most Exciting City in the World", Weekend *Telegraph* 16 April 1965. Copyright © 1965 John Crosby.

Delmer, D. Sefton, "Reichstag Fire", *Daily Express* 28 February 1933. Copyright © 1933 Express Newspapers Ltd.

Delmer, D. Sefton. "The Revolution in Hungary", *Daily Express* 24 October 1956. Copyright © 1956 Express Newspapers Ltd.

Dos Passos, John. "Red Day on Capitol Hill", *The New Republic* 23 December 1931. Copyright © 1931 Harrison-Blaine Inc.

Edgar, Donald. "The Wedding of Grace Kelly". Copyright © 1957 Donald Edgar.

Fagence, Maurice. "Sentence Day at Nuremberg", *Daily Herald* 2 October 1946. Copyright © 1946 MSI.

Fetterman, John. "P.F.C. Gibson Comes Home", Louisville *Times* July 1968.

Fisk, Robert. "It was the Christians", *The Times* 20 September 1982. Copyright © 1982 Times Newspapers Ltd.

Fisk, Robert. "The clock said 7.55 – precisely the time the missile struck", *The Independent*, 24 March © 2003. Copyright 2003 Robert Fisk and Independent Newspapers (UK) Ltd.

Frank, George. "A Member of the Manson Gang Tries to Kill President Ford", UPI 6 September 1975. Copyright © 1975 UPI.

Freedland, Jonathan. "The Homecoming", *Guardian* 1 September 1997. Copyright © 1997 the *Guardian*.

Fritz, Mark. "Back with a Vengeance", Associated Press 17 May 1994. Copyright © 1994 AP.

Gallagher, O.D. "The Loss of *Repulse*", *Daily Express* 12 December 1941. Copyright © 1941 Express Newspapers Ltd.

Gellhorn, Martha. "Justice at Night", *The Spectator* August 1936. Reprinted from *The View From the Ground*, Granta Books, 1989. Copyright © 1936, 1989 the Estate of Martha Gellhorn.

Gibbs, Philip. *Adventures in Journalism*, Heinemann, 1923.

Gott, Richard. "US Intelligence Agent In at Che Guevara's Death", *Guardian* 11 October 1967. Copyright © 1967 the *Guardian*.

Gunther, John. *Inside Europe*, Harper & Bros, 1940. Copyright © 1940 Harper & Bros. Reprinted by permission of HarperCollins Inc.

Gwinn, Mary Ann. "A Deadly Call of the Wild", *Seattle Times* 4 April 1989. Copyright © 1989 Seattle Times. Reprinted by permission of *The Seattle Times*.

Hastings, Max. "Max Hastings Leads the Way: The First Man into Port Stanley", *Evening Standard* 15 June 1982. Copyright © 1982 Max Hastings and the *Evening Standard*.

Hemingway, Ernest. "The Loyalists", *The New Republic* 1938. Copyright © 1938 Harrison-Blaine Inc, Mary Hemingway, Ernest Hemingway By-Line Company.

Herr, Michael. *Dispatches*, Alfred Knopf, 1977. Copyright © 1977 Michael Herr. Reprinted by permission of Macmillan.

Hersey, John. "Hiroshima", *New Yorker* August 1946. Copyright © 1946 New Yorker Magazine Inc.

Hersh, Seymour M. "My Lai: Lieutenant Accused of Murdering 109 Citizens", *St Louis Dispatch* 13 November 1969.

Hislop, John, "The Grand National: The View from the Saddle", *The Observer* 30 March 1947. Copyright © 1947 *The Observer*. Reprinted by permission of Guardian Media Ltd.

Hoggart, Simon. "Britannia Runs the Shop", *The Observer* 2 January 1983. Copyright © 1983 *The Observer*.

Jack, Ian. "Modern Life is Rubbish", *Sunday Times* 19 May 1985. Copyright © 1985 Times Newspapers Ltd.

James, Clive. "Drained Crystals", *The Observer* 16 September 1973. Copyright © 1973 *The Observer*.

Jenkins, Peter. "Miss Woods Puts Her Foot In It", *Guardian* 28 November 1973. Copyright © 1973 the *Guardian*.

Krakauer, Jon. *Into Thin Air*, Villard Books, 1997. Copyright © 1997 Jon Krakauer.

Laurence, William L. "A Mushroom Cloud" *New York Times* 3 September 1945. Copyright © 1945 New York Times.

Leitch, David. "Norman Mailer's Night Out", *Sunday Times* 25 April 1965. Copyright © 1965 Times Newspapers Ltd.

MacColl, R.M. "Woman Stoned to Death", *Daily Express* 11 February 1958. Copyright © 1958 Express Newspapers Ltd.

Mailer, Norman. "A Vote for Bobby K.", *Village Voice* 1965.

Marcus, Greil. "Woodstock", *Rolling Stone*, September 1969. Copyright © 1969 Greil Marcus.

Miller, David. "England Win World Cup", *Daily Telegraph* 31 July 1966. Copyright © 1966 Telegraph Group Ltd.

Miller, Webb. *I Found No Peace*, Victor Gollancz 1937. Copyright © 1941 The Estate of Webb Miller.

Mitchell, Jonathan. "Joe Louis Never Smiles", *The New Republic* 9 October 1935. Copyright © 1935 Harrison-Blaine Inc.

Morin, Relman. "Little Rock – Violence at Central High", Associated Press 4 September 1957. Copyright © 1957 AP.

Morris, James. "Everest Conquered", *The Times* 8 June 1953. Copyright © 1953 Times Newspapers Ltd.

Murray, Jim. "One Man's Sun-baked Theory on the Athletic Supremacy", *Los Angeles Times*, 30 April 1989. Copyright © 1989 *Los Angeles Times*.

Murrow, Edward R. "A Report During the Blitz", CBS radio 13 September 1940. Copyright © 1940 CBS Inc.

Orwell, George. *The Road to Wigan Pier*, Victor Gollancz 1937. Copyright (1937) the Estate of Eric Blair. Reprinted by permission of AM Heath.

Orwell, George. "The Moon Under Water", *Evening Standard* 9 February 1946. Copyright © 1946 the Estate of Eric Blair.

Parker, Dorothy. "A Book of Great Short Stories", *The New Yorker* 29 October 1927. Copyright (1927) New Yorker Inc.

Pegler, Westbrook. "Are Wrestlers People?", *Esquire* January 1934. Copyright (1934) Esquire Inc.

Pyle, Ernie. "The Death of Captain Waskow", Washington *Daily News* 10 January 1944. Copyright © 1944 Scripps Howard Foundation. Reprinted by permission of the Scripps Howard News Alliance.

Ransome, Arthur. "A Trip Up the Volga", Manchester *Guardian*, 13 October 1921. Copyright © 1921 the *Guardian*.

Rees-Mogg, William. "Who Breaks a Butterfly on a Wheel?" *The Times* 1 July 1967. Copyright © 1967 Times Newspapers Ltd.

Rice, Grantland. "Notre Dames's 'Four Horsemen'", New York *Herald Tribune*, 19 October 1924.

Schanberg, Sidney H. "American Reporters Brief Brush with Arrest and Death," *New York Times*, 9 May 1975. Copyright © 1975 New York Times Company.

Shirer, William L. *Berlin Diary*, Alfred A. Knopf 1939 Inc. Copyright © 1939 The William L. Shirer Literary Trust.

Simpson, John. "The Bombing of Baghdad", *The Observer* 20 January 1991. Copyright © 1991 *The Observer*.

Simpson, Kirke L. "Bugles Sound Taps for Warrior's Requiem" Associated Press 11 November 1921. Copyright © 1921 AP.

Smith, Merriman. "Kennedy Assassinated", UPI 23 November 1963. Copyright © 1963 UPI

Steele, Jonathan. "McDonald's in Moscow", *Guardian* 1 February 1990. Copyright © 1990 *The Guardian*.

Steinbeck, John. "Death in the Dust", *San Francisco News* 21 October 1936.

Steinem, Gloria. "I Was a Playboy Bunny", *Show* magazine 1963. Copyright © 1963 Gloria Steinem.

Tetlow, Edwin. *As It Happened*, Peter Owen 1990. Copyright © 1990 Edwin Tetwin.

Thompson, Hunter S. *Fear and Loathing on the Campaign Trail '72*, Straight Arrow Books, 1973. Copyright © Hunter S. Thompson, 1973. Reprinted by permission of HarperCollins.

Tweedie, Jill. "Letter from a Fainthearted Feminist", *Guardian* 21 January 1981. Copyright © 1981 Guardian Media Ltd.

Tyler, Humphrey. "Eye-witness at Sharpeville", *The Observer* 27 March 1960. Copyright © 1960 *The Observer*.

Vedeneeva, I. "The Ultimate Step", *Ogonyok* January 1989. Reprinted from *The Best of Ogonyok*, edited by Vitaly Korotich and Cathy Porter, Heinemann 1990. Translation Copyright © 1990 Cathy Porter.

Vidal, Gore. "A Yankee in Outer Mongolia" *The Observer*, 14 November 1982.

White, Sam. "Picasso, 75, Gets a Surprise Present". Copyright © 1956 the *Evening Standard*.

Wolfe, Tom. *The Electric Kool-Aid Acid Test*, Farrar, Straus and Giroux, Inc., 1968. Copyright © 1968 Tom Wolfe.

Other titles available from Robinson Publishing

The Mammoth Book of War Correspondents   Ed. Jon E. Lewis   £7.99 [ ]
Giving more than 100 eyewitness accounts of the reality of human conflict, this collection offers examples of fine writing by men and women who have overcome the danger and deprivation of life at the front, often boldly confronting obstructive military and perfidious politicians to show their dedication and their desire to reveal the true face of war to the world at large.

The Mammoth Book of Fighter Pilots   Ed. Jon E. Lewis   £7.99 [ ]
Relive the exploits of Manfred von Richthofen, Eddie Rickenbacker, Richard Hillary, Johnnie Johnson, Luftwaffe WWII aces Heinz Knoke and Johannes Steinhoff, and over 20 others. This is a comprehensive and fascinating book about a form of combat that has changed beyond recognition over the last hundred years. It gives vivid insights into both the daily round and the dangers, such as bailing out over enemy territory, surviving in an Iraqi POW camp, or getting shot down in a blazing Spitfire.

The Mammoth Book of Heroes   Ed. Jon E. Lewis   £7.99 [ ]
True courage is one of the most highly valued attributes of humanity. Gathered together in this volume are over 70 accounts, many of them in the words of those who were there, about men and women who showed real courage, often with their lives on the line. No fictional hero can match the true courage of Ernest Shackleton, the bravery of British soldiers at Rorke's Drift, or the spirit of Annie Sullivan teaching the deaf and blind Helen Keller to speak and read. This is an inspiring collection that celebrates the brave of heart through the ages.

The Mammoth Book of Pulp Action   Ed. Maxim Jakubowski   £6.99 [ ]
Furious action, unbridled passion, seedy lowlife and beautiful women – it's all here in this great new volume of pulp fiction stories, featuring classic noir and hard-boiled crime authors from 8 decades of crime writing.

Robinson books are available from all good bookshops or direct from the publisher. Just tick the titles you want and fill in the form below.

TBS Direct
Colchester Road, Frating Green, Colchester, Essex CO7 7DW
Tel: +44 (0) 1206 255777
Fax: +44 (0) 1206 255914
Email: sales@tbs-ltd.co.uk

UK/BFPO customers please allow £1.00 for p&p for the first book, plus 50p for the second, plus 30p for each additional book up to a maximum charge of £3.00.
Overseas customers (inc. Ireland), please allow £2.00 for the first book, plus £1.00 for the second, plus 50p for each additional book.

Please send me the titles ticked above.

NAME (Block letters) . . . .

ADDRESS . . . .

. . . .

POSTCODE . . . .

I enclose a cheque/PO (payable to TBS Direct) for . . . .

I wish to pay by Switch/Credit card

Number . . . .

Card Expiry Date . . . .

Switch Issue Number . . . .

Other titles available from Robinson Publishing

The Mammoth Book of Endurance & Adventure Ed. Jon E. Lewis £7.99 [ ]
Eyewitness recollections from the world's most intrepid adventurers. It recounts over 50 true-life adventures taken from contemporary memoirs, letters and journals of ordinary mortals who achieved extraordinary things.

The Mammoth Book of How It Happened in Britain Ed. Jon E. Lewis £7.99 [ ]
Containing over 300 accounts of the most dramatic and influential moments in British history, compiled from eye-witness sources. Here are all the myriad scenes of war, social unrest, natural disaster, political change, religious movements, society life and individual achievement which made Britain great.

The Mammoth Book of Travel in Dangerous Places Ed. John Keay £7.99 [ ]
This catalogue of cliff-hanging endeavour in the world's wildest places makes unforgettable reading. Well-known travel historian John Keay has selected and introduced the original first-hand narratives of many heroes, including Ross and Franklin's experiences in the Arctic, the classic journeys of Livingstone and Stanley and the tragic ends of Wills in Australia and Scott in Antarctica.

The Mammoth Book of Great Detective Stories Ed. Herbert Van Thal £7.99 [ ]
This huge and unique volume includes 4 anthologies by Herbert Van Thal featuring 35 of the best detective stories ever told. The stories range in style and setting from the mean streets of Raymond Chandler's New York to the classic English whodunnit by Agatha Christie.

Robinson books are available from all good bookshops or direct from the publisher. Just tick the titles you want and fill in the form below.

TBS Direct
Colchester Road, Frating Green, Colchester, Essex CO7 7DW
Tel: +44 (0) 1206 255777
Fax: +44 (0) 1206 255914
Email: sales@tbs-ltd.co.uk

UK/BFPO customers please allow £1.00 for p&p for the first book, plus 50p for the second, plus 30p for each additional book up to a maximum charge of £3.00.
Overseas customers (inc. Ireland), please allow £2.00 for the first book, plus £1.00 for the second, plus 50p for each additional book.

Please send me the titles ticked above.

NAME (Block letters) . . . .

ADDRESS . . . .

. . . .

POSTCODE . . . .

I enclose a cheque/PO (payable to TBS Direct) for . . . .

I wish to pay by Switch/Credit card

Number . . . .

Card Expiry Date . . . .

Switch Issue Number . . . .